EUROPE'S PHYSICIAN

EUROPE'S PHYSICIAN

THE VARIOUS LIFE OF
SIR THEODORE DE MAYERNE

HUGH TREVOR-ROPER

YALE UNIVERSITY PRESS
NEW HAVEN AND LONDON

Published with assistance from the foundation established in memory of Oliver Baty Cunningham of the Class of 1917, Yale College.

For information about this and other Yale University Press publications, please contact:
U.S. Office: sales.press@yale.edu   www.yalebooks.com
Europe Office: sales@yaleup.co.uk   www.yaleup.co.uk

Set in Minion by J&L Composition, Filey, North Yorkshire
Printed in Great Britain by St Edmundsbury Press Ltd, Bury St Edmunds

Library of Congress Cataloging-in-Publication Data

Trevor-Roper, H.R. (Hugh Redwald), 1914–
    Europe's physician: the life of Sir Theodore de Mayerne, 1573–1655/Hugh Trevor-Roper
    p. cm.
    Includes bibliographical references and index.
    ISBN 0–300–11263–7
    1. Mayerne, Theodore Turquet de, Sir, 1573–1655   2. Physicians—France—Biography.
    3. Physicians—France—History—17th century.
    Title.
        [DNLM: 1. Mayerne, Théodore Turquet de, Sir, 1573–1655.   2. Physicians—
        France—Biography.   WZ 100 M4688T 2006]
    R507.M39T74 2006
    610.92′24—dc22
    [B]

                                                                              2006010595

A catalogue record for this book is available from the British Library.

10 9 8 7 6 5 4 3 2 1

Contents

Illustrations

Editor's Foreword

Blair Worden

Hugh Trevor-Roper, who died in 2003, had, among so many other historical interests, an abiding one in the relationship of medicine to society. Perhaps it can be traced to his upbringing as the son of a doctor in rural Northumberland. But it took shape in a very different setting, when, at the end of the Second World War, he interrogated members of Hitler's entourage and wrote *The Last Days of Hitler*. He discovered that the quarrels among the Führer's doctors in the last phase of his life, which were ostensibly about the correct treatment of the patient, belonged to a fierce struggle for power among Hitler's courtiers. In 1980, in a lecture on 'Medicine and Politics',[1] he noted that those two activities, which are kept separate in most societies at most times, had interacted at the court of Stalin much as at Hitler's.

For where absolute power is sustained and made terrible by ideology, he observed, the habitual professional purity of medicine will be broken down and the Hippocratic rules corrupted. In the same lecture he traced that pattern in an era to whose parallels – partial parallels – with the twentieth century he was always alert: the Europe of the sixteenth and seventeenth centuries, the time of the Renaissance and Reformation, when the development of royal absolutism merged with the forces of religious dogma and persecution. There, too, medical controversy was inseparable from wider ideological debate. There, too, medical careers were also political careers.

This book is a study of one such career, that of Sir Theodore de Mayerne, perhaps the most famous physician in the Europe of his own time but a figure rarely known in our own, when the specialisation of knowledge has divided his medical achievements, which have become the preserve of experts, from his wider preoccupations in politics and religion, which have been forgotten. From a Huguenot family uprooted by the wars of religion, he became doctor

---

[1] Delivered to the American College of Cardiologists, and published in *The American Scholar*, 1982.

to Henri IV of France and then, when the Catholic reaction that followed Henri's death prompted him to leave France for England, to James I and Charles I. While building up his formidable medical practice, he acted as diplomat and secret agent and became the focus of major diplomatic episodes.

Trevor-Roper was drawn to the variety of Mayerne's eventful life, to his vivid and imposing personality, and to the arduous detective work, across national and intellectual frontiers, that was needed to reconstruct them. He was attracted, too, to the range and versatility of Mayerne's interests, among them his pioneering research, which had lasting results, into the technology of art and painting. To Trevor-Roper, however, biography was not an end in itself. Mayerne's adjustments, practical and psychological, to alterations of intellectual climate and to changing facts of power are placed within those long-term developments of politics and ideas, Continental and English, that Trevor-Roper traced in a series of collections of essays over a quarter of a century.[2]

He first encountered Mayerne during the Second World War. In Marjorie Hope Nicolson's edition of the seventeenth-century correspondence which she published in 1930 as *Conway Letters*, a book recommended to Trevor-Roper by his friend the writer Logan Pearsall Smith, he warmed to letters written by the physician to his patient Viscount Conway. But it seems not to have been until the early 1970s that the main research for the present book began. Most of the writing was completed in 1979, the year before his lecture on medicine and politics. Then – it is a pattern of his life – the book was crowded out by other preoccupations. Though he intermittently returned to it after his retirement in 1987, adding and revising passages, he was prevented by illness and near-blindness from completing it. The greater part of his text had reached an advanced or even an almost completed state, but there was much that existed only in draft. There was much that he still wanted to do and that could not be done for him, or anyway that should not be attempted in his name. He aimed, once the text was finished, to write a reflective introduction, and would have amplified and rounded the concluding passages. At many points of his manuscript he jotted notes and queries to himself, often unintelligible, enjoining the rewriting or reorganisation of material and the further pursuit and testing of evidence.

I do not think that any lover of history or literature would regret the decision to publish the book, albeit in a form that falls unavoidably short of its

[2] *Religion, The Reformation and Social Change* (London, 1967; republished as *The Crisis of the Seventeenth Century* by the Liberty Fund, 2001); *Renaissance Essays* (London, 1985); *Catholics, Anglicans and Puritans* (London, 1987); *From Counter-Reformation to Glorious Revolution* (London, 1992).

author's ideal. Even so, it cannot be published without some sense of unease. The preparation of a continuous text has involved a process of management that has necessarily risked the misrepresentation or distortion of its author's intentions. In passages which he did not polish I have sometimes amended his text to bring it into line with his declared literary principles. Occasionally I have needed to add to it, though in each case only briefly.

The pace of historical reassessment since 1979 has inevitably given to some passages of the book the air of an earlier time – but not to many of them. There are changes that he would have wished to make in the light of later writing, but others that he would not. Although I have on occasion modified statements of fact, I have sought not to amend his opinions or impair his perspective. I have however made occasional use of square brackets in notes, for two purposes: to carry brief editorial comment, and to alert readers to some recent publications of which he would doubtless have wanted to take account. One such work should be mentioned here, Brian Nance's *Turquet de Mayerne as Baroque Physician* (2001). Nance's approach, which centres on Mayerne's case-notes, is different from Trevor-Roper's. Trevor-Roper supplies a contextual account of Mayerne's medical thinking and practice, Nance a detailed study of their content and character. The two studies, which were written more or less independently of each other, as a rule complement each other and reinforce each other's findings.

In completing his book, Trevor-Roper would have wanted to check his references – no small task in a work that draws on sources in six countries and eight languages – and to supply missing ones. It has been practicable to do the greater part of this work for him, but not all of it. Slips may have got through (or been introduced in the process of checking). I would be surprised, however, if any of them affected his argument anywhere near its centre.

He would have had another wish. Some of the experts who answered queries by him are thanked in his endnotes, but he would have wanted to acknowledge those and other debts at the outset of the work. Perhaps he would have mentioned, besides living scholars, two writers from the recent past whose inspiration lies behind the book and whose work he, in turn, did so much to encourage: Walter Pagel and Frances Yates. For my part I could not have prepared the book without the selfless guidance of others. Above all I am indebted to the scholarly and editorial acumen, and the sustaining enthusiasms, of my assistants Mary Ann Lund and John Young. Laurence Brockliss, Noel Malcolm and Paul Slack commented invaluably on Trevor-Roper's text, and Giles Mandelbrote supplied indispensable bibliographical expertise. So many more people have aided me that I could not particularise my obligations to them without trespassing on the reader's patience, but all my debts to those whose names follow are significant and some of them are extensive: Crofton

Black, Jeremy Catto, Henry Challender, Pauline Croft, Linda Cross, Alastair Duke, R.J.W. Evans, Julian Goodare, Mark Greengrass, Ole Grell, Stephanie Hodgson-Wright, Peregrine Horden, James Howard-Johnston, Gillian Lewis, Sir Hugh Lloyd-Jones, Ian Maclean, Helen Payne, Jennifer Richenberg, Dennis Weller, Tony Woodman and Susan Wormell; Simon Bailey of the Bodleian Library; Iain Brown of the National Library of Scotland; and Caroline Kelly and Chris Low of the Library of the University of Nottingham.

1

Mayerne and his World

In 1605 Francis Bacon presented to King James I his book, *The Advancement of Learning*, which challenged the intellectual presuppositions of the past and sketched the foundations of future knowledge. Reviewing the axioms and rules of all the sciences in turn, he came to the science of medicine, and there as elsewhere he found the need of change. In particular, he deplored 'the discontinuance of the ancient and serious diligence of Hippocrates, which used to set down a narrative of the special cases of his patients, and how they proceeded, and how they were judged by recovery or death'.[1] This 'ancient and serious diligence', Bacon believed, needed to be revived as a precondition to the advance of medical science.

Why had the Hippocratic method, the method of attention to individual cases, been discontinued? According to Bacon, it was the result, in medicine, of that same scholasticism which had retarded the advance of all the sciences. In particular, it was the result of the long reign of Galen, 'that narrowest of minds'[2] but most prolific of writers who, in the second century AD, had reduced medicine to an academic system, divorced from observation and experience. The authority of Galen, and the weight of his writings, had extinguished the older, more tentative science of Hippocrates, and for the next fourteen centuries he had dominated the study of medicine. He had become the Aristotle of the medical world; and not only was he, like Aristotle, by now a tyrant, standing in the way of necessary change: he had also, in the Middle Ages, been transmogrified by 'Arabian' interpreters. His science had become more scholastic, more academic, more bizarre than ever. In the sixteenth century, it is true, these Arabian sophistications had been attenuated. With the revival of Greek studies, the pure text of Galen, as of Aristotle, had been restored. The medieval encrustations had been, to some extent, cleaned away. Besides, practice could and did advance independently of theory, or behind an official lip-service to theory. But still, in its pure or impure form, Galenic doctrine dominated the public teaching of medical science and inhibited that spirit of experiment and observation which had been invoked, seven centuries earlier, by the Father of Medicine, Hippocrates. It was Bacon's aim, in medicine, to destroy Galen and release the imprisoned spirit of Hippocrates, just as, in philosophy, he would destroy Aristotle and release the imprisoned spirit of the pre-Socratic philosophers.

Bacon was not the first to challenge the giant systematisers who had dominated the science of the past. The 'Hermetic' Platonists (or neo-Platonists) of the Renaissance, Marsilio Ficino at their head, had defied Aristotle, and had offered an interpretation of Nature which was entirely different from his, although to us no less bizarre. They developed the theory of the macrocosm and the microcosm: that is, the idea that the body and soul of man are a miniature replica of the body and soul of the world; and that between those two worlds, the great and the little, there are correspondences, sympathies and antipathies which the philosopher, the *magus*, could understand and control.

In medicine the attack on Aristotle was led in the earlier sixteenth century by the Swiss physician Paracelsus, the name given (although not apparently by himself) to Philip Theophrastus Bombast von Hohenheim.[3] Paracelsus made a frontal attack on the Galenist establishment. Not only did he accept the Platonist theory of the macrocosm and the microcosm. He gave it a new dimension. Out of his study of the medieval alchemists and his own experience in mines and furnaces, he evolved the view that the universe, the macrocosm, was chemically controlled – was in fact itself a gigantic chemical crucible – and that its original creation had been a chemical operation, or rather a 'separation' of the pure from the impure. From this it followed that the microcosm – the human body – was also a chemical system whose condition could be altered, adjusted, cured by medical treatment. It was by reference to this general theory, from which he deduced some new and fertile ideas, but to which he added many strange and inconsequent details drawn from his own imagination and from German peasant folklore, that he justified his medical innovations: his insistence that diseases were living parasites planted in the individual human body, not merely an accidental imbalance of 'humours'; his replacement of those four 'humours' of the Galenists by his three chemical 'principles', sulphur, mercury and salt; his search for a 'universal dissolvent'; his detoxication of poisons to convert them into cures; his homeopathic remedies; his distillations and 'projections', which made him a continuator, in the Renaissance, of the alchemical tradition of the Middle Ages.

The extremism of Paracelsus and his disciples discredited their programme of reform, and thus strengthened the official cult. To Bacon, in any case, they were no better than the old tyrants whom they challenged. For they too were dogmatists, not seekers after truth: 'heresiarchs', 'founders of schools', such as

Bacon had no wish to be. In Bacon's mind, Hermetic 'magi' like Giordano Bruno, with their extravagant claims to conjure with the world, vulgar uncritical egotists like Paracelsus, declaring all science but their own vain and useless, did no good to their cause. Whatever truth they might assert was buried, and damaged, by the messianic violence of their assertion.[4] When forced to distinguish between 'such trifles', Bacon himself preferred Galen, 'that vain babbler, the renegade from experience', to the 'monster' Paracelsus.[5]

So Galenism was not broken, perhaps rather it was fortified, by the direct impact of Paracelsian 'chemical' medicine. Paracelsian ideas might penetrate into the practice of medical craftsmen – the apothecaries and barber-surgeons to whom, in fact, they had been addressed[6] – but they did not disturb the accepted theory of the medical establishment. The Royal College of Physicians in London, whose licence was necessary to all practitioners, retained throughout the sixteenth century its corporate fidelity to Galen. It was in the works of Galen that candidates for examination were formally examined, by them that they were tested, to them that they were referred.[7] The revival of Greek studies had of course entailed the revival of Hippocrates. His works too had been edited, published and praised. Some doctors were even influenced by them. But formally it was Galenic dogma, not the Hippocratic method, which dominated the teaching of medicine. In calling for a return from Galen to Hippocrates, from the 'magistralities' of the physicians to 'the traditions of experience', Bacon, here as elsewhere, was challenging the academic establishment.

In that, at least, he resembled Paracelsus. There was much about Paracelsus for him to detest or mistrust. He hated his arrogant claim to be an inspired prophet. He repudiated 'the ancient opinion that man was Microcosmus, an abstractor or model of the world': an opinion, he wrote, that 'hath been fantastically strained by Paracelsus and the alchemists, as if there were to be found in man's body certain correspondences and parallels, which should have respect to all varieties of things, as stars, planets, minerals, which are extant in the great world'. In general Bacon was very sceptical of alchemy.[8] Yet whatever he thought of Paracelsus's character and doctrines, at least he approved the openness and empirical cast of his thinking. Indeed at one point, having urged the physicians of his time to return to the experimental methods, Bacon moved to an open commendation of chemical medicines. 'In preparation of medicines,' he wrote,

> I do find strange, specially considering how mineral medicines have been extolled, and that they are safer for the outward than inward parts, that no man hath sought to make an imitation by art of natural baths and medicinable fountains; which nevertheless are confessed to receive their virtues

from minerals; and not so only, but discerned and distinguished from what particular mineral they receive tincture, as sulphur, vitriol, steel, or the like; which nature if it may be reduced to compositions of art, both the variety of them will be increased, and the temper of them will be more commanded.[9]

In Elizabethan England, the use of medicinal baths and mineral waters had indeed become fashionable; but as yet physicians had not sought to analyse their properties or explain their effects. Indeed, the cures were often psychological, or at least non-rational. The new spas were often the old holy wells secularised. Popery had been abolished, and with it holy wells and miraculous cures; but men would not, for that, cease to visit those curative waters.[10] In calling upon science to rationalise and extend the process, Bacon was, once again, a pioneer.[11]

A year after Bacon's challenge, there came to England the man who, more than any other, was to realise the medical part of his ambitious programme. This was Theodore (or Théodore) de Mayerne, a French Huguenot, born in Geneva, and at that time physician-in-ordinary to Henri IV, King of France. His visit in 1605 was brief – brief and rather mysterious. But five years later, Mayerne would return to England, invested with new dignity, as first physician to King James I and all the royal family. England would be his home until his death forty-four years later. In the course of those years he would become the best-known, and probably the most influential, though not the greatest physician in seventeenth-century England. Paracelsus had been a wanderer, moving, sometimes fleeing, from the Baltic to the Levant, from Holland to Poland. Mayerne, like Paracelsus, was an international figure. Mayerne's life, too, was mobile – until its later part, when age and corpulence, together with the accidents of politics, made it sedentary. But he had none of Paracelsus's flamboyance, none of his urge to provoke. He worked within established systems, astutely managing his political and material interests.

It was through Mayerne that 'chemical medicine' became respectable in England, and found its way into the official pharmacopoeia. He played a large part in the organisation – the rationalisation, he would have thought it – of medical supplies. He was also the founder of clinical medicine in England. He was the first physician to keep detailed notes on his patients; and it is thanks to his careful records – of his prescriptions, his consultations, above all his clinical examinations – that we know, or can know, more about the physical condition of English kings and queens, courtiers and statesmen, in the first half of the seventeenth century than in any earlier – or some later – periods. For if Mayerne was a cautious disciple of Paracelsus, he was also a professed disciple of Hippocrates. He would quote the wisdom of Hippocrates to his patients.[12] In some of his portraits, his hands rest on a sculptured bust of Hippocrates. On his tombstone in the church of St Martin-in-the-Fields he is described as *Hippocrates alter*, a second Hippocrates.

Whether Bacon ever realised that Theodore de Mayerne was the answer to his prayer, we do not know. Probably he did not. He must have known Mayerne personally. They must have met at the court of King James. They could have conversed freely from the beginning, for Bacon, unlike most educated Englishmen, had lived in Paris and knew French. They must have known each other officially, too. As Attorney-General, Bacon was prosecutor in the *cause célèbre* of the murder of Sir Thomas Overbury, in which Mayerne was examined. As Lord Chancellor he determined the dispute between the apothecaries and the grocers, in which Mayerne was deeply involved. Bacon and Mayerne also shared intellectual interests, in chemical experiments and the history of painting. But the fact remains that Bacon, who so extolled experimental science and the labour of the artisan, had little personal contact with either. That cool, Olympian intellect laid down the laws of progress and then turned aside, to recreate itself in the exquisite gardens of Gorhambury, the library and aviaries of York House. In all Bacon's known writings, public or private, there is no mention of Mayerne, and Bacon is one of the few Jacobean statesmen who seem never to have consulted the first physician of the king.

But if Bacon never noticed Mayerne, the modern student of early Stuart England cannot avoid him. Wherever we turn, he is there, half-concealed perhaps behind strange spellings – Dr Maherne, Dr Mayard, Dr Myrne, Dr Mayhorne, Dr Magerne, Dr Meyer, Dr Myrene, Dr Meene – but unmistakable: an ample, immovable, central figure in that half-century of revolutionary change. At first he was a court figure, inseparable, it seems, from the life of courts. 'For eleven *lustres*' – that is, for fifty-five years – he wrote to Lord Conway in 1651, he had 'lived at the courts of kings and princes',[13] and his medical rivals declared that he was 'a braver courtier than doctor'. But he was never wholly a courtier: always he fretted slightly at that delicate, profitable slavery; for he never ceased to be a Huguenot, with that inner republicanism of the Huguenot which could sustain itself, independent, self-contained, inviolate, even at the most absolute or extravagant court. Behind the unfailing grace and *savoir-faire* of the perfect courtier there was always the self-command, even the austerity, of the Protestant virtuoso, 'totus teres atque rotundus' – wholly polished and well-rounded; and behind those classical attitudes there lay, and would sometimes reveal itself, the inflexible virtue, the exigent, unsparing self-sufficiency, of the authentic Calvinist who knows that he is of the Elect. So when revolution came to England and his royal patrons were swept away, Mayerne remained apparently unmoved. He stayed where he was, in his house in Chelsea, untouched (and untaxed) through every political change. Twenty-three years after taking part in the autopsy of Henri IV of France, he would perform the same service for John Pym, that great enemy of Henri's posthumous son-in-law King Charles I;[14] and in his old age he would receive from the regicide usurper Oliver Cromwell the renewal of the privileges first granted to him by his old master, King James.

It was a triumph of acceptance – acceptance not assimilation: for he was recognised largely on his own terms. In spite of his declared intention when he first settled in England, he never became an Englishman. He saw himself as a Frenchman, preserved his French connections and many of his French patients, spoke French for preference. He wrote to his English friends and patrons in French, to English doctors and clergy in Latin. When the Marquis of Newcastle insisted that Mayerne write for him in English, so that his servants in Nottinghamshire could follow his instructions, he did so, but under protest: he hated to do anything, he said, that he could not do 'de bonne grace'.[15] Others were less firm than the marquis. Even the king – both James I and Charles I – would oblige him by corresponding with him in French. Nor did he succumb to English society: English society succumbed to him. The foreigner, the intruder, the heretic brought the natives round to his way of thought.

For in his youth, Mayerne had been a controversial figure: a heretic, in science as in religion. He had found himself in the centre of bitter medical disputes in Paris and on the fringe of court scandal in London, and had been denounced in both as a pushing immigrant adventurer. In Paris the animosity against him had never entirely died down. But England was more tolerant. The enmity quickly evaporated. Against that ample, benign figure, the gusts of envy, like the tides of political passion, beat in vain. Mayerne soon became an institution. His patients – court and country, Cavalier and Roundhead, Catholic, Anglican, Puritan – all venerated him. Physicians, apothecaries, grocers, distillers, all in turn bowed down before him. He was flattered and indulged by James I, treated as a saviour by Charles I, honoured by the embattled Long Parliament, the regicide republic, the Cromwellian Protectorate. He was trusted as a secret political agent by the leader of the French Huguenots, by the King of England, by the States-General of Holland, by the Republic of Geneva, by the canton of Berne. Foreign rulers competed to lure him from England, but in the end he always preferred to stay. In England he would die, very old and very rich. Some said he was worth £100,000, others £140,000, in cash, besides property in England and a noble estate in Switzerland.[16] He was the first medical man to leave such a fortune: in this respect too he was a pioneer.

It was certainly a remarkable career, especially when we think of the hazards that must be faced by any court doctor, and above all by a reforming, foreign court doctor in that time. The 'Hippocratic oath' had been rotted by the consecration of Reason of State. No great man died without grave suspicion of poison. Mayerne was in at many famous deaths, and where there was suspicion, whether of negligence, as in the cases of Lord Salisbury and Prince Henry, or of poison, as in the case of Sir Thomas Overbury, it was always the French doctor who was most liable to be suspected. In 1625, when King James I died, the Duke of Buckingham (who was also Mayerne's patient) was accused of poisoning him, and in view of that allegation, which would be formally repeated by the opponents of Charles I for a quarter of a century, 'the French doctor' was perhaps thankful that he had been abroad at the time. After all, Queen Elizabeth's doctor, Dr Lopez, who was also a foreigner, had ended on the gallows on precisely such a charge, animated by precisely such xenophobia. Four years later, when Charles I was at war with France, a secret report from France was read to him. In it, a French spy informed him that he had learned, from a reliable source, that 'the King of England had a French doctor called Mayherne, which was as dangerous and damnable a fellow as ever was Judas'.[17] Fortunately, the report was ignored. Mayerne was, by that time, secure in the royal confidence. But the grim fate of the Portuguese Jew, Dr Lopez, less than fifty years before, serves to emphasise the good fortune of the French Huguenot, Dr Mayerne.

Mayerne came to England as a court physician. But success at court inevitably brings success elsewhere. Mayerne's private practice was enormous, and in the end – as he admitted – was the chief direct source of his wealth. A glance through his surviving records shows half the aristocracy of England, and indeed of Scotland, as his patients; and these records are by no means complete, for many of his prescriptions are anonymous, and it is from private papers – diaries, memoirs, letters – that we learn the missing names. Those who consulted him include almost all the ministers of James I and Charles I, from Robert Cecil, Earl of Salisbury, the architect of the Stuart triumph in 1603, to Attorney-General Noy, the architect, through the fatal device of ship-money, of its crisis in 1640. All the Scottish favourites, and would-be favourites, are there – those 'beggarly bluecaps' who streamed to the golden fountain of Jacobean London. So are the noble politicians of Scotland, like Lord Dunfermline, Chancellor of Scotland, and Scots who remained in Scotland, such as 'a Scotch noblewoman paralysed for the last four years' whose case was sent up to Mayerne, for his *consilium* or written opinion, by Arthur Johnston, the poetical doctor of Edinburgh. Even Irishmen are there, if grand enough, like Randall McDonnell, Lord Dunluce – the son of the old rebel Sorley Boy and himself a rebel too, but now reconciled and rich – or 'dominus Roche, Hybernus'; and of course the English viceroys of Ireland, one after another: Lord Chichester and all his family; Lord Falkland, to whom

Mayerne was hastily summoned when he fell from his horse in Theobalds Park in 1633;[18] Strafford himself, whose symptoms, as he languished in York in those fateful days before the meeting of the Long Parliament in 1640, were sent up to Mayerne for his *consilium*, by his own doctor, Sir Maurice Williams. We find almost all the English secretaries of state: Sir Ralph Winwood; Sir Dudley Carleton, Lord Dorchester; Lord Conway; Sir John Coke; Sir Francis Windebank; English ambassadors abroad, ordinary and extraordinary – Sir Thomas Edmondes, Sir Henry Neville, Sir Isaac Wake, the Earl of Carlisle, Sir William Beecher, Lord Scudamore and many others. We find foreign ambassadors in England: the Duc de Bouillon, the Marquis de Senecterre, M. de Châteauneuf. All these rely on Mayerne. So do thinkers and writers: Isaac Casaubon, the greatest of the international scholars of his age, who was his familiar friend; Thomas Harriot, the greatest of the mathematicians and astronomers – sent to him, no doubt, by his patron the Earl of Northumberland; the poets John Donne and Fulke Greville; and the sceptical philosopher and founder of deism, Lord Herbert of Cherbury, who was also ambassador in Paris, and whose heretical work *De veritate* Mayerne would read and enjoy in manuscript: 'nervosum illud tuum maioris operis fragmentum a me acute lectum' (that sinewy fragment of a larger work of yours was keenly read by me).[19]

These are all, directly or indirectly, court patients; but the list goes on, and soon we find ourselves, politically and geographically, far outside the verge of the court. Provincial doctors write to him about their patients from all England, and indeed from abroad. So we find the celebrated court doctor advising a country Catholic, Lady Stonor, 'morborum myriade affecta'; or Lady Jones in Herefordshire; or Lady Carteret, 'melancholica hysterica', in the isle of Jersey; or a Scottish professor at the Huguenot academy of Saumur, Dr Craig; or Mr William Kendrick, 'pannifex Readingensis', a clothier of Reading, the rich benefactor of his native town; or 'Mr Scottowe, alderman of Norwich'; or the Puritan divine Richard Baxter; or a Puritan squire whom, in 1628, Mayerne would find 'valde melancholicus', Oliver Cromwell.

Of course he had his detractors. He 'failed as often in judgement as any of the rest', wrote one of the more spiteful of them, John Chamberlain, the snob gossip-writer, the Creevy of the Jacobean court.[20] There was also the matter of his fees. His visits, his written letters of advice, were notoriously expensive. But his patients clung to him. Charles I and Henrietta Maria were as dependent on him as James I and Queen Anne, the Queen of Bohemia and the Prince Palatine. The Conways and Cavendishes were faithful to him for thirty years. The Duchesse de la Tremoïlle – that is, Charlotte-Brabantine de Nassau, daughter of William the Silent, Prince of Orange – first consulted him, as far as we know, in Paris in 1606. She died in 1631, but her successor was his patient in 1637 and was still consulting him in 1649. She was Marie de la Tour d'Auvergne, daughter of Henri, Duc de Bouillon, who had also been his patient forty years before. The Duke and Duchess of Richmond and Lennox are among Mayerne's first patients in England. They would become close friends, holding his children at the font. The duchess would present him with his portrait, engage in epistolary badinage with him, and come to wartime London in order to live in Chelsea, within reach of her doctor. When she died she would bequeath £100 to buy a piece of plate for 'my good friend Sir Theodore Mayerne, whom my Lord and myself did and had much cause to value'.[21] The plain fact was that he was better than any other doctor. His fees might be high, but they were worth paying. Nor did he only cure the rich or their dependants. The philosopher John Smith, Fellow of Queens' College, Cambridge, who, having tried many other doctors, finally put himself, for the whole summer of 1651, 'under the cure of the famous Dr Theodore Mahern',[22] was unlikely to afford the high fees or the handsome New Year's gifts paid to him by his aristocratic patients. And we are assured by the Reverend Thomas Hodges, vicar of Kensington, who witnessed Mayerne's will and preached his funeral sermon (and whose son became a distinguished physician under his influence), that Mayerne never declined to advise a poor patient who could pay nothing.[23] This indeed was part of his Hippocratic duty.

Mayerne's fame as a physician was not confined to England. It had begun in France, and there it continued, in spite of all the machinations and denigrations of his professional rivals and doctrinal enemies. His grand patients also carried his reputation abroad, and doctors and apothecaries in Germany and Holland, Lorraine and Switzerland, France and Italy, acknowledged his patronage or sought his advice. Some of the greatest doctors of the time consulted him: in England, William Harvey, his colleague and friend; in Switzerland Wilhelm Fabry, or Fabricius Hildanus, 'the German Paré', the greatest expert in his time on the surgery of the battlefield.[24] Foreign princes too relied on him to send medical attendants, while doctors whom he patronised would serve the King of Sweden and the Tsar of Russia.

One of Mayerne's many English patients was Lady Slingsby, the wife of Sir Henry Slingsby of Scriven, baronet. Lady Slingsby had tried many doctors, without success, but in 1639, her husband tells us, 'at last she was a patient of Theodore Meene the king's physician, and from him she hath reaped the most benefit for her health.' Sir Henry called on Mayerne for a new prescription for his wife, and incidentally, in his diary, gives us a picture of the doctor in his consulting room. He writes that he has sent down physic for her from London:

by the directions of Dr Mayerne, of whom she had taken physic the year before: for his custom is to register in a book the diseases and remedies of all his patients, if they be of difficulties, so that sending for his book he finds what he had done to her formerly, and thereupon prescribes the same. Usually I went in a morning for his advice, about seven of the clock, where I used to find him set in his study, which was a large room furnished with books and pictures; and as one of the chiefest, he had the picture of the head of Hippocrates that great physician; and upon his table he had the proportion of a man in wax, to set forth the order and composure of every part. Before his table he had a frame with shelves, whereon he set some books; and behind this he sat to receive those that came for his advice; for he seldom went to any, for he was corpulent and unwieldy; and then again he was rich, and the king's physician, and a knight, which made him more costly to deal with.[25]

Such was the 'second Hippocrates' at the age of sixty-seven and at the height of his prosperity. Five years later we have another account of him from a more distant and less admiring source. Gui Patin, doctor of medicine of the faculty of Paris and Professor of the Collège Royal, was an able doctor, of wide learning and remarkable intelligence; but he was an irreconcilable Galenist, and his mordant, satirical pen never spared those who had studied outside Paris (and especially at Montpellier), or quarrelled with his faculty, or accepted 'chemical' ideas. Mayerne was guilty on all three counts and therefore, when Patin was asked by his friend Dr Spon of Lyon for an account of this famous doctor, himself of Lyonnais origin, no mercy could be expected. After describing Mayerne's early history in Paris, and his battle with the orthodox professors – the 'honest men who exerted themselves nobly to prevent the chemists and charlatans from acquiring influence here, to sell their trash to those who gape after novelty in Paris' – he adds: 'this Mayerne is still in England today, very old, almost in his second childhood. It is said that he has left the party of the king and has put himself on the side of the parliament. I have seen one of his sons in Paris, studying medicine, who has since died in England. They say that he is very hard on his children, being so avaricious, and lets them die of hunger. He is a great chemist, very rich, and knows how to extract many a *jacobus* for a *consilium* of five or six pages.'[26]

Gui Patin's account is clearly malicious. In some respects it is wrong. Mayerne was certainly not in his dotage in 1645, or even ten years later, when he died. And yet it is not entirely untrue either. Mayerne was fond of his money and – partly on that account – unsuccessful with his children. For that fault, he ultimately paid a heavy price. But having quoted Patin, we may add, as a corrective note, the comment of a later, more objective critic, who was born in Geneva while Mayerne was still alive; who knew his relations there – he corresponded with his great-niece, Louise Windsor, a familiar figure in the literary life of the city[27] – and who drew his information from reliable Swiss sources. This was Pierre Bayle, the great sceptic, the founding father of the eighteenth-century Enlightenment. In his famous *Dictionnaire historique,* Bayle included an article on Mayerne. He there quoted the words of Patin, but he took care to warn his readers that Patin wrote 'as one who liked to denigrate and who hated medical reformers'. Therefore, from Patin's caricature, he invited them to turn to the portrait which formed the frontispiece to Mayerne's posthumously published works. It is an engraving, based on the last portrait to be painted of Mayerne, shortly before his death. Here, observed Bayle, 'we see a copperplate engraving of M. de Mayerne, as he was at the age of eighty-two. You could not imagine a more attractive figure: a lively, serene, majestic expression, a venerable beard!' This was a man who, according to Patin, had been, by that time, for ten years in his dotage.

So far, I have described Mayerne as he appeared to his contemporaries: a fashionable and successful court physician who, more than any other, introduced into England and established there 'the ancient and serious diligence of Hippocrates'. But he was also much more than that. Behind that urbane exterior, he was a man of various and sometimes secret enterprise. In the privacy of his study he was a pioneer in the technology of art. Perhaps he was himself a painter. He was interested in the manufacture of pigments, cosmetics, artificial precious metals, gems and pearls. He was in fact an alchemist as well as a chemist, a Hermetic adept as well as a Hippocratic doctor. In some of his portraits, the bust of Hippocrates rests upon a book inscribed with the name of Hermes, and in most of them there is some Hermetic symbol. And finally, in addition to all this, he was, incidentally, a secret political agent in an international cause. In all these activities he deserves our notice; but before approaching the details of his career, it may be worth while to elaborate a little on the last; for that is the area of his life which has been least noticed. And yet, in some respects, it is the most interesting.

For Mayerne, above all things, was a cosmopolitan. Born in Geneva, of French-Piedmontese parents, educated in Germany and France, living in France and England, establishing himself as a feudal baron in Switzerland, married in turn to two Dutch women, he might call himself, at one time, 'a Frenchman of Geneva', at another 'à demi Suisse', or again declare his intention to be 'à tout escient anglois'; but in fact he never belonged to any country. He was a citizen of the world, or rather, within the world, of an international society whose claims transcended those of any mere local patriotism. From his very birth, even before his birth, his career was determined by one great fact of sixteenth-century life: the brute, inescapable fact of religious persecution. It is a fact of life to which our English history owes more than we always remember.

The dispersal of European talent in the century after the Reformation is surely one of the great fertilising displacements of European history. There is nothing comparable with it until the equally fertilising – and even more costly – dispersal of the European Jews in recent times. First from Italy, especially in the 1550s, then from France, especially after the massacre of St Bartholomew in 1572, then from the southern Netherlands, especially after the fall of Antwerp in 1585 – these at least were the spectacular moments in the course of a long, persistent pressure – the 'Calvinists' of Western Europe left their homes and carried their talents to more tolerant foreign countries. Sometimes they were not Calvinists at all, in the strict sense of the word: that is, they did not accept, *ex animo*, either the theological doctrine or the ecclesiastical organisation of the Calvinist Church. They did not necessarily believe in predestination or approve of theocracy. They were intellectual reformers, 'liberals', even 'libertines', in the tradition of Erasmus, who were driven to protect themselves by assuming a 'Calvinist' armour which, once they were securely established, they would easily discard again. But if they would discard that armour, they would never discard the mentality which had caused them to assume it rather than to surrender (as other 'liberals' had done) to the exasperated Catholic society around them. They were a proud race, an élite of independent, individualist, self-contained, self-disciplined, active, modern men. They showed the force of their character by their willingness to emigrate. They needed that force in order to remake their lives in foreign countries. They often also remade the foreign countries into which they emigrated.

For by this dispersal, old countries would be changed and new ones created. Just as the persecuted and scattered Jews of our time have created the state of Israel – a practical experiment inconceivable until it was established – and have thereby convulsed the politics of the surrounding Arab world, so the persecuted and dispersed Calvinists of the sixteenth century created new political systems which disturbed the traditional balance of Europe. Italian and French *émigrés* created a new society in, or on the edge of, rural Switzerland. Flemish and French *émigrés* created a new federation in the backward northern Netherlands and turned Amsterdam from an obscure fishing town into the commercial miracle of the seventeenth century. These immigrants were a dynamic force partly because of their moral qualities. They were heretics: that is, they had chosen their own way of life and were determined to live by it. But their power sprang also from their places of origin. They came from the most advanced areas of Europe: Italy, Flanders, the Rhineland, France. Their dispersal was a displacement, for the benefit of less favoured lands, of the most advanced science, the most sophisticated techniques, of Europe.

This massive dispersal of talent presented Europe with a new international élite: mobile, self-reliant, cohesive, generating its own momentum, securing its own future. It set up its own schools, its own universities, and aimed to create a new type of man who would be everywhere at home. *Omne solum forti patria* was its cosmopolitan motto: to a brave man, every country is a fatherland. In England, in this age of sudden development, we find foreign Protestants at every point of advance. Foreign Protestants – the Swiss Martin Bucer, the Italian Peter Martyr – helped to shape the English Church. Foreign Protestants – the Genoese Sir Horatio Pallavicino under Queen Elizabeth, the Lucchese Sir Philip Burlamachi under Charles I – financed the English Crown. Foreign Protestants drained the English fens and worked the English mines. A foreign Protestant, the Italian Giacomo à Concio or Acontius, fortified Berwick-on-Tweed for Queen Elizabeth and founded the tradition of 'rational theology' which would prevail in the next century. A foreign Protestant, Alberico Gentili, would create in England the philosophic study of international law. A foreign Protestant, Isaac Casaubon, fleeing from the Calvinist bigotry of Geneva and the Catholic bigotry of Paris, would end his career as the learned ornament of the Jacobean court and would dream – as so many foreigners, and some Englishmen, would dream in those enthusiastic days – of an England that would be the capital of a third world, free of confessional domination.

To this international court of James I, from that international dispersion, would come also Theodore de Mayerne. It is important to remember that origin. The few writers who have dealt with him have tended to forget it. They have written as specialists in medical history, with expertise with which I could not venture to compete. This is a layman's book, which considers Mayerne as a social and intellectual figure, rather than as a purely medical one, in seventeenth-century history. Specialists see him as an enterprising physician who followed the call of royal patronage. That is too narrow a view. Mayerne's career is incomplete, perhaps unintelligible, if it is detached from the larger context which controlled it and gave it its form and direction.

Intellectually and politically, it was a Protestant context. There was no inherent connection between Protestantism and Paracelsianism, the two guiding principles of Mayerne's life, although in their earlier stages, as challenges to orthodoxy, they often went together. But with the advances of the Counter-Reformation in the late sixteenth century, the Roman Church became ever less tolerant of Platonism, and thus of the Paracelsian medical teaching that embraced it. Protestantism and Paracelsianism were driven into alliance. In Mayerne's mind they merged into a single ideology. It was the ideology of the Calvinist international: specifically of the chapter of its history which began in 1572, with the massacre of St Bartholomew.

2

Early Years, 1573–1598

Theodore de Mayerne was born in Geneva and emigrated, via Paris, to London. He was not the first *émigré* in his family. His father, Louis, had been born in Lyon and had emigrated to Geneva. His grandfather, Étienne, had been born at Chieri in Piedmont and had emigrated to Lyon. The family name was not Mayerne but Turquet. The grandfather Étienne was always known as Étienne Turquet, and a street in Lyon – not a very impressive street – is called after him l'impasse Turquet. However, Turquet was a plebeian name – it meant snub-nosed terrier and would sometimes be used injuriously – and those of the family who had social pretensions preferred to call themselves 'de Mayerne'. Theodore would afterwards refer to his great-grandfather, the father of Étienne Turquet, as 'Jacques de Mayerne, dit Turquet', as if Mayerne were his real name, whatever he was commonly called. The difference was significant, for the name 'de Mayerne' was 'noble'. It carried with it a coat of arms which was supposedly granted by the emperor Frederick I Barbarossa. However that claim to nobility had been acquired, the name is likely to have had more prosaic origins. It probably derived from the village of Magherno, near Pavia, where the family may have had property. At any event, by the time of Étienne Turquet (if not before) the family had forfeited its claim to nobility by engaging in trade.[1]

Étienne Turquet had a younger brother, Audinet, of whom we know nothing except that his widow was still living in 1574. Audinet left two sons. One of them, Jean, studied medicine at the University of Paris, and we find him living in Avallon in 1582, under the name of de Mayerne-Turquet; for medicine was a 'noble' profession. He probably died soon afterwards, as Theodore de Mayerne seems not to have known him. There is no evidence that Jean left any family. Audinet's other son was probably Jacques Turquet, who, being a tradesman – 'marchand joaillier, bourgeois de Paris' – could not claim nobility. He was alive in 1576. Paris Turquet, similarly 'marchand joaillier, bourgeois de Paris', who was alive in 1634, living in rue de la Grande

Truanderie, parish of St Eustache, was probably his son. Paris Turquet left two sons and three daughters. The sons, Charles and Louis, by obtaining royal office, would rise out of the bourgeois class. They could therefore reclaim their nobility and would call themselves Mayerne-Turquet.[2] The descendants of Audinet evidently remained Catholic and lost contact with the Protestant descendants of Étienne with whom we are concerned. We may therefore forget about them for the time being, and return to the senior branch, that of Étienne.

Étienne Turquet, Theodore de Mayerne's grandfather, was born in 1495 or thereabouts. By 1524, if not before, his business interests had brought him to Lyon, the commercial and banking city through whose fairs the manufactured goods of Italy entered France. He dealt wholesale in cloth, silk and salted fish. He owned two contiguous houses at the corner of the rue de Saônerie and the rue de la Chevrerie, one for the cloth and silk business, the other for the fish. He was an active and prosperous merchant, supplying the royal galleys at Marseille with fish, and he was also a useful and conscientious *notable* of the city, serving as rector of the Conseil Général de l'Aumône which handled poor-relief. He married into the commercial élite of Lyon. His wife was Claudine, daughter of Claude Clavel, a prosperous merchant and member of the Consulat, the municipal government of the city. In his business he had, as his junior partner, another Piedmontese, Barthélémy Naris.

In 1536 Étienne Turquet took an important step in the expansion of his business. When in that year the King of France, François I, passed through Lyon in order to oppose the army of the emperor Charles V in Italy, Turquet saw an opportunity of using royal favour to bring a new industry to the city. The importation into France of manufactured silk had been interrupted by the Italian wars, and especially by the defection to the emperor of the city of Genoa, the centre of the manufacture of velvet. Turquet and Naris proposed that the industry be established in Lyon – as it had been, although very briefly, in the reign of Louis XI – and they offered, if granted certain concessions, to establish it themselves, with skilled Piedmontese workmen. In this way the loyal city of Lyon would benefit and the 'rebellious' city of Genoa would be punished. The magistrates of Lyon thought well of the project, and recommended it to the king on his return from Italy. François I accepted the proposal, and by letters patent, dated October 1536, he declared his decision. He wished, he said, 'to people and increase our said town of Lyon, which is one of the principal keys and the frontier of our kingdom, and the most convenient and propitious place for the manufacture of the said velvets'. He therefore granted to Turquet and Naris the privileges which they required. The Consulat advanced some of the costs; the Piedmontese workmen were brought in and settled in Lyon; and the silk industry, thus established, became the base of those other industries – printing, porcelain, fustian – which would soon convert Lyon from a commercial into an industrial town. 'In giving the first stimulus to industry, the main cause of the wealth and greatness of Lyon,' says one of its historians, 'Turquet has deserved a place in our local hall of fame.'[3] It is possible that, after commerce and industry, Turquet moved on into finance, for his son would afterwards describe him as having been a banker.[4]

With industry came intellectual change. In the middle of the sixteenth century Lyon was a centre of French Protestantism: indeed, in 1562 the city was ruled by the Protestant party. By that time, Étienne Turquet was dead. He had died in 1560. It seems probable that he had himself become a Protestant. However, his wife, who survived him, did not, and the ferment of heresy in the city evidently stiffened her Catholic devotion.[5] It can be assumed that the children were all brought up as Roman Catholics. There were three children alive at the time of her death: Philippe, who became a nun in the nunnery of la Déserte; Françoise, who married Claude Bourbon, a royal official; and Louis, the father of Theodore de Mayerne.

Louis Turquet was born in Lyon in 1533 or 1534.[6] He was brought up in comfortable circumstances and well educated, although we do not know where. He continued to live at Lyon, but he evidently did not carry on his father's business, for his mother described him, in her will, as 'noble': he probably held some kind of office. He married into the official class: his wife was Louise, daughter of Antoine Maçon, treasurer at war first to François I, then to Henri II. The Maçon family also came from Lyon. At some time, both he and his wife were converted to Calvinism. His Calvinism was cultivated, moral and intellectual, the Calvinism of Calvin himself and of the first generation of his disciples. It was also firmly held, and total: the faith of a convert. It dominated his whole outlook. This was made clear by his later history. Of his early history, before 1572, we know nothing.

On 24 August 1572 came the massacre of St Bartholomew, that crucial episode which precipitated the great Huguenot dispersion and drove hitherto conservative men to think in radical, even revolutionary terms. After Paris, the massacre – or rather, the communal war which the massacre in Paris had unleashed – spread to the provinces. The Huguenots of Lyon, summoned by the Consulat, and arrested *en masse*, were slaughtered by organised Catholic parties under the blind eye of authority, and their corpses thrown into the River Saône. Louis Turquet and his wife escaped the immediate massacre, but narrowly. Their two houses, we are told, were burnt down. Nor could they assume that the danger was past when the first killing was over, for the communal hatred simmered on. The Consulat, reporting the butchery, seemed eager to carry it further. The chief trouble-makers, it said, were still at large, but they were now on the defensive and could be destroyed at will if the effort were made; and 'if that should be the wish of the king', they would be glad to oblige. They were the more willing because the property of the heretics could be confiscated for the benefit of the orthodox. In fact, after the massacre, the Consulat and the governor both claimed a share of the spoils.[7]

How or where Louis Turquet lived during these dangerous months we do not know. But, like many of the Protestants of Lyon, he soon decided to escape from France and seek refuge in the free city of Geneva. There he arrived in the course of the winter, with his wife and their only child, a daughter Isabeau or Elizabeth. On 16 March 1573 he was admitted as an 'inhabitant' of the city. Six months later his first son was born. He was born, as Mayerne himself twice recorded, on 28 September 1573 at eight o'clock in the morning. He was baptised in the cathedral church of St Pierre, Calvin's own church. His godfather was Calvin's successor as spiritual dictator of the republic, Theodore de Bèze, or Beza. Beza himself preached the sermon and then presented the child at the font and gave him his own name, Theodore. It was a name which Theodore de Mayerne would afterwards transmit to four godsons of his own, three of whom will appear, in due course, in this narrative.[8]

The Calvinism of Louis Turquet was obviously a source of pain to his widowed mother, Claudine Turquet. In September 1575 she made her will. After specific bequests to her three children, she left the entire residue of her estate to the children of Louis Turquet, born or to be born. But this was on condition that they be brought up 'in catholic, apostolic and Roman religion', and live as Catholics. Any who were not Catholic were not to receive a sou; 'and if all the children should be of the so-called reformed religion (which God forbid)', then the whole estate was to go to charity – half to the Aumône Générale of Lyon, half to the hospital of Pont du Rhône, although Louis Turquet was to enjoy the income for life. To emphasise her determination and ensure the fulfilment of her wishes, Claudine Turquet appointed two sound Catholics as executors of her will, and had it witnessed by seven priests and clerks of St Croix.

During their long exile in Geneva, several other children were born to Louis and Louise Turquet. Apart from Theodore and Isabeau, we know of two sons, Henri, born in 1587, and Philippe, born in 1591, and four daughters, Marie, Judith, Susanne and Louise. All were brought up as Protestants. In spite of this, the charities of Lyon did not in the end acquire Claudine Turquet's fortune. Louis Turquet long outlived his mother's executors, and by 1618 there was no means of enforcing the condition of her will.[9]

The income from his mother's estate must have been useful to Louis Turquet in his exile in Geneva. We do not know how he lived there. Apparently he had no employment, for he would complain of his 'long leisure', his 'enforced idleness'.[10] As a friend of Beza, he would naturally enjoy a certain repute, but evidently he did not involve himself deeply in the affairs of the city. Geneva was not his home, and he never became a citizen of it. He was forty years old when he came to it. He clearly regarded it as a place of temporary exile until he could return to France, 'de laquelle je suis nay humble et dévot subject',[11] and work for the reform of Church and state. Meanwhile he made occasional visits. He was at Lyon early in 1579 and he published a book there in 1580. But such visits were never long, and he felt safer in Geneva. The danger was brought home to him in or about 1586 when he had again ventured into France. That was the time when the Holy League was gathering force at Lyon and Protestants lived in fear of fresh massacres. 'I was obliged', Louis Turquet afterwards wrote, 'to abandon my house and flee from the fury of the League, and follow the fortune and adventures of Henri de Bourbon, then King of Navarre.'[12] He evidently returned to Geneva, where we find him in 1591. Only when Henri of Navarre was established firmly on the throne would he return permanently to France.

While living in Geneva, Louis Turquet occupied himself with literary work. Since he had published nothing before his first flight from Lyon in 1572, it is probable that he wrote for money. His son would recall sympathetically his father's difficult life and the misfortunes which he had stoically borne.[13] He no doubt referred to his exile; but he may also have been recalling his straitened circumstances. Mayerne certainly regarded poverty as a great misfortune, to be avoided by all means. Louis Turquet's first publications were translations of popular works of philosophy and morality: by the Spanish humanists Antonio de Guevara and Juan Luís Vives, and by the Hermetic philosopher Henry Cornelius Agrippa who had lived for a time in Lyon.[14] In 1586 he published his best-known work, *The General History of Spain*, a massive compilation from Spanish, Italian and Latin writers. This was composed, he tells us, 'in the mountains of Savoy', perhaps when he was staying with his Piedmontese cousins, the Pournas de la Piemente, the only relations with whom his family remained in touch.[15] He describes it as the first product of his pen, so it had evidently lain long in manuscript. He now dedicated it to Henri de Navarre. These translations were popular and would be reprinted: his *History of Spain* would afterwards be translated into English and recommended to Protestant readers as a sounder introduction to the subject than the famous work of the Jesuit Juan de Mariana, from which, however, it included extracts. Afterwards Louis Turquet would write a continuation of it, but this would not be published;[16] nor would his translations of the late Roman history of Ammianus Marcellinus and of the work on the decorative arts that Giorgio Vasari prefixed to his *Lives of the Painters*. This last work was completed and dedicated to François de Roaldès, a distinguished scholar who taught law at the University of Cahors; but Roaldès died in 1589 and this may have frustrated the publication. The manuscript, however, unlike that of Ammianus, survives. It was to have results to which we shall come.[17]

Between his first arrival in Geneva and his appearance before the public as a writer, Louis Turquet assumed, or resumed, the name of Mayerne. He called himself Louis de Mayerne-Turquet,[18] and his son would be known formally as Theodore de Mayerne-Turquet. Informally, however, Theodore would gradually shed the unwelcome surname. Once he had established his nobility and settled in England, he would use only the form 'Theodore de Mayerne'. The form 'Theodore Turquet de Mayerne', generally imposed on him by later writers, was never used either by him or by his contemporaries.[19]

Unlike his father, Theodore de Mayerne would always remain devoted to Geneva, the city of his birth and childhood. Although he loved France, and always spoke of it as his own country, he knew the inconveniences of living there as a Huguenot. His ultimate loyalty was always to the cosmopolitan city of refuge, the capital of French Protestantism outside France. He was also devoted to his father, and to the principles which his father had instilled into him. Perhaps he was less theologically convinced than his father. He was, after all, born and baptised a Protestant: he had not been through the agony of conversion or the fire of persecution. Calvinism was to him not theological truth – he never showed any interest in its doctrines – but a sacred tradition: sacred because of his respect, indeed veneration, for his father, who had tested it and to whom, all his life, he would remain devoted. It was also a moral discipline. Both Louis Turquet and his son were typical Calvinists of their time: proud, patrician, self-sufficient (sometimes intolerably self-sufficient), even closet republicans – the type described by their friend, the Huguenot hero-poet Agrippa d'Aubigné, as 'princes qui règnent sur eux-mêmes'.

Born a Calvinist, in Calvin's holy city, Theodore de Mayerne had a good international Calvinist education. He was first sent to school in Geneva, and he kept, all his life, a notebook of his studies there.[20] Then, at the age of fourteen, he went with a tutor to Heidelberg University. He was matriculated there on 2 December 1588, as 'Theodorus Maernius, Genevensis':[21] already, away from his home circle, he had dropped the unwelcome name of Turquet. Heidelberg was a natural choice for a French Huguenot. It was Calvinist and international: half its students were foreign and by far the greater number of those were French. The Palatinate, under its Calvinist princes, was culturally a Protestant extension of France, like Geneva; and the University of Heidelberg, under the rule of the reforming administrator John Casimir, who ruled in the name of his young nephew Frederick IV, was as attractive to Huguenots for secular studies as the Academy of Geneva for Calvinist theology.

Mayerne did not study medicine at Heidelberg. Nor would he have learned there the 'chemical medicine' which he would afterwards expound. Indeed, the medical faculty at Heidelberg had recently been dominated by the great opponent of Paracelsianism, the Swiss theologian, philosopher and physician Thomas Erastus. Theodore studied 'philosophy', that is, the course of 'liberal arts' which students took before proceeding to work in one of the three 'higher faculties' of theology, medicine and law.[22] This course lasted four years. Mayerne stayed the full four years at Heidelberg, but did not take any degree: the degree of bachelor of arts was abolished by John Casimir while he was studying there.[23] However, it was presumably at Heidelberg that he laid the foundation of his wide general culture and his familiarity with the classical languages and literature: for he knew Greek as well as Latin and liked to show his knowledge in an elegant, humanist style. Even in medical diagnosis and prescription he would not forbear to quote his favourite classical poets.

Mayerne left Heidelberg in 1591. While there, he had given proof of his learning and precocity by writing a book. It was a guidebook to France, Italy, Germany and Spain, containing details of roads, stages, distances, an account of 'the most famous fairs in all Europe', and a treatise on the currencies of the different countries. His fond father had encouraged and helped him to write it, and now, on his return to Geneva, he pressed him to publish it. It was published at Geneva in 1591, when Mayerne was still only eighteen years old.[24] Although a juvenile work, compiled almost entirely from books, it proved remarkably successful and was reprinted at least ten times in the next sixty years.[25] It was one of the earliest European guidebooks, and – in the opinion of Sir William Osler – one of the best.[26] Mayerne dedicated the book to his cousin, Jean Pournas, seigneur de la Piemente – one of his Piedmontese rela-tions. In the preface he explained his interest by reference to the travel enforced by religious persecution: he had been forced to travel, he remarked, even in his mother's womb.

But whatever literary ambitions his father may have entertained for him, Mayerne was resolved, from his earliest years, to be a physician. 'I sucked the milk of medicine in my cradle,' he would afterwards write, 'nor could any advice from parents or friends ever divert my mind to any other studies.'[27] He also knew what kind of medicine he would study. A casual note accidentally reveals that already, in Geneva, when he returned from Heidelberg, if not before, Mayerne was acquainted, through his parents, with the man who was to have the greatest influence on him and to determine the course of his intel-lectual and professional life. This note, in the register of the cathedral of St Pierre at Geneva, records the baptism, on 14 December 1591, of Philippe, third son of Louis and Louise Turquet. The child does not seem to have survived long: at least we never hear of him again; but the baptismal register records the name of his godfather, whom we thus know to have been, by then, an intimate of the family. This man was Joseph du Chesne.[28]

Joseph du Chesne, known to the learned as Quercetanus and later, in society and diplomacy, as Sieur de la Violette, is a famous figure in the history of chemical medicine. A man of quite extraordinary versatility – friends and enemies alike would describe him as Proteus[29] – he was a prolific and controversial writer whose works would be reprinted for a century after his death and read and quoted throughout Europe. His influence on Mayerne's career was so important that some account of him must be given.

His enemies were only too ready to provide one. Over forty years after du Chesne's death, Gui Patin, dean of the Medical Faculty of Paris, the scourge of all chemists, apothecaries, Paracelsians and other medical heretics, gave to his friend Dr Spon of Lyon a lapidary pen-portrait of him. Du Chesne, he said, was a notorious charlatan, a monster, a gallows-bird, who in his lifetime had killed many men with his drugs. He was killing still more after his death 'by the miserable writings which he has left under his name' but which had really been written for him 'by other doctors and chemists here and there'. An ignoramus, an impostor, a drunkard, he had begun as a mere journeyman-banker in Armagnac, a poor country notorious as the breeding-ground of charlatans, but he had afterwards 'passed in Paris, and especially in the court, for a great doctor because he had picked up some chemistry in Germany'.[30] However, we need not take the views of Gui Patin too seriously: this was his normal style. A man who was employed by Henri IV in delicate diplomatic business, who was patronised by the most learned and cultivated of German princes, and who was a close friend of the great scholar Isaac Casaubon,[31] can hardly have been either graceless or ignorant. The only true statements in Patin's tirade are that du Chesne was a Gascon and had 'picked up some chemistry in Germany'.

Du Chesne travelled in Germany, as Paracelsus and many of his disciples had done, as an army surgeon. He soon became a convert and applied Paracelsian cures to gunshot wounds. In one of his works he reveals that he spent ten months in Cologne, studying medicine with the city physician, Theodor Birckmann. Birckmann was an enthusiastic Paracelsian and the chief publisher, at that time, of Paracelsian books.[32] Du Chesne then visited Heidelberg and Kassel (or Cassel), and was patronised by the Landgrave of Hesse and other princes. In his travels he was accompanied by a young man, Johann Heinrich Cherler, the son of a school-teacher in Basel, who, du Chesne says, 'was always a *fidus Achates* to me and worked with me as an assistant in my spagyric cell'.[33]

His German experiences were of great importance to du Chesne. Sixteenth-century Germany was thoroughly penetrated and quickened by heresy. It was also the great centre of European technology. Paracelsian doctrines, which provided a philosophy for the mining engineer and the artisan as well as for the surgeon and apothecary, had a natural appeal there, and German princes and statesmen, facing practical problems, often turned with relief from the theorists of established universities to these empirical enthusiasts. At the end of the century, du Chesne would give a long list of the princes who had patronised his 'spagyric' art: the emperor Rudolf II, Sigismund King of Poland, Charles IX of Sweden, Heinrich Julius Duke of Brunswick, Ferdinand Duke of Bavaria, Maurice of Hesse, the princes of Anhalt, and others.

In 1572 du Chesne decided to improve his qualifications by seeking a university degree. He chose Basel. Perhaps he was influenced by his companion Cherler;[34] but in any case Basel, which had one of the most advanced medical faculties of Europe, was an obvious choice. Protestant but liberal, it was still the city of Erasmus, open to new ideas; and by now Paracelsian ideas, purged of their original crudity, were being received there and discussed together with the revived and reformed Aristotelianism of Padua.[35] Theodor Zwinger, the dominant professor and now rector of the university, was a recent convert to Paracelsus; Pietro Perna, an immigrant from Italy, was publishing Paracelsian texts. In 1571 the greatest continuator of Paracelsus, 'Severinus the Dane', had come to Basel, where he published a digest of Paracelsus's work.[36] Du Chesne took his doctorate there in 1573. Two years later he published his first book, defending Paracelsian ideas on metals and metallic cures. He would not swear to everything Paracelsus had written, he said – he was critical of his theology – but had not Erasmus praised Paracelsus? Many of his works were surely 'almost divine', and posterity could never admire them enough. His ideas were not novel, for they had been foreshadowed by Hermes Trismegistus, Geber, Lull, Arnold of Villanova: they were part of the wisdom of the ancients, hidden from the vulgar but known to the elect, and now recovered. Du Chesne's *devise* was a winged solar divinity rising out of a newly opened tomb, and the inscription *Omnibus sed Paucis luceo*: I shine to all, but only for some. He dedicated his book to Theodor Birckmann, his initiator into Paracelsianism, and to Severinus, its modern commentator.

After taking his doctorate at Basel, du Chesne returned to France, and at once, by his controversies, his publications, and his dashing lifestyle, became famous. He was *Alchymistarum Coryphaeus*, the prince of alchemists. Having married a rich wife, he became a landed seigneur with noble titles. He was physician to the king's brother, the Duc d'Alençon. Then he moved to Geneva and, like his friend Louis Turquet, committed himself to the cause of the Huguenot King of Navarre. By 1591, when he stood godfather to Philippe Turquet, he was an important public figure in Geneva. He too was a friend of Beza, who would be godfather to his son as he had been to Theodore Turquet. Soon he would be a member of the Petit Conseil, the executive of the republic, active in its politics and in the Huguenot cause; but for the moment we will stop at the date we have reached, 1591.

In addition to his busy life as a physician, a controversialist and a politician, du Chesne was a poet. He was an admirer – one of the earliest admirers – of Guillaume Saluste, Sieur du Bartas, a Gascon and a Huguenot like himself, whose long biblical and Platonic poem on the Creation of the World would be so popular among Protestants throughout Europe. When the first book of du Bartas's poem was published in 1578, the only tributary verses in it came from du Chesne, and soon afterwards du Chesne would himself try his hand on the same theme. His long poem 'The Great Mirror of the World' is similarly biblical and Platonic. It is also Paracelsian: in it, man is a microcosm of the universe, which is the macrocosm; he is governed by the correspondences between the two; and the functional elements in Nature are reduced to the three Paracelsian 'principles' of salt, sulphur and mercury.

Du Chesne's prose writings were both philosophical and practical. As a philosopher he attacked Aristotle on the origin of metals, defended alchemy against all its detractors, and interpreted the ailments of the body, physical and psychosomatic, by its macrocosmic correspondences. In practice he drew on his experience as an army surgeon. Against the barbarous amputations and cauterisations of the time he advocated lenitive chemical therapy and 'clean' remedies.

Such was Joseph du Chesne, the famous Quercetanus, who seems, in retrospect (for there is more to come), to have supplied a role model for his young protégé Theodore Turquet.[37] However, when that protégé moved on from Heidelberg, he did not follow du Chesne to Basel. In 1572, the year of the massacre of St Bartholomew, du Chesne, as a firm Huguenot, may well have thought it safer to attend a Swiss university. In 1591 the position in France was different. Henri III, the last Valois king, had been assassinated in 1589. The King of Navarre was now rightful King of France, though he would still have to fight for Paris against the army of the Catholic League. If Mayerne, like du Chesne, was to seek royal patronage, there were obvious advantages in seeking his doctorate in France. In the circumstances, that could not be in Paris. The natural choice would be the university of the south, in Huguenot Languedoc, protected by the King of Navarre: Montpellier.

By the 1590s the University of Montpellier had a long history behind it. Its medical school had been famous in the Middle Ages, for its position on the edge of the Pyrenees had enabled it to draw on the resources of the Muslims and Jews of Spain. In the fifteenth century it had declined, but more recently it had been revived by the patronage of the French kings. In 1498 four royal chairs had been founded there, and Montpellier in return supplied several doctors for the royal court. Far from Paris and the formidable control of

Parisian orthodoxy, Montpellier was open to new ideas. Its professors were appointed by open competition – a very dangerous system in the eyes of the Paris faculty, which kept it at bay until the Revolution. It also drew on an old tradition of pharmacy and botany, perhaps derived from 'Arab' examples; and the Hippocratic tradition had always been preserved in practice even in the times of strictest Galenist orthodoxy. Already in 1537 François Rabelais, Doctor of Montpellier, had lectured there on the *Prognostics* of Hippocrates.

By Rabelais's time Montpellier was drawing students from all France and even from abroad – at least from Protestant areas; for already the new Protestantism of Languedoc was being reflected in the university. The most famous teacher at Montpellier in the middle of the century, Guillaume Rondelet, was a native of the town, who had studied in Paris but who had been obliged to return there to avoid religious persecution. Among those who came to Montpellier to study under him or his successors were Felix Platter and the two brothers Bauhin. All these acknowledged a debt to the empirical school of Montpellier, where Galenism ruled in theory but anatomy and botany were studied. Rondelet himself persuaded the king, Henri II, to provide Montpellier with an amphitheatre for anatomy lessons. The teaching of Rondelet bore visible fruit in the botanical works of his pupils Johann Bauhin and Matthieu de Lobel and in the botanical gardens whose creation, indirectly, he would inspire: the garden at his own Montpellier, the first botanical garden in France, which Richer de Belleval would persuade Henri IV to found in 1593; and the great garden at Montbéliard, which his pupil Johann Bauhin would build for the Duke of Württemberg and where du Chesne's friend Cherler would work with him.

Rondelet had died in 1566. In the following years the University of Montpellier had suffered from the wars of religion in France. However, by 1591, when Mayerne returned from Heidelberg to Geneva, the end of those wars was in sight. With the assassination of Henri III in 1589, the Valois dynasty was ended. Henri de Bourbon, the Huguenot King of Navarre, was only kept from the throne of France by the obstinate resistance of the Catholic League, which controlled the city of Paris, and by the military intervention of the King of Spain. Against such enemies the King of Navarre could rely on the support of some foreign princes and of all Huguenots. The exiled French Protestants in Geneva could now return to France in hope of a better future. It was in 1591 that du Chesne returned to France as 'conseiller et médecin ordinaire du roy'. In the same year Louis Turquet once again left Geneva for France. He went to the court of Henri IV to present to the king his plan for the government of France.[38] Before leaving Geneva he offered his services to the Petit Conseil of the city. The Council resolved to recommend the care of their interests to him and to brief him accordingly.[39] With all Huguenot eyes turning towards France and Henri IV, it was natural for Theodore de Mayerne to reject the advice of his friends who urged him to go to Paris,[40] and to seek his medical training in the half-Calvinist University of Montpellier.

Besides, there was the matter of patronage. Thanks to its royal chairs, the University of Montpellier had long enjoyed a special relationship with the Crown of France. Physicians from Montpellier – even Protestant physicians – had already served the Valois kings. They were likely to be even more acceptable to a Bourbon king who was himself both a southerner and a Huguenot. As a Huguenot, Henri IV had naturally employed Protestants as doctors – a Catholic doctor would have been an unnecessary risk for an excommunicated ruler in a time of ideological war – and naturally he had drawn some of them from Montpellier. Such was Nicolas Dortoman or d'Ortoman, a Dutch Protestant from Gelderland who had taken his doctorate in Montpellier in 1572 and had been physician to the king since 1584.[41] Dortoman had chemical interests and wrote about medicinal baths near Montpellier.[42] He was also a man of wide general culture and a formidable member, with Agrippa d'Aubigné, Philippe du Plessis Mornay, Saluste du Bartas and others, of the Academy which Henri de Navarre founded in imitation of that of Henri III in Paris. Such also was Jean Héroard who, though a Huguenot, had been *médecin ordinaire* to Charles IX and Henri III and would live to be *premier médecin* to Louis XIII; he would die in 1627 at the siege of la Rochelle. It was probable that, once established in power, Henri IV would show favour to Montpellier – as he did, endowing it, in 1593, with a chair of anatomy and botany for Richer de Bellevel, the founder of the Jardin des Plantes, and, in 1598, with a chair of surgery and pharmacy, which went to Pierre Dortoman, the nephew of the royal doctor. Clearly, when Louis Turquet was seeking to make his political advice acceptable to Henri IV, there were advantages for his son in study at Montpellier.

Theodore de Mayerne matriculated at Montpellier on 25 October 1592, and was registered as being 'of Geneva'.[43] His *pater*, the supervisor of his work, was Jean Hucher, a distinguished doctor who, like so many of the professors of Montpellier, had himself studied there. He was now the university's chancellor. Mayerne took his bachelor's degree in 1594, his licentiate in 1596. In March 1597, after 'three months of public demonstration in the royal schools and fourteen public examinations', he was admitted doctor of medicine.[44]

Mayerne looked back with pleasure and pride on his years at Montpellier. He learned much there, and would express his gratitude for it. One particularly valuable lesson lay in the easy collaboration of physicians, surgeons and apothecaries. Elsewhere – and particularly in Paris, as he was to discover – the physicians had elevated themselves into a superior caste. They were philosophers, who had studied the ancient authorities. They looked down on such

manual workers as surgeons, who were classed with barbers as mere techni-
cians of the human body, and 'pharmacists' or apothecaries, who merely
mixed drugs as instructed by the physician. But at Montpellier there was far
greater equality and freedom among these three groups. The apothecaries
there were an old established body, of great repute: Edward III of England had
an apothecary royal from Montpellier, just as James I would do. Medical
students not only read the classical works of Arab pharmacology, collected
under the name of Mesuë. They also had practical experience, both in pharmacy and in surgery. Since 1550 the law required that four anatomies be
performed every year. A 'collector' was appointed to gather simples, or herbal
drugs, all through the summer, to illustrate the regular course of botany.

The apothecaries had to pay for their privileges and status. They were not
allowed to escape medical control, as so easily happened in larger cities, where
the grand physicians became the medical advisers of the rich and the uncon-
trolled apothecaries the unauthorised doctors of the poor. In Montpellier the
chancellor or the dean of the university had long been required by law to make
annual visits to the apothecaries' shops in order to ensure that they were
conforming to the rules and were only making up drugs properly prescribed
by the physicians. After 1550 these visits took place twice a year. The doctors
of the faculty also gave lectures to the apothecaries; there were regular meetings, both formal and informal, between the two professions; and the profits
of the apothecaries were made to depend on rules made by the physicians. In
a small, self-contained university town these regulations were more easily
enforced than in a great capital, and Mayerne may easily have learned, in
Montpellier, the need both to work with the apothecaries and to control them:
a need he would afterwards seek to satisfy in London. Certainly, all his life he
would be very friendly with apothecaries and was held in respect by them.[45]

The value of his time at Montpellier would soon be brought home to him
by his experiences in Paris. In the course of his controversy with the Medical
Faculty of Paris, which we will soon have to describe, Mayerne would contrast
the theoretical medicine, and the professional *snobisme*, of the Parisian
doctors with the practical, unconstrained teaching at Montpellier. There, he
would write, he had not been taught *ex cathedra*, or by reading commentaries,
but by visiting the sick, touching and questioning them while still a pupil:
'I learned through the dangers of the citizens and by practice among the
dead.' The physicians of Paris had accused him of degrading their profession
by manual work and so confounding the jealously distinguished ranks of the
medical profession. It was beneath the dignity of a doctor, they believed, 'to go
down himself to the furnace or to handle drugs'. But to Mayerne this was the
very substance of a doctor's life. He never made or prescribed any medicine
except after personal study and labour: 'delicately manicured hands, trailing

silken robes, shrink from soot, coal, mud; but the reward of this squalor (as you think it) is understanding, whereas your fastidious pomp leads only to reputation; of which the former leads to true knowledge, the latter to ignorance'.[46] To Mayerne, this was the distinction between the medical teaching of Montpellier and Paris.

By the time when Mayerne was locked in controversy with the doctors of Paris, he was known as a 'chemical doctor' – that indeed was a great part of his offence – and we naturally ask how much of his 'chemical' doctrine he owed to the teaching of Montpellier. At first sight the evidence, on this subject, is negative. The professors of medicine at Montpellier, in his time, do not seem to have included any known Paracelsians or iatrochemists. Nor did Mayerne ever ascribe any of his chemical ideas to them. The university drew its professors largely from its own body, occasionally from the rest of France. But iatrochemistry was still, in the 1590s, relatively little known in France, and those who professed it had almost invariably discovered it in Germany or German Switzerland. Where it was known in France, it was highly controversial. Therefore, if it had appeared in Montpellier, we should expect to have heard of it. On the other hand it is certain that Mayerne emerged from his studies at Montpellier with a strong interest in chemical medicine, and that he proclaimed this interest at Montpellier without, apparently, affronting the medical faculty.

The proof of this is to be found in the theses which he defended for his degree at Montpellier.[47] In 1596, when supplicating for the degree of bachelor of medicine, he offered the question 'whether chemical remedies are better than those commonly used?'; and answered it affirmatively. In his answer he quoted the *Paramirum* of Paracelsus and defended Paracelsus's doctrine of the three principles as being consistent with orthodoxy. Admittedly, Paracelsus seemed to affront the doctrines of Hippocrates and Galen, and some might suppose (said Mayerne) that he differs fundamentally from them. 'But I believe that he is saying either the same thing, or something analogous to it, only concealed by different words.'[48] When he was examined for his doctorate, in February 1597, Mayerne showed his chemical interests even more clearly. He then put forth a series of 'assertiones medicae', divided under the headings of anatomy, pathology and therapy, chemistry, and surgery.[49] The eighteen chemical propositions are all clearly Paracelsian. They include such purely Paracelsian assertions as that 'the elements of all things are salt, sulphur and mercury'; that 'every metal can be made potable'; that 'sulphur hardens and mercury softens metal'; that 'the essence of purgatives is in tinctures'; that 'salt added to any extract increases its strength'; that 'whatever purges, does so by reason of the salt in it'; that 'the essence of metals is in *croci*'. These propositions were submitted to Jean Varandé, a Huguenot from Nîmes who had himself studied at Montpellier and then taught at the Academy of Nîmes before coming back, as professor, to Montpellier.[50] Varandé was not a chemical doctor. He opposed chemical theories, dismissed Paracelsus as 'fumosus ille philosophus',[51] and – last proof of orthodoxy – was highly praised by Gui Patin.[52] Nevertheless, Mayerne obtained his doctorate. With such propositions he certainly would not have received it at Paris.

One conclusion at least seems safe. Even if chemical medicine was not formally or actively taught at Montpellier, at least it was not actively resisted. It is probable that Mayerne's interest in it had been acquired, in the first instance, outside France, possibly in Geneva, possibly in Heidelberg. But as Geneva was a centre of Calvinist orthodoxy rather than medical heresy, and his studies at Heidelberg were classical not medical, it seems most likely that they had been stimulated by du Chesne, who in turn had found his inspiration in Germany. In Montpellier he learned practical medicine: anatomy and pharmacy as well as Galenic doctrines and Hippocratic methods. He learned to work with ready hands and an open mind, to observe, experiment and suspend judgement. He learned, in fact, not to reject the novel 'chemical' ideas which du Chesne had preached and applied in Geneva, but to accommodate them to orthodox practice and judge them by results.

He may also have learned something else. In order to test the claims of iatrochemistry, it was necessary to have access to chemical processes. Montpellier was a centre of the manufacture of colours and varnishes for painting and dyeing: 'vert-de-gris de Montpellier' is the technical name of one of them. It may well have been in the workshops of the university city that Mayerne pursued some of his private studies of chemistry. It may have been there too that his interest in chemistry began its later refinement into an interest in the technology of art.

Finally, we must mention two personal friendships which Mayerne may have either made or renewed at Montpellier. The first was with André du Laurens, who held the chair of medicine there from 1586. Du Laurens was not, it seems, a Huguenot, but he was a personal favourite of Henri IV. Jean Hucher, Mayerne's *pater* at Montpellier, whom he must have known – for he was chancellor of the university at the time and himself a royal doctor – gave du Laurens the credit for persuading the king to found the new chairs of anatomy and botany in the 1590s. In 1598 du Laurens would become *médecin ordinaire du roi* and, as such, would prove a useful ally to Mayerne in Paris, as we shall see.

The second of these two friendships was with a much greater man who, at that time, was Mayerne's fellow-citizen of Geneva and who would afterwards be his fellow-courtier and patient, first in Paris, then in London. This was Isaac Casaubon, the prince of European scholars, the Erasmus of his age. It is probable that Casaubon knew Mayerne in Geneva, for he too was the son of a persecuted Huguenot and had been born – fourteen years before him – in the city of refuge. From 1578 to 1596 Casaubon had lived in Geneva, and for most of that time he had held the chair of Greek in the Academy. He was also a close friend of Beza. It is therefore probable that he already knew Mayerne's family. Certainly, by 1608 Casaubon could describe Mayerne as an old friend, 'veteri amicitia . . . coniunctum'.[53] In 1596, when the University of Montpellier lured Casaubon from Geneva to be its 'professor of languages and good letters', Mayerne probably witnessed the solemn entry of the famous scholar, who was met by the university regents and city magistrates a mile beyond the gates and led in triumphal procession to take up his chair. Mayerne would have had the chance to attend Casaubon's lectures, and would almost certainly have done so: for he lectured on the text of Hippocrates.

Having taken his doctor's degree at Montpellier, Mayerne went whither the road of patronage naturally led him, to Paris. For now Henri IV was secure in power; and although he had exchanged Paris for a mass, he did not abandon his old co-religionists: indeed, as he admitted, he preferred to trust them about his person. He also, naturally enough, extended his patronage to those who came from the old centre of his power, Languedoc, and to the doctors who had been trained in its university at Montpellier, which had already supplied so many court physicians to his Valois predecessors. Both as a Huguenot and as a doctor of Montpellier, Mayerne might rationally hope for favour at the Bourbon court. He might also expect enmity from the Catholic doctors of Paris, who greatly resented this heretical influx from the south. Fortunately he had a friend already established in Paris, in a position to protect him: his controversial friend from Geneva, Joseph du Chesne.

3

Paris, 1598–1601

We left Joseph du Chesne in 1591, when he was appointed *médecin par quartier* – a physician serving the king for three months of the year – to Henri IV. In the following five years, while he presumably visited Paris for part of the year, he also served the king as diplomatic agent extraordinary in Switzerland. He carried personal messages from the king to the Protestant cantons, assuring them of French support and urging them to preserve their defensive alliance with the republic of Geneva. He was sent to explain to them the political motives of the king's abjuration and to assure them that it entailed no change in French policy: Protestant or Catholic, the French crown would always protect the Protestant cantons against their immediate enemies, the Catholic cantons and the Duke of Savoy, and against the patron of both, the King of Spain. He was also sent by the French ambassador in Switzerland on a secret mission to the Duke of Savoy.

The language of Henri IV's letters shows that the king valued du Chesne highly. The relations between the king and his envoy were confidential, personal and direct.[1] However, in 1596 du Chesne abandoned his diplomatic activity. In that year he became involved in an unfortunate private scandal. His relations with a well-born French *émigrée* in Geneva were suspected; he was brought to trial; and though acquitted by the court, he found it prudent to leave the holy and censorious city. He now established himself in Paris, performed his duties as royal doctor, and acquired a large and fashionable private practice. In this he was greatly helped by yet another unorthodox Huguenot doctor from Geneva, whom he had probably known before, for their interests were very similar. This was Jean Ribit, Sieur de la Rivière, who now held the key position of *premier médecin du roi*. He was to prove a valuable friend both to du Chesne and to Mayerne. To him, more than to any other man, Mayerne would owe his public career and his lasting medical philosophy.

Jean Ribit, like Mayerne, had been born in or near Geneva, the son of a Huguenot refugee. His family had previously lived in Faucigny in Savoy, but in the 1530s at least three members of it had emigrated to avoid religious persecution. One of these *émigrés*, Jean Ribit the elder, was a Greek scholar who in 1540 succeeded his close friend Conrad Gesner as Professor of Greek in the Academy of Lausanne. He afterwards exchanged the chair of Greek for that of Theology, but the religious disputes in Lausanne caused him to resign his chair in 1559, to become rector of the College of Geneva. In his last years he moved to France, to the Huguenot centre of Orléans, where he died, as Professor of Biblical Exegesis, in 1564. This elder Jean Ribit's brother Helenus became a lawyer in Geneva, and another member of the family, Hippolyte Ribit, worked as a goldsmith in the city. Jean Ribit the physician was probably the son of Jean Ribit the hellenist. He was born about 1546 and was educated at Geneva, probably in the college of which his father was regent. Like his father, and like Mayerne, he became a fluent classical scholar; then, again like Mayerne, he turned to medicine and was attracted to Paracelsian 'iatrochemistry'.[2]

Where Jean Ribit studied medicine we do not know. We only know that his studies began in France, and that at one time he attended the lectures of Giovanni Argenterio in Turin. This must have been between 1566 and 1571. Piedmont in the reign of Emmanuel Philibert, Duke of Savoy, was a thriving centre of medical study. Piedmontese doctors were found throughout Europe; the court at Turin was a centre of alchemical experiments; and Argenterio had the reputation of being an open-minded innovator interested in chemical medicine. Whether Ribit took a doctor's degree in Turin we do not know, for the records of the university do not survive. It appears that he travelled extensively in Italy and France but, at this time, avoided Germany. He may have travelled further afield. It is said that he became a Roman Catholic, but if so it was a transient phase. The plain fact is that we have no trace of him until 1589 when we find him travelling – perhaps returning – from Genoa to the Protestant court of Henry de Navarre at Nérac. By that time he was a settled, if somewhat sceptical, Protestant, known to and respected by Catherine de Bourbon, the resolutely Protestant sister of the king. In October 1589 she recommended him to one of the most famous and turbulent of her brother's Huguenot companions-in-arms, Henri de la Tour d'Auvergne, Vicomte de Turenne.

Turenne was the Huguenot grandee *par excellence*: warrior, political adventurer, over-mighty subject, wielding anarchical baronial power, but at the same time a cultivated man of the Renaissance, a great patron, and a convinced Calvinist. He had been converted to Calvinism when young and was now a powerful chief among the Calvinist noblemen who dominated and divided the Huguenot party. In 1581 he had gone to the Netherlands, with the tacit approval of the Catholic King of France, to support the Protestant revolution against the King of Spain. He had there been wounded and captured, and had spent eighteen months in captivity as the private prisoner of the Duke of Parma. Ransomed and released, he had returned to France and to the Huguenot capital of Nérac, only to encounter fresh misfortunes. A rival attempted to assassinate him on the banks of the River Garonne, and although he escaped, it was with a shot from an arquebus in the buttock. Old and new wounds continually troubled him and prevented him from taking part in Henri IV's campaign of 1589. It was in these circumstances that he accepted the advice of Catherine de Bourbon and invited Jean Ribit, now settled in France as Sieur de la Rivière, to become his personal physician.

La Rivière remained with Turenne for five years. He soon found that this entailed further travel abroad. Late in 1590, Henri IV, now legally King of France but still opposed by the Catholic League and its Spanish patrons, sent Turenne on an extensive diplomatic mission, first to England, then to Germany, to secure the military and financial support of Protestant rulers. La Rivière accompanied him, both to care for his patron's health and for his own purposes; for, as du Chesne afterwards wrote, he was 'not content with vulgar medicine' but wished to explore the new medicine of Protestant countries.[3] In England, indeed, he had few opportunities, for there he fell seriously ill. But early in 1591 he was in Germany with Turenne, whose diplomatic duties led him, and la Rivière, to the courts of Dresden, Berlin, Heidelberg, Kassel and Stuttgart, and to the free city of Frankfurt. This was Paracelsian country: the Electors of Saxony and the Palatinate, the Landgrave of Hesse and the Duke of Württemberg were all patrons of chemical doctors, and la Rivière made full use of his opportunities. He discussed medical topics, personally and by correspondence, with the most famous German doctors, and he acquired new patients among the foreign ambassadors with whom Turenne had to deal. One of the ambassadors whom la Rivière attended was Sir Horatio Pallavicino, the Genoese émigré who had come to England to become Queen Elizabeth's financier, and who had now travelled from England with Turenne as her ambassador extraordinary to the German courts. Another was Philippe Canaye de Fresne, scholar, lawyer, traveller, 'the star of French genius' as du Chesne would call him,[4] a convert to Protestantism who believed, above all, in religious unity and was the closest friend of Isaac Casaubon. Canaye de Fresne was now Henri IV's representative in Germany, and Turenne would naturally work in concert with him. Both Pallavicino and Canaye de Fresne were treated by la Rivière for gout, and both found his treatment excellent: Pallavicino also took the opportunity to obtain from him a *consilium*, or prescription, for his old mother in Genoa. Among the German doctors with whom la Rivière corresponded while in Germany were two of the most distinguished of German humanists, Caspar Peucer, the son-in-law of Melanchthon, and Joachim Camerarius II, the son of Melanchthon's friend and biographer. Peucer had been physician to Augustus, Elector of Saxony, but had been the victim of theological intrigue and had spent many years in prison, until released by the pressure of other German princes. He was now physician to the Prince of Anhalt-Dessau. Camerarius was one of a distinguished dynasty of humanist scholars and public servants in Nuremberg. His father had been famous as a reformer and a classical scholar; his son would be the last statesman of that Protestant international which was to founder in the Thirty Years War.

La Rivière's correspondence with these German doctors, which only survives because it was obtained and preserved by Mayerne, is of interest for several reasons. It shows the world in which la Rivière moved. It shows his attitude towards Paracelsianism, which was the attitude of the new generation of French 'iatrochemists', indebted to Paracelsus, but also critical of him. And it sheds light on the attitude of la Rivière's most famous disciple, Mayerne.

The most interesting of these letters is one which la Rivière wrote from Dresden on 17 March 1591, soon after his arrival in Germany. It was addressed to Caspar Peucer. La Rivière began by saying that he had been very ill while in England – indeed had nearly died there – and that he was still in a weak state of health, so that it was difficult for him to address himself to the purpose for which he had come 'to this part of Germany, so fertile of learned and religious men'. Then he proceeded to explain that purpose. He was conscious, he said, of his loss in never having visited Germany before. He had studied in medical schools of France and Italy, and there laid the foundations of his medical knowledge. Then he had travelled through most of Europe 'to confirm the teaching of theory by the practice of medicine'. But in all that time he had, regrettably, avoided Germany. This was, on the face of it, a remarkable omission, and it needed explanation. The explanation la Rivière now gave is revealing. Hitherto, he says, he had been deterred from visiting Germany, in part, at least, because of 'the crowd of spagyrics who claimed Paracelsus as the leader of their sect'. He had had experience of these spagyrics in France, where they had insinuated themselves into all the best cities, into the houses of noblemen, even into the royal court. Once admitted, they had made themselves notorious by promising quick and easy cures for all diseases. If these cures proved successful, they then trumpeted their success abroad through a host of fellow-quacks; but more often, 'instead of cures, they offer only words, of which they have ready supply'. They refuse to argue with orthodox medical doctors, whose basic principles they reject, and they boast that they have carried the art of healing to a point which the Galenists regard as criminal. To their master Paracelsus they ascribe a series of almost miraculous cures.

In spite of all this, la Rivière is eager to show that he is not prejudiced against Paracelsianism. He has read the famous refutation of Paracelsus by Thomas Erastus, he says, but is not convinced by Erastus's arguments. Nevertheless, 'I must candidly admit that I never met a Paracelsian who was a learned and honest man: everywhere I have found them garrulous impostors.' Consequently, he now puts to Peucer a series of questions. First, are the stories that are told of Paracelsus's cures really true? Secondly, if he really effected those wonderful cures, was it by the application of his distinctive methods or was it by chance? Thirdly, has any of his numerous disciples in Germany achieved comparable results? Finally, what is the considered opinion of reputable German doctors about that whole tribe? For they surely must have thought the matter out, since Paracelsus himself lived in Germany and wrote in German, and it is from Germany, as from a Trojan horse, that all these new heroes have spilled out over Europe – or at least over the richer parts of it: for, like the Jesuits, they settle only where there is money to be made . . . Then, as if he felt that he had gone too far, la Rivière checked himself. He realised, he wrote, that established theories can easily be wrong, and that those who are trained in academic medicine often reject remedies which do not satisfy their reason even though in practice they may prove effective. For instance, there are sympathetic remedies, such as the famous weapon-salve. This was an ointment which, if rubbed upon the bloodstained weapon that had caused a wound, healed the wound 'even if the patient and medicine are many miles apart, as I have often witnessed'. So, in his perplexity, he asks for advice from one who, by common consent, among all the learned physicians and astrologers of Germany – for Peucer had written, among other things, on Divination – shines out like the moon among the meaner beauties of the night. As one cultivated humanist writing to another, he knew that he could safely end his letter with a delicate literary trope.[5]

A few months later, when la Rivière was in Frankfurt, he began his correspondence with Camerarius in Nuremberg. This time, his purpose was different: he wished to engage Camerarius in discussion about chemical medicine. In particular, he wanted to know to what extent and in what form antimony was used by respectable doctors in Germany. He explained that he was at that time prescribing chemical medicines for Turenne. In the course of this correspondence he described his own experience with antimony and the uses to which he had seen it put in Italy and France. In Italy, he said, he had watched the operations of Argenterio. In France he had seen a secret preparation of antimony used against syphilis by a respectable doctor whom he knew well; but he added, 'I myself have never used it, for I only follow safe courses, known and approved by many.'[6]

Another subject which la Rivière raised in his correspondence with the German doctors was of more immediate political concern. In the critical posture of affairs in Europe in 1591, when the fortunes of France, and indeed (as Camerarius agreed) of Germany too, hung on the survival of Henri IV, la Rivière, like many others, dreaded the possibility of a political assassination. Such fears were rational enough in the years which had seen the assassination of William of Orange, of the Duke and Cardinal de Guise, and of Henri III of France, as well as repeated plots against the life of Queen Elizabeth and Henri IV. Whenever any great man died, poison was suspected – especially if he was the enemy of the King of Spain or the Jesuits – and the ambassadors and physicians of Henri IV worked in concert to protect their master against such a fate.[7] La Rivière therefore consulted his German colleagues about effective antidotes to poison. A useful reply came from Sigismund Kolreuter, the physician of the Duke of Saxony, who, like la Rivière, had studied in Turin. Kolreuter supplied details of a famous powder which was proof against all poisons and had been sold to the duke, for a great price, by an Italian monk – the same man (it was said) who had invented the weapon-salve. The powder was now known as *pulvis Saxonicus*, the Saxon powder, and the duke had tested it thoroughly, swallowing the venom of toads, snakes and other supposedly poisonous creatures and then counteracting it with this infallible antidote.[8] The antidote may, however, have been less effective than it seemed; for snake-poison, as the ancients knew well, is not poisonous when drunk: to be effective, it requires puncture.[9] A few years later, this subject was evidently still on la Rivière's mind. For Camerarius, writing in 1594 to congratulate him on his appointment as *premier médecin du roi*, expressed his horror on hearing that the enemies of France, having achieved nothing by open war, were now seeking to destroy the king by methods that were forbidden and detested even among the heathen. Then, at la Rivière's request, he listed the best prophylactics known to him. He began by reminding la Rivière of the *pulvis Saxonicus* 'which I was, I think, the first to communicate to my friends, a few years ago'. But the best antidote, he now believed, was a mixture of quince and lemon juice. The late King of Sweden, he added (referring presumably to John III, who had died in 1593), had used extract of gentian in some liquid which could be taken when there was any suspicion of poison. Some philosophers believed that precious stones, used as amulets, could counteract the effects of poison, but Camerarius himself doubted this. Next year, la Rivière was again consulting Camerarius on the same subject. Had Camerarius, he asked, any rare or excellent information of prophylactics and antidotes against poison? What was this *Ostrutium*, or this *Cruciata minor*, of which he had heard? Was it possible to obtain some of that Saxon powder? La Rivière's studies were now devoted entirely to this urgent problem – though he complained that he had little leisure for study among the crowd of courtiers.[10]

The character of la Rivière which emerges from this correspondence is elusive, because it does not fit easily into our definitions. Clearly, he was a 'chemical doctor'. He believed in chemistry and used chemical remedies, some of which came from Paracelsus. We also know, from a remark by the Duc de Sully, that he believed in astrology. He accepted the Hermetic doctrine of sympathies and antipathies, and believed in the efficacy of the weapon-salve. In general, he thought that 'experience' was more important than 'reason', and he allowed that the irrational discoveries of the empirics could be right and the most rational academic theories wrong. All these tenets put him in line with Paracelsus, and we have seen that, in the controversy between Paracelsus and Erastus, he preferred the arguments of Paracelsus. On the other hand he was clearly disgusted by what he had seen of the vulgar Paracelsians in France, with their loud claims and magical panaceas. He resented their oracular pronouncements, their refusal to enter into open discussion or submit to fair tests. Like Bacon, he disliked all claims to secret knowledge or private inspiration. He would only use such medical discoveries as had been openly declared and publicly tested, 'plurimis cognita et plurimis probata'. Essentially he is open-minded, eager to hear both sides, prepared to learn.

He is also a natural sceptic. Like Montaigne, he prefers to suspend judgement. His contemporaries, from all sides, criticised his independence of their categories. The orthodox Galenist doctors of Paris declared him a quack. To Catholics he was a heretic, perhaps an apostate. His fellow-Huguenots deplored his lack of firm conviction. He had little religion, wrote the Huguenot Sully (who must have known him well), although he added that that little inclined more to Protestantism than to Catholicism. The stern Huguenot Agrippa d'Aubigné wrote that la Rivière was a fit doctor for an apostate Huguenot, being at once a good Galenist and a very good Paracelsian, a Catholic for profit and a Huguenot for the salvation of his soul.[11] In a series of letters to la Rivière, Agrippa d'Aubigné implicitly reproved him for his lack of faith, his rejection of supernatural explanation, his disbelief in demoniac possession, his tendency to regard the confessions of witches as delusions and thus 'to change witchcraft from a crime into an illness'. These views seemed to d'Aubigné very reprehensible and frivolous and he wrote to him censoriously of 'vos libertez et gayetez ordinaires' – your habitual liberties and jests.[12] Again they remind us of Montaigne, and lead us forward from the firm convictions of the sixteenth century to the speculative freedom, the 'libertinisme érudit', of the seventeenth.

After a few months in Germany, Turenne had completed his mission. He returned to France at the head of a German army, subsidised by Queen

Elizabeth, for the relief of Henri IV. On his return, Henri IV rewarded him
with a great marriage. In October 1591, in Sedan, he was married to Charlotte,
sister and heiress of Guillaume-Robert de la Marck, Duc de Bouillon and
hereditary ruler of Sedan. Sedan was now a Protestant fortress, standing
conveniently (or inconveniently) on the road to Germany. After his marriage
Turenne was himself created Duc de Bouillon, and his family, famous in
military history, would rule or reign there, as Protestant magnates, until the
Revocation of the Edict of Nantes a century later. From now on, therefore, we
shall refer to him by his new title, as Duc de Bouillon. La Rivière presumably
returned to France with his patron, with whom he remained for another three
years. Then, in 1594, Henri IV's *premier médecin*, the Huguenot Jean
d'Ailleboust, died, and the king, who must have known la Rivière before,
asked Bouillon to release him. Bouillon complied, and for the next eleven
years la Rivière was *premier médecin du roi*.[13]

When Joseph du Chesne finally left Geneva in 1596, and established himself
in Paris, he thus found a medical patron ready to receive him. Both
Huguenots, both from Geneva, both 'chemical doctors', both personally
favoured by the king, la Rivière and du Chesne were natural allies. Moreover,
this natural alliance was consolidated by a common danger. Whether as
immigrants or as Huguenots or as 'chemical' innovators, la Rivière and du
Chesne had to face the jealousy, not to say the open hostility, of the most
powerful medical corporation in France, the Medical Faculty of the University
of Paris.

In order to understand the struggle which we are now to relate, and the
intensity of the passions which it released, we must always remember the
historical context. Henri IV, in retrospect, is 'Henri le Grand', the creator of
the Bourbon monarchy, the unifier of France, the healer of its divisions. But
his subjects did not forget that he had come to the crown through a sharp civil
war, the climax of a generation of ideological struggle. In 1591 he was still
chief of a party, not of a nation, and no community in the nation had received
him more suspiciously, or more conditionally, than the city of Paris. For this
there was some reason. During the long period of disturbance under the last,
wayward Valois kings, when the monarchy seemed unable to preserve unity,
or order, or peace, it was the central institutions of Paris which had preserved
the continuity of government.

These institutions were, above all, the Parlement of Paris, the guardian of
public law; and the university, the guardian of orthodoxy. Throughout those
years the Parlement of Paris maintained its authority as the fearless guardian
of order against anarchy. In consequence it had gained vastly in authority,
prestige and confidence, and it was not prepared tamely to submit to the
ministers of an untried and largely unknown king, who owed his power, at

least in part, to the hazard of war, and who might prove no more satisfactory than his Valois predecessors. The same tenacity had been shown by the University of Paris, which had always expressed and enforced official orthodoxy. In the years of disorder, the Sorbonne, the college of the university that was staffed by theologians, had stood firm against every attempt to weaken the Church. By its influence in the parishes and among the people, it had acquired the power to sanction the massacre of the heretical people or impose apostasy upon a heretical king. The medical faculty – which consisted of all those who had a medical doctorate from Paris and who were resident in the capital as practitioners – had also, in those years, found itself faced by heresy, the heresy of Paracelsus. Its attitude was no less firm. The intransigence of all these institutions had been hardened by the struggles of the time, and their confidence was strengthened by a sense of solidarity and interdependence. To the medical faculty it was convenient that those medical heretics who sought to undermine its orthodoxy and break its monopoly were almost always heretics in religion too; and the Parlement could generally be relied upon to support the united view of the official guardians of spiritual and physical health.

The determination of the medical faculty to resist the new Paracelsian heresy had already been shown fifteen years before the arrival of la Rivière in Paris. At that time the doctrines of Paracelsus were new in France, and were being preached, if at all, only in the provinces outside the power of central authority. Du Chesne, their most active propagandist, had operated in Lyon – and then had retreated to Geneva. Claude Dariot, a Burgundian Huguenot who translated some of the works of Paracelsus, also retreated to Geneva after the massacre of St Bartholomew, although he emerged under Henri IV and became town physician of Beaune. Other Paracelsian adepts, such as those who had so disgusted la Rivière, were no doubt protected by local magnates, more especially by Huguenots; but these, in general, practised their art in profitable obscurity.[14] However, in 1579 one of these empirics had sought to establish himself in Paris. Immediately the guardians of orthodoxy had mobilised their heavy institutional machinery to expel him. This empiric was called Roch le Baillif, and he also, like Jean Ribit, had acquired the territorial title of Sieur de la Rivière: an acquisition which has caused some confusion to historians.[15]

Roch le Baillif was a Norman born at Falaise.[16] He seems also to have been – at least for so long as it was convenient – a Huguenot. Where he had acquired his Paracelsian doctrines we do not know. He does not seem to have studied abroad, and he had no medical degree. He may simply have read the works of du Chesne. When we first hear of him, he is a client of the ancient Breton family of Rohan, the great protectors of Huguenotism in Brittany. It was the Rohan family and its successive heads, Henri the Gouty and Louis the Blind, whom he celebrated, in the text or by dedication, in his early publications. The earliest of these, which appeared in 1577, was an astrological treatise. Next year he published two further tracts. The first was a Paracelsian tract on the antiquities of Brittany – its natural deposits, mineral waters, and its baths which cured (he said) leprosy, gout, dropsy, etc. The second, entitled *Demosterion*, was an avowed attempt to reduce the doctrines of Paracelsianism into three hundred aphorisms. In it, le Baillif declares himself to be 'sectateur, à mon pouvoir, du divin Paracelse' (a follower, as far as I can, of the divine Paracelsus) and quotes – in defence of his argument that there is no fundamental disagreement between Paracelsus and the ancient medical classics – the works of 'ce docte Quercetanus': that is, Joseph du Chesne.[17] Having thus stated his philosophy, and having (it seems) temporarily lost the support of the Rohan family, le Baillif set off in 1578 to Paris, resolved to capture, single-handedly, the citadel of orthodoxy.

The expedition was not a success. The Medical Faculty of Paris was already alarmed by the Paracelsian heresy that had been preached in France by Günther (or Winther) von Andernach (who had been a member of the Paris Faculty of Medicine but who as a Protestant had retired to Basel) and now, more recently, by du Chesne. It was determined to destroy this leaven which was fermenting in the medical world. Le Baillif, who presented himself flamboyantly in Paris as astrologer and chiromancer, 'spagyrist' and 'edelphe' or Paracelsian seer, and who claimed high protection as *médecin ordinaire* of the Duc de Mercoeur (the Catholic rival of the Rohan family in Brittany) and of the king, Henri III, seemed an ideal victim. By expelling him, the doctors of Paris would not only be defending their own monopoly and giving notice to those who might seek to break it: they would also show that they were no respecters of persons. Neither the Catholic Duc de Mercoeur nor the Valois king was to suppose that he could protect those whom the faculty condemned. After some preliminary persecution on other charges, Roch le Baillif was forbidden to practise or lecture in Paris, not being a doctor of the university. Le Baillif ignored the ban, and on 30 April 1579, at the instance of the dean of the faculty, he was hauled before the Parlement of Paris.

The trial was a memorable occasion. The faculty employed three well-known advocates, one of whom, Barnabé Brisson, *avocat du roi*, spoke so eloquently in defence of ancient medicine that the faculty, overcome by emotion, solemnly undertook to give him and his family free, non-Paracelsian medical attention for three generations.[18] On the other side le Baillif had even more distinguished counsel, the famous lawyer-historian Étienne Pasquier, who had made his name defending the university against the Jesuits in 1564. Pasquier would long remember this 'great case of the Paracelsists' which he had pleaded 'for three Thursdays, before a vast crowd of people'.[19] But all

Pasquier's eloquence on behalf of le Baillif was of no avail. On 2 June 1579 the Parlement issued its *arrêt* forbidding le Baillif to practise 'etiam inter volentes' (even among the willing) and ordering him to leave the city under pain of corporal punishment. The dean of the faculty, Henri de Monantheuil, was so pleased with his achievement in ridding the city of 'this plague' that he afterwards caused it to be inscribed on his tomb.[20]

So Roch le Baillif had returned to provincial obscurity in Brittany. The faculty had won, and had thereby established an important precedent. It was a precedent which would be vividly before them in the next reign. However, before we come to the sequel, we may make a few observations about the case of Roch le Baillif.

The essential fact is that Roch le Baillif was a mere crank, a vulgar Paracelsian not to be compared, in intellectual calibre, with Jean Ribit de la Rivière, with whom he has so often been confused, or with Joseph du Chesne, whom he cited, or with Theodore de Mayerne, who would nearly share his fate. Even making all necessary allowances for prejudice, the record of his interrogation does him little credit, and the conclusion is borne out by a reading of his published works. It transpired in the course of these interrogations that le Baillif knew little Latin and no Greek. This, we might think, was venial, and his answer has a certain innocent plausibility. He replied that diseases were not cured in Latin or Greek, that it was enough to understand the matter and know the remedy. Hippocrates and Galen, he admitted, had used Greek, for it was their own language, just as the 'Arabs' had used Arabic; and for the same good reason he used French. However, the fact remained that the technical language of medicine was Latin, and it soon transpired that Le Baillif knew no medicine either. As one of his interrogators observed, in reply to every question he always sang one of his three Paracelsian refrains, viz: of the three principles of salt, sulphur and mercury; of the separation of the pure from the impure; and of the macrocosm and microcosm. He was declared, not unfairly, to be 'a mere ape of Paracelsus'. Michel de Marescot, a distinguished physician who would afterwards serve Henri IV as *médecin ordinaire*, declared roundly that he would be happy to discuss such matters with a learned Paracelsian, but that it was a waste of time to debate 'cum hoc homine plane ignaro' (with this obviously ignorant man). Henri de Monantheuil, the dean who gloried in his expulsion, was also a distinguished scholar. He was a 'modern' in philosophy, a disciple of Ramus, teacher of Jacques-Auguste de Thou, and afterwards professor of mathematics. His opposition cannot be ascribed to mere bigotry. Others went further in denunciation: they alleged that all le Baillif's pretended cures were as bogus as his degree at Caen, which had proved to be false; that he had killed a number of patients, including one of the Rohan family; and that he deserved to be hanged, like the empiric who in 1574 'had killed the late Duc de Bouillon at Sedan with antimony'.[21] They also touched on his religious heresy, describing him as 'ce Luther', and claiming that he had recently been fined 100 livres for eating a veal pasty in Lent.[22]

In 1594 all this was in the past. But the Faculty of Medicine in Paris had not forgotten the episode; many of its members, including the formidable dean Henri de Monantheuil, were still active in its affairs; and when the new king brought in another Sieur de la Rivière – a Huguenot, allegedly a Paracelsian, and certainly a chemical doctor – to Paris as his *premier médecin*, they were naturally alarmed. They were even more alarmed two years later when la Rivière was joined by the most aggressive propagandist of Paracelsianism, also a Huguenot, the oracle of Roch le Baillif: Joseph du Chesne. Finally, next year, matters were made still worse by the arrival of yet another Huguenot Paracelsian immigrant from Geneva, Theodore de Mayerne. For already in 1597, immediately after taking his doctorate at Montpellier, Mayerne was active as a physician in Paris, using chemical medicines.[23] Doubtless it was du Chesne, his old family friend, who had encouraged him to try his fortune in Paris. It was presumably through du Chesne that he then became known to la Rivière and was patronised by him. He became, in effect, third in the apostolic succession of 'chemical doctors' now settled in Paris.

It was not only as immigrants and heretics that la Rivière, du Chesne and Mayerne were distrusted by the Paris faculty. They were objectionable on another count. None of them was a doctor of the University of Paris. We do not know where, if anywhere, la Rivière took his doctorate. Du Chesne was a doctor of Basel, Mayerne of Montpellier. To the Paris faculty, that was perhaps the worst of all. To them Montpellier was a provincial university in the Albigensian, Huguenot south, recently converted into a reservoir of royal doctors by the mere accident of patronage. Montpellier, Gui Patin would exclaim, had been nothing at all until the time of Rondelet – and Rondelet himself was a doctor of Paris 'who owed his learning to our schools'. Indeed, Patin added, Montpellier – 'a stinking marsh of ignorance and impostures' – had been part of France only for three hundred years: 'auparavant ce n'etoit que barbarie' (before that it was utterly barbarous).[24] However, if the lack of a Parisian doctorate was an offence in these immigrants, it also provided the faculty with formal grounds for proceeding against them. It was because he had dared to practise in Paris without such a degree that they had been able to proceed against Roch le Baillif. The same excuse could be invoked against the new heretics, if occasion should arise. At least it could be invoked against Mayerne who, not being a royal doctor, was the weakest of the three.

The occasion soon arose. The exact sequence of events is obscure. Precise dates are missing and cannot be established from the vague and sometimes rhetorical statements of those involved. But it seems that, on arrival in Paris, Mayerne, under the protection of la Rivière and du Chesne, and largely in partnership with them, had set up in private practice and given public lectures and demonstrations in surgery, anatomy and pharmacy. He himself states that he publicly expounded the doctrines of 'Mesuë' – i.e. Arab medicine – to the apothecaries; that he engaged in public disputations; that he dissected human corpses with his own hand, before a crowd of learned observers; and that he successfully compounded his own medicine, accompanied by a personal assistant. In other words he invaded the field of the professors of anatomy and pharmacy, and worked with his hands among surgeons and apothecaries. Among his papers there is a copy of a Latin doctoral speech delivered by 'Johannes Philippus' at the college of SS. Cosmas and Damian, the college of the *chirurgi togati,* or qualified surgeons, in Paris, 'which I composed for him'.[25] If this document goes back to this time, it is further evidence of Mayerne's interest, and interference, in the world of surgery. Almost all his activities could be construed as an invasion of the rights and privileges of the medical faculty of the university.

It happened that the medical faculty, at this time, was dominated by a powerful and aggressive character. This was Jean Riolan, a man of universal knowledge, or claims, who had written much on philosophy, medicine and, in particular, surgery. He was a stout defender of the old medicine against the new, and of the privileged position of doctors of medicine as against mere practising surgeons. He wrote books with such titles as *A Philosophical Defence of the Ancient Dignity of Medicine against the Impudence of Certain Surgeons who wish to be the Equals of the Physicians and Publicly Teach Surgery,* and *A Comparison of the Physician with the Surgeon, to Chastise the Audacity of Certain Surgeons who can neither Speak Well nor be Silent.* He made insulting puns at their expense, calling them not *chirurgi* but *cacurgi.*[26] When Mayerne came to Paris, Riolan was sixty years old and had recently published his compendium of universal medicine (*Universae medicinae compendia*) and his solid textbook on surgery. He could afford to sit back a little in his fame and take his ease. He could do so with more confidence because he had a son, a likely lad, also called Jean, who was now working for his doctorate of medicine in Paris, and who showed all the signs of following in his footsteps – as indeed he very quickly did, as we shall see.

The attack on Mayerne seems to have begun in the earlier part of 1599.[27] Mayerne himself tells us that a crowd of medical enemies, 'more accustomed to brawl than to cure', set upon him and dragged him more than once before the courts. In the presence of a just magistrate, they tried to twist the sense of the law and deprive the people of Paris of his services. Asked the reason for their hostility, they replied that they alone possessed the right of practising in the city, having bought this monopoly by two years' study and 1,500 écus. When Mayerne produced his doctor's certificate from Montpellier granting him licence to practise 'throughout the world', Dr Heron, 'with a blear-eyed man whose name I have forgotten', stuttered in reply, 'Even if you were a doctor of Rome, you could not practise in Paris. Go back to Montpellier and live with your own people'.[28] This is not very precise language, but it suggests that the doctors of Paris sought to secure an order of the Parlement against Mayerne, as they had done against le Baillif in 1580.[29] If so, they were within their legal rights: an *arrêt* of the Parlement of Paris in 1598 confirmed their sole right to grant or withhold, at their discretion, the privilege of teaching and practising medicine in Paris. On the other hand, they might have had some difficulty in a legal contest before the Parlement. They would have had to rely entirely on the formal insufficiency of a degree of Montpellier. Mayerne had not, like le Baillif, given hostages to fortune. He had published nothing. And he was far more learned, in their own kind of learning, than le Baillif. No one could have maintained that he was ignorant of Latin and Greek. No one could have described him as 'the ape of Paracelsus' or 'homo plane ignarus'. If examined, he could have stood up to his examiners. In confidence, as in learning, he could have faced the doctors of Paris.

However that may be, this first attack came to nothing. As Mayerne afterwards wrote, 'while these paid-up doctors were thus pressing upon me, the victorious King Henri IV ordered my name to be inscribed in the register of his doctors, on the recommendation of the unquestioned leader and prince of all living doctors (whatever the foul-mouthed troop of ignorant men may chatter against him), Dr Jean de la Rivière, his Majesty's physician-in-chief. In this recommendation he was seconded by the testimony of the famous Dr du Laurens.' These two leaders of the medical world, Mayerne added, were not themselves doctors of Paris – du Laurens, like himself, was a doctor of Montpellier – but the Paris faculty was obliged to revere them. So the malevolent intrigues of his enemies were eluded 'and for some time the hot fury of that thunderbolt lay hid'.[30]

There were also other reasons why it lay hid. Having appointed Mayerne a royal doctor – he was *médecin ordinaire par quartier* like du Chesne – Henri IV agreed that he should be attached, for a period, to the household of a young cousin of his who, at the age of twenty, was about to set out on a grand tour of Europe. The immediate result of this appointment was that Mayerne was for many months absent from Paris and its medical controversies. The more lasting result was that he acquired a new patron to whom, for forty years, he would be a devoted friend. For the young prince whom he was to accompany was the romantic hero of the Huguenots, one of the last of their great leaders and men of action: Henri de Rohan.

4

The Grand Tour, 1599–1601

Henri de Rohan, whom Mayerne was to accompany on a tour of Europe, had been born in 1579. By his father's death in 1586 he had become, at the age of seven, the head of the oldest and greatest family of Brittany. It was also, by that time, a Huguenot family. In his infancy, Henri de Rohan had been deprived of much of his possessions, for the Catholic League had prevailed in Brittany, where its forces were led by the rival grandee, the Duc de Mercoeur. Consequently Henri de Rohan had been brought up not at the family castle of Blain but in the château of Parc-Soubise in western Brittany, the home of his widowed mother. She was Catherine de Parthenay l'Archevesque, sole heiress of another grand Huguenot family. Her first husband, Charles de Quellenec, Baron du Pont, another Huguenot nobleman from Brittany, had been one of the victims of St Bartholomew. She was also a serious-minded bluestocking and occupied herself, in her successive castles, reading the Greek and Latin classics, writing biblical tragedies, and compiling her family history. As his tutor, the young Rohan had an even more severe Huguenot pastor; and for his health – at least after 1590 – he had the questionable advice of our old friend Roch le Baillif. For this incorrigible opportunist, having served Mercoeur and the League in the days of their success, had somehow contrived to reingratiate himself with Madame de Rohan when the tide turned, and had thus saved himself, as he wrote, 'from the venomous tooth of envious men'. In 1591 he dedicated his last known work to the young Henri de Rohan, and the prefatory poems by his friends imply that he was again living in the Rohan household.[1] However, he died in 1598, a year before Mayerne was deputed to travel in the suite of Henri de Rohan.

From his earliest youth, Rohan had resolved on a life of action, and had prepared himself to play the part. He was abstemious, ambitious, politically acute, avid for military glory. He believed he was born for great things, and made a cult of heroic virtue. His favourite reading was Plutarch's *Lives of the Noble Greeks and Romans* – but he also read Machiavelli and would write a famous treatise of secular political thought. As soon as he was of an age to do so, he took up arms. Though it was then too late to support the Huguenot cause against the League, he supported Henri IV in his war against Spain, and was rewarded for his service by the restoration of lost estates. In 1598 the peace with Spain suspended his military activity. Considering (as he wrote) that his age made him fitter, in time of peace, 'to learn than to serve his country', he proposed to go on a tour not only of Christendom but of the Ottoman empire, and thereby to 'see the diversity of these countries and peoples'.[2] He would not in fact go so far as this. Fortune, he wrote, was envious of his happiness and restricted the scope of his travels; but they were nevertheless extensive. By the late spring of 1599 he was ready to leave. With him were his younger brother Benjamin, afterwards Duc de Soubise, and three or four other young Huguenot noblemen, their friends. One of these was Armand Nompar de Caumont, eldest son and heir of the Duc de la Force.[3] The Caumonts were the leading Huguenot family in Guyenne as the Rohans were in Brittany. Mayerne would afterwards be intimately involved with them too; but at present it was as an attendant upon the Rohan brothers that he was of the party.

The details of the grand tour of the Rohan brothers are recorded for us in an account which Rohan compiled for himself on his return. It is a somewhat spare record, an itinerary rather than a personal diary. It gives no dates, but it describes the route taken, the towns visited and some things of interest seen – fortresses, buildings, important works of art. Occasionally there are personal observations, but generally the work has the dry character of Baedeker rather than the intimacy, or the sensitivity, of Montaigne. Private thoughts are not revealed. Conversations are not recorded. Persons are seldom cited. His companions are never named. Even his brother is never mentioned, far less any of his other companions. There is no reference to Mayerne. However, it is a useful record for our purposes, and its details can sometimes be expanded from other sources.

The party left Paris on 8 May 1599 and travelled, via Reims, to Sedan, the Protestant city of la Rivière's old patron, Rohan's future rival, the Duc de Bouillon. From Sedan they went through Lorraine to Strasbourg, and then, via Worms and Frankfurt, to Heidelberg, the capital of the Calvinist Elector Palatine, who entertained them nobly with hunting, tennis and *courte la bague*. They then visited Mainz and passed, through Württemberg, Bavaria and Tyrol, to Innsbruck and over the Alps to Trent and Venice. With what relief those austere Huguenots escaped from Germany, with its 'petty barbarism and universal drunkenness',[4] into the civilisation of Italy, Catholic though it was! The Germans admittedly had great qualities, Rohan allowed, but 'this great addiction to the bottle obscures all, and makes them contemptible and unpresentable to the whole world.' Rohan was himself a total abstainer, and Mayerne, though he had more epicurean tastes and liked a good claret, was severe against all excess.

In Italy the travellers relaxed. Two months were spent at Venice and its university city of Padua. Then they moved across north Italy to Milan and Genoa before turning south to Pisa, Florence, Siena, Rome, Naples. They reached Naples, the most southerly point of their travels, at the beginning of the new year, and lingered, like Hannibal, in the mild winter climate of that seductive and historic bay.

Early in the new year of 1600 the young princes and their attendants turned back. They passed through Leghorn, Lucca, Bologna, Ferrara, Mantua; then they recrossed the Alps into Austria, visited Vienna and the imperial city of Prague where Rudolf II now held his court, and continued northwards through Saxony and Hanover to the maritime cities of Lübeck, Hamburg, Bremen. Then they turned west into the northern Netherlands, still at war with Spain. There they saw all the main cities. Holland, Rohan thought, was as marvellous as anything he had seen on his travels, and Amsterdam the most perfect city after Venice. Everywhere he noted the ravages of war, the cruelty of the Spaniards, the vigour of commerce and intellectual life. At Delft he remembered William of Orange, at Rotterdam Erasmus. Finally, from Flushing, the party put to sea: 'for now', as Rohan observed, 'we must cross over to England and Scotland.'[5]

The journey to England was more hazardous than they had expected. For four days and five nights they were tossed by storms in the North Sea – it was now mid-October 1600 – and finally they were forced to make a difficult landing at Harwich and travel to London by road. There they were received by Queen Elizabeth, who at first made them good cheer; but when she heard that they were determined to visit Scotland, she was not at all pleased. Her relations with James VI, at that time, were particularly delicate and she did not like the thought of foreigners in Edinburgh. However, they were not to be dissuaded, and in November they set off post haste, on the Great North Road. After eight days of travel, they reached the Border, stopped to admire the new fortifications of Berwick-on-Tweed, and entered Scotland. In Scotland they were received by King James and lavishly entertained with hunting, hawking and feasting. They were taken, for their 'contentment' – in mid-winter – to Linlithgow, Dunfermline, Stirling, Glasgow and Hamilton. On their return to Edinburgh, Rohan and Soubise stood godfathers to the king's newborn son, afterwards Charles I.[6] Then they returned to London, were received again by Queen Elizabeth, and sailed from Dover to France, arriving back in Paris early in 1601.

In all this grand tour, the high point was, rather surprisingly, Scotland. In England, Rohan does not seem, at first, to have made a good impression on the queen and he complains that he was slandered to her, although Sir Robert Cecil stood by his friend and earned his lasting gratitude.[7] But in Scotland he found everything wonderful. It is clear that King James took great trouble to woo his guests. And he wooed them successfully. Even Rohan's dry prose is suddenly refreshed and animated once he has crossed the Border, and he breaks out into lyrical praise both of Scotland and of its king. Scotland, he writes, not only surpasses all the other countries which he has seen, but even rivals France itself. And as for King James, no words could do justice to his virtues of heart and mind: surely, Rohan exclaims, this king was sent by God, who raises up great men when he wishes to change the order of the world. For is not England, at this moment, in its crisis? Queen Elizabeth is old and her dynasty will end with her. Surely King James must succeed her, being in every way the most fit to rule. 'Dieu veuille que j'en sois prophète.' If that should happen, then this whole island will be under 'un mesme Dieu, une mesme foy, une mesme loy, un mesme roy'.[8] These words were never published by Rohan. They remained in manuscript until after his death. They cannot have been interested flattery. They must have been sincere.

Rohan's reception by King James, and the close personal relations which were then established between them, were to have great influence on his later career. He was also favourably impressed, in Britain, by two great officers, one English, one Scottish. The Englishman was Sir Robert Cecil, the Scot was James VI's intimate adviser, the Earl of Mar, who had received the French party at his castle in Stirling. After his return to France, Rohan would correspond regularly with Cecil and, through Cecil, with Mar. He would also correspond directly with King James. The correspondence was closely guarded, and most of it has perished. But we know that when George Nicholson, Cecil's agent in Scotland, delivered Rohan's 'great packets', the king and his two closest confidants, Mar and Edward Bruce, secular abbot of Kinloss, would gather together 'to secret counsel'. In view of Cecil's complicity, and the particular roles played by Mar and Kinloss at that time, we can be reasonably certain of the matter which drew them all together. They were laying secret plans for the succession of King James to the English throne, and Rohan was evidently a trusted party to those plans.[9]

He was a party because he saw, in that succession, the vital interest of the French Huguenots. Rohan, even at twenty years old, was an acute observer and a political realist. He had no illusions about his cousin Henri IV. He knew that Henri IV, after his apostasy, would protect the Huguenots where it was politically expedient for him to do so; but he was no longer one of them, or their leader, and he would as easily, for the same political expediency, betray them. If the English crown too were to fall to a Catholic – and the Spaniards were still scheming for that purpose – then the Huguenot cause, the cause of international Protestantism, would be politically headless. No great power would assume its leadership, as Elizabethan England had done. The Prince of Orange in the Netherlands, the Elector Palatine at Heidelberg, would be no adequate substitute for a royal patron, the sovereign of an independent power. Therefore the peaceful succession of the King of Scotland to the throne of England was essential. After King James had in fact succeeded, Rohan would continue his correspondence with him. To him, King James, as king of a united Great Britain, was the natural head of that European Protestantism, of which, already, Rohan saw himself as the military hero.

Such was the grand tour of the two Rohan brothers and their young friends. They went to observe the world, as men marked out for politics and, if necessary, war. Rohan's observations, in his narrative of the journey, are the observations of a soldier and a statesman. Though he is interested in ancient history, admires the Italian learned academies, and notes occasional works of art, his chief interests are modern and practical. He measures fortresses, visits arsenals, studies the forms of government, quotes Machiavelli. Mayerne's interests were different. Although he too travelled to enlarge his experience and was concerned with the fortunes of the Huguenots, his main purpose in making this journey must have been to meet medical men in Germany and Italy. He went, he afterwards wrote, 'in order to visit learned men and enrich, by their discourse, my modest store of medical knowledge'.[10] For Germany and Italy were then acknowledged centres of European medicine. It was in Germany that the new 'Paracelsian' chemical medicine was most widely preached and practised, in Italy – and especially in Padua – that anatomy had been furthest advanced. Montpellier, for all its virtues, was somewhat provincial. Just as du Chesne had discovered Paracelsian medicine by travelling through Germany as an army surgeon and meeting German adepts, just as la Rivière had learned his medical philosophy by travelling over 'most of Europe' and had completed it by visiting Germany with the Duc de Bouillon, so Mayerne, by travelling in the company of another Huguenot prince, could meet the doctors of the courts and cities of Germany, could listen to the professors of Padua and the philosophers of Florence and Naples.

In his bald account of the journey Rohan never mentions Mayerne, or indeed any of his companions. Fortunately Mayerne himself kept a record, and that record – or at least part of it – survives, copied into a volume of letters and documents of personal interest which he evidently began to compile nearly thirty years later.[11] It too is bald and impersonal; nor does he ever mention Rohan or any of his companions; but it is, for our purposes, an invaluable supplement – as far as it goes – to Rohan's account. Sometimes it gives more details, or different details; it is illustrated with numerous drawings; and it supplies what Rohan never gives, exact dates. Having already written a theoretical guide to the routes of Europe, Mayerne knew exactly how to construct a practical record. At the head of it he placed a scheme showing the information which he intended to collect at each place. This consisted of the names of the places visited; the etymology of those names; historical and geographical details; public and private buildings; forms of government; the court, the schools, the character of the people. This at least was the intention. It was not exactly fulfilled (none of his literary intentions ever would be), and unfortunately the surviving record is not complete.

However, apart from a tourist's record of castles and churches, antiquities, inscriptions and miscellaneous observations, Mayerne's diary occasionally reveals his particular interests. One of these was in Huguenot colonies. Sedan, he observes, 'has served as a place of refuge for many persons of diverse nations who have fled thither for religion's sake. Hence it has grown in means, size and strength, for their better protection.'[12] To enlarge and enrich it, the Duc de Bouillon, Mayerne recorded, had added a new university to the old college and fortified the great castle of his predecessors with new moats, walls and cannon. Similarly at Pfalzburg the Count of Veldenz-Lützelstein had founded a new town in waste land and given it to 'French, Walloons and others who were driven thither by religion'.[13] In the Palatinate, Mayerne described the new city of Franckenthal which the munificence and benevolence of John Casimir, the Calvinist prince regent, had granted to French and Walloon refugees: 'almost everyone there speaks French.'[14] Mayerne also noted the Jewish colonies in Metz, Oppenheim, Worms, Frankfurt and other imperial cities, described their customs and copied their Hebrew inscriptions.

Another particular interest of Mayerne was in works of art. At Nancy, he recorded the pictures and statues in the churches; in Frankfurt the paintings of Albrecht Dürer – the apotheosis of the Virgin Mary in the Jakobitenkirche, as well as other works and his death-mask; at Innsbruck the great bronze statues of heroes and ancestors commissioned for his tomb by the emperor Maximilian; at Munich the *Kunstkammer* and curiosities of the Duke of Bavaria; at Bassano the work of 'that remarkable painter who took his name from the place'. He also recorded mechanical devices of all kinds: Roman aqueducts, engines of war, sophisticated waterworks, clocks, planetaria and musical instruments. At Zabern he noted the epitaph of the organist Johann Schlend who, though born blind, 'was an excellent musician and expert in instrumental harmony';[15] at Strasbourg the organ in the cathedral; and at Stuttgart the musical instruments and statues of musicians in the ducal palace. Occasionally he dwells on the beauty of the country, as in Lorraine, where his party followed the road 'through the most beautiful meadows, between hills set back on either side, a delightful country, in the midst of which the Moselle has chosen its bed, and flows there gently, as if asleep'.[16]

However, Mayerne's first purpose in travelling was to learn his own art: medicine, chemistry and mineral processes. Wherever he had a chance, he examined mines and mineral waters. He gives detailed accounts of the mineral resources of Lorraine: the silver and iron mines of Ste Marie and Remiremont, the salt springs of la Rosière, the salt-mine of Moyeuvre; he describes a visit to the mineral springs at Boppingen and the 'springs of naphtha or petrol' at Tegernsee; and he writes at length on the mineral resources of Tyrol. He was particularly impressed by the salt-mines of Hall – 'the greatest in all Germany' – and by the gold- and silver-mines of Schwatz, situated at the base of the mountain precipice. Both of these were owned and operated by the Fugger family. At Schwatz, Mayerne marvelled at the labyrinthine underground channels, the elaborate system of drainage and the machinery to raise the ore and separate the metal. Two thousand three hundred men were employed there every day, he was told. It took him an hour to go down the mine shaft, by a ladder and a rope, and the whole underground surface was scanned with a magnetic needle to discover the mineral. The mine also produced green and blue marcasite, as bright as turquoise and lapis lazuli, which would be mounted in gold by jewellers.[17] Mayerne questioned the miners about 'the spirits of the mine'. He was told that there were two kinds of spirits, 'some evil, who often terrify the workers, others whom they call "Bergmänlis"' – mine-dwarves – 'and say are good. They think that they are St Daniel, whom they recognise as their patron. These are rarely to be seen, but show themselves to some persons only by a tremor which is said to indicate a great treasure. Then the miners retreat, thinking that they should leave the spirits to enjoy themselves. But they mark the place, and return to it later.'

Mayerne also noticed herbs and drugs. The Bavarian Alps, he observed, abounded in rare simples: 'among others I noticed alpine rose, *chamadrys rosea* and the white trefoil of Hippocrates.'[18] But perhaps his most interesting experience was in Strasbourg, where he was able to see a model of organised public health in an urban republic. Strasbourg was already famous in the medical world for its *Pharmacopoeia*, or list of approved medicines, including chemical medicines. Mayerne was now able to see the organisation behind that document: the public hospital with its apothecary's office supplied with every kind of medicine, including various extracts much used by the local physicians. The beds, he observed, are beautifully arranged, in three large wards (the arrangements differing in summer and winter). 'They are covered with clean straw, and each has a fire to warm the air for the benefit of the poor.' The building was well ventilated, healthy and spacious, furnished with a granary and a well-stocked wine cellar. 'Some of the wines are very old: vintages of 1519 and 1525, and even one cask of 1472.'[19]

Mayerne's journal does not record meetings or conversations. But we know, from later evidence, that he met the court and city physicians; and we can assume, since his party spent four days in Strasbourg, that he took advantage of his opportunities there. Certainly he would afterwards seek to apply its lessons in London. Another period of relaxation was in Heidelberg, which of course was well known to him from his university days. Heidelberg was now the capital of European Calvinism. It was also a centre of Paracelsian and Hermetic studies. The man who effectively wielded the electoral power was Christian of Anhalt-Bernburg, the champion of a radical Protestant policy in Europe, who was himself – like all the Anhalt princes[20] – a devotee, and an amateur practitioner, of chemical medicine. Mayerne would come to know him well a few years later, and it may well be that he pursued his chemical researches here, as he certainly did, a week later, at Stuttgart.

The party spent nine days in Stuttgart, at the ducal court. The duke was Frederick, the first of the new Montbéliard line. He had succeeded his uncle Ludwig in 1593, and was married to a princess of Anhalt. Like Christian of Anhalt, he was a strong supporter of the international Protestant cause; he was closely allied with the England of Queen Elizabeth and the France of Henri IV. He was also a man of intellectual interests, a great builder and traveller (he had recently been to England and was preparing to visit Rome), and a lavish patron of the arts and sciences, particularly natural science and alchemical speculations.[21] He had been the patron of Johann Bauhin at Montbéliard and, since moving to Stuttgart, had maintained a series of court alchemists, of whom the most famous was the great Polish adept Michael Sendivogius. Unfortunately none of them had been able to satisfy him by transmuting base metal into gold. By the time of Rohan's visit no fewer than five impostors had been exposed and either expelled or executed. One of them, Georg Honauer, after a spectacular start, had recently come to an equally spectacular end: the duke had caused him to be hanged on an iron gallows which was made out of the very metal he had failed to transmute, and which was now painted, in mockery of his efforts, to resemble gold.[22] The gallows was left standing in Stuttgart for many years, as a deterrent; but it did not deter the many alchemists who still came to offer their services to the eager, credulous duke.

In his diary, Mayerne writes enthusiastically of his visit to Stuttgart: of the delightfully situated ducal palace and gardens, with their waterworks and fountains and statues. He also mentions – and illustrates – the gilded gallows on which the unfortunate Honauer had been hanged. He does not mention his own private conversations with the duke's reigning chemical philosopher. Fortunately we have another document on that subject, which shows how bare and fragmentary a record Mayerne's journal is, even at its fullest.

It is at its fullest in France and Germany. Once the party has crossed the Alps, the entries become thinner. On 17 July they were at Bassano, on the 18th at Padua, and on the 20th at Venice. Then, for the two months which Rohan – and presumably Mayerne – spent at Venice, there is nothing until 23 September, when the journal begins again with the words 'Patavio excessimus': we left Padua. A few bald entries then enable us to trace the party moving by rapid stages to Milan, where they stayed for four days, and thence to Florence, where they lingered for twelve weeks. On 26 December they left Florence, and after passing through Radicofani and Aquapendente, and inspecting the sulphur baths of Viterbo, they arrived, on 31 December, in Rome.

On that last day of the year Mayerne's journal ceases. Perhaps he began another journal at the new year, which has been lost. Perhaps he just desisted. The only entry, on arrival in Rome, is 'vide descriptionem'. This separate description survives. It is an account – rounded off with a conventional Protestant attack on the ambitions and usurpation of the popes – of the monuments seen during a week's stay in the holy city; and it ends with the words, 'but now I leave them there to continue my journey, which matters to me more than any consideration of them.'[23] So the party went on to Naples, of which Mayerne also wrote a separate account, describing the sulphurous earth and its uses, and recording that he had personally conducted Rohan into the castle of St Elmo.[24] We can thus say that Mayerne remained with Rohan to the southernmost point of his travels.

Did he also return with Rohan? Did he accompany him through Austria and Bohemia, to the Netherlands, England and Scotland? It is tempting to suppose that he did. The imperial court of Rudolph II at Prague was the capital of the Hermetic world. The courts of Saxony and Brunswick were presided over by alchemical princes. King James VI of Scotland was to become Mayerne's greatest patron. It is pleasant to think that their association may have begun in Edinburgh in 1600. However, in the complete absence of evidence, we can only say that we do not know. At Naples the record ceases, and for a whole year thereafter the trail is lost. No journal, no later note, enlightens us, either positively, by showing him with Rohan on his travels, or negatively, by showing him anywhere else. We can only speculate, unprofitably.[25]

It is more profitable to look at the travels which are documented – that is, the outward journey. How, we may ask, did Mayerne spend his time during these long pauses in Padua, Venice, Florence and Rome? The journal gives us no help, and the darkness is only occasionally pierced by incidental allusions in his later letters or in the brief, retrospective marginal notes in his

Ephemerides. We do not know whether, in Padua, he met his future colleague William Harvey, then studying for his doctorate under the great anatomist Fabricius of Aquapendente. Mayerne would afterwards quote Fabricius in his notes and, in so long a stay, he may well have attended his lectures; but in later life he would write scornfully of the doctors of Padua: those great anatomists, he would write, were unable to diagnose disease or treat it therapeutically.[26] However, certain brief allusions give us useful hints. In particular, thanks to marginal notes, we know the names of two doctors with whom he became intimate in Venice, and who remained his lifelong friends. Both were French. Their names were Asselineau and Dansé.

Pierre Asselineau was a man of some importance both in Venice and in the Huguenot international. His father was a Huguenot doctor in Orléans – one of the major centres of Calvinism in France. To escape from the civil wars of France, the son had been sent, when young, to Venice, and he had presumably studied medicine at Padua. Delighted by the society, and the freedom, of Venice, he stayed there the rest of his life, practising medicine and continuing, from that neutral base, the struggle against the Counter-Reformation. He became the intimate friend of the greatest Venetian of his time, Fra Paolo Sarpi. In the critical years after 1606, when the Catholic friar became the intellectual and political oracle of the united front against the 'Tricatholicon' of Spain, Rome and the Jesuits, the Huguenot doctor was his most trusted agent in the Protestant world. Asselineau handled most of Sarpi's foreign correspondence; he was his regular link with the Huguenot leaders, Philippe du Plessis Mornay in Saumur and Jerôme Groslot de l'Isle in Orléans; he was the essential means of access to Sarpi for foreigners coming on delicate business from England, the Netherlands and Protestant Germany; and he would translate into French or Italian the public propaganda and secret communications of the anti-Catholic alliance.[27]

As a physician, Asselineau was of the chemical party. According to Sarpi's friend and biographer, Fra Fulgenzio Micanzio, he was among the first of physicians and anatomists and 'unequalled in the knowledge of simples and minerals and their virtues and uses for the human body'. He was in fact yet another illustration of the factual alliance of chemical medicine and international Protestantism. He was therefore a natural friend of Mayerne, and Mayerne's notebooks contain frequent references to him as his informant on medical matters during his own stay in Venice. There are similar notes about Dansé, who, however, remains a shadowy figure. He seems to have been a French physician at Castelfranco di Veneto, near Padua.[28]

Asselineau and Dansé did more for Mayerne than merely discuss chemical and herbal remedies. It seems that Mayerne was seriously ill in Padua –

evidently on the outward journey[29] – and that they took charge of him and cured him. Thirty years later, when Mayerne was sending his own son to Italy, and warning him of the dangerous fluxes and fevers of its climate, he added,

at Venice, if you should fall ill, M. Asselineau, my old and dear friend, will care for you as once he cared for me. I can never thank him enough for the kindness that I received from him and from poor M. Dansé, now deceased. Thank him from me, and as long as you live be his servant, for but for the care which he took of me when I was ill in Padua, you would never have been born.[30]

In the retrospective marginal notes which are often our only evidence, Mayerne refers to other physicians with whom he discussed cures and conducted experiments in Italy. There is a record of a discussion with one Julius Placentinus in Padua;[31] of various communications from one Reutzius and one Ottonaius in Florence;[32] of a conversation with Ottavio Boere in Genoa.[33] Most of these names mean nothing to us, but we know that Franciscus Reutzius, a Paracelsian physician from Pomerania who had settled in Florence and who there gave Mayerne an unprinted work by Paracelsus, was a friend – 'mon singulier amy' – of du Chesne;[34] and Ottavio Boere had been the host of la Rivière in Genoa ten years earlier.[35] So Mayerne was no doubt following in their tracks. The Boeri were an old Genoese medical dynasty: one of them had been physician to Henry VIII of England, and it was as tutor to his sons that Erasmus had travelled from London to Rome. The dell'Ottonaio were a Florentine family, known in the previous generation, but we know nothing of Mayerne's medical friend of that name, who told him of his private powder and how he had cured his father of the stone by injecting soap into his bladder *per syphonem*. He was probably the Cristofano dell'Ottonaio who is recorded as a member of the important College of Physicians in Florence in 1630.[36] No doubt there were many other medical discussions of which no such chance record survives. We would like to know, for instance, if Mayerne, in Naples, visited the most famous of Italian Hermetists, Giambattista della Porta, whose *Magia naturalis* he often cites. But Mayerne tells us nothing directly, and where no accidental reference occurs we are helpless. After Naples we are quite without clues. When we next pick up his trail, it is in 1601, and Mayerne is back in Paris, transcribing chemical papers. Next year he is firmly established there, following his career in court and city, attending the Rohan family, beginning to complete a manual of chemical medicine for his own use, and recording with satisfaction the cures which he has achieved, sometimes alone, sometimes with his partners, la Rivière and du Chesne.[37] It is from 1602 that his personal papers begin, from then that it is possible – though still with many gaps – to document his career from contemporary private records and not merely from retrospective marginalia.

Not that it is easy to do so. Mayerne was not concerned to help a future biographer. He was not interested in chronology. Although he was continually making notes, he was, in many ways, unsystematic; and he seldom completed any project. He would begin what was intended to be a formal work, writing his name on the title-page, and add the date. But then his interest would fade and the book would be used for other purposes. Thus the original date on any document bears no necessary relation to the bulk of its contents. He would insert new sections in old books without notice, and he would transcribe passages out of old books into new. He was continually adding marginalia. Nor were the views he recorded always his own. He was an inveterate transcriber and may not necessarily have agreed with the observations he transcribed. Sometimes he took trouble to authenticate what he wrote, signing it with his signature, or his Greek motto σὺν θεῷ, 'with God': a phrase which – sometimes varied as οὐκ ἀτὲρ θεοῦ, 'not without God' – would become his regular motto; and he took care to ascribe his remedies to their authors – and thus sometimes, of course, to himself. But often he employed amanuenses, and then it is only through an occasional correction or addition in his own hand that we can tell that the manuscript was his. Sometimes his own manuscripts, among entries that were clearly written by or for him, contain entries that have clearly been added after his death. For all these reasons, his papers must be interpreted with care. However, with care they can be interpreted and some of them can even be dated. Two documents in particular are of immediate interest to us, for they evidently belong to the period immediately after his return to France.

The first is a series of miscellaneous notes, of which two are dated 1601 and all are compatible with the period 1601–3.[38] They include alchemical and medical notes, largely from du Chesne. At the end are two lists. One of these lists is headed *Emendi libri*, 'books to be bought'; the other consists simply of nine names. Among the nine are Fabricius of Aquapendente, Asselineau, Dansé and Ottonaio, all of which point to the visit to Italy. Two other names in this list are identifiable. They are du Four and Renéaume. Du Four is known as a friend of Mayerne. He was the *médecin ordinaire* of the Duc de Vendôme, the bastard son of Henri IV.[39] Paul Renéaume was also a friend of Mayerne. He was a chemical doctor whom the Medical Faculty of Paris, in 1607, would condemn as 'impudentissimum virum' for using improper – that is, chemical – remedies.[40] Mayerne copied out remedies from the notebooks of both du

Four and Renéaume. The list is therefore probably of persons from whom Mayerne obtained valuable medical information, on his travels and soon after his return.

The list of 'books to be bought' consists of seven titles. Two are current text-books: the *Praxis* of Holler, or Holerius, the great mid-sixteenth-century Hippocratic in the Paris faculty; and the surgical manual of Étienne Gourmelen, late professor of medicine at the Collège de France. Gourmelen, indeed, was out of date: he was the 'mon petit maître' who had been so pulverised by Ambroise Paré.[41] The medical *consilia* of Crato of Crafftheim were also orthodox. But the remaining four books show a very different interest. One of them was a chemical work by du Chesne.[42] The others were the works of Paracelsus, the works of Penotus, and the *Vellus aureum* or 'Golden Fleece'. Penotus was Bernard Georges Penot, a Frenchman from Guyenne, who had studied at Basel, become a Paracelsian propagandist, and ruined himself in pursuit of the philosopher's stone. In 1596 he was practising Paracelsian medicine in Franckenthal, the new Huguenot town in the Palatinate, which Mayerne had visited.[43] He was still alive in 1600 but very old: he would die in a Swiss poor-house in 1620, aged ninety-eight. The *Vellus aureum* was presumably the Paracelsian work of that title ascribed to an imaginary 'Solomon Trissmosin', the alleged teacher of Paracelsus: this work was written in German and Mayerne's papers contain extracts from it.[44]

Thus the first of these two documents reveals that Mayerne, on his return to France, was already feeling his way into the doubtful area of Paracelsian and post-Paracelsian alchemy. The second is more decisive. It shows who was directing him in these studies – and indeed leading him further still, through chemistry and alchemy, into the yet more abstruse world of Hermetic mysticism. This second document is one to which we have already referred: Mayerne's letter to the court doctor of the Duke of Württemberg. The letter is in Latin, and the copy which Mayerne preserved is undated and unaddressed.[45] But it was obviously written in 1601 or 1602, soon after his return to Paris, and it tells its own story.

After thanking his correspondent for the civility which he has shown towards him, 'a stranger, travelling abroad in eager quest of learning', and apologising for the tardiness of this letter of thanks – but he explains that he has had few opportunities and is only just recovering from the exhaustion of his travels – Mayerne recalls with satisfaction the learned discourse which they enjoyed together in Stuttgart and the experiments which they witnessed 'in the temple of your Muses'. He reminds his German friend that, on parting, he, Mayerne, promised to write to him and give him news from the intellectual world of Paris. Now, he says, he has something to impart. And so he comes to the real cause and purpose of his letter.

Recently, when I was examining the collections and labours of our philosophers, a close friend of mine, a man of no ordinary learning, showed me a
work which is not only original in its title, method, and argument, but also
spiced with solid philosophical reasoning.

Reading the manuscript of this new book, Mayerne went on,

I marvel at the discoveries made by the earliest philosophers, when the light
of Nature was so dim and the foundation of knowledge so fragile. Our
author finds that the greatest teacher of physics was Moses: for Aristotle, he
shows, was blind and, with Plato, sunk in Cimmerian darkness. The challenging title of this new book will of itself compel the reader, and the
novelty of the matter calls for a patron who is at once cultivated, liberal and
powerful.

The author, Mayerne adds, has asked him, as one recently returned from
Germany, to which of the German princes he should dedicate his book.
Mayerne has recommended the Duke of Württemberg, as a man whose
enlightened and critical spirit was known to him.

I am sure that his Highness will not refuse a just reward, especially if he is
encouraged by you. I am sending you herewith a list of the chapter headings: by this claw you will recognise the lion. Soothe your prince's leisure
hours with this intellectual food. You can do that, no doubt, as you walk
with him in the garden, or conduct him through your laboratory ... I
eagerly await your reply and will then send you the whole book, complete
with a suitable preface.

Then, having thus recommended his friend's work, he returns to his own
credentials. Lest the philosopher of Stuttgart should have forgotten, Mayerne
reveals himself.

I will keep you in suspense no longer. The writer of this letter is your great
admirer, the man who came to Stuttgart with the French prince, Monsieur
de Rohan, and who, in your *musaeum*, took down your manuscript and
copied out from it the antiquities of Württemberg; and whose name you
wished to have inscribed in your *album*.

Who was Mayerne's close friend for whose learned book, proving Moses to
be the first scientist, he was seeking German patronage? The answer can
hardly be in doubt. Whenever we catch a glimpse of Mayerne in Paris, after his

return from abroad, he is with du Chesne. Sometimes he is dining with du Chesne, sometimes they are consulting together about their patients.[46] If anyone exactly answered Mayerne's description, it was du Chesne, and if any book answered Mayerne's account of it, it was the book which du Chesne had written precisely at this time. Indeed, Mayerne, in his letter, almost gave away 'the challenging title'. 'I marvel at the discoveries of the earliest philosophers', Mayerne had written ('Priscorum miror inventa'). The title of du Chesne's book was *De priscorum philosophorum verae medicinae materia*, 'Of the Substance of the True Medicine of the Earliest Philosophers'. To the Hermetist, the *prisci philosophi*, or *prisci theologi*, were as well known and as clearly identified as the Apostolic Fathers or the Major Prophets. They were Moses, Zoroaster, Hermes Trismegistus, Orpheus: the mythical sages who, before Plato or Aristotle, had revealed, darkly indeed, but intelligibly to those who could read their language, the secret system of the world.

The Duke of Württemberg would undoubtedly have been a suitable, and perhaps a liberal, patron for such a book. But Mayerne's attempt to secure his support for du Chesne's work did not succeed. Perhaps there were good reasons for this. Alchemy had its ups and downs at the court of Frederick I. Since Mayerne's visit, in 1599, at least two more unsuccessful practitioners had been hanged on the iron gallows of Stuttgart, and a third was now languishing in prison, apprehending the same fate.[47] This third was Andreas Reiche of Salzwedel, of whom we are told that the duke had formerly given him a laboratory in the Hospital of Stuttgart and often came himself to witness the operations. We recall Mayerne's bland words, 'as you walk with him in the garden or conduct him through your laboratory . . .' Could it be that Andreas Reiche himself had been Mayerne's host at Stuttgart? If so, he was by now in no position to help: he would linger in prison for another six years, until his unrelenting patron was dead. More probably, Mayerne's friend was Florian Kappler, the director of the ducal laboratory, whose duty it was to discover and supervise its successive operators. But by 1602 even Kappler, after so many failures, might well hesitate to expose his master's name by associating it with a new foreign alchemist. He had trouble enough with those nearer home. Soon he would find himself embarrassed by the internecine feuds of the two resident scientists, Heinrich Müller from Alsace, whom the alchemical emperor Rudolf II had ennobled as von Mühlenfels, and the famous Polish adept Michael Sendivogius, who, having acquired the true secret of transmutation by rescuing its possessor from the prison of the Elector of Saxony, soon found himself, on the same account, in the private prison of Mühlenfels. The drama would end with Mühlenfels following his predecessors on the well-trodden way to the iron gallows of Honauer. Such were the risks of chemical research at the court of an energetic modern Protestant German prince, patron of learning and Knight of the Garter.

Frustrated at Stuttgart, du Chesne sought and found a more powerful patron nearer to home. In this he was proved wise by the event. For his books, when published, would exasperate his already numerous enemies in Paris. The *brutum fulmen* of the attempted prosecution of Mayerne, which had 'lain hidden' during his absence abroad, was still smouldering, and would now break out in a fine pamphletary conflagration.

5

The Chemical Challenge, 1601–1605

After his migration to Paris in 1596, Joseph du Chesne had been, for some time, remarkably discreet. Even his enemies, even the Riolans themselves – if only to emphasise his later relapse – would pay retrospective tribute to his discretion: 'he practised medicine among us', they would write, 'amice et familiariter', as a friend and colleague.[1] It is true, they disapproved strongly of his practice and of that of his 'chemical' friends, la Rivière and Mayerne. These 'iatrochemists', they asserted, were poisoning such citizens as were foolish enough to trust them by their formidable doses of precipitate of mercury and antimony, and were ruining them by their exorbitant fees: 35 écus for two pills which had caused immediate apoplexy and permanent paralysis, etc., etc. Such stories were exchanged regularly in the Paris medical faculty and improved by circulation in the city. However, without support from the Parlement of Paris – and the failure of the first attack on Mayerne suggests that they could not count on that support: times had changed since the affair of Roch le Baillif – there was no effective means of attacking the chemical doctors, and it seemed best to make a virtue of necessity. However reluctantly, the medical establishment had to contain its mortification.

The mortification was not caused solely by the medical views of the three 'iatrochemists'. We must remember that all of them were also Huguenot immigrants; and Huguenotism was not only a way of thinking: it was a way of life. The Huguenots clung together, forming a society within society, compact, impenetrable, inassimilable. Hence the communal hatred which good Catholic citizens felt for them now – the hatred that had exploded in the massacre of St Bartholomew. La Rivière, du Chesne and Mayerne formed a cohesive group: Geneva was in the experience of them all; and even in Paris their solidarity was not dissolved. They might move freely in metropolitan society. They might have numerous Catholic patients. But their private world, into which they retreated and within which they were at ease, was irreducibly

Huguenot. They consulted with Huguenot doctors; they employed Huguenot apothecaries. Huguenots were their closest friends.

This is clearly shown by Mayerne's papers. Among them there are various notes of joint consultations. But apart from one occasion when du Chesne and Mayerne consulted together with André du Laurens, Mayerne's friend and patron from Montpellier who, by that time, had succeeded la Rivière as *premier médecin du roi* and was their formal superior at court, the consultations thus recorded are always with Huguenot doctors. Generally Mayerne consulted with la Rivière or du Chesne. On one occasion all three are found gathered round the bed of a rich patient, M. de St Ysunier.[2] Only two other doctors appear in these records as occasional partners of Mayerne. They are François Pena, who consulted with du Chesne and Mayerne in 1603, and Dr Rotmund, who consulted with Mayerne seven years later. Neither of these took him outside the closed Huguenot world.

François Pena came from a distinguished family in Provence. His father was Pierre Pena, the well-known botanist who collaborated with Matthias de Lobel. Both Pierre Pena and Lobel had studied at Montpellier. They published their joint work, *Stirpium adversaria nova*, in 1571, and dedicated it to Queen Elizabeth. By that time Pena was a Protestant. Thereafter he went to Paris, where his elder brother Jean Pena was a professor of mathematics at the Collège Royal. Soon he became 'médecin secret' of Henri III. He seems to have specialised in treating syphilis, and thus became very rich at court, dying (we are told) worth 600,000 livres. Pierre Pena's son, François Pena, was brought up as a Huguenot, studied at Geneva, and then, like his father, became a successful physician in Paris.[3] Henri IV made him *médecin ordinaire du roi*. But the Paris doctors regarded him as an insufferable impostor. In February 1601 the faculty secured an order from the Chambre Civile du Châtelet forbidding him to practise in Paris or the suburbs. Pena treated the order with contempt. He declared that he was 'médecin du roy et de Monsieur le Prince de Conty', refused to appear in court, and continued his profitable practice.[4] In September 1607 the faculty repeated its prohibition, but apparently without effect.[5] Mayerne adopted several remedies from him, and he continued to be patronised by high society. A few months after his second condemnation, one of the grandest of Huguenot *grandes dames*, the Duchesse de la Tremoïlle – daughter of William the Silent and a patient of Mayerne – stood godmother to his infant son.[6]

Felix Rotmund was also a Huguenot. He came from Switzerland. His family was settled in St Gall, and Felix had studied medicine first at Basel, then at Montpellier. He and his brother Laurence had been contemporaries of Mayerne at Montpellier and it is possible that they, or one of them, had shared lodgings with him there. After leaving Montpellier, Laurence Rotmund had succeeded his father as city doctor of St Gall, while Felix had come to Paris with Mayerne. They remained close friends: the *Antidotarium* which Rotmund compiled in 1602 was afterwards obtained by Mayerne.[7]

Outside Paris, Mayerne also dealt mainly with the Huguenot doctors. Almost all the French provincial doctors whose names appear in his correspondence are either certainly or probably Huguenots. Some of them were linked with him through the old-boy network of Montpellier; but with many he seems to have had no connection except through the Huguenot free-masonry. Some of these were the personal physicians of Huguenot grandees, like Dr Palet, *médecin ordinaire* of Henri IV's cousin and heir presumptive, the Prince de Condé, and Dr du Four, *médecin ordinaire* of the king's illegitimate son, the Duc de Vendôme. Both Condé and Vendôme also used the services of Mayerne himself. Mayerne was also often consulted, through their doctors, about Huguenot patients in the provinces – la Rochelle, Sedan, Lyon. And he seems to have had particularly close relations with the Huguenot doctors of Orléans. We have already met Pierre Asselineau, the Huguenot doctor from Orléans who had emigrated to Venice, and who remained Mayerne's friend for thirty years. Mayerne's correspondence introduces us also to Dr Poniet of Orléans, whom he advised on a delicate case of *imbecillitas ad venerem*; to M. Raboteau, surgeon of Orléans; to Israel Harvet and Guillaume Baucynet,[8] doctors of Orléans; and, finally, to the mysterious 'gentilhomme d'Orléans',[9] soon to appear in this narrative, Guillaume de Trougny.

Apart from his fellow-doctors, a physician's closest professional relations were with the apothecaries who made up his medicines and with the surgeons who, under his direction, performed his operations. The names of both surgeons and apothecaries are sprinkled through Mayerne's papers. Both of these professions tended to heresy, religious as well as medical. In France they were often Huguenot – we need only think of the Huguenot apothecaries and surgeons who became so prominent in Jacobean London: Gideon de Laune, Matthias Lobel, Peter Chamberlen – and it was precisely among these depressed classes of the medical world that Paracelsian doctrines had spread most quickly. The 'chemical doctors' were inevitably closer to their apothecaries than the Galenists, who treated them as inferior artisans. Mayerne's correspondence shows him in regular and friendly social relations with them. His earliest named apothecary in Paris was one Turquois, who lived in the rue de la Harpe. Probably he was a Huguenot and a kinsman of the Huguenot named Turquois with whom Casaubon lodged in Orléans in 1603. At that time, Turquois evidently made all Mayerne's medicines.[10] Later, Mayerne had relations with many apothecaries, for it was convenient to use the personal or local apothecaries of his grand patients. But the apothecary on whom he came to rely most was another Huguenot, Pierre Naudin.

The Naudin family came from the Protestant citadel of Saumur. Two brothers were active in Paris at this time: Pierre, the apothecary, and Jean, a surgeon. Pierre Naudin was *apothécaire et valet de chambre du roi*.[11] He was a well-known figure in Huguenot circles, and his house in rue de Seine was, and would long remain, a regular rendez-vous and boarding-house for Protestant visitors.[12] He was Mayerne's personal apothecary by 1607, if not earlier,[13] and quickly became a close friend, agent and occasional host in Paris.

Regular apothecaries prepared drugs for regular physicians; but irregular physicians, like du Chesne and Mayerne, also relied on irregular assistants. In particular, for metallic, alchemical remedies, they relied on metal-workers, goldsmiths, jewellers, who, for their purposes, can be described as amateur apothecaries. One well-known dynasty served Mayerne in this capacity. It was the Huguenot family of Briot who, like the Naudins, would remain linked with him through his life.

The Briot family came originally from Damblain-en-Bassigny in Lorraine. They were pewterers, whose industry was supplied by the mines of Lorraine. But Lorraine was Catholic and they were Huguenots, and in 1579–80 François Briot emigrated to Protestant Montbéliard, the detached principality, on the borders of France, of the Duke of Württemberg. Montbéliard was also a mining area and supplied the mint of the dukes of Württemberg. It thus attracted metal-workers, painters and goldsmiths fleeing from Catholic pressure in neighbouring countries. François Briot joined the local guild of metal-workers and became an engraver. By 1585 he was engraver to the Duke of Württemberg, and he thus became involved in the shady operations of Laurent de Willermin, a Swiss adventurer who promised to produce the philosopher's stone for that great patron of alchemy, the Duke Frederick. He also engraved a medal of Frederick's protégé, the botanist Jean Bauhin.[14]

François Briot's brother Didier also emigrated from Lorraine and also became an engraver. His early history is obscure. We only know that, apart from his interest in metal, he traded in spice and cloth to Flanders, and that he would become farmer to the Duc de Nevers's mint in Charleville in 1608 and master of the mint in Sedan in 1612. But it seems that, in the first years of the century, he was in Paris. Certainly his son was then in Paris. The son, Nicolas Briot, would afterwards be famous as a jeweller and engraver, and would come to England to be engraver to Charles I.

Nicolas Briot, and perhaps also his father, were not only minters and engravers of metal. They were also amateur apothecaries, amateur physicians, surgeons and chemists. Mayerne's notebooks often refer to both father and son as experimenters with metallic cures, eye-salves, electuaries, medicines of 'vegetable silver', metallic oils, imitation gold, cosmetics, etc. The earliest datable reference is of 10 June 1604, when 'Monsieur Briot', then aged twenty-eight, was cured by Mayerne of epilepsy. In a later marginal note Mayerne added that he was still alive, in London. This shows that the reference is to Nicolas Briot. These early references prove that Briot was a friend of Mayerne long before he came to London; they strengthen the supposition that Mayerne brought him to England; and they explain why Briot, on coming to England, set up for a time as a physician.[15]

The social circle of Mayerne and du Chesne was no less Huguenot than their professional circle. One of their close friends was Isaac Casaubon, who had been lured from Montpellier to Paris in 1600 for the greater literary glory of the court and, it was hoped, for a spectacular conversion to Rome. He was given a royal pension and in 1606 was made librarian of the royal library. He was constantly pressed to change his religion, but he resisted the pressure, and we find him dining, for choice, privately with his Huguenot friends du Chesne and Mayerne. Casaubon would play an important part in Mayerne's life, both in France and in England. Another friend was the well-known Huguenot minister and scholar Pierre du Moulin. Mayerne and du Moulin had similar backgrounds. They were both sons of Huguenot fugitives from the massacre of St Bartholomew. They would become the closest of friends in the future, when the courtly doctor would regularly protect the outspoken minister against the consequences of his own indiscretions. At present they met often in Paris, where Mayerne attended du Moulin's services at the Huguenot 'temple' and looked after his health.[16]

Such other personal friends of Mayerne as we can identify in his Paris years are also Huguenots. One such is Simon le Tourneur, the Huguenot secretary of the Prince de Condé, to whose son he stood godfather in 1602.[17] Another is Pierre de Beringhem, Sieur d'Arminvilliers, a Dutchman from Gelderland whom Henri IV had picked up in Normandy and made his *conseiller et premier valet de chambre du roi*. His family would afterwards serve the House of Orange and the Elector Palatine. Pierre de Beringhem was a universal entrepreneur at the court of Henri IV, involved in industry, commerce, mining, etc. He acted as a contact man for foreign ambassadors and would be useful to Mayerne's brother-in-law when he came to Paris as Dutch ambassador in 1614, telling him whom he could trust at the court of Marie de Médicis. He would die in 1619, but Madame de Beringhem would live on in Paris, a lifelong friend and correspondent of Mayerne.[18]

I have illustrated the social cohesion of the Huguenot doctors in Paris from the circle of Mayerne, for Mayerne's personal papers survive while those of la Rivière and du Chesne do not. But it was the same circle; and the Catholic doctors of the faculty, whose society was no less self-contained, inevitably saw it as the circle of their enemies. These Huguenot doctors were in their eyes a foreign body which, thanks to royal protection, had acquired an indecent power in Paris. They had invaded the monopoly of the university and they were corrupting the true medicine as well as true religion by their destructive, heretical notions. What had been gained, Henri de Monantheuil, now Regius Professor of Mathematics, might ask, by his glorious victory over the diabolical Roch le Baillif in 1579, if three other devils, more wicked than he, were now to establish themselves in his room?

They were more wicked, of course, because they were more successful. They were successful not only with the king but also with the élite of society. These new chemical medicines, so simple, so palatable, so palliative, were far more attractive than the old. It was in vain that the experts denounced them, declaring them both poisonous and expensive: the plain fact was that the patients preferred them and were – or believed that they were – cured by them. However patiently the doctors of the faculty closed and fortified and defended their monopoly, they could not prevent rich patients from choosing their own physicians. And the physicians whom they chose did not fail, as they collected their fees, to publish and promote their own success.

In February 1602 Mayerne began to make notes of the great success of the partnership. At that time he was evidently very close to la Rivière and had already begun to collect his papers and remedies. In October of that year he entitled one of his notebooks 'Medical Observations of what was done in certain great and desperate diseases by Sieur de la Rivière, physician-in-chief to the king, Theodore de Mayerne Turquet, and some others'; and soon afterwards he began a 'list of those persons who, having been given up by the doctors of Paris, or others, were attended by us and recovered'.[19] He then filled in details of some spectacular cases, punctuating his record with exclamations of devout triumph, sometimes accompanied by his Greek motto. He referred to it twice, and on both occasions inserted the Greek word μεγαc, 'great'. This was the case of the Duc de Bellegarde.

Roger Lary, Duc de Bellegarde, had been one of the *mignons* or favourites of Henri III. It was he who, in 1589, had organised the murder of the two brothers, the Cardinal and the Duc de Guise: the desperate step whereby the last Valois king had sought to escape from the domination of Philip II of Spain and the Catholic League. When Henri III had in turn been assassinated, Bellegarde had become the confidant of Henri IV, and he was now Grand Écuyer de France. He was also the king's competitor for the favours of the most famous, and most promiscuous, of Henri's numerous mistresses, Gabrielle d'Estrées. In this, it seems, he was successful: indeed Sully declares roundly that the Duc de Vendôme was the illegitimate son not of the king but of Bellegarde. In consequence of his varied *amours*, Bellegarde, like so many of the French upper class at the time, suffered from venereal disease – from *lues venerea* or syphilis. In February 1603 la Rivière and Mayerne consulted together about so important a patient, and Mayerne offered a selection of cures from which la Rivière was to choose one. The cure was successful. The duke recovered: 'soli Deo laus et gloria!' chanted Mayerne.[20] The two men remained friends long afterwards. Thirty years later Mayerne would write complacently in the margin of his record: 'he is still alive, safe and well, and from the time of that cure he never felt the slightest trace of that disease.'[21]

About the same time, Mayerne began to keep his *Ephemerides*, or journal of the important or interesting cases with which he dealt. The record is not exhaustive: his papers, and the private correspondence of his patients, show many cases which he did not include in his *Ephemerides*; and sometimes we find a note 'refer in *Ephemerides*' – 'enter in the *Ephemerides*' – which shows that he selected particular cases for inclusion. The surviving *Ephemerides* run in an almost continuous series from August 1603 to his death in 1655,[22] and are an invaluable historical source. Mayerne evidently went over them frequently, adding marginal notes at different times to supplement and explain his old cases. The heading of the first surviving volume is missing, but in 1645 Mayerne inserted the title of the whole at the beginning of the second volume: '*Ephemerides* of diseases and index of remedies to be prescribed to various patients over forty years by Mayerne, du Chesne, etc.'[23]

The list of patients who, in those early years, were recorded by Mayerne as having been cured by la Rivière, du Chesne and himself, when the accredited doctors of Paris had given them up, include some distinguished names. There was Antoine Séguier, *president à mortier*, afterwards Chancellor of France. There was Madame de Retz. There was Sebastien Zamet, the court financier, famous for his splendid apartments and epicurean dinners, who had also had his turn as the lover of Gabrielle d'Estrées. There was 'la Concini', the notorious Italian wife of the notorious Italian adventurer Concino Concini, who had been brought over from Florence by Marie de Médicis and was to enjoy a lurid career, during her regency, as Maréchal d'Ancre. There was Renée Burlamachi, a member of a well-known Protestant family which had emigrated from Lucca to Geneva, and which from Geneva would spread to France, England and Holland. She was the widow of Cesare Balbani, another Lucchese *émigré* to Geneva. Afterwards she would be the last wife of the Huguenot hero and poet Agrippa d'Aubigné. She too, Mayerne observed, lived happily ever after, not dying until 1641. There were many other, obscurer names. There was also one more famous than them all: Armand du Plessis, the twenty-one-year-old bishop of Luçon, the future Cardinal de Richelieu. He too suffered from venereal disease – in his case *gonorrhoea inveterata*, with a hard *caruncula* at the entry of the bladder. This was a condition on which Mayerne was to become something of a specialist. Shortly after treating Richelieu he began a tract on the subject, and his explanation of the cure, in a letter to the great Swiss surgeon Wilhelm Fabry of Hilden, or Fabricius Hildanus, was the only medical writing of Mayerne published in his lifetime. It would be published by Fabry at Oppenheim, in the Palatinate, in 1619.[24]

To the established, privileged, Catholic and Galenist doctors of Paris all this was very distressing. The unqualified immigrant Huguenot 'chemical doctors', it seemed, were not only breaking into their monopoly but threatening to take it over. For it was not only Huguenots who preferred their services: high Catholic society was equally turning to them. If a man was afflicted with vene-real disease, he did not stand nicely upon sectarian positions. Huguenot grandees like Hercule de Rohan, the cousin of Mayerne's patron, and Catholic grandees like the Prince de Condé took the same way to be healed. The princes of the Church joined the princes of the Blood in the queue. The high priests of Catholicism (the Archbishop of Sens and the Archbishop of Aix) and the high priests of Calvinism (Agrippa d'Aubigné and Philippe du Plessis Mornay) alike sought the services of the three heretics from Geneva.

For the Paris doctors this capture of their richest and grandest patients by the infamous 'iatrochemists' of the court was too much. But what could they do? Their rivals, as long as their rivals were discreet – that is, silent – were safe under the protection of the court and society. Only if they should expose themselves by some particularly flagrant action, or publication, could the heavy machinery of the faculty be mobilised against them, as it had been mobilised against Roch le Baillif in 1579. The *cri de coeur* of Job – 'Oh that mine enemy had written a book!' – must often have been on the lips of the Riolans in those days; but since their arrival in Paris, neither la Rivière nor du Chesne nor Mayerne had published anything. Then, in the autumn of 1603, the fat was placed squarely in the fire. We have described the smouldering, hungry fire; we must now come to the explosive fat, whose distant savour could be smelt at the end of the last chapter. For the fat was the very same book which had so excited Mayerne when du Chesne showed it to him in manuscript, and for which Mayerne had sought the patronage of the alchem-ical Duke of Württemberg. In fact it was not dedicated to the duke, which was perhaps just as well: a German dedication would have made the book even more provocative, if that was possible, in Paris. But its place of publication sufficiently showed its heterodoxy. The royal doctor published his work not in royalist, Catholic Paris but in republican, Calvinist Geneva.[25]

As published, the book began with a challenge. In his preface to the reader, du Chesne declared his heresy by redefining the established schools of medi-cine. According to du Chesne, there were now four such schools. First, there was the 'empiric' school of Hippocrates, the father of medicine, which proceeded cautiously, experimentally, and by regular clinical observation. Then there was the 'methodic' school, which no reputable doctor now defended. It had been founded by Thessalus of Tralles, in the time of Nero, a man, said du Chesne, 'of the utmost impudence', and its exponents taught the comfortable but disastrous theory that medicine could be reduced, by various short cuts, to a series of simple rules of thumb. The third school was the 'dogmatic' or, as some called it, the 'rationalist' school of the Galenists, who borrowed from Hippocrates but built their systematic philosophy on the hypothesis of the four elements and their correspondences in the human body. To the Galenists, disease was imbalance among the elements and humours of the body. It was cured by correcting the imbalance and restoring a healthy equilibrium. So far, although there was room for marginal disagreement,[26] there was nothing to alarm the orthodox. But now du Chesne introduced a fourth school, which he not only raised to equality with these three but even extolled above them. This was the 'spagyric' school, 'which many regard as new, but which we consider the oldest of all'. The spagyric doctors, he said, were not revolutionaries: they valued both reason and experiment – the reason of Galen, the experiment of Hippocrates – but they gave to both a new philosophical basis: they began their study not, like Galen, by examining the mixture of the elements, but at the true fountain whence all reason must flow. It was to be found not in such extrinsic and universal elements but in the innate essences of the human body, which is the microcosm of the physical world.

This doctrine of essences, said du Chesne, is the foundation of the whole spagyric philosophy. By understanding it, the spagyrists have transcended all other schools and carried medicine to the highest philosophical perfection. They have been able to do this by going back to the original source of divinely revealed truth, 'the most famous, and the oldest of all philosophers', Hermes Trismegistus, whose works had been revealed to Frenchmen in 1579 through the translation by François de Foix, Comte de Candale and Bishop of Aire. Hermes, said du Chesne, had taught men to seek out, first of all, the occult, divine property of Nature. From that property, once it is recognised, it is possible to extract, and to create artificially, Nature's own cure for all diseases. This universal cure, or *panacea*, thus artificially created, is called by various names. Some call it 'quintessence', for it is the fifth essence, not made out of a mixture of the four elements. Others call it 'elixir', for it is an incomparable medicine for preserving life and repelling disease. Others call it *aurum potabile* or potable gold, not because it must always be made from gold (for it can be made out of all things under the sun), but *par excellence*, because gold excels all things. Others call it the philosopher's stone, not because of any comparison with the talisman of the old alchemists who sought to convert base metal into gold (for that is the invention and work of avarice, not medicine), but because of its eternal durability, or because it partakes of the nature of salt – salt which (here du Chesne is paraphrasing Paracelsus) is the life of nature, the solid foundation of all its virtues. Or it is called 'balsam', as the radical, incorruptible cure of all diseases. 'And although this substance, being spiritual, heavenly, invisible and hidden, and therefore perceptible to reason rather than to sense, can hardly be discovered in itself, nevertheless we shall show, by clear and certain reasons, that it both exists and can be possessed by a true philosopher . . . and soon we shall freely exhibit a specimen of it.' For as, by art, corporeal things can be rendered spiritual, so spiritual things – or astral, as Paracelsus calls them – can be rendered corporeal, invisible can be rendered visible, 'and those things which lately lay hid in the Hades of Hippocrates, or the night of Orpheus, or the pit of Democritus, can now be made manifest. What is still can be moved, and vice versa.'

This is a declaration of Hermetic faith, and the few concessions which du Chesne offered to the critics of that faith were hardly such as to disarm them. He allowed that glimpses of Hermetic truth had been granted to both Hippocrates and Galen, and had thence been revealed indirectly to some intervening doctors, like Fernel, who had shown, in his book on hidden causes in Nature, that he had 'sniffed' the truth.[27] But this was to praise the other schools only in so far as they agreed with his own. He insisted also that he himself did not go the whole way with Paracelsus; indeed, he explicitly rejected some parts of Paracelsus's philosophy. But this was merely to strengthen his own heresy by abandoning its less defensible positions.[28] Effectively, for all his apparent concessions, du Chesne was declaring open war on the old medical orthodoxy. His preface made this perfectly clear.

The substance of the work confirmed the threat. The first section elabo rated the supposed philosophy of the *prisci philosophi*. This was in fact the philosophy of Paracelsus concerning the three elements of salt, sulphur and mercury, and the means of extracting therefrom 'aurum animatum', living gold. It involved a system of 'balsamic medicine' which surpassed all other medical systems. There followed two sections on 'signatures', the 'external' signatures of simples, and the 'internal or specific signatures' discovered by the Hermetic philosophers. The final section consisted of the beginnings of a new pharmacopoeia, in which the old Galenist remedies were criticised, reorganised, complemented, sometimes subverted. In particular, there were three chapters on distillation. This section, du Chesne made clear, was only a fore- taste of what he intended ultimately to provide: a completely new system of medicine, based on Hermetic philosophy and chemical remedies.

Such, in brief, was the substance of du Chesne's book *De priscorum philosophorum verae medicinae materia*. That its publication would enrage the orthodox Galenists of Paris was a foregone conclusion, and du Chesne, who was an old troubleshooter, well versed in the rules of controversy, knew how to take proper precautions. Failing the Duke of Württemberg, he dedicated his treatise to the two most powerful ministers of Henri IV, the faithful supporters whom the king had chosen 'to repair and restore the state of this kingdom, almost entirely destroyed by so many pernicious wars'. These were Pomponne de Bellièvre, the Chancellor of France, and Nicolas Brûlart de Sillery, who would shortly succeed him in that office. In his dedication, du Chesne boasted of his intimacy with these great patrons, who were probably his patients, flattered them well, and claimed their protection. He was offering them, he said, a garland of fragrant flowers from two main schools of medical thought. To the Hippocratic teaching, 'now familiar and used by all', he had added the Hermetic philosophy, which he had renewed, 'and which, in my judgement, is far more solid, more reliable, and more effective'. 'I know', he added, 'how perilous a work I have undertaken. Many will think that I am bringing forward innovations, and so I expect to suffer many wild attacks from those who falsely accuse Hermetic medicine of novelty. But I hope to find myself well protected, for whatever is covered by your authority will be effectively defended from all injury.'

After the conclusion of his treatise on the medicine of the *prisci philosophi*, du Chesne printed, to fill out his book, four medical *consilia*. These were separately dedicated, and with equal tact. The first *consilium*, on the gout and the stone, was dedicated to his ally la Rivière. A second *consilium*, on disease of the kidneys, was dedicated to André du Laurens, who would shortly succeed la Rivière as *premier médecin du roi*. Thus the royal doctors were properly complimented. The third *consilium*, on venereal disease, was addressed, by name, to the professors of the Medical Faculty of Paris, 'learned friends, well known to me by joint consultations or social familiarity'. The fourth, on the 'immensely complicated disease' of a noble maiden, was dedicated to the professors of the rival Faculty of Medicine of Montpellier. By such a judicious distribution of dedications, du Chesne may have hoped to mitigate the blow which he clearly expected.

He was right at least in his expectation. To the medical establishment of the University of Paris, du Chesne's book was a frontal assault, more dangerous even than the attack of Roch le Baillif a generation ago. It was a blow struck in the heart of Paris, under the protection of the king, and at an intellectual level. What particularly enraged the orthodox was the exaltation of Hermetic medicine to the status of a 'school', equal, even superior, to the established schools of Hippocrates and Galen. Hitherto, Hermetic medicine had been a foreign heresy, discredited by extremism and absurdity. In le Baillif's work the absurdity of Paracelsus had still been visible. But now du Chesne, with his deeper erudition and wider range, had cleansed it of that absurdity and raised it, apparently, to a philosophic level. To the Medical Faculty of Paris such doctrines seemed no less a threat than Protestantism had seemed to the theologians of the Sorbonne. Was not this too a German heresy, which was now becoming modified, rationalised and denizened in France? Were not its advocates – la Rivière, du Chesne, Mayerne – all Protestants? Had they not all studied in Germany? Was not this new book itself published in Geneva? The doctors of the Sorbonne had triumphed over Henri IV's personal Protestantism. The doctors of the medical faculty were equally determined to triumph over his Protestant physicians.

So, when the work appeared in the bookstalls of Paris, they at once moved into action.[29] Old Riolan, it seems, was the moving spirit, but he operated from behind, through his son. On 13 August 1603 the acting dean, Gilles Heron,[30] summoned a meeting of the faculty to discuss the whole question of their relations with the royal *médecins par quartier* who were giving them so much trouble. From this it was a short step to the case of the infamous du Chesne. His enormities were now expounded. It was said that he had now at last vomited forth the poison which he had long kept hidden in his breast. The dedication of such heresy to the dignified professors of the faculty, by name, was regarded as a particular insult. There was to be a general attack on 'spagyric' doctors. But before anything could be decided, the apparently solid front of the faculty was suddenly broken. The non-conformist who now revealed himself was Pierre le Paulmier, known in Latin as Palmarius.

Pierre le Paulmier was a personal friend of du Chesne and Mayerne. He was the nephew of Julien le Paulmier, a Huguenot who had been physician to Charles IX. Julien le Paulmier had been the pupil and collaborator of Fernel, and, through him, Pierre le Paulmier had inherited Fernel's papers, which had perhaps influenced him. For le Paulmier was a chemical doctor, and all the chemical doctors – la Rivière, du Chesne, Mayerne – claimed Fernel as a precursor. If le Paulmier was a Huguenot, like his uncle, as well as a chemical doctor, his position in the faculty must have been somewhat delicate. When his turn came to speak, he ventured to defend du Chesne. He said that he had always respected du Chesne as a learned man and the king's doctor; that he himself had often had medical consultations with him; and that he did not think that *spagyria* should be repudiated, since it was very useful in medicine, 'however much it is attacked and abused by all and sundry'. However, this faint squeak of protest was soon to be silenced. The other doctors agreed that nobody should be allowed to say anything in favour of *spagyria*; that *spagyria* itself contained 'nothing but fraud, folly and trifles alien to the teaching of Hippocrates, Galen and all sound doctors, ancient and modern'; and that no member of the faculty should presume to consult with du Chesne. The objection that he was the king's doctor was pushed aside. But before launching a formal anathema against the enemy, it was necessary to unite the faculty. Le

Paulmier was therefore given a fortnight in which to recant. Isolated, he decided to yield, and on the appointed day he duly recanted. He explained that he had commended du Chesne not as a spagyric but only as a friend, and *spagyria* not as a theory but merely in so far as he had supposed that certain oils and chemically prepared liquids might usefully be prescribed by a 'dogmatic' or orthodox physician. But now he saw his error, and he swore, between the hands of the dean, that he would never again take counsel with du Chesne, spagyrists, empirics or any other persons disapproved by the faculty.[31] Thus the appearance of unanimity was restored and the faculty could proceed to the next step in the process of the excommunication. But the affair of le Paulmier was not quite over with his recantation. It would have a sequel.

The next step was to secure an official report on du Chesne's book. Immediately after receiving the recantation of le Paulmier, the faculty appointed the young Riolan, whose views were already well known, to make such a report, together with a colleague. The colleague was not identified in the subsequent controversy: everyone agreed that he was a cipher, and Mayerne would compare him with Caesar's colleague in the consulship. Even Riolan himself would soon forget him and use the first person singular in referring to their allegedly joint work. In fact the register of the faculty reveals that his colleague was Jean Duret. Like Riolan, he came of sound, orthodox stock: his father, Louis Duret, had been one of the representatives of the faculty in its battle, in 1580, against the redoubtable scholar Joseph Scaliger, who had dared, without being a member of the faculty, to comment on the text of Hippocrates.[32] The son, Riolan's colleague, was described as 'Hippocrates *redivivus*' by an orthodox practitioner who had expressed the view that 'empirics' like François Rosset – a royal doctor, a friend of la Rivière and Mayerne – should be flayed alive. So Jean Duret's views were as sound as his pedigree.[33] On 9 September Riolan and Duret reported back. Du Chesne's book, they said, was an attempt to insinuate into the bosom of medicine a new and heretical sect which would utterly destroy the old tradition. The faculty accepted the report. They decided – sixty doctors without a single dissentient, as the Riolans could proudly declare – that the book was unfit to see the light and should be buried in eternal silence. They then agreed that a formal anathema should be launched against du Chesne and published to the world in an official refutation of his book, which Riolan was commissioned to write; and they voted to present to Riolan, for his pains, a silver salt-cellar inscribed with the words 'facultas hoc me donavit munere': presented to me by the faculty.[34]

The anathema was launched the same day. It was a formidable document, in the high tradition of ideological controversy. It announced that the Medical

Faculty of Paris, having met in solemn session, and heard the report of the censors to whom it had referred du Chesne's book, now, by a unanimous vote, not only condemned all the spagyrical books of du Chesne, but the spagyric art itself; and it exhorted all those practising physic in the whole world to follow Hippocrates and Galen only. It further ordered that no man practising medicine in Paris should consult with du Chesne or with any other spagyrist or any doctor not approved by the faculty. Anyone so doing would be deprived of his salary and of all his academic privileges, and his name would be blotted out of the Register of Regent Physicians.

Riolan's pamphlet, which conveyed this document to the outer world, was soon ready. It was entitled *A Defence of the Medicine of Hippocrates and Galen*, and it was dedicated to the faculty. It was published anonymously, but the violence of the style easily betrayed, to those who knew him, the identity of the author. There is no conservative so rabid as a young conservative, and it must have been very gratifying to the old professor to see his son coming along so nicely, even though he had not yet received his doctorate. The young Riolan began by declaring that novelty is the ruin of states and of society, as is shown by the history of Rome, whose greatness only lasted so long as it maintained its ancient customs;[35] he emphasised the unanimity of the faculty against du Chesne's 'barbarous and repulsive' book; and he launched into a wholesale attack not merely on Paracelsian extremes, or on the presentation of the 'fourth school' of Hermetic philosophers as a challenge to the other three (to which the offence of du Chesne was afterwards narrowed down), but on all who used chemical medicines. He called upon God to avert this diabolical plague from the earth, and upon men to extirpate it whenever it should be found. Chemistry, declared Riolan, was not an art or a science, because it proceeded not from high philosophic 'reason' but merely from vulgar experience. At best the chemist was the servant of the apothecary as the surgeon was the servant of the physician. Even if it should be useful, chemistry was beneath the dignity of the physician and not worth its cost to the patient. Its medicines were the seductive and therefore sinful inventions of the Devil, working through his agent Paracelsus, etc., etc.[36]

Having thus, as they supposed, destroyed du Chesne and his infamous book, the doctors of the faculty met again on 25 September to consider further measures of self-protection. They decided that a solemn oath should be tendered to all members of the faculty, who should swear, individually, that they would never consult with du Chesne or any spagyrist, or divulge the secrets of the faculty. For greater solemnity, this oath was to be tendered at a public ceremony on the day of St Luke, the patron saint of physicians, which was 18 October. This was duly done. The assembled physicians, each in turn, swore the oath between the hands of the dean, and signed the Register. After that, it seemed the battle was over, and won. The hard line had succeeded. The faculty had shown its strength and its solidarity. The 'chemical doctors', in the person of du Chesne, had been crushed.

It was at this point that Mayerne suddenly intervened. No doubt he entered reluctantly. All his life he was reluctant to publish, and his temper was, in general, conciliatory, not controversial. But he was provoked by the condemnation of chemical medicine and by the personal insults of Riolan; and if, as Riolan would state, du Chesne had solicited his support, he could hardly refuse to defend at once his old friend and patron and his own honour. In a very short time Mayerne wrote and published his *Apologia*: a work designed, as the full title made clear, to show that chemical remedies can safely be used without violating the laws of Hippocrates and Galen. The book was printed in la Rochelle, the Huguenot citadel of the west, by a Huguenot printer.[37] Thus the identity of medical and religious heresy, already illustrated by du Chesne, was re-emphasised by Mayerne. But in dedicating it, Mayerne, like du Chesne, looked for a politician who could defend him if he should, once again, be persecuted. He chose Achille de Harlay, the famous President of the Parlement de Paris, whose authority in matters of public law was unquestionable. Harlay had now held his office for twenty-one years. During the convulsions of civil war, when the royal power in Paris had disappeared, he had consistently, and at the risk of his life, upheld the continuity, the impartiality and the dignity of the law. Now, in more settled times, he was an institution in himself. Mayerne's enemies might well hesitate to bring before the Parlement a man who visibly enjoyed the favour of such a president.

Forty years later, writing to his friend Dr Spon, Gui Patin would state that Mayerne was not the author of the *Apologia* which was printed in his name: that it was 'no more written by him than by you or me'. He would add a very circumstantial account of how the work came to be published. 'Two doctors of our society worked on it,' he said, 'Séguin, our elder, and his brother-in-law Akakia . . . They did this to spite some of our elders who were honest men and made gallant efforts to prevent chemists and charlatans from gaining credit here and selling their hot air to those who gape after novelty in Paris.'[38] In spite of this confident assertion – and whatever Patin said, he said with confidence – the statement that Mayerne did not write the book must be rejected. Patin often made such statements. We have seen that he equally denied to du Chesne the authorship of his works, and he would equally seek to rob Ambroise Paré of his.[39] But in fact, on all grounds, it is clear that Mayerne wrote the book. The style is his – some of the very metaphors are his;[40] it contains personal and autobiographical details which must have come from him; and although it brought him into trouble he never disowned any part of it. We can therefore safely take it as an expression of his views.

What we can allow to Patin is that Mayerne probably called on his friends for help when writing it. This is inherently likely. It is also very interesting, for it shows that the Medical Faculty of Paris, however vigorously dragooned, was not in fact as unanimous as the Riolans insisted. We have already seen that Pierre le Paulmier had to be forced into line. Now we see two distinguished members of the faculty positively collaborating with the enemy. Mayerne himself says that two or three of the ablest doctors were absent from the faculty meeting. These no doubt were (or included) the supporters whom Patin names: Pierre Séguin and Martin Akakia. Both these men were professors of medicine at the Collège Royal and both came from well-known medical dynasties. The family of Akakia had been founded by Martin Sans-malice, *premier médecin* to François I, who, as a good humanist, had converted his name into Greek as Akakia; and it would remain powerful in the faculty for over a century. Séguin would become physician to Louis XIII and, for twenty-five years, *premier médecin* to his queen, Anne of Austria. Mayerne's correspondence and notebooks show that he was intimate with both men. He would describe Akakia as 'intimus meus' and he would write to Séguin as 'amicorum integerrimo', signing himself 'tuus ad omnia'.[41] Du Chesne tells us, at this very time, that he always consulted Mayerne and Séguin in difficult cases. Afterwards Mayerne and Séguin would laugh together at the stupidity of Séguin's colleagues in the faculty.[42] All this shows that the unanimity of the faculty which appears in the public documents was very artificial; and indeed the hysterical tone of those documents, and of Riolan's pamphlets, suggests that the spokesmen of the faculty were fighting an enemy at closer quarters than they chose to admit.

Mayerne's *Apologia* is written in a very different style. It is severe and contemptuous, but its disdain has a confident, even Olympian ring. His dedication begins by repudiating any affectation of novelty. 'Far be it from me to repeal the laws of Hippocrates', he declares, 'or to deviate from them in the least.' Hippocrates, to him, was *summum dictator*, whom he would not lightly desert. However, time was always bringing forth new discoveries and it was impious to neglect the gifts of Heaven. Our precursors are not our masters but our guides. Mayerne had been savaged by the teeth of calumniators, and he appealed to Harlay to defend the public interest by distinguishing legitimate doctors, who sought to advance their art on the basis of acquired learning, from the quacks with whom the zealots of the faculty sought to confound them.

Then he turned to his anonymous calumniator. Riolan had attacked him as *transfuga* – a deserter from true medicine to false – and as a foreigner and intruder from Montpellier into the holy circle of Paris. It was true, replied Mayerne, that he had studied at the University of Montpellier. Of that he was prepared to boast. Montpellier, he said proudly, was superior to any university in the world. It was 'the most ancient and prosperous mart of medicine'; its clear air 'purges the heavy intellects bred in other places, so that medicine thrives there as in its native soil'; and he would apply to it what the ancients had said of the Greek city of Croton in Sicily, that the last of its inhabitants was equal to the first of all other Greeks.

Having thus vindicated the University of Montpellier, Mayerne went on to vindicate his own studies both there and elsewhere: the practical courses which he had followed, the experience which he had gained, his work in the hospitals, in the mortuaries, in the pharmacy and the anatomy theatre, which had qualified him better (though at a far cheaper rate) than the doctors of Paris who had merely purchased their monopoly without soiling their hands. He described his previous encounter with these 'hireling doctors', who had been defeated by the equity of the magistrate and the favour of the king. He referred to his travels abroad, to his conversations with the learned men of Germany and Italy, who had treated him as an equal. Who then, he asked, were the doctors of Paris to dismiss him as an intruder into the hall of medicine, when he was a legitimate priest of the shrine?

Of course, added Mayerne, he did not wish to condemn all the Paris doctors. He knew well that the most distinguished of them had had no part in the attack on him. He excepted particularly Dr Martin, a true doctor, pious, learned, modest and upright, a model to all . . . This exception was somewhat ironical, for Martin, in his youth, had been the Riolan of his generation. Like Louis Duret, he had led the faculty against Joseph Scaliger, even giving rival lectures on Hippocrates. Scaliger, needless to say, had won that battle.[43] Here too, Mayerne might aptly have compared the narrow jealousy of Paris with the liberal spirit of Montpellier, where Casaubon had been invited to lecture on Hippocrates. But this would have been impolitic. Martin might not be a very distinguished doctor, but he had court favour, and he was evidently a friend of Mayerne's colleague and ally Pierre Séguin.

Having thus isolated his enemies, Mayerne set out to win over the moderate Galenists by his own moderation. His assailant he dismissed as a mere parrot or magpie who chattered without understanding: who laid down the law about Hermes, whom he could not distinguish from Moses; who thought that all alchemy consisted in distillation; who denounced antimony, which he himself had probably never seen, and precipitate of mercury, which he could not accurately describe; who condemned as 'empiric' every remedy which he could not explain, or had not tried, or even heard named; and who ascribed to Paracelsus, whose name he only knew from the Index, ideas which could never be found in his books. If the doctors of Paris really wished to know about chemistry, said Mayerne, they should listen not to ignorant polemics but to the philosophy of those who had studied the subject, as he himself had done. One day, he added, if he could ever find the time, he would write out what he knew, for the benefit of the state, the improvement of science, and the confusion of his enemies. But at present he had no such time. He was too busy, being more concerned to practise than to preach, to exercise his skill among the sick, whom other and grander doctors had abandoned, than to write books: a task which called for a man of leisure, like this scurrilous pamphleteer.

However, he would give a brief profession of faith. Since everything in this sub-lunar world was created by God for the use of man, is it not reasonable, he asked, to seek remedies for the diseases with which He has punished us, in all animals, plants and minerals? In doing this we are not tied to the past. The art of medicine was not laid down, perfect and final, even by the ancients. 'If Galen had been content with the remedies of Hippocrates, the Arabians with those of Galen, their successors with those of the Arabians, medicine would never have attained its present splendour.' And yet, even now, how little we know compared with what we still do not know! Time and the barbarity of man make war against the divine call to the improvement of knowledge. It was in answer to this call that Mayerne had travelled and studied and worked. It had always been his aim, he said, to profit all men, to harm none. So, being resolved to improve the society in which he found himself, he had often left his home, travelling far in search of learning. Sworn to no school, pursuing only truth, he had read Hippocrates and Galen, Geber, Lull, Isaac,[44] 'and among other things, I wished to know for myself what that famous man, Theophrastus of Switzerland' – that is, Paracelsus – 'had handed down to posterity, in more than thirty books, sometimes anonymous, sometimes unpublished'; in which books – says Mayerne – I found much which, if rightly used, could benefit human health. If I reject some of it as contrary to sound medicine or religion or morals, must I condemn all? Out of the dunghill of Ennius Virgil picked gold.[45] You call me a chemist? I glory in the name. The true doctor uses chemical remedies together with Hippocrates' precepts, and finds in them quicker, safer, more comfortable cures. You say that it is unworthy of the dignity of the physician to go down to the furnace or to handle drugs, and you urge the faculty not to allow such confusion of ranks. I never make or prescribe anything except after personal study, personal labour. Galen himself, Mayerne pointed out, had travelled to Cyprus, gone down the mines; he had not been afraid to enter suffocating caves and to work in furnaces in order to study mineral medicine ... If Hippocrates were alive today, he would erase all your names from the roll of doctors.[46]

Having thus stated his philosophy, Mayerne came down to detail, arguing the merit of particular remedies and disputing the case-histories which had been cited against him and du Chesne. Then he turned to the formal condemnation of du Chesne, the attack on himself. He treated these attacks as the expression of mere vulgar envy. Galen himself, he remarked, had had similar trouble with doctors of Rome. So why should we be put out by that ridiculous anathema against the spagyric doctors and their science: 'a horrible thunderclap, without lightning – no, rather a childish cracker'?[47] The doctors who condemned du Chesne were like the Athenian peasant who voted against Aristides because he was held to be too just. You yourselves use chemical extracts, provided they are already in use: hellebore, spirit of vitriol, various oils, iron, laudanum, *crocus martis* . . . And anyway, what did the doctors of Paris hope to achieve by condemning du Chesne and forbidding others to consult with him? Did they think that he, the true disciple of Hippocrates, whose range was so much wider than theirs, needed their support, their licence? The thought was absurd. It only showed the unbearable arrogance of the Paris doctors, which Mayerne now urged the doctors of Europe, and especially of injured Montpellier, to rise up and crush. In particular, he appealed to André du Laurens, doctor of Montpellier, his own friend and patron, now in Paris as royal doctor, to mobilise the king. With that last ominous appeal, Mayerne ended his work and turned away from the controversy. This, he said, was his last word. 'Expect no further answers from me to your idle scribblings. Unless you publish something more worthy of a doctor, your futile squabble shall receive from me nothing but eternal, contemptuous silence.'[48]

When the professors of Paris read this formidable manifesto, there was a scurry of feet and a flutter of gowns. If it had been right to excommunicate du Chesne, how could such a flagrant defiance by Mayerne be ignored? How could the Riolans allow such contumacy to go unpunished? Or Dr Heron, the dean of the faculty, who had put his name to the first anathema? Or 'that magnificent Dr Helin' whom Mayerne had singled out by name as the first author of all these broils, a man 'equally detested by all surgeons and apothecaries'? Clearly another, even more formidable anathema must be sent forth against the contumacious rebel. So the engineers were summoned, the catapult mounted, the explosive missile framed and fitted to the machine. On 29 November 1603, after mass (according to the official register of the faculty), 'certain doctors assembled in the Upper Schools and complained that there had come forth, under the name of Mayerne Turquet, an infamous book against the honour of the faculty, into which the author, with the utmost impudence, had thrown together all the *dicteria*, scurrilities, abuse, and calumnies which rashness, ill-temper and intoxication could have suggested to a man beside himself with rage.' After this, the ritual acts were repeated. Once again Riolan and Duret were appointed to read the book and report. Once again they reported. Once again the report was read and approved, the anathema framed, and a book commissioned to disseminate it. The terms of this new anathema were far more violent than those which had been used against du Chesne. Mayerne's *Apologia* was condemned as an infamous, lying, abusive, scandalous work, such as could have been uttered only by an incompetent, shameless, drunken lunatic; he himself was declared disqualified, by reason of his rashness, impudence and ignorance of true medicine, ever to practise; and all doctors were forbidden to consult with him, on pain of degradation and expulsion from the faculty.[49]

As before, the book which purported to answer the offending work, and which published the anathema to the world, was anonymous. It was entitled *A Reply to the Infamous Apologia of Turquet*.[50] Although it was anonymous, the author, at one point, forgot himself and used language which, to an observant reader, might have suggested that he was the elder Riolan – but for the fact that, in a later work, also ostensibly written by the elder Riolan, this *Reply* was carelessly cited as being by 'my son'. In fact, the later work too was by the son, writing in his father's name.[51] The Riolans, it is clear, operated as a team, the father providing the status and the authority, the son providing the active, poisonous pen. At first the young Riolan wrote anonymously or pseudonymously; but in 1604, having taken his doctorate, he emerged from the shadows. He was well rewarded. 'As a small testimony of gratitude to his father for his many labours undertaken in the name of the faculty' – that is, to himself for the pamphlets written in his father's name – he was excused payment of the usual fees paid by new doctors and granted a gift of 180 livres, being the fees paid by the other new doctors.[52] And next year, at the age of twenty-five, he was appointed Professor of Anatomy and Botany at the Collège Royal. After that, he could afford to drop his disguise and write under his own name and titles – except when he found it more convenient, or more tactful, to write in support of himself in his father's name. This literary agility of the young Riolan confused many of his contemporaries, as it has confused modern bibliographers. But as he could not always, in the heat of his multiple controversies, remember when he was, or had been, posing as someone else, he generally let the cat out of the bag somewhere, and those who read the pamphlets can say with confidence that they are all by him.

Not that they are worth reading. They are all violent, abusive, personal. In replying to Mayerne, Riolan made heavy play with his name Turquet. Mayerne, he wrote, was rightly called after a dog since he barked, snapped and bit at all doctors, known and unknown. Clearly he suffered from rabies . . . Riolan then proceeded to accuse Mayerne of killing his patients (except such as were saved by Riolan himself, after coming to him in the nick of time to be relieved of the poisonous 'chemical' pills) and of charging huge fees for doing so. If any recovered, it was because he had arrived too late to do them any harm: 'happy the doctor who is called when the disease is on the wane.'[53] Du Chesne and Mayerne, Riolan wrote, were very properly called royal doctors, since, by killing so many of the king's subjects, they fed the royal treasure from taxes payable at death. They were also too fond of the bottle: did they not admit to having been invited to a dinner-party by a grateful patient (whom, of course, they afterwards killed)? With these and such arguments, Riolan sought to destroy his enemies. Whether, like Mayerne, they maintained a contemptuous silence, or, like du Chesne, they answered back, he followed every blow with whoops of triumph and paeans of victory. Du Chesne and Turquet, he cried (writing under another pseudonym), had been defeated and had given up the struggle: they now lay prostrate on the ground, transfixed by the unerring darts of their anonymous assailant.[54] Again, writing more gravely, in the name of his father, he recounted how Turquet had come to the aid of du Chesne, and had rent and torn the most famous medical school of Paris; but now that aspiring Phaëthon had paid the price of his temerity: 'he repents, and will long repent, of his impudent book.'[55]

We need not follow the controversy in detail. It would go through another dozen pamphlets. Two of these pamphlets were written by du Chesne, and drew down upon him two more replies from Riolan and a second, more intemperate anathema from the faculty. Mayerne held his peace, but he was not, for that reason, forgotten. On 10 June 1604, at the same meeting at which it voted the grant of money to Riolan, the faculty ordered that the list of doctors who were licensed to practise in the city, and for whom the apothecaries were authorised to prepare drugs, should be reprinted, 'but omitting the name of Theodore de Mayerne Turquet who (though included among the king's doctors) the faculty has already, by its decree of 5 December 1603, declared unfit to practise'. This order was re-enacted by the faculty on 1 October 1604.[56]

Meanwhile the battle-front had widened. In 1604 the Huguenot chemical doctors of Orléans came to the aid of their friends in Paris. Their champion was Israel Harvet. Aided by another Huguenot doctor of Orléans, Guillaume Baucinet, he contributed three pamphlets to the controversy;[57] and he sought the patronage of the most distinguished Huguenot of Orléans, Jerôme Groslot de l'Isle, whom we have already met as the friend of Pierre Asselineau in Venice. De l'Isle was the son of a *bailli* of Orléans who had been murdered in the massacre of St Bartholomew. He himself had escaped to England, and only returned when Henri IV had come to the throne. He was a friend of George Buchanan, Janus Dousa, Jacques-Auguste de Thou, Paolo Sarpi and indeed all the scholars of the Protestant and pro-Protestant world. He was a timely ally, because he had just been cured of a violent dysentery – whose symptoms are described in remorseless detail – by such 'chemical' remedies as 'laudanum' (an invention of du Chesne) and 'tinctures of coral and pearl'. But we need not lose ourselves in these peripheral skirmishes. It will be enough to notice that Harvet, who published his first book in Paris, afterwards turned to foreign printers. His second was printed in Frankfurt, and third in Hanau. The third was his last. He uttered it, according to the genial Riolan, 'with his last gasp, and then vomited out his soul to his own and Paracelsus's master', the Devil.[58]

If we could believe that controversies are decided by the flow of literature or the claims of the writers, or even by formal decisions, officially recorded, then we might suppose, as Riolan himself supposed (or at least wished others to suppose), that by 1605 the Paris doctors had defeated their rivals, who were now silent, or, like Harvet, dead. And no doubt Riolan and his friends saw confirmation of their wishes in another event of that year. For in the autumn of 1605 his two main adversaries lost their strongest supporter at court. An epidemic was raging in Paris at the time, and it carried off, among others, the patron of them both, the *premier médecin*, Jean Ribit de la Rivière.

A contemporary, who was a friend and patient of la Rivière in Paris, Jean-Baptiste le Grain, tells a story of la Rivière's death. When the physician realised that his end was near, he sent for his servants and distributed among them all his money, plate and movable possessions. Then he told them, each in turn, to leave the house and never return. When all had gone and he was alone in his house, with no furniture except the bed on which he lay, his medical friends came to enquire after his health and attended his sickness. La Rivière asked them to summon his servants; but they replied that they had found the door open, the house empty and servantless. Then la Rivière said, 'Adieu, Messieurs, il est donc temps que je m'en aille aussi, puisque mon bagage est parti' (Farewell, then, gentlemen, it is time for me to leave too, since my luggage has gone on ahead); and so died. As we never hear that la Rivière was married, or had heirs, the story may well be true, or have a basis of truth.[59] It has a certain inherent plausibility, for the few glimpses that we can catch of his personality suggest a somewhat roguish sense of humour. We remember the disapproval of the severe Huguenot Agrippa d'Aubigné, who taxed him with unseasonable gaiety and freedom of spirit. The same character was given to him, implicitly, by the diarist Pierre de l'Estoile, who on hearing of his death described him as 'the good thief on whom the Lord had pity'.[60]

The death of la Rivière was clearly a blow to du Chesne and Mayerne, and indeed to the Huguenot party at court. It would have been different if one of them had succeeded to the vacant position – as indeed might have been expected: for unquestionably the king was fond of la Rivière and valued him as a physician, and du Chesne and Mayerne were his understudies and natural successors. But in fact this was now out of the question. The ideological war was too fierce. La Rivière, when consulted by the king, was too prudent to suggest a Huguenot successor. He proposed three names: André du Laurens, who is already familiar to us and was *premier médecin* of the queen; Pierre Milon, a physician of Poitiers; and Antoine Petit, from Gien, near Orléans.[61] All three had studied at Montpellier.[62] La Rivière clearly had no opinion of the Galenists of Paris and did not expect the king to want them either. The king would show his respect for la Rivière by taking all his three nominees in turn. Immediately, he appointed du Laurens.[63] To some extent this appointment was satisfactory to the reformers. At least the post did not go to a faculty bigot. But the death of la Rivière marked a point in the history of the court of Henri IV. The long rule of the Huguenot *premiers médecins* was now at an end.

However, in other and more important respects, du Chesne and Mayerne did find themselves the heirs of la Rivière. La Rivière is himself an elusive figure, as any physician must be who leaves no written work by which to be judged. But the respect in which he was held by Mayerne is clear from Mayerne's own papers. Mayerne preserved letters, *consilia*, notebooks and commonplace-books by la Rivière, and had copies made for his own use. Of the manuscripts which he would afterwards take with him to England, the greater part were by, or of, la Rivière.[64] In the antidotaries, lists of drugs, and formal treatises in which he would record his whole system of treatment, the method and the remedies of la Rivière would easily predominate. Indeed, it is only through Mayerne's papers that we know anything about la Rivière. If du Chesne first interested Mayerne in the new medicine of Paracelsus, it was probably la Rivière who had the more lasting influence on him. For la Rivière, on all the evidence, was far less doctrinaire in his ideas, far more eclectic in his method, than du Chesne. He was less deeply committed to Paracelsian ideas, Hermetic philosophy, alchemical mysteries. The empiricism, the patient observation, the suspension of judgement, which would make Mayerne so successful a physician at the courts of James I and Charles I, are the same qualities which evidently made la Rivière so successful at the court of Henri IV. They are different from the more provocative, controversial qualities which made du Chesne a successful propagandist and a spectacular controversialist – but never made him a royal physician-in-chief.

On la Rivière's death, Mayerne not only collected his manuscripts. He also, with du Chesne, collected his patients. After 1605 all the patients of la Rivière whom we can identify as such appear, sooner or later, on Mayerne's books. Sometimes they appear at once, like the de Lomenie family or Nicolas Harlay de Sancy; sometimes, like Rivière's former patron the Duc de Bouillon, they appear in the autumn of 1609, following the death of du Chesne. A glance at Mayerne's *Ephemerides* shows the process. It also shows how barren in fact the boasted victory of the faculty had been. For these notebooks, crowded with the names of the notables of Paris, record the practice of a doctor who, by the authority of the faculty, had been struck off the register of physicians permitted to practise. In theory, no doctor should consult with him, no right-minded citizen should employ him, no apothecary should make up his medicines. But nobody outside the faculty paid any attention to its commands. Did Riolan know, in 1605, when he dedicated one of his fiery tracts to Renaud de Beaune, Archbishop of Sens, grand almoner of France, that that orthodox prelate had been a patient of the Huguenot Sieur de la Rivière and was now a patient of the banned Huguenot Dr Mayerne?

In fact the faculty had not prevailed. But nor, for that matter, had the 'chemical doctors'. The controversy between them could not be decided in such isolation. If it could have been, it would not be worth remembering, or recapitulating. It was important because it transcended the narrow bounds of the Paris faculty and the court of Henri IV. This scientific debate was enmeshed in a European controversy which could not be detached from the political and ideological tensions of Europe. In 1605 it had come to a temporary halt in Paris; but it was not over. In the next chapters we shall see it extend beyond the frontiers of France. We shall see du Chesne calling in the forces of Protestant Germany, and Mayerne feeling his way to a refuge in Protestant England.

6

The German Dimension, 1605–1606

The controversy between the chemical and the Galenist doctors of Paris, which seemed deadlocked in 1605, was both widened and deepened in the following years. It was widened by its extension to Germany, and deepened by its involvement in the growing tension between Catholic and Huguenot in Henri IV's France, especially in Paris. The widening of the controversy gave the 'iatrochemists' an intellectual victory; its deepening ensured their political defeat, and would lead ultimately to the emigration of Mayerne to England.

The extension of the controversy to Germany was implicit in its very nature, for Germany was the original source of chemical medicine. It was thence, directly or indirectly, that all the French 'chemical doctors' drew their inspiration. In a sense, the Huguenot communities in France were channels for the communication of ideas from Germany – and indeed from the whole north European Protestant world: their Protestantism made them international while French Catholicism, since Spain had captured the political leadership of the Counter-Reformation, was self-contained, national, Gallican. We have seen that du Chesne had at first sought a German patron for his provocative book, and that Israel Harvet published his later works in Germany. Already, in his reply to the *Apologia* published by Mayerne in December 1603,[1] Riolan had forecast the shift: du Chesne, he there wrote, had employed Mayerne as his immediate auxiliary 'while waiting for an ampler and more learned reply from Germany. Thus mule scratches mule';[2] and du Chesne, in his next work, published early in 1604, had given substance to the charge. In this work, which he dedicated to Sully, the greatest of the Huguenots in the government of Henri IV, du Chesne presented an *Apologia pro vita suâ*, describing his own studies in Germany and his reverence for his German teachers. He also gave a list of the German princes who patronised the new medicine and its practitioners: the emperor Rudolf II, King Sigismund of Poland, the Archbishop of Cologne, the Margrave of Brandenburg, Heinrich

Julius Duke of Brunswick, his own particular patron Moritz Landgrave of Hesse, Ferdinand Duke of Bavaria, 'all the princes of Anhalt' and many others. Thanks to these patrons, he wrote, Germany, which had always been the fertile womb of men of genius for the whole world, was now the centre of the Hermetic philosophy and the chemical art; and he proceeded to list some of the great professors of that philosophy and that art throughout Europe, almost all of them Protestants and none of them French. Such a defence, or rather defiance, was not likely to convince his adversaries, and this second book of du Chesne brought down upon his head the second anathema of the medical faculty, in which it was described as a monstrous birth unworthy to see the light and only fit to be drowned at once, as impure, in a running stream.[3]

One of the great chemists of Germany whom du Chesne particularly named was Andreas Libau or Liebau, in Latin Libavius, 'a most celebrated doctor, a faithful and industrious investigator of Nature, a keen defender of true chemistry. If our anonymous writer' – that is, Riolan – 'had read his works, he would not have raved thus against true chemistry.' In this casual way there enters into our narrative the man who, by the sheer weight of his learning, was to flatten not merely Riolan but the whole Paris faculty and the controversy which it had raised.

Andreas Libavius was a Saxon born at Halle, a centre of German salt-mining and pietism. His father had been a clothworker from the Harz mountains. With his fellow-Saxon Oswald Croll, he ranks as a founding father of modern chemistry. Croll was from Electoral Saxony and worked in Dresden. Libavius was from 'Ernestine' Saxony, ducal Saxony, which in his time was fragmented into two, three and finally four duchies. He had received a thorough humanist education, had studied philosophy and medicine at the new ducal university of Jena, valued himself as a poet (in Latin of course), and was learned in classical literature and philology. As an author he was both prolific and prolix, a true German. By 1604, when du Chesne invoked his name, he had published at least thirty works, controversial and expository, on philosophy, theology, history and, especially, alchemy and chemistry. His most important single work was his *Alchymia triumphans*, a massive textbook of the science, of which a German chemical firm has piously published a complete translation in our own time.[4] Since 1591 he had been *Stadtphysicus* or city doctor of the free city of Rothenburg-ob-der-Tauber in the region of Franconia. In 1607 one of the Saxon dukes, John Casimir of Saxe-Coburg, would call him back as head of his newly founded Casimirianum at Coburg, and there he would remain till his death in 1616.

In invoking the authority of a German Protestant, du Chesne was taking a certain risk. In invoking that of Libavius he was taking a double risk. For

Libavius, though always ready for controversy, was a far more staid and cautious man than du Chesne. A Lutheran, the subject of a conservative Lutheran prince, he had no sympathy with the political dynamism of the Calvinist international or the advanced ideas that were nourished, especially in the West German courts of Heidelberg, Kassel and Stuttgart. Though a chemist, and a pioneer of chemistry, he was not a Paracelsian. Indeed, he was one of the most resolute and formidable opponents of 'the smoky, vapid platoon of the Paracelsists'. With his severe, rational, humanist training, he regarded Paracelsus not (with Severinus the Dane and du Chesne) as a necessary if erratic genius whose revolutionary ideas must be shifted, purged and corrected, but (with Bacon) as an impostor, a vulgar, arrogant sectarian who had done incalculable harm to the orderly advance of chemical knowledge. To Libavius, medieval alchemy, however vitiated in practice, was a serious and fruitful discipline: it contained all the material out of which modern iatro-chemistry could be developed. There was no need, he thought, of the explosive and destructive stimulant of Paracelsianism; and he had said so, forcibly, in several outspoken works of Teutonic length, depth and weight. These works had been directed mainly against a German Paracelsist of Erfurt, Johann Gramann, who had exasperated him by claiming chemistry as a monopoly of the extreme Paracelsians.[5] Nonsense, replied Libavius: true chemists fitted their chemical theories into the Galenic system of elements and humours. Even the three principles of Paracelsus – salt, sulphur, mercury – could be accommodated into that system. He admitted that Paracelsus himself had performed some 'almost miraculous cures', and that his followers had at first been welcomed by open-minded men; but then they had gone too far, and now they were generally despised. They were despised for their arrogance, their refusal to discuss with other scientists, their intolerable boasts, their scurrilous abuse of their rivals – exactly the charges that had been made against them by la Rivière in his letter to Camerarius. The 'true chemists', Libavius insisted, were not of their school.[6]

One of the true chemists, he allowed, was du Chesne who, he wrote in 1594, rejected neither the elements nor the humours of Galen, whatever rhetorical phrases he might occasionally use.[7] Libavius and du Chesne, it seems, knew each other well: du Chesne would afterwards recall how, in 1598, 'mon singulier amy Libavius' had sent him his method of dissolving gold as a panacea to restore and renew the body.[8] On the other hand du Chesne's book of 1603, with its unqualified Hermetism, its exaltation of *spagyria* into a new school, might well alarm so conservative a scientist, and in appealing to him for support against the Paris faculty du Chesne might well be courting a rebuff. This was clearly the opinion of Riolan, who was delighted to see his enemy walk into such a trap. 'You refer me to the writings of Libavius,' he retorted. 'I have read what he has written against Gramann, a man just like you. He there mentions you occasionally, but only as "the spagyrist Quercetanus". He does not dignify you with the title of doctor. He clearly agrees with us.' If you want Libavius as an umpire, Riolan concluded contemptuously, rest assured that he regards you as the greatest fool of all.[9] At this time Riolan was riding high. It seems that the faculty, not content with the condemnation of the chemical doctors and the branding of their books, had appealed, again, to the Parlement, and even demanded that the death penalty be exacted from those who used chemical medicine. But the Parlement once more refused to listen to their appeal and snubbed them openly by publishing its refusal.[10]

When the noise of the great Parisian controversy reached him in Rothenburg, Libavius at first decided to keep out of the battle. It may be that Riolan and his party took positive steps to keep him out. Certainly, about this time, they began to shift their ground, suggesting that they were not attacking chemical medicine itself, only du Chesne's alleged attempt to set up a fourth, Hermetic and Paracelsian school, independent of traditional medicine and frontally opposed to it. At all events, Libavius was at first ready to accept this interpretation and, on those grounds, to remain outside a purely sectarian battle. 'I have read all about the Parisian controversy,' he wrote to another German doctor in December 1604. 'The Paris doctors are not attacking the true Alchemy accepted and preached by our party, but the Paracelsian form of it which du Chesne has taken over from the *Idea* of Severinus the Dane, and which is opposed to the principles of Galen. This is a form which neither I nor any other Hippocratic doctor approves. So let us allow Riolan to finish off those monsters and clear the field of medicine from that bane.' 'It is true', he added, 'that Riolan sometimes attacks chemical medicine rather sharply and occasionally offends against justice and truth. But we can excuse him on account of the circumstances and of the Paracelsian doctrines.' In the eyes of Libavius, the Paris faculty was defending sound medicine not against chemical ideas but only against 'those distorting colours and fraudulent fantasies with which the Paracelsians have obscured the truth'.[11]

At least that is how it seemed at the end of 1604. But as the controversy rolled on, Libavius – prompted perhaps by du Chesne and his friends – gradually realised its fundamental character. The Paris doctors, he discovered, were not defending true chemistry, however intemperately, against the Paracelsian deviation: they were opposing all chemistry, true and false alike, and indeed exploiting the false in order to destroy, with it, the true. The tactical necessities of controversy might have driven du Chesne into a somewhat exposed position, but essentially he was on the right side. As he studied the works, and the private letters, of du Chesne and the Orléans doctors, Libavius decided that 'none of these doctors had ever deserted Hippocrates for any spurious medicine.' On the contrary, they were simply seeking, like Libavius himself, to reconcile chemical medicine with traditional teaching. In this they were following the advice of Hippocrates himself, who had looked forward to the completion of medical knowledge by later discovery. On the other hand Riolan and his friends, in spite of their protestations, were clearly shown to have attacked not only particular Paracelsian passages in the work of du Chesne and Mayerne but the whole concept of chemical medicine to which both they and Libavius, though with a difference of emphasis, were committed. By the end of the year Libavius had decided that he must emerge from his neutrality and enter the lists. 'The battle', he wrote, 'is not for du Chesne: it is for Alchemy itself.'

In that battle Riolan was now boasting of his universal victory, and no voice was being raised to oppose his claims. Mayerne had kept his promised silence; du Chesne, after three pamphlets, had turned aside; Harvet was dead. As Riolan looked around at the silent and deserted battlefield and counted his verbal victories, he could afford to feel complacent. It was therefore mortifying to him when a sudden noise from the east told him that the German auxiliary, whom he thought that he had neutralised, was coming in.

It came in with massive force. Libavius's book was entitled *A Defence of Alchemy*[12] and it was dedicated to Jacques Bongars, the French scholar and bibliophile who served Henri IV as ambassador to the German princes, and whom Libavius had known in Germany. Bongars was another Huguenot from Orléans, so here too the association of chemistry both with Protestantism and with Germany was preserved. He was also a friend of la Rivière, and he had personal interests in alchemical speculation. In the course of his dedicatory epistle to Bongars, Libavius set out his purpose and the circumstances which had caused him to interfere in the debate. He explained that at first he had intended to keep out, thinking that the Paris faculty was attacking not the true and time-honoured science of alchemy, only 'that fraudulent magical mountebankry of Paracelsianism' which all right-thinking physicians and philosophers condemn. He admitted that he did not go the whole way with du Chesne and Mayerne, but he regarded them both as honourable and learned men, and he observed that they had openly declared their independence of Paracelsus. They were not renegades from Hippocrates. They should be described not as Paracelsians but as 'Hermetic iatrochemists', followers of Severinus the Dane who had sought to winnow the wheat from the chaff of Paracelsianism. For Libavius admitted that there was something in Paracelsianism. Paracelsus himself had been a good chemist, but unfortunately he had insisted on founding his own sect, cooking up an insolent new doctrine out of every absurd paradox and lunacy, and his idolatrous followers, who 'kissed the very spittle of their monarch', had made it worse. However, if one could detach oneself from these extremes, there was room for compromise. Severinus had shown the way. Those who, following him, sought to free chemistry from mumbo-jumbo and incorporate it in the Hippocratic tradition deserved to be heard, not crucified. 'I am no enemy of Paris,' Libavius ended his prologue, 'but there is more honour in the art of chemistry than in your Faculty of Paris.' He then set to work, in the body of his book, to analyse and refute in detail the judgement of Paris.

To Riolan, who had already publicly claimed Libavius as an ally, this was a body-blow, and he never fully recovered his equipoise. He replied, but not in his own name. Having recently come into the open as the champion and leader of the faculty, he now retreated again – this time behind the authority of his old father. It was in his father's name that he published what was to prove his last work in this pamphlet war, his *Reply to the Raving of Libavius*.[13] In this work the young Riolan, through the imaginary lips of his father, praised his own writings, gloried in his victory over du Chesne and Mayerne and the two doctors of Orléans, and then turned on Libavius who, he said, had come forward as 'the fifth and most fraudulent patron of that sect'. The Paris faculty, he declared, out of its fifty doctors, could produce ten champions, the least of whom could disarm and destroy such an enemy. But being personally challenged, the old Riolan would chivalrously discharge his colleagues from the fray and take it upon himself.

Libavius easily saw through the successive transparent disguises of the younger Riolan. But he did not reply at once. He retired to his study determined to end the controversy and demolish the Riolans, father and son together, and all their allies, with one massive blow. By now he was well informed about the controversy. He had received letters from du Chesne, Mayerne and the two doctors from Orléans.[14] Clearly all these French Huguenots regarded Libavius as their champion, the man who, from the safety of Protestant Germany, could finally extinguish the arrogant pretensions of the Paris faculty.

The letters of both du Chesne and Mayerne to Libavius survive, the former in print, the latter in manuscript. Both men were eager to dissociate themselves from Paracelsus and to present themselves as conservative reformers who merely wished to incorporate chemical medicine into the sound tradition of Hippocratic and even Galenic medicine. Do not think, du Chesne begged Libavius, 'that I accept the magic of Paracelsus. I am as strenuous a defender of Antiquity as the Parisian doctors themselves. To be misunderstood is the fate of every reformer: you yourself have experienced it, from blind dolts who cannot read your work. But what of that? For every one Frenchman who attacks you there are a thousand who admire you ...' Mayerne sang the same tune. He explained to Libavius that he had seen the title of his *Defence of Alchemy* in the catalogue of the Frankfurt book-fair; that he had bought and read the book; and that, having found that they were engaged in the same cause, and that Libavius had made civil mention of his name, he was now venturing to write and to set out some of the intricacies of the battle. So he described the Parisian background. He gave an unflattering account of the Paris faculty, a venerable body now rotted by diseased members, and of the insufferable Riolan, a mere chatterbox who concealed his medical insufficiency behind a garrulous tongue. He also exposed the tactics of the enemy. He urged Libavius not to fall into their trap by saying too much about Paracelsus. 'Everyone knows from your books what you think of Paracelsus . . . Besides, the controversy is not about him but about Alchemy, which you have reduced into a science. Forgive my presumption in advising you, but having heard their mutterings, I thought that I ought to warn you.' He added that, but for his public duties as royal doctor, he would himself join the common work, but there was really no need for him to do so now that the whole subject had been taken up by the savants of Germany and adorned, above all, by Libavius. Finally, he urged Libavius to go forward. It was unfortunate that he should have to descend to battle with such unequal enemies and oppose his solid reasons to the empty bubbles of Riolan; but it is thus that science is advanced. 'I do not know what you must have thought of me when the Paris faculty launched that infamous decree against me, condemning me as a Paracelsian quack.' Happily, all had been put right by Libavius's honourable mention of Mayerne in the *Defence of Alchemy*. So Mayerne discreetly disclaimed Paracelsus and placed himself, as la Rivière and du Chesne had done, in the new, more central position of Severinus.

Thus encouraged from all sides, Libavius applied himself to his task. It was gratifying to be recognised as the ultimate arbiter, the oracle of iatrochemistry in Europe. On 10 November 1606, soon after receiving Mayerne's letter, he described his progress. 'I am at work on my *Triumph*,' he wrote to his German friend, Dr Sigismund Schnitzer of Ulm: 'it is keeping me so busy, that, for the time being, I cannot hear the braying of certain asses who are rising up against me.'[15] The result of his labours appeared next year. Its title was *The Triumph of Alchemy over the Censure of the Spurious Galenic Faculty in the University of Paris . . . a Hermetic Work*.[16] It was dedicated to two of the reigning dukes of Albertine Saxony, John Casimir of Saxe-Coburg and John Ernest of Saxe-Weimar. The former was his own immediate patron. The latter would be one of the founders of the esoteric alchemical society, the *Fruchtbringende Gesellschaft*.

With this monumental work of over 900 pages, Libavius effectively crushed not only the Riolans but the whole controversy. His blood was now up and he would give no quarter. In his preface he declared himself roundly for du Chesne and Mayerne, who, he said, had brought more credit to France than all the 'schoolmen' of the faculty, none of whom had been heard of in the world except 'their advocate Riolan, a brazen chatterbox, ready for any sophistry'. Riolan pretended that the iatrochemists were seeking to drive out Hippocrates and Galen. This, said Libavius, was absurd. True medicine nowadays was not 'Hippocratic' or 'Galenic', or of any particular school: it was the common stock to which Hippocrates and Galen, Greeks and Arabs had contributed – and the alchemists too. For true alchemy is not the rubbish of Paracelsus about the transmutation of metals. No: it is the science which concerns itself with the philosopher's stone, which teaches how to discover magisteries, principles, elements, extracts, the quintessence, curative oils, waters, alkalis, elixirs, *stibii vitrum*, precipitate of mercury, etc., and to use them medically. In defence of this alchemy, du Chesne and Mayerne on one side and Libavius on the other could agree. They inclined to Paracelsus and Severinus; he was critical of both. But there was common ground on which they could meet, in common contempt of the intemperate scolding of old women ...

In the body of his work, Libavius traced the whole controversy with patience, temperance and skill. He stripped Riolan of his disguises, exposed his contradictions, his evasions, his cheats. Then he went methodically through all the old arguments to prove that alchemy was a true science with a valid philosophical basis, proceeding from God, not the Devil, and not to be rejected merely because it had been misused; that form could be separated from matter; that the quintessence could be discovered, gold made potable; that distillation, mineral remedies, homoeopathy were legitimate in medicine; etc. He ended on a lighter note, with a 'censura societatis chymicorum' – a parody of the censure of the faculty of Paris against alchemy. In this parody, the imaginary society of chemists announced that, having taken note of the actions of the Medical Faculty of Paris, of its unjust criticisms, its spite and ignorance, its inability to distinguish true from false, chemistry from Paracelsianism, its gross dishonesty and unparalleled rage against true medicine, this censure is now declared void and worthless by the chemists and iatrochemists of all nations. They require that the scurrilous works of Riolan be destroyed, with all memory of his name, and that the monument set up to record his ridiculous attack on Libavius be cast down and trampled in sewers and dungheaps, its proper place. Let the just King of France see to it that henceforth these impudent censors are deprived of all authority. Finally, let all clergy, statesmen, doctors, physicians and other good men pay no attention to them, and, if they are ill, never consult them but go instead to sound, honest, learned chemical doctors. So justice will be done.

With his *Triumph of Alchemy* Libavius laid Riolan flat, and it was some time before he could rise again. He had appealed to Libavius, the great anti-Paracelsian chemist, and Libavius had pronounced, very heavily, against him. Intellectually, that battle was decided. But what is mere intellectual victory if the social structures behind the parties remain firm? If anything the controversy, by its violence, hardened the Medical Faculty of Paris in its postures, at least for the time being. At this point we may turn aside from it and examine the professional and private activities of du Chesne and Mayerne. Here we shall find that, while they had entrusted their public defence to their German ally, they were extending their researches into mysterious areas of which that stern anti-Paracelsian would hardly have approved; and that they were both feeling their way towards escape, in different directions, from the uncomfortable atmosphere of Catholic Paris and its powerful medical corporation.

The alchemical experiments of du Chesne and Mayerne, in these years of busy practice and literary controversy in Paris, are documented, if darkly, in Mayerne's manuscripts. The chronological chaos of those manuscripts makes it difficult to date the operations, and the obscurity of the persons involved thickens the darkness around them; but the general picture is clear enough. Du Chesne, in his Parisian *Musaeum* or laboratory,[17] was engaged in personal experiments, devising new chemical cures from mercury and antimony, producing mineral panaceas and elixirs of life, and seeking to transmute metals. Associated with him in these experiments were various other persons whose names are now meaningless, but who seem to have formed an esoteric alchemical coterie around him. Secrecy enveloped these operations, and they were described in opaque, Hermetic language. Those involved also gave each other private names, which increased the sense of mystery. The members of this circle called du Chesne 'Dryida' or 'le Druide'. Superficially this was no more than a Greek version of his surname, just as 'Quercetanus', the name under which he wrote, was a Latin version: all of them mean 'of the oak'. But it also had a deeper significance, for in France the Druids of ancient Gaul had been quietly included among the *prisci theologi* of the Hermetic tradition. Like the gymnosophists of India and the magi of Persia, they were held to have preserved fragments of antique truth which they jealously protected from degradation by vulgar minds. Was not the mistletoe, their sacred plant, a panacea such as the Hermetic philosophers still sought, growing on the tree of life, the oak from which they, like du Chesne, took their name?[18]

Another private name used in this circle was 'Neptis', the niece. Apart from her gender, the identity of Neptis is not clear. Possibly she was really a niece of du Chesne. She seems to have been his pupil, and to have carried out experiments for him, and to have recorded the results in a book. She worked closely with du Chesne from 1589 if not before.[19] Possibly she was the Mlle Sabatier one of whose chemical writings Mayerne copied out, 'from her own autograph', in 1601, and who must have belonged to his alchemical circle, since she also used the name Dryida for du Chesne: 'Dryid dit ... Dryid l'a pour un secret ... comme il m'a dit de sa bouche'.[20] Or possibly she was the 'Mad de Mart vill', or 'Madame de Martinville', who appears to have inherited some of du Chesne's papers after his death and who wrote on alchemical matters to Mayerne.[21] Du Chesne had an only child, a daughter, who at some time married Joachim du Port of Geneva and lived in Geneva, but she was with her father in Paris in 1605, and 'Mr. de Chenis Quercitan's daughter' is cited as an alchemical source by an English writer.[22] But such evidence cannot be usefully pressed and the identity of Neptis is not one of those mysteries whose solution is essential to history.

Another member of this alchemical circle was known as 'Hermes'. Such a name, in a Hermetic society, argues great respect and therefore excites interest. A chance reference enables us to identify Hermes as Guillaume de Trougny (or Trogny), a Huguenot from Orléans.[23] From other references in Mayerne's papers we know that Trougny was a friend of la Rivière and was a member of Mayerne's circle by 1604, if not earlier. He was a physician and an alchemist and shared with Mayerne his various medical and chemical experiments. He devised private cures for gonorrhoea, and other diseases, used mercury and antimony, sought to extract tincture of gold, made mercury of gold and lead, believed in the messianic prophecies of Paracelsus, and wrote on the philosopher's stone. He joined du Chesne and 'Neptis' in their experiments, supplied numerous metallic mixtures for Mayerne's dispensary, and would remain in touch with him for more than twenty years.[24]

A little more light on Trougny is shed by the private letters of another Huguenot from Orléans, the scholarly diplomat Jacques Bongars. From this source we learn that 'M. de Trougny' of Orléans was a 'cousin' of Bongars. This identifies him as the 'Gulielmus Lenormantius Trunianus' who, with his brother Jean Lenormant, a former fellow student of Bongars at Marburg and Strasbourg, had accompanied Bongars on his journey to Constantinople and is described by his brother as a pioneer in chemical mysteries. His correct name was thus Guillaume Lenormant de Trougny.[25]

'Druid', 'Neptis' and 'Hermes' are the most prominently mentioned members of the esoteric alchemical and iatrochemical circle in Paris of which Mayerne was a member. With them he conducted experiments, and their concoctions filled his dispensary.[26] Other more shadowy names hover around them. Such were Villemereau, 'Caltopus' and 'Fulica' ('the Coot'); with these Mayerne was engaged in 'a hundred experiments of transmutation' according to the process of 'Emmanuel the Cretan philosopher'.[27] Such were the even more fugitive names of 'Philipon', 'Bathodius', M. de Foupatoux, M. Landrivier, through whose hands the reports of 'Druid' and his acolyte

'Neptis' passed. Jerôme Groslot de l'Isle, the Huguenot universal man of Orléans, the friend of Sarpi and Asselineau in Venice, seems to have been connected with the circle, perhaps through Trougny. So does Pierre de Beringhem, the Huguenot courtier and entrepreneur. The arcane experiments and speculations of the group are scantily recorded and difficult to follow. We have a general impression of abstruse alchemical experiments and Hermetic messianism. Its members copied out the writings of medieval English alchemists like George Ripley and John Dastin, and the new forgeries of 'Basil Valentine' and 'Isaac Hollandus'. They explored the dark corners of the Paracelsian writings and perhaps of the Jewish Cabbala. They attempted to repeat the alleged experiments of Paracelsus and 'William the father of Paracelsus', and speculated about the fulfilment of his millennial prophecies.[28]

Such were the private researches of du Chesne and Mayerne in the years of fierce public controversy in Paris. But neither of them, in those years, confined his interest to France. The Parisian controversy, whether they prevailed in it or not, was a forcible reminder that their Genevese origin, their Protestantism, and their Paracelsian and Hermetic views separated them from the central traditions of Paris, and even of France. In those years we see them, like so many other Huguenots, turning away from the established society of France and its ever more Catholic court, and investing instead in Protestant societies: Germany, Switzerland, England. To du Chesne, it was natural to look to Germany: the Germany in which he had formed his ideas, and from which, in the person of Libavius, he had now received such decisive support.

Du Chesne's return to Germany was not due solely to his alchemical interests. It was also a continuation, in a new direction, of his old diplomatic activity. For Henri IV still used him as a secret diplomat, and his diplomacy was now needed, above all, in Germany. In the past, as a Protestant party leader, fighting against the common enemy, Henri IV had naturally had good relations with the German Protestant princes. Afterwards, when he had become a Catholic and made peace with Spain, he as naturally incurred their distrust. He therefore felt it necessary to reassure them. Protestant or Catholic, he needed their support against the traditional enemy of France, the house of Habsburg. He set out to persuade them that, though a Catholic at home, he would always be a Protestant abroad. For this purpose he found it prudent to use Huguenot envoys: first Philippe Canaye de Fresne – but he unfortunately became a convert to Catholicism – then, after 1598, Jacques Bongars, the friend of Libavius and cousin of 'Hermes', Trougny. The prince whom he chiefly cultivated was the Landgrave of Hesse-Kassel. It was on him that his German policy was centred, through him that he sought to manage the other Protestant princes: in particular, the Elector Palatine and the Duke of Württemberg.

Like these last two princes, whom we have met, the Landgrave of Hesse, Moritz the Learned, was a committed patron of alchemy. He was also much more than that. Like his contemporaries James I of England and Heinrich Julius Duke of Brunswick-Wolfenbüttel, he took all learning for his province. He was poet, musical composer, surgeon, linguist, philosopher, theologian, a patron of drama, literature, all the arts and sciences. At his university of Marburg he founded a chemical laboratory, to which he attracted alchemists from France, Germany, the Netherlands and England. The director of this laboratory, in 1600, was the landgrave's personal physician, the Paracelsian alchemist Jacob Mosanus. Mosanus had travelled in England and France, and he and the landgrave wrote to each other, often, in excellent English. The landgrave used him, as so many princes used their physicians, as a political agent. In the summer of 1602 he took him on a long secret journey through Germany, Switzerland and France. In Switzerland they stopped at Yverdun for chemical conversation with a local adept. When they arrived in Paris, the landgrave had confidential political discussions with the king while Mosanus used the opportunity to exchange alchemical views with du Chesne and Mayerne.

Nearly two years later, in 1604, the landgrave took steps to strengthen his alchemical establishment.[29] He sent Mosanus to Strasbourg, where the famous Scottish alchemist Alexander Seton – the only man whose transmutations (it was said) invariably succeeded – was reported to be accessible through a local goldsmith, one Gustenhover. All the alchemical princes of Germany, from the emperor downwards, were pursuing Seton. He was imprisoned by several of them in the hope of extorting his secret, so that his life was far from easy: Mosanus wrote, 'I would not be in the Scot his coat for no good in the world.' When he arrived in Strasbourg, Mosanus, like many other such emissaries, had to report failure. Seton, he informed the landgrave, had disappeared – probably kidnapped by the Duke of Württemberg – and Gustenhover had been lured to Prague and made a baron by the emperor Rudolf II 'and is now about to make the philosopher's stone for his majesty'.[30] However, Mosanus added, he would not despair, but would continue his travels. He was going to Paris and there, with any luck, would meet Quercetanus – i.e. du Chesne – 'and I doubt not but that I shall obtain many fine physical and medicinal matters of him'. Du Chesne, he wrote, lived partly in Paris and partly in Geneva; but he would take his chance in Paris. Probably he succeeded, for three months later the landgrave wrote to Henri IV to thank him for sending 'sieur de la Violette' – i.e. du Chesne – to Kassel on a secret political errand. Du Chesne supplied the landgrave with his alchemical secrets and carried confidential political letters back to Henri IV and his ministers, Sully, Villeroy, Schomberg. A few months later the landgrave sent another personal agent to Paris, on a political mission, but with secret messages – evidently both political and alchemical – to du Chesne.[31] The exact nature of these political messages is not revealed, but they evidently related to Henri IV's conflict with the Duc de Bouillon, who, having defied the king at Sedan, had taken refuge with his brother-in-law, the Elector Palatine, at Heidelberg and was being defended against his enraged sovereign by the German princes. Du Chesne must have been an exceptionally skilful diplomat, and his personal position must have been delicate, since Bouillon was his patient.

By now the landgrave and du Chesne were in regular communication. They corresponded in intimate terms, almost as equals, and had a private cipher for the communication of alchemical secrets. Du Chesne sent the landgrave the results of his experiments and supplied him with interpretations of Paracelsus, samples of his own remedies – his laudanum, his *pulvis catheticus*, his 'grand arcane et magistère des philosophes' – and, most precious of all, his 'grand et géneral dissolvent metallique'. He also opened his own heart to the sympathetic Protestant prince. How he longed, he wrote, to escape from Paris and the pressures of its court, and to retire to Geneva, where he could devote himself to more congenial philosophical studies. He was disillusioned with the court of the apostate Henri IV, whose Protestant sympathies were now purely political, and resented his own necessary attendance on it; and he sang the praises of the great and illustrious house of Hesse, which God had chosen, in these latter times, for the advancement of His glory.

Apart from Mosanus, the landgrave maintained several other alchemists in his laboratory. The most famous of them was Johann Hartmann, a native Hessian, who at this time was professor of mathematics at the university. In 1609 the landgrave would appoint him – much to the annoyance of Libavius, who coveted the post – as the first professor of iatrochemistry in Europe. Hartmann gathered around him a team of ten specialists to concentrate their energies on the philosopher's stone. Afterwards, Hartmann would succeed Mosanus as the landgrave's personal physician. The correspondence of Mosanus and Hartmann shows that du Chesne and his circle were involved in this collective work. On one occasion the landgrave accused Hartmann of having revealed secrets to his rivals. Hartmann defended himself by explaining that although he preserved the secrecy of his work in the prince's laboratory, there was a common stock of alchemical knowledge to which all members of his international circle contributed, and on which they could all draw. He listed those with whom he had shared his work and from whom some of his own secrets had been obtained. Among the living he cited Mosanus, Eglinus, Trougny, Dauber; and among the dead (he was writing in 1612) Quercetanus, Tranckius, Sendivogius, Ruland, Croll.[32] He did not mention Mayerne by name, although Mayerne may well be included among 'the friends of Trougny' to whom he ascribes certain discoveries: the phrase would seem to apply to the Hermetic laboratory in Paris. Mayerne was not yet a famous name: he was eclipsed by du Chesne and Trougny. But Mayerne's own notes show that he knew Mosanus personally and collected prescriptions and formulae from him, from Hartmann, and from all the Hessian circle, including the landgrave himself.[33]

Another member of that circle, one of Hartmann's disciples, was Johann Rheinland, known as Rhenanus. He was a native subject of the landgrave. Like so many of these alchemical doctors, he was a poet as well as a physician, and, like the landgrave and Mosanus, he knew English well.[34] In 1610, the year when he took his doctorate at Marburg, he prepared for publication a complete course of chemistry which, he said, was highly praised by Hartmann; but Martin Ruland the younger, then court physician to the emperor Rudolf, had unscrupulously filched his definitions 'and did not blush to insert them in his *Lexicon*[35] and sell them as his own'. Such allegations, alas, are not unique among research students. Rhenanus spent the rest of his life reclaiming his own work, as he maintained, from this plagiarism.[36] A committed Paracelsian, he was well known to Mayerne, and would afterwards visit London, where we are told that he achieved several remarkable cures with his panacea of black mercury.[37]

Moritz of Hesse was not the only German prince with whom du Chesne had close relations. He was also involved with the Elector Palatine, Frederick IV, and his fatal political mentor, Prince Christian of Anhalt-Bernburg, the radical organiser of the Protestant union in Germany. Anhalt was a highly educated scholar whose alchemical interests had been sharpened during his brief stay, in 1594, at the alchemical capital of Europe, the court of the emperor Rudolf II at Prague. He also, like Moritz of Hesse and Henri IV, used his personal physician – Oswald Croll, the most famous of the later Paracelsians – as a diplomatic agent. In 1606, at the height of the chemical controversy in Paris, Anhalt himself came to visit Henri IV. His mission was on behalf of the Elector Palatine and was very secret – the English ambassador sought in vain to discover its purpose[38] – but it was not confined to high politics. The prince took the opportunity to meet both du Chesne and Mayerne. Both of them made records of the meeting. Du Chesne recorded the prince's recipe for whitening yellow pearls by placing them in the truncated genitals of a castrated cockerel and leaving them there for fifteen days: 'then kill the cockerel and take out the pearls, which will be found in its belly, completely white.' With Mayerne, the prince discussed homeopathic remedies and exhibited a speciality of his own: an antidote against all poisons, which he had learned from a soldier newly returned from Hungary. This *theriacale viperinum Christiani Principis Anhalt* was compounded of viper's organs, dried and pulverised, in two different forms. The prince, Mayerne recorded, told him various stories of its efficacy and then swallowed both preparations in his presence, 'and I also tasted them after his Excellency'.[39] It seems very similar to Professor Kolreuter's conjuring trick for the Duke of Saxony.

The increasing involvement of du Chesne in Germany, which coincided with the savage attacks on him by the Medical Faculty of Paris, is reflected in the dedication of his last work. Between his visit to Kassel in August 1604 and his death in August 1609, du Chesne published four works. All of them were directed to Germany rather than to France. The first was a work on the diseases of the head, which he began, as he told the landgrave, 'at the time when I said farewell to you'. It was printed at Marburg and dedicated to the landgrave from Paris three months later.[40] In the dedication to his text, du Chesne praised the landgrave as the undisputed prince of all literature, a master of nine tongues, versed in the wisdom of that great sage Hermes Trismegistus. Moritz, said du Chesne, was not a vulgar gaper after gold, like so many princely patrons of alchemy, but a philosopher who used his well-furnished laboratory, with its busy forges and precious retorts, in order to explore the secrets of Nature. In the text itself du Chesne did not spare his enemies, the Galenists who were still battling against him in Paris: proud, pompous and ignorant men who raged against Paracelsus but who had to resort to his mineral remedies because their own cured nobody. Man, du Chesne insisted, is the microcosm of the world; his blood is the microcosm of the sea; true medicine is to be sought not only in the works of Hippocrates and Galen but also in the understanding of the macrocosm. Of this popular work du Chesne also wrote a French version, which he dedicated to the Prince de Condé, cousin of Henri IV.[41]

With his next work du Chesne returned to addressing the specialist, the physician. This was the complete pharmacopoeia which he had long promised and of which he had given a sample in his book on the medicine of the ancient philosophers – the book which had started the whole controversy. Libavius, in his *Triumph of Alchemy*, had explicitly praised this sample, regretting its brevity and urging du Chesne to produce a much-needed chemical pharmacopoeia, 'which he will no doubt do'. Now he had done it. The book was called *The Pharmacopoeia of the Galenists Reformed*, and the reformation consisted in the incorporation of chemical and Hermetic remedies. This too was dedicated to a German prince: to Christian of Anhalt, described as the most learned of Germans, who had patronised and honoured him even in absence. The book he described in florid terms as a medicine-chest supplied from the choicest stores of ancient doctrine and reclaimed from Hermetic obscurity.[42] It too would be translated into French and would be reprinted throughout the century: indeed it would be recommended by Boerhaave, the famous Dutch chemist of the early eighteenth century.

Du Chesne's last book, a supplement to his *Pharmacopoeia*, dealt with the plague. It too was addressed to Germany, being published at Leipzig and dedicated to Ernst of Bavaria, Elector of Cologne. The elector was a patron of Paracelsianism and had recently sponsored the publication of Paracelsus's complete works. Evidently he had admired du Chesne's *Pharmacopoeia* and had written to him to say so. From a Catholic archbishop this was a compliment indeed, and du Chesne had been flattered by this attention from 'this northern star' of learning. After long reflection he decided that the most appropriate reply was to contribute thus to the cure of the frequent plagues 'which are the curse of our time'.[43]

While du Chesne was writing and publishing book after book, Mayerne was also writing. Apart from his copious notes, he began several more literary works, which he evidently intended to publish but which he would never finish. For there can be no doubt that he intended to publish them. Several of them are clearly written out, at least in part, for such a purpose. The treatises on chemistry, on medicine, on 'mechanics', on the technology of art, all bear obvious signs of being designed for print. Even his *Ephemerides*, with their judicious omissions and later footnotes, seem to be compiled for public reading, not merely for the author's own reference. It seems that he had a psychological incapacity to complete a work. Perhaps he had been made to publish his first book – that little guidebook to Europe, which he had written as an undergraduate – too soon. Often he would speak of his plans to publish his whole medical philosophy. Often he would begin an apparently systematic treatise. But never, after his *Apologia* of 1603, would he give anything of his own to the press. Among his manuscripts we often find a chance remark which declares that unfulfilled intention. There are elaborate title-pages, magnificent *exordia* – and then, after a few pages of formal writing, the impetus fails and the book becomes a disorderly miscellany of notes. Like many men of encyclopaedic ambitions, he lacked the architectonic faculty. He was conscious of having a philosophy, but he could not organise it into a coherent form.

One of his frustrated books was the manual of chemistry which Mayerne began in 1602.[44] Another was the essay on the caruncula which he began soon after he had treated the future Cardinal Richelieu for that complaint in 1605,[45] and which he was still thinking of publishing in 1616 'if I ever have a respite from a courtier's cares' – but even so he would give his writings to more elegant writers 'to lick into shape'.[46] Another was perhaps an extension of that essay: a manual of the diseases of the reproductive system,[47] which would afterwards grow into a manual of all diseases[48] but would still remain incomplete. And then there are undated works which seem, on internal evidence, to belong to this early period: a 'Core of Hermetic Philosophy';[49] an *Acroama medicum* in which, as in du Chesne's challenging book, the chemical school is presented as a fourth school of medicine;[50] a manual of metallic and mineral cures written in Paracelsian language and ending with a paean in praise of the Paracelsian 'principle' of salt: 'a sale rerum omnium conservatio, renovatio et vegetatio. O beata viriditas cunctas res generans!': the conservation, renovation and vegetation of all things is performed by salt. O blessed greenness, generator of all things![51] All these documents reflect the Hermetic Paracelsian influence which – however he might play it down to secure the support of Libavius – inspired Mayerne in the years when he shared a practice with la Rivière and the mysterious Trougny in arcane experiments and the quest for the philosopher's stone.

However, like du Chesne, he was evidently becoming disillusioned in Paris. The controversy with the faculty was disagreeable. The pressure of orthodoxy, both religious and medical, was heavy. To protect himself against it the patronage of the king was essential, and yet the king himself was now surrounded by Catholics: his support could no longer be guaranteed. La Rivière, Mayerne's great patron at court, was dead. Like du Chesne in his last years, Mayerne could be forgiven if, under those lowering clouds, he began to look towards a safer, Protestant port. In 1606 he visited – or revisited – England.

7

Interlude in England, 1606

Precisely what brought Mayerne to England in 1606 we do not know. His own records – those that survive – are completely silent on the subject. His *Ephemerides* for that period record no English patients and give merely one hint of his absence from Paris: in March 1606, sending medical advice to Madame de Jonchères, who was planning a visit to the waters of Spa, he tells her that he hopes to have returned from his travels before she sets out and to send her further advice then. It is thus clear that he intended only a brief absence from Paris. In fact he was back there in June. Of his formal activities in England we only know one detail. The archives of the University of Oxford record that on 8 April 1606 Theodore de Mayerne Turquet, a Frenchman, medical adviser to the most serene King of France, doctor of medicine of Montpellier, was admitted by incorporation as a doctor of the University of Oxford.[1] In one of the two entries in the Register, he is described as 'Reginae medicus',[2] the queen's doctor. In the context, this clearly means doctor to the Queen of England. Over half a century later, the Oxford antiquary Anthony Wood, compiling his *Fasti oxonienses*, amplified this entry by adding that Mayerne, 'lately of the council to the King of France as to matters of physic, now physician to the Queen of England, was incorporated with more than ordinary solemnity'.[3]

What was Mayerne doing in Oxford in April 1606? No English source tells us anything. We do not know why, or whence, or with whom he came, how or by whom he was recommended for the honour. We have no evidence that he was ever appointed as physician to the Queen of England before his migration to England in 1611. Queen Anne's physician was Dr Martin Schoverus. Thirty years later Mayerne mentioned Dr Martin, in a note, as 'Reginae Annae medicus, cui ego M<ayernius> successi' (Queen Anne's doctor, whom I, Mayerne, succeeded). But he succeeded Martin in 1611: he did not supplant him in 1606.[4] If he was described as *Reginae medicus* in 1606 it was not by reason of any formal appointment or any known claim by himself.

However, Mayerne's papers do supply one interesting hint, for they include a copy of the brief Latin speech which he made at Oxford on the occasion of his incorporation. In this speech Mayerne states that he has only just arrived in England for a short visit; that he is 'obscure and unknown' to the members of the university; that he has arrived in Oxford solely as a tourist, 'eius visendae tantum causâ'; and that they must not expect a polished oration from him since he is overwhelmed by the unexpected honour and is still in his travelling clothes. Nevertheless, he contrived to turn a pretty compliment, to quote Homer in Greek, and to apply a classical metaphor which he had already used in his *Apologia*.[5] However much of rhetoric there may be in these remarks, it seems clear that Mayerne's incorporation was genuinely sudden and unexpected and owed nothing to his own initiative. This implies that, however obscure and unknown he may have been, he was recommended by, or came with, persons of importance. No letter of recommendation survives. It therefore seems probable that those who brought him demonstrated or announced his importance and caused the university to declare a special degree day in order suddenly to honour him.

Nearly a hundred years later, when the learned scholar Vincent Minutoli, Professor of Greek at Geneva, compiled his brief memoir of Mayerne for Bayle's *Dictionary*, he gave a circumstantial account of Mayerne's introduction to the court of James I in England. In 1607, he tells us, Mayerne treated and cured 'un seigneur Anglais', who thereupon took him to England, 'where he had a private audience with King James'.[6] Later writers have seized upon this statement and silently altered the date from 1607 to 1606 in order to accommodate it to the visit in Oxford. Such a convenient adjustment of hearsay evidence first uttered a hundred years after the event may seem a fragile basis for conjecture, but it may nevertheless be correct. Minutoli drew on the information of Mayerne's relations in Geneva; the rest of his account stands up remarkably well to criticism; and Mayerne's family may well have been recalling the occasion of their famous kinsman's introduction to King James, while making a trivial error of the date. Moreover there was an incident which fits happily into this supposed pattern of events. Shortly before coming to England, Mayerne did treat a distinguished 'seigneur anglais' who was seriously ill in Paris. He did not record the treatment in his *Ephemerides*, but that record is far from complete. The essential connection is revealed in the despatches of the English ambassador in Paris, Sir Thomas Parry.

The 'seigneur anglais' was Francis, Lord Norreys of Rycote, a young man of great wealth and, at that time, with promise of great influence in England; for he was closely allied with the all-powerful minister, Robert Cecil, Earl of Salisbury. In 1597–8, at the age of eighteen, Norreys had accompanied Cecil to France when Cecil had been sent thither by Queen Elizabeth as ambassador extraordinary. On his return to England he had married Cecil's niece and ward, Bridget de Vere, daughter of the seventeenth Earl of Oxford. With Cecil, Norreys had supported the succession of James I, proclaiming it in Oxford and going in person to the Scottish Border to escort Queen Anne from Berwick to London. Next year he had accompanied another ambassador extraordinary, the Lord Admiral, Charles Howard Earl of Nottingham, to Valladolid to negotiate the peace which ultimately wound up Queen Elizabeth's war with Spain. On this second embassy Norreys took with him a young diplomat, Dudley Carleton. Carleton had previously been secretary in Paris to Sir Thomas Parry, and Norreys now persuaded him to accompany him to Spain, undertaking to provide for him after their return. After the conclusion of the Spanish treaty, Norreys and Carleton returned through France, but at the end of September 1605, while in Paris, Norreys was taken seriously and mysteriously ill. By the end of the first week in October it seemed that he was about to die.

To Carleton the loss of his link with the Cecilian establishment would be a disaster, and he uttered a series of agonised cries. Norreys' illness, he wrote to his friend John Chamberlain, was 'a danger of the greatest misfortune that can befall us. Conceal it, I pray you.' Meanwhile he wrote letter after letter to Cecil telling him that he despaired of Norreys' recovery and asking for instructions 'as if the worst should happen'. He clearly expected the worst to happen, for although the four doctors who assembled round the bed of so rich a patient took the matter calmly, they did not agree in their diagnosis – some called it *febris purpuratus*, others *synochus putris* – and meanwhile 'the disease is popular and many die of it'. Among those who died were 'the two greatest physicians of this town', which showed that their art was unavailing. One of these great physicians was Dr Marescot, who had actually attended Norreys; the other was, to Carleton, 'the greatest perhaps of this time': the Sieur de la Rivière, *premier médecin* to the king and patron of Mayerne.[7]

Lord Norreys did not die. After a fortnight of extreme sickness and 'many conflicts betwixt life and death', he began to improve, and by the end of the month he was out of danger; but meanwhile the medical reports which Carleton sent to Cecil showed that a new doctor had appeared on the scene. The earlier reports had been signed by Michel Marescot, Albert le Febvre, Henri Blackwood (or Blacknuod) and Jean Duret. These had seen the patient through the critical month of October. Early in November the report bears a solitary name: it is described as 'ordonnance de Mr. Mayerne-Turquet'.[8] Norreys had appealed from the establishment to the heretic, and it was evidently to the heretic that he ascribed his recovery.

Norreys remained in Paris for some months to recover from his illness. He left for England in March 1606. The ambassador, Sir Thomas Parry, also left

Paris and was at the same time replaced by Sir George Carew, who had been there as his collaborator for several months. It seems that Norreys and Parry travelled together, and spent ten or twelve days on the journey. Mayerne may well have travelled with them, for he too left Paris in March. On 6 April, two days before Mayerne received his degree at Oxford, Norreys was at his country house, Rycote, ten miles from Oxford.[9]

From this evidence we may legitimately conclude that Minutoli's account is basically correct, even though he made a slight error of date. Mayerne did treat a 'seigneur anglais' – Lord Norreys – in Paris. Norreys did take him with him to England, and may well have presented him to the king. From the court, Norreys may also have taken him to his country house in Rycote – a delightful house which had been visited by Queen Elizabeth in the time of its builder, the first Lord Norreys, the grandfather of Mayerne's patient. From Rycote, Norreys may well have taken Mayerne to Oxford in order to see the university and, perhaps, to visit Norreys' other houses, Wytham Abbey, where he had been born, and Cumnor Place, once owned by the Earl of Leicester and made famous by the death of Amy Robsart. At the university, such a visit would have been likely to arouse interest. Mayerne's own position as *médecin ordinaire* to the King of France, his arrival from the English court in the company of Lord Norreys, the nephew of the king's great minister and himself the greatest landlord near Oxford – all this would have marked him out as a man deserving of the honour to which, by his doctorate of Montpellier, he was entitled; and if, as is probable, the echoes of the great Parisian controversy had been heard in Oxford, that would not have discredited Mayerne in the university which had itself produced such 'Hermetic' doctors as Sir William Paddy and Robert Fludd.

Thus we may plausibly explain Mayerne's sudden appearance in Oxford. But what of his description, in the official Register of the university, as 'physician to the queen'? Here we can only speculate. Perhaps, when he was taken to court, Mayerne was consulted by the queen, whose hitherto robust health was now beginning to fail and who may well have been interested in a Paracelsian doctor, since the first physician at the court of her father, King Frederick III of Denmark, had been Paracelsus's great disciple, Peter Severinus. On the basis of such a casual consultation, Lord Norreys might easily present Mayerne to the doctors of Oxford as the queen's physician, and the entry in the Register would be a natural consequence. The informal phrase 'Reginae medicus' suggests a conversational description in striking contrast to the formal statement of his position at the French court, 'serenissimi Regis Galliarum in re medica a consiliis'.

So we can explain the visit to Oxford. But the visit to Oxford was a by-product of the visit to the court. Undoubtedly, if he was presented at Oxford as *reginae medicus*, he had come with the blessing of the court, and Minutoli says expressly that he had been presented there. Of the contacts which he may have made there we know little, but some can legitimately be inferred. The most important was with James Hay, now Lord Hay, who was to become his first patron in England.

The Hays of Megginch were a Scottish family, from Fife, a younger branch of the family of the earls of Errol. They were a cosmopolitan family. Sir George Hay, the fourth son of Sir Peter Hay of Megginch, had studied in Flanders, at the Scots college at Douai, under his uncle Edmund Hay, a Scottish Jesuit, who rose to be assistant to the General of the Order for France and Germany. In spite of his Jesuit upbringing, Sir George Hay remained, or became, a Protestant and, on his return to Scotland, threw himself into every kind of business. He would become one of the most active promoters of early Scottish industry – ironmaster, colliery-owner, salt and glass manufacturer – as well as a lawyer and politician who would end as Earl of Kinnoull, Lord Chancellor of Scotland.[10] Sir George's nephew James Hay was equally cosmopolitan. He too had studied in France and, on his return, had captivated King James by his urbane manners and polite learning. In 1604 the king sent him to Paris to convey his condolences on the death of Henri IV's Huguenot sister, the Duchess of Bar, and also to plead the cause of the French Huguenots. Hay soon became the most successful of the king's Scottish favourites, the only one who, by his unfailing affability, made himself popular with the English. He was to serve James I and Charles I as a diplomat – he undoubtedly had great diplomatic gifts[11] – and would rise, through intermediate titles – Lord Hay; Viscount Doncaster – to be Earl of Carlisle. His successive embassies would be almost always to Protestant powers, or in the Protestant interest: he was the diplomat of the international Protestant cause which the Crown of England would sponsor, with wavering strength, until 1629.

Not that he was himself a Puritan: far from it. Every glimpse we have of him shows him as a man of pleasure, a spendthrift, a fop. The Earl of Clarendon, in his great *History of the Rebellion*, gave a brilliant portrait of this phoenix among Scottish immigrants: of his captivating manners which enabled him to marry two great English heiresses in spite of the opposition of both their families; of his 'universal understanding' which made him fit for any employment, had he not preferred a life of pleasure, finding that business was attended by more rivalry and vexation 'and not more innocence'; and, above all, of his extravagant expenditure which staggered even that spendthrift court. For 'he was surely a man of the greatest expense in his own person of any in the age he lived, and introduced more of that expense in the excess of clothes and diet than any other man, and was indeed the original of all those inventions from which other men did but transcribe copies.' When he died 'he left behind him' (says Clarendon) 'the reputation of a very fine gentleman and a most accomplished courtier; and after having spent, in a very jovial life, above £400 000, which, upon a strict computation, he received from the Crown, he left not a house or acre of land to be remembered by.'[12] All would go up in the fragrant vapour of the *funus medicatum*, or embalmed funeral, organised for him by Dr Mayerne.[13]

Though they may have met in Paris in 1604, it was evidently at the English court that the austere, frugal, acquisitive Huguenot doctor first became attached to this man of unparalleled expense and pleasure. For four years later, without any intervening personal encounter, Mayerne would write of Hay as his patron, and of Hay's generosity towards him, in terms which imply an established friendship.[14] Hay's education in France, his interest in the Huguenot cause, and his ability to speak French would have made him a natural contact for a visiting Huguenot who could not then – and never would afterwards, if he could avoid it – speak English. Other English connections, of which we have evidence before Mayerne's emigration to England, may also have their origin in this visit of 1606. We know, for instance, that he was already, before 1610, a friend of Lord Harrington of Exton, the governor of the king's daughter, Princess Elizabeth, and Thomas Overbury, an ambitious young man who, at this time, was seeking to make his fortune at court. Overbury too had spent some time in France and would be naturally drawn to Mayerne.

Another contact of which we have evidence, and which was also to have an important sequel, was with 'Mr de St Antoine'. Pierre Antoine Bourdin, seigneur de St Antoine, was a Huguenot who, by now, had been at the English court for three years. Originally he had been master of horse to the Duc de Bourbon-Montpensier. In 1603, having been informed that James I wanted an expert riding-master for his eldest son, Henry, Prince of Wales, Henri IV had begged St Antoine from the duke and sent him to England with a present of horses. He would spend the rest of his life in England, as master of horse to Prince Henry and then, after Prince Henry's death, to his younger brother Charles, first as Prince of Wales, then as king. Mayerne recorded his attendance on St Antoine in 1606 – i.e. when Mayerne was in England. Afterwards, when he had himself emigrated to England, he would continue to attend St Antoine and his protégés, the royal horses.[15]

Apart from his presentation at court, Mayerne spent some time in the medical world of London. Among his notes are records of cures learned by him in London from various apothecaries: from 'Garret, the apothecary of Dr Butler',[16] and from Turner, another London apothecary who would supply him with many mineral, chemical and alchemical remedies.[17] There were two Turners, father and son – apothecaries, in London as in Paris, tended to run in dynasties – and they had powders and pills for almost every disease: oil of antimony, oil of vitriol, diaphoretic mercury for syphilis, pills for gonorrhoea, magnetic ointment, *laudanum Turneri, sulphuris anodynum Turneri* and *aurum potabile pauperum,* the poor man's potable gold. They also offered some less sophisticated remedies, such as their cure for gout, a blend of frog-spawn and horse-dung.[18] Mayerne also had some profitable conversations with King James's surgeon, John Nasmyth, who assured him that he had an infallible cure for gonorrhoea even after seven years of the illness; and through Turner he discovered the works of the English Paracelsian surgeon John Bannister.[19]

It is interesting to note that Mayerne's recorded medical contacts in London were almost entirely with apothecaries and surgeons. The only physician with whom he recorded even indirect contact was William Butler, who was not a London physician. He was a Fellow of Clare Hall, Cambridge, and practised in Cambridge. He never took a doctorate, but had a great reputation both for personal eccentricity and for medical success. He is described – not quite accurately – as 'the first Englishman who quickened Galenical practice with a touch of Paracelsus, trading in chemical receipts with great success'. Mayerne was evidently impressed by Butler, whom he regarded as a natural ally. Then and thereafter he collected his remedies, and he always spoke well of him, although his civility, as we shall see, was not reciprocated.

Thus in London as in Paris, Mayerne kept apart from the established metropolitan medical establishment. Here as there his connections were with the court, the apothecaries and surgeons, and provincial physicians: Dr Butler, not the Royal College of Physicians; the Huguenot doctors of Orléans, not the Medical Faculty of Paris.[20]

No doubt, in retrospect, Mayerne was satisfied with his visit to England. Lord Norreys was grateful, and might prove a valuable patron. It was something to have been honoured at court and in the oldest university of England. These London experiences had been interesting. And yet, even so, Mayerne's journey remains something of a problem. For nothing of it was predictable. These benefits were casual profits of the expedition: they do not explain its purpose. Why then did he go? Why should a busy Parisian doctor, whose engagement book was already so full, suspend his profitable practice and undertake an arduous sea journey merely at the suggestion of a somewhat unstable foreign nobleman? For Lord Norreys did not in fact prove a reliable patron to anyone. His companion Dudley Carleton would be a far more consistent friend and patient of Mayerne. Norreys might be the nephew by marriage of Lord Salisbury, but even that asset did not last long. Within a few months of her husband's return, Lady Norreys had run away from him, and his own career thereafter was marked by eccentricity and violence: insults, duels, imprisonment, 'melancholy' and an early death by suicide. It is difficult to believe that the physician-in-ordinary of the King of France would interrupt his lucrative work in Paris merely to accompany this erratic patient on a jaunt to England. As far as enlightened self-interest went, Mayerne had far greater and more reliable patrons and patients at home.

What then could have induced him to go? Once again, as so often, we are reduced to speculation. But if we are to speculate, the natural point at which to begin is with those greater patrons in France – and, in particular, with the most important of them all, the Duc de Rohan. For Rohan was the essential figure in his career, the peculiar patron and hero to whom he would always look up, or back, the perfect pattern of virtue in morality and politics. In 1606 Mayerne was still regularly in touch with Rohan, as physician to the family, regularly attending his mother, as other *grandes dames* of the Huguenot élite.[21] The last patients whose cases he recorded before leaving for England were two such Huguenot great ladies, Madame du Plessis Mornay, the formidable wife of 'the pope of the Huguenots', and the Duchesse de la Tremoïlle, the queen of the Huguenot *beau monde*. We know, from later evidence, that Rohan used Mayerne as a confidential agent in the political affairs of the Huguenot cause; and we know that, by 1606, that cause was in need of support against the pressure of the Catholic *dévots* at the French court. We also know where Rohan looked for that support. Ever since his visit to Scotland in the winter of 1600–1, he had looked to King James and to Robert Cecil.

What survives of his correspondence is both fragmentary and reticent. His communications with the English court were generally conveyed by trusted personal emissaries, and the content of his letters is confined to compliments, briefly introducing those emissaries and leaving their message to them. Nevertheless, they hint at a consistent story.

We have seen that Rohan had been in regular touch with King James and Cecil in the years before the king's succession to the English throne, and had been privy to their plans for that succession.[22] When those plans had been realised, he was naturally delighted. He could now afford to suspend conspiratorial contacts with Scotland and deal with the king and Cecil through official English channels. Sir Thomas Parry, as Queen Elizabeth's ambassador, would not have been a correct channel to the King of Scotland, but the same Sir Thomas Parry, as ambassador of James I, was different. So, in 1603, Rohan sent a secret emissary to Parry to whom, he said, Parry could speak as freely as to himself. He offered his service, professed his loyalty to the common cause, and begged Parry to treat him as one who had no other desire than to remain, all his life, a faithful servant. He beseeched Parry to receive his confidential emissary, the Sieur de la Ferté.[23] From 1603 onwards Rohan could count on Parry as his regular link with England. But he also maintained direct, secret communication with the English court. In July 1604 it was reported that Rohan had sent another personal agent, the Sieur de la Hautefontaine, to London, to present a horse to King James – but also to propose an English marriage for himself. The report did not please Henri IV, who promptly arranged that Rohan should make a suitable marriage in France – to the daughter of his own indispensable Huguenot minister, the future Duc de Sully, who, he might assume, would control him.

That was in 1604–5. In the winter of 1605–6, however, the situation changed. First, in November 1605, came the Gunpowder Plot in England. Then, in January 1606, the Papal interdict was launched against Venice. These two events inflamed confessional differences and polarised the religious politics of Europe. In France Henri IV, struggling to stand above party, insensibly slid further towards the *dévots*, while in England James I set out consciously to rally the Protestant international, wooing Venice, Switzerland, the Netherlands – and, of course, the French Huguenots. Meanwhile Parry was recalled from his post in Paris and there was no resident French ambassador in London, for M. de Beaumont had left in November 1605 and M. de la Boderie would not arrive till May 1606. At the same time Henri IV found himself forced to lead his army against the greatest and most insubordinate of his Huguenot subjects, the Duc de Bouillon, and take possession of his city of Sedan. Only the intercession of the Protestant princes of the Rhine – the Landgrave of Hesse, the Elector Palatine: friends and kinsmen of the duke, necessary allies of the king – saved Bouillon and Sedan from the consequences of defeat. As it was, Bouillon was humbled, and never again appeared as a rebel against the Crown. From that time on, the leadership of the Huguenots, as an independent body in the state, fell gradually to Rohan. At such a juncture, Rohan may well have wished to resume direct contact with James I and Cecil. We have seen that Mayerne travelled to England at the same time as Parry, perhaps in his company. He may well have been the bearer of confidential messages from Rohan to the king, or to Hay, on the state of 'those of the Religion' in France. In such circumstances it may also have been convenient for Mayerne to have a cover story to explain his journey. Such a cover is never difficult to find for a doctor. He could travel to England as a medical consultant to attend the queen.

Thus it is at least possible that the real reason for Mayerne's mysterious visit to England in the spring of 1606 was political. He may well have gone as the emissary of Rohan. He may equally, of course, have gone as the emissary of Henri IV, who may have wished, for a particular purpose, to use a private Huguenot agent known to be in the confidence of the Huguenot grandees. We have seen how Henri had recently used du Chesne as such an emissary to the Landgrave of Hesse, as he had previously used him to the Swiss cantons. Court medicine and politics, in the seventeenth century, were seldom far apart. However that may be, Mayerne's visit to England was not long. In June 1606, if not earlier, he was back in Paris. It was probably after his return to Paris that he married. Predictably, he married within the Protestant fold. No less predictably, he made a good marriage. By it he strengthened his position in the upper reaches of the Calvinist international.

His wife was a Dutch lady, Margaretha Elburg Baroness van den Boetzelaer van Asperen, of an old and noble family of Zeeland. In the mid-sixteenth century the head of this family, Wessel van den Boetzelaer, with his whole family, had been converted to Calvinism – and radical Calvinism too. In the iconoclastic riots of 1566 they had led their own servants to destroy the monuments in their own church.[24] When the Duke of Alba came to wreak vengeance on such crimes, the van den Boetzelaer family had fled abroad. But when Alba had been recalled, the four sons of Wessel van den Boetzelaer had returned to take part in the liberation of their country, and one of them, Rutger van den Boetzelaer, the inheritor of the estates, had risen high under William the Silent and established his family at the court of the new dynasty. Rutger van den Boetzelaer's eldest son, Rutger Wessel, Lord of Asperen, married, as the first of his three wives, the daughter of William's most vigorous propagandist, Philippe Marnix van St Aldegonde. Like his father-in-law, he was a devout Calvinist and wrote religious poems and meditations on the psalms. Another son, Gedeon van den Boetzelaer, Lord of Langheraeck, having studied under Lipsius at the University of Leiden and travelled widely in Europe, became a Dutch diplomat. Their sister Margaretha, with whom we are here concerned, left the Netherlands for France. She probably came in the train of the Princess Dowager of Orange, the widow of William the Silent, who, in 1594, returned to her native country. For she was Louise de Coligny, the daughter of the Huguenot leader Admiral de Coligny, that most famous victim of the massacre of St Bartholomew. As daughter and widow of martyred Calvinist heroes, the Princess of Orange enjoyed a certain halo among the Elect, and we may assume that Margaretha van den Boetzelaer, like her brothers, was a firm believer. In France Margaretha married a French Huguenot, Captain Charles de Chéridos from Périgord, a gentleman of Catherine de Navarre, Duchess of Lorraine and Bar. He was killed at Sluys in 1604, no doubt serving in the army of the prince against Spain. As a widow, Mme de Chéridos lived in Paris, evidently in the entourage of the Princess of Orange, whose own family, the Châtillon, were already patients of Mayerne.[25] She became a patient of Mayerne, and then his wife.[26]

Of Madame de Mayerne's character we know nothing. Her family was evidently grand and dull, and she seems to have been like them. She occurs in Mayerne's papers periodically as a patient, and we obtain occasional glimpses of her in the correspondence of Dutch friends, visitors or kinsmen. But no personality appears. Perhaps we should not deduce too much from Mayerne's silence about her, for he was constitutionally reticent on personal matters. We know nothing of any romance in his private life, although he preserved occasional arch letters which he exchanged with aristocratic female patients. One document suggests an earlier attachment. It is an early notebook, probably of the years 1597–1600, containing medical observations on his cases in Montpellier and Paris.[27] On the fly-leaf are written six lines of conventional amatory verse, in Latin, and the words 'souvenes vous de Marie de Champayne, vostre affectionnée à vous servir'; and on the other side of the page is a distich in Spanish:

más non podrá el tiempo y la fortuna
dos almas apartar que ya son una

(Never will time and chance be able / To divide two souls that are already one), followed by a monogram. The de Champagne family was a noble Huguenot family, which held the title Comte de Suze. Louis I, Comte de Suze, Lieutenant-General of the armies of the King of Navarre, had been killed at the battle of Coutrai in 1587, leaving young children. His son Louis II would play an active part in the next century, both as a rebel against the French crown and as a general commanding the forces of the Swiss Federation. Marie de Champagne was presumably a daughter of Louis I. Another daughter, Catherine – for I assume they were distinct persons – afterwards married Amary de Goyon II, Marquis de la Moussaye, another Huguenot grandee. Long afterwards, when Mayerne was an old man, this Catherine, Marquise de la Moussaye, would write a friendly letter to Mayerne from Paris, addressing him as 'Monsieur mon cher amy' and signing 'votre très humble et très obligée servante', and using an almost identical monogram. The marquise reversed the usual order of things: in the time when her brother, the Comte de Suze, had been a patient of Mayerne, she sent him medical advice and chemical cures for his reported infirmities. 'I would be delighted', she wrote, 'if I could act as surgeon to the first and greatest doctor in the world and the oldest of all my best friends.'[28]

We have no record of the date of Mayerne's marriage to Margaretha van den Boetzelaer. We only know that, by the time he left Paris in 1611, two children had been born to them. One of them, a daughter called Catherine, only lived for eight months; the date of her birth is unrecorded. The other was Mayerne's eldest son Henri. He was born on 8 April 1608. His godparents were the Duc de Rohan, after whom he was named, and his mother's patroness, the Dowager Princess of Orange.[29] It is probable that the marriage and the christenings took place in a private Huguenot chapel in Paris – the chapel of the dowager princess or of the Rohan family – for none of these ceremonies is recorded in the registers of the 'Temple' at Charenton which the Huguenots of Paris used for their worship from 1606 onwards.[30] Mayerne himself frequented the Temple and acted as godfather in it to the children of his Huguenot friends. But attendance there could be dangerous, since the devout Catholic mob tended to attack the worshippers on their way to or from the Temple and beat them up. The guarantee of the law, the formal protection of the Crown, were nullified by the connivance of the magistrates, and at times the Huguenots had to send 'their women and weak persons' to the Temple by water while the men went armed, in paramilitary formation. Such episodes illustrated the growing uncertainty of the Huguenot cause, which was being forced to retreat, more and more, into defensive strongholds: fortified cities in Protestant Languedoc, aristocratic households in Catholic Paris.

This was but one sign of the increasing polarisation of religious differences, the increasing social friction between Catholics and Huguenots in the France of Henri IV. Already by the autumn of 1606 the idea of an exodus was in the air. The troubles between 'those of the Religion that go to Charenton' and 'the rascality of this town' was such, wrote the English ambassador, that the Huguenots

> begin to fear a massacre here again: and therefore many of them think of dislodging. And these humours begin to stir, and work not here alone, but in other places also. For a church of the Protestants some twelve leagues from this town hath been pulled down by night. And out of Montauban, where the Protestants are the stronger, the papists assembling themselves departed at mid-day, with the Crucifix and banner of the Cross before them, and are gone to reside at Toulouse <Toulouse being the citadel of Catholicism in the heretical south>.[31]

Shortly before this, Rohan himself had slipped away from Paris and had gone, under the pretext of escorting his younger brother Soubise, to join the army of Prince Maurice in the Netherlands. The king had been very angry when the news was brought to him, fearing Spanish reactions if a duke and peer of France, the king's cousin and Sully's son-in-law, should be engaged on the side of the 'rebels'. He had sent one of Rohan's trusted servants, 'hastily, *à la française*', to bring him back. This royal intervention was very inconvenient to Rohan, for he had arranged for the same servant to go as his secret agent to England.[32]

It is against this background of increasing religious tension that we must see the events of the last four years of the reign of Henri IV and the position of

Mayerne, the committed Huguenot courtier caught in those events. But before we turn to the religious history of those years and observe, at close quarters, the mounting pressure of religious controversy, we may close this chapter by winding up our account of the secular controversy which was still raging when Mayerne went to England: the controversy between the 'iatro-chemists' of the court and the Galenists of the Paris faculty, between du Chesne and Riolan.

When Mayerne left Paris, Riolan fancied himself in possession of the field. When he returned, the first heavy gun had been fired across the Rhine. It was in October 1606 that Mayerne wrote to Libavius, disclaiming the Paracelsianism of which he and his allies were accused, and urging a united front against the enemies of Alchemy. Next year came the massive bombard-ment of Libavius's *Triumph of Alchemy*, which finally silenced Riolan. It also seems to have weakened Riolan's position in the faculty. We have seen that the faculty was not in fact as united against the chemical doctors as it appeared in public to be. Many doctors of the faculty no doubt disapproved of the hard line represented by the Riolan faction, and two at least of them – Séguin and Akakia – secretly supported Mayerne. It is reasonable to suppose that these moderate men would gradually assert themselves as the controversy became tedious and as Riolan's aggressive tactics discredited the faculty. Some such change seems to have occurred in 1607. At the beginning of that year the faculty was still in full cry against the heretics. By the end of it a settlement was in sight.

The full cry was elicited by Paul Renéaulme, a doctor of Blois. Renéaulme was a friend of Mayerne, who used several of his remedies.[33] He was a learned man, and is described as the best Greek scholar of his time after Casaubon.[34] He was also known as 'the scourge of the apothecaries', for he complained that physicians, ignoring the advice of Galen that they should make their own medicines, had delegated the preparation of medicines to apothecaries who, for their own gain, multiplied unnecessary drugs. Renéaulme urged his fellow-physicians to learn the properties of natural remedies and to realise, as Galen did, that simple and palatable remedies could be effective. He also advocated chemical remedies, insisting that Galen approved mineral cures. All these views were shared by Mayerne. In 1606 Renéaulme published a book in which he advanced these opinions and recorded the cures which he had effected by his unorthodox practice in Blois.[35] In February 1607 the faculty rounded on him. It denounced him as 'a most impudent man', and required him to swear that he would never use the remedies set out in his printed book but would follow the rules of Hippocrates and Galen and the forms publicly approved by the faculty.[36] It is unlikely that Renéaulme suffered much incon-venience from this thunderbolt which, by now, had been hurled too often.

Besides, 1607 was the year of Libavius's *Triumph*, which made all these anathemas look foolish. A few months later we find the faculty preparing to make peace. At least, it decided to make peace – under proper face-saving guarantees – with its two most formidable enemies, du Chesne and Mayerne.

The negotiation seems to have begun in October 1607, and it is interesting to note that the proposal was put forward to the assembled doctors by Jean Duret, the hitherto sleeping partner of Riolan on the committee which had examined and castigated the successive books of du Chesne and Mayerne.[37] The proposal had been put forward twice by the end of the year, and had apparently been blocked or shelved both times. But on 8 January 1608, under a new dean, it was brought up for a third time. The proposal was that 'Violareus et Turquetus'[38] – that is, du Chesne and Mayerne – 'royal doctors (as is alleged)', should be admitted into medical consultation with the doctors of the faculty: in other words, that they be restored to the register and the condemnation of 1603–4 be reversed. When the dean was making the proposal, 'behold!' says the official Register of the faculty,

> in comes Dr André du Laurens, physician-in-chief of the King, who after speaking much in honour and in favour of the faculty, demanded our favour to the said royal doctors, saying that this was the command of the Most Christian King and of the High Chancellor of France; and the said Physician-in-Chief promised that the said Violareus and Turquetus would practise medicine according to the rules or decrees of Hippocrates and Galen and the interpretation and method used by the doctors of this faculty; of which they were willing to give sureties.

The assembled doctors discussed the proposal, and finally,

> in obedience to the Most Christian King, and moved by the persuasion and elegant speech of the Physician-in-Chief, it resolved that all doctors of the faculty should be permitted to hold medical consultations with the said Violareus and Turquetus . . . provided that it be first certified, under the hand of the said Physician-in-Chief, that their names have been inscribed in the album of royal doctors, and that they undertake, in a public document signed in the presence of the royal notaries, that in future they will practise medicine according to the rules of Hippocrates and Galen, and the interpretation, use and method approved by the doctors of the Faculty of Paris, and not otherwise, or in any other way; all which the said Physician-in-Chief, as their surety, promised on oath that Violareus and Turquetus would do; and so the matter was concluded by the Dean.[39]

With this paper compromise, the war of the faculty against du Chesne and Mayerne was formally ended. It did not, of course, make any difference to their practice. Du Chesne and Mayerne continued to recommend and administer chemical medicines; they continued to meet in their alchemical circle; and they did not disavow their chemical publications. The oath was a formula to save the face of the faculty. So was the proviso that du Laurens should certify that the names of du Chesne and Mayerne were 'inscribed in the album of royal doctors'. When first venturing to anathematise du Chesne, the spokesmen of the faculty had justified their insolence by alleging that du Chesne and Mayerne had not been officially appointed as royal doctors, that they had not been 'inscribed in the album'. Mayerne had explicitly refuted this. The invincible King Henri IV, he replied, 'had ordered that my name be inscribed in the album of his doctors'.[40] But the faculty still pretended to believe that the two names were not so inscribed; the faculty could now thus yield, without too much loss of face, if that objection were removed. The surrender was thus limited and personal. It was a surrender to particular royal doctors, on a royal command: it did not entail a surrender to chemical medicine. That struggle would continue, against other victims, for another generation. Indeed, only a few months later, the faculty would condemn, for a second time, the ally of du Chesne and Mayerne, François Pena – whom they now threatened with imprisonment – and several other 'empirics', including one Jean Thibault, 'soy-disant médecin ordinaire du roy', against whom they secured an *arrêt* of the Parlement.[41] We shall soon have to describe the persecution of another victim, even closer to du Chesne and Mayerne.

However, if we pause at the end of the year 1608, we can say that du Chesne and Mayerne had won the immediate medical battle. Having won it, Mayerne took steps to consolidate his victory by improving his social status. In 1608 he and his brother Henri applied to the Cour des Aides to confirm that, having taken up 'noble' professions – Theodore as a physician, Henri as a military officer – they had not 'derogated' from the nobility of their family. They therefore claimed that it should be formally recognised. Having established their genealogy and legitimacy, the court duly declared them 'extraits de noble race' and authorised them and their legitimate descendants to bear the coat of arms of Mayerne.[42] From this time on, Mayerne rejected altogether the 'ignoble' name of Turquet which posterity, however, has insistently fastened on him, and signed himself 'de Mayerne'.

Mayerne was magnanimous in, or at any rate after, his victory over the orthodox establishment. In the summer of 1631 his younger son James was in Paris, studying medicine. With him was his travelling tutor, Mr Burrell, to whom Mayerne, from London, sent instructions. It seems that Burrell, in correspondence with Mayerne, had expressed criticism of the medical teaching in Paris. Mayerne's reply was both sensible and generous. He urged Burrell to dismiss such doubts. 'Nowhere on earth', he wrote, 'are there more learned physicians than in Paris, at least as to theory: I wish they were as good in practice . . . Paris has the best anatomists in the whole world, including Riolan and many surgeons to whom the heir of my name will be welcome and acceptable. Only the Paris doctors both carry out and teach the surgical oper-ations to which I wish him to apply himself once he is inscribed as a student of medicine.'[43] A man who could write thus fairly both about the Paris faculty and about his old adversary Riolan had clearly either forgotten or forgiven the bitter controversy of 1603.[44]

His enemies were less forgiving. Twenty years later, in 1651, when Mayerne was seventy-eight years old and one of the most successful and famous physi-cians in Europe, Riolan, who was then seventy-one, but whose bile had not been sweetened by age, would gratuitously revive the old controversy and republish the 'censure' of the Paris faculty which, half a century before, had pronounced Mayerne an incompetent, shameless, drunken lunatic, unfit to confer with the respectable doctors of Paris. The vindictiveness of Riolan was shared, and would be continued, by his successor at the Collège de France, Gui Patin, whose malicious observations upon Mayerne, as upon all iatrochemists and doctors of Montpellier, we have had occasion to quote. Even a hundred years later still, when another royal doctor from Montpellier would deplore the violence of that censure, another doctor of the Faculty of Medicine of Paris would come forward and solemnly defend the judgement as evidence of the unremitting determination of his faculty to protect its own high standards against debasement by 'charlatanism'.[45]

If the medical controversy could arouse such lasting passions, we must not expect Mayerne's contemporary enemies to have accepted their defeat. Fortunately for them, there was another front to which they could switch their forces. They could turn from the war of medicine to the war of religion.

8

Protestants and Catholics, 1600–1610

The medical controversy was a war of ideas within a particular profession. The religious controversy within which it was involved was a war of ideas in society. As such it struck far deeper roots, and lasted longer. It had begun with the wars of religion under the last Valois kings. It was not ended till Louis XIV's expulsion of the Huguenots in 1685. In the course of this long social war there were spasms of fierce communal violence, of which the massacre of St Bartholomew is the most notorious. There were also periods when the tension was relaxed. The reign of Henri IV was a period of relaxation. But the relaxation was temporary and superficial. Politically contained, the tension still continued at a deeper level. Even on the surface it was rather formalised in a peaceful pattern than altogether suspended. That pattern was a struggle for the conversion of the Huguenot élite.

Theoretically there were three possible solutions of the Huguenot problem. One was the victory of the Huguenots, the complete reformation of the Church of France. This had been the hope of Calvin and the first Huguenots. From their 'refuge' in Geneva they hoped to penetrate the Church in France and, with royal support if possible, to transform it into a Protestant Church. This was what the English and Scottish reformers had done in their countries: in England with the support of the Crown; in Scotland against the Crown, by revolution. But in France, by the 1590s, such a solution was no longer conceivable. The Crown had not been captured. Revolution had failed. When Henri IV accepted Catholicism as the only means of securing his throne, he implicitly recognised that a complete Huguenot victory was impossible. Even a Huguenot king could not carry through a Calvinist reformation in France.

The second possible solution was the complete victory of the Catholic Church, the elimination, by whatever means, of the Calvinist heresy and of the institutions which it had created for its perpetuation in France. This had been the policy of the Sainte Ligue during the wars of religion, and it would remain the policy of many social classes and institutions in France even after the

Ligue itself had been discredited by the social violence which it had encouraged and organised, and by its own subservience to the traditional enemy,
Spain. The old *Ligueurs* recognised, after 1589, that they could no longer hope
for total victory by such means. But they remained strong enough to prevent
total defeat. They accepted Henri IV as the legitimate king of an independent
nation. But they obliged him, as the price of his throne, to conform to the
Catholic Church; and under his rule they continued, by other means, to
pursue the same ends. From *Ligueurs* they became *dévots*. Some of them
remained *Ligueurs* under the skin.

Finally, there was the possibility of compromise. Those who preferred political unity to doctrinal uniformity, those who were weary of a civil discord
which had undermined national power and national independence, those
who were increasingly disgusted by sectarian intolerance, all looked for a
compromise which recognised the necessary coexistence of Huguenots and
Catholics as equal subjects of the Crown. Some envisaged a 'plural' society,
embracing separate communities with distinctive institutions and different
ways of life. Others wished to go beyond this and looked forward to a united,
comprehensive Church of France, which would adapt itself to include many
of the Huguenots and much of their organisation and would be influenced by
their ideas: a new 'Gallican' Church somewhat similar to the Church of
England, which had contrived to preserve the Erasmian *via media* between the
old Catholic Church and its radical enemies. Collectively, these men, whether
Catholic or Protestant, and regardless of differences of emphasis, were known
as the *politiques*, and it was they whose support had made it possible for an
ex-Huguenot king to rule over a largely Catholic people.

The first of these three solutions being now ruled out, the struggle under
Henri IV was between those who supported the second – the party of the
dévots – and those who supported the third – the *politiques*. Inevitably, in these
circumstances, the Huguenots, whatever their complexion, supported the
politiques – at least so long as the *politiques* had any hope of success. But the
reign of Henri IV witnessed a continuing advance by the *dévots* and a continuing retreat by the *politiques*, so that, by the end of the reign, the Huguenots
found themselves in a far weaker position than they had been at the beginning. Then, with the assassination of the king, their weakness would be
exposed. Finding no protection at court, or in national politics, they would
either resign themselves to 'internal emigration' or fall back on their own base
and, once again, under their aristocratic leaders, take up arms in sectarian
revolt.

In this process of attrition, a central part was played by the king himself.
Henri IV had been brought up as a Huguenot, under the influence of his
Protestant mother, in the Protestant province of Béarn. He had risen to power

in France, like many other great noblemen in the south, as a Huguenot party leader. In those days of struggle he had become personally attached to many of his Huguenot comrades-in-arms. By 1589 he was conditioned, in many ways, by his Huguenot past. But Huguenotism, to him, was always an accident of his life, not a personal conviction. As the English ambassador, Sir George Carew, wrote of him in 1609, 'inwardly in his heart he is of no religion at all.'[1] This was very convenient, since it enabled him, at a critical moment, to change the religion that he professed in order to ensure, for France unity, for himself its crown.

When Henri IV accepted the logic of politics and made the 'saut périlleux' or perilous leap into the bosom of the Roman Church, he regarded it, at first, as a merely personal necessity. He did not regard it as a necessity for his Huguenot friends, and he wrote to them to say so. He begged them not to fear that this change, 'which is personal to me', entailed any alteration in the security of his Protestant subjects 'or in the affection which I have always felt for them'.[2] Similar letters were sent to his Protestant allies abroad, and it was Huguenot ambassadors who conveyed the message: du Chesne himself, as we have seen, carried it to the Protestant cantons of Switzerland. No doubt Henri IV believed that he would be able to preserve this delicate balance. He accepted the view of the *politiques* that religion was separable from politics, and that he could rule in harmony over a 'plural' society.

This, however, was not the view of the *dévots*. When the Catholic establishment of Paris insisted that France could only be ruled by a Catholic king, they did not refer only to his personal religion. They referred to his court and government. To them the conversion of the king was not an isolated episode: it was the beginning of a process which was to be completed throughout the country. And little by little they would prevail. They had powerful allies, of course. Successive popes pressed favours on the king. To them he was a returned prodigal whom it was prudent to woo; and his power, now that he was a Catholic, could be used to release the papacy from its humiliating dependence on Spain. Clement VIII allowed to Henri IV of France what Clement VII had never allowed Henry VIII of England: a dispensation to divorce his queen in order to produce an heir. So Marie de Médicis came from Florence to be Queen of France and, incidentally, to add her persuasions to those of the French *dévots*. Pope Paul V would be no less obliging: he would grant a dispensation declaring Henri IV's illegitimate son, then aged seven, a fit person to be elected bishop of Metz. Such favours naturally recommended an indulgent religion to a self-indulgent king. Little by little, Henri IV accepted the logic of the *dévots*. In Catholic Paris, surrounded by Catholic institutions, it was as natural for the king to be Catholic as it had been to be a Protestant in Navarre. And always there was that seductive argument that

Catholicism was the religion of monarchy, Protestantism the religion of republics.

Henri IV never betrayed his former co-religionists. The past still bound him to them, and the necessities of diplomacy imposed upon him – as upon some of his Catholic predecessors – the patronage of foreign Protestants against the threatening power of the Habsburgs. But the past was past; old links were gradually dissolved by time and new ones were forged to replace them. Personally too Henri IV was seduced by the well-chosen tempters of the Counter-Reformation, whose urbanity, elegance and pliancy were so much more attractive to an indolent voluptuary than the moral austerity and intellectual rigour of an Agrippa d'Aubigné or a Philippe du Plessis Mornay. So, little by little, Henri IV slid deeper into that comfortable bosom. At the time of his conversion he had refused absolutely to admit the Jesuits to France. He had then told the nuncio bluntly that they were the emissaries of Spain who had sought, again and again, to assassinate him.[3] It was against their poisoned dishes that la Rivière had sought to protect him by the esoteric antidotes of the Duke of Saxony and the King of Sweden. But gradually the king's resolution weakened. The peace with Spain, in 1598, relaxed the tension, and the irresistible missionaries crept in. In 1603, in spite of the opposition of the Parlement, they were allowed to set up colleges in France. Soon a Jesuit confessor, Pierre Coton, found his way into the royal palace; and the Huguenots, realising that their voice was no longer heard at court, would complain that the king 'avait du Coton dans les oreilles': had Coton-wool in his ears.

Once the king himself had yielded, how could the old Huguenot court resist? Individuals might stand firm, confident of their power, their integrity or their indispensability. The great Huguenot nobles held their ground – for a time. The Huguenot intellectuals were no less proud – so long as they had a patron or a base. Economically, the Huguenot Maximilien de Béthune, whom the king made Duc de Sully in 1606, and his clientele were indispensable. But when the whole machine of royal power and patronage was firmly in Catholic hands, the scales were weighted against them. One by one they were pressed, bribed, seduced into conformity, or, if they resisted, quietly shut out from profit and power. Old favourites might linger on, but no new favourites came from those ranks, no new favours came that way. And meanwhile, to ease their passage, a tribe of *convertisseurs* provided high spiritual or intellectual arguments for profitable change.

Two great men, one on either side, one a *politique*, the other a *dévot*, illustrated, by their personal histories, the spiritual and intellectual struggle of those years. One was a Catholic whom the Catholic *dévots* regarded as little better than a Protestant in disguise: Jacques-Auguste de Thou, the intellectual oracle of the *politiques*. The other was a Protestant turned Catholic: Jacques Davy du Perron, Bishop of Evreux, the greatest of the *convertisseurs*.

Jacques-Auguste de Thou came from a great legal family. His father had been *premier président* of the Parlement of Paris, and his own greatest ambition was to succeed Achille de Harlay in that office. Meanwhile he served the Crown in a series of legal offices and built up a reputation as an indispensable administrator, a scholar, and a patrician of the international Republic of Letters. Himself a Catholic, he believed firmly in toleration, not only as a political necessity but as an idea. For he was a disciple of Erasmus. Indeed, his open praise of Erasmus as *grande huius saeculi decus*, the great glory of this age, was one of the many crimes which were imputed to him by the orthodox. Conversely he detested, above all things, intolerance, and he hated the intolerance of his own party, which held power, even more than that of its adversaries, who could only express, not realise, their ferocity. His moral hatred was directed against the Catholic *Ligueurs*, his intellectual contempt against the Catholic *dévots*. On the other hand those whom he most respected were often Protestants. His closest friends included the two greatest of Huguenot scholars, Joseph Scaliger and Isaac Casaubon. His favoured correspondents and collaborators included the Huguenot leader of Orléans, Jerôme Groslot de l'Isle; the secretary of the Calvinist Elector Palatine, Hans Georg Lingelsheim; the Dutch scholar Hugo Grotius; the Anglican William Camden. De Thou's great achievement in politics was the formulation, in 1598, of the Edict of Nantes, which gave to the Huguenots a guaranteed legal status in a plural society. His great work of literature was his *History of his Own Time*, which began to appear in 1603, dedicated to Henri IV. Both the Edict and the *History* were regarded by the *dévots* as intolerable affronts to orthodoxy, for both defended Huguenot positions against the intolerance of the *Ligueurs*. But de Thou was confident of his position. He was powerful in the Parlement and in society; he enjoyed the favour of the king; and even at Rome he had highly placed supporters on whom he could rely to resist the clamours of Jesuits and friars. These supporters were the French cardinals, Cardinal de Joyeuse, Cardinal d'Ossat and, most importantly for our purposes, Cardinal du Perron.

For Jacques Davy du Perron, Bishop of Evreux, the intellectual leader of the *dévots*, was not himself a *dévot*. He too was a scholar and a man of the world, friendly with *politiques* and Huguenots. At least he was superficially a scholar and externally friendly. But his friendship was not disinterested. Nothing about him was disinterested. His courtly manners, his urbane compliments, his lavish hospitality, like his scholarship and his Catholicism itself, were all directed to an ulterior purpose: self-advancement. He was a supreme opportunist. Born and bred in Switzerland, the refuge of his Huguenot parents, he had come to Paris in 1576 and there, by a timely display of erudition and a no less timely abjuration of his errors, had earned the patronage of Henri III. A few years later, another well-timed betrayal brought him into the favour of Henri IV, still a Huguenot, and of his mistress Gabrielle d'Estrées. He was rewarded with the bishopric of Evreux. Then he set out to lead his former co-religionists on the way which he himself had taken. He began at the top with the king himself: it was after secret instruction by du Perron that Henri IV finally abjured his Protestantism at St Denis. Thereafter, the bishop turned to the court and sought, by the same arts, to bring it the same way to salvation.

Du Perron realised that, at the court of Henri IV, where the religion of the Huguenots was guaranteed, conversion must be by persuasion, not force. He also realised that persuasion, to be effective on a large scale, must begin with the élite. If the great Huguenot noblemen and the great Huguenot scholars could be induced to follow the ex-Huguenot king and the ex-Huguenot cardinal, the rest of France would follow and the victory of the *dévots* would be assured. For this purpose du Perron never omitted any civility to a distinguished Huguenot at court. His function was to maintain a continuing dialogue between the two religions: a dialogue that was conducted on a high social and intellectual level, in a dramatic public arena, and in which every episode would end in a spectacular conversion to the Church.

The varying fortunes of Président de Thou and Cardinal du Perron can be read as a barometer of the unending struggle between the *politiques* and the *dévots* at the court of Henri IV. But there was also a third person who played a particular part in that drama. This was the public representative of the Huguenot clergy, Pierre du Moulin, whom we have met as a friend of Mayerne and one of the ministers of the Huguenot church of Paris.

Pierre du Moulin was not, like de Thou and du Perron, a man of the world. He was not – he could not afford to be – polished and courtly. The son of a penniless, hunted Huguenot minister, he had narrowly been preserved, in infancy, from the massacre of St Bartholomew. He had studied at the new college of Sedan, the Protestant redoubt in which his father had found refuge, and then, with a parting gift of 12 sous from his father who could no longer afford to protect him, he had found his way first to England, then to Holland. In England, while tutor to the young Earl of Rutland, he had continued his studies at Cambridge University. In Holland, he had been a professor at Leiden and had taught Grotius himself. Then he had received a call to the Huguenot church of Paris – that is, the church outside Paris, first at Grigny, then at Ablon, then at Charenton – and had become chaplain to 'Madame' – that is, Henri IV's sister Catherine, Duchess of Bar. Madame, though married (against her will) to the Catholic Duke of Lorraine, refused to follow her brother's example. She remained an obstinate Huguenot and even insisted on bringing Huguenot ministers to preach in the palace of the Louvre. In du Moulin she found a chaplain worthy of herself. A strict predestinarian, narrow and intolerant in his views, copious and courageous in stating them, unyielding and acrimonious in controversy, he was a thorn in the flesh both of du Perron and of his own fellow-Huguenots. The smooth *dévots* despised him as a donkey. Du Perron qualified the metaphor, declaring that he was a donkey who, whenever he was stroked (du Perron was an accomplished stroker), replied with a kick. That was not strictly true. It depended who stroked him.

Such were the protagonists in the ideological drama of the reign of Henri IV. The episodes were numerous and often vivid. One of the most spectacular was the conference of Fontainebleau in 1600, when Cardinal du Perron confronted 'the pope of the Huguenots', Philippe du Plessis Mornay. Du Perron liked to stage these conferences as well-prepared publicity stunts. When a distinguished convert had been privately gained, a public debate would be organised, lavish entertainment would be prepared, and the *beau monde* would be invited to partake of it. Then the convert would appear. At first he would seem to be in a state of doubt and anguish. Then, when the debate was over, he would declare himself convinced by the Catholic argument and be received into the Church. There would be great rejoicing at the repentance of the sinner, and great encouragement to other sinners to follow his example. At the conference of Fontainebleau, du Plessis Mornay underestimated both the formality of the occasion and the severity of the test. He came ill-prepared and was unquestionably defeated. The practical outcome was the public conversion of Philippe Canaye de Fresne, the Huguenot scholar, traveller and diplomat, du Chesne's 'star of French genius',[4] who was now rewarded for his spectacular apostasy with an embassy in Venice.

One of the Protestant members of the 'jury' who had to pronounce the verdict at Fontainebleau was Canaye's close friend Isaac Casaubon. After that, Casaubon himself suffered much from the attention of the *convertisseurs*, including both du Perron and Canaye. He also suffered much from the reproaches of his fellow-Huguenots, who blamed him for having taken part in a carefully staged Catholic triumph. But we will return to the problems of Casaubon. For the moment it is enough to say that his life in Paris was rendered painful by these pressures. He sought to excuse himself to his co-religionists, declined to answer the letters of Canaye, and came to dread the flattering visits, and the stroking hand, of Cardinal du Perron.

Another dramatic episode took place in 1604. In that year 'Madame' lay dying in Paris, with Pierre du Moulin at her bedside to provide the consolations of the Protestant religion to which she had so stubbornly clung. Now, in her last hours, the king made a last effort: he sent du Perron to visit her.

Du Moulin refused to admit him. The cardinal insisted and called upon the Huguenot to retire before the emissary of the Crown. Persuasion still failing, the two ministers of Christ then fell to blows in the presence of the dying princess. But du Moulin clung to his principles and to the bedpost; the cardinal was forced to retreat; and Madame died, as she had lived, a Huguenot. Four years later du Moulin would resist another effort to displace him at a noble Huguenot deathbed. On that occasion the dying lady was the Princesse de Joinville, and the usurping priest was not du Perron but St François de Sales, the saintly bishop of Geneva *in partibus infidelium.*

Under such pressure, the conversions at court increased. Among du Perron's early converts had been Nicolas Harlay de Sancy, who in 1589 had brought to Henri IV, before Paris, the decisive support of 10,000 Swiss Protestants. The king had been so glad of this reinforcement that he had promised to make de Sancy the greatest man in his kingdom. He put him in charge of the royal bounty in order to lubricate his policy towards his old co-religionists. To the unyielding Huguenot Agrippa d'Aubigné, Sancy's apostasy was the worst of all, and he would satirise it without mercy in his *Confession de Sancy.*[5] Then Henri IV had his own heir-presumptive, Henri de Bourbon, Prince de Condé, the son of a great Huguenot leader, brought up as a Catholic. In 1600, soon after the famous conference of Fontainebleau, Agrippa d'Aubigné himself faced the redoubtable du Perron in controversy: the souls of ten Huguenot gentlemen were at stake in that contest, and d'Aubigné flattered himself that he had at least delayed the conversion of some of them for a few years. One of them was Antoine de Loménie, the son of a victim of St Bartholomew. As a Protestant, he had been Henri IV's ambassador in England; after his conversion, he would become Secretary of State. But it would be easy to multiply instances of those who were seduced by the combined force of self-interest, love of ease, and what d'Aubigné called the 'discours bien polis', the 'courtoisies excessives' of du Perron.[6] The two great scholars, Scaliger and Casaubon, stood firm; so, in general, did the Huguenot clergy, although du Perron commanded a rich fund with which to bribe them;[7] but many Huguenot courtiers and some Huguenot grandees yielded, and the *convertisseurs* would carry off renegade sons of the most stalwart Huguenot fathers: a Châtillon, a Casaubon, a d'Aubigné, a Rohan.

From 1604 until 1608 du Perron was at Rome. There he was able, as it seemed, to give valuable help to his friend de Thou in staving off the threatened condemnation of his *History.* In this alliance between de Thou and du Perron there was, of course, a fundamental contradiction. De Thou, though a *politique,* was a Catholic and, as such, did not wish to be condemned: he wished his work to be read by Catholics, to penetrate their minds and undermine their bigotry. Du Perron, equally, did not wish to see de Thou condemned: the historian was too grand, and too influential, to be lost for the Church. But du Perron, naturally enough, had no such tenderness for de Thou's *History*. He did not wish to see that corrosive work undermine the faith of the *dévots*. Rather he wished to see it corrected, expurgated, neutralised, so that it could serve as an intellectual advertisement for French Catholicism. To such correction de Thou would never consent. He was proud of his independence, which he would defend against all comers: popes, *Ligueurs*, kings and great magnates like the Guise family. However, the inner contradiction of the alliance was not revealed while du Perron was at Rome, where he exerted his diplomacy, not to avert his friend's condemnation, but to negotiate his surrender. Then, in 1608, du Perron returned to France to reside in his new archbishopric of Sens: the see in which Paris itself was situated. With du Perron's return, de Thou lost a supposed ally in Rome and the Huguenots felt increased pressure in Paris.[8]

Du Perron's return coincided with another development in France: the movement for reunion of the Churches. For some time the more liberal of the Huguenots and the *politiques* among the Catholics had been advocating such a reunion: the creation of a Gallican Church which would, like the Church of England, embrace the moderate men, and the agreed beliefs, of both parties. The king himself favoured the project, and in the years 1607–8 conferences were held and pamphlets printed in support of it. The Huguenot clergy in general opposed it. They saw only too clearly the unfavourable balance of power and realised that reunion would not be upon equal terms: the Protestant Church of France would be swallowed up just as the 'Uniate' Church in the east was being swallowed up. Besides, they noted, Cardinal du Perron himself seemed to favour the project. That could only mean that he saw it as a means to divide and absorb the true Church. In this they were unquestionably right.[9]

Among the Huguenots who were temporarily seduced by the mirage of reunion was Louis Turquet, the father of Mayerne. When we last saw him, he had been driven from his house in Lyon, to which he had evidently returned from Geneva, by the forces of the Ligue, and had committed himself to the cause of Henri de Navarre, to whom he had dedicated his *History of Spain*. That was in 1586. In the following years he seems to have spent some time in France with the king. Seeing the ravages of civil war and the apparent dissolution of government, he turned his mind to the problem of reconstruction. In 1589, when Henri III was assassinated and Henri de Navarre became *de jure* King of France, Louis Turquet's hopes rose high. He saw himself as the political philosopher of the hour, the architect of a new social order, the secret adviser of the new Huguenot king. So he composed a stout work ('trois livres assez amples') to show how the essential parts of royal government – police, justice, arms, finance – could be harmonised and how the great machine of state, composed of so many and such different pieces, could be repaired and maintained. The full content of this great work should not be prostituted to the common people.[10] It was to be submitted in secret to the king and his most faithful counsellors only. In October 1591 Louis Turquet duly presented to the king the three ample books, all written out in his own hand – a very beautiful hand. But 'in order not to distract him from the great affairs in which he was occupied' – for he was still fighting for his kingdom: Paris had not yet surrendered – he also presented a printed summary of his proposals, in the form of a letter to the king.[11] The king received the summary graciously, and told the author to keep the three fat books handy so that he could read them at leisure. Meanwhile he authorised Turquet to publish his summary.[12]

One of those to whom Turquet sent a copy of his summary was his friend Joseph Scaliger, then living at the château de Preuilly, in Poitou, the home of his patron Louis de Chasteigner de la Roche-Pozay, seigneur d'Abain. Turquet suggested that Scaliger enlist the support of his patron, and offered to come in person to Preuilly or elsewhere, even 'at this bad season' (it was March), to press his case.[13] What were bad seasons, bad roads, painful journeys, to a committed reformer? Louis Turquet had already shown that he despised mere comfort. He had travelled far in the good cause, at great personal expense and inconvenience, from Geneva to Sedan, then, following the court, from Sedan to Tours. His project, he wrote, was worthy to be undertaken by men of noble family, men of experience and credit in France, like the Chasteigner, and he himself was ready to play his part, 'according to my quality and under the name and favour of the great men who are called to handle affairs of state and enjoy the honour of it'.[14] Scaliger was delighted with the summary and urged Turquet to publish the whole work; but here Turquet was firm. It was inexpedient, he wrote, to print such things: 'you know the nature of the people.'[15] Perhaps the work could be published one day, but not now. In the meantime, the programme it recommended should be put into effect: practice, not argument, must make it acceptable by the common people. In due course Turquet joined Scaliger in the château de Preuilly. The seigneur d'Abain was absent, but the indefatigable old man set out to find him, only to be turned back by the military operations of the Ligue. Back at Preuilly, he showed the whole work to Scaliger, who once again urged him to publish it. But once again Turquet refused: these were secret cabinet matters, he said, 'choses de cabale et non de publication'.[16] However, the summary was printed and, as Turquet would afterwards claim, known and read throughout France.

What was the programme which these two distinguished Huguenot scholars recommended as a model for France? Anyone who thinks that Huguenots believed in a free, open or progressive society would be surprised by it. There was to be a strict hierarchy of classes and no question of *carrière ouverte aux talents*. Nobility was not to be usurped, and the various classes – the rich, the men of letters, the men of affairs, the artisans, the labourers (in that order) – were to be kept distinct by sumptuary laws and careful regulation. The government, like the Calvinist Church, was to be decentralised but omnipresent. Religion was to be the foundation of public order, and there was to be a moral police, with offices in every seat of government, to preserve the social hierarchy, enforce the sumptuary laws, repress extravagance, expense, games, banquets, processions, funeral pomp and other vanities. Above all, it was to ensure universal sexual morality and to regulate marriage. Women were to be firmly controlled in the interests of the stability of property. All economic life was to be regulated: there were to be *bureaux de marchands* to regulate contracts, sales, customs, guilds, etc., and *bureaux de domaine* to register land and control its sale. Charity, poor-relief, moneylending, insurance were all to be controlled by the organs of the state.

Such was the plan which Louis Turquet pressed upon the debonair, pleasure-loving Henri IV. Alas – but are we surprised? – Henri IV did not read it. Nor did any of the great men to whom it was recommended do anything to implement it. Disappointed, the author returned to Geneva. But he did not burn his manuscript, as he had threatened. He kept it, and it would re-emerge, two decades later, in an explosive form.

In the years following the submission of his programme, Louis Turquet seems to have lived partly in Geneva, partly in Lyon. In 1596 he was present, as an elder of the church of Lyon, at the fourteenth National Synod of the French Reformed Churches at Saumur.[17] In 1601 he held the same position at the sixteenth National Synod, at Jargeau.[18] It was on this last occasion that he first appeared in his new guise as a reunionist. It seems that already, at that time, the king was entertaining the ideas of reunion. Turquet drew up a paper on the subject, which he submitted to the synod. However, the king's interest soon passed; once again, no notice was taken of Turquet's paper; and Turquet returned to Lyon with yet another unpublished, and unwanted, programme for reform.[19]

When we next light on Louis Turquet he is in Paris. In March 1603 we find him borrowing books from Isaac Casaubon, who was now established at court.[20] Whether he was living continuously in Paris at that time we do not know. But in 1608 he was settled in Paris, in the rue Saincte Croix. He was now aged seventy-five. Perhaps it was the revival of interest in reunion which brought him thither. No doubt the success of his son also attracted him. He came with his wife, and appears there with a Monsieur de la Pimante, who was evidently a kinsman: we can safely identify him with 'M. Pournas de la Piemente, kinsman' who remained a patient of Theodore de Mayerne for many years afterwards. We may remember that it was to Jean Pournas, seigneur de la Piemente, that Mayerne had dedicated his juvenile guidebook.[21] La Piemente seems to have acted as an amanuensis, copying out documents of interest to Louis Turquet and to other friends. One of those who used la Piemente's services was Pierre de l'Estoile, the political diarist of Paris, and it is from his diary that we are able to learn about this new phase in the life of Louis Turquet.

Pierre de l'Estoile was a lawyer, a liberal Catholic and a *politique.* In many ways he reminds us of de Thou, whom he greatly admired. Like de Thou, he detested the Catholic League and the Jesuits more than he disliked the Huguenots. Indeed, like de Thou, he seems to have positively preferred Huguenots to most of his own fellow-Catholics, and he had many Huguenot friends. He had himself been brought up among Huguenots, and had been a fellow-pupil, in Paris, with Agrippa d'Aubigné. At a time when Paris was unsafe for Huguenots, d'Aubigné and his fellow-pupils had been brought by their Huguenot tutor, Mathieu Béroald, to the safety of l'Estoile's Catholic home at Orléans.[22] L'Estoile was indeed an irenist, an Erasmian. Like de Thou he venerated the name of Erasmus, whose whole works were now condemned by his own Church. All men of good will, he wrote in his diary, must share the opinions of 'ce grand personnage', 'the fifth Doctor of the Church', who had sought to keep the Church united.[23] With these views, l'Estoile lived, in Paris, in easy familiarity with Huguenots, and he soon became – perhaps through the copying service of la Piemente – a close friend of Louis Turquet. Their friendship, that between a liberal Catholic and a liberal Huguenot, was comparable, at a less exalted level, with that of de Thou and Casaubon.

L'Estoile's first mention of Louis Turquet is on 19 April 1608. He then records that 'P.D.L.P.' – presumably Pournas de la Piemente – brought him the *Paradoxes politiques* of 'that good man M. Turquet, written by hand', together with another political pamphlet, also in manuscript, by the Sieur de Lanssac, Captain of the Guard, urging upon Henri IV a Protestant foreign policy.[24] A few months later he records that 'M. Turquet, author of the *History of Spain*, a good and learned man, and very zealous for the reunion and reform of the Church, came to see me; and being in my study, discussing this subject, he told me many things that I did not know concerning the progress of this holy work, which I think that all good men desire.'[25] In particular, Turquet told l'Estoile of the document which he had submitted to the synod of Jargeau in 1601, and promised to show it to him. Ten days later he brought it round, and l'Estoile read it. It filled six quires of paper and was entitled *Advis sur le Synode National que le Roy vouldroit convoquer.* L'Estoile found it 'a holy and Christian proposal, proceeding from a truly open heart; loving the truth, like its author'.

But he added that, being so open and truthful, it would no doubt be ill received, and if accepted by one side would be rejected by the other.[26]

L'Estoile was right. The movement for the reunion of the Catholic and Huguenot Churches in France soon ran out of steam. Next year, 1609, showed that the Catholic party was not prepared to yield an inch. In that year the *dévots* showed their strength both in Rome and in Paris, against both Huguenots and *politiques*, in the court, in the university and in the medical faculty. They struck once again at the chemical doctors; they blocked the promotion of Mayerne; and they secured the condemnation of de Thou.

The counter-attack of orthodoxy began first in the medical faculty. When we last dealt with the controversy between the Galenists and the iatrochemists in that faculty, du Chesne and Mayerne seemed to have triumphed. Under royal pressure, the ban upon consultation with them had been lifted in exchange for general assurances that they would keep to the teaching of Hippocrates and Galen, and the faculty had contented itself with the condemnation of two less powerful royal doctors, whom it described as 'empirics', François Pena and the younger Jean Thibault. But next year it returned to the old issue which had lain dormant since the great controversy of 1603–5. The occasion of its return was provided by one of its own members, Pierre le Paulmier: the same le Paulmier who had been forced, in September 1603, to recant his rash support of 'spagyria' in general and du Chesne in particular.

In 1608 Pierre le Paulmier had published a book in which he attempted, while professing complete orthodoxy, to save at least something of alchemy and chemistry from the wholesale condemnation of the faculty. The book was entitled *Lapis philosophicus dogmaticorum*, 'The philosopher's stone of the Galenists', and in it le Paulmier undertook to 'restore' Libavius to himself: that is, to correct his recent 'Paracelsian' deviation and to re-create his old anti-Paracelsian orthodoxy. In so doing, le Paulmier did not spare Libavius. He described him as 'a man rather subtle than learned', who had shamefully deserted the honourable position which he had maintained in his earlier works in order to follow the 'tenebrous Paracelsus' and his faction, and who had thus forced the Paris faculty to state the correct position. Libavius's *Alchemia*, said le Paulmier, was death to man and metal alike. It was a rotten work in which he had not only murdered the art of medicine but also insulted the Paris faculty, the most learned medical school in Europe. Le Paulmier called upon him, by confession and recantation, to earn a generous amnesty and oblivion. If he were obstinate and insisted on growing old in error, 'you will feel how sharp and painful are the arrows of truth'. As further evidence of orthodoxy, le Paulmier dedicated his work to the great champion of sound religion, Cardinal du Perron.

Outwardly this seemed fair enough. The faculty was praised, Libavius chastised, truth vindicated. Unfortunately a close glance revealed that le Paulmier's purpose was far less innocent. What he was seeking to do was to detach the cause of chemistry from its German champion Libavius, who had been so rude about the Paris faculty, and to rest it, instead, on the authority of good French doctors, with whom the faculty now seemed to be reconciled. Du Chesne, Mayerne, the doctors of Orléans, 'ingenious Renéaulme': all these excellent doctors, said le Paulmier, were fundamentally sound; they built on the foundations of their great French predecessors, Sylvius and Fernel, 'the two brightest stars of medicine'.[27] If they had, at times, gone rather far towards Paracelsian novelty, or expressed themselves rather tartly, that was only because they were temporarily inflamed by the heat of controversy. Now all that was over. Having discovered that the Paris faculty really approved chemical medicine and only repudiated Paracelsian extremism, they had all made their peace. Only the insolent foreigner Libavius remained, so far, irreconcilable. Why, then, could not the faculty forget the exasperating name of Libavius? Why could it not recognise that true chemistry had come to stay, and that its Huguenot professors were the natural leaders of orthodoxy? Such was the real message of le Paulmier who, to make it quite clear, described himself on the title-page as 'Galeno-chymicus'.

To the doctors of Paris, who secretly hated the names of du Chesne and Mayerne and had recently condemned 'ingenious Renéaulme' as 'a most impudent man', such a defence was quite inadmissible, and they lost no time in showing it. On 24 January 1609 the familiar scene was re-enacted. In a meeting of the faculty, le Paulmier's work was denounced as an attack on the teaching of Hippocrates and Galen, which contained many errors, lies and impostures. The faculty appointed three of its members to examine it, one of them being the inevitable Jean Riolan. Four days later, after hearing the report of the examiners and le Paulmier's defence, it ruled, without a dissenting voice, that the book was a libel full of errors, frauds, impostures and lies, unworthy to see the light. Le Paulmier was ordered to acknowledge and abjure his errors, publicly and in writing, within six months, and to promise never again to deviate from the ancient authorities. If he should refuse to recant, he would be struck from the roll of doctors and deprived permanently of all degrees, honours and emoluments. Meanwhile, his emoluments were stopped.

At first le Paulmier promised to comply. But the document which he submitted in February proved far from satisfactory. Instead of submitting to censure, he dared to answer back, in strong language. He also aggravated his offence by publishing his answers, and by dedicating them, moreover, to Cardinal du Perron. These answers were held by the faculty to be not only wrong and offensive in themselves, but also a gross libel on the late M. Riolan and his son. Ultimately le Paulmier appealed to the Parlement of Paris. But here he had no more success than Roch le Baillif in 1580. Indeed, counsel for the faculty – the formidable Gallican lawyer Louis Servin – explicitly cited the case of Roch le Bailliff to show that the faculty had the undoubted right to discipline those who did not accept its rules. Servin was himself an ex-Huguenot, and he made himself famous by his defence of the university against all rivals. The Parlement agreed with him. Le Paulmier's appeal was dismissed with costs. The faculty was delighted with this award which, it noted smugly, confirmed its power to censure such insolence and obstinacy. In the margin of its manuscript register the scribe wrote a jubilant note: 'this judgement is worthy to be carefully preserved.' The dean of the faculty saw to it that it was preserved: he had it printed and circulated, so that the universities of the world might all understand it.[28]

The sentence of the Parlement against le Paulmier was pronounced on 9 July 1609. It was seen, rightly, as a blow aimed by the faculty against le Paulmier's friends du Chesne and Mayerne. Le Paulmier had always openly expressed his respect for du Chesne. Indeed, it was his defence of du Chesne which had brought him into trouble in 1603. In his book of 1608 he had sought to portray du Chesne and Mayerne as representing the true tradition of medicine against both Paracelsus and the faculty. And Mayerne showed his gratitude afterwards. He could not show it to le Paulmier living, for le Paulmier only survived his condemnation by a few months. But on his death Mayerne (we are told) bought up his books and papers. When Mayerne went to England, he listed among his most valued books *Praxis Palmarii*, 'The Practice of le Paulmier'. He also brought with him le Paulmier's notebooks; and according to Gui Patin it was Mayerne who afterwards edited and published at Geneva a surgical treatise, originally written by Fernel, which had passed into his hands with the manuscripts of le Paulmier.[29]

In the few weeks following the condemnation of le Paulmier, blow followed blow for Mayerne. The blows were caused, in different ways, by two deaths. First, on 16 August, came the death of André du Laurens, *premier médecin du roi*; then, four days later, Joseph du Chesne died of an obstruction of the stomach.[30] Both men had been Mayerne's patrons, but du Chesne had been more than a patron. He had been, first, his master and mentor, then his partner and ally. Together du Chesne and Mayerne had studied and practised the new science of chemistry; together they had conquered Paris; together they had resisted the attacks of the Galenists and the Catholics. The death of such an ally, at a time of renewed pressure against both religious and medical heresy, must have been a serious loss to Mayerne. To the end du Chesne had been a firm Huguenot and an active chemist. Isaac Casaubon, himself already being harried by the *convertisseurs*, records that du Chesne died 'in purioris religionis confessione constans', constant in the profession of pure religion.[31] Mayerne, long afterwards, would note that the prescription for *Mercurius dulcis* was the last secret which du Chesne had communicated to him.[32]

André du Laurens was neither a Huguenot nor a chemist. But he too had been a friend and patron to Mayerne – and perhaps a more valuable patron precisely because he was a Catholic and a Galenist. His Catholicism, like his Galenism, was moderate; he was bound to Mayerne by an ancient friendship in the tolerant atmosphere of Montpellier; and they had been natural allies when the doctors of Paris attacked Mayerne as a doctor of Montpellier. One of du Laurens's last acts had been to intervene personally in order to secure the restoration of du Chesne and Mayerne to the roll of physicians authorised to practise in Paris. His sudden death, at the age of about forty-eight, was therefore a personal blow to Mayerne, as it was to the king, who valued him greatly. Indeed, it was said that du Laurens's life had been shortened by his extra-curricular activities at court. For whenever the king could not sleep, he would send for his *premier médecin*, who was obliged to turn out at midnight and lull his master to sleep by reading aloud to him 'the King's bible' – that is, the romance, which turned the head of Don Quixote, of *Amadis de Gaule*.[33]

The death of du Laurens did not merely deprive Mayerne of a powerful friend. It also created an important vacancy. Who would succeed him as *premier médecin*? Henri IV was in no doubt whom he wished to have. Pierre de l'Estoile, who was well informed on all court matters, recorded what he heard in his diary. The king, he wrote, 'dearly wished to appoint Turquet, called de Mayerne, *médecin ordinaire* to his Majesty, whom he loved and esteemed; but because he was of the Religion' – i.e. a Huguenot – 'would not have him, and said these words: "I would gladly have given 20,000 écus for Turquet to be a Catholic, so that he could be my *premier médecin*." M. de Sully was approached in the matter, but replied that he had sworn an oath never to speak to the king either about doctors or about cooks' – the two categories of men who, if the king were thought to be poisoned, might be suspected and thus draw suspicion on their patrons.[34] So Mayerne saw the highest medical post at court given to another: to the Catholic Antoine Petit, of Gien, whom la Rivière had included in the short-list for the post which he had drawn up in 1605.[35] Petit, according to l'Estoile, had no desire for such an honour: he was a successful doctor who preferred the ease and liberty of a very rich private practice to the honourable servitude of the court; and indeed, within a month of his appointment, 'finding that he could not adjust his life or his manners to those of the court (to which he had come with reluctance, under pressure), he obtained leave from his Majesty to retire to his house at Gien, preferring to attend his crony the cobbler there, and drink freely with him, than to wait on the gods of the court, where he was a stranger, and incur envy and slander.'[36] In fact Petit obtained the king's permission to renounce the post of *premier médecin*, retaining only that of *médecin ordinaire*. He was succeeded by Pierre Milon, the third on la Rivière's testamentary list of three.

Perhaps it was on the abdication of Petit that an episode occurred which is recounted by the accurate Minutoli. Minutoli informed Pierre Bayle that the king had pressed Mayerne to change his religion, and had offered to do great things for him if only he would comply. In the hope of converting him, 'he set Cardinal du Perron, and other ecclesiastics, on his back, and even after his resistance, caused a patent as *premier médecin* to be made out and sent to him; but the Jesuits got wind of it and promptly had it stopped by the queen, Marie de Médicis.' Mayerne, says Minutoli, never knew of this episode at the time: he first heard of it in England, over thirty years later, from César, Duc de Vendôme, the king's natural son by Gabrielle d'Estrées. The episode is circumstantially told, and Minutoli's authority commands respect. We know from Mayerne's papers that Vendôme did in fact come to England, and saw Mayerne as a patient, in 1641.[37] We may therefore accept the story as true. At least it seems clear that Vendôme told it to Mayerne; and he had no reason to invent it.

Certainly great pressure was put upon Mayerne to become a Catholic. The arguments for surrender were strong. There was the favour of the king and the court; there was the pressure of du Perron; there were the prospects of promotion. The ladies of the court were no doubt strong persuaders, for his art was particularly appreciated by them. He was now physician to the king's new mistress, Jacqueline de Bueil, Comtesse de Moret, and stayed periodically at her château of Moret near Fontainebleau, prescribing medicines and cosmetics – ointment of water-lilies, paste of young pigeons chopped in goats' milk – and treating her infant son by the king, the Comte de Moret.[38] Mayerne was on very friendly terms with the Comtesse de Moret: they would exchange such letters under the pseudonyms 'Merlin' and 'Lucille'.[39] Kings' mistresses are commonly devout. If Mayerne wished to yield, he could find plenty of extenuating examples, not only among his grand patients but also among his medical colleagues. For instance, there was Jean Héroard, *premier médecin* of the young Dauphin, afterwards Louis XIII. Héroard was a Huguenot who had taken his doctorate at Montpellier. His enemies remarked that he had been summoned to court by Charles IX, to cure a horse, and had stayed on as *médecin ordinaire* to the last two Valois kings. The change was less eccentric then than it would be now, for the office of veterinary surgeon was not yet specialised. Indeed, Mayerne himself would tend the horses of Charles I and Henrietta Maria.[40] More damaging to Héroard are his own writings while physician to the Dauphin: his trivial treatise on the education of princes and, above all, his diary: a work which might have been instructive but is in fact a congeries of nursery futilities worthier of a nanny than of a doctor.[41] Héroard was still 'of the Religion' when he was appointed to the post, on the recommendation of the Huguenot Duc de Bouillon, in 1601;[42] but by 1609 he had seen the light – the light which would lead him to the post of *premier médecin du roi* in the next reign.

However, against these pressures to comply, there were pressures to resist. Apart from any internal conviction, Mayerne was tied to the Huguenot cause by family loyalty, by education, by patronage. He was devoted to his parents, and his father was a deeply committed Huguenot, one of the élite who had narrowly escaped from the massacre of St Bartholomew. Mayerne was also the trusted client, friend and physician of the Huguenot grandees. He was intimate with the family of Rohan, and the Duc de Rohan was now recognised as the rising leader of the unyielding Huguenot party. Rohan's only rival was the Duc de Bouillon. De Bouillon had rashly revolted against Henri IV, and in 1605 the king had appeared with an army before his 'principality' of Sedan. The duke had promptly surrendered and been forgiven, and he was now somewhat chastened. But he was still an acknowledged and powerful leader of the Huguenot cause, allied by marriage to the Prince of Orange and the Elector Palatine, and the churches deferred to him. In this very year, 1609, after the death of du Chesne, Bouillon too had become a patient of Mayerne. In his diary Mayerne noted the new appointment with some complacency: 'on 1 October 1609 I was summoned by the most illustrious Duc de Bouillon, who entrusted himself to me and asked me to take care of his health'; after which Mayerne wrote down, at great length, the complete history of the duke's health and habits, so anticipating his more famous descriptions of King James and his English courtiers.[43] With the dukes of Bouillon, Rohan and Thouars, Agrippa d'Aubigné and Philippe du Plessis Mornay among his patients, Mayerne was entrenched in the confidence of the grandees and the high priests of the Huguenot party. That confidence would be shattered if he were to desert the cause merely for the sake of promotion at court.

Whatever his motives, Mayerne stood firm against both the worldly and the spiritual temptations of du Perron in 1609. Thereby he lost the post of *premier médecin du roi*. But he did not escape from the tempters. They would soon be on his back again. Meanwhile, their zeal did not rest. They turned their attention to another victim: Mayerne's old friend, and new patient, Isaac Casaubon.

Casaubon had been lured to Paris from Montpellier in 1599, with the explicit purpose of restoring the University of Paris after the neglect, pillage and discredit into which it had fallen during the wars of religion. He was to do this, naturally, from within the university, by exercising 'la profession de bonnes lettres en laditte université'. But what Casaubon was not told in Montpellier, though it soon became painfully apparent once he was in Paris, was that there was an implicit condition in the offer. The purpose of the university, in petitioning the Parlement and the king to repair its 'decayed and almost ruinous' state, was not a disinterested zeal for learning or education but, above all, to dish its great rivals the Jesuits, who were everywhere capturing the education of the élite. In its aim of defeating the hated Jesuits, the Gallican university and Parlement had no intention of surrendering to the equally hated Huguenots. In 1601, in the new statutes which were devised by the reforming commission, and which would govern the university for the next 170 years, it was expressly provided that no one should be admitted to teach or learn in it unless he professed the Roman Catholic faith.

It is therefore clear that the invitation to Casaubon presupposed that he would be converted, and from the start steps were taken to ease the process. He was invited to attend the conference of Fontainebleau as a judge, to witness the discomfiture of du Plessis Mornay and the defection of his fellow-judge and close friend Philippe Canaye de Fresne. Rumours of his own apostasy were repeatedly spread, so that he was forced formally to deny them. He was obliged to give up his private lectures, and public appointment was withheld from him. When the royal professorship of Greek, for which he was eligible, was vacant, the most famous Greek scholar in France was overlooked, and Cardinal du Perron secured the appointment of his own protégé, a young man of twenty-two called Jerome Goulu. The cardinal declared, with sublime effrontery, that he knew no man better qualified than Goulu by his knowledge of the Greek language and the authors who had written it. His real qualifica tion, however, lay elsewhere: he was a sound Catholic who saw to it that no Huguenot ever entered the faculty. In 1606 the king made Casaubon his librarian; but it soon became clear that even this post had its price. As librarian, Casaubon found himself under the jurisdiction of the Grand Almoner, who expected him to express some gratitude for his promotion. The Grand Almoner was Cardinal du Perron. The expected sign of gratitude was conversion.

In 1609, the year in which Mayerne felt the pressure of the *convertisseurs*, Casaubon, a more sensitive, more introspective character, winced under the unremitting attacks of du Perron. He hated du Perron, 'the arch-sophist', 'skilled in all the jugglery of the sophistical art'; but he also feared him, for he was armed with overwhelming power, and by his oppressive courtesies, his parade of learning, his insistent hospitality, all backed by royal authority, he could wear out a dependent, frustrated scholar. In his diary and letters Casaubon continually lamented his predicament. He was invited to breakfast by the cardinal, visited by the cardinal, summoned by the cardinal, sometimes in the name of the king. There was 'much and serious talk of religion'. 'May God deliver me from these pressures!' Casaubon would exclaim: he was tortured 'by men who tamper with my faith'. 'I call God to witness that I go to him unwillingly.' No doubt other, more worldly considerations could also be sensed. The cardinal wanted to build up the central institutions of the kingdom, royal and orthodox. This year he had also been entrusted, as Grand Almoner, with the task of restoring the Collège Royal. He longed to capture Casaubon and show him as a trophy of the Catholic reconquest of letters. But Casaubon was not to be had. 'O wretched life!' he expostulated in his diary after yet another 'severe encounter with the cardinal': 'cannot they leave me alone? This is what makes my life a burden!' And he looked around for a refuge beyond the reach of the cardinal: to Protestant Heidelberg, Nîmes, Sedan or the Catholic but free republic of Venice, now allied to the Protestant powers and defying the pope.[44]

Casaubon, and all other Huguenots threatened by the power of the *dévots*, had one great Catholic ally at the centre of power: Jacques-Auguste de Thou. It was de Thou who had secured for Casaubon the post of royal librarian; it was he who had obtained for the Huguenots in general free access to all offices – at least in law; it was he who watched their interests at court, in the Parlement, in the world of letters. De Thou was engaged with du Perron in the reform of the Collège Royal, as he had been in the reform of the university. In this time of crisis, the Huguenots looked increasingly to de Thou to save them. Unfortunately, in this very year, their champion was shown to be powerless; he could not even save himself. With the return of du Perron to France, the spurious delaying action in Rome lost its guiding hand; the *dévots* closed in; and in November 1609 de Thou's *History of his Own Time* was condemned. According to the Roman censors, that great work was not merely marked by particular blemishes, which could be corrected or excised. It was vitiated throughout by a false philosophy. 'From beginning to end', de Thou was told, 'you have shown yourself hostile to the honour and greatness of the Church ... you never speak of Catholics without contempt or of Protestants except in praise; you even blame what your father, the late President de Thou, approved: the massacre of St. Bartholomew.'[45] In short, not even the pope could save the work from condemnation, and it was duly condemned. Its condemnation showed that the shift in the balance of parties in Paris had been noted in Rome. De Thou did not fall into eclipse because of his condemnation. He was condemned because he was in eclipse, and could safely be condemned. In Paris, du Perron hinted that, had he been in Rome, he could have prevented the condemnation. But he did not wish to halt the eclipse: the eclipse both of the Huguenots and of their protectors, the *politiques*, by the *dévots*.[46]

We may seem to have strayed far from Mayerne and the debates of the physicians. But we have strayed with a purpose. What this chapter has shown is the wider, ideological context within which the medical controversies of the reign of Henri IV were fought, and from which they cannot be isolated. If we are surprised at the ferocity of the struggle between the Galenists and the iatrochemists in the Paris of Henri IV, which had no parallel in the London of Queen Elizabeth and James I, we must remember that England had not been racked by civil war. It had had no massacre of St Bartholomew, no social war in the provinces, no terrible siege of London. For historical reasons, chemistry in France was a Huguenot industry. This was not because Huguenots were more 'modern' than Catholics: in some ways the reverse was true; it was because they were, necessarily, more cosmopolitan. Chemistry was a German science, and it was the Huguenots, not the Catholics, who had studied in German universities and served German armies and hospitals. The Catholic establishment of France was determined to break down the plural society which had emerged from the deadlock of the civil wars and had been formally guaranteed by the Edict of Nantes. To do so, it sought to destroy the separate identity of the Huguenots, to break up their separate institutions, to refute or suppress their distinguishing ideas. On a purely medical level the iatro-chemists had prevailed; but they had prevailed by emphasising, however unintentionally, their Protestant character. Therefore the struggle was not confined to the medical world. It was involved in the religious struggle, which was the expression of contending social forces. By 1609 that religious struggle was going against the Huguenots. The iatrochemists, being defeated as Huguenots, had prevailed as physicians in vain.

Was their defeat then certain? Nothing is certain in history. In fact, even in 1609 there was hope. For history does not consist only of social and intellec-tual forces. There are also political forces which can change the balance in society and reverse an apparently predestined movement. In 1609 the internal balance of social forces in France seemed to be inclining, inevitably, in favour of the Catholics. But just as intellectual and ideological issues within France were contained and controlled by social forces, so social forces within France were in turn at the mercy of European politics and of French policy towards Europe. In 1609 the foreign policy of Henri IV reached a crisis: a crisis in which the internal victory of the *dévots* seemed likely to founder and all their petty triumphs to prove vain.

For if the internal policy of Henri IV seemed a continuing surrender to the *dévots,* his foreign policy was always, in its essentials, Huguenot. It was Huguenot of necessity, for the Catholic Church, as an international force, had been captured by the traditional enemies of France, the house of Habsburg. The enemies of the house of Habsburg were the necessary allies of France, and these necessary allies, by the very fact of their hostility to the Habsburgs, were almost all Protestant. France was encircled by Habsburg power, in Spain, the Netherlands, Germany, Italy. To break that encirclement, it needed the alliance of Protestant England, Protestant Holland, the Protestant princes of Germany, the Protestant cantons of Switzerland, and, in Italy, the semi-Protestant republic of Venice. It was with such allies that Henri IV, as a Huguenot, had wrested the crown of France from the *Ligueurs*, the party of Spain. It was on such allies that he was still obliged, as a Catholic, to depend, even in the outward peace after 1598. While the *dévots* colonised the court, the Church, the universities, Huguenots still found employment in embassies abroad – a Chouart de Bouzenval or an Aubery du Maurier in the Hague, a Pierre Bongars in Germany, a Comte de Suze in Switzerland. They were the natural agents of a foreign policy which, in the eyes of the *dévots*, the old *Ligueurs*, was 'Huguenot', but which in the eyes of Gallicans and Catholic *politiques* transcended these sectarian distinctions. It was a necessary national policy: the policy which had been fitfully imagined by the Catholic Valois and would be unflinchingly realised by the Catholic Cardinal Richelieu.

In the years of peace after 1598, this 'Huguenot' foreign policy had been continued, but it had not been too obvious. It had been confined to the province of diplomacy, and had not overflowed into public controversy or distorted the pattern of religious parties. But in 1609 it broke those bounds. An episode in the Rhineland – the occupation by the emperor of the duchies of Cleves and Jülich – threatened to tighten the Habsburg ring around France. To counter this threat, Henri IV felt forced to mobilise his Protestant alliances and threaten war against the house of Habsburg. The Habsburgs were prepared. They had acquired, as an ally, the first Prince of the Blood Royal of France, the Prince de Condé, who, if he could prove the illegitimacy of the Dauphin – that is, the invalidity of the king's divorce from Marguerite de Navarre – would be heir to the throne. They also controlled a party in France: the *dévots*. They were prepared to revive the Catholic League, the civil wars of France. Henri IV decided to strike first. In the spring of 1610 he gathered his army in Champagne and prepared to march to the Rhine and to reinstate, by force, the Protestant princes whom the emperor had dispossessed.

If Henri IV had made war in 1610, who can say what would have happened in France? The Huguenots, the *politiques*, would have become the party of patriotism. Their loyalty would have been assured, and perhaps rewarded. The *dévots* would have been suspect as the friends of Spain. In such circumstances the Huguenots might well have regained, at court and in public life, some of the ground which, in the last decade, they had lost. The situation was comparable to that of 1572, when the Huguenot Admiral Gaspard de Coligny was pressing his forward policy on Charles IX. To free themselves from such a policy the Catholic *dévots* of that time had resorted to a desperate and violent act: the massacre of St Bartholomew. This time the method was the same, but the operation was more limited. On 14 May 1610, as the king was setting out to join his army, a Catholic fanatic sprang upon the wheel of his coach and, with three blows with a knife, struck him dead.

The assassination of Henri IV was one of those moments which, in the short term at least, have changed the history of nations. On the day before his death, the king had caused his queen, Marie de Médicis, to be crowned and anointed, to strengthen her position as regent in his absence at the war-front. Marie de Médicis was a *dévote*, the queen of the *dévots*. With her accession to authority, the war would be stopped before it had begun; the 'Huguenot' foreign policy would be abandoned for a generation; the victory of the *dévots* at court would continue unchecked. Whatever his faults in their eyes, Henri IV had personally protected his old Huguenot friends to whom he was tied by ancient memories of a common struggle. His successors had no such inhibiting memories. They were free to turn on the Huguenots and, if they could, destroy their power.

On the day after the assassination, the royal doctors gathered round the corpse to certify the fact, and determine the cause, of the king's death. Among them were the ex-Huguenot Héroard and the Huguenots Theodore de Mayerne and François Pena. It was the last time that Huguenot doctors would attend the body of a French king.

9

The Move to England, 1610–1611

The assassination of Henri IV marked a decisive stage in the destruction of the Huguenot party, in the change from a plural to a unitary society. From 1610 onwards the Huguenots would never exercise power or influence in the court or government of France. Their political power did not completely disappear, but it was driven back into the local positions which it had held before Henri IV advanced upon Paris. Those bases – already reduced by the attrition of his reign – were threefold. There were the Huguenot churches, held together by the tightly organised discipline of provincial and national synods; there were the Huguenot grandees, their protectors – the dukes of Rohan, Bouillon, Bourbon-Montpensier, Thouars, La Force, Sully, Lesdiguières; and there were certain powerful individuals whose authority, however, was merely personal: a du Plessis Mornay, an Agrippa d'Aubigné. In the years after 1610 this last category would be gradually worn down. Sully would be dismissed from office, du Plessis confined to his government of Saumur, Lesdiguières converted to Catholicism, d'Aubigné driven out of France to Geneva. The solid basis of the Huguenot party would be confined to the churches and the grandees, and their local strength would be confined to the area to which it had been driven during the wars of religion: the south.

With the Huguenots, the *politiques* also went, temporarily, into eclipse. For they had been, within the Catholic body, the protectors of the Huguenots, the advocates of reunion, of pluralism, of the 'Huguenot' foreign policy. Their eclipse was illustrated by the fate of their most distinguished figure, Jacques-Auguste de Thou. Although his *History* had been condemned at Rome in 1609, de Thou did not despair as long as Henri IV was alive. He still believed, or hoped, that a settlement could be reached. The pope remained personally friendly and agreed to reopen the case. Du Perron also remained friendly: there was no point in driving so distinguished a man, internationally famous, the friend of princes, the prince of scholars, into opposition or even apostasy. It was by keeping such men within the Catholic Church, as ground-bait, that du Perron hoped to lure distinguished Huguenots on to his hook. Besides, there was the question of the Parlement. The pope, the Jesuits, the *dévots* all feared the Parlement of Paris, that formidable Gallican body which had consistently opposed their more extravagant claims within the kingdom of France. The present *premier président* of the Parlement was the famous Achille de Harlay, to whom it owed much of its present respect. Achille de Harlay had succeeded Christophe de Thou, Jacques-Auguste's father and de Harlay's own father-in-law. It was generally supposed that Jacques-Auguste de Thou would follow his father and his brother-in-law in that great office. Naturally, the *dévots* did not wish unnecessarily to alienate the next *premier président* of so formidable a body. But after the assassination of the king, de Thou's hope of such succession dwindled. The *dévots* in France feared him and secretly hated his ideas, as he hated theirs; the Vatican saw its chance and used it; and in March 1611 de Thou was definitely excluded from the first presidency. Thereafter Rome saw no reason to revise its censure. The *History* remained on the Index, and de Thou, though he continued to write, published no more of it. The remaining books of his great work would be published after his death in the safety of Protestant Geneva.[1]

In the eclipse of the Huguenots and the *politiques*, the universal victors were the *dévots*. Although the assassin was executed and his crime universally denounced, it was nevertheless his cause which prevailed. Marie de Médicis was the queen of the *dévots*. In so far as she was free, she followed their policy: peace with the Habsburgs, marriage alliance with the Habsburgs, appeasement of the Habsburgs, acceptance of the Habsburg dominance of Europe. However, she was not always free. Always there were the necessities of politics Always she feared the revolt of the grandees, who sought to manipulate her and who resented the wealth and power of her upstart Italian favourites, the Concini. In particular, there was Henri de Bourbon, Prince de Condé, whom the birth of the Dauphin, her son, had excluded from the throne. Condé had been prepared to revolt against Henri IV under Spanish patronage. In pursuit of his own ambitions he would be equally prepared to revolt against Marie de Médicis in alliance with the Huguenots. The nightmare of Marie de Médicis was an alliance between the disgruntled magnates round the throne and the Huguenots, with their power base in the south. This, after all, was what had happened in the time of her predecessor and kinswoman, Catherine de Médicis, and had caused the ruinous civil wars of France.

Such were the permanent political features of the Regency. Immediately, in the shock of the crime, they were muted. But they soon revealed themselves. Already, within a week of the assassination, Agrippa d'Aubigné had protested against the manner in which the queen had been declared Regent; and although du Plessis Mornay urged the Huguenots to support the throne, and the queen officially confirmed the Edict of Nantes, the signs of distrust soon appeared. In January 1611 Sully was dismissed.

Then, in May, the national Assembly of the Huguenots met at Saumur. A struggle developed over the presidency of it. The post was sought by the Duc de Bouillon, who since his ignominious surrender to Henri IV at Sedan had been tamed in spirit and been plied with favours and promises by the queen. Sully and his son-in-law Rohan opposed his claims, and in the end du Plessis Mornay was elected President. The Assembly proceeded to exploit the weakness of the Regency by demanding an extension of the Edict of Nantes. As the rift between Sully and Bouillon widened, Rohan came to the fore as the leader of the militants. It was at Saumur that he began his career as the last great leader of Huguenot revolt.

Meanwhile, at the opposite extremity of France, others were seeking to exploit the temporary disorganisation of its government. The Duke of Savoy, who had fished in the troubled waters of France while Henri IV was alive, saw the chance, now that he was dead, of a more successful coup. He made preparations for a sudden descent upon Geneva and the pays de Vaud. The city of Geneva lived in permanent fear of attack from Savoy, and since its escape from the last attempt – the famous Escalade in 1602, which had so nearly succeeded – it had relied on the protection of France. It therefore appealed to France for support, and the government of Marie de Médicis intervened diplomatically, both in Geneva and in Turin, to preserve the peace. To Geneva she sent Odet de la Noue, the son of the Huguenot hero 'Bras de Fer', François de la Noue. Meanwhile Geneva appealed to the Protestant world for armed support. The canton of Berne, which ruled the pays de Vaud, sent 600 men for the common defence. Troops were also sent by the Huguenot churches of Montpellier and Nîmes; and there were numerous Huguenot volunteers from France, including Sully's nephew, Cyrus de Béthune, and Rohan's brother, the Duc de Soubise. Among the followers of the Duc de Soubise was Samuel de la Chapelle, Baron de la Roche-Giffart in Brittany, who is also described as a kinsman of Rohan. Among those who followed Béthune was Theodore de Mayerne's younger brother Henri de Mayerne. Henri was now twenty-four years old. He had been born in Geneva, but had long been absent from the city, presumably seeking his fortune in France. He had evidently become 'a great favourite' of Béthune and had embraced the opportunity of returning, with him, as a soldier to defend his native city.[2]

Thus in the east of France as in the west the Huguenot forces, here political, there military, were gathered in expectation of action. In Paris too they were alarmed: immediately after the assassination of the king they had expected another massacre of St Bartholomew. Nothing like that had happened, but the situation continued tense, and for months Huguenot families remained under arms in their houses. The new government, however, was eager above all to prevent any disturbance which could be exploited either by the Huguenots or by the grandees, and it sought to reassure both. At the same time the advantages of conversion were once again emphasised. A few days after the assassination, du Perron was again pressing Casaubon, and perhaps Mayerne too. All this time Mayerne was in Paris, attending his patients and waiting on events. He was still in Paris in the spring of 1611, when his patron, the Duc de Rohan, was emerging as the leader of Huguenot militancy in Saumur and when his brother, with other followers of Rohan, was in arms in Geneva. At this time a quick series of separate events occurred which were to make a radical change in his life. They involved his father, his brother and himself.

First, his father. His programme of reform had been ignored. There had been no reformation of the state, no union of the Churches. His proposals had been intended to influence the élite. The élite having shown no interest, and the king in whom he had placed his hopes having been assassinated, he now decided to appeal to the people. He was seventy-eight years old and could not afford to wait. So he withdrew from France to Holland, taking with him the three books of his project of political reform. It was thirty years since the work had been first written, and naturally it needed some revision. Turquet afterwards maintained that, on the advice of his friends, he had toned it down, making it general, not particular, a study of monarchy in the abstract, not of the French monarchy in particular. He obtained permission to dedicate it to the States-General of the Netherlands, under whose protection it had been revised. He then returned to France and obtained from the Chancellor, Brûlart de Sillery, a 'privilege' of publication and arranged for the work to be printed in Paris. It is probable that the Chancellor, like the late king, had only seen the printed summary: those of Turquet's friends who saw the full work doubted whether that protection would last. De Sillery, they thought, would prove 'mauvais garant', a poor guarantor, and such a book would be better published in some free city abroad. As the English ambassador Sir George Carew observed, the Chancellor was known as 'the Treasurer of promises' – empty promises.[3] Turquet's Catholic friend Pierre de l'Estoile (who thought the book excellent in itself and copied out a large part of it) described it as 'livre d'Estat très bon, judicieux et véritable, mais mal propre pour le temps'.[4]

It seems to have been in the autumn or winter of 1610 that Louis Turquet visited the Hague and offered to dedicate his work to the States-General.[5] By March 1611 he was back in Paris and there he found, once again, that his son was being persecuted by the *convertisseurs*. The agitation which the news caused in him suggests that this time his son seemed to be wavering – as Casaubon too had seemed to waver under the last attack of du Perron.

Mayerne's appointment as *médecin ordinaire du roi* had evidently been continued in the new reign, but it would have been open to the queen to offer him a higher post at court if she had wished, and this may have been the lure once again. The episode is known to us from the diary of Pierre de l'Estoile. On 21 March 1611 l'Estoile recorded a meeting with Louis Turquet. 'That good man M. Turquet', he records,

> gave me a copy of a letter which he had written to his son, de Mayerne, on the importunity which was being used to make him abjure his religion and profess himself a Roman Catholic. The principal agent in this matter was M. du Perron, the cardinal's brother, who gave him a book written by the cardinal on the subject. To the main points of this book Turquet replied in his letter, whose very ink shows a father truly zealous for the salvation of his son's soul: he conjures his son, with strong and judicious reasons drawn from the holy Scriptures, never to abandon the religion in which he had been bred up and in which he had lived hitherto, but to remain firm and constant in it, being the truth, until his last breath.[6]

Once again Mayerne did in fact stand firm. Neither the worldly nor the spiritual bait could seduce him. Neither the cardinal nor the cardinal's brother could persuade him to follow their example and abandon the religion for which his father and theirs had been driven into exile. But the mounting pressure must have caused him to think that perhaps he too would be driven into exile; and these thoughts must have been quickened by the experience of his friend and fellow-sufferer, Isaac Casaubon.

Casaubon and Mayerne were clearly very close to one another at this time. Their predicaments were similar, and their responses to them were similar too. It is therefore instructive to compare the personal histories of the two men in those years, which were to prove decisive to both of them.

Both Casaubon and Mayerne had been personal protégés of Henri IV. Both had been disappointed of promotion, frustrated in their legitimate ambitions because of their refusal to change their religion. Both had suffered heavily from the pressure of the *convertisseurs* in the last year of the king's reign. Both, in that last year, had felt their isolation increased by the death of their Huguenot friends and supporters. Casaubon had been shattered by the death of Scaliger, his closest friend and only peer in the world of scholarship, a few months before Mayerne had lost his lifelong ally and companion-in-arms, du Chesne. Both therefore, even before the assassination of Henri IV, had felt insecure in Paris. And both, for different reasons, when they looked for a possible refuge in case of need, looked naturally towards England. Casaubon, in 1607, had been deeply mortified by an unjust award against him in Geneva, and his increasing disillusion with the strict Calvinist Church was accompanied by a growing enthusiasm for the more liberal Protestant Church of England. As a scholar, also, he was attracted by the court of the scholar-king, James I. Mayerne, since his successful visit in 1606, had retained links with England, with English doctors and with the English court, and these links had been strengthened by later visitors from London to Paris. We have seen that Mayerne was already in with the king's Scottish favourite Lord Hay; with the governor of Princess Elizabeth, Lord Harrington of Exton, and his family, which included his daughter Lucy, Countess of Bedford, the great matchmaker of the court; and with Thomas Overbury.[7] In December 1609 we find Mayerne sending a *consilium* to Lord Harrington,[8] and his correspondence shows that he had established close personal relations with Overbury. Moreover, about the same time, a young Englishman came to Paris and lodged with Casaubon. His name was Tomkis. Probably he was Thomas Tomkis, a young Fellow of Trinity College, Cambridge, of literary tastes: his comedy *Lingua*, already published, would be translated into Latin by Rhenanus, whom we have met as the court physician of the Landgrave of Hesse, and his more famous comedy *Albumazar* would be performed before King James at Cambridge in 1615.[9] At all events, he now offered himself as a useful English intermediary for both Casaubon and Mayerne. For he knew Casaubon's admirers among English scholars, he had friends at the English courts, and he was particularly close to Overbury.

Furthermore Overbury, in the last year, had greatly improved his position at that court. Originally a protégé of Robert Cecil, Earl of Salisbury, who had used him as a secret emissary to King James in Scotland, he had there become friendly, not to say intimate, with a young man, or rather boy, who would afterwards, under the protection of Lord Hay, make his way to the English court and there, by a judiciously planned encounter, catch the roving eye of the king. This was Robert Carr, who, from that moment, would be the reigning favourite, the rapidly rising star to which all courtly wagons competed to be hitched. In such a competition, Overbury had a clear advantage. Always a pusher, impatient of hard work, confident of his own brilliance, and determined to find short cuts to the top, he detached himself from Salisbury and offered himself as political mentor to the handsome but illiterate Carr, whose broad Scottish accent he, like King James, but like few others, could interpret. By 1610 Overbury was recognised as the 'governor' of the favourite and had a share in his fortunes and prospects. He was rewarded with grants of land, office at court, and a knighthood. He could hope for much more.

Thanks to these contacts, both Mayerne and Casaubon looked to England for relief from the intolerable moral pressure of the French court. The weight of that pressure on Casaubon in the first four months of 1610 is vividly recorded in his diary. At the New Year he summarised his own condition. 'There is not a day, not an hour, hardly a moment', he wrote, 'when I am free from these attempts.' The pressure came from 'men of the highest rank' and therefore could not be evaded. After that entry, the recorded interviews with Cardinal du Perron became even more frequent, and by February 1610 Casaubon is almost at breaking-point. He asks himself whether he may not be offending God even by engaging in these long conversations with the cardinal, 'although I never accept them willingly or without a struggle'. Early in April he made up his mind: 'at last', he wrote, 'I have decided what to do about a visit to England'; and on 20 April he wrote to King James himself, clearly indicating, for the first time, that he would welcome a firm invitation.[10] He made it clear that he could only accept such an invitation with the permission of the King of France, but it is evident that he expected to receive that permission.

Meanwhile Mayerne too was looking in the same direction. On 3 March 1610, having received a message from Tomkis, he wrote a long letter to Sir Thomas Overbury which indicates that an interesting invitation had been extended to him.

After initial compliments, and thanks for Overbury's courtesy, which he promised to repay by 'every kind of service, when you provide me with the occasion, or fortune offers it', Mayerne referred to 'the important proposal which you make'. This proposal was that Mayerne should come to England as personal physician to a certain 'seigneur' whom Overbury had not named. Mayerne now states that he will accept this proposal, on certain conditions. First of all, he points out that he is already (thank God) in very easy circumstances, as servant and household officer of his king. This means that he can hardly come without approval of his master, which the seigneur must seek through the proper channels, relying on Mayerne to do all that he can on his side 'to bring this treaty to a happy conclusion'. Secondly, he must know the name of his proposed patient, and the nature of his illness, 'written with his own hand, if it is secret', so that he can come properly provided. Mayerne will anyway bring his own apothecary, 'not because I doubt the loyalty and experience of those over there, but because I will proceed with more confidence if I have a man trained in my methods and accustomed to carry out my orders'. Besides, 'the new discoveries in medicine' – he is obviously referring to chemical remedies – 'are laborious and dangerous for a stranger, and often harm the health of the patient.' Thirdly, Mayerne must know the duration of his visit, which must not exceed three months. Finally, there is the little matter of payment. The seigneur is to pay what he thinks fit to the apothecary, besides the cost of his medicines. Mayerne himself is to receive the 1,000 écus offered for his expenses in advance, 'for it is not to be supposed that I should touch my own money and leave my wide and inexhaustible practice here on future expectations, although of course the word of a man of such quality is beyond suspicion, especially to a foreigner.' Mayerne's own reward is left to the honour and nobility of his patient, to whom he will make no wild promises, preferring action to words. On these conditions, he is ready to come.[11]

Who was the anonymous seigneur in England who sought, through Overbury, to borrow the physician-in-ordinary of the King of France? We do not know. The matter is never mentioned again. The most natural guess is that it was Robert Carr. But we have no evidence that Carr was in need of a physician, and it is possible – in view of the sequel, it is even likely – that Carr was himself an intermediary and was using Overbury to discover whether Mayerne was willing, in principle, to come to England for a short time. To that question the answer was clear: he was willing, provided that it was with the permission of his master, Henri IV.

Another passage in the same letter points in the same direction. Mayerne states that he has written to Lady Harrington about one of his sisters, whom Overbury, at his request, had recommended, and whom Madame de Bourdin had retained in Paris, for the service of Princess Elizabeth; 'and it will be a great honour for me if she would send me a brief note in her hand to confirm that this choice is agreeable to her'.[12] This sister was undoubtedly Louise de Mayerne, whom we afterwards find accompanying Princess Elizabeth to Heidelberg after her marriage, in 1612, to the Prince Palatine of the Rhine. Madame de Bourdin, who had acted as the intermediary, was a relation of Pierre Antoine Bourdin, seigneur de St Antoine, Prince Henry's Huguenot master of horse, one of Mayerne's patients in England.[13] Both, as yet, were thinking of temporary visits only, with the permission of Henri IV; but we cannot be sure of their real intentions. Temporary visits are useful, perhaps necessary beginnings: one does not burn one's boats until one is over the stream.

Then, on 14 May, Henri IV was assassinated. The assassination can only have strengthened the desire to leave France, especially in Casaubon, who almost immediately after it was subjected to yet another summons from Cardinal du Perron and a long discussion on matters of religion. Du Perron knew that now was the time to strike: that 'if he were to have Casaubon, it must be now'.[14] But Casaubon, whatever appearance of wavering he may have given, was determined not to be hooked. Four days later he wrote to the Archbishop of Canterbury. On 20 July the archbishop's reply reached him. It was the firm invitation to England which he had sought. Having received it, Casaubon went straight to the English ambassador. By the end of September he had seen the queen and obtained her permission to go to England for a few weeks. He was to leave his family and his books behind and to return to France if required to do so. In October he crossed the sea with the returning English ambassador extraordinary, Lord Wotton of Marley – who was, incidentally, a patient of Mayerne. Soon Casaubon was at the court of King James, delighted with his new patron and preparing for the arrival of his family. His exile, as far as he was concerned, was to be permanent. He would stay in England, he wrote, as long as King James would have him. He left King James to deal with Marie de Médicis, should she call for his return.

Mayerne reacted more slowly, but he reacted in the same way. On 19 August 1610, a month after Casaubon had received his invitation from Archbishop Bancroft, Mayerne wrote another letter to London. It was addressed to one Dr Inglis, apparently a close friend, who, on the evidence of this letter, was a physician and astronomer, a Scot normally resident in Paris and now visiting the English court. The letter is allusive and oblique, but the general purport is clear. After general professions of friendship, Mayerne expressed his hope that 'the splendour of the court and the delights of life in that island will not drive me altogether from your memory'. Then he turned to the matter in hand. 'I have visited the ambassador today for the first time,' he wrote.

> As far as I know, he had no instructions yet concerning my affair. For this reason I do not yet dare to write to Lord Hay, and cannot decently mention, or seem to know, his many kindnesses to me. But you, being unconnected with any report of me, can safely describe me as devoted to that great and good man and longing for an occasion to serve him . . . Our friend Saint-Antoine has explicitly confirmed everything. He feeds me with hope of the future and bids me expect great things. How the affair will turn, God knows; let us pray that He will deign to bless our prosperous beginnings. So much in haste; at the first sign of progress I shall at once write again. I will prepare the hernial powders and convey them to you as soon as possible. Farewell, most loyal of friends, and may you perfectly achieve what you have so well begun.[15]

The natural interpretation of these words is that Lord Hay was arranging an invitation to Mayerne to come to the English court; that the plans had been concerted between Hay and M. de St Antoine; that Inglis was acting as Mayerne's agent in the matter; and that Mayerne's lips were sealed until the invitation should be formally conveyed to him by the English ambassador. However, by the end of the year no such invitation seems to have come. In the spring of 1611 Mayerne was still in Paris, under heavy pressure from the *convertisseurs*. Indeed, if the anxieties of his father were well founded, he would seem to have been in the same position that Casaubon had reached in the summer of 1610 when, in the words of his biographer, 'if ever there be a moment in his life on which the charge of having wavered can be fixed, it is the moment at which we have now arrived.'[16] But the moment passed, and Mayerne's attention was soon occupied by another episode which brought him into still closer sympathy with his father. This episode arose out of the rally of the Huguenots in Geneva.

On Sunday 14 April – 24 April by the French calendar – at nine o'clock in the evening, a group of young Huguenot volunteers gathered in the house of Madame de Vérace, the widow of a former syndic of the city. The reason is not recorded. On such a day, and in such a place, one would like to assume a pious purpose, although the gathering was in the lady's bedroom and she was herself there in bed. At all events, a dispute arose between the Baron de la Roche-Giffart and Mayerne's brother, Henri de Mayerne. The dispute grew warm, and la Roche-Giffart, whose recorded life was one of turbulence, 'suddenly and upon slight occasion' drew his sword and stabbed Mayerne mortally. Then the assassin fled to the lodging of his commander and patron, the Duc de Soubise.[17]

The news of the crime was carried at once to the magistrates, and at eleven o'clock that night the Petit Conseil was summoned. It immediately sent for the witnesses of the affair, who were questioned. The Petit Conseil ordered the gates of the city to be shut to prevent the escape of the murderer, and sent the Lieutenant to arrest him. At the same time representations were to be made to Odet de la Noue, the ambassador, and Cyrus de Béthune, as Mayerne's commander and patron. La Noue agreed that the demand was reasonable and undertook to accompany the Lieutenant to the house of Soubise. But Soubise protested, with tears, that the murderer was no longer there, 'and several other French gentlemen also wept and begged that the crime be concealed, so that he could escape'.[18] Otherwise, they said, 2,000 Huguenot gentlemen would all be forced to leave the city and be turned, with their friends and kindred, from friends into enemies. Unable to fulfil his orders, the Lieutenant had then gone to see Béthune. Béthune was highly distressed by the murder of his friend and used strong language. He protested that justice must be done, and that he would see it done, if not by the magistrates of Geneva then by himself or by others. He was concerned not, he said, with his private interest, even though the dead man was his officer, but with the scandal that would fall on all the French in Geneva. When these conversations were reported to it next day, the Petit Conseil informed la Noue that they would not leave the council chamber until the murderer was given up, and 'at last, after several comings and goings, the said baron was brought in.'

The culprit was now under the control of the city, but what were the magistrates of Geneva to do with him? They were in a ticklish position, obliged to decide a quarrel which was dividing into furious factions those who had come to their help. On one side the friends of la Roche-Giffart petitioned for his release. The Duc de Soubise naturally supported him; letters in his favour came from the Lieutenant-General of the Forces and the governor of Burgundy; and M. de la Varenne, sent to Turin by the French government, stopped in Geneva to emphasise that the queen herself was interested in la Roche-Giffart and hoped that he would be pardoned. On the other side Cyrus de Béthune, angered first by the murder of Mayerne, then by the refusal of the authorities to allow a military funeral, formally demanded that la Roche-Giffart be punished, and protested against the partial testimony of his friends. M. Goulart, the moderator of the Venerable Company of Preachers, the formidable spiritual police of Geneva, declared that the judgement of God would fall upon the city if due punishment were not exacted. Goulart announced that he would preach publicly on the matter, which could only inflame passions on both sides; and he added that the cause of the crime was the indecent freedom of women to circulate in the town and thereby meet and seduce its defenders. In the end a compromise was reached. La Roche-Giffart was persuaded to confess his crime and beg for pardon. On 19 April the Grand Conseil, the council of 200, met, and his plea was heard. Odet de la Noue, the Duc de Soubise, and 'almost all the French noblemen now in the town for our support', endorsed his plea. La Noue made a speech extenuating the crime as unpremeditated, the result of a sudden quarrel. He pointed out that the criminal was 'of a great house, and beloved by all the gentlemen who have come here for our support', and that the queen herself would have written in his support had there been time. The Grand Conseil, 'for good considerations moving them thereto', decided to pardon the offence and send the offender quickly back to France before private revenge should overtake him. It seems, however, that he was not immediately set free, for he did not arrive in Paris until July.[19]

The news of the murder of Henri de Mayerne reached his brother Theodore at a time when he was already turning away from the court of Marie de Médicis. Theodore was shocked by the report. He was also shocked by its reception at court. The news had been brought by a servant of la Roche-Giffart's, who had given his master's version; and on the basis of that version, Mayerne discovered, the court was already preparing to secure his pardon. On 2 May, from Fontainebleau, from the court of Marie de Médicis itself, Mayerne wrote an indignant letter to the Petit Conseil of Geneva, demanding, in respectful but firm tones, that it execute justice without regard to persons, and that la Roche-Giffart suffer 'the full penalty ordained for an act so rash, so cruel, so contrary to the laws of God and man'. 'I know', he went on, 'that his highly placed friends, the authority of the queen who has written to you for his release, the present face of your affairs, and perhaps other reasons unknown to me, may hold your minds in suspense'; but 'the crime is atrocious, the circumstances aggravate it, and although he is a subject of the king, it is reasonable that he should live under the laws of the place where he is, and submit to the penalties prescribed for those who violate them.' So far, only the murderer's version had been heard. 'Therefore I beg you, in all humility, that whatever recommendation comes from here, you will suspend judgement on the queen's request until the true facts are clear. . . . My father would not fail to add his humble entreaties to mine, but at present he cannot do so, being far from this court, in poor health, and perhaps not yet informed of the misfortune which, by destroying the peace of his old age, will end his life, if God does not take pity on his own.'[20]

There is something splendid in this last glimpse of the Huguenot court-doctor, writing from the court itself, to demand that a foreign republic show no respect to persons and should disregard the letters of his queen. It shows Mayerne not in his usual guise, as a courtier, whose perfect bedside manner carried him effortlessly into the confidence of even Catholic princes, but as an Old Testament prophet, standing firmly, even arrogantly, on his own principles or interest, and defying human power. This too was a permanent part of his character. It reminds us of his father, whose place he was now taking, for the son supposed that the old man was ill and out of reach, uninformed of the tragedy. In this he was wrong. The old man may have been ill and far from court, but the news had reached him and he too had written to the Petit Conseil, no doubt in the same strain, though his letter has not survived.[21] Nor was he inactive. At this moment he was probably inserting the last few ounces of dynamite into the literary bomb which he was about to insert under the throne of Marie de Médicis.

By now Theodore de Mayerne's secret negotiations in England had borne fruit. The message for which he had been waiting at last arrived. At the end of April, just after he had learned of his brother's murder in Geneva, Mayerne was visited in Paris by Sir George Keir, gentleman of King James's Privy Chamber.[22] Keir brought with him a personal letter from King James, under his own hand and seal, inviting Mayerne to come to England as one of his physicians-in-ordinary. If he accepted, Mayerne was to receive an annuity of £400 a year, a pension of £200 a year for his widow if he should die, New Year's gifts of money and plate, an allowance for house-rent, two horses in the king's stable, a diet of five dishes, lodgings in court 'and all other appurtenances and profits belonging thereunto, as the usual portion of their Majesty's physicians-in-ordinary'. There were also 'promises of more'.[23]

The invitation could hardly have been more timely. Mayerne was by now disgusted with the French court. He had long been blocked in his career and harried on account of his religion. He had seen his master assassinated and could prophesy that the Huguenots at court would fare worse in the new reign. Now he had seen the queen intervene on behalf of the murderer of his brother. On receipt of the king's letter, he did not hesitate. He went at once to the English ambassador, Sir Thomas Edmondes, who had recently become his patient.[24] Edmondes undertook to handle the matter with the French court, and his candid report to Lord Treasurer Salisbury shows how he did it. 'I wrote', he explained,

> unto Monsieur de Villeroy to entreat him (as it was fit in good respect) that he would move the queen to grant leave to Monsieur de Mayerne to pass into England for the use which his Majesty desireth to make of his service for the taking of some physick this spring time, without making it known that his Majesty proposed absolutely to retain him there; which may hereafter more properly and with the less exception be signified upon the liking which his Majesty shall take of him; and Monsieur de Villeroy did presently very kindly procure the queen's good allowance of his said journey, as it will appear unto your Lordship by his letter written unto me to that effect.

Villeroy, the Secretary of State, had in fact acted very promptly and in good faith. The queen, he replied to Edmondes, not only permitted but 'expressly commanded' Mayerne to go and attend the King of England, whose health was as dear to her as her own and vital to the peace of Christendom. Villeroy provided Mayerne with an immediate passport and a personal letter of recommendation to Salisbury. The letter was written on 2 May 1611, the day on which Mayerne wrote to the Petit Conseil of Geneva to stand firm against the pressure of the queen.[25]

A week later, Mayerne took his leave of the English ambassador, who also supplied him with a letter of commendation addressed personally to the king. Mayerne, Edmondes wrote, was going to England in obedience to the royal command, 'there to devote himself to your Majesty's service'. Edmondes offered his own personal testimony, as a patient, to 'his extraordinary worth and sufficiency', his 'excellent skill in his profession', and 'his entire and sincere honesty', all of which would be sadly missed in Paris. Besides, he added, he was 'of so ingenious a spirit as I presume he will also that way show your Majesty contentment'. In other words, like Casaubon, he would divert the king with learned conversation.[26] A fortnight later, Mayerne arrived in London.[27] His last recorded patient in Paris was the Comtesse de Moret, who had been the penultimate mistress of the late king.[28] His first patient in London, before he had even taken the oath of James I, was his fellow-*émigré* and close friend, Isaac Casaubon.[29]

Compared with the careful and correct migration of Casaubon, who took such pains to observe all the formalities and who went personally to take his leave of the queen, Mayerne's departure from France seems somewhat unceremonious. After eleven years at court, he disappeared as soon as he could get his passport, and did not wait for a formal leave-taking. He left all arrangements to the English ambassador in Paris, and relied on the English authorities to make his excuses afterwards. Perhaps he was soured by the murder of his brother and by the queen's attitude to it. Perhaps he had some inkling of his father's bombshell and wished to be out of reach when it burst. Perhaps he felt that he was behaving rather shabbily in pretending to go abroad for a brief visit while meaning to emigrate permanently. Whatever the explanation, he certainly avoided seeing the queen. Afterwards he did his best to rectify this omission through the good offices of King James, who undertook to write on his behalf to Marie de Médicis, and of the French ambassador in London, who wrote to Villeroy. Unfortunately, even here there was a hitch, for the French ambassador, having done his part, reported that no progress could be made since the promised letter from the king had not arrived: the queen regent was therefore saying nothing. In some alarm, Mayerne wrote to Edmondes in Paris. He was afraid, he said, that he had offended both the queen, 'making her think that I despise her service, leaving without a word to her', and the king, who would suppose 'that I am more interested in my own advantage than to perform my duty'. 'Better late than never,' he wrote, begging the ambassador to regulate the affair; and, he added sententiously, 'to know the right moment is the soul of all diplomacy'.[30]

The affair was duly regulated. Indeed, Marie de Médicis took the unceremonious departure of Mayerne better than the more punctilious migration of Casaubon. For once it was clear that Casaubon did not intend to return, there was a great resentment among the *dévots*, and Cardinal du Perron pressed for his return. He still needed Casaubon, he said, to help with the reformation of the University of Paris – which meant that he still thought him ripe for conversion, as indeed did many others. When Edmondes said that, as a Protestant, Casaubon was best kept in England 'as he himself desired', Villeroy replied – as Edmondes reported – 'that he thought him to be more inclinable to their opinions than to ours'. The same view was expressed by Casaubon's Protestant friends. 'Keep him in England by hook or crook,' du Moulin wrote to an English bishop, 'for if he returns to us, he is sure to defect.'[31] The result was a tug-of-war between the English and the French court, the queen regent ordering Casaubon summarily to return and King James stubbornly resisting. At one moment the queen yielded so far as to grant an extension of Casaubon's leave for another six months, but the king protested that he would not accept such a limitation. He declared roundly that 'the said Casaubon was not at all necessary to France', that no time-limit had been specified before, and that now that he was in England he was to stay there. When the French ambassador explained that Casaubon was a man of rare learning and culture and that Cardinal du Perron had important plans for him in France, the king cut him short, saying that there was no shortage of men of letters in France. After this the ambassador gave up the effort, and Casaubon stayed in England, to entertain the king and to demolish the pretentious learning of the Catholic Cardinal Baronius: which is precisely what King James wanted him to do and what Cardinal du Perron wanted to stop him doing.[32]

Over Mayerne there were no such undignified struggles – for reasons which soon became obvious. The French court soon realised that he intended to stay in England, and was not pleased about it, but decided that nothing was to be gained by showing resentment. King James refused to apologise for his coup: the queen regent, he said, ought to be glad of it, since it showed his love of France and the French. 'To this', the French ambassador wrote to Marie de Médicis, 'your Majesty may perhaps assent the more willingly since, in approaching the person of the said king, he will have the means, as I believe he has the inclination, to do some service to your Majesty and his country.' In other words, Mayerne, if humoured, might be useful as a French agent at the very centre of the English court. Marie de Médicis saw the force of his argument. When King James's letter was at last delivered, she decided to give a friendly answer. Her ambassador in London was instructed 'above all' to make Mayerne believe 'that the service which he will give to the King of England will give great pleasure to their Majesties'. But although King James had asked Marie de Médicis to discharge Mayerne from her service in his favour, she declined to sever that possibly useful link. Mayerne himself wished to sell his post as *médecin ordinaire du roi* and thus secure the return of his capital, and his wife called on Edmondes to ask for his help in persuading the queen; but the queen was firm. She would not release Mayerne, she said, but 'was contented to do him the grace and favour that he should be continued still in his place, to show that though he were in his Majesty's service, yet she desired to retain a joint interest in him, and for that purpose that he should still be allowed his wages and continued in all other privileges of his place as fully as if he did himself actually serve her'. Madame de Mayerne was not deceived by this flattering language. She told Edmondes that a sale of the office would have been preferable, 'for that she doubteth that his pension may be hereafter taken from him'. We shall see that her doubt was not unreasonable.

In this comedy there was one little detail which mystified Mayerne, the French ambassador and the French government alike. Why had King James's letter to Marie de Médicis been so embarrassingly delayed? The answer was ultimately supplied by Sir Thomas Edmondes. It was he who had held it up.

He had been begged to do so by Mayerne's father and friends, 'à cause de ses affaires privées'. What these private affairs were we do not know, but we may risk a conjecture. The name of Mayerne-Turquet was not very popular at the French court at that moment, and the news that Theodore de Mayerne, having been sent so formally to London on a brief visit, had suddenly decided to stay there might well have been the last straw. No one knew this better than Mayerne's father. For in June Louis Turquet had exploded his literary bomb-shell. The court and government of Marie de Médicis were still reeling from the blast.

The bomb itself was a solid work of elaborate construction. In the controversy which followed its explosion, Louis Turquet would insist that he had never expected such an effect. It was, he argued, a very innocent treatise, a mere academic generalisation of the ideas which he had formulated a generation ago for the inattentive Henri IV and which had aroused such enthusiasm in Joseph Scaliger. With the passage of time those ideas had become (he said) less relevant to France, and so he had dedicated this revision of them to the States-General of the Netherlands. The government of the United Provinces, he explained, was still somewhat fluid and experimental. He had therefore thought that his ideas on the ideal form of government might be welcome there. The reader of Turquet's book might well find his explanation unconvincing, for there were some parts of it which seemed to have no more relevance to the problems of the Netherlands than to those of Henri IV's France in 1590, but which were dangerously relevant to those of France in 1611.

The work was entitled *La Monarchie aristodémocratique*, and its content matched the title. Louis Turquet called for the old Aristotelian ideal of 'mixed monarchy', constitutional monarchy, as against Catholic royal absolutism. 'Sovereignty', he declared, 'springs from the people, to whom, in case of tyranny, it may return'; 'states-general' – parliaments – 'are the guardians of fundamental laws, the school of kings'; 'the mixture of three forms of state' – monarchy, aristocracy and democracy – is the most perfect form of government . . . These whiggish generalities were bad enough. Published in the 1570s they had fanned the civil wars of France. A generation later, in the 1640s, they would fan the civil wars of England. But Louis Turquet did not stop at generalities. He became dangerously particular. He attacked the improper power of the Roman clergy in the independent kingdom of France. He also denounced feminine rule. 'Queens do not rule in masculine kingdoms,' he told the subjects of Marie de Médicis. They have never ruled in France without disaster, for women are of themselves easily corrupted, ambitious, seducers, deceivers, deaf to reason; they corrupt the nurture of princes; women and boys are set on thrones by the wrath of God for the ruin of nations; and there were dark allusions to Agrippina, the mother of Nero.[33]

Naturally the *dévots* were enraged. If the situation after the assassination of Henri IV had seemed, to the Huguenots, dangerously similar to that of 1572, Louis Turquet's response to it seemed, to the *dévots*, dangerously similar to the revolutionary Huguenot pamphlets which had been published after 1572. In the replies which it evoked, the parallel would be plainly stated. Turquet would be linked with the pseudonymous author of that momentous work of Huguenot resistance theory of 1579, *Vindiciae contra tyrannos*; and in his rejoinders to those replies he would, in effect, accept the parallel, harking back to the great experiences of his life, which had formed and seared his mind, the massacre of St Bartholomew and the war with the League.[34] Indeed, it could be said that Turquet went even further than his predecessors, for his pamphlet did not merely revive the political doctrines of the 1570s. It combined with them an echo of John Knox's trumpet blasts against the monstrous regiment of women.

The publication of Turquet's book caused great alarm to the French government. It threatened to re-inflame the old ideological passions at a critical moment: critical for the government, critical also for the Huguenots. For at this moment the Huguenot delegates were gathered at Saumur. Great trouble had been taken to ensure that the moderates should control that assembly. But could they keep control, it was asked, if the *dévots* were provoked into action in Paris? For already the clergy were on the warpath. Almost as soon as the book had been printed, the papal nuncio had clamoured for action against the author of this 'truly impious and most seditious book'. The proper penalty, he said, was death. The matter was discussed by the leading counsellors – the Chancellor Brûlart de Sillery, the Secretary of State Villeroy, the Duc de Soissons, and the favourite Concino Concini, now all-powerful as Maréchal d'Ancre. After discussion, they decided that the best course was to conceal the facts from the queen. Apart from general reasons of political prudence, there were also some personal motives for concealment. It would be embarrassing to the Chancellor, for instance, to explain why he had given a royal privilege for the publication of such a book. So they took the necessary steps. Silence was enjoined, and it seemed that, with luck, the dreadful book would be forgotten.

Alas, there was no such luck. The counsellors had reckoned without the clergy, and, in particular, without one enterprising priest. The Abbé du Bois was a famous clerical troubleshooter and tribune of the pulpit. During the wars of religion he had cast off his monastic habit and fought as a soldier against the Huguenots. Henri III had called him 'L'empereur des moines'. In 1611 he had recently returned from Rome and, as *conseiller et prédicateur du roi*, he had privileged access to the court. Now, having seen Turquet's book, he informed the trembling Maréchal d'Ancre that, if the marshal would not take the book to the queen, he would do so himself. Unable to dissuade this turbulent priest, d'Ancre set out to forestall him, only to find that the queen had already received a copy, no doubt from the abbé. She referred the matter to the Council. There voices were raised demanding that Turquet be burnt. The nuncio added his influence on the side of severity: he would have had both Turquet and his book burnt. At one time he hoped to prevail. But in the end, as he observed crossly, 'all my hopes vanished' as the counsellors shifted their ground, 'and all for no other reason than fear of irritating the Huguenots'.[35]

Louis Turquet was not burnt, but he was arrested, and closely questioned about his book.[36] The book itself was seized in the bookshops and, as far as possible, suppressed.[37] The old man defended himself stoutly under interrogation, and after only a day in prison was released with a reprimand. The official reasons given were his age – he was now seventy-eight – and the clemency of the queen,[38] but the real reason was unquestionably, as the nuncio reported (and Cardinal Richelieu would afterwards agree with him), fear of Huguenot reactions. If only the Huguenots had not been in session at Saumur, the government might have reacted more strongly. The Vatican, of course, continued to press for severity, but the answer was always the same. In Paris, the queen assured the nuncio that she had herself demanded Turquet's punishment, but 'had been advised to put it off till after the dissolution of the Assembly'.[39] In Rome, the French ambassador told the pope (who had read the book and been much enraged by it) that it was indeed a wicked work, 'but we must dissemble for the present, and later, when the moment is right, take our revenge.'[40]

Ironically, while the heretical Louis Turquet, thanks to the coincidence of the Huguenot assembly at Saumur, escaped scot-free, the orthodox Abbé du Bois, who claimed the honour of exposing him, suffered heavily for his views. Three months after defending the cause of the Church in this affair, he returned to Rome, expecting recognition and reward. He was clapped into the Castel Sant'Angelo, and spent the last fifteen years of his life in that grim papal prison. His misfortune was that he had quarrelled with the Jesuits, who proved more formidable enemies than the Huguenots.

Thus the storm over Louis Turquet's book in the end died down.[41] After the crisis was past, Marie de Médicis was even able to extract a few small advantages from it. First, she used it to flatter Mayerne and thus keep him, as she hoped, in her interest. The French ambassador in London was informed that Turquet had published a book 'which has gravely offended their Majesties, and assuredly with good reason. However, they have been content merely to reprimand him through the Chancellor: a sign of their clemency. We say that if his son had been here, he would have dissuaded his father from publishing this book. It is a book which will be just as much disliked in England as here, for it teaches the people to bridle the authority and despise the power of kings, and above all it denounces the rule of women.' We can hardly doubt that these sentiments were intended to be passed on to Mayerne. Certainly the ambassador assumed that they were. He replied that he had hardly seen Mayerne, who claimed to be too busy attending the king, although the king (thank God) seemed in perfect health. From his behaviour, it seemed that Mayerne was preparing himself to stay permanently in England. 'I will report further when I have seen him, and I will tell him about the book.'[42]

The other episode which we may connect with this affair brings us back to the murder in Geneva. On 10 July 1611, while the affair of Turquet's book was still a live political issue, the Baron de la Roche-Giffart, the murderer of Henri de Mayerne, arrived in Paris. In deference, no doubt, to the magistrates of Geneva, who had released him for trial in France, he was promptly put in prison. But his imprisonment lasted no longer than that of Louis Turquet. On the same evening he was released 'on the express order of the queen'.[43] Marie de Médicis might have had to yield to the Huguenots over the libels of Louis Turquet, and to the necessities of politics over Mayerne's departure to England, but she was not prepared to execute justice on their behalf for the murder of their son and brother. However, the vendetta between the two Huguenot families of Mayerne and la Roche-Giffart, which began in Geneva in 1611, did not die out with the passage of time. Over twenty years later we find it breaking out again.

Meanwhile what of Louis Turquet himself? The queen had promised the nuncio that she would have him punished once the Huguenot Assembly was dissolved. Clearly it was inadvisable for him to remain in Paris. Mayerne's first instinct was to fetch his old father over to England. On 4 July he wrote to Sir Thomas Edmondes in Paris that he planned to bring over his whole family 'afin d'estre tout à fait et à bon escient Anglois'.[44] But here an unexpected obstacle intervened. King James, as Marie de Médicis had guessed, had no more love than she for the enemies of absolute monarchy, and he wholly forbade Mayerne to bring his father to England. So the old man set off in the opposite direction, and lay low for a time in his home town of Lyon. Meanwhile, in mid-September 1611, Madame de Mayerne and her son Henri arrived in England.[45] On 26 October Mayerne, his wife, and his son were all legally denizened there. Louis Turquet evidently spent the winter at Lyon.

However, Mayerne did not give up his hopes of bringing his father to England. In April 1612 he wrote to Edmondes in Paris a letter which is rendered attractive by that unmistakable warmth which always suffuses his writing whenever he refers to his father. 'I believe', he wrote, 'that my father has seen you on his return from Lyon. Please continue to oblige me. If he speaks of any matter to you, and if he comes to you to ask any favour, do not deny him. Disperse any shadow that may linger in his mind because his Majesty would not let him come here on account of his book. You know the nature of his Majesty: you know that he thinks no more of that.'[46] And sure enough, the king's indignation soon passed. By the following winter, if not earlier, Mayerne's father and mother were both in London, living with their son in the parish of St Martin-in-the-Fields and meeting their old friends the Casaubons.[47] While in London, Louis Turquet wrote a curious letter which brings us back to the cause of his recent troubles, his book.

We have seen that Louis Turquet had dedicated it to the States-General of the United Provinces of the Netherlands. It seems probable that the States-General, depending as they did, to a large extent, on the diplomatic support of France, were somewhat put out when they discovered that they had unwittingly accepted the dedication of a work which was regarded in France as an attack on the French government. However, the Secretary of the States-General, Christiaan Huygens, evidently persuaded them, not without difficulty, to express their gratitude for the dedication by a gift of money, and accordingly they voted, belatedly, the somewhat niggardly sum of 200 florins. The news of his success, and of its limits and cost, was communicated by Christiaan Huygens to a friend in England who showed Huygens' letter to Turquet. The result was another explosion of Huguenot pride, Huguenot self-righteousness, addressed directly to the unfortunate Huygens.

'I have seen', wrote Turquet to Huygens in a firm, clear hand,

the trouble you have taken to cause MM. the States-General to show their appreciation of my dedication to them of my book. I thank you, for I believe that you have acted from sincere affection and a certain idea of honour. But I would have been happy if you had given them my volumes and had then left them to their thoughts without pressing them to make me any reward; for it seems that, by importunity, you have extorted from them the money-order for 200 florins, and that they have at last, after long deliberation, thrown it at you in disdain, as a bribe, like those who wish to rid themselves of a troublesome person. Therefore I would be glad if you would make it clear to them that it is not at my request that you have been so busy. On the contrary, you ought to recall that when I was at your house at the Hague, two years ago, and asked whether MM. the States would accept the dedication of my book ... and you replied that they would indeed, although the reward would be small, for the state was involved in great expense, I answered frankly that I asked for nothing. In which answer I have persisted, dedicating it to them out of affection, having had it printed at my own expense, not without many frustrations, and without looking for any other recompense than that which men of honour expect for their services, viz: friendship and good will.

So Turquet returned their gratuity, protesting that he was not mercenary and could easily dispense with their 200 florins, and that he did not care what they thought of his book, which, he added somewhat significantly, did not depend on their approbation, 'since it does not apply exclusively to their affairs, but to those of many other countries'. Finally, he particularly demanded, and insisted 'by all the rights of civility and honour, that in returning the money-order for 200 florins you beg them, in my name, to remove it from their register, to erase and cancel the record of it, so that my name is not seen there, for it cannot remain there, in that form, without affront to my honour.'[48]

Louis Turquet was very sensitive about his honour and could ride the high horse when he felt that it was affronted. On such occasions he was no respecter of persons. At the time when he wrote this letter he was living in London as the guest of his son, whose royal patron had expressly repudiated that book as an insult to royalty. That did not deter him, or cool his indignation: indeed, two years later his views were unchanged, his power of invective undiminished. We shall find some of these qualities inherited by his son.

Since we have followed Louis Turquet so far, we may follow him a little further. His wife, Mayerne's mother, seems to have stayed more continuously than he in London, but we find him there again in March 1614. Then he was back in Paris. He was in Paris when his wife died, in London, on 15 July 1615, and was buried in the church of St Martin-in-the-Fields. On that occasion Mayerne wrote a letter to his own wife's brother which, once again, shows his invariable tenderness towards his father. The brother-in-law was Gedeon van den Boetzelaer, Baron van Langheraeck, who had recently been appointed Dutch ambassador in Paris. 'I lost my mother four days ago,' Mayerne wrote. 'I still have a father whom I honour as much for the qualities which God has planted in him as out of natural duty and obligation.' Mayerne is alarmed to think how his father, stoic though he is and accustomed to affliction, will take this new blow, and he asks his brother-in-law to console him. 'Above all, I beg you to persuade him to wind up his affairs soon and come here to be with his family, where he will find nothing but very humble obedience and every kind of contentment.' A few days later, Mayerne wrote again to thank his brother-in-law for his letter of condolence. Once again he urged him to beg his father to come and spend the rest of his days with his family.[49] But Louis Turquet stayed in Paris. Perhaps he was too old to be transplanted into English soil. He would die in Paris, aged eighty-five, and would be buried in the Protestant cemetery of Charenton on 1 April 1618.[50]

We have been led forward in time by Louis Turquet and his wife. We must now go back to their son whom, with his wife and son, we left newly denizened in England in the autumn of 1611. Their life in France is now over and they are resolved to be 'tout à fait et à bon escient Anglois'. We shall see how far they succeeded.

10

First Years in England, 1611–1613

Mayerne's emigration from France to England was caused primarily by religion. However careful he had been not to burn his bridges in France, in case he should wish to return, the fact remained that he had left a successful practice in Paris for a speculative future in London, and had done so because Paris was Catholic and London Protestant. However, mere difference of religion was not the sole motive of such decisive action. The Paris of Henri IV, after all, had been Catholic, and he had stayed there. But the Paris of Marie de Médicis was different. Under her rule the Catholicism of the court had become intolerant. Politics might still require that the Huguenot grandees be humoured, but the tendency was clear. Power and policy were now in the hands of the old *Ligueurs*, the *dévots*. This was a social fact, far more fundamental than the mere profession of a religion of state. It affected the whole character of society, and Mayerne, like Casaubon, recognised the implications. In exchanging Paris for London, the two men were exchanging a closed for an open society.

Indeed, for a particularly open society. For if the Catholic court of Marie de Médicis was more closed than that of Henri IV, the Protestant court of James I was more open than that of Elizabeth. The old queen's court had been decorous, punctilious, almost hieratic in its formality. It had an established tradition behind it, the tradition of the Renaissance monarchy of the Tudors, and in its last years that tradition had become conventional, conservative, suspicious of new ideas. But King James, coming from Scotland, where there was no court, no ceremony, no decorum, where the king was almost powerless, the puppet of barbarian chieftains, was unable and unwilling to assume this oppressive burden of ceremony. He might revel in his new-found opulence, his new liberty, his new power; indeed, he might over-estimate all these delicious gains, imagining himself richer, freer and more absolute than he really was; but he could not adjust himself to the discipline of his new position. He remained informal, unrestrained in his behaviour, unconventional in his friendships, open-handed in his generosity, uninhibited in his speech. The old courtiers were often shocked by his behaviour: this was not what they were accustomed to under the old queen. They saw the old hierarchies being broken down, their distinctions blurred, honours debased; and they looked with dismay on the parvenu courtiers, the invasion of uncouth Scotchmen, the vulgar display of new city wealth. Three hundred years later, similar sentiments would be felt when another long-lived queen died and another long-excluded successor, with his unconventional friends, his court of parvenus and plutocrats, swept aside the conventions and hypocrisies of the past age.

But James I, unlike Edward VII, was an intellectual: far more intellectual than Queen Elizabeth had been, for all her high, humanist education. He loved ideas, and men of ideas: genuinely loved them. In the evenings, after long days of business, or neglect of business, or hunting, he liked to relax in the company of scholars, to hear them talk, and to out-talk them, shine among them, as one of them. That was one reason why he was so glad to have captured Casaubon; and Casaubon (at first) was enchanted by the king's attention to him, his genuine interest in scholarship, his learned conversation. Of course (as Casaubon too was to discover) the king's interest was not entirely disinterested. His learning served his political ambitions, or at least his personal vanity. But it was genuine learning nevertheless, and learning, if carefully handled, was a sure way to his favour. No king of England, except possibly Henry VIII, has shown such personal favour to learned men, or to the universities, as James I; and if this favour was not always constant, at least its oscillations were less sanguinary than those of Henry VIII.

He was also not afraid of new ideas. Indeed, he took a positive pleasure in novelty – provided, of course, that it kept within his rules. The more ideas circulated at his court, the happier he was, though the ideas might be unorthodox, even absurd. Real thinkers, like Francis Bacon, found themselves in company with adventurers, even charlatans. But then Bacon too was open-minded: he too liked unorthodox ideas and looked, for the advancement of learning, not to established experts but to innovators, heretics, 'empirics' – that is, to amateur researchers freed from traditional scholastic discipline.

This taste for novelty was apparent also in medical matters. In Scotland, before he had succeeded to the English throne, James had appointed, as his 'mediciner', or personal physician, one John Craig. The king brought Craig with him when he came to London in 1603, and would keep him there. Craig was a man of distinction, cosmopolitan in his education. He had travelled widely, especially in Germany, studying in Königsberg, Wittenberg and Frankfurt-on-Oder, and taking his doctorate, like du Chesne, at Basel. He had accompanied King James to Denmark, when the king went thither to fetch his bride, and at Copenhagen he must have met the Danish court-physician, Peter Severinus himself. With his German education and Danish journey, Craig must have been familiar with the new European medicine, and would have had plenty to discuss with Mayerne, whom he would afterwards know well in England. They were not, we must add, very good friends in England: perhaps the long established court-doctor did not relish the phenomenal success of the newcomer who had cut him out in his last years, especially if Craig had known Mayerne in Scotland several years before, as the young travelling companion of an even younger foreign prince coming to pay court to his own master.

Meanwhile, as King of England, James needed English physicians too. His first choice was William Paddy. Paddy was already well established in the medical and social world. He was a doctor of Leiden – one of the earliest students at that new university – and had practised there for sixteen years before returning to England in 1589, where he would become physician to Lord Burghley, 'dissector of anatomies' in the Company of Barber-Surgeons, and Fellow and Censor of the Royal College of Physicians. Rich, hospitable and generous, a man of the world – he was Member of Parliament for Thetford from 1604 to 1611 and for a time was on the Privy Council – a poet and lover of books and music, his tastes were humanist and conservative. He was a friend of high churchmen – of Lancelot Andrewes, with whom he had been at Merchant Taylors' School, and of William Laud, who would follow him to St John's College, Oxford. But he also – like so many members of that college – had open, liberal views. Though an orthodox Galenist, he was sympathetic to Hermetic and chemical doctors: to Dr Robert Fludd (also a St John's man) and to the Rosicrucian Count Michael Maier. He was universally respected: the praise of Justus Lipsius would accompany him from Leiden, and in England he would be described by John Aubrey as 'an incomparable person ... one of the first learned men who made a physician's practice his study'.[1]

Paddy was made chief physician to the king and knighted in 1604. Soon he was joined by another English doctor. This was Henry Atkins. Atkins had served with Paddy on committees of the Royal College, and may have been recommended by him. He had chemical ideas. In 1604, when the king's second son, Prince Charles, was ill at Dunfermline, James sent Atkins, with an apothecary, to Scotland to attend him and to bring him to London. On his return, he made him another of his English physicians. Like Paddy, Atkins would prosper at court. He would die in the next reign, 'rich in money and land'.

Craig, Paddy and Atkins were all reputable in their profession. Paddy and Atkins were already Fellows of the Royal College of Physicians. Craig would be elected a Fellow on his arrival in England. But in 1609 James I showed the more heretical side of his character by appointing, as physician-in-ordinary to the royal household, one Leonard Poe, a notorious character whom the Royal College had again and again condemned as an ignorant charlatan. However,

Poe was evidently a plausible charlatan, for he had the backing of noblemen and Privy Councillors; he was consulted on medical matters by Francis Bacon; and he would be cited as an authority by Mayerne. The Royal College normally granted fellowship without question to royal doctors, but it drew the line at Poe, whom it had so often condemned. In the end it admitted him under protest, and changed its rules so as to be in a stronger position next time.

Thus the intellectual climate of the English court was already sympathetic to Mayerne, and the established medical world was not hostile, for chemical ideas had already penetrated the Royal College of Physicians. We shall see soon how deeply they had penetrated. Since the college was the English equivalent of the Medical Faculty of Paris, this was important. It meant that Mayerne would not find himself in open war with the medical establishment. The great battle in Paris was enough for one lifetime, and, had there been another such battle to be fought, he might well have hesitated to come to London. As a foreigner by birth he was not, by the normal conventions, qualified to be a Fellow of the College, but equally he was not likely to be persecuted by it: he would be left in peace to concentrate on his career at court.

From the start, he was kept busy. On 11 June 1611, two days after taking the oath of loyalty to James I and less than three weeks after his arrival in London, he was prescribing an elaborate distillation of hart's horn for the king at Greenwich. The prescription was sent to Gideon de Laune, the royal apothecary, to be made up. Gideon de Laune was another Huguenot, and his relations with Mayerne were to be close and fruitful. A few days later, Mayerne was prescribing medicines for the queen, and then ordering a complete dispensary to be carried with the king on his progress. Throughout that summer and autumn he was familiarising himself with the health of the royal family. The queen's health, in particular, caused him concern. He noted that she was liable to fainting fits, through a defect in her stomach and also by heredity, since her father and grandfather, her brother the King of Denmark, and her eldest son Prince Henry had the same trouble. He observed that her joints were weak from birth, and that she had been given copious purges by his predecessor Dr Martin. He prescribed 'golden elixir of life', taken from the Hermetic antidotary of Oswald Gaebelkhover, physician to the Duke of Württemberg.[2] A little later he proposed a full regime of medicines – no fewer than twelve courses – to be taken by her, and by 16 October he could note with satisfaction that on his return to London from Hampton Court he had left her in excellent health and spirits.[3]

He also made arrangements for the future. Like all chemical doctors, Mayerne was a great believer in the curative properties of mineral waters and baths. In France he had recommended the baths of Pougues,[4] near Nevers, which were favoured by Henri IV, and of course the well-known waters of Spa in Flanders. On his arrival in England he made a study of English mineral waters, and naturally turned first to those of Bath, famous since Roman times. In this summer of 1611 he went himself to Bath, together with his friend Lord Hay, in order to inspect the facilities. He saw them under the guidance of a local doctor, Dr Sherwood, a learned old man who, he was told, had formerly studied at Montpellier, under Rondelet. Evidently he was satisfied, for after his return to court he proposed that the queen should visit Bath, where 'the waters contain abundance of sulphur and sulphurous spirit, but little nitre'. The proposal was accepted by the other doctors, and Mayerne was able to write to Sherwood, in January 1612, that next year he hoped to return with a larger company. This was the origin of the queen's progress to Bath in the early summer of 1613. Mayerne also studied the baths at St Andrew's cliff, Bristol, where the royal party stopped on its way back from London. Later he would send his patients to Wellingborough, Tunbridge Wells and Knaresborough.[5]

After his return from Bath, Mayerne found himself carried off to Hampton Court, and then, after a brief period in London, to Royston and Newmarket, for the king wished to enjoy a prolonged hunting expedition. Clearly, James I was delighted with Mayerne: with his interesting new remedies, his courtly manners, his learned conversation. Mayerne recorded one of his conversations with King James: how the physician demonstrated to the king, from Avicenna, Falloppia, Realdus Columbus and others, that the heart in an embryo has no movement.[6] We are reminded of Casaubon's equally learned conversations with the king on patristic scholarship and classical philology. Indeed, between these two old friends, now together at a foreign court, there was a certain rivalry, even, reportedly, a certain jealousy. Casaubon, we are told, was put out to hear of the king's liberality to Mayerne: four times as much as he was himself receiving, in spite of the late archbishop's liberal promises.[7] However, their friendship was uninterrupted. In London, Mayerne regularly visited Casaubon, looked after his health, and often took him home to dinner. In his letters and diaries, Casaubon (who could be querulous enough) never mentions Mayerne without praise: there he is always 'vir clarissimus', 'insignis medicus et amicus', 'vir in arte suâ maximus et mihi amicissimus'. Success at the English court never caused Mayerne to neglect his old friends.

Meanwhile other members of the court competed to follow the royal example. Prominent among them were the Scots: Lord Hay, of course; Robert Carr, the reigning favourite, who had sent the somewhat mysterious message last year; Ludovic Stuart, Duke of Richmond and Lennox, the king's cousin; Thomas Fenton, kinsman and London agent of the Earl of Mar . . . But the English were not far behind. There was the Earl of Montgomery, the first

English favourite; Lord Monteagle, the discoverer of the Gunpowder Plot; Lord North, the discoverer of the curative waters of Tunbridge and the curative salts of Epsom. Indeed, the whole court were eager to exhibit their symptoms to this fashionable new doctor whom the wisest of kings had fetched from France.

Not all of them came because they were ill. Just as the queen and the great ladies of the court looked to Mayerne to supply cosmetics – face-powder, hair-dye, rouge – so the male favourites of James I sought to improve their charms by his chemical arts. Lord Hay wanted fragrant hair-powder, pastilles *ad suffitum cubiculi* (to perfume the bedchamber), paste to whiten and soften his hands, opiate dentifrice, and 'roots to carry in his purse, to polish his teeth'.[8] Carr wanted scent to counteract the bad smell which (he said) his diamond necklaces gave to his clothes, and a dressing for his hair. Mayerne obliged by providing a concoction of roses, coriander, aromatic reeds, musk, amber and civet. It had, he said, a delicious smell.[9]

One of Mayerne's great innovations in therapy was his searching case-histories of his patients – or at least of the more valuable of them. For such patients he would begin his study with a general psychosomatic profile, then proceed to a survey (*Theoria*) of the disease, and finally set out the practical cure. The most famous of these case-histories would be drawn up, thirteen years later, of James I himself. Another such history had been compiled when Mayerne accepted the Duc de Bouillon as his patient, after the death of du Chesne.[10] In 1611 Carr qualified for such a profile. From this we learn, among other things,[11] that he had recently reverted to his national food of oatmeal, with unhappy consequences for his digestion; that he drank beer, not wine; that he slept too much, and talked in his sleep; that he perspired freely, so that his hair had to be curled with hot irons every day.[12]

The favourites of James I were part of the court. They enjoyed the lavish patronage of the Crown, but as yet they had little influence on policy. That was controlled by the Privy Council, and the Privy Council was still dominated, effectively, by the old Elizabethan establishment whose undisputed leader was Robert Cecil, now Earl of Salisbury. Mayerne, as he wrote to his friend Sir Thomas Edmondes in Paris, was so busy attending the king that he had no time to pay his court to the Privy Councillors. But he evidently stood well among them, and he was especially pleased by the courtesy shown to him by the Earl of Salisbury. This courtesy he was soon to repay – at some cost to himself.

It was now eight years since Robert Cecil had managed the peaceful succession of James I. The new king, partly out of gratitude, partly out of political necessity, had kept him in power. Under Cecil the heirs of the old Elizabethans had continued the old Elizabethan policies. They had sought to maintain the agreement of Crown and Parliament at home and to support the Protestant cause abroad. It is true, peace had been made with Spain in 1604; but that peace had long been overdue: only the long life of Queen Elizabeth, and Spanish designs of imposing a successor to her, had kept the war going so long. Even so, Cecil's position was not unchallenged or unrivalled. James I had encouraged, beside Cecil, the heirs of the old families whom the Cecils, in the reign of Elizabeth, had kept out of power, or even temporarily destroyed: the Howards, whose head, the fourth Duke of Norfolk, had been executed in 1572; the Devereux, whose head, the second Earl of Essex, Cecil's great rival, had been executed in 1601. Recently the king had accused Cecil of being 'too much in love with Parliaments' and too eager to reform, and thereby reduce, the patronage of the Crown. There was also, by now, another court: the court, at St James's, of Henry, Prince of Wales. Prince Henry was, by all appearances, an 'Elizabethan'. In 1611 he was seventeen years old. His court, it was said, was better attended than his father's. It was clear that 'the reversionary interest' would soon be a distinct force in England. That reversionary interest was committed to the 'Protestant' cause.

In fact, neither Cecil nor Prince Henry was to play a part in the coming decade. By the end of 1612 both were dead, Cecil at forty-nine, Prince Henry at eighteen; and Mayerne was to be at both of those controversial deaths.

Cecil was the first to go. His regular doctor was the king's physician-in-ordinary, Dr Atkins. But when Mayerne arrived in England, he too was summoned to see him, for the Lord Treasurer, by that time, was mysteriously ill. Mayerne's first recorded visit was on 28 July 1611.[13] Cecil was then at his house at Cranborne, and Mayerne evidently called on his way to or from Bath. He then wrote a full case-history in his usual way. From it we learn, among other biographical details, the hour of Cecil's birth,[14] that he was of minute stature, and that, as an infant, he had been dropped by his nurse, who however had concealed the fact: hence his deformed back and constricted lung. We also learn about his tastes: that he ate no fish and disliked salt, except salt beef; that he liked unripe cherries, and grapes (which were bad for him), and drank ale and beer, not wine, except a little dry Spanish wine before meals for his flatulence.

Four days later, from Salisbury, Mayerne wrote a long *consilium* for Cecil.[15] It was in his most elaborate style, with large philosophical generalities and a parade of learned detail, improved by Virgilian cadences and Greek quotations from Hippocrates. In sum, he found that Cecil suffered from no serious failure of faculty or function, but that his body, 'the weak receptacle of a noble spirit', was distraught by unbalanced and contending humours. Though the body itself was hot and dry, cold and damp humours prevailed in the brain, which was exhausted by perpetual agitation of the mind. The spleen was enlarged – and how could it not be in one who bore such a burden? – and dispersed its overflow through the body, causing diarrhoea and nasal discharge. The essential work of the physician was therefore to restore the balance of temperament by a rational regime and course of medicine. So the patient was to live on a diet of tender meat, fresh vegetables, lightly boiled eggs and herbal drinks, avoiding strong meat, high spices, fat, milk. He was to seek mild air, take mild exercise: a short walk before meals, a ride on horseback or an airing in his coach, general massage in the morning, massage of the limbs in the evening. Those whose genius has raised them to high honours must correct, by such exercise, the inconveniences of their sedentary life. They should also indulge a little in Venus, to reduce the pressure of the salacious spirits which inflame man's nature and excite it to orgasm, and should find, in adequate sleep, rest for the brain, whose force is expended by perpetual agitation.

> Medicine lays down laws for the body; but the mind, especially if it is exalted, emancipated, in full command of itself, rejoices in its own magnanimity. Therefore it is not as a command, but by persuasion, that we seek to recommend tranquillity, in so far as that is allowed by great affairs and the safety of the state, which needs your firm hand on the tiller. The movements of the mind are in the power of Reason. He who commands Reason, and is ruled by it, may follow it even against the decrees of Nature.

Finally, before coming to his usual long list of composite medicines, Mayerne balances his Galenic overture with a Paracelsian coda. Nature, he says, 'whose function is to separate the pure from the impure', must be allowed, or assisted, to evacuate the daily superfluities of the body through the appropriate orifices. 'What Hippocrates says of diseases, we say of excretions. Let them be drawn out by the nearest way and the nearest aperture.'

Mayerne's rational therapy, set in its Galeno-Paracelsian context, did not cure Cecil's disease, whatever it was, though it may have improved his condition: by December he was 'well recovered', in health if not yet in spirits, and by February he was reported to be getting better every day; indeed, his illness was said to be 'nothing so dangerous as was suspected' – only scurvy.[16] However, the improvement was evidently illusory. On 13 March 1612 Mayerne saw him again and described him as suffering from both scurvy and, what was more serious, dropsy.[17]

Earlier, in France, Mayerne had made a careful study of scurvy. In that country it had become a national problem in consequence of the ocean voyages of the last century. Cartier's expedition to Canada had been ravaged by it. Although Hawkins had recognised that citrus juice was an effective cure, and the Dutch had supplied it for the East Indies fleet in 1598, so simple a remedy was discovered only to be forgotten, and had to be rediscovered in the eighteenth century. So Champlain's expeditions to Canada in 1604 and 1608 were again decimated by scurvy, for which, as he complains, 'nous ne pusmes trouver aucun remède': we could find no remedy.[18] On Champlain's return to France, early in 1610, the problem was referred to the royal doctors, and Mayerne himself wrote a full and learned *consilium* on it. But it was not until 1632 that he added, in the margin (having listened to a Huguenot officer employed by the Dutch in the east), 'N.B. le limon a une vertu miraculeuse contre le scorbut': lemon has a miraculous power against scurvy.[19] As a modern historian of medicine writes, 'perhaps one of the most bewildering aspects of the history of scurvy is the manner in which a cure was repeatedly found, only to be lost again.'[20]

Mayerne's notebooks at this time are also full of remedies for dropsy; no doubt his thoughts were stimulated by his attendance on Cecil. The cures are mainly chemical or Hermetic, taken from Paracelsus, Gaebelkhover and Mayerne's old friends la Rivière, du Chesne and Trougny. In particular there was Trougny's 'arcanum diureticum', his *Oxoronia*, distilled from human urine and vitriol.[21] Some of these remedies seem rather desperate, such as the cure of 'a certain Anabaptist who in Germany is called der Wassersucht Doktor' – the dropsy doctor.[22] But Mayerne would never reject a cure merely because it came from an unorthodox source. Nor would he ever despair. Opposite one list of cures for dropsy he wrote, '*ergo ne desperes. Vidi*': 'So do not despair: I have seen it.'[23] His pertinacity was a professional point of honour. As he wrote, in red ink, against one of his more difficult cases, 'incurable diseases are not to be left at prognosis: the physician must go on to attack them, so that he may not be held responsible for death and the patient may conform to treatment. Many conditions are thought incurable when they are not. *Ergo ne desperes*'.[24]

The health of the great Lord Treasurer was naturally followed with interest by those who feared the political consequences of his death, who looked eagerly for the division of the spoils, or who merely dealt in court news. One of the last category was John Chamberlain, an indefatigable and, to us, invaluable commentator. Chamberlain was a somewhat cynical, rather snobbish, elderly bachelor who haunted the precincts of St Paul's Cathedral, then the great mart of news, and served his friends as a regular gossip-columnist. He evidently did not take to Mayerne, this foreign intruder into the charmed circle of his familiar courtier friends: his allusions to him are generally critical. The Lord Treasurer, Chamberlain wrote on 25 March, was still improving, but slowly, 'by reason of the weakness of his body and the uncertainty of his disease . . . and yet he wants not a whole college of physicians that consult upon him every day, among whom Turquet takes upon him and is very confident'.[25] Another courtly voice echoed his sentiments: 'I pray God', he wrote, 'his physician have not practised more haste than good speed, in which course M. de Mayerne, *alias* Turquett, a French doctor, *emporta le prix*.'[26] These critics saw to it that their views reached Cecil himself: 'learned Mayerne', he was told, 'had blundered.'[27] Mayerne, it seems, was blamed for bleeding the patient, which other doctors 'generally disallowed'. At all events, he did not attend Cecil again. While Mayerne remained at court, to fulfil his duties there, the ailing statesman was carried by slow stages to Bath. But the relief which he obtained there was temporary, and he died on the way at Marlborough, attended by three physicians, Atkins, Lister and the notorious Poe, all royal physicians-in-ordinary, and by three surgeons.[28]

Mayerne was evidently shaken by the attacks made on him at the time of Cecil's illness. He wrote to his friend Sir Thomas Edmondes about 'les calomnies dont on a voulu tâcher ma reputation' – calumnies which Edmondes had rebutted 'en vray et parfaict amy'.[29] But worse was in store. Six months later came the great Jacobean family tragedy, the death of 'Oberon, the Fairy Prince', the white hope of all who looked for a continuation, or resumption, of Elizabethan traditions: Prince Henry.

Since Prince Henry now had his own establishment, Mayerne was not his doctor. That post was held by Dr John Hammond, physician-in-ordinary to the king since 1604. But when Mayerne became involved, he took account, in his usual way, of the prince's personality and way of life. Of the latter, he did not approve. The prince, he observed, regularly exhausted himself by overexertion, hunting, riding, playing tennis in the heat of the day, even in that summer of 1612, the hottest in memory. Nor did he approve of his diet: surfeits of fruit and fish, melons and unripe grapes, oysters, both cooked and raw, eaten 'sans reigles ny mesure'. Worst of all, when thus gorged, he would plunge in the river and swim for several hours. No wonder, after one such excess, he fell ill on 10 October 1612, with fever, shivers, sweating and other symptoms. Dr Hammond at first treated him with clysters (that is, enemas) and laxative pills, but although he was visibly ill the prince refused to take to his bed or to reduce his activities. On 24 October he played tennis; next day, being Sunday, he attended a sermon and ate at the king's table – once again unripe grapes – although he looked pale and thin, his eyes hollow and dull. Then he fainted – an accident, says Mayerne, not unusual in him and his family – and the disease returned, stronger than ever. It was at this point that the king sent Mayerne to visit him.

Mayerne found the prince in a high fever, his face red, his lips black, his tongue dry, tormented by thirst and unable to face the light of a candle. He ordered a *tisane* to slake the thirst and a light broth when the fever should abate. Next day he and Hammond consulted together. They prescribed medicines and a clyster. When these gave only temporary relief, they decided on 'a light purge, solely to reduce the quantity of humours'. Before giving this they suggested that the prince might call in other advice, but the prince refused point-blank: he wanted no more doctors. So the purge was given: senna and rhubarb in refreshing cordial waters and syrup of roses, which 'worked with incredible gentleness' and gave great hope of recovery.

Next day, in spite of the prince's veto, a new doctor appeared at his bedside. This was Dr Butler, the famous and eccentric Cambridge practitioner, whom Mayerne had admired since his first visit to England six years earlier. He had been summoned to see the prince by Sir David Murray, of the prince's bedchamber, who acted on his own authority, in secret.[30] Butler, according to Mayerne, approved the treatment given so far, declared the disease to be 'Hungarian fever' and advised only cordials and restoratives. However, the fever returned, the prince's nose bled profusely (he was liable to this accident too), and it was decided, since Nature herself was clearly recommending such a course, to bleed him. It seems that there was some controversy over this, at least over the timing of the operation, and Butler 'was loth to consent';[31] but in the end the three doctors agreed. The patient was bled on 1 November, 7 or 8 ounces, and next day had the best day since the illness had begun.

After the bleeding, the prince was told that a fourth doctor had arrived to see him. He was not pleased, and it was with difficulty that the other doctors persuaded him that he had need of all possible advice and that the number of learned men around his bed could not but be very salutary. So Dr Atkins was admitted and offered a new diagnosis. The disease, he said, was *febris putrida*, whose seat was above the liver; it was not malign, he said, except for the putrescence of the blood. However, the prince felt differently: his spirits were now failing, and it was time, he said, for him to die.

Next day, finding their patient worse, the doctors again debated bleeding, and again there was disagreement. It seems that Mayerne wished to bleed and that the other doctors, led by Atkins, refused. In consequence the prince was not bled. Next day he was much worse, and although his head was shaved and pigeons applied to it, the decline was not stayed. A cock, slit down the back and placed on the soles of his feet on the following day, was no more effective. At this point, we are told, when the doctors differed, the king gave 'absolute power to Dr Mayerne (his chief physician) to do what he would of himself, without advice of the rest'; but Mayerne prudently declined the responsibility. Always he insisted on consensus, protesting that 'it should never be said, in after ages, that he had killed the king's eldest son.'[32]

Thereupon, to increase the confusion, two more doctors arrived, Dr Giffard and Dr Palmer. They diagnosed plague: a manifest absurdity, thought Mayerne, since there were none of the well-known symptoms, and none of the doctors had been infected, though they had stooped over the patient and inhaled his breath a thousand times. However, in deference to the new arrivals, diascordium was given, tempered by cooler cordials. It had little effect. Next day the prince was dead.

At the last moment, yet another physician – this time an amateur, but an amateur more famous than any of the professionals – intervened. No man had a greater interest in the prince's recovery than the most famous of all surviving Elizabethans, Sir Walter Ralegh, who was now spending his eighth year as a prisoner in the Tower. Ralegh was an enthusiastic student of chemistry and he alleviated his imprisonment by carrying out chemical experiments in an improvised laboratory in a shed under the Tower wall. Like Sir Robert Killigrew, he made up cures for his friends. His most famous cure was a popular cordial – 'the great cordial of Sir Walter Ralegh' – which was still in use 150 years after his death.[33] Mayerne had already been in touch with Ralegh, and had recently sent him, at his request, a great variety of chemical substances so that he could make up medicines for his friend Sir Roger Aston.[34] Afterwards he would record, with respect, many of Ralegh's nostrums. At this time Ralegh had been assiduously cultivating Prince Henry, in the hope of securing his own release, and the prince, who admired Ralegh and maintained that 'only his father would keep such a bird in a cage', had undertaken to achieve it. It is said that, after several attempts, he had by now obtained a promise that Ralegh should be released by Christmas – only seven weeks ahead. Naturally therefore Ralegh was dismayed by the news of the prince's serious illness. At the last minute he sent him his 'quintessence' – probably his 'Diaphoreticon', a panacea for all diseases, which Mayerne himself would often use.[35] It did not work: Ralegh himself said that it had arrived too late to be effective; and when the prince died, on 6 November, Ralegh's hopes of release were shattered. He was at that time engaged on his *History of the World*, which he proposed to dedicate to the prince. He now brought that work to a sudden end. 'Besides many other discouragements persuading my silence,' explained the concluding words of the *History*, 'it hath pleased God to take that glorious Prince out of the world ... whose unspeakable and never enough lamented loss hath taught me to say with Job, My harp is also turned to mourning and my organ into the voice of them that weep.'

Ralegh was not alone in his despair. All those who wished to continue the traditions of Queen Elizabeth, now reviving in popularity, and all those who had invested in the 'reversionary interest' at court, joined in the chorus of lamentation. As Prince Henry had become a hero not only to part of the court but also to the people, this chorus was dangerously loud. There were the inevitable suggestions of poison, the scarcely less inevitable search for a scapegoat; and for those who looked for it, the scapegoat was only too obvious. Had there not been a sinister foreigner among the English doctors at the prince's bedside? Mayerne had been accused of causing the unloved Cecil's death by his 'blunders'. Now it was insinuated that he had killed the darling of the English people, the heir to the throne, at best by carelessness, at worst, perhaps, by poison. Unfortunately for Mayerne, those infamous suggestions were nourished by the irrepressible indiscretions of one of his own colleagues – and one, too, whom he admired: Dr Butler.

Dr Butler was now an old man – seventy-seven years old. Though without a real doctorate, and though unlicensed except in Cambridge, he had acquired a great reputation both as a physician and as a character. Secure in his fame and in his college fellowship, he could afford to be eccentric, and he was no respecter of persons. By 1611 he was the best-known doctor in England. No doubt, therefore, he was somewhat put out when a foreign doctor arrived and stole the limelight from him – a doctor, moreover, with whom he could not compete, for how could this rough old college codger, this 'drunken sot' with 'his dudgeon manner' as John Chamberlain called him,[36] stand up to the courtly and urbane Frenchman? Mayerne might genuinely admire Butler; he might use all his charm to woo him; but Butler distrusted Mayerne, and his distrust was perhaps tinged with envy. He also had a reputation for churlishness to maintain, and he was resolved to maintain it. He would not be wooed.

Mayerne's attempts to woo Butler had begun soon after his arrival in England. He had then written to Butler, seeking his friendship, and had invoked the support of his patron, 'my Maecenas, Lord Hay'. Butler had replied cautiously, saying that he rejected Mayerne's Hermetic doctrines, preferring a sceptical suspension of judgement.[37] Then the two men had met – or at least had the chance of meeting – during the last illness of Robert Cecil. Butler had evidently been summoned to Cecil's bedside, but seeing 'how the world went' – that is, seeing that Cecil was unlikely to recover – 'with rudeness sought to wind himself out of the business, and withal had a great tooth to Turquet, or Monsieur de Mayern (as they call him), who hath since sought his good will divers ways and by kind letters, which he will not accept, but answers doggedly.'[38] It seems that, once again, Mayerne had employed Lord Hay as an intermediary; for we have a very dogged letter from Butler to Hay stating bluntly that he will choose his own friends and that, if Hay persists in trying to bring him and Mayerne together, he will break off relations with the whole Hay family. Then came the illness of Prince Henry, and the sudden arrival of Butler to join Hammond and Mayerne. When he learned that Butler had been called in, Mayerne offered to withdraw, but was forbidden to do so by the king, who 'in the very bedroom, nay, at the very bedside of the sick Prince, composed the quarrel of the doctors and made them shake hands'.[39] However, it was noticed that Butler was very sparing of his attendance. He did not expect the prince to recover and so, as in the case of Cecil, he wished (it was thought) to evade responsibility for his death.

He duly evaded it by placing the blame on Mayerne. In particular, he blamed Mayerne for having given the prince a purge so soon after he sickened and so having 'dispersed the disease into all parts', instead of either waiting three or four days or letting blood 'before it was so much corrupted'. These imputations, being maliciously spread, were the signal for an explosion of hostility against Mayerne, who was 'much blamed' for his treatment of the prince and on whom 'the greatest fault is laid'.[40] He was declared to be an ignorant, negligent physician; the old libel of the Paris faculty, in which he and du Chesne were stigmatised as drunken, ignorant, headstrong charlatans, was revived and quoted against him; and rumours went from mouth to mouth that the prince had been poisoned by the 'French physician', who had been so imprudently called in.[41]

To defend himself against these calumnies, Mayerne decided to appeal to the king. He drew up two documents, one in French, the other – more concise but also less discreet – in Latin. In emotional language he protested against those malevolent men who 'like unclean caterpillars creep on to the choicest flowers and poison them with their stinking venom', and begged the king to protect him from the 'tempests of lies furiously raised up' against him. To prove his innocence he set out, in exact detail, day by day, the course of the prince's disease, the reasoning of the doctors, the treatment given. He drew attention to the autopsy, and to the contemporary report based on it which had been written in the presence of all the doctors and signed by them. This report showed that the prince had died 'without appearance or sign of any hint of poison'.[42]

The king responded. He provided Mayerne with an ample testimonial, signed by himself. In this he stated that he had invited Mayerne to be his first physician because of his confidence in him, and that he was entirely satisfied with his service; but that since Mayerne, on the unfortunate death of Prince Henry, had been blamed for negligent or faulty treatment, and since rumours had been spread to the prejudice of his honour and reputation, which had caused him to appeal to the king, now the king gladly certified that Mayerne had never neglected any part of his duty, and that he had always given good and faithful advice and had done nothing except with the agreement of other doctors. Similar certificates were supplied by the Privy Council and by the officers and gentlemen of the late prince.

Mayerne's full report of the prince's illness was designed only to clear his own name, and with the royal testimonial it achieved that result. But for us it has a greater significance. Thanks to that detailed case-history we know, as Mayerne and his contemporaries did not, the real cause of the prince's death, and can regard Henry as the earliest case of typhoid fever recorded in England.[43]

Thus Mayerne survived the crisis of Prince Henry's death. But he never forgot the lesson which it taught. In any medical crisis, he would always make sure that other doctors were committed to his support; and his advice to other court doctors was always to do the same. Meanwhile, he set out to win over the difficult Dr Butler. In this he was ultimately successful, but only after yet another difference, for which, this time, the fault was his own.

The episode occurred in 1613, when the king was ill. Mayerne then proposed a course of treatment to which he secured the agreement of all the other royal doctors, except Dr Craig, the senior royal physician whom he, in effect, had displaced. Dr Craig, being a Scot, did not yield easily. He expressed his dissent openly and aggressively and attacked Mayerne 'even at the royal bedside, irreverently'. Afterwards, to make matters worse, Craig sent to Mayerne a copy of Petrarch's invective 'against a certain doctor', as if applicable to him. Mayerne suspected the hand of Butler in this affair and complained to the king. He also wrote an ambiguous letter to Butler to put him in his place. This time it was Butler's turn to be magnanimous. Once again, Lord Hay was brought in as a peacemaker, and from then on all was well. Indeed – in retrospect at least – Mayerne seems to have been genuinely fond of this old curmudgeon whose abilities he admired and whose foibles he, and others, found engaging. He even referred to their quarrels as *amantium irae*, lovers' quarrels, which, in the words of Terence, are the bonds of love.[44]

Butler was also, in a new sense, a colleague. For Mayerne was now a Cambridge as well as an Oxford man, having been made a doctor of that university by incorporation. This honour was given to him in special circumstances. In October 1612 the young Elector Palatine had arrived in England to marry the king's daughter, the Princess Elizabeth. Owing to the death of Prince Henry in November, the marriage ceremony was postponed until the period of court mourning was over. So the Palatine party stayed in England longer than they had intended. At the beginning of March the court was at Newmarket, and on the 4th Prince Charles took the Elector on a visit to Cambridge, where 'they found great entertainment'.[45] Mayerne went with him, and it was on this occasion that he was given his doctorate, in the presence of the two princes.[46] As a doctor of Montpellier he was qualified for incorporation, but coming when it did, in such circumstances, the honour can be seen as a further testimonial to protect him, or at least restore his morale, after the unfortunate affair of Prince Henry's death.

Thus by 1613, after some initial difficulties, Mayerne seemed to have established himself firmly at the English court. Unfortunately the dramatic and controversial deaths at that court were not yet over. There was one more to come: the most dramatic and controversial of them all. Indeed, it was one of the most famous court scandals in English history. In it too Mayerne was involved. For it was the death of his old patient and friend, the man who, in 1609, had so mysteriously invited him to England: Sir Thomas Overbury.

11

Sir Thomas Overbury, 1612–1615

When we last met Overbury, it seemed that he could look forward to a great future. Able, polished, self-assured, he had established himself as the intimate friend and sole political adviser of the reigning favourite, Robert Carr; and as that favourite was carried upwards, by royal indulgence, so his adviser was drawn upwards, a necessary satellite, in his wake. By the spring of 1612, when Robert Cecil died, Carr had already risen high: he was now Viscount Rochester, the first Scot to sit in the House of Lords,[1] Knight of the Garter, Privy Councillor, Keeper of the Signet. All the signs suggested that he would rise higher still. For Cecil's death had opened a great void at the top. Cecil had combined, in his own person, three of the greatest offices of state. He had been at once Lord Treasurer, Master of the Wards, Secretary of State. As Lord Treasurer he had handled the finances of the Crown, as Master of the Wards its patronage, as Secretary its foreign policy. His death therefore opened a competition for all these offices.

In this competition the driving force was the ambition of the house of Howard. Ever since its eclipse, with the execution of the fourth Duke of Norfolk in 1572, for taking part in Catholic plots against Elizabeth, that family had been seeking to work its way back to the centre of power. Its active leader was Lord Henry Howard, the younger brother of the executed duke: a crafty old bachelor who concealed his unscrupulous machinations behind a parade of decorative learning and a smokescreen of portentous language. Thanks to an early but secret investment in the claims of the King of Scots, Lord Henry had ensured that the family would prosper in the new reign, and although the upstart house of Cecil could not be displaced (Robert Cecil, too, having made himself indispensable), an alliance of convenience was made, and power shared, between the two families. Robert Cecil, now Earl of Salisbury, determined policy. Lord Henry, now Earl of Northampton, guided the flock of Howards into the rich pastures of court patronage. When Cecil died, the

Howard family were thus well placed to bid for his inheritance: to move from court office to political power.

For the Howards had a policy too. The competition was not merely of personalities and parties, for patronage and profit. It was political, even ideological. The Howards were Catholic, or half-Catholic, or crypto-Catholic – Northampton himself was a crypto-Catholic – and they supported a policy of alliance with Spain abroad and toleration (at least) of Catholics at home. In particular, they advocated a Spanish marriage for Prince Henry. They were thus frontally opposed to those 'Elizabethans' who sought to maintain England's position as leader of international Protestantism. This being so, the position of Secretary of State was of particular significance. If the Howards could capture the Treasurership, they would pillage the Treasury (as they afterwards did). If they could capture the Mastership of the Wards, they would exploit its vast opportunities for patronage. But if they could capture the Secretaryship, they would change the foreign policy of England: they would shift it into the orbit of Spain.

King James, naturally enough, did not wish to see himself the prisoner of one great family. He had his own ideas of policy, and in order to preserve his independence he liked to balance the factions at the English court. Therefore, when Cecil died, he sought to keep those three great offices under his own control. He did not appoint a new Lord Treasurer, but put the Treasury into commission. He allowed Northampton and Northampton's nephew Thomas Howard, Earl of Suffolk, to be commissioners; but that was as much as he would grant to that grasping family. For the Mastership of the Wards, he was in great perplexity. He said that he had 'groped after one in the dark' and would 'make trial if a meaner man cannot perform it as well as a great' – and he duly appointed a succession of 'meaner men' to keep it out of more powerful hands. As for the Secretaryship, he was 'much troubled' by the competition, and decided, for the time, to do nothing. He said that he was 'prettily skilled in the craft himself, and till he be thoroughly weary will execute it in person'.[2] In fact, he devolved its duties on his favourite, Rochester.

In appointing Rochester, the king clearly intended to keep foreign affairs, through a docile creature, under his own control. He soon found that he had made a mistake. Rochester, being both indolent and unlettered, needed regular, detailed political guidance, which the king was far too busy to give him, and he therefore turned, naturally enough, to his constant mentor, his 'oracle of direction', Sir Thomas Overbury.[3] All the foreign despatches now passed through Overbury's hands, and Overbury, in the words of Francis Bacon, 'perused them, copied them, registered them, made table-talk of them, as <he> thought good. So I will undertake the time was, when Overbury knew more of the secrets of state, than the council-table did.'[4] In other words, Rochester, who had been appointed by the king to be his instrument, had instead become the instrument of Overbury. Since Overbury was not only thrusting and self-confident, 'always over-valuing himself and under-valuing others' – 'of an insolent and thrasonical disposition', as Bacon would put it[5] – this reversal of roles was soon widely known. It was commonly said that 'Overbury governed Carr and Carr governs the king', and this phrase was duly reported to the king. Naturally the king was mortified and took a strong dislike to Overbury. It was imprudent of Overbury at the same time, by a trivial error, to alienate the queen too. It was even more imprudent, when he had already made so many enemies, to quarrel with his only friend, the patron upon whom he had absolutely depended, Rochester.

The quarrel arose, indirectly, out of the ambition of the Howards. Although they had been frustrated of their immediate aims, the Howards saw well enough that the king's stalling operations over those great offices could only be temporary. Meanwhile they set out to strengthen their position at court. It happened that, just at this moment, fortune played into their hands. They discovered that Lady Frances Howard had fallen in love with Lord Rochester.

Frances Howard was the daughter of the Earl of Suffolk. She was young, beautiful and amorous. At an early age she had been married to the young Earl of Essex. It had been a very grand wedding, arranged and paid for by the king himself; but the parties were then children and the marriage was not a success. The husband was too grave, the wife too skittish; and now, after being the mistress of Prince Henry, she had fallen into the arms of the great favourite. As yet, the intrigue was secret; but when the Howard family learned of it, they at once saw its possibilities. If that intrigue could be converted into a marriage, Rochester, who had hitherto been associated with the opposite party, would be absorbed into the Howard family system and the Howards, having captured this postern gate, would command the court. Rochester himself welcomed the prospect of a grand English alliance. There was only one obstacle. In order to be free to marry Rochester, Frances Howard had to find means of breaking her marriage to Essex. She needed a divorce; and divorce was not easy. It required a declaration of nullity, endorsed by the Church.

So began the great Howard plot. First of all, plausible grounds must be found for divorce. Secondly, after divorce, Lady Frances was to be married to Rochester. But in order that the plot should succeed, the two stages must be kept entirely separate. If it were once suspected that the lady sought divorce in order to marry an adulterous lover, the divorce would never go through. How could a commission of bishops and lawyers agree to a divorce of convenience, a mere change of husbands? If the marriage were to be broken at all, the essential issue of nullity must not be complicated by any extraneous knowledge. Therefore the Earl of Essex must be dissuaded from contesting a charge of impotence – not impotence in general, which would obstruct a future marriage, but a particular impotence in respect of his present wife only. Then, when the bishops and lawyers had allowed the divorce on these grounds, the two partners, happily severed from each other, would be free to make other even happier arrangements.

Of course, if Essex had indeed been suffering from such selective impotence, it might have been curable. Mayerne would no doubt have been willing to cure it. He was experienced and equipped for the purpose. For instance, there was his powder of burned newt, to be rubbed on the toe of the right foot, which was said to work wonders; 'and if you wish for some respite and repose from the combats of Venus, wash the same great toe with water and carnal desire will suddenly cease.'[6] In 1607 he had a precisely similar case, in Paris, with M. Lespicier of Orléans.[7] But the Howard family, almost alone of the English high aristocracy, did not employ the services of Mayerne. Nor did they wish for a cure. They wished to exploit a fictitious, not to correct a real, disability.

Such was the plot. Could it succeed? Obviously its success depended entirely on absolute secrecy about the proposed remarriage. Only the two parties, and the Howard family, must know about that. For if that were once revealed, or even hinted, to the king, or to the bishops and lawyers whom he would appoint to decide the matter of divorce, the whole plot would founder.

It was at this point that Overbury became a key figure. As Rochester's closest confidant, Overbury already knew all the facts. Indeed, he had encouraged Rochester's intrigue with Lady Essex and had himself helped to write the love-letters of his patron. But amorous intrigue was one thing, marriage another, and to this particular marriage Overbury had the strongest objections. Its political implications were obvious to him. Once absorbed into the Howard system, Rochester would have no need of a private political adviser. Overbury would therefore become superfluous; and since his pride had alienated all alternative patrons, his prospects of a brilliant political career would suddenly vanish.

Faced with such disaster, Overbury sought by every means to dissuade Rochester from the marriage. He exhorted, he cajoled, he threatened. He denounced Lady Essex and the whole Howard family. Ultimately Rochester rebelled. He drew secretly away from Overbury and took counsel with his new friends, the Howards, and particularly, of course, with the most cunning intriguer of them all, the Earl of Northampton.

For both of them the problem was now the same. How were they to defeat, but at the same time to silence, this dangerous man who knew so much and who, at any time, by a word, could destroy their plans? The sly old politician produced the answer. Overbury must be removed from all possible communication with the court until the divorce was safely through. The king's displeasure with him must be exploited. Overbury must be offered a distant embassy, as distant as possible.

The king was only too glad to help. He too had had enough of Overbury. So Overbury was approached with a flattering offer: would he go as ambassador to Moscow? Overbury would not: such an embassy was civil death. Nearer and more comfortable embassies were then offered, but again he refused. It seems that Rochester encouraged him to refuse, in order to lead him into the trap. At all events he fell into it. His refusal of a formal royal offer was an act of contempt, and was reported as such to the king. The king reacted in accordance with the suggestions made to him. On 21 April 1613 Overbury was sent to purge his contempt in the Tower.[8]

So far so good; but even in the Tower a man could talk unless he were closely guarded. The Howards had thought of that. They arranged that Overbury be 'close prisoner', held incommunicado. They also took steps to ensure a limited and controlled system of communication, so that they, but only they, could determine what information he received or imparted. Soon after Overbury's imprisonment, the Lieutenant of the Tower, Sir William Wade (or Waad), an old and incorruptible officer, was dismissed from his post on a charge of negligence and replaced by Sir Gervase Elwes, who was thought to be more pliant. Rochester had secured the dismissal: the Howards provided the replacement.[9] Next, the personal gaoler of Overbury, who had been nominated by Wade, was also removed and replaced by another: one Richard Weston, a creature of the Howards.[10] Thanks to these precautions, Overbury could still exchange messages with Rochester; but the messages were regulated, through his gaolers, by the Howards, and even Rochester's messages to him were controlled by the Howards.

All this time, Overbury was unaware that he had lost the confidence and personal friendship of Rochester. He supposed that he had been imprisoned by the king's orders, to cleanse his contempt, and that he would soon be released. Indeed, he relied on Rochester to secure his release and advised him, in detail, on the tactics to be used for that purpose.[11] Rochester and Northampton must have enjoyed many a merry laugh over these letters as they concerted plans to prolong the imprisonment. But in small matters Rochester could afford to be indulgent. On one occasion Overbury contrived, from his window, to exchange a few words with Sir Robert Killigrew, a courtier who was not only a client of Rochester but also an amateur chemist, and who had come to the Tower to visit his friend and fellow-chemist, Sir Walter Ralegh. This conversation bred a happy idea. Why, thought Overbury, should not Rochester send him some of Killigrew's special emetic 'white powder' to induce sickness? His old friend Dr Mayerne could then be summoned to attend him, and Mayerne, as the king's doctor, would report to the soft-hearted king that Overbury was suffering from 'flatus hypochondriacus' and ought to be released on compassionate grounds.[12] Rochester accepted this suggestion, and Killigrew's powders were duly sent. Mayerne was absent from London at the time – he was accompanying the queen on her progress to take the waters at Bath; but Rochester and Northampton obtained leave from the king for John Craig junior, the nephew of the king's Scottish doctor and himself now a royal physician, to attend Overbury when necessary; and on his return to court Mayerne also visited the prisoner, or sent his apothecary. Whether Mayerne or Craig also recommended release, we do not know: all we know is that Rochester made no attempt to procure it.

Overbury's imprisonment was not abridged, it was only palliated, by the sympathetic communications of his false friend, which included regular presents of broths, venison pasties, tarts, jellies and bottles of wine. These delicacies, sent in the name of Lord Rochester, had been prepared in the kitchen of Lady Essex.[13]

So the time dragged on, and in the Tower Overbury's health soon became worse – far worse than he intended or expected it to be from Killigrew's innocent white powders, or than could be cured by Mayerne's mild medicines. Three times out of four, Killigrew's powders had the correct result: Mayerne duly diagnosed 'flatus hypochondriacus'. But on the fourth occasion this slight ailment was transformed into terrible convulsions and violent diarrhoea, which did not respond to treatment. Overbury then complained of the uselessness of Mayerne's drugs, and was reproved by Rochester for doing so.[14] Rochester evidently did not take Overbury's complaints seriously: no doubt he assumed that they were part of the act, to secure release; and for the moment at least, in spite of all protests from Overbury himself, from his father and from his brother-in-law, Rochester was determined to keep Overbury where he was.

Meanwhile, the business of the divorce dragged on too. It too proved more painful than the parties had expected. The Archbishop of Canterbury, in particular, made difficulties. He had grave doubts, both legal and religious, about the alleged nullity, and about whether the Earl of Essex was, or could be, impotent (or, as the countess suggested, bewitched) in respect of his wife but not of other women. So the commission was prolonged, while discreet tests were made of Lady Essex's virginity by selected court ladies and expert midwives who gathered round a modestly veiled female figure alleged to be the countess but thought, by sceptics, to be one of her maids. In the end, the commission being equally divided, the king intervened to help the Howards. He added two safe voters to the commission and ordered it, thus afforced, to think again. Meanwhile, by a necessary consequence, Overbury's imprisonment was prolonged too. As it was prolonged, his health steadily declined.

By the end of August, news leaked out from the Tower that Overbury 'is like to run a short course, being sick unto death'.[15] The Lieutenant of the Tower, in alarm, sent for Dr Craig and for the king's surgeon, John Nasmyth. Mayerne, still with the queen at Bath, heard the news there – presumably from the doctors or from his apothecary Paul de Lobel (or L'Obel, or Loubell), who was in regular attendance – and wrote to Rochester to commiserate with him on the imminent loss of so close a friend. In his perplexity, the Lieutenant of the Tower, who had never envisaged such an outcome, tried to control all access to the prisoner: only Lobel and his assistant were to see him. However, Overbury did not die yet. He rallied, and lived long enough to make another desperate bid for his release. He wrote to the Earl of Northampton. He wrote to the Earl of Suffolk. He offered to be their faithful servant if only they would let him out.[16] But nothing happened. Then the scales fell from his eyes. He realised that Rochester had become his enemy. In his mortification, he wrote a long, scalding letter to his old friend, telling him that, in order 'that this wickedness may never die', he had written down the whole story of their relationship 'from the first hour to this day: what I found you at first, what I found you when I came; how I lost all the great ones of my country for studying your fortune, reputation and understanding; how many hazards I have run for you; how many gentlemen, for giving themselves to you, a stranger, are now left to the oppression of their enemies; what secrets have passed betwixt you and me.' This great screed, he said, he had sealed under eight seals and sent to his friends for safe custody, thereby ensuring that 'whether I die or live, your nature shall never die, nor leave to be the most odious man alive.'[17]

That was Sir Thomas Overbury's last message to his old friend. Soon afterwards his health deteriorated again, and on 14 September the Lieutenant of the Tower called urgently for Mayerne. Mayerne sent the apothecary Lobel. Lobel found Overbury very weak, and ordered that he be given a clyster, or enema, as prescribed by Mayerne. That night the gaoler heard, from Overbury's cell, horrible groans. Early in the morning, the prisoner died in agony.

The Lieutenant quickly impanelled a jury of warders and prisoners, who pronounced that Overbury had died a natural death. The body, which was 'nothing but skin and bone', disfigured by horrible sores, and 'stank intolerably', was hastily buried 'without knowledge or privity of his friends, on Tower Hill'.[18] The Earl of Northampton, who had masterminded the whole plot – the imprisonment, the divorce, the marriage – took the news of Overbury's demise calmly. 'God is gracious', he wrote to Rochester, 'in cutting off ill instruments ... This factious crew had a purpose ... to have made some strange use of him.'[19] In particular, of course, they would have made use of him to block the divorce, which now at last sailed through the judiciously afforced committee. The Archbishop of Canterbury protested to the last, but he was now in the minority; and for decency's sake he was forbidden to state his reasons. Two months later the divorced Countess of Essex, who, since her marriage had been nullified, had reverted to her maiden name of Lady Frances Howard, was married to the Viscount Rochester, newly created Earl of Somerset in order to match her rank. This second wedding, like the first, was a splendid occasion. Now, as then, there were elaborate masques. The king, now as then, paid the cost. The same Dean of the Chapel Royal officiated. And the bride wore her hair long, as a virgin.

Thus the Howards celebrated their triumph. It did not last long. Six months later the Earl of Northampton died, full of years and iniquity, leaving the family without a political manager. Within two months of his death, the enemies of the Howards, headed by the Archbishop of Canterbury, would groom a new favourite to catch the royal eye, and George Villiers would begin his phenomenal ascent to ducal grandeur and regal power. And in the following year, a chance confession provided the enemies of the Howards with the means of undoing, or at least of beginning to undo, the Machiavellian triumph of 1613.

The confession allegedly came from a boy, William Reeve, who had been the assistant (or allegedly the assistant) to the apothecary Lobel.[20] In 1615 Reeve was taken ill in Flushing and believed that he was dying. He then confessed, or allegedly confessed, that in September 1613 he had been bribed with £20 to insert into that clyster a dose of sublimate of mercury: a deadly poison which destroys the organs and causes a horrible death. The bribe had been given by James Franklin, an apothecary with a bad reputation.[21] Reeve's confession was carried to London by a returning English ambassador and handed to the new Secretary of State, Sir Ralph Winwood, whom the king, after two years of vacancy, had at last appointed. Winwood was a strong supporter of international Protestantism and he was opposed to the Howards, who were now seeking to replace him by their own client, Sir Thomas Lake. Winwood reported the matter to the king, and the king, 'though he could not, out of the clearness of his judgement, but perceive that it might closely touch some that were in the nearest place about him', nevertheless, 'such is his love to justice', ordered the wheels of the law to turn.

The result was an enquiry by Chief Justice Coke; a feverish collection – and, on the other side, destruction and falsification – of documents; a series of preliminary trials leading to four public executions; and finally the most spectacular scene of all, the trial in May 1616, in the High Steward's court, sitting in Westminster Hall, of the Earl and Countess of Somerset for the murder, by poisoning, of Sir Thomas Overbury. The countess pleaded guilty and confessed all. The earl defended himself stubbornly. Both were found guilty – the countess as the murderer, the earl as an accessory before the fact. They were duly sentenced to death. In fact, after six years in the Tower, they were pardoned and released to live on, in total obscurity and mutual hatred, into the next reign.[22]

Their alleged accomplices were less fortunate. They were Mrs Turner, the countess's agent, who was said to have procured the poison; James Franklin, the apothecary, who was said to have supplied it; Sir Gervase Elwes, the Lieutenant of the Tower, who was said to have allowed it into the Tower; and Richard Weston, the gaoler, who was said to have ensured that it reached the prisoner and to have been personally present when the last fatal dose was injected. All these were found guilty and hanged. Other poisons, it was claimed, had been inserted into the tarts and jellies prepared in the countess's kitchen and sent, from the earl, to comfort the prisoner. These had been arsenic, 'lapis cosmatis', mercury sublimate, cantharides and 'great spiders'.[23] Not all of this poison had reached the prisoner. Sometimes the Lieutenant, sometimes the gaoler, had had scruples. Some of it had been abstracted and thrown down the privy. But arsenic had been given to Overbury in one of the white powders said to have been supplied by Sir Robert Killigrew, which explained its fearful effect and the inefficacy of Mayerne's prescription; and the last fatal clyster had been consciously permitted by all the defendants: by that time the life of Overbury had become tedious to them all, and they were glad to finish him off.

In state trials of the seventeenth century, the prosecution generally proved its case, and modern historians approach their conclusions with due scepticism. Today it is generally agreed that the countess indeed intended to poison Overbury, and that her instruments – Elwes, Weston, Franklin, Mrs Turner – by action or connivance played their part. The involvement of the Earl of Somerset is less certain. He certainly sought to have Overbury imprisoned, but probably only for long enough to prevent him from obstructing the divorce and the remarriage. As he himself put it, in his defence, 'my furthest intent in his imprisonment was to the end that he should make no impediment to my marriage.' The Earl of Northampton equally had no interest in Overbury's death, being concerned only with his political elimination. But both Somerset and Northampton were evidently relieved when he was out of the way.

There remain still many mysteries of detail. That which concerns Mayerne rises from the part played by the apothecary Paul de Lobel. This Paul de Lobel was the son of a more famous father, Matthias de Lobel (or de l'Obel), the botanist whose name still survives in the plant Lobelia. Matthias de Lobel had studied at Montpellier and had been physician to William the Silent in the Netherlands; then he had come to England and become one of James I's apothecaries. The son, Paul de Lobel, was a close friend of Mayerne and was often employed by him. When Mayerne was commanded by the king to attend Overbury in the Tower, he recommended Lobel as his apothecary for the purpose, partly because Lobel lived in Lime Street, conveniently close to the Tower. Lobel visited Overbury on 25 June 1613 and on several later occasions. At the end, he was the only apothecary admitted to attend Overbury, and it was he who had come on the last day and whose assistant, William Reeve, had allegedly given the fatal clyster.

When the enquiry into the murder began, in the autumn of 1615, Paul de Lobel was questioned. In reply, he stated that Overbury was sick of a consumption, and that he never ministered any physic to him except 'by the advice of Monsieur Mayerne'. He still had Mayerne's signed prescriptions, twenty-eight pages of them in all, covering all the physic which he had ever given to Overbury; these prescriptions he handed over. But he added that Overbury had had 'waters and other things' from sources unknown to him, and that he had seen plasters on his back which he had not applied.[24] Soon afterwards Lobel was visited by his landlord's son, Edward Ryder, who called to collect the rent, and old Dr Lobel raised with him the subject of Overbury's death. Lord Chief Justice Coke, said Ryder, was seeking to prove poisoning; but, said Dr Lobel, Overbury 'was not poisoned, but died of a consumption proceeding from melancholy by reason of his imprisonment'. As for that last clyster, 'for which his son had been called in question', it 'was prescribed by Dr. Mayerne, the King's doctor': his son had made it according to Mayerne's direc-tions.[25] Then he went on to attack those who spoke of poison, and poured contempt on English doctors, saying that they 'were all but fools, speaking wildly of Dr. Butler and others, as also of Mr. Chamberlyne, the Queen's chirurgeon, who doth not like the proceeding of Monsieur Mayerne, whom Dr. Lobel commended to be the bravest doctor, and that there was never a good doctor in England but Mayerne; to whom', says Ryder, 'I answered that I had heard otherwise in Paris, that he was a braver courtier than doctor; but he continued still in his commendations, dispraising all others; and so, after other to the same effect, we departed.'[26]

Edward Ryder noted that, in this conversation, Dr Lobel was suspiciously silent about the boy, William Reeve, who had supposedly applied the fatal clyster and who now claimed to have been bribed to insert the poison. About a week later his suspicions were increased when he and his wife met old Dr Lobel and his wife, near the Merchant Taylors' Hall. This time it was Ryder who raised the matter of Overbury, observing that, by now, it was clear that he had been poisoned. Then he added slyly that 'I heard it was done by an apothecary's boy in Lime-street, near to Mr. Garret's,[27] speaking as if I knew not that it was his son's boy'; and that the boy had since run away. At this, according to Ryder, Mrs Lobel exclaimed, in French, 'oh husband, that was William, whom you sent into France', and who, she added, had been his son's assistant; whereupon the old man looked at his wife and 'his teeth did chatter as if he trembled'. Ryder then asked him if he had sent the boy away, and Dr Lobel replied that he had sent him with a letter to a friend in Paris, saying that he did not know the cause of his leaving; which Ryder thought odd, as well he might.[28]

Ryder clearly felt suspicious of Lobel, and some later writers have echoed his suspicions. Why, they ask, was Paul de Lobel not put on trial? Why was he not at least interrogated more closely? Why was not the suspicion cast upon him more deeply probed? Why was not the history of Lobel's assistant established by interrogation of the other prisoners? Why was not Mayerne produced as a witness at Somerset's trial? In the middle of the last century, a learned lawyer raised these questions, and then, having exposed all the weaknesses in the case for the prosecution, advanced an even more sinister hypothesis. All the problems, he suggested, are soluble if we assume that James I was the murderer of Overbury and that he 'availed himself, for that purpose, of Mayerne's skill in chemistry . . . and of that physician's experience in the secret state-poisonings of the French capital'.[29] As for the king's motive, that is not very clear, but might it not be that it was connected with the death of Prince Henry? Did not Sir Edward Coke, at one of the preliminary trials, seek to make that connection, suggesting that the prince was poisoned by grapes prepared by a popish hostess? And had not the king been very angry at this digression, and stopped that particular trial? Are there not also suggestions that the prince, at the time of his death, had fallen out of favour with his father, and that the king had 'a rooted hatred' of Overbury? And why, in Mayerne's collection of cases, has all matter relating to Prince Henry been torn out of the book?[30]

There is no need for any such vain speculations. The behaviour of the Lobels can be perfectly explained by their alarm on discovering that Overbury had been poisoned and that they had been innocently connected with a political murder which had now become a matter of state. In such cases innocence was no protection against trouble, or perhaps even against conviction; the Lobels were foreigners at the mercy of English politics; and their action in enabling the boy to escape to Paris might well be misconstrued. In these circumstances they had good reason to be alarmed. If Paul de Lobel was not in fact put on trial, the explanation need not be sinister or recondite. By law, in order to try the accomplices, it was necessary first to convict a principal. William Reeve, being abroad, could not be convicted. It was therefore necessary to look elsewhere, and the gaoler, Richard Weston, who had personally supervised the last injection, was chosen for that part.[31] As for Mayerne, his only connection with that injection was an innocent prescription, which Lobel had handed over to the court. No one, at the time, expressed any doubts of his honesty in the matter. That was reserved for a Cambridge professor of law more than two centuries later.[32]

There is also a more general reason for dismissing all such speculations. Behind the personal motives for the murder – the jealousies, the divorce, the marriage – there lies also the political motive. By detaching the favourite from his 'oracle of direction', the Howards sought to bring him into their own system and use his influence at court to further their designs. In foreign policy, that meant to sever England from international Protestantism and bring about a Spanish alliance, a Spanish royal marriage. While he was independent of the Howards, and subject to the influence of Overbury, Rochester had been opposed to their faction. His candidates for the secretaryship – first Sir Henry Neville, then Sir Ralph Winwood – had been supporters of international Protestantism. The murder of Overbury was therefore part – an incidental, unintentional part – of a plan to bring England over to a pro-Spanish, pro-Catholic policy. Indeed, Sir Edward Coke had tried to represent it as a Popish Plot, and to raise, as could so easily be raised in that century, a popular scare and hysterical persecution. He was stopped by the good sense of the king. Against this political background, any suggestion that Mayerne had a hand in the death of his old friend sinks through its own absurdity. Mayerne had not left Catholic France in order to range England on the Catholic side in the ideological war of Europe. He was himself a Protestant, committed by birth, education, patronage, ideas, to international Protestantism. Indeed, we shall find that, at this very time, he was acting, in the intervals of medical duties, and under the cover of those duties, as the secret political agent of international Protestantism.

Secret Agent of King James,
1614–1615

When Mayerne shifted his base from Paris to London, he had no intention of breaking his connection with France. He continued to regard himself as a loyal subject of the King of France. But though French at heart, he was not entirely French. He was also a Huguenot, and that meant a cosmopolitan. For the Huguenots were far more international than the French Catholics. French Catholicism was Gallican, as the Church of England under Archbishop Laud was Anglican. French Protestantism was an international movement. The whole Protestant international had long been directed by Frenchmen – first Calvin, then Beza – from the French city of Geneva. It was in areas of French culture that Calvinism had directly challenged the Church, and it was men bred in that culture who had carried it abroad and enabled it to triumph in other societies: from Flanders to the northern Netherlands, from France and Geneva to the German Rhineland and Scotland. French was spoken, and French culture prevailed, in the court of the Prince of Orange at The Hague. The same was true of the courts of the Protestant princes of the Rhineland. The princes themselves were bound, by marriage, to the great Huguenot families: the Bourbon-Montpensier, the Châtillon, the de la Tour d'Auvergne, the la Tremoïlle, the Rohan. The Duke of Zweibrücken was married to the Duc de Rohan's sister, and Rohan had been delighted, on escorting her thither, to find 'une cour demi-française mais un prince tout entièrement français qui l'aime extrêmement'. The clergy of the Calvinist principalities, or at least the most active of them, were French émigrés, bound by a French culture, and by a French ideology whose headquarters, for the time being, was just outside France.

In the sixteenth century the Calvinists had hoped to conquer France and to make the French government the agent of universal reform. Thus they would combine ideology and nationalism in an imperial mission. With the conversion of Henri IV that particular dream vanished. But the imperial idea did not: it merely shifted its base. For the next thirty years the European

Calvinists, still under French leadership, placed their hopes in England: the England of James I. We have seen how the Duc de Rohan, in 1600, saw James as the new leader of the Protestant world. By that time he was the only king in Europe to whom Calvinists could look. When he had become King of England, thought Rohan, he would be the natural successor to the Calvinist King of Navarre, who, on becoming King of France, had failed.

Unfortunately, King James, on becoming King of England, would fail too. He too would be seduced by the established Church of the stronger country. He decided that London was worth a prayer-book. And like Henri IV, he not only accepted the established Church: he fell in love with it. Its clergy were so much more polished, learned, courtly than those dreadful Calvinist ministers, those 'trumpets of sedition', as he called them, in Scotland. However, the Anglican Church was at least a Protestant Church and King James was flattered by the idea of Protestant imperialism with himself as its head. Therefore he never disowned it and, throughout his reign, he accepted the homage of foreign Protestants and extended his patronage to them. Sometimes he even intervened on their behalf, or gave them orders as their temporal head. Thus London, in his reign, became the metropolis of an international movement. It contained within itself the microcosm of an international world.

It was within that movement and that world that Mayerne lived, now and always. In his professional life he was a courtier, prepared to bow towards any throne; a grand doctor, careful of the health of any patient. Catholic princes and bishops in France, Spanish ambassadors in France and England, entrusted themselves to his skill. But his chosen world was different. His two wives, his two sons-in-law, his personal confidants, the husbands whom he found for his sisters, the tutors whom he employed for his children, his assistants, his apothecaries, his amanuenses, his agents, would all come from the world of international Protestantism. Most of them were *émigré* French Huguenots like himself: M. de Hayen, from Sedan, the first tutor of his children;[1] M. Chouart, Hayen's successor; his apothecaries Lobel, le Myre, de Laune, le Pleurs, Briot; his assistants Dr Brouart, Jean Chappeau, Antoine Choqueux, Gedéon Chabray;[2] and many others. As both his wives were Dutch, he would have Dutch connections too: a Dutch maid, Anneken, a Dutch banker, Dirick Hoste;[3] and he was friendly with Italian Calvinists from Geneva and German Calvinists from the Palatinate. Calvinism was the bond which united them all.

Calvinism, not Calvinist doctrine. In none of Mayerne's writing is there any sign of personal theological interest or even of deep religious feeling. He was not a strict Calvinist, or Puritan. Nor was he particularly drawn to the clergy. He conformed to the Anglican Church, but he had very few friends among its higher clergy, though he must have met many of the bishops at court. Among them his only patients were the learned James Ussher, Archbishop of Armagh, whose stubborn urine he quickened by a diet of powdered bees,[4] and John Thornborough, Bishop of Bristol and Worcester, who saw him more often as a fellow-alchemist than as a patient: for the bishop was an enthusiastic amateur who wrote a book on the philosopher's stone and particularly impressed Mayerne with one of his transmutations.[5] On the other hand he had many friends and patients among the cosmopolitan Calvinist clergy – Pierre du Moulin, Samuel Durand, William Craig of the Huguenot Academy of Saumur, Cesar Calandrini, who became the minister to the Dutch church in London (which Mayerne's wives attended), Ezekiel Marmet, the minister of the French church and almoner of Rohan's brother Soubise. Both the French and the Dutch churches would enlist his support, when needed, against Anglican pressure.[6] These men were part of his world – indeed, the intellectual leaders of his world – and although he might not subscribe to their theological doctrines, he recognised them as essential defenders and interpreters of the same international cause to which, by family tradition, loyalty and education, he belonged.

As one of the most successful of the foreign Protestants in Jacobean London, Mayerne soon became familiar to them all. His house in the fashionable parish of St Martin-in-the-Fields became their general rendezvous. Huguenot visitors from France, Switzerland, Holland, regularly called upon him, bringing and seeking news. At his epicurean dinners one might meet international financiers such as Philip Burlamachi, who raised foreign loans for James I and Charles I, or Burlamachi's brother-in-law and partner Jean Calandrini; or immigrant physicians such as Theodore Diodati, the father of Milton's friend Charles Diodati. All these families had, like him, strong links to Geneva, and like his family they hailed originally from Italy. They too were refugees from religious persecution – Diodati's father, like Louis Turquet, had fled to Geneva from Lyon to avoid the massacre of St Bartholomew. They too, by now, were international, equally at home in Switzerland, Holland or England. Diodati's brother was a famous theologian in Geneva. Jean Calandrini was the brother of the minister in London. A later visitor was the young Constantijn Huygens, future poet and physician, whom Mayerne would first meet at dinner with the Burlamachi family, and who would be promptly invited to dine, Madame Mayerne expressing regret that he had not called on her first.[7] As time passed, Mayerne's house would become one of the centres of the Protestant international in London, a strange contrast to the giddy, spendthrift court of James I or the correct, elegant court of Charles I.

In the first few years after his arrival, his most frequent visitor was probably his old friend Isaac Casaubon. Casaubon's health was now declining – he was suffering from the stone, and painful investigations with a catheter were necessary – and he was regularly visited by Mayerne and by another immi-grant doctor, the Fleming Raphael Thory, or Thorius. Casaubon's diaries and letters show him now closer than ever to Mayerne. Only one thing might have divided them: Casaubon, who hated Geneva, had fallen in love, like James I, with the Anglican Church; and he now dreamed, with Grotius and the English Arminians, of a general reunion of the Churches. This caused some of his fellow-Huguenots to suspect, once again, that he was sliding into popery. However, there was no real danger of that: Casaubon had not escaped from the masterful du Perron in order to succumb to conversion in England. Indeed, when Mayerne suggested that Casaubon go to Spa to take the waters there, he refused: nothing, he said, would induce him to go there, to a Catholic country, where 'those enemies of God' – he meant the Jesuits – would set on him again.[8] So he remained in England, where he died on 12 July 1614. Mayerne carried out the autopsy and wrote, for his friends and the learned world, a full account of his illness and death.[9] Three days later Mayerne suffered another personal loss in the death of his mother, who was staying with him in London.[10]

With the controversial deaths of two of his most distinguished new patients, Cecil and Prince Henry; with the death, in disconcerting circum-stances, of his friend Sir Thomas Overbury; and with two deaths in his own personal circle, Mayerne's first three years in England might well have depressed him. However, he had been sustained throughout by the constant support of the king, who had shown his confidence in the most public manner after the death of Prince Henry. Now he showed it again by employing Mayerne in a more confidential matter. It was a matter which rose directly out of the death of Casaubon. In order to understand it, we must go back and examine the tragicomic history of Casaubon's relations with King James.

When Casaubon had received the flattering invitation of Archbishop Bancroft to come to England, he had naively supposed that this invitation, unlike that of Henri IV in 1600, was disinterested: that the scholar-king was offering to be his patron, so that he could continue his philological researches without other commitment. Unfortunately, he was mistaken. Kings, even scholar-kings, were not like that. After a brief honeymoon period, Casaubon discovered that, in modern courts, there was no room for mere scholarship. Just as Henri IV, having lured him to Paris to be his librarian, had then sought to convert him to Catholicism in order that he might be a learned mascot for the Gallican Church, so James I, having lured him to London to be his private scholar in residence, sought to convert him into his own historical propagan-dist and research assistant in the various controversies in which he was involved. In particular, there were two such controversies. The first was the king's private argument with Jacques-Auguste de Thou, over de Thou's great

History of his Own Time; the second was his public battle with the famous Jesuit controversialist Cardinal Bellarmine.

We have already seen de Thou locked in diplomatic battle with the court of Rome on account of his liberal religious views. That battle had ended with the condemnation of his *History* in 1609. His controversy with James I went on longer. It had begun in 1604, and was still going eleven years later. It concerned the historian's portrait of James's mother, Mary, Queen of Scots.

At the end of 1603, when he had completed his first volume, de Thou, on the advice of Henri IV, had sent a presentation copy to King James, who had acknowledged it in a letter glowing with gratitude and flattery. How refreshing, he exclaimed, to find at last a historian who had banished from his work that spirit of party which was the mortal vice of the profession; and he added that he longed to see the succeeding volumes. The inner meaning of these compliments soon became clear: the king was above all eager that the greatest living historian would not go wrong – i.e. should not differ from him – when he came to describe the stormy reign, in Scotland, of King James's mother, Mary Stuart. At present, the only printed account of Mary's reign was the brilliant propaganda of her greatest enemy, George Buchanan. In order to help de Thou towards true impartiality, the king prevailed upon distinguished scholars – William Camden, Sir Henry Savile, Sir Robert Cotton – to write to him at length, and he condescended himself to offer a personal commentary on Scottish affairs, on which he was, of course, the greatest expert. Unfortunately de Thou, eager though he was to oblige so great a king, piqued himself upon his own independence of mind and insisted on checking the king's account by reference to other sources. In particular he listened to Scottish *émigrés* living (for good reason) in Paris. When, in consequence, the second instalment of the *History*, which came out in 1607, did not entirely follow the royal instructions, the king was very angry. It was insufferable, he said, that the word of a rebel should be trusted rather than that of a king. However, since the offending volume was out, recrimination was useless: the best course now was to persuade de Thou to correct what he had published and to write more carefully in future; for there were still thirteen years of Mary's reign to come. Meanwhile, the king commissioned his own historians, Camden and Cotton, to write an objective account which would serve either to correct de Thou, if he were corrigible, or to refute him, if he were not.

It was at this point that Casaubon came to England and was seized upon by King James as a new ally. Casaubon was an intimate friend of de Thou and could be used both to convey and to reinforce the royal view. So, for four years, the continuing comedy is revealed to us by the correspondence of these two great French scholars. At one time it was nearly broken off entirely when de Thou's indiscretions were reported to the king. There were loud explosions on both sides of the Channel: accusations by the king of broken faith and protestations by the historians of insulted honour. But the king's eagerness to correct the historical record proved stronger even than his pride, and de Thou had no desire to lose the valuable English material with which the king was now supplying him, although he insisted on judging it himself. So it was agreed on both sides to put the blame on the unfortunate messenger. The French ambassador and Casaubon, between them, soon restored a somewhat uncertain peace; and communication, though suspended, was not broken off.[11] Then, in August 1614, Casaubon died, leaving the king without his essential intermediary.

The king's second controversy, his public controversy with Bellarmine, had also come to depend upon Casaubon. It had begun in 1605–6 with the Gunpowder Plot and the Oath of Allegiance which the English government had afterwards imposed on its Catholic subjects, requiring them to disown the claim of the pope to depose heretical kings. This oath, which threatened, and was intended, to divide the English Catholics, thoroughly alarmed the theorists of the Counter-Reformation. By 1610 James I found himself locked in controversy with two cardinals, the two most famous, and most extreme, Catholic controversialists in Rome, Bellarmine and Baronius, who would soon be joined by the equally formidable Cardinal du Perron in Paris. Against such a combination, he needed learned assistance; and Casaubon, when he arrived at court, soon found himself pressed into service here too. Against Bellarmine, the king had employed the pen of Lancelot Andrewes, Bishop of Chichester, who had thus qualified for promotion to the better bishopric of Ely. Casaubon's task was to refute the views of Baronius on early Church history. This he did, very effectively, in a work published in the last year of his life. His next task would no doubt have been to deal with his old tormentor, Cardinal du Perron. But here too, death intervened, leaving the king in need of another champion.

It was in these circumstances that King James turned to Mayerne. In February 1615 Mayerne was instructed to go to Paris. He was eager to go anyway, to see his French patients, but he also went with secret instructions from the king. These instructions were, first, to take to de Thou the last instalment of Camden's *Annals of the Reign of Queen Elizabeth* up to 1587 – i.e. up to the death of Mary Stuart – and obtain from him an assurance that he would be guided by it and make the necessary corrections of his own work; and secondly, to bring back a reliable Huguenot whom King James intended, in the king's own name, and in French, to destroy the arguments of du Perron against the sovereign rights of kings.

Mayerne performed both duties. Having arrived in Paris, he quickly saw the English ambassador, his old friend and patient Sir Thomas Edmondes.[12] He then called on de Thou and gave him the long awaited text of Camden's *Annals.* De Thou expressed his gratitude for this useful text, promised to be guided by it, and, as a sign of good faith, showed Mayerne his own text, in which certain passages had been erased or softened to meet the king's views. All in all, Mayerne reported to the king, 'if the results accord with his words (as I believe that they will), your Majesty's wishes will be served.'[13]

Mayerne fulfilled his other task no less successfully. The new research assistant whom he was to secure for the king was an old friend whom we have already met, and who was to play a large part in his life (and in the controversies of James I). This was the well-known Huguenot minister and scholar Pierre du Moulin.[14]

Pierre du Moulin was now in Paris, the pastor of the Huguenot church at Charenton and the defender of the Huguenot cause against the powerful pressure of the great *convertisseur*, Cardinal du Perron. In the last years of Henri IV, when the Catholic party seemed to be advancing on all fronts, he had become a supporter, in his own way, of the movement for the reunion of Churches, on the Anglican model. So when King James needed help in his controversy with the pope, and consulted Mayerne, it was natural for Mayerne to recommend his old friend. A correspondence then ensued, and although the king had to give du Moulin, through Mayerne, a somewhat peremptory lecture, to put him right on certain points of theology,[15] the minister was duly hired and in 1610 earned an easy £2,000 by writing in support of the royal argument.[16] Therefore when the king again needed a research assistant in his controversy with du Perron, he naturally turned, through the same intermediary, to the same scholar.

In his autobiography, du Moulin described how Mayerne called on him in Paris and conveyed the royal invitation to England.[17] When du Moulin consulted his church at Charenton, the consistory opposed the project, fearing that du Moulin, like Casaubon and Mayerne, would emigrate for good. Too many valuable Huguenots were now finding their way to the court of King James. But du Moulin promised to return, and on this understanding they allowed him to go. He arranged to travel to England with Mayerne, and they left together in March 1615.

While despatching the king's business in Paris, Mayerne did not neglect his own. He visited several of his old patients, both Catholic and Protestant, and some new. Among the Catholics were the Comtesse de Moret, the mistress of the late king; the Spanish ambassador, Don Iñigo de Cárdenas, whose long diplomatic career would end in the Puritan England of Oliver Cromwell; and the Cardinal de Joyeuse. With the Comtesse de Moret he scored a great triumph. She was now blind in both eyes. Mayerne diagnosed the cause as 'gutta serena', obstruction of the optic nerves. He treated her, and within a month she had completely recovered the sight of her left eye. 'The right eye', he remarked, 'remains blind, but not without some faint irradiation when the other eye is shut and the pupil pressed and dilated.' He decided to attack the disease first by way of the stomach, which was disordered; and by the end of his stay the countess was completely cured.[18] The cure caused something of a sensation in Paris. Sir Thomas Edmondes reported that the countess had been 'many days blind of both her eyes, and was abandoned of all the physicians in Paris', and that Mayerne's 'admirable cure' had made him 'very renowned' in the city.[19] Among the Protestants, Mayerne visited the houses of the two rival Huguenot grandees, the dukes de Rohan and de Bouillon.

Mayerne also saw other old friends. Above all, he was in touch – he would always be in touch – with his old apothecary, Pierre Naudin, who acted as his agent, banker and host in Paris. At the end of February, he attended the Huguenot Temple at Charenton and stood godfather to Naudin's infant son, to whom he gave the name Theodore.[20] Like his godfather, Theodore Naudin would ultimately emigrate to England.[21]

In March 1615 Mayerne returned from this highly successful visit. Du Moulin came with him[22] and, on arrival in England, was immediately set to work by the king. He duly produced the *Declaration du roy Jacques I . . . pour le droit des rois*, which was published in the same year and translated into Latin and English. For this he was rewarded with a Cambridge doctorate, a prebend at Canterbury worth £200 a year with a fine house, a benefice of equal value in Wales, and a gold chain for his brother.[23] Three months later he returned to France; but he maintained his profitable connection with the English court, and his two sons would become Englishmen – one of them a doctor patronised, for a time, by Mayerne.

Such were the avowed purposes of Mayerne's visit to Paris at the beginning of 1615. But were there others, less avowable? There is some reason to believe that there were. Already, in the preceding year, we find Mayerne engaged in dark machinations on behalf of King James. He had been giving secret instructions to a somewhat dubious political adventurer whom he had summoned from Holland to England for the king's service. This man was called Nicholas de Rebbe, and he claimed, by his 'experimental knowledge of the science of the greatest cabinet in Europe', to be able to help the king to reduce his enemies.[24] It looks as if de Rebbe was a projector with a secret weapon. In any case, Mayerne was clearly being used by James I as a confidential agent for secret affairs. Now, on his visit to France, there were other secret matters in which he was both able and willing to act. In order to envisage them, we must consider the politics of France and, in particular, of the French Huguenots.

For we are now entering into another turbulent period of French politics: the resumption, after the orderly reign of Henri IV, of the religious struggles of the sixteenth century. The scale of the conflict is not now so great, nor the stakes so high. The heroic age of the Huguenots is now over, and they are fighting not now for power, but for survival. The heroes too are fewer, for the paladins of Henri de Navarre are passing, and the great Huguenot magnates have become more cautious in the new age. Only one leader rises to dominate the last stage of militant Huguenotism in France. This is Mayerne's old patron, the Plutarchian hero whom he so admired, Henri Duc de Rohan.

Since the assassination of Henri IV, the Huguenots in France had been in a state of confusion. They saw that the tide was turning against them. They saw with dismay the dismissal of their political leader, the Duc de Sully, Rohan's father-in-law; the favour granted to the old *Ligueurs*; and finally, in 1612, the double marriage treaty with Spain. But their own counsels were divided. As before the victory of Henri IV, many of the great nobles were dissatisfied with the rule of a Médici queen, and some of them were prepared to take up arms and to ally themselves with the Huguenot churches. But would the Huguenot churches gain by such an alliance? Not all the malcontent nobles were Huguenots; and even those who were were divided in counsel. Some of them, like the Duc de Bouillon, were for temporising. He was the most experienced statesman of the party, but he had shot his bolt by his rebellion in 1606 and now he shrank from decisive action. Others were more radical. They would separate the interest of the Huguenot churches from that of the princes, and stand firm in defence of their own rights, making temporary alliances if necessary, but single-mindedly pursuing their own interest. This was the policy of Rohan, who combined a Machiavellian sense of statecraft with firm Huguenot convictions. Thanks to his single-mindedness, and his skill, he would gradually emerge as the leader of the party of action.

The first aristocratic *prise d'armes* against the regime of Marie de Médicis was headed by the next prince of the blood, the Prince de Condé, and was directed against the queen's Italian favourite, Concino Concini, now Maréchal d'Ancre, and the proposed Spanish marriages. Condé was not a Huguenot: though the son of a Huguenot hero, he had been brought up, being an orphan, as a Catholic in the Catholic court. Later the Duc de Bouillon, finding his own approaches to the court slighted, joined Condé in opposition and sought to carry his fellow-Huguenots with him; but Rohan refused to be involved in this adventure, and the rivalry between the two dukes turned to enmity. By May 1614, when peace was restored, Bouillon had lost ground. By confusing the Huguenot cause with that of the disaffected grandees, he had weakened his position as its patron, while Rohan, by keeping them apart, had improved his. Indeed, under his patronage, the Huguenots positively gained in power. The queen chose to buy peace by yielding to their demands rather than those of the princes: they were a less immediate threat to royal authority.

However, in the winter of 1614–15 this fragile peace again began to crumble. The power of the Crown was seen to have grown, and soon the princes, under Condé, were preparing a new revolt. To compensate for lack of Huguenot support, they wooed the Parlement of Paris. Once again Bouillon supported Condé. Once again Rohan stood apart, building up his distinct power base. How he would use that power in politics he had yet to decide, but his purpose was clear: either from the princes or from the Crown he would exact new concessions for the Huguenot churches, which accepted him as their patron. What the next demands of those churches would be was to be shown at their next General Assembly, which was to meet, by royal permission, next autumn, at Grenoble.

All through this period of manoeuvre, the rival leaders of French Protestantism, Bouillon and Rohan, were seeking support from England. James I was still in high Protestant mood. He was in controversy with popes and cardinals: he was correcting the theologians of the Netherlands; and he was marrying his only daughter – beneath her station as the queen complained – to the most aggressively Protestant of German princes, the Elector Palatine. The Duc de Bouillon, who was the Elector's uncle, was the maker of that match. Throughout those years both Huguenot leaders had kept in touch with King James. So did Condé. The king encouraged them, discreetly. When Condé sent his secretary, M. de la Grange, to explain his projects 'for the public good', la Grange was referred to Mayerne, who gave him an introduction to his own brother-in-law, the Dutch ambassador in Paris, whom he was eager to know.[25] The king continually urged Bouillon to persevere in his 'great design . . . for the reformation of the court and consequently of the state' of France.[26] He assured du Plessis Mornay that he was working for a union of Protestant princes 'to be ready when the time comes to overthrow the Antichrist'.[27] And he was in regular correspondence with Rohan, treating him as a sovereign prince and addressing him as 'mon cousin'.

Rohan's communication with James I, now as earlier, was secret. It did not go through the English ambassador, nor was it committed to writing. Rohan's letters to the king remained purely formal: compliments, congratulations, condolences, professions of devotion; and his letters to the English ministers – first Salisbury, then Rochester – are no different. Messages of substance were always conveyed verbally by trusted emissaries, generally from Brittany: the Sieur de la Hautefontaine, or de la Roche Popelinière, or de Boislorée, or Villieu-Charlemaigne.[28] However, on 27 November 1614, exceptionally, he sent to the king a full account of the state of the Huguenots in France. Then, a month later, he followed it up with another brief letter. The face of affairs, he now wrote, had changed, and so he had instructed the bearer to give an up-to-date account.[29] What that account was we do not know; but a fortnight later the king wrote to his ambassador in Paris telling him that Dr Mayerne was on his way, and asking him to give him all the help that he needed: 'You may without danger treat freely with him in all matters which may concern our service, both in respect of his loyalty towards our person as for the ability of his judgement and sufficiency.'

James I and Mayerne supposed that they were acting in perfect secrecy. If they had been able to read the French diplomatic correspondence, they would have known better. In fact, from the start, the French government had been watching every move. A few days before leaving London, Mayerne had dined with the French ambassador and had told him that the king had given him leave to go to France, for three weeks. He was going, he said, on purely private business: in particular, he wished 'to see his father, who is old, and to try to persuade him to come to England to end his days'.[30] Prudently, he said nothing about any royal commission, nor mentioned the suspect names of de Thou and du Moulin. But the French ambassador – Samuel Spifame, Sieur de Buisseaux – was not so easily deceived. He wrote at once to his government. All these explanations, he said, were mere 'colour': the quality of the person, the suddenness of the journey, the shortness of his proposed stay in France, and the present tension of affairs there, all pointed to a secret political purpose, 'of which I shall give you further details by word of mouth' – for the ambassador also was on his way to France; 'meanwhile it would be well to keep an eye on the said Sieur de Mayerne, and see on whom he pays his first calls.'[31]

We do not know what the ambassador said when he arrived in Paris; but the letters of his secretary, M. de Sève, whom he left as *chargé d'affaires* in England, more than supply the defect. M. de Sève was evidently a specialist in counter-espionage, and he showed both zeal and relish as he traced the comings and goings of the French grandees and their agents in England, recorded their contacts, and speculated on their secret purposes.

According to de Sève, Mayerne was going to France, partly indeed on his own account, but largely as the secret political emissary of James I. In Paris, he was to act in concert with the English ambassador, Sir Thomas Edmondes. He was to see the chief Huguenots and effect a union between them and the princes in order to wreck the Spanish marriages. In particular, he was to unite the two men he referred to as the 'Dévot' and the 'Sermon' – that is, Rohan and Bouillon – and thereby to raise a great revolt. After that, he was to be ready, if required, to go to la Rochelle 'to engage that people in their design, to raise money from it at need, and to make it a refuge on the sea and a gateway to England'. De Sève did not think that Mayerne would himself go to la Rochelle: more probably the Dévot – Rohan – would make that journey himself; 'but that would be only when the abscess is about to burst'. Anyway, the French government was to watch the Dévot closely, for it was on him that all the hopes of the rebels turned. In all his letters, de Sève emphasised the same theme. The true purpose of Mayerne's journey, he wrote, was to ensure the union of Rohan with Bouillon, and of the Huguenots with the princes, in a general revolt against the Spanish marriages. It was particularly important to discover whether Rohan spoke of going to la Rochelle; for that would be a clear sign that the revolt was about to break out, and then the 'Sermon' – Bouillon – would not be far behind. When Mayerne returned to England with du Moulin, de Sève reported that du Moulin was involved in the plot. He also remarked that Mayerne had now sent his own surgeon to France, to treat certain grandees, and that 'melons' from Sedan which had been sent by Bouillon to King James were accompanied by letters which were addressed to Mayerne.[32]

Much of this was no doubt spy-fever, but it is clear from the English evidence that it contained some truth. Mayerne had a secret commission from King James; when in Paris, he did see both Bouillon and Rohan privately, ostensibly in his medical capacity; and the written report which he submitted to the king on his return shows that his instructions were precisely what de Sève assumed them to be: he was to reconcile the two leaders with each other so that the Huguenots might make a common front with the grandees. 'As for the agreement which Your Majesty expressly instructed me to urge upon our grandees,' he reported,

> I found them very much at odds and monsieur ambassadeur <i.e. Edmondes> much vexed and eager to effect between them that good intelligence which is so necessary if they seek their own preservation and the public good. Gradually they are softening towards each other, and if I may judge by appearances, I hope to be able to bring your Majesty good news. At present I can say no more. . . . As for the state of this country, I would need volumes to describe all the disorders which are occurring daily.[33]

Moreover, on his return to England, Mayerne took with him not only du Moulin but also a confidential message from Rohan to King James. What that message was we do not know: we only have the letter which Mayerne presumably carried himself. It runs:

Sire,

Your Majesty will learn from M. de Mayerne the state of our court, and therefore I will excuse myself, for the present, from saying anything about it. He is a man whom you and I both trust, and being full of judgement, he will tell you our affairs better than I can write them. I hope, Sire, that my actions will always prove to the world, and especially to Your Majesty, that I seek nothing but to advance the glory of God, for which I will spare neither life nor goods, and to show to you that I am, more than anyone in the world,

Sire,

Your very humble and very obedient servant

Henri de Rohan

[PS]

Sire,

I have opened my heart to M. de Mayerne. I beg you most humbly that I may have your views and your promises on the important matters which he will communicate to you from me.

Paris

24 March 1615.[34]

This letter suggests that Rohan was already contemplating action by the Huguenot party; and the suggestion is supported by a remark made by Mayerne, soon after his return to England, to his patient, the king's confidant, Lord Fenton. He told Fenton 'that France was never in so miserable a state', and that rebellion could not be long delayed.[35] It is also supported by the experience of his fellow-traveller Pierre du Moulin. For although the French government did not reveal its suspicions of Mayerne, which would have caused a diplomatic rupture, it had no inhibitions about the detested du Moulin. When du Moulin returned from England to France in the summer of 1615, and landed at Boulogne, he was immediately arrested, imprisoned and searched. As he himself recalled, that was the time when the French princes had begun to revolt against the queen regent, and 'I was suspected of having passed into England to secure support for them.'[36] Nothing, evidently, was proved; but the suspicion clung. From now on du Moulin was openly, and Mayerne secretly, in the black book of the French government, and their movements were carefully watched by its agents.

We cannot say how James I replied to Rohan's message; but he continued to watch the internal affairs of France carefully. Those affairs seemed to follow the course predicted by de Sève. In July the Huguenot General Assembly met at Grenoble: later, in October, it would move to Nîmes. It found itself wooed by all three aristocratic leaders – Condé, Bouillon, Rohan – and pleased itself with the prospect of extending Huguenot power and determining the affairs of the nation. Thereupon Rohan decided to act. He supported the extreme claims of the Assembly. He and his brother, the Duc de Soubise, took up arms in the south. The abscess was about to burst.

In the south, the Rohan brothers were supported by another great nobleman, Jacques Nompar de Caumont, Duc de la Force. La Force was an old friend of the Rohan family, and his son had accompanied Rohan on his grand tour in 1599–1601. The duke himself had had a miraculous escape from the massacre of St Bartholomew, when Charles IX had personally ordered his murder. Afterwards, Henri IV had made him governor of Béarn and viceroy of Navarre, his own original kingdom. Now la Force watched with dismay the re-Catholicisation of that historic Huguenot citadel, which he had himself reconquered from the Ligue. The General Assembly of Grenoble demanded that the process be halted, and it appointed la Force as its general in Lower Guyenne. From now on the Caumont family would be firmly allied to the Rohan brothers. Through them it too would re-enter the world of Mayerne.

All these events were closely observed by King James. Officially, King James presented himself as a mediator between the Crown of France and the Huguenots. That a foreign king should adopt such a rôle was sufficiently humiliating to the King of France. It was even more humiliating when King James presented himself openly as 'Protector of the Religion' – protector, that is, of rebels against their lawful sovereign. Nevertheless, this was the rôle which he was now openly assuming. He showed it by sending out another private emissary: Gian Francesco Biondi.

Biondi was by birth a Croat from Dalmatia. His real name was Biundović.[37] His family was noble but poor. Being a Venetian subject, he had studied law at the university of Padua. In Venice he had fallen under the influence of Paolo Sarpi and of his friends Fulgenzio Micanzio and the Huguenot doctor Pierre Asselineau. He had become a Protestant and, with the English ambassador Sir Henry Wotton (who would be his constant patron) and the Genevese theologian Jean Diodati, he had worked busily to introduce Protestantism into Venice for 'the advancement of God's kingdom and the destruction of the great Babylon'.[38] In 1609 Wotton had taken him to England and had sought to enlist the king's support for this project. In the following years he had travelled to and fro in the cause – to France, Italy, Savoy, Holland. He had fed Venice with heretical books, supplied English and Venetian ambassadors with information, and sought to act as English agent with the union of Protestant princes of Germany. Now King James briefed him for a special mission. He was to go first to Sedan and there receive advice from the Duc de Bouillon. If the duke wished, he was to see the Prince de Condé too. Then he was to go to Grenoble and deliver a message from King James to the Huguenot Assembly. From Grenoble he was to go on to Savoy, where he had other commissions; for the Duke of Savoy was also stirring against Spain. Biondi duly appeared at Grenoble and addressed the assembled Huguenots in the name of King James. He urged them to keep the peace, but promised support if their liberty should be violated. God, he said, had made the King of Great Britain 'Protector of the Religion'.[39]

Thus in 1615 – when the Howards seemed to have conquered the English court and were thinking of a Spanish marriage for the future English king – James I, by means of two Protestant immigrants, Mayerne and Biondi, one sent to Rohan, the other to Bouillon, was secretly supporting Huguenot rebellion in France. Such were the contradictions, or perhaps we should say such was the balance, of his foreign policy.

The rebellion did not, in the end, achieve its full aims. The French court was able to exploit the divisions of the malcontent nobles; and the Franco-Spanish marriages were duly celebrated with great public magnificence. But the rebels received some satisfaction in a pacification which was agreed early next year at Loudun. The English ambassador was present at the conference, and Rohan wrote separately to King James from Loudun to keep him informed of its progress.[40] In due course King James replied, telling Rohan that he was sending Lord Hay to congratulate Louis XIII on the marriages and on the pacification 'so recently concluded with you and the other princes who, out of a common zeal for the good and safety of your country, have been driven to take up the defence of its liberties'.[41]

Meanwhile we return to Mayerne. He had scarcely arrived in England when he was sent to Greenwich, where the queen was suffering from gout, and there he was distressed to hear that the king, at the same time, was down with a heavy rheum at Newmarket, 'the fruit of the intellectual labours which have so oppressed him in London' – all those historical and theological controversies. As it was impossible to be in two places at once, he sent the king a letter of advice. He urged him to adjust his way of life, 'especially in the quality and frequency of his drink', so that pleasurable exercise and healthy diet, 'which is the principal article of health', should conspire for his preservation.[42]

While Mayerne was thus distracted, his wife handed him a letter from her brother in Holland which had an electric effect upon him. Mayerne's Dutch brother-in-law, Baron Wessel van den Boetzelaer, was a well-educated grandee of Zeeland, who had held public employment in his own country. He was a connoisseur of art and wrote poetry in French and Dutch. But he was evidently under economic pressure: he had already sold one property to the city of Dordrecht;[43] and now he proposed to sell his family estate of Asperen and come and settle in England, where his sister was so satisfactorily established.

Mayerne was horrified. Such a project, he declared, would be disastrous; and he wrote at once to the baron to say so. Ancient oak trees, he told him, cannot be transplanted. If the baron were to sell Asperen, he would never retain his social status. He would not find himself nearly so grand in England as he was in Holland. In England no man could be a seigneur unless naturalised by Act of Parliament. Unless so naturalised, all his goods would be at the mercy of the Crown. But if so naturalised, he would find that the marriage of his children would be determined by some courtier to whom the king had granted the right. The taxes in England were very high. So was the cost of life. In short, he must not sell Asperen.[44]

At the same time, Mayerne wrote off to his other brother-in-law, the baron's brother, Gedeon van den Boetzelaer, Baron van Langheraek, who was now Dutch ambassador in Paris. After some medical advice for the ambassador and his wife, who 'will never recover unless she follows my prescriptions', he came to the main point of his letter. 'My wife has just received a letter from M. le baron d'Asperen, in which he promises us the honour of his arrival among us. If he comes in a public capacity, I could not be happier, and I shall do all that I can to serve him; but if it is only for diversion, allow me to say that his quality and the rank which he holds at home ought to dissuade him, apart from the fact that he would not find, at our court, quite the reception and honour that he might expect or deserve.' For the honour of the family, therefore, this mad project must be stopped. Trust my local knowledge, Mayerne pleaded: 'handle this matter prudently, without mentioning my name.'[45]

Reading these letters, we are struck by a note of uncharacteristic urgency, as if Mayerne has lost his usual composure. We are reminded of his reaction to the charges about the death of Prince Henry. Some of his statements – e.g. about the marriage of children – are simply, as they stand, untrue.[46] Perhaps he was really concerned with the implicit social decline of his wife's family, if her brother were to become a mere *rentier* in England. Perhaps also he feared that his brother-in-law would be an economic burden to himself. Social status and money were both important in his eyes, and he was proud of the ancient lineage of the van den Boetzelaer. However, in the end, all was well. Social disaster was averted. Pressed on all sides, the baron gave up his foolish fancy of emigration, and preserved his dignity and his estates in Holland.

13

Medical Reformer, 1615–1616

For nearly two years after his return from France, in the spring of 1615, we know little about Mayerne's movements. No *Ephemerides* for that period survive. The last dated entry before this gap in the evidence is a *consilium* sent to the Spanish ambassador in France whom he had seen as a patient in Paris. It was sent from Salisbury on 1 August 1615. The queen was then on another visit to Bath and Mayerne was doubtless accompanying her. The next surviving volume of *Ephemerides* begins on 1 May 1617. For the intervening twenty-one months we have only a few professional jottings; but these at least show that he was continuously in England treating his patients.

One of the most interesting of his patients at this time was the greatest of English mathematicians and astronomers before Newton, Thomas Harriot. Harriot had been sent by Sir Walter Ralegh to Virginia in 1585 and was now being maintained at Sion House by Ralegh's friend and fellow-prisoner (and Mayerne's patient) Henry Percy, ninth Earl of Northumberland (known as 'the Wizard Earl' for his pursuit of forbidden knowledge). Harriot had been referred to Mayerne by Samuel Turner, the son of Ralegh's doctor Peter Turner, and Mayerne had seen him several times since May 1614. He had noted that Harriot had been the first to bring the habit of smoking tobacco from Virginia to England and was suffering from a cancerous growth in the left nostril, which was eating away the septum, and was to be removed 'if possible, but with the minimum of pain'. In November 1616 Harriot returned to Mayerne in obvious distress. 'Think of me', he wrote to him, 'as your greatest friend. The case is yours as well as mine. My recovery will be your glory, but through Almighty God, the author of all good.' He believed in God, he added, and in medicine as ordained by God, and in the physician as his minister. It was the *cri de coeur* of a believer, who was prepared for death but was eager to live. Mayerne diagnosed his affliction as 'noli-me-tangere' – cancer of the eyelids, nose or angle of the eye and neighbouring parts, and deemed incurable. He afterwards claimed that his special plaster had been very effective. At least Harriot lived for another six years before the cancer killed him.[1]

The little personal evidence that we have in this period suggests that Mayerne, though successful, was not happy. In November 1616 he recorded a new series of chemical experiments, begun, as he wrote, 'with the favour of God, who has separated me from the company of wicked men'; and he added, in Spanish and French, a pious distich, praying to be kept from anyone or anything that kept him from God:

> Dios aparta de me
> Quien me aparta de se
>
> Mon Dieu eslongue de moy
> Ce qui m'eslongue de soy.[2]

When the *Ephemerides* begin again six months later, they open with a Latin hexameter, warning himself to be prudent in misfortune. On the next page, immediately after a note about the allowance due to him for the maintenance of his horses – 172 bales of hay and 258 pecks of oatmeal – the melancholy strain reasserts itself in Latin verse:

> Si vitare voles acerba quaedam
> Et tristes animi cavere morsus
> Nulli te facias nimis sodalem
> Gaudebis minus, at minus dolebis.[3]

(If you wish to avoid all bitterness, and to guard against the biting of an unhappy soul, take none for a special friend. You will have less joy but also less sorrow.)

All this suggests that Mayerne had committed himself too closely to a friend who either had been lost or had betrayed him. We may observe that the ill-documented period from 1615 to 1616 includes those traumatic months in which a series of public trials in London was revealing the true history of the murder of his friend Sir Thomas Overbury. This certainly revealed 'wickedness' in some court circles. Mayerne could have been congratulating himself that he had not been involved with the Howards and regretting his closeness to the Earl of Somerset. But perhaps it is idle to speculate.

However, although we cannot follow him in detail, we know of one important matter in which Mayerne was involved in that period, and of which, perhaps, he was the motive force. This was the new incorporation of the

Society of Apothecaries and the production of the London pharmacopoeia: the beginning of a systematic attempt to regulate and improve the supply of medicine in London and, by example, in England.

The apothecaries, in England as elsewhere, had always been, like the surgeons, a depressed class in the medical profession. They were held to be unlearned, and were classed with tradesmen; and this classification was emphasised by the terms of their incorporation. Just as the surgeons were incorporated together with the barbers, so the apothecaries were incorporated together with the grocers. This association was resented by both surgeons and apothecaries, who regarded themselves as skilled workers, and indeed were accepted as such by laymen and by the more liberal physicians. However, the old-fashioned physicians refused to admit their claims, regarding them as unqualified empirics except when they were acting under the orders of the physician. This did not stop the apothecaries and surgeons from prospering. The physicians might seek to control them, to forbid them to practise except under orders, to write against them, and to discourage laymen from resorting directly to them. But they remained the physicians of the poor, and some of them became, by their practice, rich. No doubt there were many unskilled and dangerous empirics among them; but the physicians too had their rogue members.

In the sixteenth century the ideas of Paracelsus were particularly acceptable to the surgeons and apothecaries, and this indeed sharpened the opposition between them and the orthodox Galenic physicians. On the other hand the chemical doctors, who accepted Paracelsian ideas, or some of them, had good relations with the apothecaries, as with the surgeons. This sharpened the division between the orthodox Galenists and the chemical doctors. We have seen this division in France, where la Rivière, du Chesne and Mayerne were distrusted by the faculty of medicine, in part because of their closeness to the surgeons and apothecaries.

In England the tension was never so great as in France, because in England the opposition had not been polarised by religious difference and civil war. There was indeed a traditional antithesis, which had been institutionalised by the foundation in 1518 of the Royal College of Physicians; but the college itself proved to be far more liberal than its French equivalent, the Medical Faculty of Paris: there were no great legal cases like that of Roch le Baillif. An 'Elizabethan compromise' emerged in medicine as in religion. Paracelsian ideas had easy access to England, and translations of the writings of Paracelsus and his disciples, including especially those of du Chesne, were widely read. As in France, many of the nobility patronised Paracelsian empirics, and by the 1580s qualified physicians were prepared to accept Paracelsian ideas in alliance with apothecaries and surgeons. Where England differed from France was in the attitude of the established institution. While the Paris faculty had condemned the new ideas, and the claims of their advocates, outright, the Royal College of Physicians had been willing at least to consider them.

The period when the ideas of Paracelsus, and the claims of the apothecaries, received most consideration from the college was the late 1580s and early 1590s. This was the time when the college itself was planning a new pharmacopoeia, and it coincided with the activity, within the college, of the Paracelsian physician Thomas Mouffet (or Moffet). It was in 1588 that the apothecaries, fearing an invasion of their field by the physicians, first petitioned Queen Elizabeth for a monopoly of compounding and selling drugs and medicine; and it was in the same year that Mouffet, after being kept at bay for some years, was admitted as a Fellow of the Royal College of Physicians.

Thomas Mouffet, whose name is immortalised in English folklore by his little daughter's encounter with a spider, is the most interesting of the early English Paracelsian doctors.[4] The son of a London merchant, who was evidently of Scottish origin – the son described himself as 'Scot-Anglus' – he was educated at the Merchant Taylors' School and then at Cambridge. After taking his M.A. he went to the University of Basel and studied medicine there, staying with Felix Platter and corresponding with Thomas Zwinger. In Basel he became a Paracelsian, and his thesis on opiates was suppressed in proof because of his attack on Thomas Erastus of Heidelberg, the strongest critic of Paracelsus. After taking his doctorate, in 1578, he travelled in Spain, in Italy (where he studied silkworms) and in Germany. He then returned to England and, after a brief stay there, accompanied Peregrine, Lord Willoughby de Eresby, on his embassy to Denmark. There he met Tycho Brahe and Peter Severinus. On his return to England he published, in 1584, his most important work in defence of chemical medicines, which he dedicated to Severinus. The following year he applied for fellowship of the Royal College, and was rejected. Three years later, in 1588, he was accepted, and it was now that the apothecaries started to put pressure on the college.

In their petition, the apothecaries expressed alarm because 'some unworthy physicians' had taken it upon themselves to compound drugs for profit. In other words, the apothecaries were seeking to exploit the physicians' well-known dislike of unqualified 'empiric' doctors in order to strengthen their own control over the manufacture and sale of medicines, and to convert it into a monopoly. The apothecaries were also alarmed by the recent action of the physicians in setting up their own physic garden, under the control of John Gerard, the famous herbalist. This also looked like an invasion of the privileges of the apothecaries.

The apothecaries' petition failed. Queen Elizabeth's government was sensitive on the subject of monopolies, which were coming under attack in Parliament, and it was not prepared to increase their number.[5] But Mouffet, being now a Fellow of the college, was able to make his weight felt, especially since, thanks to his extensive practice, he had valuable political allies. He had been taken up by the Leicester–Sidney circle: Sir Francis Walsingham, the Secretary of State, was his patient; so was Sir Francis Drake; and he was a close friend of Sir Philip Sidney's sister, Mary Countess of Pembroke, who gave him a pension and persuaded him to settle at Bulbridge, close to her husband's seat at Wilton. Through Pembroke's influence he would be elected to Parliament in 1597, as member for the borough of Wilton. It seems clear that it was Mouffet's arrival at the Royal College which encouraged a party among its Fellows to propose the compilation and publication of an official pharmacopoeia.

Official pharmacopoeias – that is, lists of approved drugs which apothecaries were licensed to compound and sell – were not new. Several Italian and German towns had published such lists, which had a long history behind them. They were based on the *Antidotarium parvum* and the *Antidotarium magnum* of the School of Salerno.[6] What were new were the extension of such pharmacopoeias, and of the right to enforce their use, from the narrow limits of a city republic to a nation state; and the incorporation of chemical medicines into the lists. Some such medicines had been included in the *Pharmacopoeia Augustana*, published by the city of Augsburg, in 1564. But the categories of drugs which the Royal College proposed to its recently established Pharmacopoeia Committee in 1589 reveal (we are told) 'a remarkable and almost revolutionary modernity on the part of the college'.[7] They included liniments, unguents, electuaries, opiates, set out in distinct groups; and a subcommittee was to report on extracts, salts, chemical compositions, metals – in other words, the very subjects of controversy between the Galenists and the iatrochemists.[8]

Unfortunately we have no record of the committee's reports, and we can only deduce the forces at work in the college. But we may note that the committee contained several Fellows who had studied abroad and were of intellectual distinction. Three of them, including Mouffet himself, were doctors of Basel. It is probable (in view of his later activity) that an important part was played by Henry Atkins, whom we have met as one of the physicians of James I. Indeed it is likely that Atkins and Mouffet worked together for the new 'chemical' pharmacopoeia. If so, however, they worked in vain, for the project was defeated, or allowed to lapse. By 1594 it was dead. It may have been defeated earlier. Perhaps it lacked sufficient political patronage. Perhaps the political patrons were themselves preoccupied by more important concerns. The 1590s were a period of intense political in-fighting as the question of the succession to Queen Elizabeth became acute; the party of Leicester and Sidney was in eclipse with the death of Leicester in 1588 and of Walsingham in 1590; and their political heir, the young Earl of Essex, was now its sole leader. Perhaps it is significant that Mouffet, in 1591, and Atkins, in 1593, volunteered to serve as doctors on Essex's expeditions against Rouen and Cadiz (though Atkins was so seasick in the Channel that he had to return home). They may already have been defeated in the college, or their withdrawal may have facilitated their defeat. At all events, the project of an English 'chemical' pharmacopoeia, like the project of a new charter for the apothecaries, was shelved, and in the last ten years of Queen Elizabeth we hear no more of it. In those years Mouffet was either concentrating on his practice in London or immersed in literature in his retirement at Wilton.

Mouffet's great work was on insects. At Cambridge, he had come to know Thomas Penny, a Fellow of Trinity College who was also a botanist and an entomologist. As a prebendary of St Paul's Cathedral, Penny had offended Archbishop Parker. In consequence he had gone abroad, and in Switzerland he had come to know the famous naturalist Conrad Gesner, a main source of the reception of Paracelsian ideas into England. After Gesner's death he had helped to arrange his collections and publish his work; it seems that he had acquired Gesner's drawings of butterflies, which he took with him to England to be the basis of a work of his own. In 1589 Penny died and Mouffet acquired his unfinished work. He had also acquired the papers of an earlier English botanist and entomologist, Edward Wotton. Out of these materials, Mouffet constructed a new work, and in 1590 he had it ready for the press. He wrote for it a dedication to Queen Elizabeth and arranged to publish it at The Hague. However, this project also died. The Dutch publisher, we are told, could not face the cost of such a work, which had over 500 illustrations; Mouffet was only able to publish a poem, 'The Silk-worms and their Flies', which he dedicated to his patroness the Countess of Pembroke. His great work on insects was still in manuscript when he died in 1604.

Mouffet was in many ways the precursor of Mayerne. Like Mayerne, he was a highly civilised man of cosmopolitan tastes, wide intellectual interests and pleasing manners. He was a scholar and an elegant writer. He was fond of music – he bequeathed to his stepchildren his musical instruments including a pair of virginals – and his poetry was praised by contemporaries. Though his ideas were unorthodox, he was able to win support within the medical establishment, and he had valuable political patrons. However, he failed. The apothecaries remained as they were. The chemical pharmacopoeia was not compiled. The great work on insects was not published. His misfortune was that his attempt was made in the reign of Queen Elizabeth – and in the last, most conservative years of her reign. Mayerne took over all his ambitions, and succeeded. But then Mayerne worked in the reign of King James.

In this, as in so many other matters, King James showed his liberalism, his freedom from established ideas. We have already seen how he welcomed 'chemical' doctors even before he lured Mayerne into his service: the first English doctor whom he patronised was Mouffet's ally Dr Atkins. He also consistently supported the apothecaries against the physicians.[9] Here too he showed his hand early. On the death of Queen Elizabeth, as a matter of course, the charter of the Grocers' Company was suspended and submitted to the Crown for reconsideration. The Crown thereupon took the opportunity to alter its terms. It did not go as far as the apothecaries wished. It did not separate them from the grocers. But it did, of its own initiative, make them a distinct body within the grocers. This was not a great concession, since they still held no position on the governing body of the company; but it had its psychological value: it showed that the king favoured them. Seven years later, a bold spirit among them decided to exploit that favour. He was Gideon de Laune.[10]

Gideon de Laune (or Delanne), like so many London apothecaries, was of an immigrant family. His father, who had brought the family to England, was a Huguenot pastor from Normandy. Later, when Gideon and his brothers obtained a grant of arms, it was the arms of the family of Launey of Belmesnil in Normandy 'from whom they are descended'. Gideon was by now apothecary to Queen Anne and a man of wealth: by the end of King James's reign he would be 'opulentissimus', extremely rich – and indeed any apothecary who made up the elaborate pharmaceutical confections prescribed by Mayerne and his colleagues for the court could hardly fail to prosper. De Laune also prospered from the sale of his private nostrum, 'de Laune's pill'. He would live to be ninety-four, the venerable Founding Father of a City company.

In 1610 de Laune mobilised a party among the apothecaries and proposed that they seek to promote a bill in Parliament to separate the apothecaries from the grocers and form them into a distinct City company. When the grocers learned this, they were very angry. They summoned the offending apothecaries – all except de Laune, whom, as a foreigner, they declined to admit – and bullied them into submission. De Laune refused to be either excluded or silenced: he came to the court and was accused by the grocers of unseemly behaviour there. In consequence of this vigorous reaction by the grocers, the apothecaries' bill went no further. After its first reading it was dropped by the House of Commons.

1 Sir Theodore de Mayerne, by or after Rubens.

2 Henri, Duc de Rohan, the Huguenot soldier and thinker who was Mayerne's patron and hero.

3 Agrippa d'Aubigné, the stern and 'indomitable Huguenot warrior-poet', Mayerne's ally.

4 Henri IV of France, Mayerne's patient, whose favour protected him from the French medical establishment.

5 Marie de Médicis, Henri's devoutly Catholic widow, after whose reversal of the king's policies Mayerne emigrated to England.

6 Sir Thomas Overbury, 'determined to find short cuts to the top', whose murder by poison in the Tower was the great scandal of Jacobean politics.

7 King James VI and I, the unconventional king who delighted in Mayerne's company and remedies, and of whose medical condition he wrote a vivid account.

8 Robert Cecil, Earl of Salisbury, the leading minister of James I. His death was blamed on Mayerne by rival doctors at court.

9 A prescription by Mayerne for his devoted patient Queen Henrietta Maria. 'The only Frenchmen whom she would have about her, she said, were doctors.'

Dieu preserve leurs Ma.tés auec leur maison
& leurs subiects, & pour la santé des hommes
veuille donner efficace aux conseils & operations
de ceux qui se mettent en debuoir de les se=
courir.

De MAYERNE
Regiarum Majestatum
Medicus Primarius.

David Bethun Med.s
Regius ordina=
rius.

Matheus Lister Regiar.l
majestatū Medicus Ordinarius

10 The conclusion of Mayerne's ambitious project for the prevention and control of the plague (1631).

11 and 12 Mayerne's castle at Aubonne. 'The slit eyes of its great cylindrical dome squint
malevolently over a fresh and delightful landscape.'

AVBONÆ·

Sr Theodore Mayerne

13 Mayerne as painted in his early sixties by his patient John Hoskins. Mayerne's hands rest on a bust of Hippocrates.

However, de Laune did not give up. Four years later, in April 1614, he and his supporters petitioned the king for a royal charter granting them a separate organisation. By this time James I was confident of his own position. He had Mayerne and de Laune at his side. And his new Attorney-General was Francis Bacon who, like himself, distrusted the medical establishment. When James I referred the petition of the apothecaries to his law officers (Bacon and Sir Henry Yelverton), and instructed them to confer with the king's physicians (Mayerne and Atkins) and with the petitioning apothecaries (de Laune and his supporters), there was good reason to think that the petition would succeed.

As indeed it did. On 13 May 1614 the law officers reported to the king that the conference had duly taken place, and they now recommended that the apothecaries be separated from the grocers and subordinated to the physicians. Meanwhile Atkins had submitted a detailed plan to the Royal College and secured its approval. The opposition of the City of London held up the charter for three years. It finally passed the Great Seal on 6 December 1617.[11] In the preamble, the king stated that he had been moved to grant the Charter by consideration of the public good and by 'the petitions of our well beloved and faithful physicians Theodore de Mayerne and Henry Atkins, and also of the aforesaid Apothecaries'.

This charter established a separate City guild, 'The Masters, Wardens and Society of the Art and Mystery of the Apothecaries of the City of London'. To this guild it granted a monopoly of keeping apothecaries' shops, and it made it unlawful for grocers and others to make, sell or apply medicines or medicinal compositions, viz: distilled waters, compounds or chemical oils, *apozemata*, syrups, conserves, *eclegmata*, electuaries, *condita*, drugs, pills, powders, *troches*, oils, unguents, plasters, or by any other way to practise medicine within the City or suburbs of London, to a radius of seven miles. The grocers naturally protested, but their protests were ignored. They were told that they were tradesmen having no professional skill in the matter and not to be trusted, since they were more concerned with the profits of trade than with the perfection of medicaments, of which the physicians, not they, were the proper judges. King James was very well satisfied with this result. As a contemporary wrote, 'the Company of the Apothecaries, that have divided themselves from the ancient society of Grocers, grew so highly favoured by our sovereign Lord King James I that, as I have heard, he called them his Company.'[12]

In one respect King James and Bacon, with their distrust of physicians, were more liberal than Mayerne and Atkins. For if Mayerne and Atkins sought to free the apothecaries from the control of the grocers, it was in order that they might depend entirely on the physicians. To the apothecaries, subjection to the physicians was obviously more desirable than subjection to the grocers; but independence was more desirable still. In the proposals approved by the Royal College there were twenty 'headings'. Of these, nine dealt with the constitution and government of the new society, nine concerned the control of pharmacy, and the remaining two reserved the rights of the college over the apothecaries and those of the royal physicians to prepare and use their own secret remedies. The former of these last two headings was considerably modified in the final form of the actual charter, for Bacon 'deliberately frustrated the design of Atkins and Mayerne and of the College of Physicians to bring the Apothecaries into complete subjection to the Physicians'.[13]

The other clause, concerning the secret remedies of the royal physicians, was of course of personal interest to Mayerne and Atkins, since both of them were royal physicians and both, as chemical doctors, had their own secrets. Mayerne in particular, as a Hermetic doctor, had a whole range of secret receipts which he had no intention of divulging. His experiments with 'Hermes', 'Dryida' and 'Neptis' were all secret sessions, and the composition of the 'universal dissolvents', 'elixirs', panaceas and *panchresta* which they devised was jealously kept within that esoteric circle of adepts. Mayerne's notebooks are full of dark references to such secrets. There was the secret of contrayerna, the American plant which was his panacea; and there were many others. These secrets might be divulged to intimate friends, or in exchange for equally valuable formulae: 'be assured', he would write to such a friend, the physician of the Duc de Bellegarde in Paris, 'that the most secret cabinet of my most refined researches will never be closed to you';[14] but it was not to be thrown open to the apothecaries of London. In this too Mayerne dissented from Bacon, who, if he would have admired the Hippocratic side of Mayerne's technique, was unsympathetic to Hermetism of any kind, believing that science was advanced by open exchange and public verification, not by private revelation or esoteric mystery. However, he evidently did not think it prudent to challenge the royal doctors on that matter.

One of the recommendations of Mayerne and Atkins accepted by the Royal College and by the Crown in 1614 was that the college should prepare, for the guidance of the apothecaries, a London Antidotary. This was clearly an attempt to revive the project of a pharmacopoeia which had foundered in the last reign. This time it was carried through; and once again the driving force was provided by Atkins and Mayerne.

In order to carry it through, the Royal College appointed a new committee. Atkins, of course, was on it: he was indeed president of the college in the vital years 1616–18. Another prominent member of it, who had also been on the old committee, was Sir William Paddy, also a royal doctor. If Paddy and Atkins had supported Mouffet when they were young, and thereby launched the idea of the pharmacopoeia, they were far stronger now that they were well-established grandees of the college, royal physicians, and had the support of the king's first and favourite physician, Mayerne.

It was presumably to strengthen their hand in this matter that Mayerne's friends, at this point, secured his election as a Fellow of the Royal College. Hitherto he had been excluded, as a foreigner; but in 1616 the college agreed that a royal physician-in-ordinary, whatever his country of origin, might be admitted as a Fellow. The measure was clearly intended for his benefit, and he was promptly and unanimously elected on 26 June. He was thus able to work for the pharmacopoeia within the college. At the same time he must have learned the full history of the previous attempt, and have discovered, if he did not already know, the part played by Mouffet.

For it was in 1617 – that is, precisely while the pharmacopoeia was being drawn up – that Mayerne recorded that he had made contact with one Darnell, a London apothecary who had worked for Mouffet and who had become 'very well known to me'.[15] Darnell had somehow acquired all Mouffet's papers, and Mayerne exploited this advantage. He acquired the secret of Mouffet's 'blue water' or eye-lotion, which had cured desperate cases and, being sold at 2 shillings an ounce, had made Darnell's fame and fortune.[16] He also acquired the 'miraculous', 'celestial' powder, commonly called 'Captain Green's powder' but actually Dr Mouffet's, for ulcers, fistulae, bone-decay and eye-infections. In Mayerne's hands, this powder would work wonders on the queen,[17] and by a single application, after 'infinite remedies' had failed, would cure the itching anus of the great London merchant Sir Nicholas Crisp.[18] These were notable acquisitions, qualifying for red-letter entries and other marks of emphasis in Mayerne's notebooks; but there were also numerous more ordinary chemical preparations, plasters, cosmetics, etc., which Mayerne found in Mouffet's papers and of which Darnell would teach him Mouffet's own method of application. To Mayerne, Darnell was obviously a great find: through him he was to become the heir of Mouffet.

More important for us, Darnell sold to Mayerne the unpublished text of Mouffet's great work on insects. As a service to learning, and perhaps as a gesture of gratitude to Mouffet, Mayerne decided to publish this work. At first, according to his own account, he too, like Mouffet himself, could not find a printer to undertake so costly an enterprise, and so it 'lay many years unpublished in his study'.[19] But at last the difficulty was overcome, and it appeared in 1634, a beautiful book, beautifully illustrated, with an introduction by Mayerne which lauded Mouffet's eminence and learning. It is thus due to Mayerne that Mouffet has obtained recognition, and that one authority can describe him as 'the prince of entomologists before John Swammerdam (1637–1680)'.[20] In the eighteenth century Mouffet's manuscript as prepared for the press – a ravishing volume, even more beautiful, with its delicately coloured illustrations, than the printed text – would be acquired, with them, by Sir Hans Sloane, among whose papers it can still be seen in the British Library.[21]

Mouffet had intended to dedicate his work to Queen Elizabeth. On her death, he transferred the dedication to King James. King James was dead when Mayerne published it, but he did not transfer the dedication to his successor: he dedicated it to Sir William Paddy. In his dedication, Mayerne looked back to the year 1616, when he had been elected to the Royal College, one imagines on Paddy's recommendation, and recalled with gratitude the civility of the English doctors on that occasion. They had received him, he said, 'not with sidelong glances and eyes swollen with viperish poison' – a clear reference to the hostility of the Paris faculty – but in easy friendship, taking him readily into consultation and supporting him in his methods.[22]

Although thus elected, and welcomed, into the Royal College, Mayerne played little part in it after 1618, and he would decline the eminent position of 'Elect' when it was offered to him in 1627. His duties at court, he said, absorbed all his time. It is clear that his election, coming when it did, and as it did, was closely related to the preparation of the pharmacopoeia. His participation in that work was essential if it were to fulfil its purpose and include the new chemical medicines. Mayerne had already compiled long lists of drugs for his own use and for the dispensary of the court, and among his papers there are lists and drafts which clearly look forward to the official pharmacopoeia. Among them is the 'court antidotary' which he drew up on his arrival in England in 1611, followed by a draft of the sections for the London pharmacopoeia; a 'catalogue of medicines necessary for the preparation of a royal dispensary', with their description; a catalogue of chemical medicines to be prepared for such a dispensary in December 1616; and notes on previous pharmacopoeias – 'The Florentine Antidotary' (i.e., presumably, the *Nuovo receptario composito* of 1498) and the *Antidotarium Augustanum* (i.e. notes on the Augsburg pharmacopoeia of 1564).[23]

The text of the new pharmacopoeia was ready for publication in the spring of 1618, and Mayerne was requested to write the dedication of the published version to the king. The publication appeared on 7 May, but seven months later it was superseded by another, fuller text. The official explanation given by the college was that the printer had been too hasty and had 'snatched away from our hands this little work not yet finished off'.[24] This may or may not have been true. In any case the differences between the two versions need not concern us, for the texts have the same traditional base, the later edition having more matter in each category. Both versions have lists of chemical remedies, many of which – preparations of iron and antimony, *tartarus vitri-*

olatus or potassium sulphate, *mercurius vitae* and, especially, *mercurius dulcis* or calomel[25] – had almost certainly been supplied by Mayerne. Mayerne's own copy of the work, now in the British Library, has his marginal notes which show his own part in its preparation.

Thus the two years during which, for a large part, we lack the guidance of Mayerne's *Ephemerides* were years in which he was particularly active, not merely at court, but also in the reform of the English medical profession. The new charter for the independent Society of Apothecaries, which freed them from the embrace of the grocers and placed them under the control of the physicians, and the new London pharmacopoeia, the first such document in English medical history, were due partly to the exceptional interest of King James, but also to Mayerne's own efforts and influence. With all his self-confidence, he was a man of great tact. This is obvious enough from his correspondence. It was stated explicitly by one of his colleagues in the Royal College, Dr Baldwin Hamey junior. Hamey was the son of an immigrant doctor from the Netherlands, and was himself a traditionalist in medicine. He is chiefly remembered because he compiled brief lives of his colleagues which have been very useful to historians.[26] His comments on those colleagues are often astringent, but of Mayerne he writes nothing but lyrical praise. He dwells on Mayerne's exact clinical methods, his personal charm, his unfailing courtesy. Mayerne, he says, never tried to score off other doctors: he always thought first of his patient's health, and if he differed from his colleagues he was careful not to embarrass or humiliate them. He always acquiesced in sound advice. Look, for instance, at 'our *Pharmacopoeia*' or at his edition of Mouffet's book on insects. 'In the former you will never see the name of Mayerne, except in the list of his colleagues,[27] although from the very beginning his style, his work and the symbols that he used are everywhere obvious; for he regarded nothing as his own, to the exclusion of the other Fellows. In the latter, he shows the same candour towards Mouffet and the illustrious Paddy, to whom he dedicates the book.'

To conclude this chapter, we may record a few other episodes in Mayerne's life during the period which it covers. In 1616 he was appointed Ranger of Horne Park, near the royal palace of Eltham, Kent.[28] This was a royal park, formerly the property of the Roper family of Well Hall, Eltham, who, being Roman Catholics, had been obliged to part with it. As Ranger, Mayerne had a residence at Eltham, which he occasionally used. He was responsible for the deer in the park and he found it convenient as a nursery in which to grow medicinal herbs. But the normal duties were presumably carried out by a deputy. The office was essentially a sinecure, such as was used to reward most of James I's doctors, and a modest sinecure at that: the salary was £6.1s.8d, though no doubt there were also perquisites. The grant would be renewed in 1625, and the parliamentary survey of Eltham in 1649 shows that he still held it in that year.

In 1617, the year after that appointment, Mayerne accompanied the king on a progress which carried him further than his regular journeys to Bath and Newmarket. He went, perhaps for the second time, to Scotland.

King James had not been in Scotland since 1603, when he had left that barren wilderness for the Promised Land of England. Thanks partly to his absence, which preserved him from the violence of the resident Scottish nobility, and partly to his new wealth, which enabled him to bribe, manage or cow their leaders, he had been able, from a safe distance, to impose his will, and even to reduce the truculent ministers of the Kirk to some semblance of order. There were now real bishops again in Scotland, and decent church services. He had therefore decided to pay a formal visit to his native country. Mayerne accompanied him.

The royal party set out on 7 May and arrived in Edinburgh on 16 May. During that visit Mayerne received, with almost the whole court, the freedom of the City of Edinburgh,[29] took on a new Scottish assistant (whom he brought back to England),[30] and treated a series of Scottish patients: Lady Abercorn; the Earl of Dunfermline, Chancellor of Scotland, and his secretary; the Bishop of Galloway; Mr Hay, town clerk of Edinburgh; and his host in Edinburgh, Gill Gourlay, whom he cured of a well-known Scottish disease, the itch.[31] He also treated some of the attendant English courtiers. One of them was the new favourite, George Villiers, now Earl of Buckingham. Buckingham had never recovered from a cold caught two years earlier, 'when he was accompanying the king out hunting in the winter cold, bare-headed all day, as his Majesty's inseparable companion'; but this, added Mayerne, is the misery of court life, from which even the greatest courtier is not free.[32] Such sentiments now become frequent in Mayerne's notes. Weariness of court life, and impatience with the frivolity of courtiers, become a recurrent undertone in the record of experiments, concoctions and cures. A few weeks later, when back in England, he would be complaining of Buckingham's protégé Endymion Porter, who, it seems, would not follow his advice. 'Remedies are vain and labour wasted', he wrote in emphatic red ink, if the patient indulges himself freely, as courtiers do, in every excess, and keeps no measure in diet, sleep and exercise.[33]

Mayerne also took advantage of his visit to Scotland to talk to Scottish doctors and pick up some miscellaneous Scottish wisdom. He learned that the women of Scotland made great use of the herb *digitalis*, or foxglove, both internally, to kill worms, and externally, as sedative plasters and fomentations.[34] It was from the Scottish surgeon James Kinloch – presumably a relation of David Kinloch, the king's Scottish physician at this time (since Craig now lived in London), a literary man whose long Latin poem *De procreatione hominis* is perhaps the most elaborately obscene work ever to have been veiled in a learned language[35] – that Mayerne learned that the herb *senecio* (ragwort) mixed with beer was useful against scabies.[36] With these acquisitions of knowledge he returned to England on 23 August 1617.

Soon after his return, he was called to see an important politician who had been taken suddenly ill. This was Sir Ralph Winwood, the Secretary of State who had been inserted into that sensitive office by Robert Carr, three years earlier. Mayerne visited him and caused him to be bled. The blood was 'very bad and foul' and the loss of it caused him to faint several times. Mayerne never saw him again, being summoned by the king. Meanwhile the Secretary died. Once again, Mayerne was blamed for letting blood too soon. 'Of all men, I have no fancy to him', wrote John Chamberlain, for 'I have observed he is commonly unfortunate in any dangerous disease'. However, he added, the autopsy revealed that the Secretary could not have lasted long, 'having his heart withered almost to nothing, his spleen utterly rotten, one of his kidneys clean gone, the other perished, his liver full of black spots, his lungs not sound, besides divers other defects, so that it was a wonder how he held out so long and looked so well'.[37]

The death of Winwood opened once again the critical office of the Secretary of State. Winwood had been committed to a Protestant, anti-Spanish foreign policy. Indeed, he had over-committed himself, personally securing the release of Sir Walter Ralegh and encouraging his projects for an attack on Spain, whether in the Mediterranean, or on the French coast in alliance with the Huguenot rebels, or in America. James I was prepared to entertain such ideas, if only to preserve his position at the head of European Protestantism. But he was essentially a man of peace, seeking to balance the ideologically opposed forces in Europe; and at this moment he was negotiating also for a rich Spanish marriage for his son, Prince Charles. On that subject he was in regular contact with the Spanish ambassador, the famous Gondomar. Within a year, Gondomar would have secured the ruin and execution of Ralegh; and if Winwood had still been alive, he would no doubt have shared in that ruin.

In these circumstances, the succession to Winwood was of great importance. The Howard family, in spite of the Overbury scandal, were still in office, and their client, Sir Thomas Lake, was Winwood's assistant. Gondomar had established a position of influence at court. The Spanish bait tempted the king. And yet the king wished to preserve his freedom, to maintain relations with the foreign Protestants, the enemies of Spain. Once again, as in 1612, he was in a quandary, and he extracted himself in the same way. Then he had decided to be his own Secretary of State. He had put his favourite, Rochester, in charge of the office, and Rochester had left the correspondence in the hands

of Overbury. Now, forgetting some of the inconveniences of that arrangement, the king declared that he had never been so well served as in the days
when he had been his own Secretary; and he put his new favourite,
Buckingham, in charge of that office. Buckingham left the correspondence to
Lake. However, this experiment, like that one, soon proved unsatisfactory, and
in January 1618 a successor to Winwood was found. This was Sir Robert
Naunton, a creature of Buckingham, scholarly and harmless. This, it was
thought, would leave the direction of foreign affairs in the hands of the king.

Such direction was badly needed, for in that year the great crisis of
European Protestantism was to begin.

14

The Protestant Revolution,
1616–1622

The idea that the great struggle was imminent was now a firm conviction of the Calvinist churches. It had been worked into their intellectual system: their chronology, their cosmology, their eschatology. It had been integrated with modern science, Hermetic and Paracelsian, alchemical and astrological. It had been accepted as true and necessary doctrine by their Assemblies. And by now the very date and place had been discovered. It had been discovered, by a happy accident, through a defector at the end of the year 1601.

The defector was a Catholic priest, Gaspar (or Brocalo) Baronius, the nephew of the famous cardinal whose Catholic *Annals* King James was so anxious to see refuted, and who himself would very nearly become Pope. Gaspar Baronius was well placed to know Roman policy, for he was – thanks to his uncle's patronage – a powerful figure in papal circles. But he had been shocked by the execution of three Englishmen and a French Capuchin friar for heresy. While on an official journey from Rome to Madrid he had defected to the Huguenots in France. He was brought to Paris, and there, in the house of that great political operator the Duc de Bouillon, he revealed to the assembled Huguenot élite the documents in his possession. They included two files entitled, respectively, 'Arts of Peace' and 'Arts of War', which together set out the strategy of the Roman Church for the final conquest of Protestant Europe. They showed – at least as d'Aubigné recalled them afterwards – that the great crusade of reconquest was to begin with a persecution in the Grisons or Graubünde, then a distinct federation linked with the Swiss confederation but not yet part of it. The inhabitants of the Grisons were Protestant, but they ruled over the resentful Catholic peasants of the Valtelline, the Alpine pass which was regarded as vital, strategically and economically, to both sides in the holy war: for it linked Catholic Austria with Italy, Protestant Switzerland with Venice. A massacre in this combustible area (according to Baronius's documents) was to give the first signal; 'the standard of the crusade' was then to be raised, and a full-scale war of reconquest launched. It was to be launched in 1622.[1]

Whether the story was true or not, developments in the following years certainly seemed to confirm it. The court of Spain might seem intent on peace, but Spanish governors in Milan and Naples, Spanish ambassadors in Venice, Prague and Vienna, were pressing for a forward policy; the Counter-Reformation was gaining ground in Flanders and the Rhineland; the Duke of Savoy had his eyes on Geneva and the pays de Vaud, whose loss he had never digested. Admittedly the emperor Rudolf II was unsound; but Spanish diplomacy was to ensure a more reliable successor.

How could European Protestantism defend itself against this threatened crusade? Was it to retreat into itself, rely on toleration or permanent deadlock? Certainly not. The only possible course was to organise defence, perhaps even aggression, a pre-emptive strike before the enemy was ready. To do this it was of course essential to mobilise a great power whose secular interest was opposed to that of Spain. That power could be England, which had been the natural protector of European Protestantism under Elizabeth. But James I, though theologically sound, and willing to accept this titular role, was politically rather unpredictable. The traditional enemy of the house of Habsburg was the Crown of France. Henri IV might now be Catholic, but his secular interest impelled him to oppose the old enemy by all means. So he would seek to mobilise and use the European Protestants. They, on their side, would seek to mobilise and use him.

In any case, the front line of operations, whether diplomatic or military, was not in doubt. It was to be found in the string of Protestant states, French in culture and religion, that lay across the French frontier. In 1596 the then Elector Palatine gave asylum at his French-speaking court at Heidelberg to his cousin the Duc de Bouillon, who had fled the wrath of Henri IV. Guided by his guardian, Christian of Anhalt, the present Elector, Frederick V, was the leader of Protestant action in Germany. Then there were the Calvinist cantons of Switzerland and the great citadel of Calvinism, the French city of Geneva. Behind these Calvinist strongholds lay the Lutheran principalities of Germany, of which the nearest – Hesse and Württemberg – were penetrated by Calvinism. The Landgrave of Hesse, Moritz the Learned, was himself converted to Calvinism. So was the new Duke of Cleves – the Elector of Brandenburg – in 1609. In Geneva the French Calvinists were joined by the *émigré* Calvinists from Italy: the Burlamachi, the Calandrini, the Turrettini, the Diodati, inter-related dynasties of entrepreneurs, scholars, preachers – a cosmopolitan freemasonry which linked the European Calvinists not only, economically, with London and Amsterdam but also, being Italian, with Venice; and in Venice another Huguenot, Mayerne's medical friend Pierre Asselineau, more radical even than Paolo Sarpi, handled the secret foreign relations of the heretical republic.

On this front-line of European Calvinism, both the Catholic French crown and the Protestant French Huguenots sought their foreign allies, the one against a Spanish, the other against a Catholic hegemony. The period of their greatest collaboration was in the last years of Henri IV, the period from 1606 to 1610 when the 'Great Design' of a renewed frontal war was being planned. Since their priorities were different, neither could absolutely trust the other; and so there were, in effect, two separate but overlapping diplomatic systems, sometimes supporting, sometimes spying on, sometimes even betraying, each other. We are concerned with the Protestant system, into which we happen to have an invaluable window in the correspondence of its great organiser, 'the pope of the Huguenots', Philippe du Plessis Mornay.

After his defeat in the great public debate with Cardinal du Perron in 1600, Mornay had retired to his governorship of Saumur. He was regarded as one of 'les prudents', moderate in his beliefs and politics: was he not an irenist, a Platonist, a rationalist? But in those years 1606–10 his political aims were radical. So was his language. It was then that he wrote his work on *The Mystery of Iniquity*, proving the pope to be the Antichrist who must be utterly destroyed, then that he set out to create a secret, ideological alliance behind the more public secular alliances of Henri IV. Through his correspondence we see him at the centre of an elaborate web whose filaments are fixed in four points: the Netherlands, the Rhineland, Geneva, Venice. And what a vibrant web it is! Letter after letter is sent out, report after report comes in; secret agents set out for The Hague, Sedan, Heidelberg, Geneva, the Valtelline, Venice. Mornay operates at all levels: he is himself on equal terms with the princes and the great ladies who can manipulate them – the Dowager Princess of Orange, the Duchesse de la Tremoïlle. He can command the churches and the pastors. His trusted secretary, David de Liques, travels everywhere for him: how convenient that he has a brother who is a physician in The Hague. Foreign ambassadors, or their secretaries, or their chaplains, are secretly wooed; new diplomatic links are forged, particular envoys are proposed, new agents are recruited: 'I am looking everywhere for persons who can serve in this work.' 'I leave nothing undone,' Mornay assures his allies, 'in Germany, in England, in the Netherlands, through letters, through friends, in season, out of season, to right, to left', for now is the time to found the bell which will sound the tocsin of war. It must be rung soon, for time is running out and, if we do not act now, 'these great plans will die with us.'

Mornay's chief agent in Geneva was the pastor Jean Diodati: he was 'the key in this business'; but the door that was to be opened in 1610 was Venice. Through that door, it seemed, the Gospel could now enter Italy and bring Antichrist down; and not only Italy, for Venice had an Austrian border. In Venice his most trusted agent was of course Dr Asselineau. To Asselineau

Mornay reports everything; to him he sends his other secret agents; to him he reports every success elsewhere: how the Dutch peace of 1609 will liberate Dutch ships for war in the Mediterranean; how the King of England, like himself, has shown the pope to be Antichrist; how the German princes and the Prince of Orange have been fixed, and will send agents, personally approved by him, to Venice; and how these agents will correspond directly with him. Early in 1610 Asselineau is confident of a successful war, which must not be confined to Venice and Savoy: it must be extended to Austria and Bohemia, where Mornay is in touch with the Moravian quasi-Calvinist magnate Karel Žerotín. 'Meanwhile those who manage affairs here are constantly pushing the wheel, and especially the two good fathers'[2] – that is, Paolo Sarpi and his friend Fulgenzio Micanzio. 'Certainly', he writes a month later, 'this Great Beast is now near his end in Italy', and 'war cannot be renewed here without his total ruin. The more he is attacked from all sides, the sooner he will be destroyed.'[3] In Geneva, and in secret visits from Geneva to Venice, Diodati pushed the same policy. He too looked forward to the imminent fall of the great Antichrist. And that fall was to be precipitated by war: a war of aggression, a pre-emptive crusade, to be launched before the Catholic crusade of 1622. As Diodati's biographer writes, after reading his numerous, often enciphered letters, 'far from looking with anxiety at a horizon heavy with clouds, the Calvinists nourished the secret hope that war would hasten the progress of Reform.'[4]

The pre-emptive strike was not launched in 1610. The assassination of Henri IV suddenly stopped that great adventure. Mornay was desolated: 'our hopes vanished with the death of the King,' he exclaimed: 'in one moment it has changed the face of the world and eclipsed the stars.' With it, the policy of the French crown changed: under the regency of the queen mother, alliance with Spain and the rule of the *dévots* at home replaced alliance with international Protestantism and war against the Habsburgs. The dream of a Calvinist Venice sank gradually out of sight. As Asselineau wrote, Paolo Sarpi himself grew 'cold'. Without the French motor the machine ran down. But the Huguenot activists did not abandon hope. In 1611 they rushed to the defence of Geneva against the threat from Savoy. That was the occasion when Henri de Mayerne was killed by the Baron de Roche-Giffart. Then the scene changed again, as a new crisis arose in Germany. In the same year, 1611, the Habsburg family joined to depose the unsatisfactory emperor Rudolf II, the patron of Protestants and chemists, Hermetists and Paracelsians, from the Bohemian throne, and replaced him by his brother Mathias. Mathias was an elderly man, also childless. But that had its advantages: as Mornay wrote, it would give a breathing space during which plans could be laid to secure 'some more salutary election'. To Mornay that meant, of course, the election of an emperor who would not support Spain and the Counter-Reformation, perhaps not a Habsburg at all, at least someone other than the Habsburg candidate, the Archduke Ferdinand of Styria.

The ideal candidate was there in waiting. He was the young Elector Palatine Frederick V. For many years the Electors Palatine had been the political leaders of aggressive Calvinism. The present elector was nephew of the Duc de Bouillon and of the Prince of Orange, bound by treaty to the Netherlands. Soon he would be the son-in-law of the King of England. Dynastically and diplomatically he had all the necessary qualifications. So, during the short reign of the Emperor Mathias, he was groomed for his part. Then, in 1618, the conspirators struck. A revolutionary Protestant party seized power in Prague and threw the Habsburg ministers out of the window of the Hradschin Palace. Next year, when the emperor died, Frederick was elected King of Bohemia. That incidentally gave the Protestants a majority of the electors to the impe-rial throne. The Calvinist revolution, it seemed, had been carried into the heart of Germany.

It was a rash adventure, a gamble for the highest stakes. To succeed, it needed the support of the greater powers: of England, France, the Netherlands. The Duc de Bouillon, who, with the Prince of Orange, had masterminded the plan, sought this support, but it did not come. The new king found himself supported only by the Calvinist international. To it, of course, the election was a great coup – and not a political coup only. It was a decisive step in the fulfilment of the divine plan of history, the beginning of the great 'shakings' prophesied in Scripture which were to herald the fall of Antichrist and set in motion the drama of 'the Last Things'. To the Paracelsian enthusiasts this drama included the return to earth of the Prophet Elijah – 'Elias Artista', 'the chemical Elias' – announced by Paracelsus himself and by his two most famous modern apostles, Oswald Croll and Michael Sendivogius, who would 'make all things new'.[5]

One of those who was exhilarated by these events was Agrippa d'Aubigné, the most universal, but also the most inflexible, of the Huguenot heroes of the wars of religion. After the assassination of Henri IV, d'Aubigné would not be a party to the compromises which other Huguenot leaders thought necessary to the survival of their cause. He therefore retired into splendid isolation and devoted himself to literature. He denounced the defectors from the cause, and the waverers in it. He polished and updated his great sanguinary poem, Les Tragiques, in which the Valois court, the papacy, the Jesuits, with all their sins upon them, are handed over to divine vengeance and the martyrs of St Bartholomew receive their reward in heaven. And he worked on his Universal History, a work of majestic propaganda which, like the History of de Thou, would cause its author a great deal of trouble. D'Aubigné stated that he had been encouraged to write this work by Henri IV – no doubt in his Huguenot days. After 1610, however, it was unlikely to be welcome in France. Christian of Anhalt offered to have it published at Heidelberg, but d'Aubigné was unwilling to send his 'treasure' so far away. In the end he had it printed at a private press on his country estate in France. It was promptly condemned and burnt by authority in Paris. In his isolation, d'Aubigné retained his respect for only one of the present Huguenot leaders: the Duc de Rohan. Disdaining his feeble contemporaries, he preferred to look back to the heroic age of which he himself was a survivor and Rohan the worthy heir – and forward to the great struggle in which, as he knew, Antichrist would fall. He also knew when that would happen – or at least when the process would begin. It was to begin, as revealed by the defector Gaspar Baronius, with trouble in the Grisons, in Switzerland.

However, d'Aubigné's calculations proved inexact. That great European war, in which the last struggle of the French Huguenots was enveloped, broke out – as a result of the forward policy of his friend, Christian of Anhalt – not in 1622 but in the summer of 1618.

When we left the French Huguenots, they had improved their position by joining the second revolt of the princes, which had been ended by the Pacification of Loudun in May 1616. Unfortunately the princes were less satisfied than the Huguenots by the results of that treaty, and in September they took to arms for the third time since the assassination of Henri IV. This time Rohan and the Huguenots kept aloof; the princes were defeated; and the queen mother's favourite, the Maréchal d'Ancre, seemed about to emerge as the absolute master of France. However, once again, as so often in the last forty years, a timely assassination changed all. On 24 April 1617, d'Ancre was murdered in the Louvre; the queen mother herself was imprisoned; and the government was assumed, in the name of the young Louis XIII, by a junta of grandees dominated by Charles Albert, Maréchal, now Duc, de Luynes. Luynes set out on a policy of Catholic restoration, both at home and abroad, and of good relations with Spain. In particular the Catholic Church was to recover all its rights in Protestant Béarn. A royal edict was published, and rejected by the States of Béarn. The Huguenots of France raised the alarm. Technically, they had no right to interfere – Béarn was an independent kingdom – but they could not fail to read the signs. Rohan, who had not been forgiven for his refusal to join the grandees, and who himself had claims to the kingdom of Béarn, retired to Brittany and placed himself on the side of the queen mother, now a prisoner at Blois. Then, in February 1618, the queen mother was liberated by the Duc d'Epernon, and appealed to Rohan and the Huguenots, now gathered in assembly at la Rochelle, to support her. By a new reversal of alliances, the queen mother, and the Huguenots led by Rohan, seemed about to challenge the Catholic rule of Louis XIII and the princes, led by de Luynes.

In this tense situation, in June 1618, Mayerne decided to revisit France. It was now three months since his father, Louis Turquet, had died in Paris. There were also his French patients to be seen. He therefore applied for leave of absence. King James not only granted the leave: he also gave him a personal letter of recommendation to the King of France, stating that Mayerne was travelling for his private affairs and asking his brother monarch to grant him his help, 'for which we ourselves will gladly assume the obligation and shall be ready to requite it another time'.[6]

In order that there should be no doubt of the private character of the visit, and no grounds for suspicion, Mayerne took care to inform the representatives of both France and Spain. The Spanish ambassador was Gondomar, the most famous enemy of the Protestant international. He was at the height of his influence in England: at this very moment he had forced the king to agree that 'the pirate' Sir Walter Ralegh, newly arrived from Guiana, should be executed. However, Mayerne enjoyed good relations with Gondomar, who was one of his patients: like his predecessor Dr Alonso de Velasco and his colleague in Paris Don Iñigo de Cárdenas, this Catholic Spaniard preferred a heretical doctor. Mayerne and Gondomar exchanged little civilities: for instance, Gondomar presented Mayerne with a dog called Turco, for hunting partridges. Mayerne was fond of dogs: he had a dog called Harlequin and a bitch called Madrille, which he had recently boarded out with a Scottish tailor in Tottel Street.[7] Mayerne was also indebted to Gondomar for a useful remedy against open-air draughts.[8] It was therefore as an old friend that Mayerne now called on Gondomar to take leave of him, and explained that he was going to France to settle the affairs of his late father – and also to perform a small service for King James. The king had instructed him to see his old friend Pierre du Moulin and get him to correct a book which he had recently published, and bring it into line with the practice of the Church of England.[9] About the same time, Mayerne called on the French agent, M. Leclerc, who was standing in for the ambassador, recently recalled to France. To him he gave the same explanation, but he did not specify the nature of his mission to du Moulin. This was perhaps prudent, for the French government thoroughly distrusted du Moulin as a dangerous radical and an English agent. King James, we may note, in his letter to the King of France had not mentioned du Moulin.

Evidently neither Gondomar nor Leclerc was entirely satisfied by Mayerne's parade of innocence. No doubt they remembered his previous visit in 1615, and the suspicions it had aroused. Now, as then, the situation in Europe was tense. Now, as then, the Huguenots and their patrons were stirring in France,

Rohan was on the move, du Moulin, as usual, was at the centre of trouble, and here was Mayerne coming to France to confer and collude with him. All this was very sinister. The French government must have known that Mayerne was close to Rohan, probably his agent at the English court. Only six months earlier, on his return to Paris after a suspicious visit to Savoy, Rohan had written to Mayerne urging him to engage James I in the Huguenot cause: for the rapprochement between France and Spain 'should be of great concern to His Majesty of Great Britain. He must see that there is a party here fomented by Spain, which seeks to draw France in that direction, and which will find a pretext to destroy our religion in Christendom.'[10] In all the circumstances we must allow that the French government had some reason to be suspicious.

Leclerc certainly was. He told the French Secretary of State, Brûlart de Puysieux, that Mayerne, when describing their meeting, had sought to engage him in political discussion, without success. 'According to my information,' he added, 'he is going to la Rochelle and to Basel in Switzerland. I think I should tell you this so that you can keep an eye on him.'[11] La Rochelle, of course, was an emotive name, like du Moulin. Three weeks later Leclerc sent a further despatch on the same subject. 'I have already warned you', he wrote, 'that it would be well to watch the behaviour of the Sieur de Mayerne when he is among you. I can now tell you, as a certain truth, that he has been expressly charged, while in France, to see those of the Religion, and to give them assurances from here. That is why he must be watched, for I can assure you that this is gospel-true.'[12]

Mayerne, of course, knew nothing of this. He did not even know that his cover had been blown in 1615. Confident in his status, and in his royal protection, he arrived in Paris and began to see his grand Huguenot patients. However, the French authorities, having been alerted, were watching. As the English agent, William Beecher, afterwards reported (for here too there was no ambassador, Sir Thomas Edmondes having returned in November 1617), they 'have a most curious espial upon M. de Mayerne, even upon his ordinary actions'.[13] Then suddenly, at the end of July, they struck. Mayerne was ordered to leave France at once. No delay was allowed, no reason given, and requests for either only caused a reiteration of the peremptory command: he must be gone.

This rough expulsion of so distinguished a visitor, a visitor personally warranted by the King of England, caused a sensation in Paris. Beecher, who was taken completely by surprise, reported that 'there is nothing that hath been so much agitated in discourse'; that 'the conjectures and advices that have been given me of this matter . . . would not be contained in a sheet of paper'; and that the Huguenots were greatly indignant at a step which implicitly 'accused' them 'of making a faction in the state'. He could not penetrate the mystery, for men who had discussed the affair with the ministers of state came away convinced 'that either they have nothing to say or are most resolute not to declare it'.[14] The episode was the talk of the town in London too. Beecher reported it to his friend William Camden, the historian, who recorded it as an important item in his projected *Annals* of the reign of King James; the court gossip John Chamberlain, who had weekly meetings with Camden at St Paul's, got hold of the story; it was transmitted from England to Scotland;[15] and of course it became the subject of diplomatic *démarches* in both London and Paris.

Mayerne was outraged at the insult to his honour. Back in London, he mounted his high horse and from that elevated posture protested loudly. All through the months of August and September the courts and corridors reverberated with the noise of the *affaire* Mayerne. In London James I, the Marquis of Buckingham, and Mayerne himself, kept up the heat. Mayerne told the trembling French agent, M. Leclerc, that he would ask the king to send him back to Paris to defend his honour, to demand the punishment of the offender, and receive public apologies. Leclerc begged him not to do any such thing: it would only do harm. But behind Mayerne stood King James. He too was enraged. The insult, he insisted, was to himself, and if no adequate explanation was produced he would break off diplomatic relations. In Paris Beecher kept busy. He pressed the French ministers, both jointly and severally, tackling the Duc de Luynes himself in the garden of the Tuileries. It was an unheard-of act, he said, an insult and injustice to both Mayerne and the King of England. If Mayerne's presence in Paris was inconvenient, why could he not have received a private hint, and a civil explanation, from the Chancellor, M. de Sillery, who knew him well, instead of being expelled 'with such solemnity as had made a noise not only over Paris and France but peradventure over all Christendom?'

To these protests the French ministers gave varying and inadequate answers. At first they had tried to isolate the affair, saying that it need not disturb the good relations between England and France. That line had clearly failed. So now they declared that the affair was of such importance that they would explain it to no one except the King of England himself – to whom indeed, they said, they had already explained it; which the king denied. Sometimes they indicated that it was an unfortunate necessity imposed upon them by the present infirmities of their state, for which they deserved pity rather than censure. But then they would retreat into the clouds again, saying that they 'had proceeded upon good and sure ground and such as would justify them before all the world when it should be time to disclose it which for great considerations they might not yet do'. Sometimes they tried to separate Mayerne from King James, who, they pretended to believe, had been unaware of Mayerne's activities. When King James would have none of that they fell back on the argument that, though a great king, he was surrounded by 'malicious spirits' who pushed him into radical courses. 'Nay,' quoth Luynes, 'and I know that there are those of the Religion *qui soufflent.*'

Meanwhile, to strengthen their hand, the French ministers pressed Leclerc to supply them with further evidence from London. Leclerc set to work. He fished for hearsay evidence, bribed Huguenot visitors, listened to the gossip of Mayerne's enemies and critics at court. Queen Anne was reported to have said something which might be usefully interpreted. Secretary Naunton's cautious phrases might conceal sinister knowledge. Best of all was the information supplied by a Huguenot gentleman, the Sieur de Guillerville, whom Leclerc enlisted as his informer and whom he sent off to Newmarket when Mayerne was there with the king, with instructions to observe Mayerne's actions and mark his words. Guillerville promised to be back in two days and to report. On his return he reported that he had attended a dinner party at which Mayerne, led on by him, had spoken very freely of his experiences in Paris: how he had had secret meetings by day and night 'in an inn where he took his meals'; how 'sometimes, between the pear and the cheese,' he had had discussions with 'those of the Religion'; how he had feared, when exposed – he could not imagine who had exposed him – that he would find himself lodged in the Bastille. He also confessed (said Guillerville) that he had sought an occasion to go as a deputy for the Huguenots to Sedan, to visit the Duc de Bouillon. This was a change from the earlier agent's information that he was going to la Rochelle and Basel, but Leclerc did not worry about that, for he was now, he felt, hot on the trail. He would cultivate an English milord who had been at the alleged dinner party, and whom he knew well. In this way he would put it about that there were good reasons for Mayerne's expulsion, and make trouble between him and the king. In other words, he was no longer collecting evidence: he was making propaganda, causing difficulty. The Sieur de Guillerville, he told the French Secretary of State, was the Duc de Bouillon's trusted agent: an excellent man who deserved to be rewarded; for he was leaking all the duke's secrets too.

Encouraged by this information, the French ministers stood their ground. They were sure that Mayerne had been up to no good in Paris, and anyway, they could not now retreat without loss of face. So they simply declined to answer further questions, hoping that the problem would then go away. Neither Mayerne nor the king would allow it to go away. On the advice of the king, Mayerne wrote directly to the King of France. The letter does not survive: all that we know is that Beecher, on receiving it, was afraid to deliver it. It would do no good, he said – the French ministers were weary of the affair, and it would only reduce his own value as an intermediary: 'I understand they complain of me to others that I do too much embrace M. de Mayerne's cause. And besides,' he added mysteriously, 'there is another reason private to M. de Mayerne which makes me resolve to attend his Majesty's pleasure yet once again concerning that letter.'

One reason why Beecher was reluctant to pursue the matter was that it had now become involved in a new cause of diplomatic friction. During these same months the English government was concerned with the case of Sir Walter Ralegh. He was now back in the Tower, and a Commission of Inquiry was considering the case for his execution. In the course of its work the commission discovered that Leclerc had conspired with Ralegh to smuggle him out of England to France. The facts were indisputable: Ralegh himself admitted them; and early in October the government acted. First a French 'domestic' of Leclerc, one Hugon, was arrested and imprisoned. Then Leclerc himself was summarily banned from the royal court and left the country. Effectively, he was expelled. Beecher remained in Paris long enough to observe the reactions of the French ministers. As he foretold, they saw the expulsion of Leclerc as 'a revenge for that of M. de Mayerne'. Unable to deny the facts, they declared that Leclerc had acted without their knowledge, and suggested that Mayerne had engineered the whole affair: 'that their agent was drawn artificially into this business, and they suspect M. de Mayerne to be the contriver of it'. After that, King James carried out his own threat. Beecher was recalled from Paris and all diplomatic relations between England and France were suspended. In his final summary of his services while he had filled that post, Beecher included the claim that 'he acted in the affair appertaining to M. de Mayerne'.

The complete diplomatic rupture between England and France caused by the expulsion of Mayerne lasted seven months. In those seven months much happened. All over Europe – in the Netherlands, in Bohemia, in Germany – war-clouds were gathering. A controversial imperial election was pending. The Protestants in Béarn apprehended a disastrous change in their status. The French Huguenots, assembled at la Rochelle, were threatening mutiny. France, it seemed, was sliding into civil war, and England was moving into the Spanish orbit. In the spring of 1619 the French government decided that it was necessary to repair the breach. After intense activity in the corridors – especially by Mayerne's friend Biondi, now acting as agent of the Duke of Savoy in London – arrangements were made. The occasion was provided by the death of Queen Anne. She had died in January, at Greenwich, with Mayerne in attendance, who recorded the event with an elegiac Virgilian line. In May Louis XIII sent M. des Ursins, Marquis de Tresnel, as ambassador extraordinary to offer his condolences. James I responded by sending Sir Edward Herbert, afterwards Lord Herbert of Cherbury, the learned and gladiatorial philosopher of deism.

He too was to go in, in the first instance, as ambassador extraordinary, with particular instructions. These were, first, to obtain a renewal, by the young Louis XIII, of the oath of alliance with Britain made by his father, Henri IV, and, secondly, to settle 'the business of M. de Mayerne'. The ice having been thus broken, regular diplomatic relations could be resumed. Herbert would stay on as ambassador in ordinary and Tresnel would return to France and be replaced in London by the Comte de Tillières.

Tresnel returned in May. Before he left, he had an amicable private conversation with Buckingham at Greenwich. He assured Buckingham that M. de Mayerne would be satisfied. And he received in return an assurance that the case of Hugon, who was still in prison, would not be overlooked. Herbert followed him to France; and there, at the French court, then at Tours, the two ambassadors met and exchanged private assurances of cooperation. Soon Herbert felt able to write to King James that all was in hand. The king's two specific commandments – the renewing of the oath and 'the business of Mr. de Mayerne . . . are both accorded'. The former matter would be dealt with when the king returned to Paris, the latter 'when Mr. de Mayerne will'. The assurance given Herbert had been unconditional; however, no doubt 'a gracious hearing of the French in their suits' – i.e. especially concerning Hugon – would lubricate the general amnesty.[16] The king was naturally delighted by this assurance. Unfortunately, in a separate letter to Mayerne, Herbert was more particular. He told him that all was now well, for he had secured a promise of his 'pardon'.

A promise of pardon indeed! That was not at all what Mayerne meant by 'satisfaction'. It implied that he had been at fault, and, moreover, that the king, in supporting him, was conniving at his fault, and was therefore an accomplice in it, and that his royal word was disbelieved: honour was at stake. When a casual postscript to a later letter caused the king to send for Mayerne and thus brought the two letters together, the royal wrath exploded. Herbert, by this time, had now retired from the heat and plague of Paris to the rural ease of the Duchesse de Ventadour's château of Merlou, where he had stayed, during her father's time, to perfect his French and his horsemanship.[17] These nostalgic memories were rudely shaken by a severe letter from Secretary Naunton, transmitting, in more controlled form, the royal explosion. His Majesty, said Naunton, was 'much displeased at the miscarrying of Mr. Mayerne his business'; and after setting out the facts, he concluded,

> I am commanded to write unto you that, 'if you have indeed transgressed his Majesty's instructions so far as to sue for Mayerne's pardon, implying him by that means confessedly to be guilty of some fault, . . . there is no other way for you to make it straight again, but to tell that King that you

must ask both him and the king our master pardon for that mistake, his Majesty's directions to you being expressly these: to let that king know that if they would lay any fault to Mayerne's charge, his Majesty would see it punished as it deserved. Otherwise he desired that he might be restored to the king's favour, and have leave to pass to and fro between England and France as his occasions should require.'[18]

Scarcely had Herbert received this letter when it was followed by another, from Mayerne himself. He was particularly outraged because, in the general disclosure of documents, he had discovered, from Herbert's letter to the king, that the king had offered, if Mayerne should be proved at fault, to 'punish' him.[19] That of course was yet another insult, and since the phrase about punishment had been cited by Herbert, he ascribed it to him. Herbert now had a busy time writing emollient letters from the château de Merlou. He wrote to Naunton, to the king, to Mayerne. To Naunton he set out the facts and 'satisfied all objections'.[20] To Mayerne he apologised, for having written in misleading language.[21] To the king he explained that the whole fuss was due to a misunderstanding: it 'hath no other ground but the mistaking of Monsieur de Mayerne', whose sensitivity in his own cause showed 'more of the sick man than the physician'; and he offered to take upon himself the responsibility for the unfortunate phrase about punishment, 'that I may not leave any dislike in one so near your Majesty's person'.[22]

So gradually – very gradually – the great affair died down. Everyone was weary of it except Mayerne, and he could hardly keep the battle going for ever, especially in those dramatic months when all Europe was in commotion. Besides, there were those other reasons, 'private to M. de Mayerne', which Beecher had mentioned and to which we will come. So, by February 1620 the new French ambassador, the Comte de Tillières, could write that 'M. de Mayerne is now settling down and wishes, for the future, to give no cause for suspicion in France.' Three months later, having received an informal assurance through his old patient the Maréchal de Bassompierre that the King of France regarded him as his faithful subject and would grant any reasonable request, he decided, after a good deal of smouldering and spluttering, to accept what was offered, at least as a first instalment. The Venetian ambassador also reported that Leclerc had been expelled in retaliation for the expulsion of Mayerne. Since he had to swallow the bitter drink quietly, he said, he would do so – while reserving his right to go on grumbling, which he did, to some tune, for several years. In long, obsequious letters to the French ministers, he would dwell on his absolute, hereditary loyalty to the French crown, expose the still bleeding wounds in his honour and his pride – wounds which still needed to be anointed with the balm of compensation and revenge. He would demand assurances that he would be welcome if he should seek to revisit France, and protest his exaggerated gratitude for benefits still to come: he was 'only an atom' in the world, but 'the memory of a benefit would never perish in his heart.'[23]

This gradual, self-righteous surrender had its reasons. Mayerne's breach with the French government damaged him not only in his pride but in his interests. He still held an office at the French court, as *médecin par quartier*, and this office entitled him to a salary. His tenure of that office had for some years been contested by a rival claimant, who naturally exploited Mayerne's absence, and the salary had by now fallen into arrears. Moreover, he was also engaged in certain economic speculations for which the good will of the French government was necessary. We shall describe them in due course. These two material concerns – what Mayerne summarised as 'l'advancement de mes affaires'[24] – were never far from his mind when he lamented the great insult of 1618; they are perhaps the 'other reasons private to M. de Mayerne' mentioned by Beecher; and they may explain his slow and tortuous retreat from his first demand of unconditional surrender to the ultimate acceptance of a compromise peace.

On their side, the French ministers were also eager to settle the diplomatic breach with England which had been precipitated by the unfortunate affair of 1618. Their reasons were political. For Mayerne had only been back in England for a month when the Protestant military leadership in Europe carried out its great coup: the revolution in Prague, the 'defenestration' of the Catholic ministers, and the offer, to the Elector Palatine, of the crown of Bohemia. With that offer, by the Bohemian estates, and its acceptance, by the titular leader of the Protestant union, Christian of Anhalt scored, it seemed, his greatest triumph. Not only was there a Protestant King of Bohemia: there was also, if his election was accepted as valid, a Protestant majority in the imperial diet which elected the emperor. The Habsburg domination of Europe was threatened; and as the Habsburg domination was the secular base of the Counter-Reformation, Antichrist himself must tremble on his throne. All over Europe the Protestant enthusiasts crowed in triumph. The ancient prophecies, they cried, were now to be fulfilled. The millennium was at hand.

The city of Heidelberg, in that year, became the capital of an international revolution. The German elector – grandson of William of Orange and his French wife Charlotte de Bourbon-Montpensier, nephew of the Huguenot Duc de Bouillon, son-in-law of the King of England – ruled over a cosmopolitan court. We happen to see a sample of that cosmopolis in the *album amicorum* of a Breton gentleman, a client of the Duc de Rohan, who was there in this very year, immediately after the elector had accepted the Bohemian crown. Among those who signed his album are Elizabeth, the new English

Queen of Bohemia; Christian of Anhalt, the political adviser of the coup; the Duke of Zweibrücken, Rohan's brother-in-law, who administered the Palatinate while the new king was in Prague; the old Duchess of Rohan and two of her daughters; the Swiss Christian Wolfgang von Erlach; three Danes; and Louise de Mayerne, Mayerne's younger sister, whom he had placed, through Lady Harrington, with the Princess Elizabeth while the princess was still in England. There is also a cosmopolitan group of scholars: Georg Michael Lingelsheim; the humanist tutor and secretary of the elector; David Paraeus, the Heidelberg theologian; Denys Godefroy, the Swiss jurist, now at Heidelberg; Janus Gruter, the Dutch scholar, now librarian of the great Palatine Library; and Matthias Pasor, the orientalist from Herborn, the avant-garde university of the house of Orange-Nassau. The album is a record of the élite of Protestant Europe, gathered in Heidelberg to witness the triumph of the cause.[25]

A year later, on 31 October, the new King and Queen of Bohemia entered Prague, with Louise de Mayerne in their train, and prepared to solemnise their coronation amid Calvinist rejoicing which included Puritan iconoclasm and millenarian enthusiasm. They reigned for one winter. Then came the Catholic and Habsburg revenge. The Duke of Bavaria, as general of the emperor, invaded Bohemia. The government of France, for all its traditional jealousy of the house of Habsburg, supported the Catholic cause: it was now dominated by Luynes and the *dévots*. King James, for all his Protestantism and love of his daughter, refused to help: he wished to maintain the balance in a peaceful Europe, not to overthrow it by a reckless adventure. On 8 November 1620, at the battle of the White Mountain, that adventure came to an end. The Bavarian army occupied Prague. Bohemian Protestantism, and Bohemian independence with it, were destroyed – destroyed for three centuries. The dethroned king and queen fled through Germany to find a final exile in The Hague; and soon the Palatinate itself would be given over to the plunder of Spanish and Bavarian armies.

Meanwhile, in France, the Huguenots were caught unprepared. In April 1620 the queen mother had challenged the rule of Luynes. Rohan imprudently committed the Huguenots to her cause. At that time the Protestants were still riding high, and Rohan could write to James I as the royal patron of a victorious cause, 'the greatest king of those who call upon his name in purity at a time when he is performing miracles for the increase of his Church'.[26] But the queen mother, betrayed by her adviser Richelieu, was defeated in battle at Pont-de-Cé; Luynes and Richelieu were reconciled; and the discarded Huguenots were left to pay the price. Luynes was now able to turn the whole force of the Crown against the last stronghold of the Huguenots in the south. The royal army entered Pau; Catholicism was restored by force in Béarn; and on 7 November 1620 – the day before the battle of the White Mountain – Louis XIII returned in triumph to Paris.

Such was the inglorious débâcle of the great Protestant crusade of 1618–20. Next year, when the twelve-year Truce of 1609 ran out, and the Spanish government renewed the war against its 'rebels' in the Netherlands, it seemed that international Protestantism was doomed. Its prophecies had been exploded. Its defeated remnants were gathering in disconnected citadels of defence: in the southern massif of France and the Huguenot city of la Rochelle; in Geneva and the Protestant cantons of Switzerland; and among the swamps and dykes of Holland. How long, it might be asked, could it hold out even there? The French crown was determined to eliminate the Huguenots in the south; the Spaniards were determined to crush the rebels in the north; and the pope saw his chance of destroying at last the unprotected heretical capital of Geneva.

Of those three redoubts, the last seemed now the weakest and the most exposed. In the past, Geneva and the Protestant cantons of Switzerland had relied on the protection of France, while the Catholic cantons were bound by treaty to Spain. It was a French expert who had designed the fortifications of Geneva, a French army which had defended the city in 1610, and there was a resident French ambassador to the cantons in the Catholic town of Solothurn. After 1610, when French policy was uncertain, the Protestant cantons began to look closely at their defences. Zürich and Berne, the two strongest cantons, took the lead, and in 1612 entered into an agreement with an elderly but reliable German condottiere, Georg-Friedrich, disinherited Margrave of Baden-Durlach. The margrave was a sound Protestant, who claimed to have read the whole Bible fifty-eight times, and a great strategist, who would write a three-volume work on the theory of war. He now undertook to organise the defence of the cantons. At the same time the cantons looked further afield for diplomatic support: to the recently formed Union of German Protestant princes, and beyond them, to England.

The canton of Berne and the city of Geneva had both been in contact with the English government since the beginning of the century; but the contact had been intermittent and casual. Geneva had made use of the services of Étienne le Sieur, a French Huguenot who had begun as secretary to the French ambassador in London and would end as Sir Stephen Lesieur, English ambassador to the emperor. King James, immediately after his accession, had relied on one John Craig, who was then in Geneva. Perhaps this was his Scottish court doctor of that name. In Berne, Queen Elizabeth had relied on one Paul Lentulus, who was also one of her court doctors.[27] We have already seen that Henri IV had used his court doctor du Chesne as diplomatic agent in Switzerland. There were thus good precedents for the use of royal physicians as intermediaries in Swiss diplomacy, and in 1615 Mayerne found himself drawn into that diplomacy. The man who drew him in was a Swiss patient, Hans Rudolf von Erlach von Riggisburg.

Hans Rudolf von Erlach came from a prominent Bernese family. His elder brother, Franz Ludwig von Erlach, Freiherr von Spiez, was a member of the Inner Council of Berne and a regular ambassador for the city. In 1615, Hans Rudolf von Erlach was sent as Bernese envoy to France, but his overtures were not welcomed by the French government, which would show its distrust by interfering with his despatches. No doubt it suspected him too of complicity with its Huguenot rebels. Erlach thereupon moved on to London. Ostensibly, he came to consult Mayerne, to whom he had been recommended by a famous German surgeon, Wilhelm Fabri von Hilden, best known as Fabricius Hildanus, who was physician to the city of Berne and also to its military protector, the Margrave of Baden-Durlach. He was suffering from an unfortunate complaint which Mayerne customarily described as *caruncula*, a urinary obstruction caused, in this instance, by 'a particularly energetic copulation'. Mayerne was an expert on the *caruncula*, of which he had cured Cardinal de Richelieu. However, although his medical needs provided the occasion of Erlach's visit, there was also a political purpose. He was seeking English support for the Swiss confederation. The French ambassador in London, who was deeply suspicious of this 'soy-disant ambassadeur' and spied on him busily, noted that, in spite of all his own attempts to discredit him, Erlach was received by the king and defended by Mayerne, who 'parades him here and would have us believe that he is the best man in the world'. The Venetian ambassador similarly reported that the 'baron d'Arlac' had called upon him with a letter of introduction from Mayerne. Erlach, he added, had come to England in order to place himself under the treatment of Mayerne for stricture of the urethra, but had used the opportunity to have many long interviews with the king, seeking his intervention with the Duke of Savoy to maintain the peace in Switzerland.[28]

James I responded warmly to Erlach's overtures. He urged him to work for a defensive union with the German princes[29] and instructed his ambassadors in Venice and Savoy (which was then at war with Spain) to cooperate; as they did – Sir Isaac Wake in Savoy acted as a firm friend and mediator for the Swiss cantons and Geneva,[30] and it was largely through his efforts that a treaty of mutual defence between Berne, Geneva and Savoy was at last hammered out in June 1617. This treaty – the treaty of St Julien – was claimed as a great coup for Jacobean diplomacy. For the immediate future it gave a new sense of security to Geneva and the Protestant cantons. The French government was mortified: the French minister Villeroy protested that Geneva had sought the protection of the King of England 'au mépris de Sa Majesté très chrétienne', and stopped the annual subsidy which had been paid to Geneva since 1600. In spite of many alarms, the treaty of St Julien proved a great success: it would preserve Switzerland in peace throughout the Thirty Years War.

At first, this could hardly be guessed. For within a year of the treaty the whole European balance of power was convulsed by the Protestant coup in Prague. Two months later, in July 1618, it was followed by another Protestant coup in that vital Alpine pass, the Valtelline. Next year Christian of Anhalt was in Savoy and a close alliance was made between Savoy and Venice. It was an alliance against the Habsburgs. However, this Protestant advance was short-lived. In 1620 came the reaction. The Catholics massacred the Protestant rulers of the Valtelline and handed the vital pass over to Spain. Then came the battle of the White Mountain. With France still hostile and German Protestantism in total disarray, the delicate machinery of Swiss security was shattered. How could the Margrave of Baden Durlach alone stand up to victorious Bavarian and Spanish armies? What help could England give? How could that notorious opportunist, the Catholic Duke of Savoy, be trusted to keep the treaty he had signed? In the total collapse of European Protestantism, Geneva itself seemed an easy prey. To those who believed the revelations of Gaspar Baronius, it was clear that the Catholic crusade had begun. And sure enough, in July 1621, amid the jubilation of universal victory, Pope Gregory XV sent a special emissary to the courts of Savoy and France to prepare for the final reckoning with the infamous city of Calvin.

The instructions which the Pope gave to his emissary, Father Corona, glow with complacency at the prospect before him. Geneva, he points out, has no territory or dignity. It is a cramped city swarming with plebeian and mechanic people, living a free and disorderly life, careless of military glory or true learning: in short, 'the cess-pit of Europe'. That such a centre of infection should be tolerated, and should discharge its poisonous refuse over neighbouring countries, is a public scandal. It must be destroyed. To destroy it is the duty of the pope and, next under him, the Duke of Savoy. Now an opportunity has arisen such as may not recur for another century. Father Corona is to go to Turin and deploy every argument. He must dwell on 'the tears of the pope, the salvation of the Church, the military ambition of the Duke of Savoy'. He must not take no for an answer. Then he must go on to Paris and woo the King of France. There he must deploy different arguments. He must speak of the pope's desire to contribute to the unity of France by reducing the Protestant enclaves of la Rochelle, Sedan, Orange. In return, the king must allow Geneva to be conquered by Savoy. Geneva is the Rome of the heretics, but now that the heretics have their backs to the wall in their several lairs, they cannot come out to save it. Therefore let the king now give up for good 'the policy of Henri IV and the damnable protection of Geneva'. Let him concentrate on the conquest of la Rochelle, and leave Geneva to its fate. There is no room for jealousy here. The gain to Savoy will be slight, Geneva having become famous only for the evil that is in it. If the king should agree in principle, but should wish to lead the attack himself, Father Corona is to praise his zeal but answer firmly, No: that would not do at all. Corona is to cultivate Luynes and the Cardinal de Retz, and to work on the king's confessor – to promise him a college for his order in conquered Geneva. 'In one word, try everything and do not allow yourself to be put off by one or two refusals.'[31]

Such were the dramatic events of the years 1618–21: years which saw the brief triumph and catastrophic fall of the Calvinist international, the total loss of the Palatinate and Bohemia, the deadly peril of Geneva itself. And yet in the very midst of this crisis, Theodore de Mayerne made a remarkable decision: he took steps to transfer his base from England and establish it in Switzerland, a few miles from Geneva.

Why did he make this dramatic decision? Was he weary of England and the courtier's life? Was it social ambition: the desire to found a dynasty in the region of his birth? Or was it loyalty to the cause of international Protestantism: a wish to be at the centre of affairs in such decisive times? Was it indeed connected with these events at all, or was it a mere coincidence? And why did he choose to be not a citizen of French Calvinist Geneva, the place of his birth, but a subject of Lutheran German-speaking Berne? For the property which he bought was the castle of Aubonne, a feudal barony in the pays de Vaud, then (and until the French Revolution) a subject territory of the canton of Berne. He bought it, unvisited, unseen, on 7 October 1620, just a month before the fatal battle of the White Mountain.

15

Baron d'Aubonne, 1620–1621

As far as we know, Mayerne had no early association with the canton of Berne. His first contact with the governing oligarchy of that canton seems to have been with his patient, the special ambassador, Hans Rudolf von Erlach, who had visited England in 1615. It seems that Erlach became a close friend of Mayerne. He was also grateful to him, for Mayerne completely cured his complaint. When Erlach was returning to Switzerland in order to represent Berne in the negotiations for Sir Isaac Wake's treaty with Savoy, Mayerne wrote to Fabricius, the Bernese doctor who had sent Erlach to him, boasting of his triumph: 'the royal highway of seed and urine is now wide open, and the liquid which, until lately, was exuded with great effort and drop by drop is now delivered in a copious, continuous, direct stream.'[1] 'Your friend', he added, 'will tell all on his arrival in Berne.'[2]

From this little urinary rectification many other results were to flow. Mayerne, we have already noticed, seems to have been in low spirits in 1616, and in the course of his professional attendance on von Erlach he released some of his inhibitions. He was uncomplimentary about life in England. The English nobility, he said, gave no example except in eating, drinking, smoking tobacco and wasting time.[3] In writing to Fabricius he also expressed a certain frustration. 'My letter would swell into a volume if I were to tell you all,' he wrote – he was still preening himself on his cure of von Erlach's ailment – but alas, he had no leisure to dilate upon his medical discoveries, let alone to publish them.[4] It is clear that in 1616 Mayerne was beginning to tire of England and life at court. He longed to continue his researches and enjoy the civilised company of Europe. Like du Chesne at the end of his life, he began to hanker for the spirit of republican freedom. Especially he must have hankered in that spring of 1616, when the Overbury scandal was at its height. On the other hand, he liked money and he had his social ambitions. His wife came from a grand family, and knew it. He had to keep up with the van Boetzelaers.

The other court doctors, his models, had become landed proprietors in France: the Sieur de la Rivière, the Sieur de la Violette. However, Mayerne did not want an estate in France: the time when a Huguenot landlord could feel safe in France was past. Nor could he be tempted by an estate in England: his remonstrances to his Dutch brother-in-law show that. Geneva was his real home. If he was to found a landed dynasty it must be in Protestant Switzerland near Geneva. That meant, in effect, in the pays de Vaud: the territory between the Jura mountains and the Lake of Geneva, which had been wrested from Savoy in 1535 and was now ruled as a subject territory by the canton of Berne.

To the Berne oligarchy, 'MM. de Berne', 'Their Excellencies of Berne', this must have been an acceptable hint. Their city was now taking the lead in Swiss affairs, and with the growing dangers around them they were glad to welcome influential immigrants. They particularly needed reliable feudatories in the pays de Vaud, which the Duke of Savoy still hoped to recover. To them, therefore, Mayerne would be a welcome immigrant. He was a man of great influence: the confidant of kings and princes, the familiar friend of the élite of Protestant Europe. But would he really come? In 1616 it must have seemed unlikely. Then, in 1619, he received a reminder of royal mortality – one of those dynastic accidents which had caused him to change countries once, and might cause him to change again.

For in 1619 one of his royal patients died. Queen Anne had long been ailing: indeed, on 11 January 1618, between dropsy, scurvy and gout she had almost been given up, and Mayerne, who had resorted to an alchemical remedy of 'Trougny[5] – vitriol of iron – had uttered, in his notebook, a topical reflexion: 'NB: always call in colleagues to a royal person, even if the patient refuses . . . but while this is done, the infirmity increases and it is too late for iron potions.' It is a reminiscence, no doubt, of the case of Prince Henry. Then follows, in red, the Virgilian valediction

Nox ruit Aenea, nos flendo ducimus horas.[6]

The queen recovered then; but it would clearly not be for long, and a year later she died in her sleep, 'exhausted by scurvy, with many bleedings through the nose'.[7] At the time of her death, the king was ill at Newmarket, and was thought to be dying too. Mayerne may well have supposed, at that time, that his own future in England was uncertain. For the time being, he took rational steps to ensure that the family income did not suffer. He secured the continuation of his salary in respect of the queen, though she was dead, and a grant of £100 down and a pension of £60 a year, from the Court of Wards, to his sister Marie, for good and faithful service as one of the queen's ladies.[8] But it would have been imprudent not to look ahead; and to look ahead, for him, was to look abroad.

Looking abroad, he might also note another prominent migration. Two months after the death of the Queen of England, the most famous of the old Huguenot heroes, Agrippa d'Aubigné, renounced his own country, France. Dismayed by the opportunist alliance of Rohan – the one leader whom he respected – with the queen mother, he decided to retire (he was now sixty-seven) to the place of his education, the one true city of the faith, Geneva. So he handed over his governorship of Maillezais, and his impregnable château of Dognon, to Rohan, whom he told that he was not willing to be of the queen's 'party', though he added that he would be of Rohan's party to the end.[9] He went first to the Huguenot stronghold of St Jean d'Angély. From there he had his *Histoire universelle* printed at his own expense. He 'held it a great honour to see it condemned and burnt at the Collège Royal in Paris'.[10] Then he made his way to Geneva. He arrived there, to a solemn civic reception, on 1 September 1620. Soon he would be building himself a fine house in Geneva, Le Crest, and would marry a lady from one of the most international of Genevese families, Renée Burlamachi, the widow of Caesar Balbani.

It was at this moment that Mayerne – doubtless through Erlach – received the news that the canton of Berne would be willing to sell to him the castle and barony of Aubonne. This was a property which had been confiscated in 1615, when its last owner, François Vilain, bourgeois of Geneva, had been convicted of high treason.[11] The resale of such a barony was a ticklish matter. There were very few private baronies in the pays de Vaud, and it was essential that they should be in reliable hands; for the country, being French and Calvinist, did not always submit quietly to its remote German and Lutheran overlords; and the case of Vilain was fresh in memory. After him, Mayerne must have seemed a very suitable feudatory. So, on 7 October 1620, the sale was agreed, for 24,300 *écus bernois*. The formalities of transfer would take another ten months. Mayerne's possession would be finally confirmed on 21 August 1621.[12]

Mayerne's attitude, at the time of his purchase, is illustrated by a long letter which he wrote, four days later, to his friend Samuel Durant, Huguenot minister in Paris and protégé of the Rohan family. Durant had evidently informed Mayerne of an important convert to Protestantism – one Granier, nephew of the late Catholic Bishop of Geneva[13] – and had suggested that Mayerne should find employment for this valuable proselyte somewhere where he could be an advertisement for the faith. Perhaps, Durant suggested, he could be placed in the household of the even more spectacular convert, Marcantonio de Dominis, Archbishop of Spalato, who had recently been welcomed and liberally rewarded in England. In reply, Mayerne expressed doubt about the archbishop, who, he said, was rather stuffy and would only take Italians, and very dubious Italians at that. He advised that Granier should announce his conversion not in England but in 'the theatre of Europe' – that is, in France – both for public effect and to avoid any difficulty with 'the suspicious humours' of the English, who are 'never at a loss for carping criticism when there is any question of promoting foreigners'. England, he added, somewhat ungratefully, was 'very sterile' in posts for foreigners, and those available are 'poor and menial, intolerable to a generous spirit'. Sometimes something better turned up; but the problem then was how to net such a post for one's protégés. So he gave exact advice: ambassadors must be mobilised; concerted letters must be sent to well-chosen peers; the greatest finesse must be used; and thus a mine could be sprung which would have the desired effect ... Then, having put the English in their place, Mayerne turned to his own affairs. God willing, he would be in Paris in the spring 'with my eldest son, whom I wish to transplant entirely from this country': could the minister find a good lodging for 'an alert little chap, quick tempered, no lover of books, very good natured, easily won by kindness, never by force'?[14] This was his heir, Henri, the godson of the Duc de Rohan, now twelve years old; and Mayerne, whatever his own plans, wanted to plant his dynasty outside England – in Aubonne.

After the purchase had been agreed, one of the first to congratulate Mayerne was his medical friend in Berne, Fabricius Hildanus. Fabricius had evidently known Mayerne earlier, and had probably himself been one of his agents in the matter. He expressed his pleasure that all had turned out as Mayerne had wished, and that they would now be able to continue their learned discussions in person. 'I am sure that you will be charmed by the place. It is quite delightful. I doubt whether, in all that area on the north of Lake Leman, you could find anywhere more attractive, healthier or more fertile . . .'[15] Fabricius dated his letter 3 November 1620. A few days later came the battle of the White Mountain.

The catastrophic consequences of that great defeat were not at first apparent. It was, after all, only a local battle in a far-off country, little known. Only when the victorious Bavarian armies moved to the Rhine and the Spaniards renewed the war against the Dutch did the Bohemian disaster come to be seen to be the beginning of a general war. On 27 December Mayerne received first-hand news of the battle from M. de Martines, the secretary of Francis Nethersole, the Queen of Bohemia's English adviser. He reacted calmly. The defeat, he agreed, was very unfortunate, but it did not altogether surprise him, since the house of Austria could hardly be expected to accept such an affront lying down, and the King of Bohemia was singularly ill-equipped for serious war: he had no allies, no military leaders, and only a ragged mutinous army. We must hope, said Mayerne, that God will now come to the rescue. 'I have no taste for meddling with affairs of state,' he went on, implausibly, 'in which private persons find only danger and frustration, and then, when they have worn themselves out by the effort, receive scant reward.' We are reminded that Mayerne was writing only five months after his misadventure in Paris. Then he went on to personal matters. His sister – that is his youngest sister Louise, maid of honour to the ruined queen – had lost all, just when she was due to be married to a Huguenot retainer of the electoral family;[16] but on Mayerne's advice she would continue to serve the queen in adversity. He could give no other advice, for

> although I may have my faults, at least I never abandon my friends in need
> ... Throughout all these tempests, I have steadily pursued my project of
> Aubonne and now, thank God, I have been lord of the place for three
> months, and am preparing to go there as soon as possible and put my
> family in possession. I had been looking forward to having M. d'Estoy as a
> neighbour there,[17] but I hear that he is dead in Bohemia: a great pity. But I
> shall have plenty of other friends there, and am promised every civility. It is
> a great blessing to have a place of one's own in some corner of the world.[18]

A little later, he wrote to thank Fabricius for his letter of congratulation: 'May Almighty God grant, to me and mine, a long and peaceful enjoyment of my purchase ... I am planning (God willing) to fly off and visit it very soon; for although it is mine, I do not yet know it.'[19]

If Mayerne was to fly off from England to Aubonne, the natural route lay through France. He had not set foot in France since the humiliation of 1618, for which he had not yet (as he thought) received adequate amends. However, it seems that he was now determined to return to Paris. For some months he had been preparing the ground. He had written to Brûlart de Puysieux, the French Secretary of State, requesting an assurance that he would be welcome there and could travel in safety and honour, as a good and faithful subject and servant of the king;[20] he had told Samuel Durant that he hoped to see him in Paris in the spring of 1621;[21] and in March 1621 he made practical arrangements. He applied to the French government for a passport, and the French ambassador warmly supported the application.[22] He arranged for his wife to go to Holland, to stay with her relations while he went through France.[23] And it seems that he planned to meet, in Paris, the survivors of his old Hermetic circle, and, in particular, 'Hermes' himself – his old Huguenot friend from Orléans, Guillaume de Trougny.

In fact, for Mayerne, this 'iter Albonense', this journey to Aubonne, was to be something of a Hermetic pilgrimage. For the first time since his schooldays he was to revisit the city of his birth, and on the way he was to renew old acquaintances and discover new secrets. In preparation for the visit, he compiled a book, written in his own hand throughout, and entitled 'Viaticum, or formulae for medical experiments: the traveller's handbook, *anno* 1621'.[24] Although, like all Mayerne's notebooks, it has many later entries, so that we can never be sure when updated passages were written, the original character of the book is fairly clear. It is a list of mineral remedies and experiments, together with arcane Hermetic poems, citations from alchemists old and new, apocryphal and real; speculations, projections, transmutations. The dominant names throughout are those of his alchemical friends in Paris: Quercetanus, 'Neptis', Trougny.

However, in spite of all these preparations, it seems that, at the last minute, Mayerne changed his plans. He did not go through France; instead, he seems to have diverted his wife from Holland and sent her, as his representative, with their family, to Paris, where of course she could stay with her brother the Dutch ambassador.[25] What had caused the change, we do not know: his note-books are silent, and for a whole year there is a gap in his *Ephemerides*. Perhaps the guarantees from France, if they came, were insufficient for that proud spirit: for he was still demanding public apologies and an opportunity, by his presence in Paris, to expose 'the bad conscience' of his enemies'.[26] Or perhaps public events – the renewal of religious war in France which caused a flight of Huguenots from Paris – made such a journey inopportune. For once again, in spite of his public professions, he was not travelling in a purely personal capacity. As the Venetian ambassador reported, Mayerne, though he was still going to Switzerland 'ostensibly on his private affairs', 'is thought to have some commission from his Majesty for the said cantons'. The ambassador himself was sceptical of this belief.[27] Yet Mayerne was in fact secretly supplied with formal letters from King James to the canton of Berne and to the city of Geneva.[28] In these circumstances he could not risk another misadventure in France.

Of the details of his journey, we know nothing. Probably he went to Holland, and then travelled up the Rhine. All that we can say for certain is that at the end of March 1621 he was still in London, expecting to leave, and that he was in Geneva by 18 June.[29] He arrived to find a letter from Agrippa d'Aubigné.[30] It was a letter which was to mark the beginning of a new intimacy, and a new sphere of political activity. It also illustrated the radical transformation of European politics which had taken place since Mayerne set out.

For now the Bohemian affair could no longer be regarded as an isolated event in central Europe, a temporary internal disturbance of the Habsburg empire. Now the armies were everywhere on the move. The King of France had declared open war on the Huguenots. La Rochelle stood firm in defiance.

Rohan was organising the defence of Languedoc. His brother Soubise was holding out in St Jean d'Angély. The Rhineland was in commotion. The pope was savouring the thought of the conquest of Geneva. Mayerne, who had set out for the 'peaceful enjoyment' of his Swiss château, had arrived to find all Switzerland, and Geneva itself, in a state of alarm; and there was his fellow-Huguenot, like some Hebrew prophet sent from God, in a posture of command, beckoning him to share the burden of the holy war.

'I would ask', d'Aubigné wrote to Mayerne, 'for some correspondence between us, as a sign that the honour and friendship in which I hold you are acknowledged by you. This honest bearer will give you an account of our condition more freely than my pen would dare.' For now the standard of the crusade which had been prepared for 1622 – that is, the crusade revealed by Gaspar Baronius in 1601 – 'has been hoisted a year and a half earlier by the tug of Bohemia'. The citizens of Geneva, he lamented, had forgotten what it was to fight, and shrank even from preparation for war. Those of the Grisons, surprised by the Habsburg coup in the Valtelline, were flapping their wings only to discover their own weakness. The Duke of Savoy was an enigma, but his ambitions were not: in return for supporting France, he wanted Geneva and the whole French-speaking area; 'and then you shall have him for your sovereign and I shall be dispossessed.' The Protestants of France now had their backs to the wall. King James's moderation did but serve the Habsburg cause: 'God grant that this new treaty with Spain' – that is, the treaty of a Spanish marriage for his son the Prince of Wales – 'does not open the way for the assassination of his sacred person and machinations against his kingdom.'

Mayerne responded willingly to d'Aubigné's approach. They met, and they corresponded.[31] They discussed diplomacy and fortifications. At one of their meetings, d'Aubigné showed Mayerne an interesting engine on which he had been working, and to which we shall return.[32] At the same time, Mayerne was in direct touch with the Petit Conseil, the rulers of the city of Geneva. Immediately on his arrival – perhaps immediately on receiving d'Aubigné's letter – he sought out one of the syndics of Geneva, M. Larchevesque, and told him that he was charged by the King of Great Britain, his master, to assure the city of his good will; and he then offered, out of his own sincere and cordial affection, to act as the agent of the city at the English court. When this was reported to it, the Petit Conseil agreed to thank him and to invite him, next day, to dinner.[33]

From now on, d'Aubigné and Mayerne worked together for the defence of Geneva and Switzerland against the imminent danger of a final conquest. The indomitable Huguenot warrior-poet, whose experience of ideology and war went back fifty years, beyond the massacre of St Bartholomew, had retired to spend his old age in Geneva just in time to become the animating spirit of a new resistance; and the energetic, acquisitive Huguenot doctor, dreaming of leisure for research and writing, had come to take possession of his rural château just in time to be swept into his wake. Mayerne might declare, in his letters, that he did not meddle with affairs of state; but who could believe that? In fact, he loved to be in the centre of things; and now, once again, he was. Expelled from France, and chary of returning to that scene of his humiliation, he discovered, in the agonising autumn and winter of 1621–2, a new centre of activity in Switzerland.

In the face of the threat of conquest, the city of Geneva, on 4 September 1621, set up a Council of War, with seven members. One of them was d'Aubigné, who was in charge of the fortifications. Two days later, two of the syndics – MM. Colladon and Chasteauneuf – had a long conversation with Mayerne, who suggested that, before writing to King James, they write to the Duke of Savoy asking him to explain his levy of troops and the extraordinary military preparations that were visible from their walls. Next month, we find Mayerne regularly closeted with the governors of Geneva, drafting letters from them to King James, advising them about diplomatic representation, suggesting names of generals. James I should be reminded (he said) that previously he had helped the Duke of Savoy against Spain: now it was time to restrain him and help Geneva against Savoy. It was essential, he insisted, that a regular envoy be sent to London: it was not enough to give a commission to Philip Burlamachi, already there; nor would he dare to accept the post himself. As for a general, there was much to be said – if King James agreed – for a proposal to hire the English soldier of fortune Sir Henry Peyton, who was at present commanding the English forces of the Republic of Venice. But the immediate need was money. Collections could be organised in England. In all this, the city should enlist the support of Isaac Wake in Turin, 'if only to impress on His Majesty your present danger'. In the end, the decision about the envoy to be sent to London was left entirely to Mayerne.[34] Meanwhile a special emissary, Benedetto Turrettini, was sent to the Netherlands, to seek advice from that great military authority, the Prince of Orange. The prince would duly send an expert to join d'Aubigné, and the city walls would be strengthened on their recommendations. It was also agreed to seek advice from the prince's brother-in-law, the Duc de Bouillon, in Sedan.

'Your imminent danger will spur me on,' Mayerne wrote to the Petit Conseil of Geneva, 'and I shall always prefer the public good to my own.' However, he naturally expected his own good to be considered, and he added that he would expect, 'while I work for you', that the city would protect his interests and would advise his family what to do 'if things should hot up'. 'By the favour which my wife and children receive from you', he added, 'I shall judge your good will to me.' Evidently Mayerne intended to place his family permanently at Aubonne even while he was in England.[35]

For now he was at Aubonne and could survey the property which he had bought unseen. It was indeed a seigneurial estate, more appropriate to a medieval warrior baron than to a modern, avant-garde court-physician; but then it is a great mistake to see Huguenots, Calvinists, Protestants as necessarily more 'modern' than their ideological rivals. The castle of Aubonne still stands: a huge *château fort*, surrounded by high circular stone ramparts and dominated by a great cylindrical, domed stone tower, rising from its underground dungeon, grim, high and blind except for occasional narrow slit eyes which squint malevolently over that fresh, delightful land.[36] And that land now belonged to Mayerne: a fine estate of cornfields, vineyards and pasture on the southward slopes of the Jura mountains, with feudal rights and jurisdiction, taxes and rents, tithes of wine and corn, tolls of roads and bridges, rights of mills and of butchery ('all the tongues of all the beasts slaughtered there'), 'noble' lieges and vassals, profits of justice, perquisites of all kinds, obedient peasants in his fields, obedient Calvinist ministers in his four parsonages.[37] Mayerne surveyed it with pleasure. He was now a nobleman, 'Baron d'Aubonne'. The phrase 'dominatio tua', 'your lordship', tinkled musically in his ears as he read it in the grave Latin letters of his fellow-doctors, among learned discussions of bowels and bladders, the itch and the stone. Now he could hold his own with the grandees among whom he moved at the English court, and with the van Boetzelaers too; and he intended to relish his new status, to use his rights, and to exact all that was due to him from those whom he now regularly called 'my subjects'.

Of course, everything depended on politics – politics and war. In his zeal for the cause, Mayerne was also protecting his own investment. When he looked abroad, he could see ominous portents. Already, in conquered Bohemia, the Protestant castles were being confiscated, and Protestant 'barons' driven out, as the Habsburg administrators and the Jesuits poured in. Always there was the danger that Mayerne, having taken such care to find a barony in a safe Protestant republic, would wake up to find himself the subject of a Catholic duke. Sometimes it seemed to him that only a miracle could save Geneva and the pays de Vaud. Fortunately the pays de Vaud was not only the essential hinterland of Geneva: it was also the forward bastion and colony of the canton of Berne; and Berne was now the acknowledged leader of the Swiss confederation. Therefore, after Geneva, Mayerne and d'Aubigné turned their attention, and offered their services, to Berne.

In November 1621 d'Aubigné paid his first visit to Berne. It was a visit of reconnaissance, to inspect the fortifications of the city and to examine the prospects of resistance if the confederation should be attacked. In the same month, Mayerne began his journey home, and he too decided to pass through Berne; for Berne too was using him as its unofficial diplomatic agent. When he left, he carried important political messages from both Geneva and Berne. There were messages for King James in England. There were also messages to be delivered, on the way, at Sedan. For Mayerne had agreed to go in person, as the envoy of the two cities, to that great politician of the Huguenot movement, its essential link with the princes of Germany and the house of Orange in the Netherlands, the Duc de Bouillon, who was also his patient.

In the letter which he carried from Geneva to James I, the magistrates of that city thanked the king for his good will towards them, which he had proved by keeping their firm friend Sir Isaac Wake in Turin 'and again, more recently, by sending M. de Mayerne', whom they now asked to represent the gravity of their present situation.[38] The letter from the magistrates of Berne was more explicit. The assurance of royal support brought by the Sieur de Mayerne, Baron d'Aubonne, *premier médecin de Vôtre Majesté*, they wrote, 'overwhelms us with obligations'. Now, since an irresistible torrent was over-whelming the common cause, making it essential for all Protestants to unite, they turned naturally to King James. The said baron, in whom all parties had complete confidence, would present their case freely and faithfully, according to their instructions.[39]

Those instructions survive, in the archives of Berne. They are written in German. In them, Mayerne was requested to convey the greetings and compliments of the city of Berne both to the Duc de Bouillon and, especially, to the King of England, as the declared patron and protector of the true Evangelical Church. He was to set out the critical state of the Confederation, especially in the Valtelline, whose Protestant overlords had been forcibly robbed of their rightful sovereignty and possession by the Spaniards and the Austrians. He was to show that this act of aggression affected all Protestant princes, since the Valtelline was the most vital pass in Europe, the link between Austria, Spain and Italy, and the means whereby the house of Habsburg sought to establish a universal monarchy. And he was to ask the King of England and the Duc de Bouillon for diplomatic support and military help and advice.[40]

Thus briefed, Mayerne left Berne at the end of November 1621. He passed through Catholic Solothurn, the seat of the French ambassador. Whether he had a commission to perform in Solothurn, we do not know. We only know that Fabricius sent a patient, Johann Jacob Diesbach, of a Bernese family, to catch him there as he passed through. But Diesbach arrived too late: Mayerne had already left for Sedan. The journey to Sedan, Mayerne afterwards wrote, was difficult and slow, through severe winter weather. He arrived there in mid-December and stayed there until after the New Year.

There were many temptations to stay, apart from the bad weather and the hospitality of the duke. Over twenty years earlier, when Mayerne had first passed through Sedan, he had found it a general refuge of Protestants, fleeing from persecution: a second Geneva. Now, more than ever, it fulfilled that role. After the disastrous battle of the White Mountain, the defeated King of Bohemia had taken refuge in his uncle's castle. With him were the relics of his army, and its commanders Ernst von Mansfield and Christian of Brunswick. He would stay there for over two years. At the same time another stream of refugees was pouring in from France, fleeing from civil war and Catholic persecution. In consequence of this influx, Sedan had replaced Heidelberg as the capital of the militant Protestant international: a military citadel, thanks to the great castle which overshadowed the town; an intellectual citadel, thanks to the Protestant academy, founded and protected by the duke. So Mayerne was sure to meet many old friends there. Among them were some who are already familiar to us.

One of them was the Huguenot minister Pierre du Moulin. The immediate cause of his flight was a rash letter which he had written, in the previous year, as president of that revolutionary Huguenot gathering, the synod of Alais, to King James. Encouraged by the Duc de Bouillon and by the English ambassador – Mayerne's friend the philosophical Lord Herbert of Cherbury – du Moulin had urged James I to support the King of Bohemia. Unfortunately the letter had fallen into the wrong hands; the French government was very angry at this impertinence by one of its subjects; and du Moulin, on Herbert's advice, had bolted to Sedan. From Sedan he had written to Mayerne seeking his mediation. Mayerne had duly approached the French ambassador in London, but had received a short answer. Du Moulin, the ambassador told him, had not only written an improper letter to a foreign prince: he had also – what was worse – taken part in an illegal assembly, and was therefore a rebel against his king. Du Moulin therefore thought it prudent to stay where he was appointed to be, as the tutor to the duke's heir in Sedan. Sedan would remain his base for the rest of his long life.

Another visitor to Sedan was Louis de Champagne, Comte de Suze-Bernet. He was the brother of Mayerne's old friends Marie de Champagne and Catherine, Marquise de la Moussaye, and was himself – needless to say – a patient of Mayerne. His château at Suze had been an intermediate refuge for du Moulin on his flight from Paris. Now he too arrived at Sedan. A third refugee from France was Mayerne's old friend Trougny. Thus, if Mayerne had originally intended to meet him in Paris, he was disappointed only in the place. The alchemical discussions which he had hoped to enjoy with him were merely transferred to Sedan.

In Sedan, Mayerne performed his commissions for the city of Geneva and the canton of Berne. On behalf of both of them, he sought the advice of

Bouillon, both as to diplomacy and as to defence. Bouillon was now old, and he had long been cautious; but he was an authority on both subjects, and he was in charge both of the foreign diplomacy and of the foreign auxiliaries of the Huguenots. He gave his answer to the two cities, at some length. Mayerne summarised it in two long letters, which, in view of their importance, he sent back by special express messenger from Sedan. The letter to Berne survives, in a German version, in the archives of that city.[41]

According to Mayerne, Bouillon expressed his full moral support for the Swiss in their struggle, but urged MM. de Berne to realise that the struggle was not ideological, for religion – i.e. against Catholicism – but for the existence or dissolution of the body politic of Switzerland – i.e. of the confederation, which included Catholic as well as Protestant cantons. Unless firm action was taken immediately, the Swiss were likely to lose their liberty – not necessarily through external attack but through internal dissension on petty issues. Therefore they must unite against the common enemy, regardless of internal differences, and appoint sound patriots to essential posts. A general assembly of the confederation must be called, and the cantons must not be represented by pensioners of foreign powers. Defence must be organised for the whole confederation: there must be no separate confessional unions 'such as the Germans have made'. Those had ruined Germany, and they would ruin the Swiss confederation, which was a microcosm of the German federal empire. This was the duke's first and essential recommendation: internal cohesion, regardless of religion – for the enemy was not Catholicism but the house of Austria – and common measures of defence.

Defence entailed foreign aid, and that foreign aid (said the duke) must come, essentially, from France. Let the confederation send able ambassadors, with clear instructions, to the court of France. They must tell the King of France that they were resolved to defend their freedom, and that they needed French support, both money and men; for otherwise other princes – the Duke of Savoy, or the King of Spain from Milan – would intervene. Perhaps they should seek support from Venice too; but if any foreign troops are enlisted, they should be French, preferably Huguenots, and be raised with the permission of the King of France; and the confederation must be prepared to act firmly against any ambitious military man who seeks to bring in enemy armies. Thus the confederation, internally united, will be externally strong.

But what if such internal unity is unattainable, if inner disunity makes it impossible? Then, and then only, the Swiss Protestants should go it alone, having first made their position clear to France and other powers. And they must have special care to support Geneva (which was not in the confederation), for their own good, as the protective shield of their land.

Such were the duke's recommendations for the common good of the confederation. But he also had a special message for the rulers of Berne. Let them prepare a treasury and arsenal for war. Here the duke would help. Let them send an experienced gunfounder to him for instruction, and a map, so that he can advise on the strategy of defence. Let them call in an experienced engineer. They must fortify not only Berne but their frontiers. Let them use only native Bernese to protect their forts, and keep foreigners under surveillance in towns. German and Flemish soldiers should be kept apart, under their own officers. Places not to be defended should be stripped of arms. Let the soldiers be trained by those who have been in Holland, or can be fetched thence. Let there be a captain-general, one of the governors of the republic, with full power to execute the orders of the war council. The duke recommended for this post the Vidame de Chartres. He made other recommendations too, to other posts. Monsieur d'Aubigné too would be a good maître-de-camp, though not if that meant robbing Geneva of 'so essential a means of its preservation'.

Such, concludes Mayerne, is the duke's advice. Mayerne urges MM. de Berne to take it, 'for the conservation of their state, for which (in so far as his own preservation in the tumult of France allows him) he will stand unfailingly by you. And so, having discharged my duty to your Lordships, I continue my journey, by God's grace, to England, promising, on my arrival there, to execute your whole commission to his Majesty, and to report back to your Lordships.'

Mayerne's letter to Geneva does not survive, but it is summarised briefly in the Register of the Petit Conseil. According to the Register, Mayerne wrote that he had described to the duke the state in which he had left Geneva, 'both as to fortifications and as to our resolution to defend ourselves bravely, with the aid of God and our friends, if we are attacked'. The duke had replied that he had an accurate plan of the fortifications in Geneva, as they were left by M. de Béthune, who had constructed them in 1611; but that he needed a plan of later additions, with measurements of bastions, horns and trenches, in order to give his advice. He had also ordered Mayerne to write to MM. de Berne to recommend that they give full support to Geneva in the common cause.[42] Mayerne wrote, too, a full report to Agrippa d'Aubigné, who now took over the organisation of military defence, while he himself continued his journey to England to win the diplomatic support of King James.[43]

MM. de Berne accepted the advice of Bouillon, with which d'Aubigné substantially agreed. They took the lead in the confederation, pressed for its unity, and prepared for its defence. They also begged d'Aubigné to come back to Berne and advise them. D'Aubigné was already advising Geneva, whose fortifications he wished to complete, so making the city as impregnable as 'Malta, Corfu, Palmanova, and Sluys';[44] but he yielded to their importunity, went to Berne, travelled over the whole area, and wrote to Mayerne, now in

England, to describe his visit. At first, he said, his friends in Geneva had ridiculed the project: it was impossible, they thought, to awaken 'that sleeping bear'. But he had gone, prodded the bear, and woken it up. After eleven days in secret session with six of the principal men, he had secured a resolution to raise an army and fortify the city. He was impatient of those who doubted its natural strength. 'On the contrary,' he wrote, 'it is a marvellously strong site, which, at half the cost of Geneva, could be made stronger than la Rochelle, if you exclude the advantage of the sea.' I know, d'Aubigné added, the inconstancy of the people, and the tares which are sown in our wheat by those enemies among us, who, as I learn, have sought to traverse your negotiations also. But such malice must drive us to greater effort: it is but further proof of the 'grand design' of the enemy, the plan to reduce all Christendom to slavery 'under the red standard of the crusade which is to be raised in this year 1622'.[45]

The year 1622 would certainly be a year of action for d'Aubigné. To him it was the year of destiny, in which 'all the princes who have abased their sceptres under the yoke of Rome' were resolved to extinguish both God's truth and political liberty. So he urged MM. de Berne to 'wake up after your long Capuan repose . . . I pray God that in my extreme old age He may give me the honour to be your best soldier . . . and see your valour break the insolence of Antichrist.' And, referring to Rohan's resistance in France, 'we are now all in arms, la Rochelle continues to fortify itself by sea, and all the towns of Guyenne and Languedoc by land.' Later in the year, Heidelberg, the capital of the Elector Palatine, would fall to the Bavarian army. But d'Aubigné would not be dismayed. This new disaster would only spur him to still greater endeavours. Every defeat, to him, was an incentive to resistance; and he would throw himself into the task of fortifying the northern bastion of Switzerland, the city of Basel.[46]

How could even the torpid oligarchy of Berne resist such an indomitable old man? They offered him, as Bouillon had suggested, the post of captain-general. He declined, pleading ignorance of the German language, and recommended three other names. One was Bouillon's own nominee, the Vidame de Chartres. Another was Mayerne's old friend Louis de Champagne, Comte de Suze-Bernet, the protector of du Moulin – who indeed acted as his messenger to d'Aubigné in Geneva. De Suze was chosen. With the permission of the King of France, he would become the general of the Swiss armies, acting in concert with d'Aubigné. He would serve the republic well, and when he died, in 1636, would be buried in a mausoleum in Berne.

Such were the consequences of Mayerne's diplomatic activity in Sedan in that Christmas season of 1621–2. But perhaps it was not diplomacy which gave him the greatest pleasure. His own records say nothing of it. What he remembered was rather his meetings with his alchemical friend, the high priest of his old Hermetic circle, the man whom he knew by the almost sacred name of 'Hermes', Guillaume de Trougny.

With Trougny, in Sedan, Mayerne enjoyed, once again, long Hermetic sessions. By him, he was initiated into new alchemical secrets. Among other things, Trougny wrote out for him, in his own hand, the 'Occult Art' of one of the founding fathers of Hermetic doctrine, Elias the Artist, who was said to be exempt from original sin and to possess the fruit of the tree of life and the secret of immortality, which he would disclose in the last days. Mayerne was so impressed with Trougny's document that he copied it out in his own hand.[47] It was a treatise on minerals and the means of extracting their 'spirit', a spirit more abstruse than the spirit of animals and vegetables; 'but there is nothing so hidden that it cannot at last be discovered.' At Sedan, Mayerne recorded a whole series of sessions at which 'Hermes' was the teacher, he the pupil taking notes at his master's 'dictation'. Hermes spoke of universal medicine; of 'the universal ferment which is the vitriol latent in all metals, and is elicited from them by the acid spirits of vegetables or, better still, by spirits of vitriol and sulphur'; of medicines of the first and second order; of the three philosophical stones. Together, Mayerne and Trougny rehearsed the ideas of medieval and mythical alchemists, of Ripley and 'Basil Valentine'; and Hermes reported the important discoveries of a noble Pole, Goraysky de Goray. Mayerne would afterwards correspond with this noble Pole, with whom he would agree an alchemical code. But 'Hermes' would then have second thoughts about him: the Pole, he would write to Mayerne, knew something about theory but had never himself put hand to crucible; 'therefore his speculations must be tested.'[48] Hermes and Mayerne, of course, were constant at their crucibles, and they were helped, at Sedan, by an 'excellent apothecary and good chemist', M. Bonne, from whom Mayerne would adopt many recondite cures.[49]

Soon after the New Year, Mayerne left Sedan for England. He arrived before the end of January 1622.[50] He found King James in poor health and an ill temper; as well he might be: for in England too, during Mayerne's absence, things had changed for the worse.

16

Protector of Switzerland, 1622

King James had some grounds for ill humour in January 1622. Events were out of control. His policy was in ruins. His credit had collapsed. It was very mortifying for the senior king in Europe, born in the purple, and the most learned, the British Solomon, who had aspired to be absolute at home and the umpire of Europe. What, he might ask himself, had gone wrong? His policy had been neither dishonourable nor unintelligent. Born in revolution, brought up in anarchy and civil war, when Europe was convulsed by ideological struggle, he had dreamed of stability: of a Europe at peace and himself as its arbiter, holding the balance between the two ideological powers. To this end, he had married his daughter to a Protestant prince and had hoped, by a Spanish match for his son, to exercise influence with the Catholic powers. But now his Protestant son-in-law, by his Bohemian adventure, had spoiled it all. The delicate balance of power had been shattered, Europe was at war, and his daughter was a penniless exile. Meanwhile his claims of absolutism at home had been disputed by a Parliament which he had just dissolved in a temper, having torn out of its Journal, with his own hands, the page on which the members had vindicated their rights. In consequence he had lost a parliamentary subsidy and fallen into complete dependence on Spain and its imperious ambassador Gondomar. He had also fallen off his horse into the New River and been pulled out by the boots, in the nick of time. Naturally he was in a bad mood, and hardly likely to welcome proposals that he should send armies to support the Protestants of Switzerland.

So the first reports which Mayerne sent back to Geneva and Berne were not very encouraging. 'I arrived', he wrote, 'to find the Parliament dissolved and more dissension than I would have liked, so that I am afraid that domestic affairs may distract us from foreign.' Consequently, 'I have had no opportunity to pour your complaints into the bosom of His Majesty, nor to represent your needs, as I shall not fail to do as soon as he is pleased to give me audience.'[1] A fortnight later, having been jogged by a letter from the Petit Conseil, he could only repeat his protestations of frustrated zeal: 'His Majesty's health has been bad and his affairs are so numerous and pressing that he puts me off from day to day.' However, he had orders to set out for Newmarket next week. There the king had promised to receive him and 'to listen patiently and reply to all my proposals'.[2]

In such circumstances, Mayerne thought, it was perhaps just as well that the city of Geneva had not sent an official envoy, as he had himself proposed. Clearly the time was not yet ripe for that. Besides, as soon became clear, it was not necessary. Early in February, before he had seen the king, Mayerne received a document from Berne. It was a letter from the magistrates of the city to King James, and it was accompanied by a formal commission appointing Mayerne as the official agent of the canton at the English court, with power to negotiate in its name. Mayerne purred with pleasure at this tribute to his zeal and efficiency. The king, when he at last granted the audience, was pleased to allow the appointment. He also expressed the closest interest in the affairs of both Geneva and Berne, and seemed delighted to handle them through the agency of Mayerne. Soon Mayerne would be assuring the Petit Conseil of Geneva that it could forget the idea of a special representative in London: 'Wherever I am, you shall have no need of agent or solicitor.'[3]

In the early months of 1622, Mayerne wrote regularly to the rulers of both Berne and Geneva. The common interest of the two cities was in the policy of the unpredictable Duke of Savoy. Formally, the duke was allied to both by the Treaty of Asti. But could he be trusted to keep that treaty? Could he resist the temptation to join the Catholic powers, who were now so successful, and seek to reconquer Geneva and the pays de Vaud? His ambitions were well known; his past record was one of unscrupulous opportunism; and the recent mission of Father Corona was no secret to the diplomats of Europe. From their windows the citizens of Geneva could now see Savoyard troops drilling as if for action. Such mobilisation, so close to the frontier, was contrary to the treaty, and naturally caused alarm both in Geneva, fearful for its very existence, and in Berne, fearful for the pays de Vaud.

How fortunate that the Treaty of Asti was guaranteed by the King of England, who, by his past diplomacy, had won a remarkable personal influence over the Duke of Savoy! And how doubly fortunate that both Berne and Geneva now had a reliable agent who had won remarkable personal influence over the King of England! Nor was that the end of their good fortune. For Mayerne was not only influential in England: he was also in direct personal touch with all the men whose support was most essential to them. He was intimate with the Duc de Bouillon, with Agrippa d'Aubigné, and with the new general of the Swiss army, the Comte de Suze. Suze's liaison officer with d'Aubigné was Mayerne's old friend Pierre du Moulin.[4] Mayerne was a close personal friend of Isaac Wake, the architect of the Treaty of Asti, in Turin, and he had an anonymous but well-informed private correspondent in Piedmont. He also had an invaluable source for the politics of the Duke of Savoy in another old friend, whom we have already met as his colleague in secret diplomacy, and who was now to become more intimately involved in his life: Gian Francesco Biondi.

Since his visit to Grenoble and Turin in 1615, Biondi had taken on a new role. He had been engaged, with the permission of King James, as official agent of the Duke of Savoy in London. He was thus in a position exactly parallel to that which Mayerne held in respect of Berne and Geneva. Indeed, the similarity went further: for each professed natural loyalty to a third state – Mayerne to France, Biondi to Venice – of which neither was a true native, one being of Piedmontese, the other of Croatian origin. Biondi sometimes professed disquiet at his multiple allegiance, so contrary, as he remarked, to the Gospel; and it seems that he had some reason for self-examination: for according to Mayerne the duke revealed all his plans frankly to his agent, who then passed them on privately to him.[5] Mayerne carried the burden more easily. With King James seeking to keep the peace between Savoy, Geneva and Berne, these two cosmopolitan agents naturally saw much of each other, and in this very year, 1622, their collaboration was cemented by a family alliance: Biondi married Mayerne's sister Marie, who lived with Mayerne in London. It was not, perhaps, a very good match: Biondi had only a somewhat precarious pension from King James as well as whatever he might receive from Savoy; but equally the lady's attractions were not great. She was elderly and, it was said, ugly; like her brother, she was of substantial bulk ('a very lump or great piece of flesh' according to the unchivalrous John Chamberlain);[6] and her portion was small, though she too had a pension from the Crown, paid from the Court of Wards. After the marriage, Mayerne secured a knighthood for his brother-in-law, and provided him with useful aphrodisiac aids.[7] Biondi, now Sir Francis Biondi, repaid him with useful confidential information from the Duke of Savoy.

Thanks to this central position, Mayerne was able to send regular information and advice to Geneva and Berne. His immediate problem was to correct the prevailing opinion in England, which was that the fears of Geneva were illusory; that the Duke of Savoy would observe the treaty; and that, even if he did not, the city was in no danger, thanks to its own defences and the mutual jealousies of its neighbours. Mayerne did not share this comfortable view, 'seeing the progress already made throughout Europe for the fulfilment of the General Design aiming at our destruction'.[8] The General Design was now a term of art among the Huguenots, and Mayerne was using, automatically, the tabloid language of d'Aubigné. In his audience, he was able to convince King James that the apprehensions of Geneva were not mere panic. After all, the Duke of Savoy was still the same duke who had made the treacherous attack on Geneva – 'the Escalade' – in 1602. How then could he be trusted? Even at this moment, Mayerne had news that the duke's ambassador in Paris had twice sought to persuade the King of France to drop his protection of Geneva. Happily the King of France had refused, but the situation was still ticklish. Prompted by Mayerne, King James wrote to Wake in Turin to read a lecture to the duke, reminding him of his obligations, and Mayerne sent copies of the letter to both Geneva and Berne, 'so that you can see how this great king loves you and has your safety at heart'. 'His Majesty's authority with the duke', he added, 'is not small, for he has proved himself a good friend and helped him in his hour of need.'[9] Nevertheless, the two cities were to take no risks. They were to stand firmly together and look to their defences. 'Since we are in an age of miracles, in which no novelties should surprise us,' who could predict 'the adventurous humour of that prince, your neighbour', especially when the King of France was distracted by these unhappy civil wars?[10]

Wake's lecture, it seems, had its effect. By April 1622 Mayerne could assure the two cities that the immediate danger was over. Wake had reported from Turin that the Duke of Savoy, pressed once again by the pope to invade Switzerland and capture Geneva, had replied that he had other fish to fry and had no intention of breaking his treaties. So those armies, which were visible so near Geneva, were not, after all, directed against it. 'Nevertheless,' added Mayerne, 'do not drop your guard.'

To Geneva and to the pays de Vaud, the most direct threat came from Savoy; but to Berne itself, and to the confederation generally, the more immediate danger lay in Germany, where Spanish and Bavarian armies were gradually overpowering the forces of the Elector Palatine and his few allies. Here too Mayerne was liberal of advice. The Swiss confederation, he declared, or at least the Protestant cantons, should ally themselves with the new union of Protestant powers in Germany. 'God grant that it may be a phoenix, reborn from its ashes, and more fortunate than the old. . . . By union the Swiss are what they are, and would be what they once were if they could stay united in will.' Would Berne like him to mobilise King James for such a union? 'If you need advice, tell me, and I shall do your bidding and my duty.'

The two cities were grateful for advice, but they had hoped for some more solid assistance, 'some fruit of his Majesty's liberality'. Here, unfortunately, they were disappointed. Having quarrelled with his Parliament, while committing himself to the support of his son-in-law, King James was in no state to pay up. As Mayerne explained to Geneva, the king was determined to maintain their republic, 'and if the present state of his affairs allowed him to gratify you with a subvention worthy of his quality and proportionate to your needs, he would not wait to be asked'. Unfortunately, being hard pressed for cash, and his family being in such need, that was out of the question, and Geneva was advised to apply for the customary subsidies from France.

Reading Mayerne's letters to Geneva and Berne, we have the impression of a man who thoroughly enjoyed the exercise of influence and power. He is no longer merely the suave, successful medical pioneer, the friend of apothecaries and surgeons: he is the masterful politician, instructing rulers and ambassadors, wielding authority, dictating policy. A servant in name only, he recommends, patronises, even commands his distant masters: for he speaks to them in the name of a greater prince, their protector King James. So his tone of voice is peremptory. He must have full information on all subjects. Letters must be sent by such and such means only. A particular person – a servant of his friend Hans Rudolf von Erlach – must be used as messenger. Why has General Steckius been sent to France? 'Your Excellencies must kindly take care to inform me on this and on all other events which I may need to know, whether in your state or in those of your neighbours which may concern you, however slightly. Otherwise I cannot advise His Majesty correctly, and my negotiation will be vain and fruitless.' There is no room here for argument. If Berne and Geneva wish to be saved, they must obey the orders of the King of England's new Secretary – as it were – for the Central Department: Dr Mayerne.

Mayerne's sense of his domination of foreign policy was most obvious in April 1622. By that time, he believed, the immediate danger from Savoy had been averted and a new opportunity had presented itself. This arose from the outbreak of yet another civil war in France.

For while Mayerne had been in Switzerland, events had moved fast in France. In 1621 the Huguenots, for the first time, found themselves isolated in revolt. The grandees – even some of the Huguenot grandees – stood aside, and the French government of the Duc de Luynes resolved to crush the defiant rebels of la Rochelle and Languedoc as it had already crushed those of Béarn. On 17 April, at Fontainebleau, with the princes of the blood and his councillors around him, Louis XIII formally declared war on them. Then he set out in person, with his army, to enjoy the victory. At first, it was an effortless victory. At Saumur, he dismissed the Huguenot governor, du Plessis Mornay. At Thouars, the Huguenot Duc de la Tremoïlle obediently opened the gates. Sully's town of St Maixent surrendered at once. The first resistance came at the citadel of St Jean d'Angély. There Rohan's brother, the Duc de Soubise, refused to open the gates, and the royal army was forced to sit down and besiege the town. Meanwhile, in the south, Rohan himself, supported by the Duc de la Force, organised the defence of Languedoc. When St Jean d'Angély fell, Soubise escaped to la Rochelle and organised its fleet. He became 'the admiral of the Churches', while his brother was their general. These two brothers – *les frères Antichristi* as Richelieu would call them – were the animating spirits of the revolt. They held together the miscellaneous forces of southern Protestantism, uniting the radical urban republic of la Rochelle with the old Albigensian towns of Languedoc. So began a new religious war, uncompromising on both sides: a crusade against the Protestants of France parallel and contemporary with the crusade against those of Germany; and the threat of one against those of Geneva and Switzerland.

As always in such a crisis, Rohan turned to King James, 'the Protector of the Religion'. His letters to the king, in those months of agony, sound a note of despair. He appeals to religion and to kinship. He reminds the king of the scene at Holyrood, over twenty years ago, when 'I had had the honour to hold the Monseigneur your son at his baptism'. He protests that he and his house 'are now on the brink of ruin, solely for the sake of our religion'. 'In short, Sire, we face a general and premeditated persecution throughout Christendom.'[11]

Such an appeal was not very welcome to James I – or indeed to Mayerne. James was concerned to support as cheaply as possible the hard-pressed Elector Palatine in Germany. Mayerne was on his way to Switzerland to give moral support to Geneva and Berne and to encourage the Duke of Savoy to keep the peace. But such a policy, to be effective, required the support of France. Only France could really protect Geneva, or frighten Savoy. James therefore needed to keep on good terms with the French government. He could hardly do this if he should support a rebellion against it. So the Huguenots of the south were left to fight for their cause alone.

They were willing to do so. Three months later, in August 1621, the army of Louis XIII was poised, as it thought, for the kill. Its commander, the Duc de Mayenne, laid siege to Montauban. The town held out for three months. In the course of the siege Mayenne was killed. When the news of his death reached Paris, the Catholic mob burned down the Huguenot Temple at Charenton, and the Huguenots fled for safety to Sedan. But even in Sedan some of them did not feel secure. Du Moulin, in a panic, wrote to King James that the Church was threatened with ruin even there; and he proposed to flee to England with his family.[12] In the end, the resistance of Montauban was successful. The siege was raised, and Rohan's desperate energy kept the Huguenots of the south united against the royal power. They were still united, and still in arms, in January 1622, when Mayerne returned, via Sedan, to London, where he reported that the Protestant cities of Switzerland, like those of Languedoc, were fortifying themselves against threatened conquest.

At this point James I bestirred himself. He turned, as so often in those years, to his old favourite, Mayerne's most faithful friend and patron, the sophisticated, prodigal, French-speaking Lord Hay, now decorated with a new title as Viscount Doncaster.

King James had already sent Doncaster on special embassies to Germany and France. His last embassy had been to France, at the time of the siege of Montauban. As always, the king presented himself as a mediator between Louis XIII and his subjects. That indeed was his interest. His mediation had not been successful, but now he would try again. Doncaster was to go to the royal camp in south-western France and seek to preserve Rohan from destruction. But at the last minute, new instructions were issued to him, and it seems probable that these were suggested by Mayerne. Mayerne had heard – perhaps through Biondi – that the King of France was preparing to visit Lyon, where the Duke of Savoy was to meet him. The duke, he understood, would urge the king to give peace to his Huguenot subjects and turn his arms against the Spaniards in the Valtelline. This, of course, would be welcome both to Rohan and to the Swiss. Mayerne at once saw a new opportunity. Why should not Doncaster follow the French court to Lyon and lend his support to the Duke of Savoy? Together, they could then press upon Louis XIII a return to the policy of Henri IV – that is, accommodation with his own Huguenot subjects and protection of Protestant Geneva and Protestant Switzerland.[13] Such a change of policy seemed more practicable now, for in December 1621 the Duc de Luynes had died and the new French ministers, being uncommitted to his pro-Spanish, Catholic policy, could contemplate a return to the past. It seemed the ideal solution, and King James evidently agreed to an extension of Doncaster's mission. In the circumstances, and in view of what followed, we can hardly doubt that the proposal came from Mayerne.

On 4 April 1622, Mayerne wrote to both Berne and Geneva to inform them of this favourable development. Doncaster, he told the Petit Conseil of Geneva, had left two days ago, carrying letters of credence and powers to treat with the Duke of Savoy 'on any subject. . . . Do not let slip this opportunity to serve yourselves. Use him boldly: he is a vigorous and zealous intermediary for our religion. He will be able, in our king's name, to extract from the duke a promise to live in friendship with you, to keep the treaties, and to remove any grounds for discontent. You could not have a better agent at court. I have given the said lord ambassador some notes on this subject for your service.' If the journey to Lyon should not take place, the ambassador could still be used as a channel to King James, 'with whom he is in very good odour; and if you think that I can help, let me know. Apart from his public office, which obliges him, I have the honour to be his close friend, and I can serve you.'[14]

To the Avoyer and Council of Berne, Mayerne was even more explicit. He urged them to send a special envoy to Lyon, nominally to wait on the King of France but in fact to treat with Doncaster and, through him, to put pressure,

in King James's name, on the Duke of Savoy. 'Do not miss this unique opportunity. . . . I have given the said Lord Ambassador some notes for this purpose.
He is my special patron and friend and has promised me to do everything
possible for your benefit. . . . His own inclination carries him that way, but
beyond that I shall push him on, and I shall give orders that the king our
master (I mean, his and mine) shall command him.'[15]

'Je l'y pousseray et doneray ordre que le Roy . . . le luy commandera . . . .'
The language is somewhat surprising. We are a far cry from the unpolitical
court-doctor. Rather we seem to hear the voice of Cardinal Wolsey, 'Ego et Rex
meus'. But Cardinal Wolsey at least held a responsible office. He was Lord
Chancellor of England, not an immigrant foreigner at the English court. Nor
did Mayerne stop here. As he informed the two cities, he had given the
ambassador certain notes for his guidance. These notes, which still survive
among Doncaster's diplomatic papers in the British Library, are even more
surprising. They are headed 'memorandum of the articles which my lord
viscount Doncaster, ambassador extraordinary of His Majesty of Great Britain
to the King of France, will please to take as instructions', and they are written
throughout in French, in Mayerne's own hand.[16]

And what are these 'instructions'? First, the ambassador is to support and
encourage the proposed reconquest of the Valtelline and the restoration to the
Grisons of their ancient liberty – that is, their control over the valley. He is to
incite the King of France to this laudable enterprise by appeals to the honour
of his crown and to the sworn alliance between France and the Grisons.

Secondly, he is to make it plain to the King of France that he must return to
the policy of Henri IV, who always valued his alliance with the Swiss cantons
and gave them French protection. Recently, this protection has been withheld
and the Swiss have been exposed to the machinations of Jesuits, papal
nuncios, Spanish ambassadors, 'powerful sowers of tares and prodigal distrib-
utors of coin'. This policy should now be changed. French ambassadors should
be told that their task is not to spread the Catholic faith but 'to manage the
hearts and affections of the Swiss for the benefit of the Crown of France'.
Recent French ambassadors have been 'men born rather for the oratory than
for the embassy'; hence the loss of the Valtelline and the seduction of the Swiss
Catholics by Spain. The King of France must mend his ways and send, as
ambassadors, not Catholic bigots but sensible men of the world, who will
recover the old influence and extend the old protection. The Swiss, on their
side, must resolve their differences, restore the unity of the confederation,
guarantee it by new oaths, 'and make this great body move for the good of
France, which will support it on this side with immeasurable force'. In particular, the King of France must cultivate the Protestants, and especially
Messieurs de Berne and the city of Geneva, 'observing diligently the comings

and goings and the plans of the ambassador of his Highness of Savoy'. That duke, 'for all his fine pretences, and in spite of all his protestations to the contrary, always has his eye on those states', seeking to dull the edge of their vigilance and to exploit their trust in the treaties which Sir Isaac Wake has made for the King of Great Britain, and which the duke has signed and confirmed in the high court of Savoy.

Thirdly, the ambassador is to speak up, if necessary, for the states of Berne and Geneva, as one specially charged to do so by the king his master. In any case he is to express his Majesty's particular affection for them, as shown in those treaties. He should also encourage any agents of Swiss cantons at the French court, receiving them freely and saying that his Majesty has expressly charged him to serve them with all his power. Knowing his Majesty's desire to further the good cause and to gratify these republics, I have (adds Mayerne) given them notice of it and have advised them not to let slip this opportunity of helping themselves.

Such are Mayerne's political instructions to the ambassador. Although he uses the king's name, he speaks in his own person. He steps forward as maker of English policy, the protector of Switzerland, a minister, at least, of the Crown. But he has not yet finished. There are some additional instructions which reveal, even more clearly, his own hand.

First, since the ambassador will doubtless wish to help the afflicted, he must enquire after Granier, the unfortunate nephew of the late bishop of Geneva. Granier, recalls Mayerne, came to England to adopt our religion. Having been sent back to Paris to make public profession of it, he has been thrown into the Bastille on suspicion of having gone abroad, as a spy, in order to treat of affairs of state to the detriment of the king's service – even though he is a subject not of the King of France but of the Duke of Savoy. Since his imprisonment we have had no news of him. If he is alive, the ambassador is to secure his release . . . It was Mayerne who had proposed sending Granier back, to announce his conversion in a more public theatre than London – with this unfortunate result. In fact, Mayerne soon learned, he had already been freed and was back in England.

Secondly, 'if M. de Trougny of Orléans and M. Naudin, my apothecary, present themselves to him, and beg his help and a safe-conduct for their persons in order to seek refuge in England, away from the perils which daily threaten them', the ambassador is to receive them kindly. He is to protect them by the favour which he enjoys from the king, and, if necessary, to declare them to be his own servants, entrusted with his despatches, and covered by diplomatic immunity. Thus they will be able to cross the sea without danger of arrest at the ports or any other inconvenience.

Thirdly, the ambassador is to thank M. le Président Jeannin for having been the only person to disapprove of 'the manner in which I was maltreated on my last journey in France', and to assure 'all the great ministers' now in power 'of my humble and unalterable devotion to the good of France, for which I pray for a peace as constant and flourishing as that which I saw it enjoying under the reign of my good master, Henri the Great of august memory'.

Finally, the ambassador is to 'say a word *en passant* to M. Schomberg for the payment of the arrears that are due to me in my capacity as *conseiller et médecin ordinaire du Roy*'.

To the modern reader, there is something bizarre in this document. The French doctor of the King of England, having dictated French policy to the King of France, in the name of the King of England, through the English ambassador and having instructed the ambassador to use his diplomatic privileges for various private purposes, then uses the services of the same English ambassador to declare his own unalterable devotion to the interests of France. However, it is clear that Mayerne himself saw nothing inconsistent in his actions. To serve two, or even more, masters entailed no inconvenient conflict if one were confident that the interest of all was the same, and that the true interest of Catholic France lay in the defence of the Protestant international.

The King of France thought differently. He did not accept Doncaster's mediation, nor did Doncaster go, after all, to Lyon. In fact, there was no need for him to go. Even without English pressure, the new French government was returning to the foreign policy of Henri IV, and Geneva and Berne could feel safe from attack by Savoy. However, if the cloud from the south retreated, that in the north became more threatening. Spanish and Bavarian armies were now closing in on the Rhineland: closing in for the kill.

In London, Mayerne watched these events with alarm. In June 1622 he wrote again to the Petit Conseil of Geneva, warning it of this new danger. A private source in Piedmont, he wrote, had informed him that the Duke of Savoy had at present no intention of attacking Geneva or Berne. 'However,' he added, 'not only Geneva but MM. de Berne and all the Protestant cantons are threatened by a great and perilous storm.' The Catholic armies were now preparing for the final assault in the Palatinate; the whole Rhineland Circle of the Empire was at risk; and if that should fall, the Protestant cantons of Switzerland would be the next victims. The Habsburgs and the Catholic cantons would fall upon them, and, in that case, 'we must suppose that the Duke of Savoy would claim his share of the cake'. So all efforts must be made to save the Rhineland, 'for if it goes, the rest follows: *actum est*' – all is over. 'So you see,' commented Mayerne, 'sentence has been pronounced on us, and we must now turn every stone to prevent its execution. We are working powerfully, and not unsuccessfully, to save the Rhineland Circle.'[17]

The Rhineland Circle was not saved. In September its bastion, the Elector Palatine's capital of Heidelberg, was captured and sacked by the Bavarian troops of Tilly. With that disaster, Mayerne's nightmare had become true. Protestant Switzerland was now surrounded by armed enemies, and the knife was poised over the cake. Too late, the torpid burghers recognised their plight. In the hour of crisis it was not they but the old Huguenot *émigré*, the warrior-poet of the civil wars of France, Agrippa d'Aubigné, who roused them to belated resistance.

The key to Switzerland in the north, the point of entry from Germany, was the city of Basel. That autumn d'Aubigné appeared in Basel. He threw himself into the new task of fortifying it as he had previously fortified Geneva and Berne. Basel, he wrote, with its great arsenals and its bridge over the Rhine, was now ripe for conquest. The loss of Heidelberg had not sufficiently alarmed its citizens, or those of Geneva either. God had struck them with a spirit of insensibility, or lethargy. But if the Swiss had forgotten their ancient valour, we, he wrote to the Comte de Suze, have not. We must defend the Swiss until they recover the spirit of their fathers. If, with our weak arms, we cannot prevent that heavy body from falling to the ground, at least we should prepare ourselves to raise it up again ... 'We', of course, are the indomitable French Huguenots, who, Mayerne observes, bear the brunt of the struggle everywhere. For evidence, one need only look at France, where 'la Rochelle continues to fortify itself on the sea, and all the towns of Guyenne and Languedoc by land: they boast now that they have thirty Montaubans.'[18]

D'Aubigné and Mayerne remained in regular contact. D'Aubigné's side of the correspondence shows the incredible energy of this indefatigable septuagenarian, who refused to despair of the Huguenot cause and who, if he was not allowed to defend it in France, would defend it abroad. All through the next year, while Rohan sustained the revolt in France, d'Aubigné saw to its physical defence in Switzerland and acted as its propagandist abroad. His letters flowed out in all directions, hortatory, comminatory, imperative: to kings and statesmen, generals, men of letters, city magistrates. The struggle against Antichrist was, to him, indivisible: no country was too distant, no means too inconsiderable, to be thrown into it; and since he was a universal man, equally at home in philosophy, poetry, history, fortification and technical invention, he applied his mind not only to ideology and diplomacy, bastions and ramparts, but also to the details of military intelligence and secret weapons.

One letter shows d'Aubigné and Mayerne discussing one such weapon.[19] It was a clandestine telephone ('engin pour parler de loin'), whose first version they had tried out together during Mayerne's visit, and about which Mayerne had asked for further news. D'Aubigné replied that he had now tested it again, twice, and that it functioned perfectly. It could be used to send secret messages to a prisoner in a cell, provided he was equipped with a receiving box six inches long. By means of it, the commander of a relieving army could communicate with the government of a besieged city,

> and even if you were not sure of the man who handled the machine, you could use it in a language which he did not understand. I reckon that for 12,000 écus we could make machines to speak from my house, Le Crest, to yours at Aubonne. They are nine Savoyard leagues apart, more than from Paris to Étampes or from France to England ... I may add that the mystery-machine is so powerful that it can speak as easily from London to Paris, or even to Madrid, as through three walls, which it did when we tested it together.

The only possible objection was its cost, which was proportionate to the distance covered. To speak across the Lake of Geneva would cost 1,200 écus, from France to England 12,000, and so on. There was also a little practical difficulty: there must be a hut where the operator is safe and cannot be seen through a door or a crack in the wall. It seems that this hut had to be in enemy territory. Unfortunately we have no further details about this secret weapon, which, d'Aubigné insisted, was not magical but scientific, and which he had vowed never to use for low or evil purposes, but only for the Cause.

In one respect, the attitude of Mayerne differed from that of d'Aubigné. This was in respect of France. D'Aubigné had been rejected by France. He had been condemned to death there, and his book had been burnt. Consequently, he felt little loyalty to his own country and its Catholic government, and he supported the Huguenot resistance *à l'outrance*. Mayerne was more prudent. Whatever his loyalty to Rohan, whatever his hopes for Rohan's success, he would not damage his own ultimate aims by such self-exposure. Politically, he wished for a return to the system of Henri IV: a French monarchy which, even if itself Catholic, would guarantee the liberties of the Huguenots at home and their Protestant kinsmen abroad. He also had private reasons to humour the French government: his office, his salary, his investments. After the unfortunate affair of 1618, he was eager for peace: peace with honour; peace also with profit. All his communications with the French government, direct or indirect, dwell on this theme. In these circumstances he could never, like d'Aubigné, have written defiant letters to Louis XIII, accusing him of complicity with Antichrist.[20] If he sought the same ends as d'Aubigné, he sought them by different, and more politic, means.

This was shown in the summer of 1622, when Rohan's brother Soubise came to England, seeking support for the revolt in Languedoc. At the same time, Benedetto Turrettini, the special emissary whom Geneva had sent to Holland, visited England seeking financial support for the defence of Switzerland.

Mayerne saw them both – Soubise was an old friend and a regular patient – but he was careful to keep them apart. 'We thought it best, M. Turrettini and I', he wrote to Geneva, that there should be no meeting with Soubise, 'for fear of irritating the tutelary gods under whose protection you live, since they are angry with him'.[21] The tutelary gods were the ministers of France, whom Mayerne wished to see returning to their old rôle as protectors of Geneva. For that purpose Soubise, for the time being, must be kept at arm's length. This was anyway the view of King James, who had no intention of becoming involved too deeply with Rohan's war of religion.

Fortunately, he did not need to. In the autumn, Rohan, having ignored the timorous advice of King James, forced the King of France to concede peace on Huguenot terms. By the peace of Montpellier, in October 1622, the rights of the Huguenots, where they had been withdrawn, were restored, and Rohan himself returned to the royal favour and provincial power. It seemed that the old coexistence was re-established, and that Geneva and Switzerland, having survived the threat from Savoy, could now face the danger in the north with the assurance of support from a reunited France. This was what Mayerne wanted. He could be satisfied with his work as a political agent.

He could also be satisfied with his other, non-political activities. For all this busy diplomacy did not stop his medical work. Even as he travelled – in Aubonne, in Geneva, in Berne, in Sedan – he was constantly seeing patients; and if he could not prescribe for them on the spot, he would send them long *consilia* from London. So Fabricius's patient Johann Jacob Diesbach, who had missed him in Solothurn, was not overlooked. He was suffering from gout and suppression of urine – two complaints on which Mayerne was particularly expert. Diesbach was advised to take a purge consisting of juice of cassia with turpentine and powdered rhubarb when the moon was three-quarters full; then, for the next four mornings, vitriol of tartar as described in Croll's *Basilica chymica*. 'After drinking liquid seasoned with this salt and with aperient roots, together with the tips of young mallows and stinging nettles, let the patient (if his condition precludes other exercise) ride on horseback; then scour his belly with emollient cooling clysters, including Quercetanus' anti-nephritic electuary.' Since Diesbach had previously been a patient of la Rivière and du Chesne, no doubt he was used to this sort of thing.[22] More serious was the case of the Duc de Bouillon. He had always suffered, at least in the eyes of his doctors, from a complex of diseases and now, according to Mayerne, he was suffering from 'extreme weakness and universal prostration of the faculties'.[23] This was alarming in one who was the necessary protector of so many Huguenot refugees and the political adviser of the whole international movement. No wonder du Moulin, and now Trougny in Sedan, lived in a state of alarm, and periodically cast eyes in the direction of England, as a safer refuge.

So much for Continental patients. But of course, after so long an absence, Mayerne's English patients too were queuing up for appointments. Prominent among them was the young Marchioness of Buckingham, who wished to ease the labour of childbirth. That presented no problem. In her ninth month, on going to bed and rising, she was to anoint her pudenda with emollient unguent, and to keep in readiness a long list of ingredients, including water of stag's head (as prepared for the king), confection of Alkermes of Montpellier, finger-bones, Cretan dittany, *crocus martis corallinus*, and dried testicles of horse. This worked. 'A happy and successful treatment,' Mayerne noted, and added piously in Greek, 'to God alone be the glory.'[24]

Less successful was the prescription for the Duchess of Lennox. She was the third wife of the duke, who was now fifty years old and had no heir. Mayerne was consulted on this delicate matter. He recommended that, on going to bed, the duchess anoint her big toes and the soles of her feet with ointment of green lizards, 'rectified' – that is, distilled; and he prescribed a liniment also 'pro veretro mariti': for the husband's genitals. 'If she does not conceive then', Mayerne noted, 'she is totally sterile.'[25] She did not conceive, and the dukedom went to the duke's brother; but the family kept its faith in Mayerne.[26]

So the fatal year 1622, the year of the great Catholic crusade, had passed off without total disaster. Heidelberg indeed had been lost, but Geneva was still safe. Father Corona's mission had failed. The rulers of France were not prepared to see the city taken over by Savoy: they were reverting to 'the damnable policy of Henri IV'. The Duke of Savoy decided that without French support he could not take the risk: anyway he had no desire to weaken his own title by readmitting the rival authority of the bishop of Geneva.[27] So he kept, and would continue to keep, the treaty negotiated by Wake, who had great influence with him.[28] In France, too, the Huguenots had preserved, even improved, their position. And in 1623, after the fiasco of Prince Charles's Spanish journey, there was a change of mood at the English court: a change from appeasement to resistance as the only means to recover the Palatinate. It was in these changed circumstances that Mayerne decided, in the winter of 1623–4, that it was time to revisit his barony of Aubonne.

17

The Last Years of King James, 1623–1625

For his second visit to Aubonne, Mayerne decided to be firm. He would take the bull by the horns and travel through France. So, having sent his family on ahead of him, he conveyed a message to Paris through the French ambassador and, on being assured that Louis XIII regarded him as a good subject, proceeded to the next, more formal step. In December 1623 he wrote a letter of elaborate civility to the French Secretary of State, Brûlart de Puysieux, thanking him for his good offices with the King of France and feeling his way towards a dignified return to Paris. He hoped, he wrote, to thank him soon in person, 'especially if you deign to assure me, by a word in your own hand, that I shall be welcome. I shall never give you any cause for regret: be sure of that.'[1] At the same time he wrote out a long document 'for the physicians-in-ordinary of the king, for their future deliberations on the cure of his Majesty's present ailments and the preservation of his health'.[2] It was a document to which he attached great importance: he wrote it out in his own register and in red ink. It was designed to guide his colleagues during his own absence.

This document is the most famous of Mayerne's psychosomatic portraits.[3] If no other evidence survived, it would suffice to ensure his reputation as a 'Hippocratic' doctor. It illustrates his patient observation, both physical and psychological, and his careful adaptation of remedies not only to the disease but to the temperament of his patient. It also, indirectly, portrays the character of James I: his human weaknesses and eccentricities, his lability, his disorderly habits, his resentment of discipline. At the end of it we know not only the liver and the spleen, the gout and the diarrhoea, the medical history and the dietary habits, but also the personality and the mind of one of the most elusive of our kings.

The document is divided into sections. First, there is a purely physical account of the king's bodily health and habits. Then there is his medical history, reconstructed from infancy and illustrated from Mayerne's own previous records. Then we learn the medicines which, by practice, have been found both useful and acceptable. Finally, Mayerne sets out the problems facing the royal doctors in the foreseeable future, and defines the decisions that must be taken. The whole document breathes a rational, tentative, empirical spirit. There is no Hermetic language, there are no recondite or elaborate prescriptions. It is Mayerne at his best.

Without following him through the labyrinth of the royal anatomy, we may note a few of his salient points. King James had had a bad start in life, having been entrusted, for his first year, to a tipsy Scottish nurse whose alcoholic milk made him so weak that he was six years old before he could walk. His legs, especially, remained weak and thin, hardly able to support his body; his crooked gait made one leg weaker than the other. Hence came the gout which had afflicted him since 1616 and now disabled him from exercise. On the other hand, his head was strong and was never upset either on the sea, or in a coach, or by drink. His natural organs too were sound, but he suffered from catarrh, was extremely sensitive to cold and wet weather, and his naturally sound faculties and functions were liable to be disturbed by accident or perturbation of mind. His early passion for the chase had led to many accidents: falls from his horse, galling boots or stirrups, legs crushed against posts; and his volatile mind, darting with incredible rapidity between elation and gloom, violent rage and sunny geniality, reacted perceptibly on his health. 'Melancholy' was accompanied by heart-ache, palpitation, vomiting and interruption of the pulse. Conversely, these physical symptoms disappeared when gaiety returned. The spleen, Mayerne explained, easily mopped up the plentiful melancholic juice and, when things went well, disposed of it 'through appropriate channels'.

Unfortunately, the king still further abused his health by bad habits. Having lost teeth through catarrh, he swallowed his food greedily without chewing it. His diet was unexceptionable, except that he would eat no bread, but

in drink he errs in quality, quantity, frequency, time and order. He drinks promiscuously beer, ale, Spanish wine, French sweet wine, and especially, his ordinary drink, thick white muscatel; whence diarrhoea. Sometimes, when his stomach is loose, he takes red Alicante wine, but he does not care whether the wine is good so long as it is sweet. He hates water and anything watery.

He would eat fresh fruit at all times of day or night, sparingly indeed, but without order; also juleps, syrups, juice of pomegranates, oranges, lemons, always sweetened with sugar. These dietary irregularities affected the health. His stomach was not good, and he suffered all his life from diarrhoea and wind. Diarrhoea was also precipitated by the melancholy to which that sensitive mind was so prone. In 1610, just before the end of his first Parliament, his extreme dejection led to a terrible bout of diarrhoea, lasting eight days. Similar bouts followed the deaths of Prince Henry in 1612 and the queen in 1619.

King James's most striking feature, according to Mayerne, was his sensitivity, both of body and of mind. His stomach, his skin, his whole system was of excessive tenderness and he suffered torments from the slightest irritations. 'He is of the most exquisite sensibility and cannot bear pain'; when in pain 'his mind is tossed by the most violent motions and the bile surges around his heart, aggravating instead of soothing the evil'. When he vomited, his whole body was affected and his face was spotted with a red rash for the next two days. After a day in the saddle his urine was often bloody – 'turbid and red like Alicante wine (these are His Majesty's own words)'.[4] He could not stand the application of plasters to the skin, 'which is so thin and tender that it itches very easily'. He refused all clysters until a grave illness in 1613. He would never allow himself to be bled, and only once permitted the application of leeches. He was 'impatient of sweat, as of everything else'. He was also a very bad sleeper: he would wake up at all hours, 'nor would sleep overtake him again, unless a book was read to him'. His ailments came and went with equal fickleness: colds would cure themselves before the apothecary had made up the prescription; jaundice would appear in the eyes and then disappear.

So difficult a patient required careful handling, especially since, as we have noted in the case of the apothecaries, he had little use for physicians. 'He laughs at medicine', wrote Mayerne, 'and regards physicians as not only unnecessary but positively useless. He says that their art rests on mere conjectures, which are uncertain and therefore invalid.' The king believed in the curative power of nature, rejected purges and drugs of all kinds as contrary to nature, and refused almost all of them. On the other hand, when he yielded, the mind commanded the matter. When a doctor – presumably Mayerne – expressed surprise that his stomach accepted, for the first and only time, a particular purge, 'he replied that he found anything easy when he had once decided that it had to be done.' In other words, what he wants, he really wants.

Having set out the problems, Mayerne did not offer authoritative answers. He simply stated the facts and marked out the limits within which his colleagues were to judge. His advice was given in the form of a series of specific questions, which would have to be answered in each hypothetical case; and since the answer would depend on circumstances, he left it to them. At present, all seemed well: 'the causes of disease, being stilled in this winter season, are suspended.' Therefore the royal physicians should exploit their respite in order to reflect seriously and individually on their work, consulting their own experience and records, 'those mute doctors', in order to protect the life of the best and most august of princes, who was also the least easy of patients.

So Mayerne prepared for his second expedition to Aubonne. He had reason to be concerned for King James's health, which had been seriously imperilled in 1619 and had shown some alarming symptoms only two months earlier, in October 1623: violent diarrhoea, weakness, piercing pains in the hip, muscular spasms in the right leg. Why then, we ask, did he go? And why did the king so easily grant him leave? Can it be that, once again, the visit to Aubonne was only partly for private business: that, in part at least, it was cover for another exercise in royal diplomacy?

It could. For now, once again, the city of Geneva was, or thought itself, in danger; the actions of the Duke of Savoy were again causing alarm. The city appealed to James I; and James I, in the new conjuncture of affairs after the failure of the Spanish match, was eager to help. He wrote two letters, one to the duke, to remind him of his treaty obligations, and one to the city, to reassure it. Mayerne, on the king's instructions, sent a copy of the first letter to the city, for information.[5] In his covering letter, Mayerne rubbed in the value of his own intervention and the thanks that were due to the king, who, in the midst of his weighty affairs, always watched over the interests of Geneva. 'Rest assured that you have here in me an indefatigable agent who, apart from his natural duty towards your state, will always be pleased to serve you and honoured to obey your commands . . . it may well be that my private affairs will call me over this summer. If so, I shall be very happy to bring you good news.'[6]

In fact, Mayerne did not arrive in the summer. His journey was delayed for a few months. This delay may have been due to the arrival, in March 1624, of an old friend, Pierre du Moulin, who had once again been summoned by King James to act as his research assistant in his long controversy with Cardinal du Perron.

Du Moulin was now thoroughly unpopular in Catholic France. His actions in 1620, which had forced him to take refuge in Sedan, had not been forgiven, and he had good reason to keep clear of French soil. He travelled from Sedan to London via the Spanish Netherlands and Holland. On his arrival in London he reported to the king at Theobalds, and the two were closeted together, doubtless discussing the arguments of du Perron. The French ambassador naturally suspected the worst. 'I do not know what happened at this conference,' he wrote, 'but those of the Religion tell me that he promised them to give the king a full description of the affairs of France, and to incite him to support the mutinous plans of the Huguenot rebels.' However, the ambassador knew where power now lay in England. 'If he tries to play this game,' he commented, 'I shall appeal to the Prince of Wales and the Duke of

Buckingham to send him out of England; for his presence here alienates this King from us.' Twelve days later, the ambassador reported that du Moulin had tried to call on him, but that he had put him off until he could be told whether the King of France wished him to receive so notorious a rebel.[7]

Soon afterwards, du Moulin fell ill. It says much for Mayerne's personal loyalty and independence of spirit that, although he had just succeeded in repairing his own relations with the French government, he at once took its *bête noire* into his own house in order to care for him. He diagnosed the disease as sciatica, complicated by acute 'melancholy'. He took great trouble with his treatment. He even offered to accompany du Moulin personally back to Sedan, if he could recover in time.[8] Meanwhile, he prepared for his own, somewhat deferred, visit to Paris and Aubonne.

He prepared it in close concert with the king. On 14 July he was knighted by the king at Theobalds.[9] Five days later, he was granted leave of absence from his duties at court. At the same time his brother-in-law, Sir Francis Biondi, was similarly granted leave.[10] As before, while Mayerne was heading for Switzerland, Biondi was bound for Savoy. Clearly the familiar pair was being sent on a diplomatic errand which, in Mayerne's case, was disguised, as usual, as a private visit. Mayerne's departure was planned for the first days of September, the necessary assurances having been given by France.

On the eve of his departure, Mayerne wrote another long document for the king's physicians-in-ordinary. Written only eight months after the previous document, it naturally has much in common with it. But it also has certain differences, both in style and in substance. It can be seen as a postscript to the former document: a postscript which intervening time has rendered at once more urgent, more authoritative and more concrete.[11]

'I am now going away', the document begins, 'and shall perhaps be absent from you (though with our royal master's permission) longer than either duty or necessity may seem to require.' Therefore he had thought it good, in conjunction with 'our most experienced colleague Dr Atkins' – the same Dr Atkins who had joined him in framing the *Pharmacopoeia* – to select, from his copious notes, such prescriptions as had, in his long experience, proved useful and acceptable for the usual ailments of 'a master who refuses all unpleasant remedies'. But before coming down to these details he laid down, in his most majestic style, the essential rules to be observed in any crisis.

The first commandment, on which all others depended, was that all amateurs, whether laymen or unqualified doctors, must be absolutely excluded. In the treatment of kings, only *artis proceres*, the heads of the profession 'whose number is very small and select', must be admitted. There was no room for those 'cranks and triflers, the fraudulent parasites of the great'. That done, six further rules were laid down in order to preserve medical solidarity.

There must be free and open deliberation. All others being removed (unless a surgeon is required), only the doctors must decide. Any disagreement among the doctors must be totally and rationally resolved, before they separate, so that no doubt remains to be exploited by those who deal in futile scholastic blather. Decisions are to be recorded in writing on the spot. Prescriptions are to be signed by all the doctors and handed to the apothecary. Finally, 'if you wish to live in peace', nothing must be said in public about their discussions: only the decision should be uttered, as an oracle. Thus, and only thus, will the physicians ensure the health of the king, the dignity of their profession, and their own peace. Of course, Mayerne adds, the royal physicians do not need this advice. He presents it so that they might prudently avoid those rocks with which the stormy sea of the court is everywhere beset, and on which his own reputation, more valuable to him than his life, had nearly been wrecked. He was thinking, of course – as so often – of the death of Prince Henry.

After this exordium, Mayerne again goes through the king's ailments: his weak stomach, obstruction of the liver attended by 'fugitive jaundice', his catarrh, his arthritis, his piles; from which were to be feared dropsy, scurvy, ulceration of the kidneys, corruption of the lungs, apoplexy. There was danger from the 'purple fever' now epidemically raging in the hot summer. And there was that constant fear of princes, poison. Basic to all prevention and cure, says Mayerne, are *victus ratio, pharmaca, chirurgi manus* – a rational way of life, correct drugs, good surgery. This patient has a delicate body, of exquisite sensation; he is unfortunately impatient of medical advice and hates drugs. So we must prescribe gingerly. Perhaps we can start by emending his deplorable drinking habits – but gradually, to avoid shock to nature. Perhaps his sleep can be improved, either artificially or by edible cures placed under his pillow. Perhaps we can minister to the disease of his mind, charm or reason away his gloom, reduce the number and fire of his brief but nevertheless painful rages. Of course, if we had a prince whom we could manage by the rules of our art, prescription would be easy; but since we may not do what we ought, let us do what his Majesty allows and prescribe as best we can, listing those remedies which he will take, and which have proved useful.

So the remedies are listed: vomitories of metallic mould in wine followed by restorative possets; laxative infusions; mineral diuretics in sweet broth, 'cream of tartar', 'vitriol of tartar', diuretic powder compounded of crab's eyes, fish heads, crickets, grasshoppers, millipedes, etc. 'which I pass over lest the list of remedies swell beyond reason'. Sudorifics are good for the king, but will he take them? The best sudorific for bad fits of melancholy is antimony fixed by spirit of nitre, but many are (quite wrongly) afraid of it; so gentler vegetable potions can be used. For the king's intestinal complaints the best cures are metallic: iron peroxide, to be made thus and thus; mineral waters from Spa,

Wellingborough and Tunbridge; and, for paroxysms of diarrhoea, *chalybeata*, iron drinks which unfortunately the king hates, so that it is a waste of time to describe them. For gout, Hippocrates requires an exact regime, 'for which, in our master, I would not dare to hope'. Thus, while recording the need, we must fall back on more traditional remedies: arthritic powder compounded of scrapings of an unburied human skull, herbs, white wine, whey, etc., to be taken at the full moon, when the humours are most swollen. But since the king hates eating human bodies, an ox's head can be substituted. For extreme pain, there are narcotics, which only timid doctors are afraid to use. For piles, lenitive applications and blood-letting are necessary. Against purple fever, if it cannot be nipped in the bud by bleeding, Mayerne sets out all the old nostrums – bezoar, contrayerva, oil of scorpions. Against poison, the sovereign remedy is still the Saxon powder – that great secret of Dr Kolreuter[12] – compounded of organs of vipers and honey. These, in brief, are the remedies: the great problem is to persuade the king to take them, or even to take physicians and their advice seriously. For this an effort of propaganda is needed. It must be directed not only against the irreducible scepticism of the king but also to his councillors and servants, who must persuade him, not so much by reasons (which his acute intellect is always able to refute) as by prayers and conjurations, to take greater care of his health, to hold physicians in greater esteem, and to pay more heed to their instructions. On this somewhat despairing note Mayerne took leave of his colleagues and prepared for his second journey to Aubonne.

If Mayerne had any apprehensions about leaving his king for several months, King James was equally apprehensive about being left without his doctor. His anxiety shows through the last document that he wrote for Mayerne before Mayerne's departure – the last document he would ever write for him. It is a formal letter from the King of England to 'our good friends the Avoyer and Council of the City of Berne', and it was written at the very last moment before Mayerne left. Seldom can a formal letter from a king to city magistrates have revealed such personal concern, such warmth of feeling. It can be seen as a last testimonial to a valued friend and, at the same time, the expression of personal foreboding that he might need him most of all when he was out of reach.

'The Sieur de Mayerne, Baron of Aubonne, our faithful and well-beloved counsellor and chief physician,' the king wrote,

> having asked our leave to go beyond seas in order to visit his house of Aubonne in the lands that are subject to you, and to settle his private affairs, we have asked him to carry with him our most express recommendation, in keeping with the measure of his fidelity to us and ours and the value that

we place upon him. The good treatment which he received from you, on the strength of the letters which he brought from us on his first journey, remains fresh in our memory, and we believe that these second letters will be even more effective, if that is possible, whether for the granting of his just requests, or the furtherance of his affairs, or for the justice which our servants, and especially those who are so close to our person, may reasonably expect from you. . . . His duties make his presence so necessary to us that our temporary suspension of them is no small proof of our favour. Contribute to his prompt return by shortening, as far as you can, the interruption of his service. We shall be grateful to you, and shall prove it to you in like and greater matters. For the rest, be assured of our love to your state, whose prosperity and preservation will always be close to our heart. The said sieur de Mayerne will renew these assurances to you on our behalf, and you may entirely trust his words. So we pray God, Messieurs, to keep you in his protection.[13]

The worst apprehensions, both of Mayerne and of the king, were soon to be confirmed.

Mayerne's original plan was to sail from Dover to Dieppe, taking with him his ailing guest, du Moulin. Another companion on the voyage was to be a young Swiss pastor, Antoine Léger, the secretary of the Genevese emissary Benedetto Turrettini. Léger had been on a short visit to England and was now returning to Geneva. He would afterwards play a significant part in the Protestant international as the agent through whom the Greek Church in its captivity would be swung over, temporarily, to Calvinism. However, in the end it was decided that du Moulin was too ill to travel. He was therefore transferred from Mayerne's house to that of Philip Burlamachi, where he would soon be joined by his wife and children. Mayerne then left for France with Léger. He went via Amiens,[14] and by the beginning of October was in Paris for the first time since his humiliating expulsion in 1618.

From the moment when Mayerne left England, his *Ephemerides* are silent. We do not know how he spent his time in France. But in his letters to the French ministers he had declared his intention of waiting on Louis XIII, and on them, to express his gratitude for favour past and to come. This intention had also been reported to Louis XIII personally by the French ambassador in London, the Marquis d'Effiat, who had added his own testimonial. Mayerne, he wrote, was a good Frenchman; his claim for arrears of salary was 'worthy of the justice of your Majesty'; and he had the support of King James.[15] We may therefore assume that Mayerne not only saw his French patients in Paris but also waited on the king. We know, from a later letter, that he was received by the king's ministers and that he believed he had secured at least some promise about his economic interests.[16] The ministers, incidentally, had recently changed. In August the Marquis de la Vieuville, *chef de conseil*, had fallen from power and been replaced by Mayerne's old patient, Cardinal de Richelieu, who now began his nineteen-year rule in France.

Can we assume anything else? It is tempting to note that this was precisely the moment at which the hand of the Prince of Wales, rebuffed in Spain, was being accepted for Henrietta Maria, Princess of France. The negotiations had been in train for several months. The policy was that of Buckingham, who hoped to complete it by an Anglo-French alliance, as the driving force of a great coalition against Spain. To Mayerne, such a marriage would obviously be welcome. It would ease the strain of his double loyalty, and the alliance, if it were made, would forward his political aims: it would have the effect which he desired in Switzerland, it would defend the Protestant interest in Germany, and it would be some protection to the Huguenots of France. If a private contact were needed in these delicate matters, he was clearly fitted for the task. However, we can only speculate. We have no evidence of any political activity by Mayerne in Paris; the memory of 1618 was not yet obliterated. We do not know how long he stayed in Paris – probably at least three weeks. Then he went on to Geneva, Aubonne and Berne.

How did he spend his time in Switzerland? He kept no records of those months. The public archives are silent. But the chance survival of a single document shows that he was not idle. The document is a private letter sent from Geneva, in November, to the Duke of Buckingham who, at that time, as a sequel to the marriage treaty, was planning a new Anglo-French campaign on the Continent. A joint army, under Count Ernst von Mansfeld, the defeated commander of the Palatine army, was to enter Germany from France and reconquer the lost Palatinate. On this subject Mayerne had ideas; and since he had been treating the duke on the eve of his departure, and had agreed with him to exchange information, he now took the opportunity of a professional letter to set them out.

After a few preliminaries about his medical remedies and instructions, which he heard had been very effective, and somewhat unctuous congratulations on the French marriage and the prospect of a French alliance, he came to the main point. Everyone, he wrote, was now eagerly awaiting the arrival of the English army under Count von Mansfeld, poised to strike 'wherever the wise directions of the king our master will take it'. On this subject he had had some conversation in Geneva with his old friend the Margrave of Baden-Durlach, and he now wrote to suggest that the margrave should be invited to play a part in this grand strategy – perhaps by a diversionary attack on the enemy base of Bavaria. The margrave, he pointed out, had a promise of help from France and Venice; he had particularly close relations with Messieurs de Berne, who were now alone among the Swiss in showing 'that they have some blood in their fingernails and some courage'; and his personal qualities were exceptional. He had always shown himself a man of his word, even when others had broken theirs; he had always fought on when others had surrendered and 'had never bent the knee in servile obedience'; he was a professional at his trade, recognised by all as an expert – captain-general, *maréchal de camp, castramétateur, sergent de bataille, maistre d'artillerie*; his own lands and fortresses were strategically placed as 'a curtain before the Palatinate, on the side where danger threatens'; and he was the only Lutheran prince who cooperated with Calvinists. In short, he would be an ideal ally – let Buckingham consult Lord Belfast who had seen action with him in Germany – and was eager to be employed and to give satisfaction. Mayerne also enclosed with his letter a report on the latest events in the Grisons, where there had been a most satisfactory coup by the anti-Habsburg party. Altogether, the Habsburgs 'would find nothing to laugh at anywhere. Forgive me for acting as your counsellor: if I should err in it, blame yourself who invited me to do so.'[17]

All we can say about the rest of Mayerne's visit to Switzerland is that he was at Berne in December, where he treated his old patient Hans Rudolf von Erlach;[18] that he received from his friend Fabricius Hildanus a presentation copy of his latest work on surgery, containing Mayerne's own writings on the *caruncula;* and that he then returned to Aubonne. He was at Aubonne late in March, when his rural peace was suddenly shattered by a letter from his faithful apothecary and banker, Pierre Naudin. It brought alarming news concerning Mayerne's post as *médecin ordinaire* to Louis XIII.

We have seen that, on his migration to England, Mayerne had contrived to retain his office, which he exercised by deputy, himself keeping the title and the salary, both of which he valued. The French court had accepted this arrangement partly because it thought that he might be useful as a political agent. In fact his political services had been negligible: in 1618 he had indeed been accused of being a spy, but on the wrong side. So we are not surprised that his salary had fallen into arrears. Mayerne's elaborate protestations of devotion to France, the French monarchy and the French interests were not entirely free of economic motives, and his visit to Paris on the way out to Aubonne had, he thought, settled that matter. However, apart from the mere question of arrears, there was also another, far graver threat which had occasionally sounded ominously in his ears: a threat not merely to the regularity of his salary but to the title itself, by which the salary was justified. For naturally, since Mayerne had taken up a full-time post in England, there were those who claimed that his appointment at the French court had lapsed, and was at the disposal of the Crown. The Crown, which sold such posts, had an interest in a regular turnover; and of course there were aspirants ready and eager to purchase them.

The first challenge to Mayerne's post came from one Paul le Maistre, whom Mayerne had succeeded as *médecin par quartier* to Henri IV in 1602.[19] Le Maistre was *premier médecin* of the Prince de Condé[20] and *médecin ordinaire* to Louis XIII.[21] He was evidently a protégé of Jean Héroard, the *premier médecin* of Louis XIII. Fortunately Héroard was a friend of Mayerne, and seems to have kept le Maistre under control. Then le Maistre died, and Mayerne, writing to Héroard to condole on his death, remarked that at any rate his own post was presumably now unchallenged.[22] More recently, in March 1624, another competitor had arisen, one Rodalsé. Fortunately his claim was expressed in such violent language that it was not taken seriously. Mayerne had mobilised the French ambassador in London, and the impertinent Rodalsé had been duly squashed.[23] Thus when he left Paris for Aubonne, having exchanged compliments with the king and his ministers, he had assumed that this particular danger was now extinct.

It was therefore with some dismay that he now learned from Naudin that a new claimant – the physician of Gaston d'Orléans, the king's brother – had arisen and was actually bringing a legal action against him, demanding that he produce his legal title to the office. Mayerne reacted vigorously. He wrote magisterial letters to the Chancellor of France, M. d'Aligre, and to the Secretary of State, M. Ville-aux-Clercs. The case, he declared, was *un vis sans fin*, an endless screw: he had thought that, 'after seeing you' – that is, on his way through Paris – 'one word would have settled all'; but no doubt these grand ministers had other things on their minds. As for his title-deeds, he could not produce them: they were in England 'in a place accessible only to me, and I have the key with me here in Switzerland'. So he relied on the French ministers to put an end to all this nonsense . . .'[24] Then he packed his bags and prepared to leave Aubonne at once and to return to England – via Paris.

Before leaving Switzerland, he paid a formal visit to their Excellencies of Berne. From them he received a letter to James I, acknowledging the king's interest in the re-establishment of Christendom and thanking him particularly for having allowed M. de Mayerne to visit them.[25] From Berne he returned to Geneva. There he was greeted with sombre news from England. His worst apprehensions had been realised. King James was dead.

He had died on 27 March while his chief physician was absent in Switzerland. To be sure, Mayerne had left careful instructions how the other royal physicians were to act if a crisis should arise. Unfortunately, in his absence, none of these instructions were obeyed. The result was a scandal whose repercussions would be heard for the next thirty years.

For what had been Mayerne's instructions? He had demanded that laymen and unqualified doctors be kept away from the royal bed, that decisions be made by the established royal doctors only, that any disagreement between them must be resolved before they separate, that their collective decisions be recorded and signed, and that no preliminary discussions or disagreements be published. Only thus could scandal such as had followed the death of Prince Henry be averted. But what had in fact happened? The courtiers and the amateur doctors had thronged the royal bedchamber, recommending their private nostrums; the doctors had been divided among themselves; nothing had been recorded; and, worst of all, the disputes had been carried outside the bedchamber and a tendentious account, with malicious insinuations, had been printed and published to the world.

The king had been in uncertain health for some time, and at the beginning of March he himself began to feel that his end was near. On 2 March one of his favourite Scottish courtiers, the second Marquis of Hamilton, Lord Steward of the Household, was carried away, like many others, by a malignant fever, then raging. 'If the branches be thus cut down,' sighed the king, 'the stock cannot continue long.' Three days later he too went down with the same fever. He recovered sufficiently to attend Hamilton's funeral on 23 March, but his health failed again thereafter, and four days later he was dead. In the course of his illness he had been attended by the royal doctors, but, as usual, had paid little attention to them. Divided among themselves, and lacking the overpowering authority of Mayerne, they could not prevent him from taking amateur remedies and, in particular, while they were away at dinner, from taking a posset drink prescribed by the Duke of Buckingham and from having a plaster – the nostrum of a country doctor at Dunmow – applied to his wrists and stomach by Buckingham's mother. The royal doctors, on their return from dinner, naturally resented this interference, and one of them, Dr John Craig, the son and successor of the king's first Scottish 'principal mediciner', broke yet another of Mayerne's rules by revealing all, and perhaps more than all, to a dubious compatriot, George Eglishem.

George Eglishem was a Scot who, by his own account, had always been on familiar terms with the great. As an infant, he had been brought up with his contemporary, the Marquis of Hamilton (their fathers being – he said – the closest of friends). At the age of three he had been presented by him to King James, then King of Scotland. Later, he had studied medicine in Leiden, and after several years of practice abroad had returned, about 1616, to his own country. There King James had not only made him his personal physician but had also showered him with honours, gifts and offices, and had submitted patiently to his most vulgar impertinences.[26] So at least Eglishem would claim, when the king and the marquis were both safely dead. Unfortunately not one of these claims is corroborated by external records. From them, all that we learn is that Eglishem had indeed spent some time abroad, where he had made himself ridiculous by extravagant claims and bombastic controversies; that he was alleged to have been guilty of coining false money; and that his marriage, in 1617, had taken place in the Clink prison. There is no evidence that he had any medical qualifications, though apparently he did dabble in astrology. Since he described himself, in print, in 1618, while King James was alive, by the vague title of *regius medicus*, the king's doctor, it is possible that he had some casual connection with the court, although the court seems to have been unaware of it. His controversial writings – extravagant attacks on scholars whom King James was known to dislike[27] – were presumably designed to attract royal favour. They could certainly serve no other purpose. Among scholars, they only excited ribald mirth and gained him such irreverent nicknames as Thunderer, Windbag and Ass's Fart.[28]

This was the man to whom, it appears, Dr Craig divulged his doubts. Eglishem converted them to further uses. A year later, when the House of Commons was impeaching Buckingham, Eglishem (from abroad, at a safe distance) published a pamphlet in which he claimed – with a wealth of circumstantial detail, as if he had himself been present at the time – that both King James and Eglishem's supposed patron the Marquis of Hamilton had been poisoned by the Duke of Buckingham.[29] Indeed, he alleged that there was a long list of important men whom Buckingham intended to have murdered, and that he, Eglishem, was also on the list. And he called, severally, on the king and the Parliament to put the duke on trial for murder.[30] The Parliament, of course, was sympathetic; but even it did not, as yet, take up Eglishem's charge: it merely accused the duke of impropriety in interfering with the medical treatment of King James. The king was less sympathetic: he dissolved the Parliament and ordered the prosecution of Eglishem and his accomplices. As Eglishem was in Brussels[31] – enemy territory – he was not prosecuted. He simply disappeared from history.

His pamphlet did not. Indeed, it was to have a remarkably long life. Published in Latin, English and German, it scattered the seeds of a very useful myth. Originally inspired (we must assume) by Buckingham's enemies, who were mortified by his political survival into the new reign, it fed his impeachment in 1626 and was cited by his assassin in 1628.[32] Then, when Buckingham was out of the way, it was turned against King Charles. For had not King Charles too profited by the death of his father? Had he not clearly been in league with Buckingham against James I who, in his last months, was wearying of the insolent favourite? Had he not afterwards protected him by frustrating this impeachment? The charge of poisoning his father would be insidiously revived during the Puritan Revolution: by the House of Commons as a reason for breaking off negotiations with the king in 1648; and as justification for the king's execution by the most eloquent hack-writer of the Revolution, John Milton.[33]

Mayerne's instructions, if they had been enforced by his presence, would at least have prevented this scandal. As it was, he was helpless in Geneva. All that he could do was to accept a new commission from that city. Instead of letters of thanks to King James, such as he was carrying from Berne, he took with him letters of condolence to King Charles, accompanied by secret verbal instructions. Then he set off for Paris, where he had work to do *en route* for London.

In Paris no doubt he saw the French ministers again, to fix, finally as he hoped, the unending screw of his title as *médecin ordinaire du roi*. But he also saw other old friends. In particular, he was once again closeted in alchemical experiments with Guillaume de Trougny, now back in the capital; and he renewed his acquaintance with another old Huguenot friend, Nicolas Briot.[34]

We last met the Briot family in Mayerne's earliest days in Paris. Lorrainers by birth, engravers and metal-workers by family tradition, import–export merchants in Flanders, they were also apothecaries as a sideline. It was evidently in this capacity, and as members of the immigrant Huguenot colony in Paris, that they were known to Mayerne. Since then, they had experienced many ups and downs. In 1608 Didier Briot had leased the right to mint money for the Duc de Nevers, but he had been squeezed out by his own engraver and had withdrawn, like so many other Huguenots, to Sedan. There, for a time, he minted the money of the Duc de Bouillon. Meanwhile his son Nicolas had established himself as *tailleur-général des monnaies* of France (principal engraver of the Mint) – and also of his native Lorraine. Although forbidden to work for other princes, he occasionally obtained licence to do so. He also engraved prints for private patrons, among them the great botanist Caspar Bauhin.

To outward appearance, Nicolas Briot was a successful and prosperous man. However, there were rivalries in the Mint, and wherever he went he had a genius for making enemies. Perhaps his techniques were really defective, as was said; perhaps his religion, as well as his temper, made him unpopular. At all events, his ambitious plan to re-mint the coinage of France, though supported by the king, was opposed by the experts and the Cour des Monnaies. In September 1624, after a long struggle, he was deprived of his office. When Mayerne visited him on his return to Paris in the spring of 1625 he found him defeated and riddled with debts.[35] It was while he was in this state that Briot decided to emigrate, as Mayerne had done, to England. The sequence of events makes it almost certain that it was Mayerne who encouraged him to do so.

Mayerne himself returned to England late in June 1625. He at once took steps to ensure that his economic interests would be protected in the new reign. He also sought to perform his duties on behalf of the city of Geneva. On 15 July he wrote to the city to report his success. Apologising for his delay, he explained that he had waited for the right moment and had finally caught the king in his bedchamber, at his *levée*, 'when his grandeur was laid aside'. He had made all the necessary protestations, recommendations, remonstrances and appeals, without omitting any detail of his verbal instructions. The king (he said) had received the formal letter from Geneva with a smiling, friendly countenance which bore witness to his inner thoughts and gave assurance of his good intentions towards the republic. A few days later, being solicited for an answer, the king instructed Mayerne to thank the city for its congratulations, and to assure it that its preservation was close to his heart, as he would show whenever necessary: he only regretted that it was not nearer in space, so that he could show his good will towards it more easily.[36]

That was the last message which Mayerne would ever pass between the King of Great Britain and a foreign government. Times, he was soon to discover, had changed.

One other change must have been apparent to him at once. When he left England, he had been much concerned with the health of his friend and house-guest, Pierre du Moulin, who had been too ill to accompany him to France and had stayed behind in the house of Philip Burlamachi. It seems clear that du Moulin, at that time, had intended to settle permanently in England, and that his proposed return to Sedan was simply to wind up his affairs and fetch his family; for Protestantism in Sedan did not seem so secure now that its old patron, the Duc de Bouillon, was dead. In fact, since he was unable to travel, his family came to England and joined him there, thus making his own journey unnecessary. In October 1624 du Moulin showed the nature of his plans by a letter which he wrote to Sir Edward Conway, the Secretary of State. In it he noted that the Bishop of Gloucester had just died; and he took the opportunity to ask Conway to remember him to his Majesty, 'so that, by his command, the Lord Keeper may give orders that I be appointed'.[37] The Lord Keeper, at the time, was that agile and cultivated Jacobean trimmer, John Williams, Bishop of Lincoln, who, no doubt, would happily have helped one of his master's intellectual protégés into an English bishopric. But alas, it was too late: that bishopric was bespoke; and by the time that another was vacant, du Moulin had read the signs of the times correctly. When King James died, he packed his bags and returned to Sedan:[38] for the rest of his long life – he would live to be ninety – he would never see England again.

However, to compensate for the loss of one friend, Mayerne was soon able to welcome another. In September 1625, only three months after they had parted in Paris, Nicolas Briot arrived in London. He arrived without funds and without promise of employment, and it is probable that he lived, at first, with Mayerne. We are told (and Mayerne's papers bear it out) that in his first months in England 'he practised medicine and made some excellent cures'; also that he engraved seals for the King and Queen of England.[39] Certainly he was working for the king very soon, and it must have been Mayerne who introduced him at court. Briot showed his gratitude in tangible form. One of his first works in England is a medallion, which is also the first known portrait, of the friend and patron who had rescued him from France and brought him to begin a new career in England. Mayerne's profile appears on the obverse, in furred gown and straight shirt collar, with a Latin inscription 'Theodore de Mayerne, Kt, Baron of Aubonne, chief physician to the Kings of France and England'. On the reverse is Hermetic symbolism and a Latin version of Mayerne's Greek motto, 'non haec sine Numine':[40] these things were acquired not without divine will.

For Briot too was a Hermetist. This many-talented man, who was to become, within three years, the chief engraver to the King of England[41] – in England, as in France, he was supported by the king against the violent opposition of the officers of the Mint – was also an alchemical philosopher whose views (like his cures) were respected by Mayerne. Among Mayerne's papers is a treatise which in November 1626 Mayerne copied out, with his own hand, with headings in silver ink, 'from the miscellanies of M. Briot' in London.[42] It is a succinct exposition of the theory of Paracelsian chemistry, beginning with the creation of the world as the separation, by the Divine Chemist, of the pure from the impure – that is, from the Soul of the World above, which operates on the Four Elements below and creates the three principles out of them. From an understanding of these processes comes the art of alchemy and alchemical medicine, whereby in terrestrial things too, and in the body of a man, pure is separated from impure, subtle from thick and gross, so that the active spiritual forces of Nature, refined and delivered from corporal bonds, can realise their purposes: for 'all virtue and active power come from Heaven, which is the Soul of the World, and this Soul dwells in the universal Spirit which injects it into bodies.' So we come down to medical application: to the use of antimony, sulphur of gold, laudanum, magistery of pearls and 'the blood-purifying syrup of Dr. Mayerne'. At this point Mayerne himself afterwards added a proprietary marginal note in his private red ink: 'I once ordered this syrup for Jean Martin, Brother of the Rosy Cross, nephew of M. Briot, suffering from incipient leprosy . . . When he was cured, he went to Moscow, where he died.'

This Jean Martin, goldsmith, jeweller and apothecary, went to Moscow soon after Mayerne had copied out his uncle's text. Mayerne was behind that journey too: his influence reached out even to the court of the Tsar. The key figure here was Arthur Dee, the son of the great English Magus, the founding father of Rosicrucianism, John Dee. Arthur Dee was a professed Rosicrucian, and a Hermetic physician. He had trouble with the Royal College of Physicians because of his unorthodox panaceas. But in 1615, probably through Mayerne's influence, he became physician to Queen Anne. He went to Russia in 1621 with a recommendation to the Tsar Michael Romanov by James I, and was one of those who introduced chemical medicine there. In December 1626 he returned to England to visit his family – and with a secret commission from the Tsar: for the Tsar also used doctors as amateur diplomats. In London, he found Mayerne working in close contact with Briot. When he returned to Moscow, he took with him Briot's nephew, together with John Gilbert, chief engraver of the royal mint. Four years later, Mayerne sent another member of Briot's family to join Dee in Russia. This was Briot's son Philippe, who arrived in Moscow with a letter from Charles I to the Tsar. He was employed in Russia as an apothecary and surgeon. Unfortunately he proved a bad hat, and gave Dee a great deal of trouble, producing, 'instead of grain, thistles and barren wild oats'; but Mayerne would ask Dee to forgive all for the sake of his own love of the Briot family.[43]

That was in the future. Meanwhile Mayerne and Briot, two Huguenot *émigrés*, collaborated to inaugurate the new reign in England. On 2 February 1626 Charles I was crowned in Westminster Abbey. The coronation largesse – the special coins distributed as commemorative tokens by the king – was minted by Briot. The coronation oil with which the king was anointed – that magic balm which not all the water in the rough rude sea could wash away – was manufactured by the royal apothecary, another Huguenot, Nicholas le Myre, according to a new recipe devised by Theodore de Mayerne. It contained orange and jasmine flowers distilled in Benjamin oil, oils of rose and cinnamon, benzoin, ambergris, civet, musk and spirit of rosemary, and had a rich and peculiar fragrance. It was evidently satisfactory, for it has been used ever since, and was compounded, in 1953, by Messrs Savory and Moore, for the coronation of Queen Elizabeth II.[44]

18

Charles I and the Protestant Débâcle, 1625–1630

The death of James I, like the death of Elizabeth, transformed the English court – and not only the court. To moralists, the change was for the better. As the Puritan Lucy Hutchinson would put it – and as the widow of a regicide she had no love for Charles I:

> the face of the court was much changed in the change of the king, for King Charles was temperate, chaste and serious; so that the fools and bawds, mimics and catamites of the former court grew out of fashion. . . . Men of learning and ingenuity in all arts were in esteem, and received encouragement from the king, who was a most excellent judge and a great lover of paintings, carvings, gravings and many other ingenuities, less offensive than the bawdry and profane abusive wit which was the only exercise of the other court.[1]

Mrs Hutchinson did not, of course, approve of art – to her it was merely 'less offensive' than profane wit; nor did she allow that King James had been a great patron and encourager of science.

King Charles's court was certainly more orderly, more correct, formal and decorous than that of his father. But behind this superficial improvement in 'the face of the court' there was a deeper change. The intellectual openness, the ready acceptance of novel ideas, even of heresy, was over. Heresy now had too dangerous a mien. In the universal convulsion of Europe, it looked too like subversion. *Stare super antiquas vias* – to stand upon the old ways – would be the motto of King Charles's reign. In the world of learning, King James had presided over the founding of new libraries, new scientific studies, new university chairs. King Charles would preside over new disciplinary statutes and a redirection of learning into the safe study of the Fathers. The correctness of the court was a model for the correction of society.

There was also a change in politics. King James had not given much thought to the government of England. Delighted to have come at last into so rich an inheritance, he spent freely, declared himself an absolute king, and in fact allowed the old machinery to run on. But in foreign affairs he had a policy. However weakly and erratically he may have pursued this aim, he sought to be the arbiter of Europe, the pacifier of ideological strife. He saw himself, as others saw him, as the patron of the Protestant international. But he was a pacific patron, who sought to protect European Protestantism, not to lead it on aggressive crusades. He would support the French Huguenots, but only so that, by standing firm, they could effectively demand, and he could secure for them, equal rights: rights of peaceful coexistence. His Alpine diplomacy – the treaty between Switzerland, Geneva and Savoy – had secured such coexistence in the nodal point of Europe. Admittedly, at the end of his reign, such aims appeared chimerical, but they were still his aims. The embassies of Lord Doncaster, the first and ablest of his favourites, were the last vain gropings for that lost ideal. They were lost in the noise and shambles of the Thirty Years War.

King Charles's policies were very different, indeed opposite. He had firm views about government at home. His father had talked about absolute monarchy by divine right, but had done nothing to realise it. His son would realise it by re-establishing the authority of the Crown over Parliament, of the Privy Council over local government, of the bishops over the Church. He did not believe in pluralism. Rather he believed in a unitary state and a unitary Church. In 1625 these could only be aspirations. If they were to be realised, hard work was needed – by somebody. As for foreign affairs, they were already out of control, and it was too late for a King of England to seek to determine them. King James had sacrificed real power in England to the pursuit of illusory power in Europe. King Charles would reverse this process. He would put his own house in order. Foreign policy, to him, had only one aim. It was not to restore European peace or to hold the balance of European power, but to recover, one way or another – either by compliance with the victorious Catholic powers, or by support of Protestant resistance – the lost inheritance of his brother-in-law and sister, their electorate on the Rhine. To his subjects, this struggle for the Palatinate was an ideological crusade. They saw Protestantism crushed, its ministers persecuted or exiled, the Jesuits moving in; and they subscribed money freely and clamoured for action. To King Charles it was purely dynastic, the cause of his family, which had been dispossessed, and must be restored; and restoration by treaty would be cheaper, and more agreeable, than restoration by war.

These were King Charles's ideals, from the outset of his reign. But they could not be immediately expressed in action. With the crown he had inherited its present problems, which had first to be disposed of. He had also inherited a dominating minister, the man whose personal authority, for over three years, would mask the abruptness of the change and prolong, until it was disastrous, the political anarchy of the declining years of King James. This was the last favourite of King James, George Villiers, Marquis, now Duke, of Buckingham.

Whatever we think of Buckingham's politics, we cannot resist the evidence of his personal charm. To have held, for ten years, the wayward affections of King James and yet, at the same time, to have completely bewitched his son, and so preserved his influence undiminished, even increased, in the new reign, argues no mean powers of fascination. Nor was that fascination exercised only on successive kings. Until the political disasters of his rule had become obvious, and had drawn upon him almost universal obloquy, all men admitted it and yielded willingly to him. The patriot Sir John Eliot and the future Archbishop Laud cannot be regarded as mere toadies of power; the clergy of all persuasions succumbed to him; and even after his unlamented death the future Earl of Clarendon would praise the 'noble nature and generous disposition', the 'flowing courtesy and affability to all men', of the great favourite.

Unfortunately, personal charm and political sense do not always go together. In the first three and a half years of the new reign, when Buckingham was, to all intents and purposes, Regent of England, his vanity and irresponsibility carried Jacobean foreign policy, already aimless from the loss of its helmsman, and fatally holed on the uncharted rocks of Germany, into final shipwreck on the shoals and sandbanks of Cadiz and la Rochelle.

The turning-point came in the year 1624. It was then that Buckingham, having returned with Prince Charles from the visit to Spain, which was the last, most dramatic episode in the long and futile project of the Spanish marriage, and having made a royal marriage treaty with France instead, committed the weakening King James to war with Spain. In vain the king protested at this rejection of his policy, this abandonment of all hope of being the mediator of Europe. Buckingham, carrying the prince with him, and riding the crest of parliamentary enthusiasm for a Protestant war, was irresistible. War was declared. A German condottiere was employed to lead a landforce to the Palatinate. A naval expedition against Cadiz was prepared. Unfortunately, in the same year, a new minister came to power in France also; and Buckingham and Prince Charles, having committed themselves to dependence upon France, in order to fight against Spain, found themselves involved with a statesman whom they could never match, the Cardinal de Richelieu.

The crisis arose because Richelieu was determined to bring the French Huguenots to heel and, wielding the whole weight of a united France, to resume the European policy of Henri IV. When he came to power he found the Huguenots stronger than ever, Rohan's resistance having forced the French government to restore their rights and to confirm their ecclesiastical assemblies. Rohan himself had been received into favour. He was the victor of the civil war, the guarantor of the treaty, the man of the hour; and his power in the south was now firmly based. It rested on the impregnable maritime city of la Rochelle, the defensible land massif of the Auvergne, and the formidable organisation of the churches. It was now increased by his governorship of numerous strong Protestant towns. But Richelieu had no intention of allowing this power to remain unbroken. His purpose was made clear by the building, in defiance of the treaty, of a new fortress opposite la Rochelle. It was called Fort Louis. When the Huguenots saw that the work on Fort Louis had not been suspended they knew that Richelieu was determined to break the treaty. They believed that 'either la Rochelle must take Fort Louis or Fort Louis will take la Rochelle'; and when remonstrances failed, they decided to strike first: to make, from their present position of strength, a new war of religion.

The initiative, this time, came not from Rohan but from his brother Soubise. Soubise, the sea captain, called in by la Rochelle, dragged his brother into the war. Then, by his indiscriminate piracy, he enabled Richelieu to call on his allies, first the Dutch, then the English, for aid. Rohan had appealed for English support, but Charles I – that is, Buckingham – was committed to the chimera of a French alliance, and in September 1625 Soubise, defeated at sea, fled to England which, from now on, was to be his base and his home.

With the destruction of Soubise's fleet, Rohan was left to fight on alone by land. At first his position seemed desperate, and Richelieu believed that he could detach him from la Rochelle, leaving that obstinate city unprotected by land as by sea. However, Rohan refused to be detached, or to make any separate agreement with Richelieu. In the end Charles I interposed to secure peace. By the Treaty of Paris, on 5 February 1626, Richelieu undertook to raze Fort Louis 'in reasonable time'. The treaty was guaranteed by Charles I. It was accepted with relief by the towns of Languedoc, but the citizens of la Rochelle were not confident. They could only be confident when they saw Fort Louis razed to the ground.

Fort Louis was not razed: instead the building was resumed. Nor were the other terms of the treaty kept. For Richelieu hated the treaty, imposed as it was by foreign mediation, which he saw as foreign intervention in the affairs of France. Now he was determined to end such intervention. Rohan in France and Soubise in England, when they saw the treaty broken, naturally appealed to Charles I as its guarantor; and Buckingham, who had himself, by now, quarrelled with the Crown of France, persuaded Charles to promise military support. He was prepared to make war not only against Spain, but also against France.

How could he – even he – contemplate so wild a venture? His war against Spain had been disastrous. In Germany, nothing had been gained. The war at sea had been a failure: the English fleet had returned broken and mutinous from Cadiz. The English Parliament, which had so recently supported his bellicose gestures, was now crying for his blood. But he was not alarmed. While King Charles protected Buckingham's rear by dissolving Parliament, the duke set out to recover his own prestige and popularity by extending the war: by making it a conflict not only for the Palatinate but for the Protestant cause: the cause of the French Huguenots. If Rohan would maintain the Protestant revolt in France, the English fleet would carry Soubise to the relief of la Rochelle. Meanwhile a great coalition would be raised to distract the power of France. The dukes of Savoy and Lorraine would be persuaded to attack in the east, and the Prince de Condé and the nobility of France would be invited to resume their old rebellion against the Crown.

So began the last of the French wars of religion: the final struggle for the distinct political rights of the Huguenots within France. It was a struggle which Richelieu could not afford to lose and in which England, being involved as a belligerent, could no longer appear as a mediator, and could end only victorious or defeated. In fact, for Buckingham, it would end in total defeat: defeat and annihilation. His grand coalition never materialised. His envoy to Savoy was seized in France and thrown into the Bastille, where he revealed to the French government that Rohan was in league with England. The French princes hung back. The Duc de Bouillon was dead. The Prince de Condé, bribed by the promise of Rohan's estates, commanded royal, not rebel, troops. The Rohan brothers were isolated. Rohan himself was proscribed as a rebel. The Parlement of Toulouse, always savage in its bigotry, condemned him, fortunately in his absence, to be torn apart by four horses; and it offered 50,000 écus and a patent of nobility to his assassin. His mother and sister fled for refuge to la Rochelle. Soubise, serving under Buckingham's command, shared in his defeat and ignominious return to England. On 23 August 1628 Buckingham, who was preparing, with Soubise, to lead another fleet to rescue his lost reputation, was assassinated at Portsmouth. Two months later, la Rochelle, after a long siege, was starved into surrender. Its great walls were razed, its special privileges cancelled, its autonomy ended. Protestantism was not rooted out, as in conquered Bohemia or the Palatinate. 'The Religion' could still be freely practised. But the whole concept of Huguenot 'places de sureté', safe havens, as guaranteed by the Edict of Nantes, was now obsolete. Henceforth royal officers would rule the provincial Huguenot town.

With the fall of its maritime citadel, the cause of the Huguenot rebellion was doomed. For another eight months, Rohan sought to maintain the struggle in his southern redoubt. Betrayed by Protestant England, he turned to Catholic Savoy, and even, in despair, to Catholic Spain. At last, in June 1629, he accepted defeat. By the Peace of Alais, the Huguenots bought their survival as a tolerated sect by surrendering their political claims, their public representation, and the General Assemblies which had been the means of their unity. As for the Rohan brothers – Richelieu's *frères Antichristi* – the cardinal, seeking not revenge but unity, would gladly have employed them, as Henri IV had continued to employ his Huguenot warriors, in the service of France – but not, after such a struggle, within France. Indeed, neither of them was willing to live in the country of their defeat. Soubise would spend the rest of his life as an exile in England, a restless, perpetual intriguer against the hated cardinal. Rohan, restored to his property but never fully trusted by Richelieu, would continue to combine his old ideals of French patriotism and active Huguenot virtue by serving the suspicious cardinal where alone they could still be combined: abroad.

The year 1629 thus marked the end of a chapter in the history of the Huguenots of France. It also, by a necessary consequence, closed a chapter of English history. No longer could the King of England dream of protecting the liberties of the Huguenots, for there were now no such liberties to protect. They had been swept away, as so many Protestant liberties had been swept away in those years of universal disaster. By 1629 the whole concept of international Protestantism had become a chimera, with the Catholic Church resuming all its lost lands in Germany and victorious imperial armies on the shores of the Baltic sea. The old Jacobean policy, which King James himself had articulated rather than applied, had been carried to bankruptcy by Buckingham. Now, with the removal of Buckingham, it could be wound up. In 1629 Charles I sought peace with France and Spain. From now on he wished to forget about the Protestant international, to forgo foreign adventures which needed parliamentary subsidies. He wanted to dispense with Parliament, and to concentrate on the more congenial task of making real the 'absolute monarchy' of which his father had only spoken. The decade of Buckingham was over: the decade of Strafford and Laud was to begin.

To Mayerne, the collapse of both the Huguenot cause and the Jacobean policy must have been a double blow. His life at the court of King James had been based on Jacobean assumptions. There he had been the link between two courts, the unofficial mediator of the Protestant international. Secure in the personal confidence of King James, he had built up a unique position as the trusted agent in England of the French Huguenots, the Swiss cantons, the city of Geneva. With a brother-in-law in Holland, another brother-in-law as Dutch ambassador in Paris, a sister at the court of the Electress Palatine, and another sister married to the agent of the Duke of Savoy, he was the most international figure at the English court. In France, he was still titular physician to the king, but at the same time he was trusted by all the Huguenot leaders. In England all foreign ambassadors, even the successive Spanish ambassadors, were his patients, as were almost all English ambassadors abroad. But all these contacts were politically valuable only if there was peace and friendship between England and France, and if England was the active head, or at least centre, of European Protestantism. Of these two conditions, the first was destroyed by Buckingham, the second was renounced by Charles I. Therefore, although Mayerne was confirmed in all his medical functions and perquisites in the new reign, we must expect to find a change in his political position.

The greatest strain was brought by Buckingham's war. From the beginning, Mayerne seems not to have yielded to Buckingham's charm. Buckingham was his patient, of course, and Mayerne noted his various ailments. His notes disguised the duke's identity – as they generally did with his more famous patients, until they were dead – and gave him the cover name 'Palamedes'. But his occasional comments never suggest the personal sympathy which he showed with the earlier royal favourites, Hay and Carr. Buckingham's death is recorded by him with cold epigrams and ingenious acrostics. On one occasion Mayerne did write with some feeling about Buckingham's health. But that was in a letter to the king, 'knowing that your favour towards him makes your Majesty impatient to expect and eager to hear good news'.[2] Of course, Mayerne cultivated the great favourite at the height of his power, and he naturally approved the marriage alliance between the English and French courts.[3] That was the only part of Buckingham's policy that he would have approved: a brief moment of sanity between the impetuous follies of the visit to Spain and the war against France: a war which was ruinous to the Huguenots and to his patron Rohan; which broke the common front between France and England in support of European Protestantism; and which was very inconvenient to a French doctor at the English court.

For of course, as relations deteriorated, all Frenchmen at court were suspect. The first to feel this were the new queen's French attendants. Henrietta Maria had brought with her a company of French ladies and French Catholic clergy, headed by her almoner, Mgr du Plessis, Bishop of Mende. The bishop was a kinsman of Cardinal Richelieu and seems to have been, like him, a worldly cleric. Mayerne found him a bad patient: 'he refuses medicine', he noted, 'and lives a disorderly life, as courtiers do.'[4] Next year, after a series of disagreeable scenes, King Charles put his foot down. All the French servants were dismissed. The bishop protested, the queen made another scene, and the French women, we are told, 'howled and lamented as if they had been going to execution'. However, the king's orders were obeyed, and the poor ladies were carried to Dover and shipped back to France. This was no doubt just as well, since war followed. When the war was over, Richelieu proposed to replace them; but by now the queen had digested the affair and, on her husband's advice, refused to accept any French attendants, lest they should act as spies. The only Frenchmen whom she would have about her, she said, were doctors. She was happy with Mayerne.[5]

Mayerne also suffered from the spy-fever of the war years. It was now that an Englishman who had been in a French prison reported, on his release, how he had heard from a fellow-prisoner that 'the King of England had a French doctor called Mayherne, which was as dangerous and damnable a fellow as ever was Judas':[6] indeed, the Englishman's informant had seen such letters of Mayerne 'as made his hair to stand upright'. However, Mayerne does not seem to have been inconvenienced by these rumours. He was, after all, a Huguenot, and his sympathies were with the Rohan brothers, whom English support, as he well saw, was driving forward to their ruin. For this revolt, by tying the hands of Richelieu, was preventing him from acting firmly against the Huguenots' real enemy, Spain.

In these circumstances the most that Mayerne could do was to seek to soften the misfortunes of the Rohan family. In the autumn of 1625, when Soubise had been defeated at sea and Rohan's position in Languedoc seemed desperate, we find Mayerne conspiring with Lucy, Countess of Bedford to marry Rohan's sister, Anne, into an English noble family: perhaps the Stanley family, whose heir had recently married the Huguenot Charlotte de la Tremoïlle, daughter of the Duc de Thouars. The Countess of Bedford was the daughter of Lord Harrington of Exton, the 'governor' of the Princess Elizabeth. She was also the friend and patroness of poets – and Anne de Rohan was herself a poetess. Writing to an unknown correspondent, the countess said that she had entrusted the project to Mayerne. 'Considering the present condition of the house of Rohan, and the future danger of the whole party of the Religion in France,' she went on, 'I think it might be a happiness to Mlle de Rohan, and of great use to her friends, if she were lodged in so noble a family.' There would be no difficulty in arranging the match, she added: she and the Lord Chamberlain, the Earl of Pembroke, would easily fix it. 'I have enjoined my father' – i.e. my father-confessor, Mayerne – 'not to break the seal which I have set on his lips, except it be to open them to my Lord Chamberlain.'[7] However, the matchmakers did not succeed, and Anne de Rohan died unmarried.

While Mayerne, from his refuge in England, watched the Huguenot débâcle and the catastrophe of the house of Rohan, another old ally of Rohan, Agrippa d'Aubigné, watched it from his refuge in Geneva. D'Aubigné had been the last and most resolute supporter of Rohan in resistance to Catholic reconquest in France. The Catholic court of France had pursued him even in Geneva. He too had been condemned to death in his absence, and Geneva did not dare to honour him too much for fear of irritating the government of France. But in Geneva he saw, as Mayerne also saw, that French power was necessary to the safety of the city, the only check on the far more dangerous ambitions of the Habsburgs, Rome and Savoy. Therefore he could not approve the distraction of that power by those two perpetual agitators, as he now saw them, Rohan and Soubise. Like Mayerne, he wished to see England as a stabilising force, protecting the Huguenots in their legitimate aims, restraining the Catholic zeal of France. So, when James I died, he looked hopefully towards his successor and wooed him with what he hoped would be a welcome offering: a presentation copy of his great work, *L'Histoire universelle.*

Since arriving in Geneva, d'Aubigné had prepared a new edition of his works, to be published there. However, the Petit Conseil, again afraid of offending the French government, which had banned and burned his *History,* afterwards withdrew the licence which it had granted. D'Aubigné had then turned to Sarpi's friend Fra Fulgenzio, seeking, through him, to have the book printed in Venice; but again there had been difficulties. In the end he had had it printed secretly in Geneva in 1626, with a false imprint of Amsterdam. This was the edition which he now offered to Charles I. To accompany it, he wrote a fulsome letter which assumed that the king, like himself, disdained flattery and loved the republican virtues of freedom, candour and truth. Prudently, he sent the book, unbound, and the letter, unsealed, to Mayerne, together with another copy of the book for Mayerne himself. He explained to him that he had not dared to have the book bound in Geneva, lest the secret printing be discovered. So he asked Mayerne to have it bound handsomely in London. He also asked him to read the covering letter to the king, for he had heard 'that the book of M. de Thou, excellent though it was, was very ill received' by King James, the author having written too innocently about the king's mother, Mary Queen of Scots. D'Aubigné too had written about her, soberly, frankly, without animosity. 'I mention this in case my book should too be unwelcome. If so, I beg you to change course and give it to seigneur Philip Burlamachi, to whom I would have sent a third copy if I had one to hand.'[8] We cannot know how Mayerne handled this commission; but knowing his prudence (and his personal acquaintance with the affair of de Thou), and knowing also King Charles's views on candour, truth and freedom, we may suspect that the book went to Philip Burlamachi.

Buckingham's disastrous wars were formally ended after his death by two treaties: the Treaty of Susa with France, signed in April 1629, and that of Madrid with Spain, signed in November 1630. Both affected Mayerne personally. The peace with France left him with a long grievance against the French government. That with Spain brought him a new friend, another amateur diplomat like himself: Peter Paul Rubens.

The grievance concerned Mayerne's post in France as *médecin ordinaire du roi*. We have seen how his arrears of salary had been unpaid and his title to the post challenged. In 1624, after a patient and tortuous cultivation of the French ministers, he thought that he had settled that matter, only to discover, in Aubonne next spring, that this 'endless screw' was being turned again. No doubt he took further steps when in Paris on his way home. But then had come the war between England and France which undid all his patient diplomacy. Moreover, in the course of that war, he had also lost an old friend and ally in the French court: the *premier médecin* Jean Héroard, who died at the siege of la Rochelle. Héroard's successor was one Charles Bouvard, an arrogant and controversial doctor who would bully the medical faculty, the court, and his royal patient for the rest of his reign. He was chiefly famous for his insatiable bleeding of his patients. His appointment was a heavy blow to Mayerne, for he was no friend. This became clear when the war was over. Mayerne then found, not only that he had been denounced in Paris as 'a firebrand of war meddling in affairs of state', but that, on this pretext, his appointment at the French court had been formally cancelled. His post had been given to Dr Cousinot, a strict Galenist who had just qualified himself for it by marrying the daughter of the new *premier médecin*, Dr Bouvard.[9]

Mayerne's reaction was predictable. A spate of letters, swollen and foaming with virtuous indignation, rolled out from the house in St Martin's Lane. It was like the affair of 1618 all over again. Mayerne wrote to the French ministers. He wrote to Richelieu himself. He mobilised the English ambassador in Paris, his old friend Sir Thomas Edmondes, and the new French ambassador to England, the Marquis de Châteauneuf. He engaged the Queen of England to write to her mother, the Queen Mother of France. Was this, he asked the French ministers, a fair return for all his past services, 'and those which I am continuing to give to the Queen of Great Britain, sister of his Majesty'? Had he not faithfully carried out his duties for thirty years? If he had been absent for the last eighteen of those years, what did that matter? Had he not paid M. Carré, a resident *médecin ordinaire*, to act for him? The objection that the two countries had been at war was equally empty, for physicians are not subject to the laws of war: they fight only against disease. Of course, he insisted, he was not concerned with the trifling profits of the office, 'having never been moved by desire for gain'. It was a matter of honour. Perhaps, he wrote to Richelieu, this 'shameful plunder' had been justified by the 'original sin' of his religion; but 'I cannot be washed clean of that, given the claims of birth, education, constancy.' And then there was the manner of the deed, the brusque indignity of his dismissal. These things, if they were to be done at all, should be done in a certain style and in certain conventional forms: 'when Polyxena was sacrificed, she took care to fall decently.'[10]

Meanwhile, similar letters were pouring out to Mayerne's professional friends, to doctors and apothecaries in France. To them, he was less restrained. To a French colleague he wrote that he was about to accompany the Queen of England to certain mineral waters, 'almost as good as those of Pougues, and of the same properties' – doubtless at Wellingborough, the favourite spa of Henrietta Maria – but that on his return he would appear in France to demand restitution of his stolen office. He would do such things – what they should be he knew not: 'how, I cannot yet say; but if the only knot which ties me to your court is cut, I shall say adieu to you for ever. It will be no great loss, but even the smallest reed casts a shadow. *Inest formicae sua bilis*' – even the ant can be angry. 'At least I shall live freely in Switzerland, whither I shall retire to give to the world the works which I have long owed to it.'[11]

Thus pressed, Mayerne's friends moved into action. Sir Thomas Edmondes did his best: 'every letter from M. Naudin attests your affection . . . and your diligence' in the matter, Mayerne would write gratefully.[12] The Marquis de Châteauneuf, bombarded with further letters now that he had returned to France to be Keeper of the Great Seal, pulled his full weight. He secured a royal *brevet*, which did not indeed reinstate Mayerne but at least awarded him 10,000 francs compensation. Unfortunately, nothing then happened. The royal letter was a dead letter, or, as Mayerne put it, a trick. So, after two years, a new spate of letters from London would regurgitate the whole scandalous history. 'During the siege of la Rochelle,' Mayerne would write to Richelieu, 'the *premier médecin* robbed me of my office as *conseiller et médecin ordinaire du roy*', giving it to his son-in-law as his daughter's marriage portion. Now, after all the efforts of ministers and ambassadors, even of royalty, this wretched *premier médecin*, 'who, as I hear, is already over-gorged with wealth', had fobbed him off with a 'piece of parchment'.[13]

But in the end, it seems, even the imperious *premier médecin* was forced to yield. We have no record of his payment, but by 1638 Mayerne had forgotten his animosity against the French court. When, in that year, his sister Madame du Mesnil was passing through France to Switzerland in order to put the château of Aubonne in order, he wrote to his faithful apothecary and banker, Pierre Naudin, to lend her, for her travelling expenses, 'the moneys received or to be received' on his behalf. Among them he specified the 10,000 francs 'compensation for my office'. Presumably those moneys were by now in, or almost in, the bag.[14]

Mayerne suffered yet another misfortune in those distressing years of Buckingham's wars. He lost his wife. Lady Mayerne is a shadowy figure and it is difficult to say much, or indeed anything, about her. She seems to have spent some time, in her last years, at Aubonne, even when Mayerne himself was not there: we know, from a letter of Agrippa d'Aubigné, that Mayerne's children (the eldest of whom was then fifteen years old) were at Aubonne in March 1623,[15] and in May 1625 'la baronne d'Aubonne' was selling the wine of the estate in Geneva – profitably, since the city, in view of her husband's services, exempted it from the normal taxes.[16] She died in London on 17 November 1628, soon after the fall of la Rochelle. From Geneva, d'Aubigné wrote to condole with Mayerne: 'we touch your hand in sympathy, but are too weak to raise you up. The storms which roll over our heads, the gulfs which open, one after another, before us – in a word, the three scourges of God which over-whelm us together – all this has left us insensible to common losses. . . . All that we can say is to urge you to lower your head against the hailstorm from behind and open your eyes to the precipices in front.'[17] In front lay the last stand of Rohan in Languedoc, the débâcle of Protestantism in Germany.

How did Mayerne react to the successive disasters? How did he respond to the universal and, as it must have seemed, final destruction of that Protestant international which was the public context of his life? Reading his letters and papers of this period, we can see an orderly retreat into a new bastion of self-defence against the outer world. If European Protestantism was everywhere in agony – an agony precipitated by the aggression of its leaders, the Elector Palatine, the Rohan family – then he would fall back on his old loyalty to Geneva and his new loyalty to the canton of Berne. He would become a Swiss patriot, the advocate of unity among the cantons, of alliance with Geneva, and of national self-defence. Hitherto he had described himself as French: French of Geneva, that French city. Now, as Baron d'Aubonne, he described himself regularly as Swiss, and Switzerland as his country. In England he had treated English patients, but his private world was always that of the Protestant international. Now he was resolved to settle his family permanently in Switzerland, to found a dynasty there. His eldest son, whom he called Henri d'Aubonne, was, Mayerne resolved, to be a grand seigneur in the pays de Vaud, the ancestor of a long line of territorial magnates who would protect the heartland of European Protestantism.

From the beginning Henri had been brought up in a French, not an English world. He had a French Protestant tutor, and in 1618, at the age of ten, he was evidently living in France, probably in Paris with the invaluable Naudin. Two years later, having bought Aubonne, Mayerne wrote that he intended 'entière-ment despaïser' – wholly to transplant – his son.[18] Henri was no scholar, but he would be a gentleman, a soldier, a landlord in Switzerland. Early in 1628, when he was twenty, he was sent on a grand tour to see the world. Pulling the strings which already lay at his hand, Mayerne arranged that Henri should accompany Lord Doncaster, Mayerne's old friend, now Earl of Carlisle, who was about to embark on yet another embassy. For in the agony of the Protestant cause, when England was being defeated by both France and Spain,

Charles I and Buckingham were still looking desperately for Continental coalitions, and Carlisle had been instructed to go to the Netherlands, to the dukes of Lorraine and Savoy, and to Venice, to rouse them all against the common danger. He was also to go to Switzerland, where, he was told, the Margrave of Baden-Durlach 'keeps yet some life, some hope, and great resolution', and was to be given every encouragement. It was not a very hopeful embassy: Carlisle's instructions were to sound a general alarm rather than to make concrete proposals; but he was told that further instructions would come from the king 'or in our name, from the Duke of Buckingham, our High Admiral, or one of our principal Secretaries of State'.[19] Young Henri was to benefit from accompanying this embassy as his father had done from his youthful journey with Rohan.

Mayerne's instructions to his son, on this occasion, still survive. They belong to a well-known literary genre, immortalised by Shakespeare in the advice of Polonius to Laertes. In this genre they deserve a high place. In view of Henri's character, as it would be revealed in the following years, they are a poignant document.

It begins with an exhortation to economy. The world, says Mayerne, thinks those children happy whose fathers have worked themselves to death to acquire riches for them to spend in idleness, 'supposing that a fortune acquired without labour is much sweeter than one that is scraped together, bit by bit, by the sweat of the brow and continual toil'. Such an attitude is only fit for those idle drones who, in a well-ordered commonwealth, 'ought to be exterminated by fire and sword'. As for Mayerne himself, he thanks God for two infinite mercies: that he has never disobeyed his mother or father, and that he has earned everything that he owns by honourable toil.

After these first two general commandments come the particular instructions for the journey. The Earl of Carlisle has accepted Henri above other candidates: therefore he must be conscious of his good fortune and show it by assiduous and respectful attention. He must listen, not speak. He must never be idle. 'Paint with pencil and pen, since you have a natural gift for it. . . . Keep away from wine, especially at Berne and Aubonne. . . . Always put plenty of water in your wine, especially in Italy, where the wines are *forts et furieux*. . . . Flee from women as from reefs upon which body and soul are pitifully shipwrecked . . . gambling is a plague which ruins all who indulge in it. . . . To my great regret, I must reproach you for your tendency to borrow money from everyone without ever thinking of paying your debts'; also for prodigality, quickness of temper, etc., etc.

An additional instruction shows great solicitude for Henri's health and gives some expert medical advice. He was to abstain not only from wine but from violent exercise, and to keep indoors during the heat of the day. He was not to rely on his youth or natural strength, for it is the strongest who are attacked by these fevers and fluxes. He was to be moderate of fruit, especially melons. He was to take with him his father's panacea, the 'stone' of Contrayerva, and, if wounded, to remember his 'eau des harquebuzades'. He would also be able to call on his father's medical colleagues. 'Being recognised as my son, I am sure that the doctors of the places through which you pass' will always help. 'Among others, you will find at Nancy MM. Fournier, father and son, doctors to his Highness, and M. de Meny, his chief surgeon: they will not neglect you if you are in need.' And at Venice there was Mayerne's dear friend M. Asselineau, who had saved his life.[20]

Since Carlisle was going to be in Berne, and to see the Margrave of Baden-Durlach, Mayerne took the opportunity to write to his old friend, the former ambassador, Hans Rudolf von Erlach, now a member of the Council of the Republic. Erlach had deserved well of Mayerne, ensuring that the title-deeds of Aubonne were made legally secure, and Mayerne now wrote to thank him and to introduce his son 'whom I have vowed to the service of our country'. He had had him educated, he wrote, according to his natural bent, and was now sending him on this grand tour in order that 'he should see other countries and become qualified, one day, worthily to serve his own'. He asked Erlach to present Henri to the governors of Berne, and to assure them 'that it is to defend their rights that he is preparing to make himself a man of action. If we live, and are left in peace, in a few years I shall bring him myself and settle him in Aubonne, to spend the rest of his days there, with some wife whom we shall find here or there.'[21]

But the future, he had to admit, was very obscure. At that moment an Austrian army of 24,000 men was hovering on the northern and eastern frontiers of the confederation, poised, it was widely said, to reduce 'the Swiss rebels' to their ancient obedience.[22] 'Here we are told', Mayerne went on, 'that all Switzerland is surrounded by men of war, led and paid by our ancient hereditary enemies' – that is, by the house of Austria; and shall we sleep, lulled by fair words? 'Let us unite, Trojans and Rutulans alike' – i.e. all the cantons, regardless of old differences[23] – 'and show our teeth to those who show us their claws. Switzerland is not a little morsel, or easy to swallow, provided it will take the trouble to know its own strength.' Therefore, let us stand firm: we have arms; 'let us have good leaders, and if we do not breed them, let us import them. We shall have peace when they know that we are ready for war.'[24]

In these documents we see the growing Swiss patriotism of Mayerne, his identification of the now shrunken Protestant cause with Switzerland, as its last, irreducible, redoubt. But we also see his strong dynastic sense, and a real tenderness towards his son, comparable with the tenderness which he had also shown towards his father. For Mayerne was a loving father. Dorothy Osborne, who knew the household of his second marriage well ('Sir Theodore did me the honour to call me daughter'), recalled that the family was 'so passionate' on the death of a son that 'I never failed to see them all crying'.[25] But the tenderness evidently blinded him towards one obvious danger. For is it not strange – comically, tragically strange – to see this practised man of the world choosing to send his son, at an impressionable age, to discover the world, and to learn frugality, puritan sobriety and strict accounting, in the company – of all men – of James Hay, Earl of Carlisle, the most extravagant of all the extravagant courtiers of James I: Carlisle who had ridden into Paris on silver horse-shoes, scattering ostentatious largesse; whose exquisite banquets were a by-word for conspicuous waste; who had 'no bowels in the point of running in debt and borrowing all he could'; and who, in his 'very jovial' life, dissipated the entire fortune thrust upon him by an equally prodigal king? Carlisle, behind his Petronian hedonism, was an able diplomat; he was a good friend and patron to Mayerne, who for his part had discovered the world in the company of the austere, Spartan hero Rohan; but was he the ideal choice as 'maistre, patron, amy et censeur tout ensemble' to a young man of eighteen whom his father had already recognised as a reckless prodigal?

To retreat to a Swiss redoubt, and a Swiss patriotism, was one possible response to the disasters of the 1620s. Another was to retreat inwardly, upon oneself. As the outer world of Protestantism collapsed, so we see Mayerne drawing back, more and more, into a proud, personal reserve. Outwardly, he is still the urbane courtier of a Catholic queen, but inwardly he is a solitary figure, resting firmly on his own Huguenot values, his independence, his pride. Such a withdrawal is a form of 'interior emigration', a consequence of defeat. We see it in Rohan; we see it in Agrippa d'Aubigné; we see it, in compa-rable form, in the great court-Jews of the Diaspora. Outwardly, these men comply with the world which they have been unable to change, but inwardly they know that their own values, their own traditions, are better, and they will not desert them. It was d'Aubigné who once described the Huguenots of the heroic age as 'princes qui règnent sur eux-mêmes'. To the end of his life, though he was not a great feudatory like Rohan or Bouillon but a mere gentleman, d'Aubigné remained such a prince. Louis Turquet was another. In middle age, and in defeat, Mayerne became more and more like his father, who feared no man and was quick to resent any slight to his honour. He was also, as their letters show, increasingly respected by d'Aubigné. These two formidable men, so different in many ways – one the universal man of mili-tant Protestantism, man of letters and man of war, the other the prosperous court-doctor, sedentary, affable and urbane – showed, when they converged on the shores of Lake Leman, one from an island-fortress in embattled Languedoc, the other from the royal palace of England, that they were both survivors from a heroic age of individualism. Whether that inheritance could be passed on to the next generation was another matter.

Switzerland and the maintenance of an internal Protestantism: these bound d'Aubigné and Mayerne together. The new friendship which Mayerne derived from the peace negotiations with Spain had a very different basis. For Peter Paul Rubens was not a Protestant. He had left his early Protestantism far behind him, with his childhood in Cologne, and now, when he came to England as Spanish ambassador in April 1629, he was the official artist, even the propagandist, of the *Pax Hispanica* and the Spanish domination of Europe. However, he was already known to several of Mayerne's friends among English diplomats – to Sir Dudley Carleton, to Carlisle himself, who had met him while on his last embassy – and, once in London, he was a familiar figure at court, often engaged with the king in artistic conversation. Mayerne seized the opportunity to commission his own portrait from Rubens, and Rubens painted a sketch from the life. It shows him seated in a leather chair, with a bust of Aesculapius, the god of healing, in an alcove beside him, and, on the other side, through an open window, a seascape and a light-house with burning torch guiding a ship into harbour as Mayerne's art guided his patients to safety through the hazards of life. Mayerne acknowledged it in a fulsome letter. Rubens, he wrote, was 'the true paragon in all that you under-take', in whom there was perfect harmony between the spirit and the hand. Mayerne was delighted both by the portrait and by the flattering imagery in it.[26]

In his letter, before coming to the portrait, Mayerne refers to the 'particular favours' which he had received from Rubens. This suggests that the favours were not confined to the portrait. Unfortunately they are not specified. We can only say that the two men must have had plenty to discuss while Mayerne sat as Rubens painted. Both were active in diplomacy. As diplomats, both were amateurs, foreigners whose local loyalties gave a personal slant to their formal diplomatic duties: Mayerne, the old emissary of the King of England, was a patriot for Geneva and Berne; Rubens, the new emissary of the King of Spain, was a patriot for Flanders. And the patriotism of the two men was similar. Mayerne looked for a Switzerland, both Catholic and Protestant, preserved in peace by the agreement of France and England: Rubens looked for a united Netherlands, both Catholic and Protestant, preserved in peace under its own monarchy. Indeed, at this very time, while in London, Rubens paid a secret visit to the Dutch ambassador (with whose country his master, the King of Spain, was at war) in order to sound him about the terms on which the Netherlands might be reunited. The Dutch ambassador was Albert Joachimi, who did not agree with him. The only way of uniting the Netherlands, he replied, was by driving out the Spaniards from Flanders.

Mayerne too was in treaty with Joachimi at this same time, on another more personal matter. For on 14 August 1630, he married Joachimi's daughter Isabella. Like her predecessor, she was a widow. Her previous husband had been a Dutchman, Francis van den Berg, resident at Chelsea. The Bishop of London, in whose diocese both parties lived, licensed the marriage to take place in the parish of Chelsea, or of St Martin-in-the-Fields (Mayerne's own parish), or Fulham, the bishop's own church. They chose to be married at Fulham – probably by the bishop himself.[27] Such an arrangement for the marriage of a French and a Dutch Calvinist, members of the French and Dutch churches in London, is somewhat surprising, and can only be explained as deference to power or to politeness. For the bishop was William Laud, who would soon become known as the persecutor of the Huguenot and Dutch congregations, while Lady Mayerne would become the patroness of those extreme enemies of Laud, the radical Anabaptists.[28]

As for Rubens, diplomatic affairs were not the only interest that he shared with Mayerne. For Mayerne was himself an amateur of art, with special interests in it. Indeed, in one sense his most lasting significance is, ironically, not in the history of medicine but in the history of art – of the decorative arts. That interest did not begin in 1629 and his association with Rubens, but it received a great impetus from it. That, however, is a separate subject, which can be left for later.[29]

19

A New Regime, 1630–1631

Mayerne began his *Ephemerides* for the year 1630 with the words 'Annus quem D.O.M. fortunatum esse velit': a year which, please God, will be fortunate. Certainly the previous years had been very unfortunate from his point of view: unfortunate for his cause, for his friends, for himself. But now, although much had been lost, the future began to look brighter. The Huguenot revolt in France had been crushed, but at least 'the Religion' was not to be persecuted, and the restored power of a united France would be used by Richelieu against the real extirpators of Protestantism, the house of Habsburg. At the same time a new Protestant champion had arisen in the north: Gustavus Adolphus, King of Sweden, had entered Germany and, for the next two years, would hurl back the hitherto victorious Habsburg armies. Meanwhile, the danger to Switzerland had receded; the incalculable and always suspect Duke of Savoy had died; the Calvinist cause, though abandoned by England, had found a steadier base in the Netherlands; the Anglo-French war was over; and Mayerne was repairing his recent bereavement by a new marriage, which, since his father-in-law was Dutch ambassador in England, preserved his connection with the Protestant international.

Not that he would use that connection so much in future. The traumatic events of the 1620s had destroyed many of the old ideals of that Protestant international which had been organised and inspired by the French Huguenots. Above all, it had destroyed the intellectual coherence of those ideals: the 'world picture', the all-embracing ideology which had inspired it, and which was now irremediably fragmented. The victories of Gustavus Adolphus might break the power of the house of Austria. They might save German Protestantism from extinction. But they could not restore those grandiose illusions of a new universal enlightenment, Platonic, Hermetic, millenarian, which had inspired a radical generation, now dying out. In 1630, Agrippa d'Aubigné would die in Geneva, aged seventy-eight. In 1631 the exiled Duc de Rohan would acknowledge defeat by accepting a commission from his conqueror Richelieu: he would go to the Grisons as French ambassador extraordinary to organise and command a Protestant army for the recovery of the Valtelline from Spain and Austria. His brother, the Duc de Soubise, would live permanently in England. In 1632 Gustavus Adolphus himself would perish at Lützen; and soon afterwards, having lost that last hope of restitution, the Elector Palatine, the 'Winter King' of Bohemia, the rash precipitator of the war in which he and his cause had foundered, would die, ruined and disconsolate, at Mainz. His adviser – his Mephistopheles, some would say, the architect of those grandiose projects – Christian of Anhalt had already died, in 1630. From now on, the war would change its character. Its ideological force was spent. It would become a mere contest for power. On the ruins of that discredited 'world picture', a new synthesis would be built up, above all in France: a rational, orderly, unitary system, gradually purged of millenarian and Hermetic fantasies: the system of Descartes.

In England, in the first years of the decade, the Protestant gentry, roused to indignation by the misgovernment of Buckingham, and left impotent by the dismissal of Parliament, found a new hero in Gustavus Adolphus. Now was the time, they said, to revive the glories of Queen Elizabeth's reign, to support the Swedish crusader and, while he restored Protestantism in Europe, to make profitable inroads into the Atlantic empire of Spain. The great champion of this policy was Sir Thomas Roe, diplomat and seafarer, who could claim some credit for having launched Gustavus on his German adventure. He hoped now to be Secretary of State and to direct the new Elizabethan foreign policy. But Charles I was not interested. He had settled for a policy of economy, neutrality and peace: impotence abroad in order to concentrate on the reconstruction of monarchy and Church at home.

Mayerne accepted the new course without pleasure but without complaint. What else could he do? He was now fifty-seven years old, universally respected in his profession, which had made him very rich. He had his family and his property to consider. He would remain always a Huguenot, but, as his patron and hero Rohan had shown, it was too late to defend that cause except as a personal philosophy and way of life. Rohan, having ceased to be an independent force, now looked with admiration to Gustavus Adolphus, the new pattern of a Protestant warrior hero; but he served Richelieu. What Mayerne thought of Gustavus we do not know: he was prudently silent. But he kept his international political contacts. When opponents of Richelieu tried to raise a coalition against him, Mayerne's patient Sir Isaac Wake, ambassador in Savoy, wrote to the Secretary of State, Lord Conway, urging him to consult Mayerne; and Conway, another patient, assured him that this would always be done in such cases.[1] Mayerne also showed his Huguenot spirit in private actions. Now and always, he was the patron at the English court of those Huguenots who were driven to seek refuge in England from persecution abroad.

As such, he was often in demand. In his own house he constantly entertained and employed Huguenot *émigrés*. He sought relief and employment for others. We have seen him seeking to rescue Trougny and Naudin, bringing over Briot, advising Granier, entertaining du Moulin. He had a constant stream of Huguenot tutors, assistants, amanuenses, servants. In 1624 he wrote to Conway, on behalf of five Protestant fugitives from the massacre in the Valtelline, 'une partie des restes du feu et du cousteau qui ont ravagé ces montagnes que l'on croyait jadis inaccessibles': a part of the remnant left by the fire and sword that have devastated these mountains, once thought inaccessible. He urged Conway to present their petitions to the king, and offered himself to advise on the letter to be sent to Archbishop Abbot.[2] Now there were more such 'restes', and the Virgilian phrase 'reliquiae Danaum' – the remnants of the Greeks – would drop often from his pen. We shall meet some of the refugees. Unfortunately, the new ruler of the Church would be less sympathetic to them than the old. That new ruler was William Laud. He did not like foreign Protestants at all.

For although he had not yet succeeded to Canterbury, Laud was already, since 1628, exercising all the powers of the archbishop, and from that date onwards English Puritans and foreign Protestants of any kind were at a disadvantage. With Laud, Mayerne's personal relations were minimal. He was not Laud's doctor – or that of the king's other leading adviser, the Earl of Strafford (although Strafford's doctor would consult him in a moment of crisis)[3] – and we know only two letters from Mayerne to Laud, neither of which suggests any warmth in their relations. The first is in support of a Frenchwoman, Mme de la Mare, the wife of one of the royal musicians, whom Laud had caused to be imprisoned for unorthodox religious utterances. Mayerne protested that she was a harmless woman and that her wild remarks were merely the effect of 'melancholy'.[4] The other is in response to Laud's demand for a contribution to the archbishop's great prestige project, the rebuilding of St Paul's Cathedral. The letter ('I send you, but at your command ...') makes it clear that Mayerne's contribution of £20 was not voluntary. His stilted compliments and ornate Latin suggest a distant and formal relationship.[5] In order to secure patronage for his Huguenot protégés, Mayerne had to turn elsewhere: to Sir Thomas Roe, for instance, who agreed, somewhat reluctantly, for he was himself in disfavour – 'docked up', as he put it, like 'Drake's ship' at Deptford – to recommend one of them as physician to Gustavus Adolphus.[6]

Laud's policy of enforcing rigid conformity to the episcopal Church of England did not merely reduce the patronage available to new Protestant immigrants: it also created difficulties for those already established. In 1634, being now archbishop, he launched a campaign to impose conformity on the Dutch and French Calvinists long settled in England. The campaign began in his own diocese of Canterbury, where there were three foreign churches, French in Canterbury and Dutch in Sandwich and Maidstone. The threatened churches at once appealed to their *Coetus*, or joint organisation in London, and on 3 February 1635 a deputation from this body waited on Mayerne as an influential Huguenot whose wife was a member of the Dutch church in London. Appeal was also made to the Dutch ambassador, Mayerne's father-in-law, Albert Joachimi, and to his friends the Duc de Soubise, as the champion of the French Huguenots, and the king's foreign banker, Philip Burlamachi. There were at least two other meetings with Mayerne, who did his best and was thanked for his help. As a result of these appeals, some small concessions of detail were obtained, but the policy was not altered: Charles I had already promised his support to Laud, and was not to be deflected.[7]

However, if the new course of government was unwelcome to Mayerne in the religious sphere, there was an area where a strong central government could help him to realise his aims: that of public health. The late sixteenth and early seventeenth centuries were periods of plague – bubonic plague – and when plague fell on great cities, only a strong government could hope to handle the problems which it created. There had been serious outbreaks of plague in London, as in most of Europe, in the 1590s and again at the beginning of the new century. In 1603 King James had arrived in his new capital to find it racked by plague. King Charles equally had succeeded to the throne at a time of plague; he had had to hold his first Parliament in Oxford to avoid it. The year 1630 saw the worst plague (it was thought) since the Black Death. It was a plague which had spread throughout Europe. In England it would be known, until it was eclipsed by the last outbreak of 1665, as 'the Great Plague'. The problems created by this epidemic, which coincided with economic depression and high prices, were great. Since the government was at last undistracted by either war or parliament, it now felt free to tackle them – or at least to think of tackling them – in a radical way. Though it reissued old orders, it also countenanced new measures. It looked abroad to foreign examples, and in England it sought the advice of the best physicians available: that is, of the Royal College and of the senior court physicians, who, of course, were members of it.[8]

The Royal College gave its advice early in 1630 and again in March 1631. In its first document[9] it drew on the experience of 'Paris, Venice and Padua and many other cities'; in its second it dwelt on the social and environmental causes of plague and advocated a new institution, a 'commission or office of health' with penal power, such as had been 'found useful in Spain, Italy and other places'. We do not know what part, if any, Mayerne may have taken in formulating these documents. Though a Fellow of the College, he was not as active in it as his colleagues Dr Bethune and the newly recruited physician-in-ordinary Dr Harvey.[10] Mayerne had of course experience of the plague in Paris in 1606–7, and he had recorded his treatment of it in his contemporary 'anti-dotary'.[11] But such experience was not unique to him. The evidence from Spain could hardly have come from him. It may have been supplied by Dr Bethune: for Bethune had travelled in Spain, where the great epidemic of the 1590s had led to one of the most famous treatises on the plague, *El Libro de la peste* by the royal physician Luís de Mercado.[12] The measures taken in Venice and Padua would be familiar to Mayerne, from his visit in 1599–1600, but would also be known to the many physicians – including Bethune and Harvey – who were doctors of Padua. One of the recommendations of the college was for a special team of doctors to care for the victims of plague in London: a similar institution, on a permanent basis, was proposed for Paris by Mayerne's hated rival Dr Bouvard, the new *premier médecin* of Louis XIII. So on the whole it is unsafe to assume that Mayerne was particularly involved in the report of the Royal College. He expressed his views in a separate document: the report submitted by the three senior royal physicians: himself, Bethune and Dr Lister.

This report survives: a long document of thirty-eight pages, dated 19 March 1631 and signed by all three. Mayerne's signature comes first, a bold, majestic flourish, followed by his title in Latin and his Greek motto. The text is in French, and is written throughout in Mayerne's hand. The style also is unmis-takably his. So are some of the details. The whole document, in fact, was clearly composed and written by him and represents his ideas, as discussed with and confirmed by his colleagues.[13]

As usual, Mayerne begins with Olympian generalities. The plague, he writes, was one of the scourges wherewith God, of his justice, punishes the sins of men, and in many cases it can be neither prevented nor cured. But that is no reason for submitting weakly to it or awaiting divine judgement 'with a resolution that is more superstitious than Christian'. Rather, it is our duty to use those remedies which Reason and Nature show to be effective, knowing as we do that our good Father in Heaven chastises us not always for our destruction but sometimes for our correction.

How does the plague, this 'queen of maladies', come to men? Either it comes direct from the finger of God, like the plague which suddenly destroyed 70,000 Israelites from Dan to Beersheba in the days of King David, or it is mediated through the human senses, by infection of food and other matter needed to repair the daily waste of 'the triple substance of sublunary creatures'. In the former case, there is no remedy but prayer and amendment of life, according to the rules and example of the theologians. In the latter, the physicians, 'who are the assistants and ministers of Nature', must march out, armed with valour, learning and prudence, to do battle against this devouring monster: a monster which can be destroyed only by rational, scientific methods, determined by the physicians and faithfully applied by the magistrates. For order is the essential soul of all things, whether in the great world, the macrocosm, or in the microcosm, man.

After this magisterial exordium, Mayerne comes down to the practical steps to be taken. First, the Privy Council must set up a special body to control and coordinate all measures for the prevention, containment and cure of the disease. Secondly, since we are now in the old age of the world, and the golden age of innocence is past, that body must provide a steady source of income, without which 'all the fine speeches in the world are but wind'. Thus Mayerne urged the Privy Council to set up, in London, a perpetual body which was to be known as the Chamber or Office of Health, and which was to be supplied by 'a spring which will never dry up'. To devise such a source, without which 'our idea is only a dream', should not be beyond the wit of the king's learned counsellors. The Office of Health was to consist of twelve regular members or councillors: the Lord Mayor and Recorder of London, two privy councillors, two bishops (one being the Bishop of London), two aldermen, the king's first physician, the President of the Royal College of Physicians, a third senior and experienced physician 'who shall have travelled abroad', and an expert surgeon. They were to be assisted by a staff of treasurers, receivers, collectors, clerks, messengers.

Having taken an oath before the Archbishop of Canterbury, the twelve councillors of the Office of Health were to enter on their duties. They were to devise laws, choose lower officers, interview and select architects, and build hospitals. Their authority under the Privy Council was to be absolute, in the whole area from Brentford to Blackwall and from Richmond to Greenwich, before, during and after outbreaks of plague; and it was to be enforceable by imprisonment and fine. One of their first acts was to be the construction of at least four or five permanent hospitals (three or four north of the river and one in Southwark) including, in particular, one 'superb and magnificent' brick building, simple in design, built to last, for both ill and convalescent. This grand hospital was to be placed in Chelsea, near King James's College of Controversy, 'or towards Paddington, on the stream which flows there' – for running water was essential. It was to be called Charles Godshouse or The House of Health of King Charles, and was to be imitated, on a smaller scale, in provincial towns: for the Office of Health was to be a model for the whole kingdom.

Having unfolded his plan and devised his instruments, Mayerne described the administrative measures necessary to control the plague. On the first sign of plague on the Continent, English merchants were to report to the Office of Health, which would then impose restrictions. At the ports, entry was to be controlled by certificates of health, as in Italy. The control of vagabonds was to be enforced. Unruly, base people were to be driven from London (as they were from Paris); in particular the Irish, who were notoriously poor and dirty, were to be removed. Unemployed persons were to be taken away to work on rural projects. Slum buildings, newly erected in contravention of law, were to be pulled down, as breeding-places of the plague, and only neat and spacious buildings, fit for the better sort and persons of quality, to be permitted. Drains were to be cleaned out, all carrion to be destroyed, slaughter-houses and rubbish heaps to be removed from the city, prisons to be kept clean, butcheries and breweries to be inspected, alehouses shut. Since famine almost inevitably bred the plague, steps must be taken to punish the cornering of food, to maintain its quality, and to control its price.

Such a policy required a police, and a police needed to be maintained. Mayerne urged that the services of those who, whether as clergy or as doctors, risked their lives in centres of plague should be properly recognised. Patrons of livings – the bishops, the Lord Keeper and others – should take care of the clergy. Doctors should be paid, and their widows, if they died, pensioned. And to begin with, interpolated Mayerne, who would never overlook a deserving Huguenot, 'we recommend to the Lords of the Council a Frenchman named Isaac le Sueur, a man of good life, pious and religious, one of several from the *débris* of la Rochelle, who did good service to the city in the year 1625, during the great conflagration of the plague, of which he cured an infinite number', as can be shown by testimonials . . . We know a little about this Isaac le Sueur. He was a Hermetic doctor who, on his arrival from la Rochelle, had appealed to Mayerne for support. He claimed to have studied over 200 volumes by Hermetic philosophers and to have carried out successful alchemical experiments, both alone and with others. He interested Mayerne by his ideas on universal medicine, and he made for him, in 1630, the 'snake-root' which had been effective against the plague of 1625.[14] Mayerne also recommended a Spanish doctor, Nicholas Sacharles, who had been appointed and paid ('though very little') by the City of London in the same year, 1625. Some of these plague-doctors and plague-clergy were to reside in the plague-hospitals, and the doctors were to draw up 'un petit antidotaire chasse-peste' – a list of plague remedies, in Latin for themselves and their apothecaries, in English, 'under common and intelligible names', for others.

If the plague, in spite of these precautions, should reach England, the Office of Health was to take further steps. All unnecessary assemblies were to be forbidden: stage-plays, bear-baiting, bullfights, raree-shows. Taverns, cabarets, eating-houses were to be suppressed. Violent exertions, especially in summer, were to be discouraged. Stray dogs and cats, as carriers of the disease, must be put down: those dogs that were to be spared as hunting hounds or watch-dogs (like Mayerne's dogs Turco and Harlequin) must be identified by metal tabs attached to their collars. Pigeons and rabbits in the city must be destroyed. Houses must be fumigated, windows kept open. Churches too must be fumigated, and worshippers should carry disinfectant sponges.

To cope with those who had caught the plague, a corps of specialists was to be organised. Each of the five Departments of London was to be served by at least one doctor, one surgeon, one apothecary, one midwife and twelve *corbeaux* or bearers of the dead. In each parish there should be a minister, two or more female visitors, one or two sextons, and guards as required. All those who dealt with the infected should be clearly identified: red crosses on their clothes, or a red staff in their hands, should warn the healthy to keep their distance. The *corbeaux*, in particular, should be conspicuous by their long black cloaks with red crosses before and behind, by their red staves, and they should always go about in companies. The cemeteries for the dead should be far from the town. A system of quarantine should separate the healthy from the sick. The price of drugs and antidotes should be controlled.

When the plague had receded, the Office of Health would still have work to do, for 'the seeds of the plague', as Mayerne remembered from his experience in Paris, lingered in houses and clothes. So these were to be thoroughly cleaned and fumigated.

Of course, many of these proposals were not new: they were conventional measures dictated by the accepted medical views of the time. Many of them had previously been imposed, by order of the Privy Council, on local author-ities. What was new, in Mayerne's plan, was the centralised, authoritarian machinery: the Office of Health, the organisation of hospitals, the continuous activity, the specialised officials. Here the model was supplied by the cities of the Continent: by the Health Boards of Italy,[15] with which he had become familiar on his grand tour, and, above all, by Paris as he had known it. The proposed new London hospitals were clearly based on the two hospitals which Henri IV had caused to be built in Paris in 1606–8: the hospital of the Faubourg St Marcel on the south side of the city and the Hôpital St Louis to the north – the latter designed expressly to prevent the spread of the plague of 1606–7.

When these two documents – that of the Royal College and that of Mayerne and his colleagues – were delivered to the Privy Council, they were at first taken very seriously. They were referred to a committee of named councillors, who were to consider them and advise the king. Because Mayerne's document was in French, Dr Lister, being one of its signatories, was ordered to translate it into English 'with all convenient expedition, to the end that no time be lost in a matter of so great importance and necessity for the public good'.[16] Lister duly complied, and his translation survives among the State Papers.[17] About the same time, the Privy Council sent to the City of London 'directions for erecting of an hospital or workhouse, to be set up in London, according as was said to be at Paris'. These directions contained a detailed and graphic description of the hospitals of St Marcel and St Louis.[18] However, as the plague receded, these radical proposals for dealing with it were soon forgotten. No Office of Health was established, no new hospital built. As their author admitted, such a programme would cost money; and whence was that money to come now that Charles I had dispensed with Parliament? So Mayerne's project of a model health service in England, like his father's for a model society in France, dissolved. Without finance, his fine words were 'but wind', his idea 'only a dream'.[19] When the plague returned to England in the later 1630s, he would be wiser: he would retreat to the well-appointed country house of the Countess of Bedford and there devise expensive prophylactics for his rich patients. Frustrated in international politics, unsympathetic to the new religious orthodoxy, disappointed in his plans of medical reform, Mayerne can hardly have welcomed the change from Jacobean to Caroline England, and we may reasonably ask why he did not now carry out his repeatedly expressed plan of retiring to Aubonne and preparing his works for publication. All that was needed was a period of undisturbed peace and leisure for writing; and where could he better enjoy such freedom and such leisure than in his castle, which he had bought with such high hopes, at Aubonne? There too he would be free of court life, where a royal doctor, he said, was a mere pack-horse.

Mayerne's thoughts were often in Aubonne in those years. They were also often among his unfinished notes and on the great work on Hermetic medicine which he longed to write. At the end of 1630 he found himself in correspondence with one of the *médecins ordinaires* of the King of France, François de Monginot. After the death of the *premier médecin* Héroard and the succession of the infamous Bouvard, Monginot was Mayerne's closest friend among the French royal doctors. A native of Langres and graduate of Montpellier, he had been *médecin ordinaire* of the Prince de Condé before entering the service of the king. Once established as *médecin ordinaire*, he did an unfashionable and indeed unprofitable thing.[20] After witnessing one of the public religious disputations which were a feature of the time in France,[21] and which were designed to convert Huguenots to Catholicism, he was convinced that not the Jesuit but the Huguenot had the better case. The Huguenot was our old friend Pierre du Moulin. So Monginot was converted to Protestantism. After his conversion, he published a pamphlet justifying his action and dedicated it to the Roman Catholic gentry of Langres. He remained *médecin ordinaire du roi* (the post was for life, and he would have to be bought out), but of course further promotion at court was out of the question. He was evidently a Hermetic doctor, and an admirer of Mayerne, to whom he now wrote offering to dedicate to him a new book on the quartan ague.

In his reply, Mayerne acknowledged Monginot's treatise on dropsy and 'your *Paradox on the Quartan Ague*, on the title-page of which you wish to honour my name. Although I am not so puffed up as to suppose myself worthy to buttress a new doctrine, however reasonable, or so ambitious as to wish to feature as a patron, please do what you wish. . . . I have read and re-read your *Paradox*, and am pleased by its originality: you seek to penetrate to the inmost secrets of Nature. It is a very bold and very useful speculation, to try to discover, in the little world' – the microcosm, man – 'by analogy and even by truth, much of what is engendered in the great one' – the macrocosm, the universe – 'especially in mines and salt'. Then, after offering to return the compliment of a dedication, Mayerne added, 'for it is high time that I take up my pen if I want to leave to the world after me some of the fruits of my genius, as my conscience obliges me and my friends invite me'.[22]

However, Mayerne never did complete any of his projected medical works. Nor did he ever see Aubonne again. For the last thirty years of his life, he would never leave England. His own explanation was that he was always too busy: his constant practice, and his genuine devotion to it and to the interest of his patients, denied him the time to write. But under King Charles there was another restraint. The king would not let him go.

At first the veto was not absolute. The king would simply maintain that the time was inconvenient: that the queen was in poor health, or was expecting a child, and that Mayerne's attendance on her was essential. Aubonne was far away, the journey took time, communication was difficult; and how could the king forget the unfortunate consequence of Mayerne's last journey, which had left James I to die without his help? So at least he would say; but it is difficult to believe that these were the true reasons. After all, Charles I, like his father, had a considerable medical establishment. There were Sir Martin Lister, Sir William Paddy, Dr Atkins, Dr Craig junior, Dr Chambers, Simon Baskerville, men whom he had inherited, and David Bethune and William Harvey, whom he appointed or promoted and whom he seems to have preferred to Mayerne. The king does not seem to have insisted on Mayerne's personal attendance.[23] The queen also had another doctor, Sir John Cademan, a Catholic. When Cademan wished to travel to France, there was no difficulty,[24] and later Harvey, whom the king greatly valued, was allowed to accompany the Earl of Arundel on a long journey to Vienna with a detour into Italy. When Charles I continually refused Mayerne's applications to visit Aubonne, and finally, in 1633, put his foot down firmly and forbade him ever again to raise the subject, he must have had stronger reasons than mere desire for his occasional services.

We can hardly doubt what those reasons were. Mayerne was far too political a doctor; he had far too many grand contacts abroad; and his foreign contacts were precisely those which, after 1630, were being cut. Charles I honoured and flattered Mayerne; he was genuinely anxious to keep him at court; he knew that the queen, in particular, depended on him; but he distrusted him in politics. He did not want that busybody to be out of control, on the Continent, re-mobilising that Protestant international on which he had turned his back.

There was also, from now on, a new style in diplomacy. James I had liked amateur diplomats, who indeed had been necessary for secret negotiations with Protestant 'rebels' in Catholic countries. Charles I's tidy mind preferred official channels and correct procedures. For Switzerland, he now sent an accredited envoy to reside at Zürich.[25] The day of the amateurs was over. Not only Mayerne but his brother-in-law Sir Francis Biondi now disappeared from European politics. He too would remain in England, forced to turn to light literature, as Mayerne would turn back to medicine – and art.[26]

Unaware, at first, that he would be permanently prevented from revisiting the estate of which he was so proud, Mayerne busied himself, in the early 1630s, with his dynastic projects. Rich with the profits of his profession, he intended to go out to Aubonne and there, even if he did not write his great work, at least to establish his son Henri, fresh from his grand tour with the Earl of Carlisle, as the young baron. Henri was to live at the château as his father's lieutenant and successor, to become known to his 'subjects' there, to make a suitable marriage, and to establish in the pays de Vaud 'la racine de ma posterité'.[27] For his second son, James, Mayerne had other plans. James was the godson of King James, who had been represented at the ceremony of his baptism by the Duke of Lennox, by Robert Carr, Earl of Somerset, and by Lady Hay, the wife of the future Earl of Carlisle. He was to follow his father's career and become a doctor; and the stages of his education had been well thought out. Having been prepared, like his brother, by an *émigré* Huguenot tutor, who had accompanied him to the fashionable school run by Dr Farnaby in London, he was to begin his higher education at Oxford and then move on to study medicine in Paris. 'I wish him', Mayerne would write, 'first to lay the solid foundations of ancient medicine, and then to build on them the super-structure of Hermetic wisdom, quarried from the minds of the true sages.'[28] In other words, he was to follow Mayerne's own course: for those very words – 'Hermetica aedificia ex auctorum veridicorum medullâ deprompta' – raise up the ghost of Joseph du Chesne.

The first part of this programme was punctually carried out. In 1628 Mayerne persuaded the Bishop of Winchester, Richard Neile, to recommend

James for a place in Trinity College, Oxford. He asked the bishop to write personally to the president, the formidable Dr Kettel, so that the boy might be noticed by the Fellows 'even though he is the younger son'. He requested Neile, too, to recommend the grant of an Oxford degree to the French 'preceptor and supervisor of his studies and morals' who would accompany him: for young James was not to be left solely to his English college tutor, Mr Faringdon, although he too had been personally chosen by Mayerne. The French tutor, M. Benoît,[29] needless to say, was a Huguenot; he had a degree from the sound Huguenot academy of Montauban. Mayerne also himself wrote to President Kettel, explaining that he had chosen Trinity College on the advice of his friends, rather than other, perhaps grander establishments, because he had heard that Dr Kettel was a great guardian and censor of morals: 'I beg and pray that you will have him at your table' – i.e. as a gentleman-commoner – 'so that while his body is fed, his mind may be seasoned by your wit and wisdom'. And he wrote to an old medical friend at Oxford, Dr Ashworth, asking him to prod all the parties with the spur of friendly admonition, to watch over the boy's health, and to keep him supplied with his special cough-lozenges.[30]

In November 1628, when James was settled at Oxford, receiving heavy paternal advice, and his elder brother Henri was on his way back from his grand tour, their mother died. In conveying the sad news to her brother, the Baron Wessel van den Boetzelaer, Mayerne was able to say that he had done all that he could, 'by an extraordinary care for their education', to make them worthy of their grand Boetzelaer ancestry. The baron, he added, might be seeing Henri soon, for 'I have begun to make him a foreigner, by sending him on a tour to Italy with the Earl of Carlisle, and now he is about to return': so he might well drop in at the castle of Asperen.[31]

Henri duly returned, and in 1630 Mayerne took the next steps for his education. In that year Mayerne was consulted by a new patient, M. Malaguet, an elderly military man from Brittany – presumably a dependant of Rohan.[32] Malaguet was serving, like many Huguenot officers, in the army of the United Provinces at Utrecht, and Mayerne, after discussion with Rohan's brother Soubise (who was in London and consulted him regularly for his gout), arranged for Henri to serve under him and learn the military art. However, prolonged life in camp and barracks in the Netherlands was dull, and after more than a year of it Mayerne became alarmed at reports of his son's idleness and dissipation. Clearly a change was needed. So, belatedly, he remembered his own early years: while young James was imbibing wit and wisdom at the high table of Trinity College, Oxford, why should not young Henri learn the same lessons of honour and sobriety as he himself had done under that paragon of all the virtues, his own godfather, the Duc de Rohan?

20

Planting a Dynasty, 1630–1639

Rohan was now in Venice, commanding the land forces of the city and still seeking to serve both the true interest of France, as he saw it, and the Huguenot cause. Now that Richelieu had resumed the foreign policy of Henri IV, this, he believed, was again possible. At least it was possible outside France, where the suspicious cardinal was determined to keep him. He would gladly have lived in Geneva, as Agrippa d'Aubigné had done, but the cardinal had vetoed that too, and the cautious republic, not daring to alienate its chief foreign protector, obediently forbade Rohan to reside on the property which he had bought there. In Venice, the exiled hero turned to literature. He read the classics of Roman virtue. He also wrote. The pen, he told his mother, was now seldom out of his hand. He wrote his memoirs; he wrote, under the title *Le parfait capitaine*, a eulogy of Julius Caesar; he also wrote his most famous work of political thought, his treatise on *The Interest of Princes* – an implicit justification of Henri IV's (and Richelieu's) 'reason of state' and the absorption of religion by politics. But literature alone could not satisfy him. Always he longed for action. At one time he thought of selling his lands in France and buying the kingdom of Cyprus from the Ottoman Sultan: the Greek patriarch, Cyril Lucaris, had offered to arrange the sale. There, as successor of the medieval French kings of Cyprus, he would found a French colony, a *France d'Outremer*, a 'refuge' for the exiled Huguenots.[1] Nearer home, he followed, with nostalgic admiration, the German victories of that other Protestant hero, the King of Sweden. Then, in 1632, his opportunity came. Richelieu wished to see the vital Alpine pass of the Valtelline recovered from Spanish control and restored to the Protestant Grisons. For this purpose a Protestant army must be formed in the Grisons; and what Frenchman was fitter to command it than the hero of Languedoc? The offer was made, and accepted. So the last stage of Rohan's career began, as a Protestant warrior serving the foreign policy of the Cardinal of France.

It was at this moment that Mayerne saw a new opportunity of reclaiming his wastrel son. He wrote to Rohan asking if he would accept Henri as an officer under his command. He wished his son (he said) to live for two years as their servant 'as I myself once did, and to receive from the conversation, teaching and example of my lord such a tincture of honour and virtue as will cling to him to the last moment of his life'.[2]

Rohan agreed, and Mayerne overflowed with gratitude to his old patron. 'No check to your fortune, however great, can halt my respect for you,' he wrote, 'far less efface the memory of my debt to you. If my sons do not inherit this resolve, I shall disavow them for ever.' Not, he hastily added, that Henri would ever incur such a fate: in spite of 'the crudities of his youth' he had progressed too far in the school of honour and virtue for that. So Mayerne would send him to Venice, or wherever Rohan was, 'to be your servant and drink from their source the precepts and examples of honour and virtue'.[3]

In the spring of 1632, Henri de Mayerne had his marching orders. His old tutor, another Huguenot, M. Chouart, now one of Mayerne's medical assistants,[4] would come to Utrecht and escort him to Venice or the Grisons. They were to go via Paris, Berne and Aubonne. At Paris, they were to call on young James, who was now studying medicine there, accompanied by his tutor M. de Berolles. Chouart was to report on him and his studies, for the boy was a bad correspondent and Mayerne did not trust Berolles' judgement. At Berne, Henri was to pay his respects to their Excellencies, the magistrates of the city. At Aubonne he was to meet his future 'subjects' and make it clear, by his visit, that their baron, though unfortunately prevented from visiting them, had them very much on his mind.

For neither in Paris nor in Aubonne were events going according to plan. Indeed, Mayerne had had most disturbing reports from both places. Nor had he any confidence that Henri could deal with the crises that had arisen: rather, he was likely to aggravate them. Mayerne relied on Chouart to act as his agent in Paris and on their Excellencies of Berne to represent his interests in Aubonne.

First, we turn to Paris. Here Mayerne had settled James comfortably, as he thought, in the house of his old friend and apothecary Pierre Naudin, under the double surveillance of his host and tutor, in order to study at the medical faculty, with which Mayerne had evidently forgotten his past differences. Not all his adversaries had forgotten it, and Mayerne had other enemies in Paris too. Particularly there was the family of la Roche-Giffart. It was now twenty years since Mayerne's brother Henri had been killed in Geneva by the Baron de la Roche-Giffart. The assassin had escaped the just punishment which Mayerne and his father had demanded, thanks to the protection of the queen mother, but afterwards he had been accidentally killed by a servant. The servant had then fled to England, where he had continued to live and where Mayerne admitted that he had seen him. The Roche-Giffart family had therefore chosen to assume that he had been hired by Mayerne to murder his master. They impressed upon the dead man's sons the duty of revenge. Now the sons were grown up, and Mayerne's son James had rashly come to Paris and was at their mercy. They let it be known that, since they could not reach Mayerne himself, they would avenge their father's blood by murdering his son. When Mayerne learned of this threat, from a Parisian friend, in July 1631, all his old spirit of defiance was aroused. He wrote at once to declare it. Roche-Giffart, he said, had been 'justly swept from the face of the earth solely by the finger of God, without any human premeditation', and his sons should leave vengeance (if there were any cause of it) to the Lord, for it was His. 'These young gentlemen have no need to draw more blood on their house. Their father has stained it deep enough by the murder of my brother in full view and knowledge of a whole city. . . . His wounds bleed still. My family, in my absence, demanded justice from men, but when this was refused by authority and prevented by violence, God chose to show that he could catch the evil-doers, who could not escape his all-powerful arm.' Therefore the Roche-Giffart family should contemplate God's judgements with fear and trembling, and realise that good men do not fear, knowing that the Devil and wicked men have only so much power as is allowed to them by God, who visits the sins of the fathers on the third and fourth generation.

As for himself, he added, nothing that they might do would deflect him one inch from his path, for his conscience was clear and 'a good conscience is a perpetual feast.' Let them seek him out in England if they wished. His friends urged him to fetch his son home, or at least to change James's address, and to keep him indoors; but Mayerne would not heed such craven advice. Let the boy continue his studies, only taking reasonable care. 'God will preserve him, or, if it pleases God to afflict me with some misfortune to him, all the habitable earth shall not save the authors of it. The king is too just and his chief ministers are too much my friends.' However, he asked his French contacts to keep an eye on the boy and not to let his brother know of these threats, lest, being a soldier, he should act precipitately, 'and I dread nothing more than to see blood in my house'. At the same time he wrote to his son's tutor giving similar advice – and also some admonition. The boy, he had heard, was not giving satisfaction: M. Naudin had complained bitterly of his irregularities; he must study virtue and medicine and write to his father – not familiar letters but such as may occasionally show him to be a philosopher imbued with physics, metaphysics, ethics and logic.[5]

James was not murdered in Paris, but neither did he write to his father or imbue himself with science and philosophy. Six months later a formidable

letter was brought out to him by the faithful Chouart. In it Mayerne told
James that he was tired of complaining of his silence; that when a father has
performed his duties to his children, he is discharged before God and the
world; and that if James showed no amendment in his behaviour, he should
look out: 'I have other children on the way' – the first, a daughter, Dorothea
Theodora, was already three months old – 'from whom I hope for comfort if
I should be so unfortunate as to be neglected by their elders.' So James was
urged to study, and then, on his return, his father would teach him 'the last
and greatest secrets of the profession in which you have chosen to follow me'.[6]
In other words, Mayerne's will was being shaken.

So much for James in Paris. Meanwhile there were Mayerne's 'subjects' in
Aubonne, who were also in need of a wigging. Two letters, despatched on the
same day, and clearly intended to be delivered by Chouart, prepared them for
the worst. One was addressed to the officers of the barony. In it Mayerne
regretted his absence from his beloved subjects. He explained that he had been
obliged, by royal command, to postpone his intended journey; but that he was
sending his son, 'who will one day, God willing, be your lord', and who was at
present heading for the Grisons to serve the Duc de Rohan and to learn to
fight for his country and defend it if attacked. Meanwhile, Mayerne has heard
of grave abuses of justice in his absence, which he will not tolerate. He has
always been a father to his subjects, he writes, and if they think that they can
exchange him for a better master, they are wrong: 'whatever happens, I shall
not give up one iota of my rights.'[7]

These dark hints were made a little clearer in the second letter, which was
addressed to the senators of Berne. To them too Mayerne lamented his
inability to come out in person, as he had planned. He asked them to support
him in maintaining his seigneurial rights. His subjects, he explained, had
taken advantage of his absence to fish in troubled waters. In particular, there
was the case of one Gideon Grivel, who had fled from justice to avoid a charge
of attempted murder. His goods had been confiscated by the baronial officers,
but, Mayerne points out, 'they belong to me, who am, under your Excellencies,
the lord.' He protests that he is a mild ruler, 'especially in the country in which
I have chosen to establish the root of my posterity'. So he expects to receive
justice, and in order to do so is sending his eldest son, whom he could easily
have made a courtier but whom he prefers to make a soldier, to be useful to
the Republic of Berne.[8]

How useful would Henri be? To judge from Mayerne's letters to the friends
who were to receive him *en route*, there was room for doubt. 'He is young and
farouche,' he wrote to one of them, but he will be better 'when his Mercury is
fixed'. 'He needs good examples of honour and virtue,' he told another, 'to
settle the froth of a licentious and unbridled youth.' If Rohan cannot reclaim

him, he exclaims to a third, 'I cannot torment myself with him further. . . . When I die, and not before, I shall leave him Aubonne, if he makes himself worthy of it.' Until then – 'for I shall remain always Baron of Aubonne till my last gasp' – he would give his son an allowance from it, but no more. To Rohan himself, he put a good face on the matter. His late wife, he explained, being of a grand family in Holland, had insisted on having their two sons educated with more freedom and more money than was good for them, and Henri had become, through idleness, a spendthrift and a debauchee. But he was a good horseman – acknowledged by M. de St Antoine to be his best pupil. He had studied mathematics, the lute and fencing. He was improving now, and he had the root of the matter in him . . .[9]

Meanwhile, in a last attempt to bring about such improvement, Mayerne wrote firmly to Henri himself. The tone was no longer that of the letter of advice which had speeded him on the embassy of Lord Carlisle. Like the letter to James, it was a commination. Henri was informed that Chouart was coming to Holland to pick him up and travel with him. He would bring orders which Henri must obey implicitly if he did not wish to be cut off for ever. His disorderly life must cease. He must shed all his vices before presenting himself to Rohan, for two opposites cannot live together, and Rohan is a man of unmixed virtue, who drinks only water and detests tobacco, that *fumée infernale*. Henri must be like the fish whose flesh is saltless though it swims in brine. There will be no need to spend anything. Shun women . . . etc., etc.[10]

Chouart duly set out; Henri was duly collected in Holland and delivered to Rohan in the Grisons; and in July 1632 Mayerne was relieved when Chouart returned, having stopped for some time in Paris on the way back, and reported that Rohan had received his son graciously and offered to have him taught German, mathematics, horsemanship and fortification. Once again Mayerne wrote to express his thanks to Rohan, 'mon premier maistre'.[11] Now at last, he thought, Henri was settled with the best possible patron; James had been straightened out in Paris; and he could turn his mind to other things. He could even take notice of his remoter relatives, his Catholic cousins in France, who now, in his grandeur, had turned to him.

These were the descendants of Audinet Turquet, the brother of Étienne Turquet of Lyon. For two, or perhaps three, generations (for we do not know the profession of Audinet) they had been tradesmen – goldsmiths in Paris – and so had forfeited their claim to nobility. But now the great-grandson of Audinet, Charles Turquet, was established in the royal service, as *conseiller du roi*, second *avocat* at the royal salt-house at Issoudun, and *bailli* of the town and country of Buzançois. He was also contemplating marriage with the daughter of another royal official, controller of the salt-house at Selles. In these circumstances he could reclaim his long-lost nobility; but being uncertain of the correct procedure, either he or his father decided to seek advice from the head of the family. It was the first time that Mayerne had heard from these obscure kinsmen. He replied in his most majestic style. 'He who takes note of his friends', he began sententiously, 'should expect a return. It is true that those of my name have shown so little concern to have relations with me (although I am head of the family and God has been pleased to honour me with the titles and talents with which his bounty has endowed me) that until this hour I have taken no notice of them, and would have continued to do so, if your letters had not aroused me.' He admitted that he was not familiar with all the details of such business, 'our family having long been exiles in foreign lands'. But he set out the necessary genealogical and administrative facts, and gave some rather haughty advice:

> if any of your family has done anything incompatible with nobility, as prac-tising trade or merchandise, then even if you can prove your identity, you must apply for letters patent. Our coat of arms, which I bear in full, but which the cadet branch must bear with a star in one of the bars of the escutcheon, are: two bars *or* in field *azure*; the coat divided in half, with, in chief, an eagle *sable* field *or*; helmet open, and on it a scroll *or azure*, from which comes a savage raising in both hands a club, as if to strike, with this motto or device: *audentes fortuna juvat*: fortune favours the bold. Tell me in detail who you are, and whether it is you whom I once knew in Paris, and expect all assistance from him who is, Monsieur mon cousin, your most humble servant . . .'[12]

We hear no more of these re-ennobled kinsmen in Paris, but one at least of them was to acquire some small distinction. Louis de Mayerne-Turquet, the brother of Charles, became geographer royal to the young Louis XIV and in 1648 presented to the king the design of a map of the world, in which the whole terrestrial globe was presented in a flat circle. This new projection was not indeed the invention of Louis de Mayerne: it had been drawn earlier (as he freely admitted) by Ottavio Pisani in Italy and by Guillaume Postel in France; but his advocacy of it, which was supported by the two professors of the Collège Royal, Jean-Baptiste Morin and Pierre Gassendi, secured the approval of the king; and in 1668, when work was begun on the splendid new Observatory of Paris, the map was engraved on the floor of its eastern tower by Jean-Dominique Cassini, newly arrived from Italy. It was afterwards effaced and had to be re-engraved twice. It was still visible in the eighteenth century, but has since been destroyed.[13]

For Mayerne, the problem of Aubonne would not go away. How could it ever be solved in his absence? It is clear that Mayerne resented Charles I's refusal to allow him to go there. Almost every letter which he wrote to his friends abroad in the spring of 1632 bewailed the postponement – for as yet he saw it only as a postponement – of that long-deferred and, after seven years' absence, essential journey. He had hoped to put his son personally 'in possession of the land which I have bought for him' and himself to spend six months in his château, enjoying, 'in full liberty, the sweet conversation of my friends'. Especially, he wished to see his old friend Sir Isaac Wake in Turin (now about to leave for the embassy in Paris), 'and to discuss with you, *tête à tête*, the work of which you have kindly sent me the details'; for Wake was an enthusiastic amateur alchemist, deeply read in the unintelligible works of the great Polish alchemist Sendivogius. He had also hoped to see his relations and various friends at Geneva, and of course, once again, to set down, before it was too late, 'the fruits of my philosophy'. But it was no good. 'Me voylà, frustré encore,' he exploded.[14] To his sister and brother-in-law, at least, he could speak freely. He had been stopped, he told them: brutally blocked, flatly forbidden; 'but those who serve princes have no redress: they are forced to abandon all and sacrifice themselves for others. ... I now realise how true was the prophecy of our late father, who warned me that in serving princes I would be a slave all my life.'[15]

Mayerne had good grounds for his resentment, for there was clearly much to correct at Aubonne. His officers had been exploiting his absence in every way. As he put it in a letter to an unidentified 'cousin' in Geneva, 'until now I have been unfortunate with this property, which is a beautiful and noble estate but needs the presence of its lord.' Expenses had swallowed up income and left only paper instead of hard cash. Hitherto Mayerne had farmed out the revenues. Now he decided to change course: he would keep the estate in hand, and manage it through a deputy. He had meant to visit it last year (that is, in 1631), he wrote, and then again this year, but both times he had been prevented: 'the good opinion which I enjoy with their Majesties has deprived me (at least for a time) of my liberty.' So, in the spring of 1632, since he could not trust his son, he sent out a young man 'on whose fidelity I can rely, knowing him to be entirely devoted to my service'.[16] This young man, who was to play an important part in Mayerne's later life, was Jean Colladon.

The Colladons were an old and distinguished academic and professional family in Geneva. Germain Colladon, a celebrated jurist, had been the legal assistant of Calvin and had drawn up for him the civil and political edicts of the Holy City. His son Esaïe Colladon was a professor of philosophy at Calvin's Academy. Jean Colladon, the son of Esaïe, had been born in 1608, and in 1631, at the age of twenty-three, he had been invited to England by Mayerne in order to act as his assistant and to study medicine under his tuition. Now Mayerne used him as his agent to go to Aubonne and regulate his interests there. On receiving his report, Mayerne's first thought was to leave Colladon there as his manager, but he felt scruples about wasting the time of his protégé and diverting him from his medical studies, 'in which I can be of great help to him'. So he recalled him to London and selected another young Huguenot protégé to replace him. This was Isaac le Sueur, the Hermetic physician and plague-doctor, whom Mayerne had sought to establish in London as part of his scheme of a permanent health service. Having failed there, he now sent him, armed with a letter of introduction to his cousin, 'to Aubonne, with his little family, to be my deputy, my lieutenant, my receiver, my steward, and to look after my interests as if I were there myself'. Le Sueur and his wife, Mayerne reported, were 'vigilant, incorruptible and frugal, and will go about quietly to procure my profit. They are' – a phrase he used for a second time of Isaac le Sueur – 'of the *débris* of la Rochelle.'[17]

Another ally whom Mayerne called in to his help was the *châtelain* of the neighbouring barony of Morges, M. de Goumouins. In a letter of thanks for his help, Mayerne again lamented the difficulties of an absentee proprietor. 'I know', he wrote, 'that if your good advice and assistance had been seconded by good fortune, my miserable estate, which till now has yielded only thorns, would have been more fruitful.' Would he ever now see a profit from it? Probably not, he sighed, thanks to that wretched *fermier*, 'this man who has reaped where he has not sown and so unscrupulously wasted my purse' in full view and with the full connivance of Mayerne's agents and officers. 'That is what comes of living far from one's estate and trusting it to third parties.' Ruin, he now believed, was inevitable: plague, war and famine had undermined the will and means to good work.[18] Unfortunately, the helpful M. de Goumouins died soon afterwards, so that there seemed no means of staying the slide to ruin. Then, suddenly, Mayerne received news that the process was being unexpectedly accelerated. Henri de Mayerne had had enough of Spartan virtue and frugality with the Duc de Rohan and had arrived, unannounced, at Aubonne.

His father was outraged. His whole purpose had been to give his son two years of strict discipline and salutary example. Now, after only two months, Henri had deserted his post, turned up at the family château, bearing arms and ready 'to go I know not where and do I know not what'. 'Now my estate of Aubonne (which would be for him if he does not disqualify himself) is a dungheap, having suffered terribly, like those of my neighbours, from the scourges which have ravaged our country.' A year later, Henri was still at Aubonne, planning to make a dreadful *mésalliance*, quite unsuitable to his baronial status. Mayerne bombarded him with protests. He deplored his idle wastrel life. Why did he not go to Geneva and live *en pension*, for two years, with some honest man like the famous theologian Jean Diodati, who had been such a valued ally in the heady days of the Calvinist international? Then he could converse with his social equals and take away the reproach of Rohan that he consorted only with servants. Why did he waste his time with his mania for hunting, and fill Aubonne with parasites?

Alas, Henri had no intention of spending two years with a respectable Calvinist minister in the holy city of Geneva. He much preferred his rakish life at Aubonne. The next thing that Mayerne heard was that Henri was still at Aubonne, and ill. Once again he wrote to rebuke and advise. Henri's whole life, he complained, had been a series of irregularities. Wine and tobacco had now brought him to such a state that, unless he changed course, he must prepare 'not to beget children but to pass to another life'. 'I see well', Mayerne went on, after giving medical advice, 'that I must cross the sea, which I shall do as soon as possible' – as soon, that is, as Lady Mayerne had been delivered of her third child. 'You can tell this to all those who think that they shall never see me again, and make merry and play at robbing the absent king.'[19] Thus Mayerne's subjects had fair warning: the furious lord of the vineyard, having sent his heir in vain, was now about to come out himself and take his revenge on those naughty husbandmen who had denied him the fruit of his property while he was detained in a far country. Of course it was *brutum fulmen.* Mayerne did not cross the sea. He would not have been allowed to do so. The ban had been declared. Henri crept home and died in London in January 1634, aged twenty-five.

There remained James. Three months after his elder brother's death, while James – now the heir to the barony – was still in Paris, studying medicine, Mayerne received yet another shocking report. The faithful Chouart had sent out to James's tutor, M. de Berolles, a small sum of money, which James had intercepted and diverted to his 'friponneries renaissantes'. At once a swingeing letter sailed out from St Martin's Lane. James, it now seemed, was irredeemable. Was this the way to reward Chouart's services to his late brother? Then, once again, Mayerne shook his will. Lady Mayerne had now borne her third child, a son. Let James beware, lest the inheritance be diverted to this new claimant. 'Miserable youth, what are you up to? Will you never come to your senses? . . . But to wash the head of an ass is a waste of soap.'[20]

Two months later James was back in England, and Mayerne persevered in his plans to make him a doctor. He sent him to Sir William Paddy, with the presentation copy of his edition of Mouffet's book on insects and with a letter requesting Paddy to accept him as his student.[21] Paddy agreed. But it came to nothing. Two years later, James was on his way, with Chouart and servants in attendance, to Aubonne. [22] The last we hear of him alive is in April 1638, when Mayerne reported to his old host in Paris, Pierre Naudin, that 'by the kindness of Their Majesties, whom I have the honour to serve', James was *escuyer tranchant* (carver) to the young Prince of Wales: 'God make him an honest man.'[23] James's lessons in the best school of surgery in Europe had at least qualified him to carve the royal beef. Next year he too was dead, aged, like his brother, in his mid-twenties.

The history of Mayerne's relations with his sons is a melancholy story. He himself blamed the grand ideas of the van Boetzelaer family: he had yielded to their social rather than to his own humanist ideal of education. We may see it somewhat differently, as Nature's revenge against a powerful and exacting father, and we may note that he was not the only great Huguenot individualist to suffer this revenge. Isaac Casaubon, the Duc de Rohan, Agrippa d'Aubigné, all saw their severe pattern of life, the high ideal on which they had modelled themselves, and which they sought to impose on their family, repudiated by sons who could not carry such a burden. Nothing that Mayerne wrote to his sons in private letters (which, however, he carefully copied out for preservation) was as excoriating as d'Aubigné's description, in the memoirs which he wrote for 'posterity', of his own disinherited only son, Constant. He had begun those memoirs by dedicating them to his son, who was to see in them a model for himself. He ended them with a blistering attack on that 'wretch' who, having first been debauched by gaming and drunkenness at Sedan, had then abandoned the study of literature to lose himself at the gaming-tables of Holland; whom his father had then sought to rescue by sending him to command a regiment under the Prince de Condé; but who, since 'nothing could satisfy the insolence of a lost spirit', had returned to his old ways and, being put in charge of his father's castle, had turned it into 'a gambling hell, a brothel and a den of thieves and sharpers'.[24] We seem to be reading the history of Henri de Mayerne again. It is the syndrome of the puritan hero's rebel son.

For Mayerne it was a double tragedy because he had invested such hopes in his sons. He was capable of great affection and he had a strong dynastic sense. It was to 'establish the root of his posterity' that he had bought that distant castle in Switzerland, outside the reach of English taxes, so that his family might become as grand as the van Boetzelaer. In fact, it was all a terrible mistake. Mayerne's words, 'Aubonne est une ornière' – Aubonne is a dungheap – could be the final epitaph on the whole adventure. In the end, Mayerne would have no heir to his name, no posterity to root there. The two sons of his second marriage, Albert born in 1634 and Louis born in 1635, would both die before him, Albert at three,[25] Louis, his last hope, at seven.[26]

Fortunately he found a substitute for his paternal affection in the young man who had become his assistant, Jean Colladon. Colladon became his most devoted disciple, served him in all his activities, shared his interests, and was treated as his son: Mayerne addressed him as 'mon enfant'.[27] In 1636 Mayerne obtained royal letters which caused Colladon to be incorporated as a doctor of medicine at Cambridge, and this enabled him to set up in practice in Norwich, working with one of Mayerne's own apothecaries who was established there.[28] However, at the end of the year Mayerne fetched him back from Norwich to go on an errand abroad. A marriage had been arranged for him, to legitimate his position in the family. He was to go to Geneva to visit Mayerne's sister Judith – his favourite sister 'que j'aime uniquement' – and to marry her daughter Aimée. He was also to carry a letter from Mayerne to the City of Geneva.[29]

For Geneva, at that time, was in the throes of another crisis. In 1636 a Spanish army, under the imperial general Clam Gallas, had approached the Pont de Grésin, and its commander had made a secret agreement with the new Duke of Savoy, Victor Amadeus, to seize that 'seminary of heresy', Geneva itself. That particular threat had come to nothing, for the imperial army had been forced to retreat, but the pressure from Savoy continued, and the Petit Conseil decided to appeal both formally to Charles I and his Secretary of State and, less formally, to Philip Burlamachi and Mayerne. The letter which was delivered by Colladon was Mayerne's answer to this appeal. In it he 'humbly kissed the hands of Messeigneurs' and offered them all the services within his power. The Petit Conseil wrote back to him, informing him of all the breaches of the Treaty of St Julien by the Duke of Savoy, and wrote too to Lord Fielding, the English ambassador at Venice, who had been instructed to watch over the interests of Geneva. It also wrote formally to Charles I, to the Secretary of State Sir John Coke, and to Philip Burlamachi in London. All these letters to London were sent, as usual, through the Burlamachi network.[30]

Having delivered Mayerne's letter, Colladon stayed on in Geneva and returned slowly through France. His marriage with Aimée de Frotté was solemnised at the Huguenot Temple at Charenton in July 1637. On arrival in England, Colladon evidently returned to Norwich for a time, and then rejoined Mayerne in London. When a son was born to the Colladons, he was called Theodore, and we can assume that Mayerne was his godfather. Colladon would remain with Mayerne, an invaluable and devoted supporter, for the rest of Mayerne's life.

Later in the same year, Mayerne was again in touch with the city of Geneva. By this time Archbishop Laud was at the height of his power. The high Anglican clergy were disowning Calvin and disclaiming any communion with his followers. The foreign Protestants in England were being persecuted; and in Paris the English ambassador, Laud's friend Lord Scudamore, ostentatiously refused to attend, as his predecessors had done, the Huguenot services at Charenton. England, it seemed to many, was repudiating its historic role – its Elizabethan and Jacobean role – as leader of the Protestant international: indeed, repudiating Protestantism altogether. Reports of these sinister developments naturally reached Geneva and caused alarm among the ministers there. So in November 1637 two of them – the famous Jean Diodati and his colleague Abraham du Par – brought the matter before the Council. They reported that the bishops and clergy of England were publicly denouncing the Calvinist clergy of Geneva as enemies of monarchy and episcopacy, hardly different from the radicals among the Jesuits. The Venerable Company of Pastors at first proposed to write to Dr Davenant, the anti-Laudian Bishop of Salisbury, as a 'personnage très docte et d'une grande probité'. But in the end, after discussion in the Council, it was decided 'to write to M. de Mayerne to discover his opinion on the subject and on the remedy to be adopted'.[31] Though we do not know the letter or the reply, it is unlikely that Mayerne could have helped. A Huguenot at court, however influential, was in no position to compete, in church matters, with the formidable Archbishop of Canterbury.

Cut off from his property in Switzerland, and from his political base in Geneva and Berne, unable to help his foreign friends, a powerless witness of England's retreat from international Protestantism, Mayerne can hardly have felt at home in the England of Charles I. Nor were his personal relations with the king, as far as we can see, very close. It was the queen, Henrietta Maria, who depended on him – no doubt, in part, because he was French. He accompanied her regularly to the baths at Wellingborough and prescribed remedies for her arthritis, her red face, her swollen eyelids and constant sneezing fits. He supplied her with elaborate cosmetics and rich ointments of puppy-dogs, worms and bats. But after the end of 1628, there is no evidence that Charles I personally used the services of Mayerne at all. In the register in which he records his attendance on the king, there are notes of some early prescriptions and precautions against the plague in 1625–6 – pills, inhalations, fumigations of royal rooms, smelling-balsam, etc. Then, on 24 December 1628, comes an entry which shows that Charles I, like his eldest son, was a practised tree-climber: 'the king, having caught a heavy cold from standing in a tree for a long time, waiting to shoot deer, began to suffer from *crudor* of the brain, with pain in the teeth and gums of the lower jaw, on the right side.'[32] Later than that, all references are merely to the queen and the royal children.

On the other hand, he often attended the king's horses. Mayerne collected cures for horses and had learned discussions about them with his old Huguenot friend, the king's stable master, M. de St Antoine. Strong-smelling human dung, dissolved in white wine, was good for pleurisy in horses, as, reciprocally, was horse-dung, similarly 'rectified', for men. Mayerne cured a nine-year-old black horse of epilepsy in 1627 and another – a hackney – in 1632 ('who is still alive and very strong' in 1638); he cured another very valuable horse by an arcane liniment in 1626; and he hardened the fragile hooves of one of the king's horses with ointment of boiled snakes.[33] He also treated the king's mad dogs – presumably in the interest of those whom they seem regularly to have bitten.[34]

King Charles no doubt treated Mayerne, as he treated everyone, with courtesy and consideration, but the physician was no longer, as in the previous reign, a close personal friend of the monarch. He no longer moved with him from palace to palace: if he took country air, it was sometimes at the queen's palace of Oatlands, but otherwise it was at Moor Park, Waltham Abbey, or Twickenham Park, the country houses of his grand patients. It was in 1633 that Mayerne, when he at last published the book on insects which Thomas Mouffet had intended to dedicate to Queen Elizabeth and then to James I, transferred the dedication not to Charles I but to a fellow-physician, Sir William Paddy.[35] About the king, he expressed himself seldom, and when he did the note of complaint, though discreetly muted, is often audible. 'Princes', he wrote to his colleague Sir Martin Lister in 1635, 'do not easily digest the word "recompense".' Forty years of royal service had forced him often to meditate on the verse of the Gospel which says that, having done everything in our power, we are 'unprofitable servants' and have done no more than our duty.[36] Mayerne never refers to Charles I with the warmth that he always showed towards King James, 'mon bon maistre', as he described him, in retrospect, to the Queen of Bohemia, 'l'oeuil duquel n'a jamais esté que très favorable envers moy':[37] who never looked on me but with a favourable eye.

Discreet though he was, Mayerne must occasionally have expressed his feelings. One of those who must have known, or guessed, his views was the French ambassador, the Marquis de Senecterre, a former patient of Mayerne. Such may be the background to a communication which Mayerne received in June 1638, after Senecterre had returned to Paris, from his apothecary in Paris, Pierre Naudin. It was an invitation to return to France, with an assurance that he would be very well received there; for Richelieu was now in full power, and the Huguenots, their political independence having been crushed, enjoyed the protection, even the personal patronage, of the cardinal. Naudin's letter has not survived: its content must be inferred from Mayerne's long and elaborate reply.

'Let me assure you', Mayerne wrote,

that although my plans and hopes, in the winter of my age, are entirely confined within the bounds of this happy island, where what charms me most is the sweetness of peace, so long as it may please God to allow us to enjoy it, nevertheless, in truth, I always remember my dear country, and I confess that even now I would be very glad to see it again before I die. However, every time that this desire has encouraged me to seek means to cross the sea, I have encountered so many difficulties, arising from the good opinion which their Majesties, whom I have the honour to serve, are pleased to hold of my person and of the necessity of my services, that every effort to obtain leave of absence has been vain, even when my little property at Aubonne and my poor family concerns in Paris clamour for my presence, threatening me with ruin and desolation. Princes look after their own interests, not the convenience of their servants.

He did not know why the marquis, 'to whom I have many obligations', wished him to come to Paris, though he evidently had some suspicions; but in any case he needed clarification. 'It does not suit my white beard, nor the position that I hold in the world, to jump out into the street, deserting my post like a shipwrecked sailor' ('comme un matras désemparé'). 'I am well, thank God, and having recovered from a painful and dangerous illness' – he had been suffering from the stone[38] – 'I ask only to be allowed to pass my few remaining days in gentle repose.' For what was worldly advantage to a man of his age? 'It is like bread offered to a man without teeth to chew it.' He was rich, thanks to nobody but God, who had endowed him with industry: why then should he risk a journey overseas 'when I ought to be thinking only of missing my journey to Heaven?' So if he were to be persuaded, Naudin must offer rather more attractive bait than he had yet dangled before him. 'Cumbrous heavy machines like me can only be moved by powerful springs, and you know well that we do not return from the fair as quickly as from the market.' Of course he was devoted to the King and Queen of England, and would not do anything without their consent. Nevertheless ... if the bait were tempting enough, perhaps he could wangle two or three months, being drawn, of course, solely by the prestige of the post, 'to sniff a gust of that wind which we call honour', before retreating into 'the Parmesan cheese in which I have built myself a hermitage'. 'There', he concludes, 'you have the fruits of my philosophy. Do not be surprised if the sixty-five years which I have spent on this earth can change, eight times in a day, the temperament of my body and the keenness of my spirit. Reply when you like, soon or late, I do not care.' However, he hastens to add, do not think me irresolute in my business affairs: *assez tost si assez bien* – if the offer is good enough it will have to come quickly enough.[39]

Watching this magnificent charade, so tortuous but so transparent, we are reminded of the invitation to England which had come twenty-eight years ago, from the unfortunate Sir Thomas Overbury, acting for an anonymous 'seigneur anglais' (Lord Norreys). Who, we asked then, was the figure lurking behind that English lord?[40] Who, we now ask, was lurking behind the French marquis, de Senecterre? Someone, clearly, who could compete with the King of England as a patron; but not, surely, the King of France: the dreadful

Bouvard would never have allowed that. Was it then, perhaps, the cardinal himself, another old patient, who had a liking for heretical thinkers, unorthodox doctors, alchemists, Hermetists, visionaries, and did not care if they were Huguenots?

However that may be, there was no sequel, or none that we know. Mayerne stayed in London. He still dreamed of his 'hermitage' at Aubonne: only two months earlier his sister, Madame de Frotté, who had been staying with him, had set out to Aubonne to put the château in order, 'for it is there', Mayerne had then written, 'that I hope we shall finish our days together, *doucement, parmi les nostres.*'[41] But always, in spite of everything, London held him back. After all, whatever its incidental drawbacks, he had an office for life, with a high salary and numerous perquisites; he had a large and profitable private practice; he was established in a grand social world, visiting a round of great ladies; and he had his own well-organised private world, with his numerous Huguenot assistants, servants and friends. And then there was 'the sweetness of peace' in 'this happy island', that delicious Caroline peace which contrasted with the ever expanding war in Europe. Like others, Mayerne would often dwell on the happy peace of England in the 1630s. 'I pass my life here very comfortably,' he had written to his sister a few years earlier, 'for we live in a profound peace, contemplating the afflictions of those who are beyond seas.'[42]

And anyway, was the France of Richelieu really so attractive? The power of Richelieu looks firm enough to us – in retrospect. At the time it was maintained against deep hatred and continual plots. Nothing seemed firm there except the established corporations; and those corporations included the Gallican Church, still intolerant of Huguenots, and the Medical Faculty of Paris, still strong against medical heresy. In this very month in which he received Naudin's letter, Mayerne would have heard that his closest and most cherished link with France – the France to which he belonged, 'Gallia periens', as he had once called it,[43] the France that was perishing – was snapped. Rohan, his first patron, the hero whom he venerated all his life as the pattern of all virtue, was dead.

Rohan, in the phrase of Sainte-Beuve, was 'the last great man produced by the Reform in France'. His revolt had been the death-struggle of French Protestantism as an independent force. After his defeat, it would never be the same: it was left dependent on toleration, exposed to the threat which would be so easily realised by Louis XIV. By that defeat, France was set free for the external struggle, the struggle for power in Europe, but the plural society within it was at an end. In his exile, after 1629, Rohan had served Richelieu's 'Protestant' foreign policy well. He had raised an army and reconquered the Valtelline for the Grisons. But then the suspicious cardinal had let him down; the Grisons, finding themselves duped, had revolted; and Rohan, for accepting their terms, had been disowned. Distrusted and distrusting, he had refused to set foot in France and had left Switzerland to fight, as a volunteer, for Bernard of Saxe-Weimar, the successor of his dead hero, Gustavus Adolphus. Now he had himself died of wounds received in the battle of Rheinfelden. He had been buried not in France, not on his ancestral estate, but in the city of refuge, Geneva. The senators, who had hesitated to receive him alive, gave him a pompous funeral, and set up, over his grave in the cathedral of St Pierre, a monumental effigy: an honour (or superstitious observance) which they had allowed to no other man, not even to Calvin himself.

To Mayerne, Rohan's death must have seemed the end of part of his life. For forty years Rohan had embodied for him the ideal of an aristocratic Huguenot France. Now that ideal had been destroyed. However, though important in Mayerne's life, the ideal was only a part. There was another part, no less important to him, and more immediate. He was a doctor, a chemist, a philosopher. That part of his life still remained; and in it, even at the age of sixty-five, there was still much to do.

For let us not be deceived by Mayerne's rhetoric about the winter of his age, the need for repose, his physical immobility, his toothlessness, his thoughts of Heaven. He was still as active as ever – and as convivial as ever. His diet, we are told, was 'something more than liberal'.[44] 'If it were not improper to prescribe to a doctor,' Sir Simonds D'Ewes wrote, in 1639, to Mayerne's father-in-law Joachimi, 'I would recommend to Dr. Mayerne rest and abstinence.'[45] But Mayerne had no intention of trying either. He enjoyed his liberal diet; and he had work in hand.

21

Entrepreneur and Virtuoso

According to his protégé Jean Colladon, Mayerne was physically active until his sixtieth year – i.e. until 1633 – but thereafter, when he was 'heavy with age', he was 'overburdened by his weight' and found movement difficult.[1] Difficult, not impossible: we have seen him contemplating emigration at sixty-five, and he would threaten it at seventy-one. But if his physical activity was reduced, mentally he was as vigorous as ever. Indeed he compensated for his restriction in one field by an extension of interest in another. While remaining as busy as always in his medical practice, he became more active than ever on other fronts: as an entrepreneur, and as a patron of the arts.

Mayerne had always had entrepreneurial interests. At the court of Henri IV he had lived among economic adventurers. His patients and friends had included Sebastien Zamet, the great financier, and Pierre de Beringhem, a universal projector. Calvinists in general were active in economic affairs simply because, in an age of persecution, they had to be mobile: they could not afford to be tied to landed property. Mayerne's own family was accustomed to migration – from Piedmont to Lyon, from Lyon to Geneva, from Geneva to Paris and London – and therefore used to living on its wits. His grandfather had been a merchant and banker. His father, lacking an economic sense, had lived uncomfortably. In England, Mayerne had found himself at a court which has been described as 'a lottery of unearned fortunes': the courtiers competed with each other for grants of monopoly, leases, wardship, confiscations, fines, for these were the means by which officers were paid. Court doctors were treated no differently from other court officers: they received a salary, but that was a mere retainer; for their real income they relied – in addition to private practice – on indirect profit. All the Jacobean court doctors expected such remuneration: the State Papers show them applying for forfeited recusants' lands, the confiscated goods of outlaws, offices of profit. Dr Chambers was receiver of fines on penal statutes. Sir William Paddy and Matthew Gwinn, the Regius Professor of Medicine at Oxford, were garblers of tobacco. Dr Grent, physician-in-ordinary, applied for a patent for the hot-pressing of silk and a new method of shooting with longbows, both his own inventions.[2] Mayerne would have been eccentric if he had not sought similar means of enrichment. He was not eccentric – at least not in that sense.

As a foreigner at the English court, Mayerne needed a native partner, and he soon found one through his first and most constant patron, Lord Hay. For presumably it was through Hay that he discovered Hay's cousin, Sir George Hay, of Nether Lith and Kinfauns. Under King James, Sir George prospered in Scotland, where he became Lord Clerk Register and ended as Earl of Kinnoul and Lord Chancellor. But he also had other interests, and it is with these other interests that we are now concerned. He has been described as 'one of the most active promoters of early Scottish industry'. In 1607 he had established iron-works at Letterewe in Ross-shire, and had imported a colony of Englishmen to work in them, 'making iron and casting great guns until the wood of it was spent'. In 1610 he had obtained a gift (afterwards confirmed by Parliament) of the manufacture of iron and glass throughout Scotland for thirty-one years. In 1616 he was moving into a new commodity: the manufacture of smalt. And in May of the same year we find him, with two partners, possessed of a monopoly, for twenty-one years, of the export of Scottish coal to the mouth of the River Seine and thence to Rouen and Paris 'or to any other place on the said river'.[3] His two partners, named in this last grant, were Robert Hay, gentleman of the bedchamber, and Theodore de Mayerne.[4]

Mayerne's function was, no doubt, to arrange the French side of the business. A month after the grant he wrote personally to the King of France, stating that the King of Britain had given him this monopoly of export and asking for a similar monopoly of import from the mouth of the Seine to Paris, free of all tolls and taxes. By this means, he offered to provide for the heating of Paris with Scottish coal. The affair, he added, was one of very great expense and incredible risk, and he did not doubt that it would be granted.[5] Mayerne's letter was sent to Paris by the French ambassador in London, who, at his request, wrote a personal letter to the French Secretary of State, Villeroy, asking him to forward the affair, and referring him, for further details, to Mayerne's old father and to Pierre de Beringhem, who no doubt had a subsidiary interest in the matter.[6]

Mayerne evidently had great hopes of this venture, which, on the face of it, could have been very profitable. The provision of coal to London at this time made the fortune of the Newcastle Hostmen, who enjoyed a monopoly of the trade. A similar monopoly for the provision of Paris would presumably have made the fortune of those who had acquired it, even if only to sell to more active entrepreneurs.[7] Mayerne may of course have come in as a sleeping partner, simply on account of his supposed influence with the French court;

but equally he may have envisaged a more active role. As an alchemist, he had a genuine interest in minerals, and he seems to have acquired a particular knowledge of Scottish coal. Scottish coal, he noted, had a brighter flame than English, and burnt with less smell: it might well be richer for medicinal purposes – in particular, to cure strangury. He also thought it the best ingredient for black paint.[8] In other words, he was interested in it in three distinct categories: as an entrepreneur, as a physician, and as a technologist of art.

However, it seems that the project never materialised. For several years Mayerne pressed his case at the French court; but no doubt there were other interests, there as in England, which were opposed to such a monopoly. No progress had been made by 1618, when Mayerne was expelled so ignominiously from France. In his elaborate attempts to restore his relations with the French court after that humiliation, the affair of the coal monopoly was never far from his mind. Thus in February 1620 the French ambassador wrote to his government that Mayerne wished to be at peace with it, and free from suspicion, adding, 'he has asked me to write to you touching his letters about the import of Scottish coal into France, which he begs you to expedite. This will be a benefit for Paris and an opportunity to increase his desire to be of service.'[9] In later letters, Mayerne returned to the same theme: he wanted peace with honour; and he coupled honour with economic concessions – arrears of pay and 'advancement de mes affaires'.[10] In December 1623, when peace had been restored, Mayerne wrote to Puysieux to thank him for his effective intercession with the king, and then went on to the necessary details of a final settlement: 'to come down to particulars . . . I understand that, by the orders which you have procured from the mouth of the king concerning my salary, past and to come, and my affair of the Scotch coal, things are proceeding, though very slowly. He has solicited often, waited long, and now hopes for some profit.'[11] However, it does not seem that anything was done. Sir George Hay had by now given up industry for politics; war with France suspended Mayerne's claims on the French crown; monopolies were resented in England; and the project of heating Paris with Scottish coal for the profit of the courtiers in London sank quietly and finally out of sight.

It was succeeded, in Mayerne's life, by other initiatives. They began, for reasons which will soon appear, in 1633. On 26 June of that year Mayerne wrote direct to King Charles, enclosing a petition. The petition does not survive, but Mayerne made a copy of the covering letter, with which he was no doubt pleased: for it combined a flowing courtly style with a tone of haughty independence and unmistakable innuendo. In the preamble, which was long and florid, he protested that he was not seeking a reward for his services, and that he did not presume to think himself indispensable. Long experience in royal courts (he added acidly) had taught him not to do that. He merely wished to beg a favour. But he begged it somewhat peremptorily. His life, he pointed out, was now in its evening, and so he could not afford to wait. The favour would cost the Crown nothing in cash, little in future revenue, and perhaps it would anyway bring nothing to anyone: for the gleam of hope – which he describes as a hope of treasures hidden under the waters in the bowels of the earth – might well be extinguished by the event, showing once again that all that glisters is not gold . . . He then asked for 'a prompt, frank and decisive answer, authorising me to pluck the rose without the thorns'.[12]

The substance of the petition is clear from a letter which Mayerne wrote next day to his old patron Lord Hay, now Earl of Carlisle, soliciting his support. What Mayerne was seeking was the lease of a lead-mine which had been flooded for over a century and had now reverted to the Crown. If it were now drained, it could, Mayerne maintained, be brought back into production.[13] At the same time Mayerne wrote to Will Murray, gentleman of the king's bedchamber and master of the back-stairs at court, asking for his support and giving the background to this application. He had, he explained, repeatedly applied to the king for leave to go abroad, to visit Aubonne, but his applications had been invariably refused. On the last three occasions the king had refused with his own mouth. He ordered Mayerne not to raise the matter again: he was 'no longer even to think of parting from himself, the Queen and their children'. But the king had encouraged him to ask for some other sign of his favour, as a recompense for this ban. So now he asked for the rent of this drowned lead-mine.[14] A further reference to the project may perhaps be contained in an undated letter from Mayerne to Meric Casaubon, the son of his old friend Isaac Casaubon, which has survived among Casaubon's papers. Evidently Casaubon was going to visit lead-mining country – perhaps the actual mine in which Mayerne was interested. Mayerne wrote to him in his usual imperative style:

M. Casaubon will please to remember, when he is at the lead-mines, to enquire either of the miners or, preferably, of the master of the mine, which is the richest vein and which, after being fired, leaves most fine silver – how many grains per ounce, or how many ounces of ore are needed to produce a grain of silver – and to write to me what they report. From this mine he is to detach some of the mineral, without fire or water, together with the earth or stone, and the purest part of it, freshly taken from the earth, is to be placed immediately in a little cork which is then to be tightly bound and firmly closed and sent immediately to me by the carrier of the place or other convenient means, and this, please, as quickly as possible. I wish the mineral to be taken directly from the ground and not to consist of pieces which have been extracted long ago and exposed to the air. The cask can weigh up to 200 pounds. He is to send me a note of the cost and what I must pay here proportionately.[15]

It thus seems that Mayerne's interest in the lead-mine was in the yield of silver that he could expect; and that he wished to operate the mine himself, and not merely to use his monopoly, if he should obtain it, as a source of rent. However, we hear no more of this project, and subsequent events suggest that it too came to nothing.

A few months later, Mayerne applied for another monopoly, this time in the animal kingdom: a monopoly to lay oyster-beds. In his petition, he states that although there is great plenty of oysters on the coasts of England and Wales, the trade in them has been cornered by foreigners, who choose the fairest and best, even before they be fully fed and grown, and sell them abroad by the hundred, leaving only 'the refuse and worst' to be sold, at artificially high prices, to the king's subjects. So Mayerne requested that, 'for the greater increase of oysters within this kingdom, and for the restraining the exportation of them into foreign parts by strangers', he be granted exclusive rights for thirty-one years to lay the beds and export the oysters under licence.[16] His petition was duly referred to the Lord Keeper and the Lord Privy Seal, but soon ran into trouble. Objectors pointed out, somewhat sardonically no doubt, that if Mayerne intended to lay oysters freely, for the benefit of the fisherman, that would be 'a good charity'; 'but if he intend to have any propriety' – property – 'in those oysters', then he was invading existing rights. The oysters growing in inland creeks belonged to the landlords; those in 'channels and shoals of the sea which are in the king's hands, not yet passed away by letters patent', belonged to the fisherman who 'have ever had common of fishing for their living' there. Besides, the cultivation of oysters was already well regulated under the good order of the Admiralty. There were existing orders to restrain the Dutch from exporting Kentish oysters, and those orders would be traversed by Mayerne's proposal to export under licence.[17] Mayerne's petition was finally turned down as an invasion of the jurisdiction of the Admiralty.

Scottish coal-mines, English lead-mines, English oyster-beds – what have these three enterprises in common? One thing, of course, is the hope of profit. Mayerne's applications can be seen as mere financial speculations. On the other hand, all three are connected with alchemy and alchemical medicine – coal for his furnaces, lead for transmutation, oysters for pearls: 'magistery of pearls' was one of the favourite prescriptions which he had taken over from du Chesne. Probably, therefore, Mayerne was speculating in the area in which he had personal knowledge and personal interests: he wished, while exploiting a profitable investment, to apply his own expertise and to supply his own needs from his own resources. How far his applications were taken, we do not know. It is by mere accident that the few documents which inform us of these enterprises have survived, scattered haphazardly in different archives; and he may well have been involved in other such enterprises which we cannot now trace.

Thus no contemporary document tells us, what we know from retrospective evidence, that Mayerne also held the office of Garbler of Spices and Seeds under Charles I.[18] Once again, the office reflected his interests: he was a botanist, interested (as all Paracelsians were) in medicinal herbs, and he engaged in a regular traffic in seeds, exchanging them with and on behalf of other botanists, English and foreign.[19] It was through Mayerne that the famous botanist John Parkinson was appointed botanist royal to Charles I;[20] Mayerne wrote in praise of Parkinson's two great works, *Paradisi in sole paradisus terrestris* (1629) and *Theatrum botanicum* (1640).[21]

This summary of Mayerne's entrepreneurial activities up to 1633 reveals a certain pattern. They had begun in 1616, when he had survived his early difficulties, had been accepted as a Fellow of the Royal College of Physicians, and had started work on the new pharmacopoeia: in other words, when he had committed himself to life in England. After 1620 his interests shifted. Having compromised himself in France and failed to corner the Franco-Scottish coal-trade, he had become involved in the affairs of Switzerland and had bought his barony of Aubonne, which became the new centre of his interests. In these circumstances he allowed his English projects to lapse. However, in 1633 it was finally made clear to him that he would not be allowed to leave England. Thereupon his mind returned from Swiss to English investments. The lease of the lead-mine was projected in 1633 and was explicitly related by him to the ban on foreign travel. The monopoly of laying oyster-beds was projected in the same year. If Mayerne was forbidden to develop his estates and expound alchemical secrets from his feudal tower in the pays de Vaud, he would exploit present opportunities from his house in St Martin's Lane.

So, when lead and oysters failed, he did not desist. In the summer of 1635 he tried again, though again in vain. This time his project was nearer home. It was to be a monopoly of distilling. All his working life he had been an active distiller. His notebooks, even the earliest of them, contain notes and drawings of methods of distilling. Alchemy consisted largely of distillation. By that process 'projections' were made for the transmutation of metals. By it chemical medicines were produced. Therefore, when new processes and new products needed to be regulated, it was natural for him to enter into the affair. Just as he had encouraged the formation of a reputable Society of Apothecaries, free from the mercantile embrace of the grocers and effectively controlled and protected by the physicians, so he would naturally wish to see the distillers made respectable and regulated; and he did not disdain the profits of their regulation. In 1638, in partnership with Sir Thomas Cademan, his fellow-physician to Queen Henrietta Maria, he founded a new company, the Distillers of London. They set about the establishment of rules, which were published in 1639,[22] for the making of strong waters and vinegars. Their initiative was resisted by the Society of Apothecaries as a threat to their monopoly, but the physicians prevailed.[23]

Mayerne's enthusiasms, outside his medical work, were wide and varied. Economic motives informed some of them, but not all. He compiled a cookery book, in one of the many desperate efforts made by foreigners to improve the English cuisine. He invented a cordial, the secret of which remained the valuable property of his sister's family in Geneva, and which would be offered to Napoleon when he entered Geneva as a conqueror. He kept deer and grew medicinal herbs at Horne Park, near Eltham, where he was Ranger.[24] He examined means to catch carp; a means of keeping wine from going off; a method for inducing wolves, foxes and other carnivores to follow one (for what purpose is not clear) by rubbing one's boots with an ointment of boiled cockchafers, galbanum and pig's dung, 'as old and smelly as possible'; and for making that elusive nostrum, the elixir of life.

Of Mayerne's interests outside his medical studies and practice, there is one to which posterity is indebted: his energetic study of the technology of art. Its most imposing result has outlived his medical work and reputation, for medical science dates more quickly than art. In his own time it was the other way round: his fame was as a physician, the most admired physician in Europe, while his artistic interests were a private hobby known only to a narrow circle. Intellectually, however, the two pursuits were to him insepa-rable. Both were applications of the science of chemistry. His notes on the two subjects follow the same method – observation, cross-examination, 'specula-tion', experiment – and are expressed in the same form: the same scrupulous acknowledgement of source where derivative and the same proprietary symbols where original.

For the chemistry of painting belonged to a larger chemical theory held by the disciples of Paracelsus. The Paracelsian doctrine was more than a branch of science: it was a revelation, a world-system, which embraced all sciences, from metaphysics to household gadgets. Thus it is that we find, in the scien-tific activity of Mayerne's time, the combination in the same persons of large and, to us, fantastic cosmological beliefs with an intense interest in the smallest aspects of Nature and apparently trivial technical 'improvements'. Paracelsus himself had explicitly emphasised this connection: to him the divine chemistry of the universe, the macrocosm, provided the inspiration to explore the intimate recesses of the human microcosm, and the whole science of iatrochemistry presumed that connection. In the seventeenth century we find the same phenomenon in Samuel Hartlib and his friends, whose zeal for the communication of knowledge and the improvement of rural and house-hold economy was fired by messianic and millenarian conceptions. Although there is a great difference between the humble altruist Hartlib and the grand, acquisitive courtier-physician Mayerne, it is a difference of personality, not of policy. Mayerne's philosophy was total, and if he was sometimes, like Bacon, the Olympian patron, he was also, at other times, himself the experimenter who worked, as he had claimed in his *Apologia*, with his own hands.

Perhaps the best and most succinct expression of the connection of paint and Paracelsianism is the essay by Mayerne's friend the Paracelsian apothe-cary, physician and engraver Nicolas Briot, which Mayerne copied out in 1626. Having established his 'doctrine générale', which explains the Creation of the World by the Divine Chemist, Briot comes to the realisation of this doctrine in the human arts and medicine, and to its practical application, within those arts, in the use of medical and chemical remedies. Within twenty-eight pages we have moved from Briot's Paracelsian philosophy to his concrete specialised interests: colours, dyes, inks, gilt, varnish.

Reading through Mayerne's papers, we are astonished by the time and the vigour that he gave to his artistic interests. He experimented with pigments, varnishes, enamels. He studied the techniques of painting, jewellery (real and imitation), metalwork, sculpture, marquetry, gilding, glass-work, tapestry, dyeing, waterproofing, the concoction and erasure of coloured inks. He examined methods of colouring and varnishing wood; of preparing acids for etching; of extracting mineral colours; of making and applying lacquer; of purifying oils and varnishes; of repairing pictures and frames and canvases. He investigated the trade secrets of the porcelain-makers of China and of 'le maistre de Foulam', the chemist and potter John Dwight of Fulham. He preserved a document, by unknown hands (for the authors write in the plural), which describes a 'curious method of using enamel and colours in illumination', 'as it is done in Limoges', and 'new and different colours' to be used in enamel painting. This method, say the writers, is 'private to ourselves and must not be indulged'. In the margin, opposite the formula for the red colour, Mayerne placed his possessive monogram and wrote 'my invention'.

Mayerne's interest in the technology of art produced a document that has been of keen interest to art historians, who have used it since the time of Horace Walpole. They know it as 'the Mayerne manuscript'. It is Sloane MS 2052 in the British Library. It is an indispensable document in the history of Baroque painting, and indeed in the technique of oil-painting from the time of the Flemish primitives to the time of Rubens.

Mayerne himself described the volume, on a formal, not to say flamboyant, title-page, in his own majestic handwriting, with his proprietary Greek motto concealed like a rebus in the last flourish of his pen, as 'Pictoria, Sculptoria et quae subalternarum artium . . .'. After this ambitious start, and many folios carefully written out by him, and enriched by later marginal notes, sometimes in his own special red ink, the volume gradually sinks in status. Characteristically it dissolves into a miscellany of notes, written by various hands, on paper of varying size, interspersed occasionally with alien matter. Finally, and again characteristically, it stops, without notice or ceremony.

The text consists of a series of observations, based partly on reading but largely on conversations with artists and craftsmen with whom Mayerne discussed their techniques, about the mechanical aspects of those arts: the materials used, the kind of oil preferred, the mixing and application of paint, the composition of varnish, the best means to preserve colour, avoid cracking, etc. No detail is too small for inclusion, and in line with his usual practice there are marginal notes by Mayerne, sometimes dated, which add details from later information or his own experiments.

In spite of its disorderly character, the manuscript has been recognised, ever since its discovery in the 1840s, as a document of great importance for the techniques of North European art in the Baroque era.[25] The first English scholar to use it described it as the most important of all original sources on that subject.[26] The German scholar who first printed it declared it 'a historical record full of lively charm, an incomparable and invaluable source for the technique of painting'.[27] To a modern Dutch scholar it is 'one of the most important sources for the technique of painting in the seventeenth century'.[28] French editors have pronounced it 'a document of capital importance' for those who would revive the pictorial methods of the Old Masters.[29] A recent authority has pronounced it 'one of the most fascinating documents of its kind'.[30] No student of the artistic techniques of the age of Rubens can overlook it, or, on studying it, fail to be impressed by what one such scholar has called 'the all-embracing interest in art subjects' of its author.[31]

Scholars have examined, as I am not qualified to do, the technical content of this famous document.[32] Instead I shall describe the origins of the manuscript, its compilation and its significance in Mayerne's crowded life.

There is nothing eccentric in Mayerne's interest in the techniques of painting and decoration. The function of a physician at that time, and especially of a chemical physician, was not narrowly specialised. Many physicians had experimented with pigments, jewellery and the decorative arts. In medieval monasteries, the same dispensaries had supplied both paint and stained glass for the chapel, and ointments, drugs and plasters for the infirmary. Many earlier manuscripts contain, indiscriminately, like those of Mayerne, recipes for both such categories. The de Ketham manuscript of the fifteenth century – an important source for pigments – was evidently compiled by a physician.[33] Other physicians – Richard Haydocke, John Bate – interested themselves in artists' pigments and varnishes. Mayerne was operating within a recognised tradition.

How and when did he discover this interest and decide, in the course of an exceptionally busy career as physician, chemist, courtier, diplomatist and entrepreneur, to devote time and energy to personal research in it? It seems to have been a comparatively late discovery. No early document suggests it. In his notes on his grand tour of 1599–1600 he mentioned a few pictures.[34] There too he recorded the sight of 'Bergblau' – that is, the azurite or blue bice which provided painters with their most popular blue pigment – in Schwatz in Tyrol; and he would recall that experience later in his manuscript.[35] But those were commonplace observations. It was in 1620 that he drew the elaborate title-page of the manuscript. No observation on the decorative arts, either in that volume or in any other of his manuscripts, bears an earlier date.[36] From then onwards, however, there are dated entries for almost every year until 1646. It appears, therefore, that Mayerne took up the study of art, and directed his chemical experiments into its materials and methods, only in middle age; for in 1620 he was forty-seven years old.

One other fact may deserve mention at this point. Among Mayerne's surviving papers there is one (I think only one) document which demonstrably came from his father.[37] This is a translation into French, by 'Louis de Mayerne, dict Turquet', of the first part of Giorgio Vasari's *Lives* of the great painters – that is, of the introductory chapters on 'the three arts of Design: Architecture, Painting, and Sculpture'. These chapters have often been treated as a separate work: Vasari's *Lives* have generally been printed without them. This manuscript is in Louis de Mayerne's own hand, and is complete in itself, with illustrations and a much-corrected draft dedication by the translator to 'M. de Roaldès' who, we are told, had suggested the work. That dedicatee is almost certainly François de Roaldès, a distinguished jurist whose scholarly interests and liberal religious views made him a friend of Jacques-Auguste de Thou and Joseph Scaliger. Roaldès had been in Lyon in 1572 and had probably known Louis de Mayerne there. He died in 1589, so the dedication was written before that date. But – perhaps because of that death – the translation was not published, and it was still in manuscript when Louis de Mayerne himself died in 1618. There is also, among Mayerne's papers, a fair copy of this translation, complete with the corrected text of the dedication and an index, ready for publication.[38] Presumably Theodore de Mayerne acquired at least the first of these documents when he went to Paris in 1618 with the purpose (among others) of dealing with his late father's affairs. Perhaps he himself caused the fair copy to be made, intending to publish it. In any case he was clearly interested in it, for, in his father's holograph copy, he inserted marginal notes which included a long note correcting Vasari on the chemistry of niello work.

Perhaps it was this document which stimulated Mayerne to further work in the same subject. The title which he gave to his own manuscript, 'Pictoria, Sculptoria et quae subalternarum artium . . ', echoes Vasari's division of the arts, and the first entry in it also points indirectly at him: 'Quaeratur liber tractans de Pictura cui titulus est *Il riposo di Raphaell Borghini Fiorentino*':[39] the book on painting entitled *The Repose of Raphael Borghini of Florence* is to be sought after. Raffaele Borghini was the nephew of Vincenzo Borghini, prior of Florence, who was Vasari's most intimate friend. His *Riposo*, published in 1584, is a treatise, in the form of an imaginary dialogue, on the technology of the arts: in effect, a companion volume to the work of Vasari. In one of his marginal notes to his own manuscript, Mayerne refers enigmatically to his father's book – 'ex libro patris mei' – which presumably means his father's translation of Vasari.[40]

However that may be, having drawn his title-page, Mayerne set to work to collect his own material. He must have started promptly, for there are several contributions from Paul van Somer, the court painter of James I and Queen Anne. Somer died early in January 1621; but Mayerne had known him as a neighbour – they both lived in St Martin's Lane – and had seen him as a patient in the autumn of 1620,[41] and perhaps before. From then on Mayerne collected detailed information wherever he could find it, on priming, pigments, oils, varnishes, repair and conservation. Sometimes he used printed sources: the German *Illuminierbuch* of Valentin Boltz von Rufach, the *Secreti universali* of Timoteo Rossello, the popular work of the mysterious Alexius Pedemontensis, the *Chirurgia* of Paracelsus, Gerard's *Herbal*; sometimes artists' and manufacturers' manuals, or merely 'an old manuscript'. But his best information came from living sources. They are often named: Mr Heriot, the king's Scottish jeweller; Mayerne's Huguenot friends the two Briots, father and son; his brother-in-law Sir Francis Biondi; a master-dyer in Paris; a master-potter in London. There is advice on etching from Callot, on clouded glass (as in the church at Bourges), and from Dr Asselineau at Venice. Among the practitioners who advised him there are not only painters, engravers, miniaturists, but 'subaltern' workers: apothecaries, goldsmiths, clock-makers, cabinet-makers, artisans of all kinds, most of them, like the artists for whom they worked, Dutch, Flemish or French Huguenot immigrants to London.

Some of these men, like Somer, were his patients. Them he could question from a position of strength: he had them at his mercy. One Bouffault, for instance, 'très excellent ouvrier', yielded, when dying, his 'secrets' concerning the laying of gold-leaf on glass, terracotta and stone.[42] Sometimes the roles were reversed. John Hoskins, painter and miniaturist – 'pictor et illuminator nulli secundus', Mayerne called him: the greatest of painters and miniaturists – was indeed a patient, but it was while he was engaged in painting Mayerne's portrait that he explained some of the mysteries of his art: on the composition of his colours, especially the best white paint, and the secret method whereby Holbein ensured that his silver paint would not be blackened by exposure to the sun; 'and in fact,' he added, 'look at Holbein's portraits: they are a century old, but the silver looks as if it was laid on only two days ago.'[43] Hoskins moved to a studio close to Mayerne's house in 1634. The two men had many conversations in 1634–5,[44] and it was through Hoskins, and at the studio, that Mayerne met Hoskins's young nephew Thomas Cooper, who would afterwards eclipse his uncle as a miniaturist. It was from Hoskins that Mayerne learned 'tout le secret de l'enluminure'.

Another, greater artist advised Mayerne. In 1629, when Rubens came to London as the ambassador of the King of Spain, Mayerne, like Charles I, saw and seized his chance. It was then that he commissioned a portrait of himself: the splendid portrait which Rubens sketched in London and completed in Antwerp. While he sat for it, Mayerne obtained some useful tips on the master's technique: how he preserved the fluidity and vitality of his colours by dipping his brush lightly, from time to time, in spirits of turpentine, and what drying oil he used to render his varnish waterproof. Waterproofing, whether of works of art or other objects, was a problem of much concern to Mayerne. One of his sources – Captain Salé, a versatile military man in the service of the Duc de Soubise – invented (among other things) a means of waterproofing the ducal gaiters: which also found its way into Mayerne's manuscript.[45] We can envisage Mayerne, as he sat for this portrait, questioning the greatest artist of his age about his methods; and we can hear the answers. 'Il signor cavaliere Rubens', he noted,

> says that all colours should be applied quickly, with acqua di ragia (that is, with oil extracted from the soft white bix <resin> which is gathered from the pine tree: it has a pleasant smell and is distilled in water like white turpentine). This is better than *oglio di spaci*, and not so strong. To make the surface fair and clear, it must be diluted with varnish quickly and applied gently – and one must not trouble to mix it too much, while the colour is wet, for this stirring spoils the colour; but when the work is dry, one can work over it as one likes . . .[46]

Rubens spoke to Mayerne, as he usually wrote, in Italian, and Mayerne recorded his statements in that language. In general he quoted his informants in the language which they used to him: generally in Latin, French, Italian, sometimes in German, Dutch, English. The Fleming Cornelius Jansen ('bon peintre'), having become English as Johnson, spoke and was recorded in English. Van Dyck, who arrived in England to stay in 1632, varied fluently from French to Italian to Dutch. Daniel Mytens, who succeeded Somer as court painter and was displaced in turn by Van Dyck, and who was easily accessible to Mayerne since he too lived in St Martin's Lane, used French. 'M. Sorreau, en allemand Sorg' – that is, Hendrik Martens Zorg, a pupil of David Teniers – varied between French and German.[47]

Van Dyck and Mayerne, the greatest painter and the grandest doctor at court, had close personal relations from the start. Mayerne even invited Van Dyck to try his own special varnish, to be mixed with the colours on the palette 'in the manner of Gentileschi' – that is, of Orazio Gentileschi, that 'excellent peintre florentin' who was another of his informants. Charles I had persuaded Gentileschi, then an old man, to come to England, and Mayerne was impressed by his special green pigment – as also by the work of his talented daughter Artemisia. She lived mainly in Rome and Naples, as famous (we are told) for her gallantries as for her pictures, of which, Mayerne wrote, 'I have seen several'; for she spent the years 1638–41 in England. Van Dyck did not take to Mayerne's varnish: he found it too thick, the thickness imped-ing the flow of colour, and was not persuaded by Mayerne's offer to improve it by the addition of oil. Mayerne and Van Dyck had other interests in common. Both were keen alchemists. Both conducted experiments with their common friend Sir Kenelm Digby; and Van Dyck, while in England, married the daughter of the Scottish alchemist Patrick Ruthven, another neighbour of Mayerne in St Martin's Lane and a source of many of his alchem-ical formulae.

Two men who played a large part in bringing Van Dyck to England were Nicholas Lanier, the Master of the King's Music, one of Gentileschi's many lovers, and, says Mayerne, 'excellent musicien qui se plait à la peinture'; and Lanier's brother-in-law Edward Norgate, the miniaturist and herald who was also employed at court as illuminator of royal missives to exotic oriental monarchs. It has been said that it was Van Dyck's portrait of his friend Lanier that determined Charles I to capture such an artist. When Van Dyck duly arrived in England, it was Norgate who was his first host. Lanier was a friend of Mayerne. So was Norgate, who had become attached to the royal court in the same year as Mayerne, 1611. Norgate has left an account of his cooperation with him. It is in the dedication of his long-unpublished work, *Miniatura, or the Art of Limning.*

'There are now more than twenty years passed', Norgate wrote, some time in the 1640s, 'since, at the request of that learned physician Sir Theodore Mayerne, I wrote this ensuing discourse. His desire was to know the names, natures and property of the several colours of limning commonly used by those excellent artists of our nation who infinitely transcend those of his; the order to be preserved in preparing and manner of working those colours so prepared, as well for picture by the life as for landscape, history, arms, flowers, etc.; and that *propriis coloribus* and otherwise as in *chiaroscuro*', a species of limning frequent in Italy but a stranger in England. It was 'to gratify so good a friend, so ingenious a gentleman' that Norgate wrote his book, which is second only to Mayerne's manuscript as a source-book for the artists' pigments of the time.[48]

Another artist with whom Mayerne was to be involved, and who would owe much to his patronage, was the famous French miniaturist Jean Petitot. Petitot, like Mayerne, had been born in Geneva, of *émigré* Huguenot parents. He had been trained as a goldsmith and then spent two years in Paris, perhaps in the shop of Jean Toutin, a Huguenot goldsmith from Châteaudun and Blois. Toutin is well known as having revived and improved the art of enamelling on gold – an art which had been practised in Limoges in the sixteenth century but had been disused. He revived it with a difference: instead of triptychs, goblets and dishes with clear enamel, he produced watches and boxes with decorative patterns or flowers painted on opaque enamel. This technique Petitot acquired, and about 1635 he came to London, no doubt attracted by the reputation of Charles I as a patron: it was in 1635 that Jean Toutin's son Henri executed the first signed and dated enamel portrait of Charles I.

In London, Petitot presented himself to the royal jeweller, who gave him rings and other ornaments to enamel. This he did with such skill that the king sent for him and, recognising his talents, suggested that he might produce portraits in enamel. He was referred for guidance on portraiture to Van Dyck and for the technical problem to Mayerne. The problem was one of colour: there was a limited range of colours which could be vitrified, and a red suitable for the human complexion was not one of them. Petitot was established as one of the queen's household, and he lodged near Mayerne in St Martin's Lane. By 1640 Mayerne had developed, from calcined peroxide of iron, a new red pigment which solved the problem. Petitot, using Mayerne's pigments as colouring and Van Dyck's portraits as models, went on to become the greatest portrait enamellist of his time.[49] Petitot also perfected, while in England, a new method of enamelling on copper. Since he gave this valuable 'secret' to Mayerne, who described it in detail in his papers, it too was presumably worked out in collaboration with him. Mayerne kept the secret. 'Ceste façon de préparer les esmaux', he noted, 'est particulière à nous et ne doibt estre divulguée.' His note on the discovery of the method of enamelling on copper is emphatically headed 'secret de M. Petitot, inventé le 28 Octobre 1640'.[50]

Jean Petitot was joined in London by two compatriots from Geneva: his brother Joseph, described by Mayerne as 'sculpteur' – a very loose term which covered engraving and most of the 'subaltern' decorative arts – and his collaborator in enamel-work, Jean Bordier, who afterwards became his brother-in-law. Mayerne worked closely with both these men, especially with Joseph Petitot, with whom he carried out research and experiments in the gilding of leather, apparently a subject of consuming interest to him. In 1640, when Bordier was in Italy and was arrested by the Inquisition in Milan, the city of Geneva appealed, as it had often done before, to Mayerne. Mayerne went into action at once. He sought to mobilise the crypto-Catholic Secretary of State, Sir Francis Windebank, to put pressure on the Spanish ambassador, and, when that failed, appealed to the queen. The queen sent for the pope's agent at court, Count Rossetti, and, through him, begged the pope's nephew, Cardinal Barberini, as 'protector of England', to intervene. Bordier, she said, was her servant 'and also a great friend of her chief physician, whom she desires to please'. The result was satisfactory. Bordier, she was told, had now 'escaped' from prison: no doubt a tactful compromise which saved faces all round.[51] Joseph Petitot also benefited from Mayerne's patronage: in 1644 he would write to him from Geneva expressing his gratitude for 'les infinies obligations que j'ay receu de vostre personne'; and he repaid him by freely passing on the discoveries he had made abroad.[52]

The 'Mayerne manuscript' is informative on many artistic fronts. It opens a window into the artistic underworld created by the patronage of Charles I and his court: the mobilisation of craftsmen, the creation in London of a new economic activity, the convergence there of groups of immigrant artisans, the diversion of the royal apothecaries, largely under the influence of Mayerne, into the search for pigments and varnishes. Mayerne watched the building up of the great royal collection – many of its organisers, like Sir Isaac Wake and Nicholas Lanier, were his patients and friends – and was able to see the state in which some of the best paintings from the great Mantuan collection arrived in England. The ship which brought them, he had observed, carried a cargo of currants and several barrels of mercury sublimate; the fermentation of the former had vaporised the latter; and the pictures were found, on delivery, to be 'as black as ink'. A painter, unnamed by Mayerne, but in fact Jerome Lanier, the cousin of Nicholas,[53] undertook to clean them. He succeeded well enough with the oil paintings, but not with those in tempera: soap did them no good. Mayerne believed that he himself could have done better. His manuscript contains many recipes for the cleaning and restoration of paintings discoloured by time or dirt, carefully checked by experiment, as also for the bleaching and repair of prints. He derived them from 'Mark Antony, peintre bruxellois', from the royal apothecary Louis le Myre, and from M. Anceau, a bookseller in the Huguenot citadel of Sedan. Mayerne himself had visited Sedan during the crisis of French Protestantism in 1621–2, and Anceau visited London, and gave him his 'secrets', in 1631.[54]

Although art historians mostly confine themselves to the 'Mayerne manu-script', it is only the most striking of the many papers of Mayerne that reveal his artistic interests.[55] Other volumes, similarly disordered, disclose the range of his enthusiasms and contacts.[56] They show his quest for a new scarlet pigment (scarlet, he observes, on the authority of the books of Exodus and Leviticus, being different from crimson), for the orange-red colour 'Nacarat', and for a new red dye for silk from cochineal; his method of extracting such a pigment from poppy-heads; his account, derived from the Belgian painter Mark Antony, of 'the true secret of ultramarine', that inimitable but expensive blue pigment, made from powdered lapis lazuli, which kings rationed so carefully to their painters; and the personal demonstration of pen-and-ink portraiture given to him by that skilful artist in mezzotinto who visited England in 1637, the young Prince Rupert of the Rhine.[57] They indicate, too, the breadth of the world in which Mayerne moved. Beside the famous names of Rubens and Van Dyck, Somer and Mytens, Callot and Vorsterman, Briot and Petitot, Hoskins and Cooper,[58] we find dozens of obscure copy-painters, jewellers, apothecaries, dyers, clock-makers and bookbinders, generally with French or Dutch names: the immigrant or itinerant artists among whom the grandest doctor in Europe was perhaps more at home than among his obsequious and profitable patients, the insouciant, spendthrift courtiers of James I and Charles I.

With these men Mayerne was a different person, a fellow-workman in his shirt-sleeves, at the furnace and the crucible. For he did not merely listen and question: the text of his manuscripts is accompanied by an intermittent marginal commentary which shows his constant supervision and frequent participation in the practical tests and experiments there recorded: 'Vidi', 'Feci', 'Expertus sum: optimum', 'inventum meum', 'Mayerne inventeur', or, alternatively, 'falsum est: expertus sum', 'ce procédé n'a pas réussi', 'mauvais', 'fantaisie', 'ne vault rien casse'; or perhaps only his Greek motto or his own special red ink and monogram, to show his proprietary interest. Many of his documents are written or copied by amanuenses, of whom he employed several, most of them, like himself, rather untidy in their records. Perhaps it would have been better, at least for us, if he had had a single powerful secre-tary to organise these disorderly notes; but the personality and the methods, or lack of method, of the formidable master imposed themselves on a team of docile, colourless disciples: all of them Protestants, of course, mostly from Geneva, drawn by his patronage, or 'the *débris* of la Rochelle', rescued by him from the Huguenot débâcle of 1628.

Even in his old age, after 1642, when civil war has dispersed the artists of Charles I's court – when Van Dyck is dead and Petitot and Bordier have returned to France – the indefatigable old physician is still at work, organising and recording research into the methods of dyeing silk and gilding leather, seeking to extract new pigments from tropical earths, plants, beetles, barks, and adding new notes to his 'Pictoria, Sculptoria'.[59] But to what end? He was not himself an artist or a craftsman: he did not intend to exercise the arts which he studied. It is difficult to detect an economic motive in this case. Rather, it seems that he was animated by a real thirst for knowledge and a desire to leave a record of the chemical discoveries to which he had been inspired by the teaching of Paracelsus, and which he had now realised in both medicine and the arts. He would write a book. It was the doomed ambition of his life.

I have argued that Mayerne took up his interest in the technology of art in 1620. Why then? His writings leave no hint of explanation. He was moving into the later part of his life, when the active pursuits of travel and amateur diplomacy were over. Perhaps the development was related to his frustration with the courtier's life. It was in 1620 that he wrote to the German surgeon Fabricius Hildanus, yearning for 'some respite from these duties at court'. It was in the same year that he bought Aubonne, and perhaps, looking forward to a placid retirement there, he was enlarging the scope of his interests. I have speculated, too, that the discovery, in 1618, of his father's translation of Vasari may have stimulated Mayerne's interest. Perhaps, since we can only speculate, we may speculate a little further. For the years 1618–20 were after all a critical period both in public affairs and in the personal life of Mayerne. The year of 1618 saw his expulsion from Paris and the outbreak of the Thirty Years War. In 1619, when the Elector Palatine was declared King of Bohemia, the Calvinists of Europe were cock-a-hoop. Their triumph was short-lived. In 1620 the battle of the White Mountain not only ended, for three centuries, the independence of Bohemia. It also shattered an intellectual tradition. In 1619 the Hermetic, Paracelsian ideologues declared that their apocalyptic new age had dawned: Elias Artista, the chemical Elijah, was about to return. The overthrow of the Protestant cause in 1620 not only sealed the fate of the Calvinist international. It discredited the Hermetic Paracelsian philosophy. To give precise dates to major intellectual change is, of course, always impossible. Intellectual systems do not dissolve at once. Paracelsianism would survive and revive, especially among the radicals of the Puritan Revolution in England. Yet in general we can say that the total philosophy of Parcelsianism, the philosophy which claimed to answer all the major questions of religion, cosmology, science and politics, crumbled in the 1620s. The severance of chemistry from ideology had begun.

In Mayerne's own mind the Calvinist cause had merged with chemical pursuits. He had been engaged in alchemical sessions with Hermetic and Paracelsian adepts, seeking to achieve 'the Great Work' of transmutation. As late as 1621 he discussed with the Huguenot Hermetic physician Guillaume de Trougny the imminent coming of Elias Artista, 'Elijah the Alchemist', and he sought to secure for Trougny asylum, if necessary, in England.[60] But three years earlier Mayerne's cover as a political agent was blown, and in 1619–20 he saw international Calvinism first hijacked, then ruined, by its extremists. In such circumstances it would not be surprising if he decided to reduce his commitment to it. While Mayerne would never disavow his Huguenot loyalties or his Hermetic ideas, they would no longer involve him in a political programme. He seems to have had no contact with the socially and politically radical English Paracelsianism of the 1640s and 1650s. Instead he had found other, more private interests.

For now the Huguenot world, and the dominant Huguenot character, were changing. Under the impact of events, the era of great enterprises and grand illusions was passing. The next generation would be represented not by the universal men, the turbulent politicians, warrior heroes and ideological poets of his youth – a Rohan, an Agrippa d'Aubigné, a Saluste du Bartas – but by *bons bourgeois*, artisans and craftsmen, jewellers, goldsmiths, enamellists, clock-makers, engineers. In turning from Hermes Trismegistus and Elias Artista to pigments, oils and varnishes, dyed silks and *cuirs dorés*, Mayerne was moving with his co-religionists, and with the turning historical tide.

22

The Physician and his Late Years,
1640–1655

In the 1620s and 1630s Mayerne was at the height of his fame. The princes of Europe competed for his services. The doctors of Europe acknowledged him as their chief, and competed with each other in their elaborate compliments to him. He was 'Hippocrates alter', 'ce grand et illustre flambeau de la médecine',[1] 'the oracle and ornament of the healing art'.[2]

He himself disdained, or affected to disdain, these grandiloquent titles, just as he also disdained the courtly life. These things, he now realised, were vanities, the ritual of piffle before the wind – as he indicated often, and, in particular, to his old friend Dr Rumpf.

Dr Rumpf was court physician to the Elector Palatine, titular King of Bohemia, and as such, in December 1629, he had a disagreeable experience. His princely patient was suffering from an ulcered face which Dr Rumpf and his colleague Dr Valentine thought malignant and were treating accordingly. The prince, however, had ignored their recommendations and had gone out hunting. That was bad enough, but worse followed. A French surgeon appeared from nowhere – 'a man of whom I had never heard before, and who promised to cure the prince completely in four days. Secretly and behind the backs of the accredited doctors, he prescribed inhalations of smoke from live sulphur, three times a day.' Now the prince was worse. It was a shocking affair, as well as a shocking breach of professional etiquette. What was Dr Rumpf to do? He wrote a worried letter to Mayerne, addressing him as Prince of all the Doctors in Europe.[3]

Mayerne replied in his most majestic style. 'The experience of many years spent in the courts of princes', he wrote, 'has taught me that the doctors who attend the great have a wretched life. . . . In kings' courts he lives best who is least seen.' Then, after a long lamentation, and an equally long answer to the professional questions, comes the postscript: 'you are so civil as to address me as "Prince of the Doctors of all Europe". Far be it from me to claim such a title. I live at home and know how scanty is my furniture.[4] If you should honour me with further letters, pray drop (if you will forgive the phrase) those gilded trifles, which may serve to feed the chameleons of the court, but not me. It's enough for you to address me as your friend.'[5]

Mayerne could afford to be majestic, for his authority was beyond dispute. He had always been confident in his skill – it was the characteristic which had been most noted, and most resented, when he first came to England. Now criticism had dissolved before his extraordinary success, and he could lay down the law to the grandest of his patients. When the Queen of Bohemia consulted him about her little daughter, and did not provide sufficient detail, she received an Olympian demand for further and better particulars. 'It is not my custom', wrote Mayerne, 'to give professional advice without some foundations upon which I can build my opinions without fear of reproach, and being a little jealous of my honour, I demand ample and very exact information before I put my hand to my pen to work for the health of another. . . . Madame, I begin to grow old, and I have grown grey in my profession among kings and princes.'[6] If monarchs were thus lectured, lesser persons could not expect to be humoured; and they were not.

For instance, there was Sir William Gordon, a Scot, stone-deaf from syphilis. He had been to many doctors, including Dr Cademan, the queen's doctor, and all agreed that only Mayerne could cure him. Dr Cademan had prepared the way, and Sir William had evidently approached Mayerne with proper deference. In September 1628 Mayerne replied, in French of course – for even to royalty he never made linguistic concessions – and in his most florid style. Gordon, he said, must first come and live near him. 'The autumn of my age, like that of the year in which we are, makes me heavy, and from now on I must look to my comfort.' He then demands 'une obeïsance aveugle', blind obedience, 'and that you cease to be a philosopher' – i.e. to have any ideas of your own – 'until I say goodbye to you'.[7] In a letter of the same year to his Huguenot colleague in Venice, Dr Asselineau, he explained his grand method. Lady Wake, the wife of Mayerne's friend Sir Isaac Wake, ambassador to Savoy, was on her way to Italy, and Mayerne had given her a letter of introduction to Asselineau, to whose unforgettable kindness to him 'quand j'estois par delà' – i.e. in 1599 – he again refers. Meanwhile he wrote direct to Asselineau to give some relevant background information. Lady Wake, he explained, like so many people in England, was melancholic. In such cases, says Mayerne, my method is to demand and impose absolute obedience; then, if they play the slightest trick on me, I take six steps back, or I may even withdraw altogether. Mayerne recommended Asselineau to adopt the same artifice: 'Tu quoque fac simile; sic ars eluditur arte'[8] (do you likewise: thus guile will be outwitted by guile). Clearly, the Elector Palatine would soon have been brought to heel.

Mayerne could justify his authoritarian methods by the infinite care which he took in treating his patients. This care, which they all recognised, comes out in his notes. He regarded every symptom as possibly significant, the whole medical history of his patients as relevant to diagnosis. He refused to despair of their recovery; he watched over their progress; he recorded with pride their restoration to health; he counted the years of their survival; and he often reminded himself, as well as others, of the necessity of constant vigilance, attention to detail, devoted work on every case. Many a Latin or Greek quotation, many a pious, perhaps sanctimonious, ejaculation, records this devotion,[9] and he was very contemptuous of those physicians who simply prescribed according to the book, sometimes without even seeing the patient. He even ventured, in his letter to Asselineau, to criticise the august school of Padua on this account. Asselineau had written about one of his own cases (although we do not know the details, for the letter is lost). Diagnosis is difficult enough, replies Mayerne, even if one is present, far more if absent. 'It is very easy, in such cases, to mistake the marten for the fox. I am astonished that your Paduan pillars of medicine are so inexact in their enquiries and so ready to say that diseases which they have not correctly diagnosed are incurable, lightly and prematurely giving up their patients. However, I do not blame them,' he adds, somewhat ironically: 'anyone prefers to get rid of a disagreeable task as soon as possible.'

Perhaps the most attractive instance of Mayerne's genuine care for his patients is the case of Breban, a page-boy who had been sent from France to take part in the Queen's Music, and who had been so unfortunate as to arrive in the summer of 1628, during the war between England and France. Mayerne's *Ephemerides* contain several documents about Breban, and they all show great tenderness towards him. The story is summarised in a letter which he sent to François de Monginot, *médecin ordinaire du roi*, and a close personal friend, when Breban was sent back to France in the hope of recovery.

As usual, Mayerne gave a full case-history of his patient. Breban was a young boy, 'full of fire, although also intelligent beyond his age', who, through his eagerness to come to the English court, had braved a terrible Channel crossing, tossed by storms in a little boat. He was dreadfully seasick, and after landing in England was wet for three days. He caught cold, and contracted a fever, which he concealed. 'At last, this delicate little body, unable any longer to put a good face on a bad affair, was forced to surrender.' Mayerne examined him and found him suffering from consumption and empyema. As he told Monginot, he had attended him regularly, employing for his cure 'all means, internal and external, which his weak stomach, his delicate body, and his low spirits could or would admit. I know you do not regard me as a novice in my trade, and so you can imagine that I have omitted nothing that his illness required or that he could take.' But alas, treatment had proved vain. It was partly the fault of the boy's profession, which was 'vocal music. His having to sing, high and continually, as he has done with the greatest pleasure for several years, must weaken the lungs and cause them to receive defluxions from the brain, which, in this delicate creature, is large and damp.' So, in the end, since Mayerne could no longer attend him, having to take the queen to Wellingborough, and since the English climate was so bad for consumptives ('the bills of mortality show that more die of it than of anything else'), and since it was still summer, and the sea was calm, he was sending him back to breathe the air of France and, under Monginot's care, to recover his health. There then followed five pages of detailed instructions for the care of his 'fragile body, weakened by a rough crossing'. All this was during the war between England and France. 'When the storms which shake these two states are over,' Mayerne concluded, 'we shall entertain each other more freely, and perhaps even see each other again, which however can never be sooner than I wish.'[10]

We have a portrait of Mayerne, painted (apparently) in 1636.[11] It is a less formal portrait than that by Rubens, and it shows him in a somewhat graver mood. His hands are resting on the base of a sculptured marble head, equally grave, equally bearded, and life-size. Both Mayerne and his marble friend have an abstracted look, as if in meditation. The head, as the Greek inscription on the base shows, is that of Hippocrates. The equality of the two heads, in size, appearance and expression, suggests an equality of status: we see Mayerne as *Hippocrates alter*, the second Hippocrates.

However, Hippocrates, though the most obvious, is not the only other presence in that painting. For the base of the marble head is itself supported by another base. That other base is a book, and the book is inscribed, along the edges of its pages, 'Hermes'. Later commentators would forget the Hermetic inspiration of Mayerne's work. His editors, after his death, would never mention it. Nor would they publish any of his writings which reveal it. Rubens, who drew his symbolism from Catholic or classic sources, had shown no trace of it in his portrait: the great artist of the Counter-Reformation and neo-Stoicism had no sympathy with Hermetic ideas. The portraits of Mayerne which were commissioned by a later generation, perhaps after Mayerne's death, do not show it. By then, the old Protestant world-picture was extinct everywhere. But the Huguenot Nicolas Briot had included Hermetic symbols in his medallion of Mayerne in 1625, and the unknown artist of 1636 was not allowed to omit the obscure but essential basis of his philosophy.

For always, Mayerne was a Hermetist. It was the Hermetic truth, the philosophy of those ancient sages, communicated to him by du Chesne and Trougny, which animated and coordinated his 'modern' chemical ideas. His cry of excitement on reading du Chesne's exposition of the Hermetic philosophy, 'I marvel at the discoveries of the earliest philosophers',[12] never died away completely. To the end, his notebooks, his letters, contain Hermetic allusions. He hoped to see his son James crown his technical preparation – physiology, anatomy, surgery – with Hermetic philosophy. Mayerne was the great patron of Hermetic doctors. We have seen him as the champion of Isaac le Sueur, who had steeped his mind in Hermetic medicine. Another such doctor writes of 'private, sweet, most familiar and long colloquies', when Mayerne laid aside other business and discoursed of 'occult philosophy and most sacred medicines'.[13] And then there was the son of the greatest Hermetist of them all, one of 'the legitimate sons of Hermes' as Mayerne would call him: Dr Arthur Dee.

When we last saw Arthur Dee, he was acting as Mayerne's agent in Moscow, where he planted Mayerne's Huguenot protégés in the court of the Tsar Michael.[14] That was in the early years of Charles I's reign. Since then, Dee had grown weary of his well-paid exile in Russia, so far from European civilisation. He had written a book – a handbook on the practice of alchemy – but he had had to send it to Paris to be printed.[15] He longed to return to England, where he could discuss, with his equals, the mysteries of projection, transmutation, and 'the great work'. So he wrote to Mayerne begging him to secure his recall and find him a post at the English court. Mayerne evidently put his case to the king and, finally, prevailed. In December 1633 Charles I wrote to the Tsar asking him to send Dee back. In reporting the good news to Dee, Mayerne touched lightly on some of the hazards of royal ingratitude, both in England and in Russia, but promised to do his best – which he did, effectively, for Dee would soon become physician extraordinary to Charles I. Before he left Moscow, he received a typical last request from Mayerne: to place, in Russia, two more of his protégés: one an English captain, the other a Huguenot military engineer.[16]

Nothing makes the age of the Renaissance so remote from us as its Hermetism. Precisely for this reason, nineteenth-century historians, when they rediscovered the Renaissance, turned a blind, or sometimes a transforming eye on that aspect of its thought, which, however, until the mid-seventeenth century, was central to it. By and large they could ignore it, for their predecessors of the Enlightenment had already conveniently dismissed it as rubbish, and pushed it out of sight. So the historians of science and philosophy in the nineteenth century could see past it and observe, in the philosophy of Copernicus or Bruno, Bacon or Harvey, only those elements which looked 'forward' to themselves. What could not be overlooked was dismissed as 'quaint'. For the totality of the Renaissance 'world picture' had, by then, disintegrated: it was no longer held together by an animating philosophy, and its organs could be separated, either to be discarded as mere intellectual refuse or labelled 'progressive' and incorporated into a new world picture. Today we recognise that this separation is illegitimate: that the general 'world picture', the ideology, nourished the particular investigations, the ideas, and that 'the Hermetic core' (as Frances Yates has called it) of Renaissance philosophy may have been the necessary condition of scientific advance. For this reason we cannot dismiss Mayerne's Hermetic ideas as mere obscurantist fantasy, blocking scientific progress. They were perfectly compatible with views which we regard as rational, enlightened, modern.

For instance, there is Mayerne's attitude towards witchcraft and demoniac possession. This was a live issue in his time, and several cases were brought to his attention. Invariably, he treated them as cases of physical illness – for he insisted that even mental illness was caused by physical disturbance. We have seen him intervening with Archbishop Laud on behalf of a religious devia-tionist.[17] 'Demoniac possession' was, to him, a similar matter. In France a patient was brought to him who was 'convulsed by worms and thought himself possessed by demons'. He was 'miraculously cured by calomel of mercury': 'having rejected all other remedies,' says Mayerne, 'he recovered after evacuating a number of nests of tiny worms.'[18] Later, at Aubonne, 'I cured many melancholic persons who insisted that they were possessed by demons', by medical means: hellebore, antimony, powder of lapis lazuli and other strong laxatives, together with bleeding and lancing of piles. 'Colocynth', he remarks, 'proved the most effective.'[19]

But the clearest expression of his philosophy, in this matter, was elicited by the case, in 1620, of the six-year-old son of the Earl of Perth. This boy had mystified the family doctors in Scotland by sudden violent pains in the head and by excreting what appeared to be wool. The Scottish doctor sent to Mayerne a long history of the case, and suggested a series of alternative explanations. His first suggestion was that the disease might be caused by witchcraft and that it ought 'to be exorcised by incantations'. Only after positing this theological diag-nosis did he descend to possible physical explanations. Mayerne went through the Scottish document making marginal comments on the various suggestions. Then he summarised his conclusions and wrote his own considered opinion in the form of a *consilium*. Against this suggestion of witchcraft he wrote in the margin, 'medico vix credendum' – 'hardly to be believed by a physician'. In his summary, he amplified this: 'A physician ought not to suspect witchcraft either if he has seen similar symptoms produced by natural causes or if he can offer physical causes for the present symptoms.' Finally, in his *consilium*, he wrote: 'as for witchcraft, although I allow it in certain (but rare) cases, nevertheless, so long as he can discover natural causes, I would not wish to see a physician resort to metaphysical explanations, or a doctor exorcising diseases by incantations.'[20]

Nearly thirty years later, in 1647 – two years after the activities of the notorious Matthew Hopkins, 'witchfinder-general', had led to the great witch-trial
at Chelmsford – Mayerne had another opportunity of expressing his view of
the matter. An English doctor had consulted him about a woman thought to
be possessed. Mayerne replied in his magisterial style.

> I have seen the history of the girl whom certain credulous enthusiasts
> declare to be demoniac, being persuaded that they hear the devil speaking
> from her belly. I know well enough that a melancholy woman supplies the
> Devil with his seat and his bath, and long experience in many cases has
> taught me that the Prince of Darkness, hiding himself in the thick mist of a
> black humour, can mingle his power with various natural diseases and
> rouse a wild turbulence. But my mind is not so facile that it can be bowled
> over by the first impact of any phenomenon, however remarkable, nor is
> my reason so waxen as to receive any and every impression.

There are, he goes on, only two signs of demoniac possession. The first is, 'if
uneducated and illiterate persons speak in various tongues unknown to them
and reason soundly and forcefully about arts and sciences which they have
never studied'; the second is 'if a heavy body is carried up and remains for a
long time suspended in the air'. Except in these two cases, what is vulgarly
thought to be possession is always mere 'melancholy'. 'Black bile heaving in the
spleen, brain or womb, can stir up a thousand symptoms which ignorant men
regard as miracles.' Besides, there is always human fraud: 'if the Devil is full of
wiles, men too have many, which can be detected and unravelled only by sharp
wits and great patience. I remember, thirty-eight years ago in Paris, the case of
a young woman by whose public exorcism the monks sought to prove a
miracle. But that wise and perspicacious King Henri IV, whose physician I
then was, ordered that she should first be handed over to the doctors', who
soon 'unloosed the knot and deprived the exorcists of their pretended miracle.
So the heaving mountains give birth to a ridiculous mouse. Of such things,
many are fabricated, a few come from diseases, from the Devil, none.' In the
margin of his copy of this letter, Mayerne has written the name of the girl,
'Marthe Brossier', and a note: 'see the *Ephemerides* of la Rivière, the chief
physician.'[21] He would never forget the case of Marthe Brossier.

Mayerne's critical spirit often appears in his notes. He rejected theory
unconfirmed by experiment. He insisted on checking sources and would only
accept first-hand evidence.[22] He dismissed some of the arcane wisdom of the
alchemists as superstitious follies to be noted only for the purpose of refutation.[23] On the other hand his open-mindedness was sometimes dangerously
near to credulity. He recorded the most surprising cures and was prepared to

credit the most unorthodox empirics. Following the advice of Paracelsus, he collected the nostrums of old women. He also listened to amateur scientists like Sir Walter Ralegh and Sir Robert Killigrew. Another such amateur to whom he showed respect was the famous virtuoso of medicine, as of all other sciences, Sir Kenelm Digby.

There is something odd in the association of Mayerne, the elderly, austere Huguenot who was so intolerant of his irresponsible sons, with Sir Kenelm Digby, the Italianate Catholic dilettante, oscillating between erotic hedonism and baroque mortification. But then it is equally odd that Digby was a friend of Archbishop Laud, the Earl of Clarendon and Oliver Cromwell. We can only conclude that Digby had an irresistible personality. Digby broke upon the London scene in 1629, having previously been abroad, first making the grand tour of Europe, then commanding his own squadron of pirate ships, nominally against Spain, in fact against innocent Venetians, in the Mediterranean. He broke upon it with some effect, for his huge stature, striking beauty and heroic attitudes commanded attention. He was a universal man *manqué*. He was a pagan humanist of the Renaissance who slid easily from Catholicism to Anglicanism and back, a deist or libertine, only superficially religious, easily attracted – and as easily repelled – by large, seemingly stable, intellectual systems. He dabbled also in the physical sciences, and in 1633, being disconsolate from the death of his wife, the famous *femme fatale* Venetia Stanley, he retired to Gresham College, where he studied chemistry, 'wore there a long mourning cloak, a high crowned hat, his beard unshorn', and 'looked like a hermit'.[24]

It was probably at this time that he became known to Mayerne. They exchanged many arcane prescriptions. Mayerne gave Digby aphrodisiacs and – since he was *gonorrhoeae valde obnoxius* – cures for venereal disease; and he received from him in return an electuary of vipers to unclot blood and 'a marvellous secret' for making diamonds.[25] The two men also shared the services of a very appropriate assistant. This was Johannes Bánfi Hunyadi, known as Hunniades Hungarus, a Hungarian from Transylvania, who had settled in England in 1619 and who became a professor at Gresham College. He was a Hermetic alchemist and astrologer who claimed great success in transmutations. Later, he worked as alchemical operator for Dr Arthur Dee, who at last had escaped from Moscow.[26] Digby remained a close friend of Mayerne, and during the civil war, when he was imprisoned in the former Bishop of Winchester's house in Southwark, he imitated Sir Walter Ralegh in the Tower in resorting to chemistry – Digby was seeking to manufacture precious stones – and in writing an ambitious work: in Digby's case a *Treatise on Bodies*. On his release, he went to France and there sought out the papers of Mayerne's chemical mentor du Chesne. Those that he found were copied for Mayerne and are preserved among Mayerne's papers.[27] Later, in Bologna, he would seek to visit the famous French chemical doctor Pierre de la Poterie, or Poterius, who was well known and respected by Mayerne; but who had probably, by that time, already been murdered.[28]

Very few of Mayerne's personal letters survive, but those which do are the expression of a genial, friendly character, cultivated, sociable and benevolent. Most of his surviving letters come from his last years, and are addressed to his patients; but even his letters of medical advice are enlivened by the warmth and vigour of his personality. Some of the best of them were sent, between 1648 and 1655, to his patient Lord Conway. Conway was an old friend of Mayerne, who had attended his father, the first Viscount Conway, Secretary of State to James I and Charles I, since 1623, if not earlier,[29] and had been the family doctor ever since. He attended Lord Conway's famous bluestocking daughter-in-law Anne, the friend of Henry More and Francis Mercury van Helmont, though her perpetual headaches defied his 'mercurial ointment' just as they defied the attentions of William Harvey and the Irish 'stroker' Valentine Greatrakes. The second Lord Conway was a civilised, epicurean character, of great personal charm, and the circle of his friends and correspondents – for he was a voluminous and entertaining letter-writer – included some of the most interesting men of his time.[30] Mayerne was physician to many of them: to the Earl of Northumberland and to the Finch family, as well as to Sir Kenelm Digby. With Conway, Mayerne exchanged books, news, philosophical observations. When nearly eighty, his letters are as cheerful as ever. He may conventionally lament his old age, but high spirits keep breaking in.

> What use to have bread when one has no teeth, and music when the ears are deaf to the sound of a trumpet? Time when it is past is irrevocable: if there is joy for an old sinner it must be sought in memory – which is too often full of repentance to the wise, and regret to the spiritless among whose number I have never been. Let us seize all the best we can and leave the rest to the good God. Thus we shall live until we die in spite of physicians!

And again: 'Be merry, my Lord, first of all from natural inclination, and then upon the order of him, at once your physician, and always Your very humble servant, Theo. Mayerne.'[31]

Another colourful patient, shallower and more pretentious than Lady Conway, was Margaret, Marchioness (afterwards Duchess) of Newcastle. She too was a patient of Mayerne and we have several letters from him to her husband, whom Mayerne had attended from 1636 if not before. Mayerne's difficulty with the marchioness was that, fancying herself an expert in medicine, as in all other matters, she insisted on bleeding and purging herself, and doing both too much. Mayerne urged her husband to control her, as others urged him too, but he had little hope of success.[32] In 1649 he prescribed no bleeding and only mild purges, 'for by too often scouring a kettle it is at last worn out to holes.' He recommended her to take liquorice and iron water (rather than 'the excrements of a ram' recommended by a rival doctor), 'but I am afraid my lady will do nothing at all, or shall do it by piecemeal, according to her custom.'[33] A year earlier the marquis expressed concern that his wife had provided him with no heir. Mayerne's letter of advice is humane; again it contrasts well with the witches' brew recommended by the rival physician, Dr Farrer; and it recalls Mayerne's own domestic disappointments. 'Touching conception', he wrote, 'I know not if, in the estate she's in, you ought earnestly to desire it. It is hard to get children with good courage when one is melancholy, and after they are got and come into the world they bring a great deal of pain with them, and after that very often one loses them, as I have tried, to my great grief, and am sorry to have had them. Be in good health and then you may till your ground, otherwise it will be but time lost if you enter that race frowningly.'[34]

Mayerne found England altogether more agreeable a land during the calm and prosperity of the 1630s than amid the turmoil of the 1620s. Now, in 'this most happy isle', he could look back on a career of success. He was very rich and widely honoured. It is true, his relations with his children were not happy; but his relations with his patients seem to have been uniformly so. It is true, his political ambitions had failed. The Huguenot cause, in which his father had so strongly believed, and to which he himself had always been loyal, was now lost. Even so, he had prospered hugely. He had achieved, in England, everything that he had once wished to do in France. He had seen his ideas accepted, 'chemical medicine' adopted by the medical establishment, and the medical hierarchy of physicians, apothecaries and distillers organised accordingly. He had established himself at the summit of that hierarchy. He had built up a huge and distinguished practice. He had been first physician to successive reigning kings. But the peace of the happy isle was about to be shattered. The Long Parliament met in 1640, and in 1642 civil war began.

When the war broke out, Mayerne refused the king's order to his physicians to join him at York. He stayed firmly with his rich patients. Although personally dependent on the court, he probably sympathised with the 'Puritan' opposition, at least in its early, aristocratic form. His views are likely to have been those of the Earl of Bedford, and of all those 'Puritan' reformers who, in the 1630s, sought to recreate the old ideal mixed or limited monarchy of Queen Elizabeth – the same mixed monarchy that Louis Turquet de Mayerne, who like his son had been no friend to courtly life, had advocated in France – and to restore England to the leadership of the Protestant cause in Europe. With such views, he would serve his royal patients faithfully without feeling in any way alienated from those of his friends who, in the years from 1640 to 1642 and even beyond, took the other side: the Earl of Northumberland, the Earl of Leicester. Although there were occasional embarrassments, no one as yet foresaw the degeneration of normal politics into civil war and revolution.

The first moment of embarrassment came in the summer of 1641, when the judicial murder of the Earl of Strafford opened an irreparable breach between Crown and Parliament. The king then prepared to go to Scotland, and all men knew why he was going: it was to seek, in the troubled politics of Scotland, some advantage over the Parliament in England. At the same time the queen applied for a pass to go abroad for her health. She wished, she said, to take the waters of Spa. The Parliament was sceptical of her reasons: they believed – with good reason – that her real purpose was to raise foreign arms and money to enable her husband to make war on Parliament: as she would do, without their leave, a year later. They therefore applied to Mayerne for a medical certificate. Mayerne, like all 'chemical physicians', was a great believer in medical baths and waters. He had urged Casaubon, at the end of his life, to go to Spa – which Casaubon had refused to do, as he did not wish to be surrounded by the God-hating papists of Flanders.[35] Other patients he sent to take the waters of Bourbon, Forges, Rouen, Bath and Knaresborough.[36] But on this occasion he could not honestly certify that the queen was in need of that cure. Spa water, he noted, 'is not fit for her at present, her body not being prepared'. However, he managed the situation with his usual adroitness. The queen, he said, whatever her physical condition, was in a state of mental disturbance; 'any change of air would do her good, be it what she will'; since she had convinced herself that such a visit would cure her, it was at least a psychological necessity for her to go; and he duly made out a prescription for her while travelling abroad 'tam animi quam corporis curandi ergo' (as much for the good of her spirit as of her body). However, the Parliament was not convinced by this psychological reasoning, and the pass was refused.[37]

Next year, when the king left London, Mayerne stayed on in the capital. Both his professional interests and his advanced age justified such a decision. Nor is there any reason to suppose that it was questioned: after all, no one expected the king's absence to be long. In fact it lasted more than six years, and he would only return as a prisoner for his trial and execution. Inevitably, in these circumstances, Mayerne's daily life, like that of every Londoner, fell under the control of Parliament. His salary from the Crown, which was paid out of the Court of Wards, was suspended, and he relied entirely on his income from private patients – which was substantial. If we may trust his own figures, the loss of his payments from the Crown cost him over £1,000 a year.[38]

He was also threatened with parliamentary taxes to sustain the war against the Crown. This was too much, and in March 1643 he evidently decided to leave England. He obtained a pass to go to Holland, taking with him his wife, his children, his servants, his money and plate.[39] His wife was of a distinguished Dutch family, and Charles I's daughter Mary was married to the young Prince of Orange. He was therefore sure of a friendly welcome in The Hague. By the summer everything was ready. His bags were packed: the books, the bust of Hippocrates, the massive medical notes, records of cases, alchemical and pictorial experiments; and on 9 August the House of Commons passed an order allowing his trunks to pass freely from England to Holland.[40]

Then suddenly there was a change. The very next day, the order allowing Mayerne's trunks to pass was held up for three days: three days, presumably, for negotiation.[41] What negotiation ensued we do not know, but less than a month later the House of Commons, without a division, passed a resolution 'that Sir Theodore Mayerne, a stranger born, who hath testified a good affection to this kingdom, shall be exempted from payments of assessments upon any ordinance of one or both Houses'.[42] Nine days later, on 15 September, the same resolution came before the House of Lords, who were even more explicit in their testimony. 'The House of Peers,' they resolved, 'taking notice, and being well satisfied, of the good affections which Sir Theodore de Mayerne, upon all occasions, doth and always hath testified to this kingdom, . . . and to show the value this House holds of the affection of a stranger, and to encourage and tie the affection of strangers, men of quality, to this state, do order that the said Sir Theodore de Mayerne shall be discharged, freed and exempted from all payments of assessment upon any ordinance of one or both Houses.'[43]

Evidently the threat of emigration had sufficed. Parliament was not prepared to drive away the royal doctor, one of the most famous physicians in Europe, who was also doctor of so many of its own members. Mayerne himself, satisfied to have shown his power, and to have secured his economic interests, unpacked his trunks and settled down again in parliamentary London. A few months later he was able to show that he was equally indispensable in royalist Oxford.

For all through the war Mayerne in London had easy communication with the court. He was still chief physician to the royal family, and was responsible for the health of the king's two youngest children, Henry Duke of Gloucester and the Princess Elizabeth, who remained in St James's Palace, under the protection of Parliament.[44] Because of his position, he was allowed free access to the court and his patients at Oxford. He could send letters of advice, or plasters for wounded royalists;[45] or he could, if summoned, go himself, with a parliamentary safe-conduct, through the lines of war. In April 1644 he made such a journey. At that time Oxford itself seemed in danger, and the queen left it for the greater safety of Exeter to give birth to her youngest child, Henrietta, afterwards Duchess of Orléans, 'la belle Stuart'. At Exeter, she was taken ill, and wrote an urgent personal appeal to Mayerne to come to her relief. Her letter was reinforced by an even more urgent, more personal letter from the king at Oxford, smuggled past the parliamentary censorship in the diplomatic pouch of Mayerne's father-in-law, the Dutch ambassador. It was brief, simple and eloquent in its brevity. 'Mayerne,' it read, 'pour l'amour de moy allé trouver ma femme':[46] for love of me, go to my wife. Parliament gave the necessary leave and the seventy-year-old Mayerne, with another royal doctor, Sir Martin Lister, set out from London, in the queen's coach, on the seven-day journey to Exeter.[47]

This privileged neutrality of the royal doctor lasted unchallenged for another year; but in the spring of 1645, with the rise of Oliver Cromwell and the creation of the New Model Army, the radicals in Parliament made it clear that the civil war was to be fought to a finish, regardless of old conventions and personal considerations. To achieve this they needed money, and needed it urgently; and the sight of this sleek medical plutocrat sitting untaxed in his fine house in Chelsea, corresponding with royalists, interceding for royalists, serving the king and queen, was too much for them – or at least for those of them who were not his patients. So once again they resolved to end his invidious exemption from war taxes, and on 25 April, shortly after the passing of the Self-denying Ordinance, which struck at their own privileges for the sake of a more vigorous prosecution of the war, they struck at those of Mayerne. They moved an order formally cancelling his exemption from personal taxes and demanded immediate payment of his war assessment, £500 of which was to be paid at once to the garrison of Henley-on-Thames.[48]

Mayerne had been forewarned by his friends, and he lost no time in preparing his defence. On the very next day he drew up a petition to both Houses. In it he declared his case, emphasised the losses caused to him by the war, and dwelt on his present services in looking after the health of the royal children 'strictly recommended to my charge'. He then set out 'the true history of my being here in England', and offered to produce documents showing the conditions which had been agreed before he came. In particular, he dwelt on the 'exemption from all taxes and charges whatsoever' which had been granted by James I and Charles I and had been so recently confirmed by both Houses of Parliament. 'This is my case,' he confidently ended, 'which how it can be called in question, I do not see.' Privately he offered to pay half his assessment; and he clearly hinted that unless his petition were granted he would again pack his bags for Holland or France.

Fortunately the first step, this time, was taken by the House of Lords. The Lords, now reduced to nineteen peers, referred Mayerne's petition to a committee headed by the Earl of Northumberland. Northumberland (like most of the other peers) was a patient of Mayerne: he had also, very recently, been appointed by Parliament as guardian of the two royal children whose health had been committed to Mayerne. This committee produced a report, expressing the desire that 'a man so eminent in his profession, and so useful to very many persons in this kingdom, may receive all encouragements to reside still here amongst us'. The Lords accepted this document and invited the Commons 'to join with them in expressing their esteem of a man whose extraordinary abilities would make him welcome in any part of Christendom; and as he is singular for his knowledge in his profession, so he may be singular in being (by the favour of the Houses) exempted from all payments which others are subject unto; it being but a continuation of that favour which he hath enjoyed for above 30 years without interruption'.[49] This impressive testimonial had a rougher passage in the House of Commons, where the proportion of Mayerne's patients was no doubt lower and where the radical party was stronger. The House divided on it; but in the end, after a debate lasting an hour and a half, it was carried by a narrow majority of three votes: 69 to 66. The tellers for the majority were Denzil Holles and Sir John Clotworthy, two of the acknowledged leaders of the 'Presbyterian' party, the party of accommodation with the king; those for the minority were more radical. They were Sir Edward Ayscough, who had been indicted for treason, and Sir Henry Mildmay, former Keeper of the king's jewels, now particularly hateful to the royalists as a renegade courtier.[50]

A few months later, Mayerne's position was regularised by Parliament. On 4 December 1645 an ordinance of both Houses reduced the establishment of the king's two young children in London. By this ordinance, Mayerne was placed formally on the parliamentary establishment with a salary of £200 a year and an assistant who was paid £100 a year. The assistant was his own nephew, who had been acting in that capacity for some years, Jean Colladon.[51]

So Mayerne continued to practise and to prosper in the parliamentary capital. Foreigners inferred that he had deserted the king for the Parliament. Mayerne was not, indeed, a 'Cavalier'. He never had been an absolute royalist, a devotee of monarchy, or of the court. As a foreigner, he was an outsider in the complex politics of England; as a Huguenot, he admired Rohan more than Charles I; as a professional, proudly conscious that he had made his own way by his talents and his industry, his philosophy was nearer to that of the English aristocratic Puritans than to that of the 'courtiers' whom he served but secretly despised. So, when civil war broke out, he was essentially a 'neuter'. His ideal was still the old ideal of the Protestant international whose interests he had served (after his own) in his prime; but now, in his old age, when that ideal had been shown to be illusory, he was content to wait on events, hoping for an 'accommodation' between the Crown, which was his patron, and the Parliament, whose original aims resembled his own. In this cause, he would even – when he saw the chance – become active again.

For even in his old age, the veteran intriguer could not be kept from foreign intrigue. Through his father-in-law, the aged ambassador Joachimi, who remained in London throughout the war, he could correspond with the Netherlands. Through his Swiss friends, relations and agents he was in touch with the canton of Berne and the city of Geneva. And he let that fact be known. In 1643, and again in 1645, during the parliamentary debates on his exemption from taxes, it was stated, as a reason for keeping him in England, and humouring him, that 'he had a great estate and great power in Switzerland, and particularly in the canton of Berne, and that he was both able and willing to do good offices with the Protestant cantons there if we should stand in need of their assistance.'[52] What kind of assistance was to be expected from the canton of Berne – finance, mediation or theological advice – is not clear; but we may recall that Berne was the most sympathetic of cantons to the English Puritans and provided a last refuge for some of the English regicides.

Holding these views, we are not surprised to find Mayerne, in the crisis of the English revolution in 1648, placing his hopes in the English 'Presbyterian' party and in the Treaty of Newport, in the Isle of Wight, whereby that party made its last, nearly successful attempt at accommodation. 'As for the Treaty in the Isle,' he wrote to his patient Lord Conway, 'it is only in the bud: let it grow, then we may ask of it. You will greatly oblige me by letting me have word, what you hear of it. If we beat too much about the bush, a third will carry off the prize.'[53]

The 'third', of course, was the Independent Party, the radical party which would have taxed Mayerne, and whose leader, Oliver Cromwell, would in fact carry off the prize. In 1649, Mayerne saw his royal master tried and executed, the monarchy destroyed, and England governed by an oligarchy in which he had few or no friends. The change also brought him some painful experiences, both personal and economic.

With the abolition of the monarchy, the status of the two royal children still in England shrank. Their household was reduced and they were no longer allowed the privilege of their own medical establishment. Mayerne and Colladon were therefore dismissed. However, they had scarcely been dismissed as servants of the state when they had to be called in again as private practitioners. In July 1650 the unfeeling Council of State called upon Mayerne to certify whether the fourteen-year-old Princess Elizabeth was really ill.[54] She was indeed. She had never recovered from the shock of her father's execution. She had a frail constitution before, Mayerne recorded, and 'after the death of her father, she fell into great sorrow whereby all the other ailments from which she suffered were increased.' Now, on being told that she was to be removed from the comfort and company of Penshurst, where the Countess of Leicester was her guardian, to the prison of Carisbrooke Castle, with its grim memories of her father's captivity, her spirit broke. Mayerne's report was unavailing. The unfortunate princess was removed to Carisbrooke, where she immediately got worse. In alarm, the Council of State sent to Colladon 'to go with all possible speed to the Lady Elizabeth at Carisbrooke and to take care for her health, and the Council will see that he is well satisfied for his pains'.[55] But before Colladon could reach her, the princess was dead. She had not survived a week at Carisbrooke. At the bottom of his last prescription for her, Mayerne wrote a melancholy Latin quotation and added an explanatory note: 'she died on 8 September, about three o'clock in the afternoon, from a malignant fever then raging, in the Isle of Wight, far from physicians and medicines.'

In the years following the execution of the king we hear little of Mayerne in public life. However, he was not disturbed, and after Cromwell turned out the Rump Parliament in 1653 there were some signs of improvement. On 4 July the new Council of State continued Mayerne's exemption from taxes as a mark of their 'esteem of his qualities and abilities, and to manifest how acceptable his residence here is to them'.[56] The last entries which Mayerne made in his copious notebooks show him taking a close interest in the current relations between the Cromwellian regime and the Protestant rulers in the Netherlands and Switzerland, and in the protector's attempts to recreate that Protestant international, under English patronage, which had been the ideal of the Duc de Rohan, which Queen Elizabeth had seemed to cherish, which King James had inherited from her, and which had been betrayed by Charles I and Archbishop Laud.[57]

Mayerne was active as a physician to the end. His papers contain prescriptions, some of them with firm autograph signatures, within a few months of his death.[58] In 1654, in response, no doubt, to a written request, he was sending advice to the exiled royal court for the cure of Sir Edward Hyde's gout.[59] A last glimpse of him at work is provided by a sardonic writer whose chief purpose in writing was to discredit the great Dr Harvey, and who shows, incidentally, that age had not diminished the well-known confidence of Mayerne. This writer tells us how Mayerne, shortly before his death, was visited at his house in Chelsea by 'one Mr Farwel, barrister of the Temple', whose tumour in the stomach was declared by other doctors, including Harvey himself, to be incurable. Mayerne was by this time bed-ridden; but the patient was brought into his bedroom, and there Mayerne, 'upon no long *examen* of the matter', told him genially that he could easily cure him, 'but with this inconvenience, that he could throw the cause of the disease either into his arms or legs, according to the choice he would make of those limbs which he could best spare . . . without consulting the will of God Almighty: an arrogancy unheard of and savouring more of the atheist (as too many of 'em are)[60] than a pious physician, as then especially he ought to have been, being not many stages from his journey's end.' The patient (we are told) having considered the matter, and reflected that his was a sedentary profession, resigned himself to the loss of his legs, but happily recovered completely, by unaided Nature, just in time to save them.[61]

Mayerne died on 22 March 1655, at the age of eighty-two. His faculties were unimpaired to the end.[62] He was buried in his old parish church, St Martin-in-the-Fields, with his wife, mother and five of his children. A monument was erected on the north wall of the chancel, with a florid Latin inscription composed by his godson Theodore de Vaux.[63] He died a very rich man. Yet the ambition which had driven him to acquire his wealth – his desire to plant a noble dynasty in Switzerland – was doomed to failure. When he wrote his last will, on 8 March 1655, all but one of his children were dead without issue. Of the two children of his first marriage, the first, Henri, had died in 1634 aged twenty-five, the second, James, in 1639 aged twenty-six. Of the two sons of the second marriage, Albert had died aged nine, Louis aged eight. The same marriage had produced three daughters. His daughter Elizabeth, also of the second marriage, was betrothed to Lord Hastings, the royalist son and heir of the Earl of Huntingdon, to whom she was deeply attached, but who died of smallpox in 1649, on the eve of the day of marriage. Ideological enemies of Mayerne said that he unwittingly killed his intended son-in-law by bleeding him – 'a just reward for a butcher-like phlebotomist'.[64] Andrew Marvell's poem on Hastings's death, however, reflects

> how immortal must their race have stood,
> Had Mayerne once been mixed with Hastings' blood!

In 1652 Elizabeth married a French Huguenot nobleman, Pierre de Caumont, Marquis de Cugnac,[65] but she died the following year. After her death, all Mayerne's hopes of posterity were concentrated in Elizabeth's sister Adriana, his youngest daughter, who had been born in 1637.

One other member of his family remained close to him: his sister Judith, one of his seven siblings, 'une soeur que j'aime uniquement'. She was married to Pierre de Mesnil, seigneur de Frotté, a Huguenot with an estate in Normandy; but after his death she lived in Geneva. She kept an eye on Aubonne for Mayerne, who had hoped, in his retirement, to have her live there. She was evidently dead by 1655, but three daughters survived her, Susanna, Aimée and Louise. Susanna was the widow of Charles de la Matairie, whose son inherited the Mesnil estate in Normandy and was known as Henri de Mesnil. Louise had been married to, but had apparently separated from, one Richard Windsor. She also now lived in Geneva, where she would become a famous bluestocking. Aimée, Mayerne's favourite, was married to Jean Colladon of Geneva,[66] Mayerne's protégé and pupil and, for the last thirty years of Mayerne's life, his amanuensis, collaborator and general factotum. Both Mayerne and Lady Mayerne seem to have depended heavily on him, and he seems to have become a substitute for their lost sons.[67] The Colladons were attentive to Mayerne in his old age and hoped, not unreasonably, to benefit by his will.

They were to be disappointed. By his last will, drawn up on 8 March 1655,[68] Mayerne showed once again that his first concern was to endow a noble dynasty in Switzerland. Apart from trivial bequests, he left his entire estate to Adriana. Only if she should die without issue, 'which God forbid', were the Colladons to come in. In that case his personal estate was to be divided among the three daughters of Judith de Frotté, half of it to go to Aimée Colladon, the rest to be divided equally between the other two. Adriana and her mother, Mayerne's widow, were nominated executrices. But Lady de Mayerne died six months after her husband. Adriana thus found herself, at the age of seventeen or eighteen, both sole executrix and sole beneficiary of his will, and thus 'the greatest marriage in England'. In 1657, two years after her father's death, the King of France sent to the Lord Protector of England to secure her hand for Armand Caumont, Marquis de Montpouillan. He was the younger brother of the husband of Adriana's sister Elizabeth, the Marquis de Cugnac. He was a Huguenot like his brother, and was a kinsman of the great Huguenot general Turenne. The marriage of Adriana and Armand was strenuously opposed by Colladon, who used all the interest he could muster to block it.[69] In 1660, when he hoped to succeed his uncle at the Stuart court, Colladon was denouncing Montpouillan in English royalist circles.[70] He wanted Adriana to die childless so that he could inherit the estate. They were nevertheless married in 1659. By the marriage contract the marquis renounced all claims to the estate of Aubonne, so that if he should die without heirs it would remain in the hands of his widow and pass to any heirs of hers by a later marriage.

But it was she who died without heirs, in 1661, at The Hague, where her husband was serving, like so many Huguenots, in the Dutch army. Even then Colladon failed to collect his share. Adriana had a mind of her own, and in her last illness she signed a will which traversed the arrangements of her father's and her own marriage contract. She bequeathed Aubonne and almost everything else to her husband. Of her de Frotté cousins, Susanna de la Metairie and Louise Windsor were to have £5,000 between them, but not a penny went to

Richard Windsor. Jean and Aimée Colladon were to receive one jacobus each, 'pour memoire', 'et plus rien'.

Naturally there were protests, both in the pays de Vaud and in England, and a series of lawsuits followed. We do not know how the ultimate settlement was reached, but the result is clear. The Marquis de Montpouillan obtained Aubonne, which after a few years he sold. He had found it, as Mayerne had done, a hot property. His 'subjects' were a rough lot. 'Monsieur le marquis', observed an official of the government of Berne, 'est très brave homme', 'mais il a à faire avec des gens qui le traiteront assez rudement.'[71] Montpouillan's successor, Admiral du Quesne, would discover this too: he gave up after fifteen years, 'dégoûté peut-être', says the historian of the place, 'par les longs procès qu'il a eus'.

The fate of Mayerne's writings is likewise a melancholy tale. They were inherited by Adriana, but after legal disputes passed to the Colladons. In his last years Mayerne arranged some of his *consilia* with a view to publication. These were duly sent to the medical publisher Theophile Bonet in Geneva. But the quarrels among his heirs prevented publication, and the papers returned to England. Some miscellaneous writings by Mayerne, or ascribed to him, were published by outsiders, using casual copies, but his own papers, with his books and pictures, remained undisturbed in the Colladons' hands. They were still undisturbed in 1674, when Jean Colladon, who had become Sir John and a royal doctor, died.[72]

Then, in 1690, there was movement. For by then it seemed clear that the name of Mayerne was doomed to extinction. Death and sterility had reduced the posterity not only of Mayerne himself, but also of his seven brothers and sisters, to the single family of Colladon, and now it too seemed destined to die out. Jean and Aimée Colladon left a son, Theodore (presumably Mayerne's godson), who inherited the papers, and two daughters. In 1690 Theodore – also a physician and knight – was an elderly bachelor. Of the two daughters, one, Susanna, was married to John Wickart, a Huguenot who had become an Anglican clergyman in England; the other had married a French Huguenot banker and lived in Geneva; but both were childless. In these circumstances there was nothing to do with their inheritance but liquidate it, and in that year the process of liquidation began.

By now, a generation after Mayerne's death, interest in him was reviving; and since the Colladons had done nothing to publish his writings, another physician, with the encouragement of the college, had stepped in. This was Sir Theodore de Vaux, another Huguenot godson of Mayerne, who from his own notes compiled a scholarly work entitled *Mayernii praxis medica*, in two volumes, the first in 1690, the second in 1696. Sir Theodore Colladon, who like his father before him was sitting on Mayerne's manuscripts, was now stirred to action. He decided to over-trump de Vaux and publish a more authentic and substantial collection of them. He still had the *consilia* arranged by Mayerne and returned by Bonet. He added to these a selection of other manuscripts and handed the whole collection to a bookseller's hack in London, Joseph Browne, the son of a Norwich surgeon. The Colladon family had connections in Norwich, where Sir John Colladon had practised as a physician in 1636;[73] perhaps this explains the choice of Browne as editor. Browne published the collection, sloppily, as *Mayernii opera medica* in 1699–1700, a work prefaced with pompous dedications to the great and with incidental attacks on Sir Theodore de Vaux and the Royal College.

Thus were Mayerne's hopes thwarted, his fortune dispersed, his writings overlooked and then inadequately published. By the end of the century, more than his belongings had suffered decline or neglect. The shaping influences of his thought and outlook had disappeared. The Calvinist militancy and the ideological confrontations of the era of the wars of religion were over; and the Paracelsian and Hermetic ideas which in Mayerne's time had prompted innovative thought and practical experiment had become, in the scientific revolution, separated from it and discredited by it. Mayerne's mental world had passed.

Appendix A: The Name de Mayerne

Why did Louis Turquet and his son adopt the name de Mayerne? The question was never answered by them. Theodore, when he deigned to refer to it, was grandiloquent but vague, hinting at ancestral grandeur in Chieri in Piedmont, 'ancien siège de la maison de Mayerne'. Joseph Browne, the editor of his medical works, stated that the name was taken from a noble estate – 'villa non ignobilis' – near Geneva which Louis Turquet bought on arrival there in 1573 and in which his son was born. The statement was repeated in Pierre Bayle's *Dictionnaire historique* and then by later writers. But the learned eighteenth-century Genevese librarian Leonard Baulacre looked for this property and could not find it. Browne's statement is anyway disproved by the fact that Louis Turquet's cousins also assumed the name 'de Mayerne-Turquet', although they had no contact with Geneva and – until 1630 – no contact with their heretical kinsmen. This implies that the name was ascribed by both families to their common ancestors, the last of whom was Louis, Theodore's great-grandfather. Theodore believed, or wished it to be believed, that in Louis's time the family still lived in Piedmont.

The most probable answer to the question was given in the later seventeenth century by the Genevese scholar Vincent Minutoli. He told Bayle, who recorded the account in a footnote, that Turquet was a nickname, given to a particular lady of the family, who affected a 'Turkish' style of dress, and was thence transferred to her children, who were known in Chieri as 'I turchuetti'; after which the name stuck to the family and became its nickname. Minutoli knew Mayerne's nieces in Geneva and his evidence in other details has proved correct.

If Minutoli's statement is accepted, we can perhaps answer the question which Louis de Turquet and his son – both proud, self-important men – preferred not to face. We may speculate that the family were originally immigrants to Piedmont from Magerno in Lombardy, possibly drawn, like many other such immigrants, to the growing silk industry of Turin; that they were known, in the Italian style, simply as 'da Magherno' until the name Turquet was imposed upon them; and that when they had moved on to France, and prospered there, they decided to convert the humble Italian 'da Magherno', which merely indicated local origin, into the 'noble' French 'de Mayerne', which suggested seigneurial status. The change, however, was never fully accepted in France, where both Louis and his son continued to be known as Turquet. A further emigration, to England, was needed to purge that unwelcome sobriquet.

Appendix B: Portraits of Mayerne

The best-known portrait of Mayerne is the great one by Rubens (above, pp. 301, 342). This painting, or a version or a copy of this painting, is in the North Carolina Museum of Art, and an earlier version is in the Chicago Institute of Art. Here a word may be said about less well-known ones.

1 The Hoskins Portrait

This picture presents Mayerne as the scholarly physician. He holds, with both hands, a bust of his master Hippocrates, whose base rests on a book bearing the name of his other master, 'Hermes'. The painter is almost certainly John Hoskins. In an isolated note preserved among his disorderly papers, Mayerne describes a conversation in which Hoskins gave his opinion on Holbein's technique 'dum Dominum Mayerne depingeret' – while he was painting Master Mayerne – '17 September 1635'.[1] Mayerne saw Hoskins regularly in 1634–5 and greatly admired him (above, pp. 341–2). In the British Museum there is an etched portrait of Mayerne whose head is clearly based on the painting, although the bust, being incompatible with the oval frame, has been replaced by a human skull – equally part of a physician's equipment. Around the frame there runs a Latin inscription giving the date 'Anno Domini MDCXXXVI'; and in the hatched background of the portrait Mayerne's age is inscribed 'Aet. 63', i.e. 1636–7.[2] The etching is the model for later engravings from which the inscription has been left out, and for the (reversed, and very inferior) version by W. Elder printed in the posthumous edition of Mayerne's medical works (*Praxeos Mayernianae . . . syntagma*, London, 1690), in which an erroneous and misleading inscription has been inserted. It was this engraving that was cited in Bayle's *Dictionary* to offset the description of Mayerne by Gui Patin (above, p. 10). The same can be said of the original painting. An engraving by W. Elder, based upon it, is printed as a frontispiece to the posthumous edition of Mayerne's medical works.[3]

Two identical copies of the painting survive; presumably Mayerne had more than one copy made, for presentation. One of them is at Longleat House. It is recorded in the Longleat inventory of 1706, the time when Sir Theodore Colladon was winding up the Mayerne inheritance, and when the first Lord Weymouth was creating the library at Longleat and acquiring portraits for it. The second copy of the portrait belongs to me.[4] Its provenance is unknown until it was offered for sale at Christie's on 5 February 1971.

2 The Petitot Portrait

This picture, of a much older Mayerne, is in the Royal College of Physicians and is probably by Jean Petitot.[5] Petitot is also likely to have produced the only surviving miniature of Mayerne, of which two copies are known, one in the National Portrait Gallery, the other in

Ham House.[6] Ham House was created by Will Murray of the Bedchamber, Mayerne's essential intermediary in seeking favours from Charles I. Murray's possessions have remained in the house. Perhaps the miniature was a present from Mayerne to him.[7] There is also a medallion of Mayerne by Nicholas Drist, another Huguenot protégé.

3 *The Geneva Portrait*

This posthumous portrait by the Geneva artist F. Diodati is now in the University of Geneva. This picture raises many problems which have been compounded by ill-informed attempts to solve them.[8] It has been said that it was 'bequeathed' by Mayerne to his niece, Louise de Frotté, Mme Windsor, and that after his death it was taken to Geneva, either by her or by Lady Mayerne, who is said to have retired to Geneva and died there. All these statements are false. Mayerne did not bequeath it specifically to anyone, and there is no evidence that it was his to bequeath. Lady Mayerne never went abroad after her husband's death: she died in London six months later.[9] All that is certain is that the portrait belonged to Mme Windsor in Geneva at the time of her death in 1687; that it passed from her to her niece Isabella de Cambiagne, née Colladon; and that on her death in 1711 her husband gave it to the Public Library of Geneva.

There have been erroneous attempts to ascribe the painting to Rubens.[10] An engraving of it, printed as a frontispiece to the Geneva (but not to the Frankfurt or the London) edition of Mayerne's *Tractatus de arthritide*, shows that it was in Geneva by 1674, and that it had been both painted and engraved by François Diodati, a Genevese artist who engraved portraits of several famous physicians. Since Diodati was only eight years old when Mayerne died, the painting must be posthumous.[11] Presumably it was commissioned by Mme Windsor as a record. The head is clearly (if very clumsily) based on the portrait by Rubens, as are the symbolic details – the lighthouse, the ship, the Hermetic emblems. Diodati had presumably seen the Rubens portrait in the London house of Sir John Colladon, Mme Windsor's brother.[12]

[On the pictorial representation of Mayerne see too Oliver Millar, *Tudor, Stuart and Early Georgian Painting* (1963), no. 280.]

Appendix C: Mayerne's Papers

Whether Mayerne preserved his personal papers, apart from those necessary to his profession, is unclear. Barely a single original letter addressed to him is known to survive. Perhaps they are lost, or destroyed. Sir Theodore Colladon, who inherited the papers that do survive (above, p. 367), died in 1712, after which they and Mayerne's books were sold. The papers were bought by the fashionable doctor and new squire of Chelsea – the Mayerne of his age – Sir Hans Sloane, and passed from him to the British Museum.

The most important collection of Mayerne's papers, among them twenty-five volumes of his medical records, is therefore among the Sloane MSS in the British Museum. It includes most of the *Ephemerides*, his famous case-notes, which are, on the whole, well organised, for he needed to refer to them regularly. But even they – such were his disorderly habits – contain much extraneous matter, and some of this is of a personal kind. The other MSS are chaotic, mostly without order or dates or rational arrangement.[1]

The other most important MS in the British Library is Addit. MS 20921. This is an album into which Mayerne transcribed, or caused to be transcribed, copies of documents which he evidently thought important for his own life. The first entry can be dated 1629, and for a few pages a chronological order is maintained. But soon, as usual, all order is lost: documents datable, or dated, to 1610, 1605, 1600, 1598 come in, and the series goes forward, irregularly, to the last year of his life. On what principle, if any, such documents were included, and others omitted, is not apparent. But the volume is of great importance to the biographer: it supplies the nearest thing that we have to a connecting link among the *miscellanea* of the Sloane MSS.

What is the history of this MS? For some time I pleased myself with the idea that if I could discover its history I might be able to trace the missing personal archive of Mayerne. I have given up this hope. Whatever happened to that archive, I believe that this manuscript became detached from it and had a separate history of its own. All that can be said with certainty of the history of Addit. MS 20921 is that it was bought by the British Museum in January 1853 at the sale of the books and MSS of Lord Stuart of Rothesay, and that an inscription on the first page, 'ex libris adv. l'archevesque 1719', shows that it had been acquired in 1719 by an *avocat* named l'Archevesque.[2] The l'Archevesques were a well-known Huguenot family in the sixteenth century – the Duchesse de Rohan, the mother of Mayerne's patron, was *née* l'Archevesque and a branch of it settled in Geneva; but this Genevese branch was, by all accounts, extinct by the later years of the seventeenth century. Although the name is still borne in Geneva, the present bearers of it are, I am assured, of recent immigration. I therefore presume that the *avocat* who acquired the book in 1719 was a member of the l'Archevesque family living in France; and since Lord Stuart de Rothesay, a professional diplomat, was ambassador in Paris from 1815 to 1830, it is possible that he acquired the book there. These facts suggest to me that Addit. MS 20921 is identical with a manuscript of Mayerne which was taken to Paris by the Rev. John Wickart, the husband of Mayerne's great-niece Susanna, in 1697 and there disappeared from view.

Of Dr Wickart's manuscript our only information comes from Martin Lister, the eminent naturalist. Lister had gone to Paris for an extended visit, for his health, and there met Dr Wickart. Wickart was a political clergyman, used in diplomatic affairs by William III and by his confidant Hans Willem Bentinck, Earl of Portland. Portland was himself coming to Paris in that year to negotiate the Treaty of Ryswick and had sent Wickart ahead of him. Both Lister and Wickart had an interest in Mayerne: Wickart because he was very proud of the family connection, and Lister because he had been brought up by his uncle Sir Matthew Lister, Mayerne's colleague and friend as physician to James I and Charles I. So when they met in Paris, Lister was excited to learn that Wickart had brought with him a 'bundle of original papers of Sir Theodore Mayerne and his friends who corresponded with him'. Much to Lister's delight, Wickart 'presented' this document to him, and Lister, who describes his 'good fortune' in obtaining it as the climax of his visit to Paris, assures 'those who know the work of that great man' that the work would be published. That, indeed, was clearly the reason why Wickart had brought the 'bundle' – which had been found among legal documents in his wife's possession – to Paris, and why he had now given them to Lister. Mayerne's correspondence was in French, and Lister, who was a physician himself (he would become physician to Queen Anne) and who was at leisure in Paris, was obviously better able to oversee publication there than Wickart who, as Dean of Winchester and canon of Windsor, had duties in England.

However, that is the last time that we hear of this important document. When Lister died, in 1712, he left all his manuscripts to the Bodleian Library at Oxford, but it is not among them. Nor was it returned to the Wickarts. In his will Dr Wickart (who survived his wife) refers explicitly to his books and his portrait of Mayerne but makes no reference to them. If my surmise is correct, it was already, by that time, in the library of the *avocat* l'Archevesque.

What had happened to it? I suspect that, on closer examination, the document which at first sight had so excited Dr Lister was found, like so many of Mayerne's papers, to be unpublishable as it stood; that it would have required an explanatory context, a commentary, a connecting history which no one, at that time, in France or England, was able to provide; and that therefore it had lingered in Paris in the hands of some printer or potential editor until Lister was dead and Wickart had forgotten it, and was finally acquired by a private collector, M. l'Archevesque, who had it bound, and whose heirs or successors had owned it, until it was bought, and brought back to England, by Lord Stuart de Rothesay.

This at least is my provisional conjecture. It may be wrong. Critics can say that Dr Lister's description of Dr Wickart's 'bundle of papers' implies that it consisted (partly, anyway) of letters *to* Mayerne, whereas Lord Stuart's bound volume consists of letters *from* Mayerne. But the present binding is probably of later date and Lister explicitly states that, at the time of writing, he had 'not yet had the leisure to peruse' the document. If my surmise is wrong, the problem which it seeks to solve is doubled: the provenance of Addit. MS 20921 and the fate of Dr Wickart's manuscript are alike mysterious. My solution at least has the merit of economy.

Some manuscripts clearly escaped from Mayerne's archive and were lost in the half-century after his death through the litigation or carelessness of his heirs: indeed, Addit. MS 20921 would presumably have been destroyed with the other legal documents had it not been noticed by Mrs Wickart. Some of the manuscripts used by Joseph Browne for his edition of works by Mayerne found their way to the antiquarian clergyman Thomas Tanner, a notorious pilferer of documents, then beneficed in Norwich. They are now among the Tanner MSS in the Bodleian Library. Others were obtained by Dr John Moore, the bibliophile Bishop of Norwich, who was a great admirer of Mayerne. They are now, with the rest of Moore's library, in the Cambridge University Library. Another smaller batch of documents, which probably escaped from the archive at the same time, was afterwards acquired by the great collector Sir Thomas Philipps and is now in the library of the Royal College of Physicians. It contains a section of Mayerne's *Ephemerides* for the years 1634–8 (MS 444). A volume with autobiographical material is in the Royal College of Surgeons (MS 0065).

Mayerne was an excellent letter-writer, with a vigorous personal style, but very few original texts of his private letters survive. A few to Lord Conway passed, with Conway's papers, to the Public Record Office. An interesting batch of letters to the Marquis of Newcastle was preserved by the Cavendish-Bentinck family at Welbeck Abbey and is now in the library of the University of Nottingham. These letters, the only surviving ones by Mayerne written in English (above, p. 6), were written in the 1650s, when the marquis, after his defeat at Marston Moor, was living abroad, in Paris and Antwerp.

Further Reading

Blair Worden

Specialist readers will know where to find the wealth of recent work on the medical history of the Renaissance. Readers new to the subject may wish to read among the handful of studies listed below, all of which bear directly or indirectly on Trevor-Roper's themes. (Some other recent publications are referred to within square brackets in the notes to this book.)

Mayerne is approached from a different angle to Trevor-Roper's, but with compatible results, by Brian Nance, *Turquet de Mayerne as Baroque Physician* (2001). On the intellectual foundations of medical study and practice see Allen Debus, *The Chemical Philosophy: Paracelsian Science and Medicine in the Sixteenth and Seventeenth Centuries* (2nd edn, Mineola, New York, 2002); Bruce Moran, *The Alchemical World of the German Court: Occult Philosophy and Chemical Medicine in the Circle of Moritz of Hessen (1572–1632)* (Stuttgart, 1991); Moran, *Distilling Knowledge: Alchemy, Chemistry, and the Scientific Revolution* (Cambridge, Mass., 2005), esp. ch. 3 on Paracelsianism; William Newman, *Promethean Ambitions: Alchemy and the Quest to Perfect Nature* (Chicago, 2004); Charles Webster, 'Paracelsian Medicine as Popular Protest', in Ole Peter Grell and Andrew Cunningham, eds, *Medicine and the Reformation* (London, 1992), pp. 57–77; Webster, *From Paracelsus to Newton: Magic and the Making of Modern Science* (New York, 1996 edn).

Fundamental work on Paracelsianism was undertaken by Walter Pagel: especially *The Smiling Spleen: Parcelsianism in Storm and Stress* (Basel, 1984); *Religion and Neoplatonism in Renaissance Medicine* (Variorum edn, 1985); *From Paracelsus to van Helmont in Renaissance Science and Medicine* (Variorum edn, 1986).

On France see L.W.B. Brockliss and Colin Jones, *The Medical World of Early Modern France* (Oxford, 1997). On the social and institutional background to Mayerne's medical career in England see Harold J. Cook, *The Decline of the Old Medical Regime in Early Stuart London* (Ithaca, 1986), and Margaret Pelling (with Francis White), *Medical Conflicts in Early Modern London: Patronage, Physicians and Irregular Practitioners 1550–1640* (Oxford, 2003).

Bibliographical Abbreviations

Addit.	Additional (manuscript)
APC	*Acts of the Privy Council of England*
Apologia	*Theodori Mayernii Turqueti in celeberrima Monspeliensi academia doct. medicinae, & medici regii, apologia* (La Rochelle, 1603)
D'Aubigné, *Oeuvres complètes*	*Oeuvres complètes de Théodore Agrippa d'Aubigné*, ed. E. Réaume and F. de Caussade (Paris, 1873; repr. Geneva, 1967)
Bacon, *Works*	J. Spedding, R.L. Ellis and D.D. Heath, eds, *The Works of Francis Bacon* (London, 1857–74)
BFMP	Bibliothèque de la Faculté de Médecine de Paris
BL	British Library
BN	Bibliothèque Nationale
Bodl.	Bodleian Library
BSHPF	*Bulletin de la société de l'histoire du protestantisme français*
Cal. S.P. Dom.	*Calendar of State Papers, Domestic Series*
Cal. S.P. Ven.	*Calendar of State Papers . . . Venetian*
Casaubon, *Ephemerides*	Isaac Casaubon, *Ephemerides*, ed. John Russell (Oxford, 1850)
Chamberlain	N.E. McClure, ed., *The Letters of John Chamberlain* (Philadelphia, 1939)

CUL	Cambridge University Library
Heyer	Th. Heyer, 'Lettres de Théodore Turquet de Mayerne au Petit Conseil de Genève', *Mémoires et documents de la société d'histoire et d'archéologie de Genève*, xv (1865)
HMC	*Historical Manuscripts Commission Report*
Kassel MS	Gesamthochschulbibliothek, Landesbibliothek und Murhardsche Bibliothek der Stadt Kassel, 2° MS. chem. 19 (correspondence of Landgrave Moritz of Hesse)
L'Estoile	*Mémoires-journaux de Pierre de l'Estoile*, 11 vols (Paris, 1875–83)
Nance	Brian Nance, *Turquet de Mayerne as Baroque Physician: The Art of Medical Portraiture* (Amsterdam, 2001)
ODNB	*Oxford Dictionary of National Biography*
Opera medica	Theodore de Mayerne, *Opera medica*, ed. Joseph Browne (London, 1700)
PRO	Public Record Office (National Archives)
RCP	Royal College of Physicians
RCS	Royal College of Surgeons
RPC	Registres du Petit Conseil, Bibliothèque Publique et Universitaire, Geneva
Sloane MS	Sloane MS, British Library

Notes

Material within square brackets has been inserted by the editor.

Chapter 1   Mayerne and his World

1. Bacon, 'The Advancement of Learning', in *Bacon, Works*, iii. 373–4.
2. Bacon, 'Temporis partus masculus', in ibid., iii. 531.
3. The impact of Paracelsus and his followers is described in Trevor-Roper's essay 'The Paracelsian Movement', in his *Renaissance Essays* (London, 1985), pp. 149–99. See too the recent literature on Paracelsianism mentioned below.
4. For Bacon's attitude to Hermetism see especially Paulo Rossi, *Francesco Bacone, dalla magia alla scienza* (Bari, 1957; 2nd edn, Turin, 1974) [translated into English by Sacha Rabinovitch as *Francis Bacon, from Magic to Science* (London, 1968)].
5. Bacon, *Works*, iii. 532.
6. As noted by Hugh Kearney, *Science and Social Change 1500–1700* (New York and Toronto, 1971), p. 203.
7. Sir George Clark, *A History of the Royal College of Physicians of London* (Oxford, 1964), i. 165–6, etc.
8. Bacon, *Works*, iii. 366, 370, 605.
9. Ibid., iii. 376–7.
10. See the excellent account of the beginning of English watering places by R.V. Lennard, ed., *Englishmen at Rest and Play: Some Phases of English Leisure 1558–1714* (Oxford, 1931).
11. For Bacon's views on chemistry see J.C. Gregory, 'Chemistry & Alchemy in the Natural Philosophy of Francis Bacon', *Ambix*, ii (June 1938), 93–113.
12. 'Hippocrates saith, *saepe optima medecina est non uti medicina*: this is the counsel of a friend and of a servant.' Mayerne to the Duke and Duchess of Newcastle: Nottingham University Library, Portland (Welbeck) MS PW V. 90: 'Sir Theodore's advice for my lady and myself'.
13. Marjorie Hope Nicolson, ed., *Conway Letters* (London, 1930), p. 23.
14. Sloane MS 2074, fo. 70ᵛ.
15. Nottingham University Library, Portland (Welbeck) MS PW V. 90: 'Sir Theodore's advice'; CUL, MS Dd. 4–21, fo. 26. His advice to the marquis is nonetheless in almost perfect idiomatic English – though it is not in his own hand.
16. Edward Nicholas, ed., *The Nicholas Papers* (Camden Society Publications, new series 1, 1892), ii. 257; Margaret Verney, ed., *Memoirs of the Verney Family*, iii (London, 1894), p. 195.
17. *HMC Cowper*, ii. 400.

18. Elizabeth Cary, Lady Falkland, *The Tragedy of Mariam . . . with The Lady Falkland: Her Life by One of her Daughters*, ed. Barry Weller and Margaret W. Ferguson (Berkeley, 1994), pp. 218–19. The other names, except where a distinct source is given, are from Mayerne's papers in the Sloane MSS and Royal College of Physicians.
19. BL, Addit. MS 20921, fo. 68.
20. Chamberlain, i. 341.
21. In 1613, the Duke of Richmond represented the king as godfather to Mayerne's second son, James, to whom the duchess was godmother: RCS, MS 0065, private record, p. 3. (This manuscript, formerly MS 129a 1.8, is in two, separately foliated parts, the first being the – brief – private record, the second a 'Viaticum' or traveller's book.) The duchess also deputised for her niece, the Countess of Westmorland, as godmother to his son Albert in 1634. For the picture and the correspondence, see BL, Addit. MS 20921, fo. 52ᵛ. For the bequest see *Archaeologia cantiana*, xi (1877), 243.
22. J.H. Parker, ed., *The Auto-biography of Symon Patrick* (Oxford, 1839), p. 19.
23. According to Hodges's sermon, *Inaccessible Glory* (London, 1655), p. C₃, 'He was very compassionate to those who were not able to retribute aught to him, refusing none that sought for help, though their condition were never so loathsome and deplorable.'
24. A *consilium* from Mayerne to Harvey, of 1636, is in Mayerne's *Ephemerides*, RCP, MS 444, pp. 108–9 (printed in *Opera medica*, i. 361–2). Two *consilia* to Fabry, of 27 Jan. 1616 and 6 Feb. 1622, are in the Berne Bürgerbibliothek (cod. Bern 497). After a wandering life, Fabry had become city doctor in Berne.
25. Daniel Parsons, ed., *The Diary of Sir Henry Slingsby* (London, 1836), pp. 48, 69–70. Lady Slingsby's visits are recorded in Mayerne's *Ephemerides* (Sloane MSS 2067, fo. 120; 2074, fo. 78 etc.).
26. Paul Triaire, ed., *Lettres de Gui Patin 1630–1672* (Paris, 1907), pp. 481–4. Unfortunately only this volume, intended as the first, of that excellent edition was published.
27. A letter (1 Mar. 1676) of Louise Windsor to Gregorio Leti, the Italian Protestant writer, is published in Leti's *Italia regnante* (Geneva, 1675–6), iv. 65–8. For Bayle's source on Mayerne see appendix A, below.

Chapter 2   Early Years, 1573–1598

1. On the history of the family, below and appendix A.
2. The genealogy of this branch of the family can be derived from a number of MSS in the Bibliothèque Nationale: Carré d'Hozier 423, fos 52 (nobility of Jean de Mayerne-Turquet, médecin), 55–56ᵛ (copy of letter of Théodore de Mayerne to an unnamed 'cousin'), 57 (marriage contract of Charles Turquet, 1 Oct. 1634); Pièces Originales 2900, group 64415; and from a notarial document in the Archives Nationales, viz: Minutier Central, liasse 301, 1 Feb. 1661: inventory after death of Louis de Mayerne-Turquet, *géographe ordinaire du roy*.
3. Vital de Valous, *Étienne Turquet et les origines de la fabrique lyonnaise* (Lyon, 1868), p. 60.
4. *Scaligerana* (Cologne, 1667 edn), p. 244 ('Suisses').
5. De Valous, *Étienne Turquet*, p. 63.
6. The brothers Haag, *La France protestante* (Paris and Geneva, 1846–59), s.v. 'Mayerne', say that the date of his birth is unknown; but the record of his interrogation in 1611 describes him as 'natif de Lyon, âgé de soixante dixhuit ans'.
7. R. Doucet, in A. Kleinclausz et al., *Histoire de Lyon* (Lyon, 1939), i. 427–30.
8. Mayerne's godsons were (1) Theodore Le Tourneur, son of Simon Le Tourneur, secretary to the Prince de Condé, baptised at the Huguenot Temple at Charenton on 3 Mar. 1602–3 (Jules Delaborde, 'Copie des fragments des registres de l'état civil des Protestants, détruits par l'incendie du Palais de Justice en 1871', *BSHPF*, xxi (1872),

224); (2) Theodore Naudin, son of Pierre Naudin, Mayerne's apothecary in Paris, baptised there on 26 Feb. 1616 (ibid.); (3) Theodore de Vaux and (4) Theodore Colladon, who both declared themselves as such.

9. De Valous, *Étienne Turquet*, p. 64.

10. Louis de Mayerne Turquet, *Epistre au roy* (Paris?, 1590), p. 4.

11. Louis de Mayerne Turquet, *Histoire générale d'Espagne* (Lyon, 1586), dedication 'au Roy'.

12. Louis de Mayerne Turquet, *Apologie contre les detracteurs des livres de la monarchie aristodémocratique* (Paris?, 1616), p. 29.

13. Mayerne to Gedeon van Boetzelaer, heer van Langheraek, 19 July 1614: BN, MS Fonds français 17934, fo. 115.

14. Antonio de Guevara, *Mépris de la cour et louange de la vie rustique* (Geneva, 1605 edn); J.L. Vives, *L'Institution de la femme chrestienne* (Anvers, 1579); H.C. Agrippa, *Déclamation sur l'incertitude, vanité, et abus des sciences* (Paris, 1582).

15. *Histoire générale d'Espagne*, dedication, fo. Aiij.

16. The published work ends in 1583; but according to its English translator, Edward Grimeston, in 1612, Turquet afterwards continued it 'unto these times. I myself have seen it in his study in Paris, but he hath not yet put it to the press': *The Generall Historie of Spaine* (London, 1612), preface.

17. The translation of Ammianus is mentioned by Turquet's friend J.J. Scaliger in *Scaligerana*, p. 149, s.v. 'Marcellin'. For Roaldès see *Actes de l'académie nationale des sciences, belles-lettres et arts de Bordeaux*, III série, xlvii (1885), 377–477.

18. It is as Louis Turquet that he was ennobled as an inhabitant of Geneva and recorded in the register of the church of St Pierre and the Acts of the national synod in France. His friend l'Estoile regularly calls him Louis Turquet. But he published his books as 'Louis de Mayerne Turquet' and his last known letter is signed 'de Mayerne T'.

19. In Mayerne's two early books, the *Sommaire Description de la France, Allemagne, Italie et Espagne* (Geneva, 1591) and *Apologia* (1603), and in his manuscript 'Antidotarium' (1606), he names himself 'Theodore de Mayerne Turquet'. It is thus that he is described in the Oxford records when he took his degree in 1606, and in the Letters Patent appointing him first physician to James I in 1611. His detractor John Chamberlain called him Turquet as long as he could. His friend Casaubon, from his first mention of him in his *Ephemerides* in 1608 (p. 588), called him 'Mayernius', and thus distinguished him from his father, whom he called 'Torquetus': e.g. Kal. Dec. 1613: 'hunc diem cum amicis magna ex parte ego et uxor eimus, praesertim cum uxoribus D. Turqueti et filii eius D. Mayernii' (p. 1022).

20. Now Sloane MS 2013.

21. Gustav Toepke, *Die Matrikel der Universität Heidelberg*, ii (Heidelberg, 1886), p. 141.

22. That Mayerne studied 'philosophy' at Heidelberg is stated in his *Apologia*, p. 24.

23. For the course of study at Heidelberg see J.F. Hautz, *Geschichte der Universität Heidelberg* (Mannheim, 1862–4).

24. *Sommaire Description*.

25. See Sir H. George Fordham, 'The Earliest French Itineraries, 1552 and 1591: Charles Étienne and Théodore de Mayerne-Turquet', *Transactions of the Bibliographical Society*, 4th series, i (1920–1), 193–224.

26. Harvey Cushing, *Life of Sir William Osler* (n.p., 1925), ii. 640. Osler was a great admirer of Mayerne and collected books and MSS of his. The MS volume of Mayerne's *Ephemerides* now in the Library of the Royal College of Physicians (RCP, MS 444) was bought by him and bequeathed to the college.

27. 'Ad solam medecinam natus, ab incunabilis quasi medicum lac suxi, nec quicquid monuerint parentes vel amici, ad alia studia unquam animum potui applicare': *Apologia*, p. 23.

28. The entry is cited in Heyer, p. 184. Du Chesne's early familiarity with Mayerne's family is attested also by an entry in one of du Chesne's notebooks, which Sir Kenelm Digby

obtained in Paris, and of which Mayerne's nephew Jean Colladon made a copy. Du Chesne there cites a remedy recommended to him by 'la soeur de M. Turquet, nonnain a Lyon'. Mayerne himself has added the note 'ma tante' – i.e. his aunt Philippe, the Catholic nun (Sloane MS 2079, fo. 97ᵛ).

29. Liminary poems by 'TDM' in Joannes Antonius Fenotus, *Alexipharmacum* (Basel, 1575), p. 92, and 'M.L.M.' in du Chesne, *Le Pourtraict de la santé* (Paris, 1606), unpaginated preface: 'Discours sur le pourtrait de la santé'. 'TDM' is an enemy, 'M.L.M.' a friend.

30. T.H. Reveillé-Parise, ed., *Lettres de Gui Patin* (Paris, 1846), i. 510.

31. For Casaubon's friendship with du Chesne see Casaubon, *Ephemerides*, pp. 577, 684.

32. Du Chesne (or his printer) names him as 'N. Brithman', but since he describes him as city doctor of Cologne, he is clearly referring to Birckmann, who held this post. Birckmann was a member of the Cologne publishing firm of that name.

33. Du Chesne's early history and travels can be deduced from his own works, especially his *Sclopetarius* (Lyon, 1576) and his *Ad veritatem hermeticae medicinae ... stabiliendam ... responsio* (Paris, 1604).

34. Cherler (whom du Chesne calls Kerler) also returned to Basel, his home town, where he married the daughter of one of its professors, Johann Bauhin, and assisted his father-in-law to produce his famous *Historia plantarum*, finally published at Yverdun in 1619. For Cherler see H.G. Wackernagel, ed., *Die Matrikel der Universität Basel*, ii (Basel, 1956), p. 326. Wackernagel conjectures that Cherler was born about 1570, but he must have been older.

35. For the University of Basel see H. Thommen, *Geschichte der Universität Basel* (Basel, 1889), esp. pp. 239–40. For the Paracelsian movement there, see Johannes Karcher, *Theodore Zwinger und seine Zeitgenossen* (Basel, 1956).

36. Petrus Severinus, *Idea medicinae philosophicae, fundamenta continens totius doctrinae Paracelsicae, Hippocraticae et Galenicae* (Basel, 1571).

37. I know of no serious study of du Chesne. There is a brief account of him in Léon Gautier, 'La Médecine à Genève jusqu'à la fin du XVIIe siècle', *Mémoires et documents de la Société d'histoire et d'archéologie de Genève*, 2e série, x (1906), 192–201. The thesis by J. Dubédat, 'Etude sur un médecin gascon du 16e siècle, Joseph du Chesne, sieur de la Violette, dit Quercetanus', Paris, 1908, is superficial. [See now the discussions of him in Bruce Moran, *The Alchemical World of the German Court: Occult Philosophy and Chemical Medicine in the Circle of Moritz of Hessen (1572–1632)* (Stuttgart, 1991), esp. ch. 8, and the thesis by Didier Kahn, 'Paracelsisme et alchimie en France à la fin de la Renaissance', University de Paris IV, 1998.]

38. Louis Turquet's approach to Henri IV in 1591 is described in the preface to his *Apologie contre les détracteurs*, and his programme, which he had written out in several volumes, is summarised in the *Epistre au roy* (Tours, 1592) which he presented to Henri IV in October 1591.

39. The entry in RPC, 1591, fo. 153 (19 Aug.) is cited in Heyer, p. 184.

40. As Mayerne said in his doctoral speech (BL, Addit. MS 20921, fo. 90ᵛ–91ᵛ).

41. See Henri Drouot, 'Nicolas Dortoman, médecin de Henri IV', *BSHPF*, lxi (1912), pp. 423–4.

42. Nic. Dortomannus, *Libri duo. De causis et effectibus thermarum Belilucanarum ...* (Lyon, 1579).

43. Marcel Gouron, ed., *Matricule de l'université de médecine de Montpellier 1503–1599* (Geneva, 1957), p. 197.

44. *Apologia*, p. 25.

45. For the apothecaries at Montpellier see the thesis by A.P. Marty, *La Pharmacie à Montpellier depuis son origine jusqu'à la révolution* (Montpellier, 1889).

46. *Apologia*, pp. 24–6, 29–30.

47. These were kept by Mayerne and written out for him, in 1636, in his letter-book: BL, Addit. MS 20921, fos 83–90.

48. Ibid., fos 85ᵛ–86ᵛ.
49. Ibid., fos 89ᵛ–90.
50. For Verandé or Varandal (in Latin Varandaeus), see Jean Astruc, *Mémoires pour servir à l'histoire de la faculté de médecine à Montpellier*, ed. M. Lorry (Paris, 1767), ii. 14, 241–2, 259–60, 335, 504, 506.
51. *Joannis Varandaei . . . opera omnia* (Lyon, 1658), p. xii.
52. Reveillé-Parise, ed., *Lettres de Gui Patin*, i. 210.
53. Casaubon, *Ephemerides*, p. 588.

Chapter 3   Paris, 1598–1601

1. For du Chesne's diplomatic activity see Edouard Rott, *Histoire de la représentation diplomatique de la France auprès des cantons suisses*, ii (Berne, 1902), pp. 405, 465, 472, 581–3.
2. For the career of Jean Ribit, Sieur de la Rivière, see my essay 'The Sieur de la Rivière, Paracelsian Physician of Henri IV' in my *Renaissance Essays* (London, 1985), pp. 200–22.
3. Jos. Quercetanus [du Chesne], *De priscorum philosophorum verae medicinae materia* (St Gervais, 1603), p. 214.
4. In his dedication to Ribit de la Rivière of *De arthritide et . . . calculo* (1603), where he cites de Fresne as a fellow-admirer.
5. Sloane MS 2089, fos 77–8: the letter concludes 'inter caeteros Germaniae viros doctrina eximios medicos et astronomos tantum elucere quantum micat inter ignes luna minores.' The last six words are from Horace, *Odes* I, xii.
6. Sloane MS 2089, fos 74ᵛ–75.
7. See, for instance, the correspondence of Henri IV's ambassador Jacques Bongars with Joachim Camerarius: *Viri illustris Jacobi Bongarsi epistolae ad Joachimum Camerarium, medicum* (Leiden, 1647). Bongars forwarded and supported the letters of la Rivière (pp. 22, 201, 229).
8. The substance of Kolreuter's letter to la Rivière was transcribed by Mayerne into his 'Antidotarium' in 1606, where it forms the first item (Bodl., Rawlinson MS C. 516, p. 1). See also Mayerne's notes of various cures, including *pulvis Saxonicus*, sent by Kolreuter to la Rivière in 1590–1, in Sloane MS 1989, fos 125–35; and in *Opera medica*, ii. 77, 95–6.
9. Cf. Lucan, *Pharsalia*, IX, 614–16:

   Noxia serpentum est admixto sanguine pestis;
   Morsu virus habent, et fatum dente minantur,
   Pocula morte carent.

10. *Bongarsi epistolae*, pp. 201, 229.
11. Agrippa d'Aubigné, 'Confession du Sieur de Sancy', printed in Pierre de l'Estoile, *Journal de Henri III . . . ou mémoires pour servir à l'histoire de France* (The Hague, 1744), v. 384.
12. D'Aubigné, *Oeuvres complètes*, i. 423; letters in this vein addressed to la Rivière occupy pp. 422–45.
13. L'Estoile, *Mémoires-journaux*, vi. 219.
14. Even at the end of the century Étienne Pasquier could write that Paracelsianism 's'exerce aujourd'huy à l'ouvert tant en Allemagne que Suisse, et à couvert en plusieurs endroits de ce royaume': *Les Lettres d'Étienne Pasquier* (Paris, 1619), ii. 559.
15. I have dealt with this confusion, and attempted to resolve it, in my 'The Sieur de la Rivière'.
16. For the career of Roch le Baillif, see ibid., and Emmanuel Philipot, *La Vie et l'oeuvre littéraire de Noël du Fail, gentilhomme Breton* (Paris, 1914), pp. 345–64.

17. *Le Demesterion de Roch le Baillif edelphe médecin spagiric* (Rennes, 1578), dedication (to Loys de Rohan) and preamble 'au lecteur'.
18. BFMP, MS VIII, fos 108ff.
19. Philipot, *Noël du Fail*, p. 357; *Lettres d'Étienne Pasquier*, i. 455; ii. 752, 787.
20. Claude-Pierre Goujet, *Mémoire historique et littéraire sur le Collège Royal de France* (1758), ii. 92.
21. It was widely believed that Henri Robert de la Marck, Duc de Bouillon, had been poisoned by antimony. Protestants (including the Haag brothers) have accused Catherine de Médicis. There is no reason to believe this: see Pierre Congar, Jean Lecaillon and Jacques Rousseau, *Sedan et le pays sedanais* (Paris, 1969), pp. 195–7.
22. For the trial of Roch le Baillif see *Vray discours des interrogatoires faictes en la presence de MM de la cour de parlement par les docteurs régents en la faculté de médecine en l'université de Paris, à Roc le Baillif, surnommé la Rivière* (Paris, 1579).
23. In an MS note Mayerne remarks that he had tried certain chemical remedies 'in filia Guenault Pharmacopoei et aliis pluribus ann. 1597' (Sloane MS 2046, fo. 174). Jacques Guenault was an apothecary in Paris (Sloane MS 2058, fo. 25ᵛ). I suppose he was father of the physician Guenault, the 'grand empoisonneur chimique' and general *bête noire* of Gui Patin: see T.H. Reveillé-Parise, ed., *Lettres de Gui Patin* (Paris, 1846), esp. i. 175; ii. 61.
24. Reveillé-Parise, ed., *Lettres de Gui Patin*, i. 210, 344.
25. BL, Addit. MS. 20921, fo. 111.
26. [The latter term might be translated as 'crap-doctors', in parallel to the term 'piss-prophets' that was commonly aimed at the 'empiric' doctors who diagnosed maladies on the evidence of urine. 'Chirurgi' are sugeons.]
27. There is no direct evidence to show whether the attack began before or after Mayerne's travels with Rohan, but we know, from an explicit statement in Mayerne's *Apologia*, that the attack preceded his appointment as doctor to Henri IV. Unfortunately, the date of this appointment is itself obscure. According to a list of appointments in BN, MS Fonds français 7856, p. 1460 ('Officiers domestiques de la maison du roy Henry IV'), 'M. Théodore de Mayerne dit Turquet' was appointed *médecin par quartier à XIIc écus* in succession to Paul le Maistre in 1602. This would place the whole affair after Mayerne's return from Italy. However, this list is in many respects inaccurate and defective (e.g. it gives la Rivière's death as 1606 instead of 1605) and shows signs of having been compiled much later; and it is inconsistent with Mayerne's own evidence. Thus in his account of the affair of the pretended demoniac Marthe Brossier, in 1599, Mayerne writes that he was then already a royal doctor ('Rex Henricus quartus (cui tunc a consiliis medicis eram)': Sloane MS 2074, fo. 146ᵛ). In two distinct documents – his private record in RCS, MS 0065, p. 3, and his formal petition to the Long Parliament in Bodl., Tanner MS 60, fo. 134 – he states that he had been physician to Henri IV for eleven years; in the RCS MS he says 'a full 11 years' – i.e. from about May 1599. This accords with the note of his life compiled for the record by his nephew Jean Colladon in 1655 (BL, Burney MS 368, fo. 121), which states that Mayerne was appointed physician to the king and by him assigned to Rohan: i.e. that he was appointed before Rohan left Paris in August 1599.
28. *Apologia*, pp. 11, 110–11.
29. This is suggested also by Mayerne's subsequent dedication of his *Apologia* to Achille de Harlay, President of the Parlement.
30. *Apologia*, p. 12. Astruc, followed by August Hirsch, *Biographisches Lexikon der Hervorragenden Ärzte* (Berlin, 1929–35), s.v. 'Laurens', says that du Laurens only came to court in 1600, which, if true, might disturb my dating; but in fact, he was influential at court before this. Jean Hucher, who, as professor and chancellor of the University of Montpellier and himself a royal doctor, must have known, ascribes Henri IV's founda-

tion of the two new chairs in 1593 and 1597 to du Laurens's personal influence with the king even then. See Jean Hucher, *De febrium differentiis* (Lyon, 1601), dedication to du Laurens.

Chapter 4   The Grand Tour, 1599–1601

1. Roch le Baillif, *Traicté de la cause de la briefve vie de plusieurs princes et grands, et le moyen d'y pourvoir* (Rennes, 1591), dedication.
2. *Voyage du duc de Rohan faict en l'an 1600* (Amsterdam, 1646), p. 1.
3. For Armand de Caumont's presence in the party see Marquis de la Grange, ed., *Mémoires authentiques de Jacques Nompar de Caumont, duc de la Force* (Paris, 1843), i. 307. That he was still with Rohan in England is clear from the despatches of the French ambassador there (Boissise to Henri IV, 31 Oct. 1600: BN, MS Fonds français 4128, fo. 213ᵛ).
4. *Voyage du duc de Rohan*, p. 27.
5. Ibid., p. 180.
6. For the journey of Rohan and Soubise to Scotland, see Joseph Bain, ed., *The Border Papers: Calendar of Letters and Papers Relating to . . . the Borders* (London, 1894–6), pp. 714, 718, 726; also the reports of the French ambassador in London (BN, MS Fonds français 4128, fos 213–214ᵛ).
7. PRO, SP78/44, fo. 397; SP78/45, fos 13, 14, 82, 130.
8. *Voyage du duc de Rohan*, p. 208.
9. Rohan's own papers were all destroyed during the French Revolution and so we do not possess the letters which he received. His letters to King James and to Cecil are in the State Papers, France (PRO, SP78/45ff.). His letters to Mar do not survive, but the regularity of the correspondence is shown by the letters between Cecil and Nicholson preserved in the State Papers, Scotland. For Rohan's secret correspondence with Cecil, see *Calendar of State Papers Scotland 1597–1603*, pp. 869, 872, 889, 899, 906, 907, 909, 934, 968, 1001; *HMC Marquess of Salisbury*, xii. 98, 109–10.
10. *Apologia*, p. 28.
11. Mayerne's diary is in BL, Addit. MS 20921, fos 93–110ᵛ, headed 'Voyage de M. de Rohan le viii de May, 1599'.
12. BL, Addit. MS 20921, fo. 93ᵛ.
13. Ibid., fo. 97ᵛ.
14. Ibid., fo. 99ᵛ.
15. Ibid., fo. 97ᵛ.
16. Ibid., fo. 94ᵛ.
17. Ibid., fos 103ᵛ–104ᵛ. Twenty years later, writing in his 'Viaticum', of 'Bergblaw' or 'Vert d'azur', Mayerne noted, 'Vidi in fodinis argenteis Tirolensibus in pago Schwatz': RCS, MS 0065, p. 77.
18. BL, Addit. MS 20921, fo. 103ᵛ.
19. Ibid., fos 97ᵛ–98.
20. There were five such princes – the five sons among whom the dominions of Joachim Ernst von Dessau had been divided at his death in 1586.
21. On him see Frances Yates, *The Rosicrucian Enlightenment* (London, 1972).
22. See, on this subject, Chr. Friedrich Sattler, *Geschichte des Herzogthums Würtenberg unter der Regierung der Herzogen*, v (Ulm, 1772), pp. 196–230; and the two articles 'Herzog Friedrich und seine Hof-Alchymisten', in Johann Memminger's *Würtembergische Jahrbücher* (1829), pp. 216–33, 292–310.
23. BL, Addit. MS 20921, fos 108–10.
24. Ibid., fos 106ᵛ–107ᵛ.
25. In his *Apologia* of 1603, Mayerne mentions his travels in Germany and Italy and his familiarity with their doctors, but does not mention visits to the Netherlands or

England. This might suggest that he did not go to the Netherlands or England. On the other hand Germany and Italy, as the acknowledged centres of medical science at the time, were relevant to his case, as the Netherlands and England were not, so the argument is not conclusive. More forcible is the phrase, in *Apologia*, p. 99, 'ex Italia rediens', as if he came back from Italy straight to Paris. Yet when describing his travels he states that he had 'undergone various perils by land and sea' (p. 28). The only sea journey made by Rohan on this expedition was the crossing to England, which had indeed been very dangerous. The plain fact is that there is no real evidence one way or the other, and we can only leave the question in suspense. [In an essay written after this chapter, Trevor-Roper wrote that Mayerne 'travelled with Rohan as far as Naples but seems to have returned independently to Paris, while they went on to Austria, the Netherlands, England and Scotland': Trevor-Roper, 'The Huguenots and Medicine', in Randolph Vigne and Ralph Littleton, eds, *From Strangers to Citizens* (Brighton, 2001), p. 199. The reason for this change of emphasis is not apparent.]

26. Sloane MS 2069, fo. 65.
27. Sarpi's modern biographer Gaetano Cozzi describes Sarpi's link with Asselineau as 'forse il più solido e duraturo che il Sarpi abbia avuto nella sua esistenza' (perhaps the most solid and enduring of Sarpi's life): Paolo Sarpi, *Opere*, ed. Gaetano and Luisa Cozzi (Milan and Naples, 1969), pp. 10–11. See also Signor Cozzi's article on Asselineau in *Dizionario biografico degli italiani* (Rome, 1960–). Asselineau's activity as political agent is well documented in the letters of du Plessis Mornay. Between 29 September 1608 and 25 May 1612 there are fifty-six surviving letters between Mornay and Asselineau: *Mémoires et correspondance de Philippe du Plessis Mornay* (Paris, 1824–5) pp. x–xi.
28. Mayerne mentions Asselineau in Sloane MSS 304, fo. 26; 2047, fo. 64; 2048, fos 117, 139; 2049, fo. 80; 2050, fos 2, 57, 97, 122^v, etc.; Dansé is mentioned in MS 2048, fo. 7^v etc.
29. I deduce this from the facts that Mayerne's diary is remarkably empty during the two months' stay in Venice and Padua, and that Rohan's party did not return by that route.
30. Bodl., Tanner MS cxi, fo. 185.
31. CUL, MS Dd. 5–25, fo. 32.
32. Sloane MSS 1996, fo. 46; 2049, fo. 4^v; 2050, fos 64, 131.
33. Sloane MS 2017, fo. 15.
34. Sloane MS 2079, fo. 80.
35. Sloane MS 2089, fos 75^v–76.
36. Carlo M. Cipolla, *Public Health and the Medical Profession in the Renaissance* (Cambridge, 1976), pp. 98n, 124.
37. Mayerne attended Mme de Rohan, Henri de Rohan's mother, from 1602 (Sloane MS 2058, fo. 40). Sloane MS 2089 shows him working in partnership with la Rivière in 1602–3.
38. Sloane MS 283, fos 21–61^v.
39. Sloane MSS 2020, fo. 93^v; 2051, fo. 45.
40. Sloane MS 2129, fo. 140; BFMP, MS X, fo. 49.
41. On Gourmelen's rash attack on Paré see Geoffrey Keynes, ed., *The Apologie and Treatise of Ambroise Paré* (London, 1951), pp. xii, xvii, xix, 70–1. Gourmelen was – needless to say – a hero of Gui Patin.
42. Mayerne describes the work as 'Quercetanus *de remediis chymicis*'. No known work by du Chesne has this title. Mayerne probably referred to du Chesne's 'De ... medicamentorum spagyrica praeparatione et usu', printed in *Ad Jacobi Auberti Vindonis de ortu et causis metallorum contra chymicas explicationem Josephi Quercetani* (Lyon, 1575), pp. 77–186.
43. See his *Theophrastisch Vade Mecum* (Magdeburg, 1597) which describes him on the title-page as 'beider Artzney D. zu Franckenthal'.
44. Sloane MS 2097, fo. 93^v.

45. BL, Addit. MS 20921, fo. 54.
46. For their joint activities, both medical and convivial, see *Apologia*, p. 100; du Chesne, *Jos. Quercetani . . . ad veritatem hermeticae medicinae . . . stabiliendam . . . responsio* (Paris, 1604), 'Praefatio ad lectorem'.
47. See Bruce Moran, 'The Alchemist's Reality', *Halcyon* (Reno, Nev., 1986) [and, now, Moran's *The Alchemical World of the German Court: Occult Philosophy and Chemical Medicine in the Circle of Moritz of Hessen (1572–1632)* (Stuttgart, 1991)].

Chapter 5   The Chemical Challenge, 1601–1605

1. *Ad Libavi maniam, Joannis Riolani responsio pro censura scholae Parisiensis contra alchymiam lata* (Paris, 1606), p. 3.
2. The consultation with du Laurens is recorded in Sloane MS 2059, fo. 84ᵛ. The case of M. de St Ysunier is in the *Ephemerides* of 1604: Sloane MS 2058, fos 141–4; la Rivière, Mayerne and du Chesne are all mentioned as being in attendance. A consultation some eighteen months later with du Laurens and du Chesne is recorded in Sloane MS 2059, fo. 84ᵛ.
3. For Pierre Pena see L. Legré, *La Botanique en Provence au XVIe siècle. Pierre Pena et Mathias de Lobel*, i (Marseille, 1899), ch. 1. Legré loses sight of Pena in Paris, but I presume he is identical with 'le vieil bon homme Pena, médecin' who was a friend of l'Estoile and died in June 1611 (l'Estoile, *Mémoires-journaux*, iv. 90, 97, 227; xi. 226). L'Estoile also refers to 'Pena le jeune, médecin du roi', who is clearly the son of 'le vieil bon homme' (ibid., ix. 101), and Mayerne refers often to both 'Pena senior' and 'Pena junior'. That François Pena studied at Geneva is clear from the diary of the Huguenot pastor Jacques Merlin, his 'compagnon d'estudes et bon ami', published by J. Gaberel, *Histoire de l'église de Genève*, ii (Geneva, 1855), pt 2, p. 182. François Pena died in Feb. 1626: *BSHPF*, xii (1863), 279.
4. BFMP, MS IX, fos 320–9.
5. Ibid., MS X, fo. 130.
6. *BSHPF*, xxi (1872), 264.
7. Sloane MS 678, fos 75ᵛ-76.
8. Baucynet was a graduate of Montpellier. He appears under various spellings: Baucynet, Baucinet, Baussinet, Bossinet, Boissinet; but in print he writes himself Baucynetus. He appears together with la Rivière and Mayerne in April 1602 (Sloane MS 1994, fo. 20ᵛ).
9. Sloane MS 2079, fo. 104ᵛ.
10. Casaubon, *Ephemerides*, p. 297; *Apologia*, p. 55.
11. The pedigree of the Naudin family can be reconstructed from the details given in the MSS 'Tables alphabétiques sur l'histoire des familles protestantes' in the Bibliothèque de la Société d'Histoire Protestante, Paris.
12. J.A. Worp, ed., *De Briefwisseling van Constantijn Huygens, 1608–1687* (The Hague, 1911–17), v (The Hague, 1916), p. 383.
13. CUL, MS Dd. 5–24, fo. 111ᵛ.
14. On François Briot see Alexandre Tuetey, 'Le graveur lorrain, François Briot, d'après des documents inédits', *Mémoires de la Société d'émulation de Montbéliard*, xviii (1887), 45–77. That Didier Briot and François Briot were brothers is not certain, but is assumed by Tuetey. Another member of the family, Pierre Briot, also an engraver – he is described as 'graveur de monnaie et effigies du roi' – is recorded in the Haag MSS in the Bibliothèque de la Société de la France Protestante, Paris. He married Esther Petau and his children Jacques and Esther were baptised in the Huguenot Temple at Charenton in 1612 and 1614.
15. On Nicolas Briot see M.F. Mazerolle, 'Nicolas Briot, tailleur général des monnaies (1606–1625)', *Revue belge de numismatique*, lx (1904), 191–203 and 295–314. The

reference of 1604 is in Sloane MS 2058, fo. 112; other references are scattered through Sloane MSS 1984, 1989, 1990, 1999, 2045, 2046, 2049, 2078, 2080; CUL, MSS Dd. 5–25, 5–26; etc.

16. Later Mayerne referred to his 'amitié ancienne' with du Moulin (BL, Addit. MS 20921, fo. 6ᵛ).

17. Jules Delaborde, 'Copie de fragments des registres de l'état civil des protestants, détruits par l'incendie du Palais de Justice de Paris en 1871', *BSHPF*, xxi (1872), 224. Mayerne refers to this connection in his *Apologia*, p. 96: 'Simeon le Tourneur, mihi vel eo nomine amicissimus quod eius filium sacro baptismatis fonte lavandum obtulerim.'

18. For Pierre de Beringhem see *BSHPF*, xii (1863), 277; Jacques Pannier, *L'Église réformée de Paris sous Henri IV* (Paris, 1911). The names of members of the family often occur in Mayerne's MSS. For Langheraek's use of Beringhem see BN, MS Fonds français 17934, fo. 122. For letters of Mayerne to Mme de Beringhem see BL, Addit. MS 20921, fos 41, 66; *BSHPF*, xii (1863), 277.

19. Sloane MS 2089, fos 23, 27ᵛ.

20. Sloane MS 1996, fo. 55ᵛ.

21. Sloane MS 2089, fo. 57ᵛ; cf. BN, MS Fonds français 18767, fos 160–3: Mayerne to Dr Grangier, the duke's physician, 3 Jan. 1626.

22. Sloane MSS 2058–76 cover the years 1603–52, except for the years 1634–8 which are covered by RCP, MS 444. The last volume of the series, covering the years 1652–5, strayed to the Cambridge University Library, where it is MS Dd. 4–21.

23. 'Ephemerides morborum et elenchus remediorum variis aegris praescribendorum per annos XL Mayernio, Quercitano &c.': Sloane MS 2059, fo. 1.

24. Mayerne's treatment of Richelieu is recorded in Sloane MS 2059, fo. 45, and 2089, fo. 27ᵛ. For Mayerne's treatise see his 'Encheiridion ad Praxin Medicinae, anno 1607' (Sloane MS 2105A, fos 17, 20). His 'De gonorrhoeae inveteratae et caruncula et ulceris in meatu urinario curatione epistola' is printed in G. Fabricius Hildanus, *Observationum et curationum chirurgicarum centuria quarta* (Oppenheim, 1619), pp. 455–8.

25. *Jos. Quercetani . . . liber de priscorum philosophorum verae medicinae materia* (St Gervais, 1603).

26. Others, including Mayerne (Sloane MS 1997) and Libavius, put Hippocrates and Galen together, as founder and continuator, in the 'dogmatic' school, and treated the empiric school as a deviation from it, founded by Philinus of Cos.

27. The reference is to Jean Fernel, *De abditis rerum causis* (1548), 'Praefatio', where Fernel says that, some twenty years ago, he had sniffed ('odoratus') that something divine lay hidden in medicine. On Fernel see Sir Charles Sherrington, *The Endeavour of Jean Fernel* (Cambridge, 1946; repr. 1974).

28. Du Chesne always disowned the specifically religious philosophy of Paracelsus. See his *Ad Jacobi Auberti Vindonis* (Lyon, 1575).

29. The primary sources for the controversy are the MS Registers of the Faculty of Medicine and the literature in which it found vent. Narratives of the events, from opposite sides, are included in J. Riolan, *Ad Libavi maniam . . . responsio*, and in A. Libavius, *Alchymia triumphans* (Frankfurt a/M, 1607). The former is fiercely partisan, the latter moderate and reasoned.

30. The dean was Pierre l'Affilée; he was ill, and died on 6 Sept., when Heron succeeded him (BFMP, MS IX, fos 419, 422).

31. BFMP, MS IX, fos 420–1. Part of this record was published in the official record of le Paulmier's own trial before the Parlement in 1609 (when his *Lapis philosophicus dogmaticorum* was condemned): *Arrest de la cour de parlement . . . 6 Juillet 1609 . . . en la cause d'entre Mre Pierre Paulmier . . . et le doyen, docteurs régents de ladite faculté . . .* Some biographical details are given in T.H. Reveillé-Parise, ed., *Lettres de Gui Patin* (Paris, 1846), i. 280–1.

32. See Jacob Bernays, *Joseph Justus Scaliger* (Berlin, 1855), pp. 239–51.
33. See Jacques Marchant, *In Franc. Rosseti apologiam . . . declamatio* (Paris 1598), p. 32.
34. BFMP, MS IX, fos 421–3.
35. A reference to the line of Ennius: 'Moribus antiquis stat res Romana virisque'.
36. [J. Riolan], *Apologia pro Hippocratis et Galeni medicina adv. Quercetani librum de priscorum philosophorum verae medicinae materia* (Paris, 1603). The text of the 'Censure' of the faculty is also printed in Marchamont Nedham, *Medela medicinae* (London, 1665), p. 22.
37. Its title is *Theodori Mayernii Turqueti . . . apologia. In qua videre est inviolatis Hippocratis et Galeni legibus, remedia chymicè praeparata, tutò usurpari posse* (1603). The title-page gives the place ('Rupellae') but not the printers, who were the firm of Haultin. The firm had moved to La Rochelle from Lyon in 1571, which may explain Mayerne's use of it. See Louis Desgraves, *Les Haultin 1571–1623* (Geneva, 1960: vol. ii of *L'Imprimerie à la Rochelle (Travaux d'humanisme et Renaissance*, no. 34), p. 124.
38. Reveillé-Parise, ed., *Lettres de Gui Patin*, i. 366–7.
39. Ibid., i. 448–9.
40. Thus the metaphor of the Trojan horse out of whose belly emerge the heroes who will capture the city, used here of Montpellier, is deployed again in Mayerne's speech acknowledging his doctorate at Cambridge (BL, Addit. MS. 20291, fo. 92).
41. Sloane MSS 2129, fo. 128ᵛ; 2061, fo. 68.
42. *Jos. Quercetani . . . ad veritatem hermeticae medicinae . . .* (Paris, 1604), sig. A. 6.
43. For the Paris faculty's attack on Scaliger, and the controversy which it caused, see Bernays, *Joseph Justus Scaliger*, pp. 239–51.
44. Presumably this was 'Isaac Hollandus' whom Mayerne's contemporary Augustus Sala named, with Arnold of Villanova, Raymond Lull and Paracelsus, as 'one of the most celebrated Hermetic philosophers of Europe'. Like Basil Valentine, he is a timeless character, supposed to have lived before Paracelsus; but in fact the works ascribed to him and to his supposed son John Isaac Hollandus were evidently written in the late sixteenth century. See J.R. Partington, *A History of Chemistry*, ii. (London, 1961), pp. 203–8. Among Mayerne's papers is an MS of 'Cabala von Isaac den Hollander', in Dutch (Sloane MS 2097).
45. *Apologia*, p. 28: 'E stercore Ennij legit aurum Virgilius'.
46. *Apologia*, pp. 29–33.
47. Ibid., p. 105.
48. Ibid., pp. 108–11, 115.
49. BFMP, MS IX, fos 448–9.
50. *Ad famosam Turqueti apologiam responsio . . .* (Paris, 1603).
51. The later work is Riolan, *Ad Libavi maniam . . . responsio*. This is ostensibly by the elder Riolan (and is ascribed to him by Gui Patin and in the catalogue of the Bibliothèque Nationale), but in fact, as Libavius himself pointed out in *Alchymia triumphans*, p 65, it can be proved by internal evidence to be by the son.
52. BFMP, MS IX, fo. 458.
53. [J. Riolan], *Ad famosam Turqueti apologiam responsio*, p. 85.
54. *Joannis Antarveti [i.e. Riolani] medicinae candidati apologia, pro judicio scholae Parisiensis de alchimia* (Paris, 1604), pp. 3–4.
55. Riolan, *Ad Libavi maniam . . . responsio*, p. 4.
56. BFMP, MS IX, fos 458, 466. The right to issue such a list, and to issue it every year, was given to the faculty by an *arrêt* of the Parlement of Paris of 12 Sept. 1598.
57. *Israelis Harveti medici Aurelianensis defensio chymiae . . .* (Paris, 1604); *Animadversiones in Joannis Antarvetim medicinae candidati, apologiam . . . de alchymia* (Frankfurt, 1604); *Demonstratio veritatis doctrinae chymicae* (Hanau, 1605).
58. Riolan, *Ad Libavi maniam . . . responsio*, pp. 5–6: 'Furiosus Haruetus conuitiando extremum spiritum efflauit, eumque suo, id est Paracelsi magistro, reddidit.'

59. The story is quoted by the Abbé Goujet from a manuscript journal of le Grain. See the Abbé's Paris *Supplement au grand dictionaire historique . . . de M. Louis Moreri*, i (1735), s.v. 'Bailli' (for the story) and s.v. 'Grain' (for details of the MS). Goujet damaged the story by confusing la Rivière with Roch le Baillif, who had heirs, but le Grain clearly referred to our la Rivière.

60. L'Estoile, *Mémoires-journaux*, viii. 94. La Rivière's death is usually dated 5 Nov. 1605, the date on which it is recorded by l'Estoile. But Dudley Carleton, who was in Paris at the time, writes of it as a recent fact on 14/24 Oct. 1605 (*HMC Salisbury*, xvii. 454); so there is an element of uncertainty. L'Estoile is often wrong in the dates, recording events when he heard of them, not when they happened; but equally Carleton may have anticipated the fact.

61. L'Estoile, *Mémoires-journaux*, ix. 335.

62. Pierre Milon had matriculated at Montpellier in 1577, Antoine Petit in 1572 (Marcel Gouron, ed., *Matricule de l'université de médecine de Montpellier 1503–1599* (Geneva, 1957), pp. 180, 174). A. Leenhardt, *Montpelliérains, médecins des rois* (Largentière, 1941), seems to assume that it was Jean Petit (matriculated 1596: Gouron, p. 205) who became *premier médecin*; but this is a mistake. Jean Héroard, *premier médecin* of Louis XIV, explicitly refers, in his diary, to Antoine Petit as 'premier médecin du feu roi' (E. Soulié and E. de Barthelemy, eds, *Journal de Jean Héroard* (Paris, 1868), ii. 89), and l'Estoile clearly and circumstantially states that the *premier médecin* came from Gien, thus further identifying him with Antoine Petit, who is described in the Register of Montpellier as 'Genabiensis'. Jean Petit was from Paris.

63. Some later writers (e.g. Charles Read, in a note to his edition of the *Journal* of Daniel Chamier (Paris, 1858), p. 30n, and Paul Triaire (*Lettres de Gui Patin, 1630–1672* (Paris, 1907), p. 393) state or imply that Michel Marescot was *premier médecin* of Henri IV between la Rivière and du Laurens. Both Read and Triaire are scholars from whom it is rash to differ, but I have been unable to find evidence for their statement. L'Estoile clearly implies that du Laurens succeeded directly to la Rivière. Moreover l'Estoile (viii. 193) records the death of Marescot on 12 Oct. 1605, i.e. before he records the death of la Rivière on 5 Nov. 1605. The list of *premiers médecins* in BN, MS Fonds français. 7856, fo. 1460, gives du Laurens as the direct successor of la Rivière.

64. The list is in Sloane MS 2046, fo. 42.

Chapter 6   *The German Dimension, 1605–1606*

1. For the fuller title of Mayerne's *Apologia* see below, p. 389 n. 37. It can be translated as 'The Apologetic of Theodore Turquet de Mayerne, doctor of medicine in the famous Academy of Montpellier and physician to the king'.

2. [J. Riolan], *Ad famosam Turqueti apologiam responsio* (Paris, 1603).

3. *Jos. Quercetani . . . ad veritatem hermeticae medecinae . . .* (Paris, 1604). The second anathema is printed in J. Riolan, *Incursionum Quercetani depulsio* (Paris, 1605), pp. 67–8.

4. *Alchemia, Andreae Libavii . . . opera* (Frankfurt a/M, 1597), translated by Friedemann Rex and others as *Die Alchemie des Andreas Libavius: ein Lehrbuch der Chemie aus dem Jahre 1597* (Verlag Chemie, Weinheim 1964), under the auspices of the Gmelin-Institut für anorganische Chemie und Grenzgebiete in Frankfurt.

5. The title indicates the tone: J. Gramannus, *Apologetica refutatio calumniae qua Paracelsistae, philosophi ac medici saniores, nimis violenta, corrosiva et delateria aegris propinare a quibusdam Galenicis, pseudomedicis ac logiatris . . . dicuntur* (n.p., 1593): An apologetic in refutation of the calumny, maintained by certain Galenists, false physicians and wordmongers, that those more wholesome philosophers and physicians the Paracelsians prescribe exceedingly violent, corrosive and harmful substances to the sick.

6. Libavius's hostility to Paracelsus is expressed in all his works. His attacks on Gramann are in his *Neoparacelsica* (Frankfurt, 1594) and his *Antigramania secunda* ... (Frankfurt, 1595): the first 'Antigramania' constitutes part 2 of *Neoparacelsica*.

7. *Neoparacelsica*, p. 202.

8. Sloane MS 2079, fo. 80.

9. [J. Riolan], *Brevis excursus in battalogiam Quercetani* (Paris, 1604), p. 17.

10. Libavius, who was exactly informed of the whole affair, says explicitly, and several times, that the faculty had demanded the death penalty, and he makes it clear, in *Alchymia triumphans* (Frankfurt a/M, 1607), that this was in a petition to the Parlement. He also states that in 1604 a book was printed in Paris, 'cum privilegio regio' to show 'non tantum regiam autoritatem stultitiae Parisiensi sese opposuisse, verum etiam senatum eius urbis ... contempsisse' (ibid., p. 61): that royal authority not only set itself against the stupidity of the Parisans but indeed held the Council of that city in contempt.

11. Libavius to Sigismund Schnitzer, 3 Dec. 1604, printed in Joannes Hornung, *Cista medica, quâ in epistolae clarissimorum Germaniae medicorum, familiares ... asservantur* (Nuremberg, 1625), p. 58. We may observe that Libavius has no doubt that Riolan is the author of the attacks on the chemists, although as yet Riolan had not emerged from pseudonymity.

12. A. Libavius, *Defensio alchymiae et refutatio objectionum ex censura scholae Parisiensis* ... (Frankfurt, 1606). The preface is dated February 1606.

13. *Ad Libavi maniam, Joannis Riolani responsio pro censura scholae Parisiensis contra alchymiam lata* (Paris, 1606).

14. Libavius mentions all these letters in the preface to his *Alchymia triumphans*. He prints du Chesne's letter, which is undated, on pp. 15–18. The draft of Mayerne's letter (dated 12 Oct. 1606) is in his *Ephemerides:* Sloane MS 2060, fos 1–2ᵛ.

15. Hornung, *Cista medica*, p. 65.

16. *Alchymia triumphans de iniusta in se collegii Galenici spurii in Academia Parisiensi censura et Ioannes Riolani maniographia, falsa convicta, & funditus eversa. Opus hermeticum, vere didacticum* (Frankfurt a/M, 1607).

17. Mayerne refers to du Chesne's *Musaeum* in his letter to the Württemberg philosopher (above pp. 56–8). Du Chesne himself addresses the dedication of his *Tetras gravissimorum totius capitis affectuum* (Marburg, 1606) to the Landgrave of Hesse 'ex Musaeo nostro Lutetiae Parisiorum' (from our laboratory of Paris).

18. That 'Dryida', 'le Druide', who appears in several of Mayerne's papers, is du Chesne is proved by two passages in Sloane MS 693. One of these (fo. 131) reads 'vide Druidam in Tetrade cap. 30' – i.e. du Chesne's *Tetras*; the other (fo. 153) reads 'Le Druide en son livre de priscorum philosophorum medicinae materia', which clinches the matter. For the Druids as 'prisci theologi' in France, see D.P. Walker, 'The Prisca Theologia in France', *Journal of the Warburg and Courtauld Institutes*, xvii (1954), 204–59.

19. 'Primum opus Neptis tyrunculae ex instructione Druidae', Sloane MS 693, fo. 134; cf. ibid., fo. 139, where Neptis reports to Druid and refers to 'la demye once de poudre que me donnastes en l'an 1589'.

20. Sloane MS 283, fos 21–8; the remarks are ascribed to 'Madle Sabatier. Descripsi ex ipsius αὐτογραφῷ Lutetiae 1601.' For Sabatier cf. Sloane MSS 2048, fo. 75ᵛ; 2105B, fo. 77.

21. Sloane MSS 1984, fo. 1ᵛ; 2079, fo. 47ᵛ); and she is mentioned in Sloane MS 693, fo. 194ᵛ (maybe also fo. 159).

22. Bodl., Ashmole MSS 1440, pp. 48–98; 1459, p. 465. In a letter of the summer of 1605 (Kassel MS, fo. 263), du Chesne sends greetings from his wife and daughter.

23. MS Sloane 693, fo. 173. In one of his notebooks (a copy of which Mayerne acquired through the services of Kenelm Digby) du Chesne refers to 'un gentilhomme d'Orléans', and Mayerne has noted, with his own hand, in the margin: 'Mr. De Trougny'.

24. For Trougny and la Rivière see MS Sloane 1992, fo. 32ᵛ. 'Mr. du Mesnil nepveu de M. de Trogny' was a patient of Mayerne in 1604 (RCS, MS 0065, Viaticum, p. 178). 'Opera Trogniana' of various kinds are recorded in Mayerne's papers: see especially 'Medulla operationum variarum Druidae, Neptis, Hermetis et aliorum philosophorum': Sloane MS 693, fos 131ff. Trogny's treatise on the philosopher's stone is printed in Lazarus Zetzner's *Theatri chemici volumen sextum* (Strasbourg, 1661), pp. 439–40.

25. Carl Schultess, 'Aus dem Briefwechsel des Französischen Philologen und Diplomaten Jacques Bongars 1554–1612', in *Wilhelm-Gymnasium zu Hamburg Beiträge zur Gelehrtengeschichte des 17ten Jahrhunderts* (Hamburg, 1905), pp. 177, 179. For Bongars' diary see Hermann Hagen, *Zur Geschichte der Philologie* (Berlin, 1879), pp. 144–60. The clinching document is the dedication of 'Transilvanicae inscriptiones veteres nonnullae et annales de templis Leutschoviensi et Coronensi exscripti a Joanne Bongarsio' (printed in J.G. Schwandtner, *Scriptores rerum Hungaricum veteres, ac genuini* (Vienna, 1746), pp. 874–88), in which Trougny's brother describes him as a master of the alchemical sciences whose active genius has successfully opened the locked gates of Nature, etc. etc.

26. A document in the Cambridge University Library (MS Dd.– 5–26) gives a list of 'medicaments to be prepared for the setting-up of our medical dispensary' in Oct. 1607. The drugs have been devised, especially, by la Rivière, du Chesne, 'Neptis' and Trougny.

27. Sloane MSS 2055, fos 8, 65.

28. Most of these names occur at various points in Sloane MS 2055, which seems to be a record of these activities. For Villemereau see also Sloane MSS 2045, fo. 12; 2046, fos 25, 46; CUL, MS Dd. 5–26, fo. 8. For Philipon also Sloane MS 2085, fo. 25ᵛ; for 'Caltopus' also Sloane MS 2058, fo. 215ᵛ. Cabbalistic interests seem to be implied at Sloane MS 283, fo. 22.

29. For the landgrave's alchemical circle I have used, especially, two sets of manuscripts, viz: (i) the Kassel MS; (2) Staatsarchiv Marburg 4a. 39, no. 52 (letters of Mosanus to the landgrave 1602–5, 1608). The existence of the former source was noted by F.W. Strieder, *Grundlage zu einer Hessischen Gelehrten . . . Geschichte*, v (Marburg, 1785), p. 283; xvii (1819), p. 285; and it was used by Chr. V. Rommel, *Neuere Geschichte von Hessen*, vi (Kassel, 1837), pp. 493–4, 523.

30. Mosanus's letter from Strasbourg (dated 29 May 1604) is in the Marburg document cited above. It confirms the account of Seton's connection with Gustenhover given by Jacob Zwinger two years later and cited by John Ferguson, *Bibliotheca chemica* (Glasgow, 1906), ii. 375.

31. For the political missions of du Chesne (always here described as la Violette) see Chr. V. Rommel, *Correspondance inédite de Henri IV . . . avec Maurice-le-Savant, landgrave de Hesse* (Paris, 1840), pp. 201, 211. This has to be supplemented, for the enciphered parts of the documents, by Moriz Ritter, 'Quellenbeiträge zur Geschichte König Heinrichs IV', in *Sitzungsberichte der Philosophisch-Philologischen und Historischen Classe der Königl. Bayr. Akademie der Wissenschaften zu München*, v (1871), pp. 567–602. The alchemical side of these relations is shown by the private correspondence of Mosanus and du Chesne with the landgrave.

32. Kassel MS, fo. 111 (4 Jan. 1612). Hartmann was mistaken in supposing that Sendivogius was dead in 1612: he died in 1636.

33. e.g. Sloane MS 1989, fo. 62ᵛ: 'a Domino Mosano Landgravii Hassiae Archiatro'; CUL, MS Dd. 5–24, fo. 102ᵛ: 'Sic Mosanus mihi dedit'; RCS, MS 0065, Viaticum, p. 82: 'Sic fecit Mauritius Landgrav. Hassiae'; Sloane MS 1988, fo. 78ᵛ: 'Mauritius Hassiae Landgrav. Propria manu haec descripsit anno 1604'; cf. Mayerne, *Opera medica*, ii. 87.

34. On Rhenanus see Philipp Losch, 'Johannes Rhenanus, ein Casseler Poet des 17ten Jahrhunderts' (dissertation, Marburg, 1895); Hans W. Gabler, 'Tourism and Theatre: or

Some Links between Kassel and London in Jacobean Times', in *Grossbritannien und Deutschland . . . Festschrift für John W.P. Bourke* (Munich, 1974), pp. 280–92.

35. i.e. in his father's *Lexicon alchemiae,* posthumously published by the son in 1612.
36. Johan. Rhenanus, *Opera chymiatrica* (Frankfurt, 1635), epistle dedicatory.
37. Sloane MSS 2045, fo. 55; 2047, fo. 58ᵛ.
38. PRO, SP78/53, fos 138ᵛ, 149, 154.
39. Du Chesne's record is in a notebook acquired in Paris by Sir Kenelm Digby and copied for Mayerne (Sloane MS 2079, fo. 47ᵛ). Mayerne's is in his 'Antidotarium' of 1606 (Bodl., Rawlinson MS C. 516); see also his *Opera medica,* ii. 99–100.
40. *Tetras gravissimorum totius capitis affectuum* (Marburg, 1606, repr. 1609). For its publication see Kassel MS, p. 263; also the preface by Hartmann to the 1609 edition.
41. *Diateticon polyhistoricon* (Paris, 1606); *Le Pourtraict de la santé* (Paris, 1606). Du Chesne refers to his work on it in letters to the landgrave and to Mosanus (Kassel MS, pp. 248, 263).
42. *Pharmacopoeia dogmaticorum restituta . . . selectis hermeticorum floribus illustrata* (Paris, 1607).
43. *Pestis Alexicacus sive luis pestiferae fuga* (Leipzig, 1609).
44. Sloane MS 2041.
45. Sloane MS 2105A, fos 16ff.
46. 'si quando ab aulicis curis respirare mihi licuerit . . . quos informes foetus politioribus ingeniis, & peritioribus . . . lambendos tradam': Mayerne to Fabricius Hildanus, 1 Feb. 1616 (*Guilhelmi Fabricii Hildani . . . observationum et curationum chirurgicarum centuria quarta* (Oppenheim, 1619), p. 457). But it was not elegant Latinity that Mayerne lacked, as this letter shows, with its happy reminiscence of the description of Virgil in Aulus Gellius, *Attic Nights,* XVII.10.2–3. Fabricius took Mayerne's hint and published the commentary in *Guilhelmi Fabricii Hildani . . .* (p. 118) three years later. Fabricius's presentation copy of this book to Mayerne is in BL, shelfmark 1170.k.1.
47. Sloane MS 2051.
48. Sloane MSS 2044, 2047–50.
49. Sloane MS 2053.
50. Sloane MS 1997.
51. Sloane MS 2045, fo. 153ᵛ.

Chapter 7   Interlude in England, 1606

1. Oxford University Archives, NEP/Supra/Register M (1595–1606), fo. 212ᵛ.
2. Ibid., fo. 202ᵛ.
3. Anthony Wood, *Fasti Oxonienses* (London, 1813–30), under the year 1606.
4. *Cal. S.P. Dom. 1603–10,* pp. 99, 205, 233; Sloane MS 2050, fo. 72ᵛ; Sloane MS 2063, fo. 56ᵛ: 'Regina abunde purgata fuit a Dr Martino' (note dated 1611).
5. 'Oratiuncula habita Oxonii post receptionem in numerum doctorum et admissionem ad privilegia universitatis, 8 Aprilis stylo vet. 1606' (BL, Addit. MS 20921, fo. 91ᵛ).
6. Bayle, *Dictionnaire,* s.v. 'Mayerne', note C.
7. Carleton's letters to Cecil are in PRO, SP78/52, fo. 280; *HMC Salisbury,* xvii. 447–8. Cecil's reply is in *Cal. S.P. Dom. 1603–10,* p. 235; cf. *HMC Salisbury,* xvii. 454 (Carleton to Sir Walter Cope), and SP78/52, fo. 286, Sir Thomas Parry to Cecil.
8. SP78/52, fos 288, 388.
9. Norreys was expected in England some time after 23 Feb./5 Mar. (Chamberlain, i. 215–16). Mayerne wrote a letter from Paris on 25 Feb./7 Mar. (Sloane MS 2059, fo. 135), after which there is no dated entry in his *Ephemerides* until 16/26 June (Sloane MS 2059, fo. 153ᵛ). Parry left Paris carrying a letter from Villeroy to Cecil dated 28 Feb./10 Mar. (SP78/53, fo. 36). Norreys and Parry were reported by Chamberlain (i. 217) to be

still at sea on 12/22 Mar. That Norreys was still at Rycote on 6 Apr. is shown by a letter of that date in *HMC Salisbury*, xviii. 100.

10. See Pierre Paul Laffleur de Kermaingant, *L'Ambassade de France en Angleterre sous Henri IV. Mission de Christophe de Harlay comte de Beaumont 1602–1605* (Paris, 1895), i. 185; ii. 203–7.

11. Even S.R. Gardiner, who was no friend to frivolity or extravagance, wrote respectfully, in his article on him in the *Dictionary of National Biography*, of Hay's diplomatic activity.

12. Clarendon, *History of the Rebellion*, ed. W.D. Macray (Oxford, 1888), i. 77–8.

13. Mayerne's *Ephemerides* of 1638, RCP, MS 444, p. 201.

14. Sloane MS 2062, fo. 143ᵛ.

15. For St Antoine's emigration to England, see Kermaingant, *L'Ambassade de France en Angleterre*, i. 135–6, 175; PRO, SP14/57, fo. 188; SP 14/70, fo. 173; for Mayerne's attendance on him in 1606, Sloane MS 2110, fo. 146. Many attendances, both on St Antoine and on the horses, are recorded later. St Antoine appears in Van Dyck's famous equestrian portrait of Charles I, belonging to HM the Queen.

16. Sloane MS 1996, fo. 135.

17. Sloane MS 2041, fo. 32.

18. Sloane MS 2049, fo. 14ᵛ.

19. Sloane MSS 1992, fo. 57ᵛ; 2041, fo. 32; 2051, fo. 74.

20. Although he does not name them, at Oxford Mayerne probably met the Regius Professor of Medicine, Matthew Gwinn, who would normally have presented him for his degree, and perhaps Sir William Paddy, who, like Gwinn, was of St John's College. Both were Fellows of the Royal College of Physicians. But both had sympathy with chemical medicine. Gwinn, though he attacked the Paracelsian empiric Francis Anthony, called himself *Galenochymicus* and agreed with Libavius about the compatibility of Galenic and chemical medicine. Paddy was afterwards a close friend of Mayerne.

21. Sloane MS 2059, fos 113, 122. Mayerne had attended Madame de Rohan since the beginning of 1602: Sloane MSS 2058, fo. 40; 2059, fo. 28, etc.

22. Above, p. 47.

23. BL, Cotton MS Caligula E. X., fo. 225 (Rohan to Parry, 1603); cf. PRO, SP78/50, fo. 187 (Rohan to Cecil, 1603).

24. Alastair Duke, 'An Enquiry into the Troubles at Asperen, 1566–1567', *Bijdragen en mededelingen van het historisch genootschap*, lxxxii (1968), 207–27; [also, for the family, J.W. de Tombes, *Het Geslacht van den Botzelaer* (Assen, 1969)].

25. François de Châtillon, Admiral de Coligny, the princess's brother, and his wife feature as patients in Sloane MS 2129.

26. Sloane MS 2046, fo. 181ᵛ. For the van den Boetzelaer family see Martinus Beekman, *Beschreiving van de Stad en Baronnie Asperen* (Utrecht, 1745); C.W.L. Baron van den Boetzelaer, *Het Geslacht van den Boetzelaer* (Assen, 1969), ch. 11.

27. Sloane MS 2129. On internal evidence, this notebook (or at least the first part of it) seems to date from Mayerne's early years in Paris, if not in Montpellier. The book is inscribed on the title-page 'Théodore de Mayerne Turquet P. Lagneus s. ex animo'. P. Lagneus is presumably Philippe Lagneau, who studied medicine with Mayerne at Montpellier, having matriculated there in 1591: Marcel Gouron, ed., *Matricule de l'université de médecine de Montpellier 1503–1599* (Geneva, 1957), p. 194. The early entries show numerous connections with Montpellier and the court of Navarre.

28. Sloane MS 2078, fo. 24: 'sic ad me M[ayerne] Marchionissa de la Moussaye scripsit Lutet. 21 Sept. 1641.' There is another letter from the Marquise de la Moussaye to Mayerne, of Mar. 1646: CUL, MS Dd. 5–25, fo. 84. The marquise died in 1649, aged sixty-nine.

29. RCS, MS 0065, private record, p. 3.

30. The records of the Temple at Charenton were destroyed in the time of the Paris Commune in 1871, but they had previously been transcribed and arranged alphabetically by the brothers Haag as material for their work *La France protestante* (Paris and Geneva, 1846–59). These transcripts are now in the Bibliothèque de la Société de l'Histoire du Protestantisme Français, rue des Saints Pères, Paris.
31. PRO, SP78/53 fos 178ᵛ, 190 (George Carew to Salisbury, 4 and 31 Oct. 1606).
32. PRO, SP78/53, fo. 121.
33. 'Sequentia sunt D. Reneal.', Sloane MS 2129, fo. 140&ᵛ; cf. Sloane MSS 2049, fo. 68ᵛ; 283, fo. 61ᵛ.
34. L'Estoile, *Mémoires-journaux*, viii. 337.
35. Paulus Renealmus, *Ex curationibus observationes quibus videre est morbos tuto ... posse debellari: si praecipue Galenicis praeceptis chymica remedia veniant subsidio* (Paris, 1606).
36. BFMP, MS X, fo. 49.
37. Ibid., X, fo. 64.
38. As a writer, du Chesne is Latinised as Quercetanus; as a person, he is Latinised from his territorial title, Sieur de la Violette.
39. BFMP, MS X, fo. 105.
40. Mayerne, *Apologia*, p. 12.
41. BFMP, MS X, fos 130, 141.
42. The *arrêt* of the Cour des Aides was dated 30 Aug. 1608. BN, MS Carré d'Hozier 423, fo. 53.
43. BL, Addit. MS 20921, fos 69ᵛ-70.
44. [Riolan and Mayerne are likely to have met in England in the 1630s, where Riolan was physician to the exiled queen mother, Marie de Médicis. William Harvey, though he disputed with Riolan over the circulation of the blood, called him 'the leader and doyen of all contemporary anatomists'. See L.W.D. Brockliss and Colin Jones, *The Medical World of Early Modern France* (Oxford, 1997) – a magisterial work – pp. 100n, 140.]
45. See Jean Astruc, *Mémoires pour servir à la faculté de médecine de Montpellier* (Paris, 1767), pp. 360–1.

Chapter 8   Protestants and Catholics, 1600–1610

1. Sir George Carew, 'A Relation of the State of France', in Thomas Birch, *An Historical View of the Negotiations ...* (1749), pp. 445–6.
2. Henri IV to 'certains gentilshommes de la Religion', 25 July 1593, in L. Dussieux, ed., *Lettres intimes de Henri IV* (Paris, 1876), pp. 190–1.
3. Raymond Ritter, ed., *Lettres du cardinal de Florence sur Henri IV et sur la France 1596–1598* (Paris, 1955), pp. 114–15, 161, 241–2.
4. Above, p. 32 n. 4.
5. On the significance of Sancy's conversion see A. Garnier, *Agrippa d'Aubigné et le parti protestant* (Paris, 1928), ii. 254–5.
6. D'Aubigné, *Oeuvres complètes*, i. 380, 387.
7. See Jacques Pannier, *L'Église réformée de Paris sous Henri IV* (Paris, 1911), p. 212; cf. the remark of du Moulin: 'Qui est fidèle ministre à qui on n'a offert de bénéfices ou de l'argent pour le corrompre?' (cited ibid., p. 225).
8. On the diplomacy concerning de Thou's *History* at Rome see Alfred Soman, ed., *De Thou and the Index: Letters from Christophe Dupuy (1603–1607)* (Geneva, 1972).
9. On the movement for reunion see A. Coquerel, 'Précis de l'histoire de l'Église réformée de Paris sous l'Édit de Nantes, 1594–1685', *BSHPF*, xv-xvi (1866–7); and Garnier, *Agrippa d'Aubigné*, ii. 332ff.

10. Turquet to Scaliger, 16 Feb. 1592 and 14 Mar. 1592, in *Epistres françoises des personnages illustres et doctes, à Monsieur Joseph Juste de la Scala* (Harderwyck, 1624), pp. 333–5, 515–16.

11. Ibid., p. 334.

12. Louis de Mayerne Turquet, *Epistre au roy* (Tours, 1592). Further details are in his *Apologie contre les detracteurs des livres de la Monarchie aristodémocratique* (Paris?, 1616), pp. 33–5.

13. *Epistres à M. J.J. de la Scala*, p. 516.

14. Ibid., p. 334.

15. Ibid., p. 516.

16. Scaliger to N. de Thou, Sieur d'Émery, 26 Aug. 1592: BN, MS Dupuy 838, fo. 33.

17. Jean Aymon, *Tous les synodes nationaux des églises réformées de France* (The Hague, 1710), i. 195, 205, 208.

18. Ibid., i. 234.

19. L'Estoile, *Mémoires-journaux*, ix. 133.

20. Casaubon, *Ephemerides*, p. 472.

21. 'M. Pournas de la Piemente' (also spelt 'Piemante' and 'Piedmante') was in Paris in Nov.–Dec. 1642, when Mayerne prescribed medicine for him (Sloane MS 2074, fos 39^v, 40^v; CUL, MS Dd. 5–24, fos 3, 179^v). He was then sixty years old, so he would have been nine in 1591. The dedicatee of Mayerne's book, being described as 'seigneur de la Piemente', was probably his father.

22. Garnier, *Agrippa d'Aubigné*, i. 47–9.

23. L'Estoile, *Mémoires-journaux*, viii. 352.

24. Ibid., ix. 67.

25. Ibid, ix. 133.

26. Ibid, ix. 138.

27. Sylvius, one of the leading anatomists in Paris in the mid-sixteenth century, had pioneered the use of arterial and venal injections in dissections. For Fernel see above, p. 71.

28. The case of le Paulmier can be followed in BFMP, X. 251^v–257^v) and in his two published works, *Lapis philosophicus dogmaticorum* (Paris, 1608) and *Laurus palmaria fugans ventaneum fulmen cyclopum aliquot . . .* (Paris, 1609). The decree of the Parlement against le Paulmier was published as *Arrest de la cour de parlement . . . 6 Juillet 1609 . . . en cause d'entre Mre Pierre Paulmier DM, appellant des deux ordonnances de la faculté . . . et les docteurs régents de ladicte faculté et Mre. Georges Cornut, doyen d'icelle.*

29. *Enchiridion practicum medico – chirurgicum . . .* (Geneva, 1644), 'Lectori candido'; T.H. Reveillé-Parise, ed., *Lettres de Gui Patin* (Paris, 1846), i. 280; Sloane MSS 2046, fo. 42; 2100, fo. 46. Other references by Mayerne to le Paulmier are in Sloane MSS, 1999, fo. 71; 2080, fo. 8v; 2105B, fo. 53; etc.

30. L'Estoile, *Mémoires-journaux*, ix. 344–5.

31. Casaubon, *Ephemerides*, pp. 684–5.

32. Sloane MS 2081, fo. 65.

33. L'Estoile, *Mémoires-journaux*, ix. 135, 344; x. 33.

34. Ibid., ix. 390

35. Above, pp. 81–2.

36. L'Estoile, *Mémoires-journaux*, ix. 334; x. 33.

37. Sloane MS 1992, fo. 34^v.

38. Mayerne's attendance on the family is recorded in Sloane MSS 2059, fo. 51; 2060, fo. 67; 2061, fos 100, 115; 2062, fos 175, 179^v, 204; etc. For his cosmetics see Sloane MSS 1989, fo. 84^v; 2020, fo. 93; 2088, fo. 9 (the pigeon paste recipe).

39. Letter from Mayerne to the countess, 19 Nov. 1630 (BL, Addit. MS 20921, fos 10^v–11), and another of 4 June 1633 (fo. 35&^{v}), both signed 'Merlin' and addressing her as 'belle et chère Lucille'.

40. e.g. Sloane MS 1989, fo. 177. Héroard was the author of a work on the anatomy of the horse, *Hippostologie* (Paris, 1599).
41. J. Héroard, *De institutione principis* (Paris, 1617, but evidently published in 1619). Héroard's journal was published by E. Soulie and E. de Barthélémy, 2 vols (Paris, 1868). [There is now an edition by Madeleine Foisil (Paris, 1989).]
42. L'Estoile, *Mémoires-journaux*, vii. 305.
43. Sloane MS 2062, fo. 1.
44. Mark Pattison, *Isaac Casaubon 1559–1714* (London, 1875), ch. 4; Casaubon, *Ephemerides*, pp. 655, 666–7, 699–702, etc.
45. Soman, ed., *De Thou and the Index*, pp. 23–4.
46. Ibid., p. 20.

Chapter 9   The Move to England, 1610–1611

1. Alfred Soman, ed., *De Thou and the Index: Letters from Christophe Dupuy (1603–1607)* (Geneva, 1972), pp. 24–6.
2. That Henri de Mayerne had been 'long time a stranger' to Geneva is stated by the English agent George Rooke (PRO, SP78/57 fo. 173ᵛ) and implied by Mayerne's words to the Petit Conseil, 'mon frère, que le désir d'exposer sa vie pour la deffence de nostre commune patrie, avoit porté par de là' (Heyer, pp. 193–4).
3. Sir George Carew, 'A Relation of the State of France', in Thomas Birch, *An Historical View of the Negotiations . . .* (London, 1749), p. 482.
4. For the composition of Louis Turquet's book see his later work *Apologie contre les detracteurs des livres de la monarchie aristodémocratique* (n.p., 1616), pp. 33–5; L'Estoile, *Mémoires-journaux*, ix. 67, 133; xi. 131; and Turquet's letter to Christiaan Huygens of 12 Nov. 1612 (below, pp. 159–60 n. 48).
5. In his letter to Huygens of 12 Nov. 1612 he speaks of having been in Huygens' house for this purpose 'il y a deux ans passées'.
6. L'Estoile, *Mémoires-journaux*, xi. 88.
7. Above, p. 106.
8. Sloane MS 2062, fos 41–42ᵛ.
9. Tomkis is mentioned by Casaubon in a letter to Richard Thomson of 31 Jan. 1609 (T.J. van Almeloveen, ed., *Isaaci Casauboni epistolae* (Rotterdam, 1709), pp. 339–40) and by Mayerne in the letter to Overbury quoted below. For biographical details of the Tomkis family see Hugh Dick's edition of *Albumazar* (Berkeley, 1944).
10. Casaubon, *Ephemerides*, s.v. 'Perronius'; *Isaaci Casauboni epistolae*, p. 347.
11. Sloane MS 2062, fos 111–113ᵛ. The letter is supplemented by a further one of 7 Mar. 1610 (ibid., fos 113ᵛ–115ᵛ).
12. Sloane MS 2062, fo. 115.
13. Above, p. 106.
14. Casaubon, *Ephemerides*, p. 740; Mark Pattison, *Isaac Casaubon* (London, 1875), p. 301.
15. Sloane MS 2062, fo. 143ᵛ–144.
16. Pattison, *Isaac Casaubon*, p. 269.
17. For the murder of Henri de Mayerne, as recounted in the archives of Geneva, see Heyer, pp. 186–91; also the account sent by George Rooke to Sir Thomas Edmondes (PRO, SP78/57, fo. 173ᵛ).
18. RPC, 1611–12, fo. 141 (cited in Heyer, p. 187).
19. L'Estoile, *Mémoires-journaux*, xi. 128.
20. Heyer, pp. 194–5.
21. Ibid., p. 190.
22. Henri de Mayerne was murdered on 24 Apr., and Mayerne, writing to Geneva on 2 May, said that he had delayed writing owing to the shock of the news. We do not know

the date of Keir's visit to Mayerne, but it was presumably just before 30 Apr., the date on which Villeroy wrote to Edmondes conveying the queen's consent to Mayerne's journey.

23. The visit of Sir George Keir is described by Mayerne in his MS account, 'the true history of my being here in England', in his letter to Speaker Lenthall of 26 April 1645 (Bodl., Tanner MS 60, fo. 134).
24. Sloane MS 2062, fo. 181.
25. PRO, SP78/57, fos 147, 150ᵛ, 152.
26. BL, Stowe MS 172, fo. 39.
27. RCS, MS 0065, private record, p. 3.
28. Sloane MS 2062, fo. 204.
29. Casaubon, *Ephemerides*, p. 842.
30. BL, Stowe MS 172, fo. 115; and see fo. 112.
31. 'Facite et quocumque modo vester sit, nam si nos redierit, certa est defectio': du Moulin to Bishop Montagu (*Isaaci Casauboni epistolae*, 'Vita', p. 55).
32. The battle over Casaubon is recorded in the diplomatic correspondence of the time: that of the French ambassador Samuel de Spifame, Sieur de Buisseaux (BN, MS Fonds français 15985, 15986) and that of Sir Thomas Edmondes (BL, Stowe MS 172; PRO, SP78/57–8).
33. Louis Turquet, *La Monarchie aristodémocratique* (Paris, 1611), pp. 63, 502–6.
34. Louis Turquet, *Apologie*, pp. 441–61.
35. Ubaldini to Borghese, 21 June, 7 July, 2 Aug. 1611 (Vatican Archives, S.S. Francia 54, fos 288ᵛ–289ᵛ, 299–300, 316).
36. The record of his interrogation of 20 June 1611 is in BN, MS Fonds Dupuy 558, fos 40–66ᵛ.
37. L'Estoile was nevertheless able to buy two copies on 21 July and 30 July 1611 (*Mémoires-journaux*, xi. 131, 133). The Catholic l'Estoile found the book 'si beau que j'en ay extraict une grande partie nouvellement'.
38. 'La Royne ne voulut, par sa bonté, que l'autheur en eust d'autre peine.' Jean Richer, ed., *La Continuation du Mercure François* (Paris, 1613), fo. 87ᵛ.
39. Giustiniani, Venetian ambassador in Paris, to Serenissima, 13 July 1611 (BN, MS Ital. 1764, fos 75–6).
40. Borghese to Ubaldini, 3 Aug. 1611 (Vatican Archives, S.S. Francia 294).
41. Several books or pamphlets by clergy, *dévots* and old *Ligueurs* were written against Turquet's book. He replied in his *Apologie contre les detracteurs* . . .
42. BN, MS Fonds français 15986, fos 82, 92ᵛ–93.
43. L'Estoile, *Mémoires-journaux*, xi. 122.
44. BL, Stowe MS 172, fo. 112.
45. They were reported to have reached Dover 'Prid. Eid. Sept.', i.e. 12 Sept. (Casaubon, *Ephemerides*, pp. 878–9).
46. BL, Stowe MS 172, fo. 242
47. Casaubon, *Ephemerides*, pp. 948–9.
48. This letter of 12 Nov. 1612 was formerly included in the collection of Alfred Morrison at Fonthill, Wilts., and is printed in *Catalogue of the Autograph Letters and Historical Documents formed . . . by Alfred Morrison*, iv (privately printed, 1890), p. 223. Both there and in *HMC Morrison* it is wrongly described as being by Theodore de Mayerne, and as such it was bought, when the Morrison collection was dispersed, by the Wellcome Institute of the History of Medicine, where it now is.
49. BN, MS Fonds français 17934, fos 115, 119.
50. Ch. Read, 'Cimetières et inhumations des Huguenots', *BSHPF*, xii (1863), 277.

Chapter 10   First Years in England, 1611–1613

1. *Brief Lives*, s.v. 'Paddy'.
2. Sloane MS 2063, fo. 48; for Gaebelkhover as the ultimate source see *Opera medica*, ii. 83.
3. Mayerne's notes on and prescriptions for the royal family in 1611 are in Sloane MS 2063. On hart's horn see *Opera medica*, ii. 79.
4. Sloane MSS 2059, fo. 135; 2066, fo. 158ᵛ; cf. *Opera medica*, ii. 121.
5. Sloane MSS 174, fo. 23; 2063, fos 157ᵛ, 179ᵛff; 2080, fo. 7; 2065, fo. 28ᵛ; *Cal. S.P. Dom. 1637–8*, pp. 526, 600.
6. Sloane MS 2063, fo. 70ff.
7. Chamberlain, i. 317.
8. Sloane MSS 2063, fos 66ᵛ–67ᵛ; 2071, fos 70–1.
9. Sloane MSS 2063, fo. 142; 2074, fo. 107.
10. Sloane MS 2062, fo. 1 (*Opera medica*, i. 43).
11. e.g. the year of his birth, which was 1585.
12. Sloane MS 2063, fo. 102 (*Opera medica*, i. 90).
13. Sloane MS 2063, fo. 84ᵛ.
14. The date (1 June 1563) is noted by Burghley in his diurnal (*HMC Salisbury*, v. 69), but Mayerne was more specific: it was at 2 a.m.
15. Sloane MS 2063, fos 87–99.
16. Chamberlain, i. 324, 336, 338.
17. [On Mayerne and Cecil's illness see also *ODNB*: Robert Cecil, first Earl of Salisbury. An English translation of Mayerne's notes on Cecil is to be made available online by the Wellcome Trust's 'Health of the Cecils' project ('The Mental World of the Early Cecils 1560–1660') at Royal Holloway College, University of London: www.rhul.ac.uk/history/research/cecils.]
18. *Les Voyages du Sieur de Champlain* (Paris, 1613), p. 54.
19. Sloane MS 2063, fo. 8; the *consilium* itself is dated 9 March 1610. Cf. Sloane MS 2062, fo. 77.
20. J. Keevil, *Medicine and the Navy*, i (London, 1957), pp. 100–2, 150.
21. Sloane MS 2063, fo. 203ᵛ.
22. 'Curatio Hydropis cuiusdam Anabapistae qui in Germania vocatur der Wassersucht Doktor': Sloane MS 2064, fo. 202.
23. Sloane MS 2063, fos 203ᵛ–204.
24. Sloane MS 2065, fo. 113ᵛ.
25. Chamberlain, i. 341.
26. *HMC Marquess of Downshire*, iii. 249.
27. *Cal. S.P. Dom. 1611–18*, p. 119.
28. Chamberlain, i. 346.
29. BL, Stowe MS 172, fo. 242.
30. BL, Addit. MS 20921, fo. 61ᵛ. Mayerne calls him Sir Henry Murray, but this is clearly a slip.
31. Chamberlain, i. 384.
32. 'The Manner and Death of Prince Henry', in F. Peck, *Desiderata curiosa* (London, 1779 edn), i. 201.
33. On this cordial (which was used by Mayerne: Sloane MS 2078, fo. 15) see N. LeFebvre, *A Discourse upon Sʳ Walter Rawleigh's Great Cordial*, translated by Peter Belon (London, 1664). Ralegh's cordial was used regularly by the Earl of Chatham in the eighteenth century. However, Ralegh's cures were not always so successful. In this very year, 1612, when Sir Philip Sidney's daughter, the Countess of Rutland, died, Ralegh was 'slandered to have given her certain pills that despatched her'.
34. Sloane MS 2063, fo. 218.

35. Chamberlain, i. 389; Sloane MSS 2019, fo. 55^v; 2067, fo. 114. Other remedies from Ralegh are in Sloane MSS 1959, fo. 79; 1989, fo. 77^v; 2046, fo. 110; 2048, fo. 34; 2078, fo. 115; 2080, fo. 38^v.
36. Chamberlain, i. 389.
37. BL, Addit. MS. 20921, fo. 59&^{v}.
38. Chamberlain, i. 346.
39. BL, Addit. MS 20921, fo. 61^v.
40. Chamberlain, i. 388.
41. Roger Coke, *A Detection of the Court and State of England* (London, 1694), i. 61.
42. *Opera medica*, i. 103–23. [Mayerne's original Latin and French manuscripts of his defence have been removed from his *Ephemerides*. Nance, p. 189 n. 47, suggests that they were taken by Joseph Browne, the editor of Mayerne's *Opera medica*, in preparing the edition.]
43. See Sir Norman Moore's pamphlet *The Illness and Death of Henry Prince of Wales in 1612* (London, 1882). Typhoid fever was first recognised as a distinct class by Sir William Jenner in 1850.
44. Mayerne described the history of his relations with Butler, and cited much of the evidence (BL, Addit. MS 20921, fos 59–63). Unfortunately the documents are seldom dated, but I have reconstructed it as best I can. The other two letters are in Sloane MS 2065, fos 6^v–8^v, 32&^{v}.
45. Chamberlain, i. 434.
46. Mayerne's Cambridge doctorate is recorded in the University Grace Book (*Liber Gratiarum*) E. p. 184: 'M. Maiern incorporatus prout in Acad. Marspol'. Curiously, Mayerne is not mentioned in Venn's *Alumni Cantabrigienses*; but Dr Zutchi, the Cambridge University Archivist, who found the record for me, writes that this is probably because 'Venn used the original *supplicats* for the degrees, not the Grace Books, and no *supplicat* for this degree survives.' Mayerne's Latin speech on receiving the degree is in his records (BL, Addit. MS 20921, fo. 92): the date there given, 1611, is a mistake by the transcriber. In it, Mayerne refers to the august presence of 'serenissimi principes', confirming the grandeur of the ceremony. The visit of the two princes is described in Chamberlain, i. 434.

Chapter 11   Sir Thomas Overbury, 1612–1615

1. James Hay had preceded him to an English peerage, but his patent had explicitly excluded him from the English House of Lords.
2. Chamberlain, i. 354–5.
3. As Francis Bacon put it in his speech at the trial of the Earl of Somerset: William Cobbett, *Complete Collection of State Trials and Proceedings for High Treason and Other Crimes and Misdemeanours*, ii (London, 1809), p. 973.
4. Ibid.
5. Ibid.
6. Sloane MS 1989, fo. 100.
7. Sloane MSS 2059, fo. 153^v; 2060, fo. 70.
8. Ralph Winwood, *Memorials of Affairs of State in the Reigns of Queeen Elizabeth and King James I* (London, 1725), iii. 447–8.
9. Cobbett, *Complete Collection*, ii. 984.
10. PRO, SP14/82, fo. 40.
11. Copies (in some cases partial) of Overbury's letters to Rochester are in BL, Harleian MS 7002, fos 281–8.
12. Ibid., fo. 281; Cobbett, *Complete Collection*, ii. 917.
13. PRO, SP14/82, fo. 23; Cobbett, *Complete Collection*, ii. 922, 939.

14. BL, Harleian MS 7002, fos 287–8.
15. BL, Harleian MS 7002, fo. 280, printed in Thomas Birch, ed., *The Court and Times of James the First* (London, 1848), i. 269 (letter of Rev. Thomas Lorkin to Sir Thomas Puckering). In her searching study which supersedes previous accounts of the Overbury affair, Anne Somerset, *Unnatural Murder: Poison at the Court of James I* (London, 1997), suggests (p. 168 n. 55) that Birch's dating of the letter is mistaken, but the manuscript vindicates it.]
16. BL, Harleian MS 7002, fos 289–91; see also Northampton's account of the episode in a letter to Rochester: CUL, MS Dd 3-63, fos 48–9.
17. Winwood, *Memorials*, iii. 478–9.
18. PRO, SP14/82/2, fo. 2.
19. CUL, MS Dd. 3–23, fo. 53ᵛ.
20. [On Reeve see also Somerset, *Unnatural Murder*, esp. pp. 191ff, 239–40.]
21. *HMC Buccleuch*, i. 160–1.
22. The Earl of Somerset died in 1645. Mayerne attended him to the end: Sloane MS 2074, fo. 88.
23. PRO, SP14/83/38, fos 62–3.
24. PRO, SP14/82, fo. 27; Andrew Amos, *The Great Oyer of Poisoning* (London, 1846), p. 167.
25. PRO SP14/83, fo. 16, printed in Amos, *Great Oyer of Poisoning*, pp. 168–70.
26. Ibid.
27. Presumably the same Garret who was Dr Butler's apothecary.
28. PRO, SP14/83, fo. 16.
29. Amos, *The Great Oyer of Poisoning*, p. 494.
30. [For an answer to that last question see above, p. 175 n. 42.]
31. This argument is advanced by S.R. Gardiner in his careful and fair-minded study of the Overbury affair, *History of England . . . 1603–1642* (London, 1895–6), ii. 186n, 338.
32. The speculations are those of Amos, *Great Oyer of Poisoning*, esp. pp. 491ff. Amos was a legal scholar of distinction and he published (though not always accurately) many previously unprinted documents on the Overbury affair, but his historical method is pure special pleading and is exposed by James Spedding in Bacon, *Works*, v. 343–6. S.R. Gardiner, in his article on Robert Carr in the *Dictionary of National Biography*, describes Amos's book as 'of no critical value'.

Chapter 12   Secret Agent of King James, 1614–1615

1. Hayen entered Mayerne's house in 1618, when the eldest son Henri was ten years old, at a salary of £10 a year: Sloane MS 2066, fo. 71ᵛ.
2. Dr Brouart, according to Mayerne's contemporary the physician Baldwin Hamey, accompanied Mayerne to London and died there in 1639 ('Bustorum aliquot reliquiae': RCP, MS 307, item 27). Jean Chappeau returned to Geneva from London in 1627 'having spent some time here with Dr Mayerne' (*Cal. S.P. Dom. 1625–49*, p. 227). Antoine Choqueux was employed, on Mayerne's advice, as surgeon to attend the king's servants in London in 1634 and became surgeon-in-ordinary in 1643 (*Cal. S.P. Dom. 1664–5*, p. 241). Gedéon Chabray (1619–99) was a doctor of Geneva, a son of a pastor at Geneva 'mihi amicissimi'. He lived in Mayerne's house as amanuensis and assistant and was recommended by him as doctor of medicine at Oxford in 1649 (BL, Addit. MS 20921, fo. 116; CUL, MS Dd 5–25, fo. 20; Sloane MS 174, fo. 16).
3. Aubrey, *Brief Lives*, s.v. 'Bovey'. For Hoste see J.H. Hessels, ed., *Ecclesiae Londino-Batavae archivum (Cambridge, 1887–97)*, i. 855–6, 860, and iii., s.v.
4. Sloane MS 2050, fo. 154; also perhaps by an infusion of white soap in white wine: Sloane MS 3428, fo. 31.

5. He reduced all metals, including gold, to vitriol, first with oil of antimony, then with distilled vinegar, 'and from these vitriols extracted red oil'. Sloane MSS 693, fo. 63^v; 2083, fo. 17.

6. Mayerne supported the French church in the case of a Huguenot physician, Dr Duval, whose desertion to the Church of England caused him to be excommunicated: Baron F. de Schickler, *Les Églises du refuge en Angleterre* (Paris, 1892), i. 411–12. On Marmet see ibid., ii. 9–10. For Mayerne's correspondence with Marmet see BL, Addit. MS 20921, fos 8–9.

7. J.A. Worp, ed., *De Briefwisseling van Constantijn Huygens 1608–1687*, i (The Hague, 1911), p. 63. Mayerne's social life is reflected in Huygens' correspondence. Huygens' father corresponded with Mayerne's, then in London, through Caesar Calandrini (see Louis Turquet's letter to Christiaan Huygens, above, pp. 159–60). Mayerne adopted several remedies from Theodore Diodati (e.g. Sloane MSS 1991, fo. 78^v; 2020, fo. 132; 2077, fos 46–53) and would act as a referee for him in 1628 (*Cal. S.P. Dom. 1628–9*, p. 421). He had prescribed for his elder brother Joseph Diodati in Paris in 1607 (Sloane MS 2060, fo. 55). (A.G.H. Bachrach, *Sir Constantine Huygens and Britain 1596–1687* (Leiden, 1962), pp. 138, 145, arbitrarily identifies an unnamed surgeon whom Huygens visited in London, and whom he describes as 'le drôle chirurgien', 'un homme rude et grossier', with Mayerne. Mayerne was not a surgeon; he had not met Huygens at this time; and no one could describe him with such adjectives.)

8. P.C. Molhuysen, ed., *Briefwisseling van Hugo Grotius*, i (The Hague, 1928), p. 318.

9. BL, Burney MS 367, fos 107–11; *Opera medica*, i. 144–54. Ralph Thory also published an account in Holland.

10. BN, MS Fonds français 17934, fo. 115.

11. I have described this episode more fully in an essay on Camden in my *Renaissance Essays* (London, 1985), pp. 125–32.

12. PRO, SP78/63, fo. 47.

13. BL, Addit. MS 32092, fo. 224, Mayerne to James I, 17 Feb. 1615. This is the MS that was previously calendared among the papers of Sir A. Malet (*HMC Fifth Report*, p. 312).

14. On du Moulin see Lucien Rimbault, *Pierre du Moulin, 1568–1658* (Paris, 1966).

15. Mayerne informed Edmondes of the project on 20 Apr. 1612 (BL, Stowe MS 172, fo. 242^v) and conveyed the king's orders to du Moulin on 23 May 1612. Du Moulin had displeased the king by going too far in opposing the errors of his fellow-Huguenot, the 'Arminian' Daniel Tilenus. The king's ruling was that they were both wrong and must shut up: the Church of England disliked 'ces inutiles subtilités' (BL, Addit. MS. 20920, fo. 50^v). Du Moulin expressed suitable gratitude for this correction. See also National Archives of Scotland, Denmilne MS XVI, fos 32–5.

16. Du Moulin's book was *Defence de la foy catholique, contenue au livre du très puissant et serenissime Jacques I* . . . (Paris, 1612 edn).

17. 'Autobiographie de Pierre du Moulin d'après le manuscrit autographe', *BSHPF*, vii (1858), 342–3.

18. Sloane MS 2065, fos 178, 180–6, 193–194^v, 197.

19. PRO, SP78/63, fos 55^v-56.

20. The brothers Haag (*La France protestante* (Paris and Geneva, 1846–59), viii. 8) recorded the date of birth, from the registers of Charenton, as 26 Feb. 1616 (MSS of Bibliothèque de la Société de l'Histoire du Protestantisme Français, Paris). However, this must be a slip of transcription. Mayerne was in England in Feb.–Mar. 1616 (Sloane MS 1993, fos 133–49). It is impossible to check the registers, which were destroyed in the revolt of the Paris Commune in 1871.

21. See Bodl., Rawlinson MS D. 828, being the record of fraternal and sororal strife in the church of which 'brother Naudin' was a prominent member.

22. Chamberlain, i. 591.
23. 'Autobiographie de Pierre du Moulin', pp. 342–3; cf. D.H. Willson, 'James I and his Literary Assistants', *Huntington Library Quarterly*, viii (1944), 35–57.
24. *Cal. S.P. Dom. 1611–19*, p. 224; cf. Logan Pearsall Smith, *Life and Letters of Sir Henry Wotton* (Oxford, 1907), ii. 66.
25. BN, MS Fonds français 17934, fo. 122.
26. Thomas Birch, *An Historical View of the Negotiations . . .* (London, 1749), pp. 358–61, 364.
27. James I to Ph. du Plessis-Mornay: National Archives of Scotland, Denmilne MS XXI, fo. 10.
28. Rohan's letters are in PRO, SP78.
29. PRO SP78/62, fo. 246. The earlier letter to which Rohan refers is probably SP78/60, fo. 260, which is undated.
30. On 22 June or July (the MS is damaged) 1614, Mayerne similarly urged his brother-in-law Gedeon van Boetzelaer, the Dutch ambassador in Paris, to persuade Louis Turquet to come 'passer le reste de ses jours parmis les siens' (BN, MS Fonds français 17934, fo. 119).
31. BN, MS Fonds français 15988, fo. 9.
32. BN, MS Fonds français 15988, fos 15, 20, 22, 24, 26, 28, 39, etc.
33. BL, MS Addit. 32092, fo. 224.
34. National Archives of Scotland, Denmilne MS XXVI, fo. 8. This letter is not included in the list of Rohan's correspondence given by George Serr, *Henri de Rohan* (Aix-en-Provence, 1946).
35. *HMC Earl of Mar and Kellie, Supplementary Report*, p. 59.
36. 'Autobiographie de Pierre du Moulin', pp. 343–4.
37. On Biondi in general see *Dizionario biografico degli italiani* (Rome, 1960–), s.v.; *Cal. S.P. Ven.*, passim; G. Benzoni, 'Giovanni Franceso Biondi, un'avventuroso dalmata del Seicento', *Archivo Veneto*, s.v., lxxx (1967), 19–37.
38. The phrase is Diodati's: E. de Budé, *Vie de Jean Diodati* (Lausanne, 1869), p. 85.
39. Biondi's reports from France are in PRO, SP78/63, fos 251, 318; SP78/64, fo. 43. His address to the Assembly at Grenoble is in SP78/64, fo. 63. Cf. *Cal. S.P. Ven. 1613–15*, p. 542.
40. PRO, SP78/65, fo. 95.
41. PRO, SP78/66, fo. 16.
42. National Archives of Scotland, Denmilne MS XXI, fos 2, 3.
43. See C.W.L. Baron von Boetzelaer, *Het Geslacht van den Boetzelaer* (Assen, 1969), pp. 198–204.
44. BL, Addit. MS 20921, fo. 50. The copy of this letter is unaddressed and undated, but the addressee is obvious and the date is supplied by Mayerne's simultaneous letter to Langeraek.
45. BN, MS Fonds français 17934, fos 124–5.
46. They would only be true if the baron had become a tenant-in-chief of the Crown and had then died leaving his children unmarried.

Chapter 13   Medical Reformer, 1615–1616

1. Harriot's letters are in BL, Addit. MS 6789, fos 446–7 (cf. 442).
2. Sloane MS 3428, fo. 25^v.
3. Sloane MS 2066, fo. 3.
4. On Mouffet see A.G. Debus, *The English Paracelsians* (London, 1965), pp. 71–6, etc.; Manfred E. Welti, 'Englisch-Baslerische Beziehungen zur Zeit der Renaissance in der Medizin, den Naturwissenschaften und der Naturphilosophie', *Gesnerus*, xx (1963),

105–30; R.-H. Blaser, 'Un rare témoignage de fidélité envers Paracelse à Bâle . . .', in R. Blaser and H. Buess, eds, *Aktuelle Probleme aus der Geschichte der Medizin/ Current Problems in the History of Medicine: Proceedings of the XIXth International Conference for the History of Medicine* (Basel and New York, 1966); [and *ODNB*].

5. See C. Wall, H.C. Cameron and E.A. Underwood, *A History of the Worshipful Society of Apothecaries of London* (London, 1963), p. 9.

6. George Urdang, ed., *Pharmacopoeia Londinensis of 1618* (repr., Hollister Pharmaceutical Library no. 2, Madison, Wisconsin, 1944), 'Introduction', pp. 7–8.

7. Ibid., p. 15.

8. On the movement for an English pharmacopoeia see Debus, *English Paracelsians*, and Urdang, 'Introduction' (n. 6 above); also Mr Urdang's article 'How Chemicals Entered the Official Pharmacopoeias', *Archives internationales d'histoire des sciences*, xxxiii (1954), 303–14.

9. Wall, Cameron and Underwood, *History of the Worshipful Society of Apothecaries*, pp. 39, 45.

10. On de Laune see F.N.L. Poynter, *Gideon Delanne and his Family Circle* (Wellcome Historical Medical Library, Lecture no. 2, 1965); Leslie G. Matthews, *The Royal Apothecaries* (London, 1967), pp. 98–100.

11. Wall, Cameron and Underwood, *History of the Worshipful Company of Apothecaries*, pp. 11–17.

12. John Stow, *A Survey of the Cities of London and Westminster and the Borough of Southwark*, ed. John Strype, 6th edn, ii (London, 1755), p. 320.

13. Wall, Cameron and Underwood, *History of the Worshipful Company of Apothecaries*, p. 20.

14. Mayerne to Grangier, 1626: BN, MS Fonds français 18767, fo. 163.

15. Sloane MS 1999, fo. 90^v.

16. Ibid.; Sloane MS 2048, fos 89^v–90.

17. Sloane MS 2049, fo. 124.

18. Sloane MSS 2050, fo. 60; 2074, fo. 185^v.

19. Mayerne's dedication (to William Paddy) of *Insectorum sive minimorum animalium theatrum . . . ad vivum expressis iconibus super quingentis illustratum* (London, 1634), fo. A$_2$^{v}.

20. A. Haller, 'Introduction', to H. Boerhaave, *Methodus studii medici* (Amsterdam, 1751), i. 110.

21. MS Sloane 4014.

22. Mayerne's presentation copy to Paddy is now in the library of St John's College, Oxford. Mayerne sent it personally, by the hand of his second son James. For his accompanying letter see BL, Addit. MS 20921, fo. 43.

23. Sloane MS 2056, fos 27, 29, 45–56, 57, 73–4, etc.

24. Urdang, 'Introduction', p. 24.

25. Since Mayerne made calomel famous, he was long and widely regarded as its inventor, but in fact, as he himself noted in his own copy of the *Pharmacopoeia Londiniensis*, 1618, the prescription came from Oswald Croll's *Basilica chymica* (Frankfurt, 1608). See Urdang, 'How Chemicals Entered the Official Pharmacopoeias', p. 310, and Urdang, 'Introduction', p. 61. In one of his notebooks Mayerne describes his own *mercurius dulcis* as 'the last secret which Quercetanus imparted to Mayerne' (Sloane MS 2081, fo. 65). This may of course be a refinement of Croll's receipt. After Mayerne's death, his pupil Nathaniel Hodges told Seth Ward 'that that which <Lazarus> Riverius so often styles Calomelanos was nothing but *Mercurie dulcis*, and he writ it so, and so did most of the London doctors; that Sir Theodore Mayerne was the publisher of it; and that he had it of one Browne'. We can forget Browne; but Mayerne was certainly 'the publisher' of what would be for centuries the most popular chemical remedy for internal use.

26. Baldwin Hamey, 'Bustorum aliquot reliquiae', RCP, MSS 307–9. This document is the basis of W.R. Munk's *The Roll of the Royal College of Physicians of London* (London, 1861), the standard dictionary of the Fellows for the period concerned.
27. This is not quite correct. Mayerne and some others were mentioned by name in the first (May 1618) edition, though the names were suppressed in the second (Dec. 1618) edition which replaced it.
28. Henry H. Drake, ed., *Hasted's History of Kent, Corrected, Enlarged and Continued*, i (1886), p. 179; *Cal. S.P. Dom. 1625–6*, p. 56; BL, Addit. MS 5716, fo. 9; Sloane MS 2074, fo. 167 (a reference by Mayerne, dated 4 Aug. 1647, to herbs grown 'in vivario meo Horne Park').
29. Edinburgh City MSS, Register of Burgesses and Guild Brethren, iii (1617–69), 27 June 1617.
30. Sloane MS 2066, fo. 3, where Mayerne gives the asssistant's name as 'Jehan Roucastel'. He entered Mayerne's service on 15 July 1617.
31. Sloane MS 2040, fo. 87.
32. Sloane MS 2066, fo. 17.
33. Ibid., fo. 38ᵛ.
34. Sloane MS 3428, fo. 31.
35. It is printed in *Delitiae poetarum scotorum*, ed. Arthur Johnston (Amsterdam 1637) – a work approved for faith and morals by the Archbishop of St Andrew's.
36. RCS, MS 0065, Viaticum, p. 23; Sloane MS 2044, fo. 13.
37. Chamberlain, ii. 106, 108.

Chapter 14   The Protestant Revolution, 1616–1622

1. Agrippa d'Aubigné, 'Traitté sur les Guerres Civiles', in d'Aubigné, *Oeuvres complètes*, ii. 13ff.
2. *Mémoires et correspondance de Duplessis Mornay* (Paris, 1824–5), x. 549.
3. Ibid., xi. 5.
4. E. de Budé, *Vie de Jean Diodati* (Lausanne, 1869), p. 71.
5. Walter Pagel, 'The Paracelsian Elias Artista and the Alchemical Tradition', in Rosemary Dilg-Frank, ed., *Kreatur und Kosmos. Internationale Beiträge zur Paracelsusforschung* (Stuttgart, 1981).
6. BN, MS Fonds français 15988, fo. 273.
7. Sloane MS 2066, fo. 71ᵛ. We happen to know about Turco because he afterwards swallowed a bone which caused an unfortunate obstruction of the bowels and Mayerne recorded his own successful surgery on it.
8. RCS, MS 0065, Viaticum, p. 178. Another treatment of Gondomar is recorded in a marginal note in Sloane MS 2074, fo. 36ᵛ.
9. *Documentos inéditos para la historia de España. Correspondencia oficial de Don Diego Sarmiento de Acuña, conde de Gondomar* (Madrid, 1936), i. 365–6.
10. This letter, which was sold by a Bonn bookseller in 1979 (see catalogue no. 32 of Antiquariat Konrad Menschel, item 159), is the only original letter from Rohan known to me.
11. BN, MS Fonds français 15988, fo. 278&ᵛ.
12. Ibid., fos 282ᵛ–283.
13. PRO, SP78/68, fos 86ᵛ–87.
14. Ibid.
15. Chamberlain, ii. 138, 167; Camden, 'Annalium Apparatus', in *G. Camdeni . . . epistolae* (London, 1691), p. 34.
16. PRO, classmark PRO30/53/1, fo. 39.

17. As is mentioned in a letter from Puysieux to Herbert of 10 Aug. 1619, PRO, classmark PRO 30/53/1, fo. 84.
18. Ibid., fo. 116&^{v}.
19. Ibid., fo. 39.
20. As he told the king in his letter to him, ibid., fo. 122.
21. Ibid., fo. 120&^{v}.
22. Ibid. fos 122&^{v}.
23. BN, MS Fonds français 15988, fos 413–15, 458^v.
24. Mayerne to Puysieux, 26 June 1620 (ibid., fo. 476).
25. Bodl., Rawlinson MS D.935.
26. PRO, SP78/68, fo. 292^v.
27. Wolfgang Schneewind, *Die Diplomatischen Beziehungen Englands mit der Alten Eidgenossenschaft zur Zeit Elisabeths, Jacobs I und Karls I 1558–1649* (Basel, 1950), pp. 40–4.
28. Erlach's embassy is ill-documented. According to Schneewind (ibid., p. 71) the original sources are all lost. But there are some documents in Berne, Bürgerbibliothek MS H.h.XV. Mayerne's part in the story is revealed by his correspondence with Fabricius and by the despatches of French and Venetian envoys in London (BN, MS Fonds français 15988, 17975: PRO transcripts, 9 Nov., 22 Dec. 1615, 3 Jan. 1616; *Cal. S.P. Ven. 1615–17*, pp. 51, 52, 100).
29. James I to Erlach, 21, 24 Jan. 1615–16, in Berne, Bürgerbibliothek MS H.h.XV, fos 55, 96. There is a copy of the first of these letters in PRO SP96/1, fo. 211.
30. Apart from the State Papers in the PRO (SP92/14 and 96/2), Wake's diplomacy is shown in his own papers (BL, Addit. MSS 18639–42) and in his letters to the City of Geneva (Archives d'État) and to Jean Sarasin, syndic of Geneva, preserved in the archives of the Sarasin family in Geneva. I am indebted to M. Olivier Fatio for his kindness in giving me copies of these letters, the property of the family. Wake gave an account of the treaty of 1617 in his 'Discourse concerning the Thirteen Cantons of the Helvetical League' (*c.*1625) in his *Threefold Help to Political Observation* (London, 1655).
31. 'Instruction concernant Genève . . . ', 18 July 1621, printed in J. Gaberel, *Histoire de l'église de Genève*, ii (Geneva, 1855), pt 2, pp. 255–60.

Chapter 15   Baron d'Aubonne, 1620–1621

1. 'Patet regia seminis & urinae via atque amplo, continuo, recto filo redditur lotium, quod nuperrime stillatim, magno etiam conamine, exprimebatur.'
2. Mayerne's letter to Fabricius is in Berne, Bürgerbibliothek, Codex Bongars 497, fos 394–5, and is printed in *Guilhelmi Fabricii Hildani . . . observationum et curationum chirurgicarum centuria quarta* (Oppenheim, 1619), pp. 455–8. The patient is there described anonymously as 'nobilis et generosus ille'. His identity is proved by Mayerne's notes: Sloane MSS 1989, fo. 273; 1993, fo. 136; RCS, MS 0065, Viaticum, p. 171.
3. Erlach's notes on his embassy, Berne, Bürgerbibliothek MS H.h.XV, fos 66ff.
4. Berne, Bürgerbibliothek, Codex Bongars. 497, fo. 395; *Guilhelmi Fabricii Hildani . . . observationum*, p. 457; above, p. 67 n. 24.
5. CUL, MS Dd. 5–26, fo. 46^v.
6. Sloane MS 2066, fo. 61; *Aeneid* VI. 539 (Night falls, Aeneas, and we spend the hours in weeping).
7. Sloane MS 2065, fo. 50.
8. J. Nichols, *The Progresses, Processions, and Magnificent Festivities of King James I* (London, 1828), iii. 541; Bodl., Rawlinson MS D. 918, fos 54^v, 63.

9. As d'Aubigné recalled in his autobiography, 'Sa vie à ses enfants': d'Aubigné, *Oeuvres complètes*, i. 96.

10. Ibid., i. 95.

11. D. Martignier and Aymon de Crousaz, *Dictionnaire historique, géographique et statistique du Canton de Vaud* (Lausanne, 1867), p. 38, s.v. 'Aubonne'.

12. The details of the sale, and subsequent lawsuits concerning the property, are in Archives Cantonales Vaudoises (Chavannes-près-Renens), côte IB300, nos 1172 (anno 1621) to 1200 (anno 1661).

13. Mgr de Granier had been Bishop of Geneva from 1579 to 1602. He was succeeded by St François de Sales.

14. Leiden University Library, MS BPL 885 (Mayerne to Durant, 11 Oct. 1620).

15. *Guilhelmi Fabricii Hildani . . . opera quae extant omnia* (Frankfurt, 1646), p. 454.

16. She was married in 1620 to Zacharie de Jancourt, Sieur d'Ausson, of a Burgundian family, who had been at the prince elector's court since 1599 and was tutor of his children. He would follow the elector to Holland and was drowned at Haarlem in 1621. See the brothers Haag, *La France protestante* (Paris and Geneva, 1846–59), vi. 44–5.

17. Theodore de Coucault, seigneur d'Estoy, in the district of Morges, near Aubonne, had accompanied Hans Rudolf von Erlach on his diplomatic mission to France and England. The Coucault family, like Mayerne, were Huguenots; they had acquired the lordship of Estoy (now Étoy) in 1573. See Eugène Mottaz, *Dictionnaire historique, géographique et statistique du canton de Vaud*, i (Lausanne, 1914), p. 709; H. Vuilleumier, *Histoire de l'église réformée du canton de Vaud sous le régime bernois*, i (Lausanne, 1927), p. 748; J.-C. Biaudet, 'La famille de Coucault au pays de Vaud', *Revue historique vaudoise*, lix (1951). M. Biaudet quotes, only to doubt, a statement by Dom. P. Benoît that Théodore de Coucault died in Hungary, about 1620, in the service of Bethlen Gabor, and says that he 'probably' died in Paris in 1618. But Mayerne's letter supports Benoît. Mayerne would have known if Coucault had died in Paris two years earlier.

18. BL, Addit. MS 20921, fo. 44^v.

19. *Guilhelmi Fabricii Hildani . . . opera*, p. 456.

20. Mayerne to Puysieux, 9 May, 26 June 1620: BN, MS Fonds français 15988, fos 458, 476.

21. Leiden University Library, MS BPL 885.

22. Tillières to Puysieux, 9 Mar. 1621: BN, MS Fonds français 15989, fo. 40.

23. J.A. Worp, ed., *Het Briefwisseling van Constantijn Huygens 1608–1687* (The Hague 1911–17), i. 63.

24. 'Viaticum, sive medicorum experimentorum formulae; peregrinantis encheiridion anno 1621': RCS, MS 0065.

25. On 3 May 1621 the Privy Council gave a pass to Madame de Mayerne, her children and servants, to go to France 'for the ordering and settling of divers businesses concerning Dr Mayerne's estate': *APC 1619–21*, p. 379.

26. BN, MS Fonds français 15988, fo. 476.

27. *Cal. S.P. Ven. 1621–3*, p. 30.

28. The king's letters are mentioned in the formal replies which Mayerne carried back with him: PRO, SP96/2, fos 63 (Geneva), 65 (Berne).

29. That Mayerne, in spite of his detailed preparations, did not in fact travel through France, on his way to or from Aubonne in 1621–2, seems clear from his statement in his instructions to Viscount Doncaster, only three months after his return (see below, pp. 262–4), about his ill-treatment (i.e. the expulsion of 1618) during 'mon dernier voyage en France'. A remark by d'Aubigné (*Oeuvres complètes*, i. 214) shows that he returned via The Hague. He probably went out that way too.

30. The letter (d'Aubigné, *Oeuvres complètes*, i. 206–7) is undated, but it was written to Mayerne before he had reached Aubonne ('en attendant qu'Aubonne vous reçoive, et que nous vous y voyons') and was presumably delivered to him in Geneva.

31. Unfortunately only d'Aubigné's letters – or some of them – have survived. They are in the Bibliothèque Publique et Universitaire de Genève, Archives Tronchin, and are printed in d'Aubigné, *Oeuvres complètes*.
32. Below, pp. 265–6.
33. RPC, MS (1621), fo. 161.
34. Ibid., fos 229, 264, 278, 281, 289 (= Heyer, p. 317).
35. Heyer, p. 196.
36. The tower, in its present form, and some other features, were built by S.-B. Tavernier, who bought the estate from Mayerne's son-in-law, the Marquis de Montpouillan, in 1670; but there had been a medieval tower recorded in 1197. On the château see L. Blondel, 'Châteaux de l'ancien diocèse de Genève', *Mémoires et documents de la Societé d'histoire et d'archéologie de Genève*, vii (1856); for Montpouillan's inheritance of Aubonne see Archives Cantonales Vaudoises (Chavannes-près-Renens), cote IB300B, no. 1199.
37. Mayerne's privileges as Baron d'Aubonne are set out in Archives Cantonales Vaudoises, cote IB300B, nos 1172–3.
38. PRO, SP96/2, fo. 63.
39. Ibid., fo. 65.
40. 'Dess Herren Früherren von Aulbonne Instruction', Berne Staatsarchiv, Q 251/252.
41. There are three copies of the German text in the Bürgerbibliothek in Berne (MSS H.h. I.15, fos 193ff; I.102, fos 21–8; I.109, no. 3). These are no doubt official translations: the original letter was presumably in French. Mayerne was particularly solicitous for its delivery, since it was, as he wrote from England, 'de poids pour les advis utiles et necessaires qu'elle contient' (Berne Staatsarchiv, UP52, fo. 67).
42. RPC, MS (1622), fo. 4.
43. D'Aubigné, *Oeuvres complètes*, i. 137.
44. Ibid., i. 583.
45. Ibid., i. 216.
46. Ibid., i. 145.
47. Sloane MS 693, fos 52–61: 'Ars occulta detecta ab Elia Artista ex ipsius Trougny [αὐτογραφῷ autographou]; mihi dato Sedani et in mei gratiam ab ipso authore conscripto Januar 1622'.
48. The 'auditiones Hermetis', 'confabulationes Hermetis', 'dictationes Hermetis' at Sedan in 1621 can be found in Sloane MSS 693 and 2083.
49. For Bonne at Sedan, see RCS, MS 0065, Viaticum, p. 125; Sloane MS 2051, fo. 31. Other references to Bonne are in Sloane MSS 2069, fo. 54; 2071, fo. 3ᵛ; RCS, MS 0065, p. 107. He was apothecary to Charlotte de la Tremoïlle, afterwards Countess of Derby.
50. He was still in Sedan in 'January 1622' (Sloane MS 2083, fo. 1). He wrote to the Petit Conseil of Geneva from London on 12 Jan. 1622 (Heyer, p. 198). He used the Continental calendar while abroad and had probably switched to the English on arrival in England, so an extra ten days can be assigned to the interval.

Chapter 16   Protector of Switzerland, 1622

1. Heyer, p. 198. Heyer's collection includes all the surviving letters from Mayerne to Geneva (letters 1–7, 9–10 and 13). Those to Berne are in Berne Staatsarchiv, UP52, fos 67, 69; ibid., England-Buch E (1514–1622), fos 32–5. He always wrote to both cities on the same day.
2. Heyer, p. 199.
3. Ibid., p. 202.
4. D'Aubigné, *Oeuvres complètes*, i. 138, 233, 290.
5. Heyer, p. 200.

6. Chamberlain, ii. 479.

7. Sloane MS 2051, fo. 7.

8. Heyer, p. 198.

9. Ibid., p. 203.

10. Berne Staatsarchiv, England-Buch E, fo. 33.

11. PRO, SP78/69, fo. 102&^{v}; cf. Rohan to Doncaster, BL, Egerton MS 2594, fos 37, 79, 154.

12. PRO, SP78/69, fo. 174.

13. On Doncaster's proposed journey to Lyon see also *Cal. S.P. Ven. 1621–3*, p. 276.

14. Heyer, pp. 205–7.

15. Berne Staatsarchiv, UP52/69 (4 Apr. 1622).

16. BL, Egerton MS 2594, fos 198–9.

17. Heyer, pp. 207–9.

18. D'Aubigné, *Oeuvres complètes*, i. 145, 152, 220.

19. Ibid., i. 299–302. Only part of the letter survives in d'Aubigné's MSS (now in the Tronchin MSS in the Bibliothèque Publique et Universitaire, Geneva), but it can be completed from Mayerne's copy (Sloane MS 1990, fo. 101^v).

20. D'Aubigné, *Oeuvres complètes*, i. 501ff.

21. Heyer, pp. 208–9.

22. *Guilhelmi Fabricii Hildani . . . opera quae extant omnia* (Frankfurt, 1682 edn), p. 558.

23. Sloane MS 2067, fo. 18.

24. Ibid., fo. 6.

25. Ibid., fo. 79.

26. Ibid.; above, p. 9. Mayerne was more successful with the next Duchess of Lennox, for whom he prescribed an even more recondite means of conception (Sloane MS 2074, fo. 120^v) after which she bore an only son, who however died aged eleven. The dukedom thereupon became extinct. She was the daughter of the first Duke of Buckingham – another child whose birth was thus facilitated; so it could be said that her own birth and that of her son were due, or at least could be ascribed, to Mayerne's nostrums.

27. Wake to Secretary of State, 2/12 Oct. 1621 (PRO, SP92/8, fo. 202).

28. The duke, at this time, took no decision without the agreement of Wake (Moriz Ritter, 'Die Pfälzische Politik und die Böhmische Königswahl von 1619', *Historische Zeitschrift*, lxxix (1897), 248–9.

Chapter 17   The Last Years of King James, 1623–1625

1. BN, MS Fonds français 15989, fo. 582.

2. Sloane MS 1679, fo. 42.

3. It is reprinted in full in Latin in Sir Norman Moore, *History of the Study of Medicine in the British Isles* (Oxford, 1908), pp. 162–76.

4. Mayerne's notes on King James's urine have been cited as evidence that the king suffered from porphyria and that this disease, conveyed by heredity through five uncontaminated generations, broke out again in George III: a somewhat slender basis for so confident a conclusion. See Ida Macalpine and Richard Hunter, *Porphyria – a Royal Malady* (London, British Medical Association, 1968), pp. 26–33.

5. Heyer, pp. 209–10.

6. Ibid., p. 211.

7. BN, MS Fonds français 4509, fos 202, 244.

8. Du Moulin's visit to England and the plans for his return are described in the life of du Moulin by his son, quoted by Lucien Rimbault, *Pierre du Moulin, 1568–1658. Un pasteur classique à l'âge classique* (Paris, 1966), pp. 227–8, and in a letter from Antoine Léger to Benedetto Turrettini of 2 Sept. 1624, in Bibliothèque Publique et Universitaire, Geneva, Ami Lullin MS 54, fo. 24.

9. RCS, MS 0065, private record, p. 3; cf. Chamberlain, ii. 571.
10. *Cal. S.P. Dom. 1623–5*, p. 307.
11. Sloane MS 2067, fo. 127ʳff. Printed (with the usual numerous inaccuracies) in *Opera medica*, i. 288–307.
12. Above, p. 35.
13. PRO, SP104/166 (unfoliated: 30 Aug. 1624).
14. He was in Amiens on 9 Sept. 1624 (Sloane MS 1999, fo. 1). Léger was detained at Abbeville by the illness of his companion M. du Chat (Bibliothèque Publique et Universaitaire, Geneva, Ami Lullin MS 54, fo. 25).
15. Effiat to Louis XIII, 8 Sept. 1624: BN, MS Fonds français 4510, fo. 137ᵛ.
16. BL, Addit. MS 20921, fo. 47. Mayerne there refers to a discussion with Ville-aux-Clercs 'avant vostre voyage d'Angleterre'. Ville-aux-Clercs was sent to England in connection with the royal marriage late in Nov. 1624.
17. Bodl., Tanner MS 73, fos 485–6.
18. Sloane MSS 1991, fo. 106; 2077, fo. 107ᵛ.
19. BN, MS Fonds français 7586.
20. David l'Aigneau, *Traicté de la saignée* (2nd edn, Paris, 1635), p. 61.
21. He kept Héroard's diary for him from 15 to 30 Apr. 1611. Héroard there describes him as '*médecin*' – not *médecin ordinaire* – '*du roi*' (E. Soulié and E. de Barthélemy, eds, *Journal de Jean Héroard sur l'enfance et la jeunesse de Louis XIII* (Paris, 1868), ii. 60).
22. BL, Addit. MS 20921, fo. 56ᵛ. The letter, as here copied, is dated 'Londres ce dernier de l'année 1610', but this is an error of transcription. At that time Mayerne was not yet in London, nor le Maistre dead.
23. Villières to Ville-aux-Clercs, 12 Mar. 1624: BN, MS Fonds français 4509, fos 79ᵛ-80.
24. BL, Addit. MS 20921, fos 46ᵛ-47 (to d'Aligre), 47&ᵛ (to Ville-aux-Clercs).
25. PRO, SP96/2, fo. 109.
26. Eglishem claimed to have 'often rubbed into King James that honesty was the best policy' ('Domino meo felicis memoriae Jacobo Regi saepius inculcavi optimam politiam honestatem'): *Prodromus vindictae* (Frankfurt a/M, 1626), sig. A2ᵛ.
27. He attacked Buchanan not only as a bad subject, but also (what no other man ever dared to do) as a bad poet – far inferior to himself; and he accused the Dutch theologian Conrad Vorstius not only of heresy but of atheism, Judaism, 'Turkism', etc., etc.
28. 'Brontes', 'Aeolus', 'Onopordus': see the poems of Arthur Johnson and others printed in *Musa latina Aberdoniensis*, New Spalding Club, new series, ix (Aberdeen, 1892).
29. It was suggested, at the time of his death, that Hamilton had been poisoned, 'because he swelled unmeasurably after he was dead', but an autopsy had revealed no signs of poison (Chamberlain, ii. 604).
30. Eglishem, *Prodromus vindictae*; and in English, *The Fore-runner of Revenge* (Frankfurt, 1626). A document in *Cal. S.P. Dom. 1625–6*, p. 337 shows that it was published shortly before 20 May 1626. The parliamentary attack on Buckingham had begun in March 1626.
31. *Cal. S.P. Dom. 1625–6*, p. 377.
32. Izaak Walton, ed., *Reliquiae Wottonianae* (1672 edn), p. 232.
33. *A Declaration of the Commons of England in Parliament assembled expressing their Reasons and Grounds for Passing the Late Resolutions touching No Further Addresses* (London, 1648), pp. 13–16; Milton, 'Eikonoklastes', in *Complete Prose Works of John Milton*, iii, ed. Merritt Y. Hughes (New Haven and London, 1962), pp. 351–2.
34. On Trougny, see Sloane MSS 693, fos 122ᵛ-123ᵛ; 1984, fo. 31; on Briot, Sloane MS 1999, fo. 23ᵛ.
35. F. Mazerolle, 'Nicolas Briot, tailleur général des monnaies (1606–1625)', *Revue belge de numismatique*, lx (1904), 309.
36. RPC, MS 124 (1625), fo. 152.

37. PRO, SP78/73, fo. 254.
38. Rimbault, *Pierre du Moulin*, p. 229.
39. Evidence given before the Cour des Monnaies, Jan. 1628, cited by Mazerolle, 'Nicolas Briot', p. 311.
40. The cast of this medallion is in the British Museum. It is illustrated in H.A. Grueber, ed., *Medallic Illustrations of the History of Great Britain and Ireland to the Death of George II* (London, 1904–11), plate XIX, no. 14. The medallion is dated 1625 and could have been made from the life either in Paris in May 1625 or in London between Sept. and Dec. 1625. I have plumped for the latter date as more likely.
41. On Briot's career in England see Henry Symonds, 'English Mint Engravers of the Tudor and Stuart Periods, 1485–1688', *Numismatic Chronicle*, 4th series, xiii (1913), 367–8; Helen Farquhar, 'Nicholas Briot and the Civil War', ibid., xiv (1914), 169–235.
42. Sloane MS 3426, fo. 2.
43. Two letters from Mayerne to Dee are in BL, Addit. MS 20921, fos 40ᵛ–41, 42. Mayerne there refers to a regular correspondence between them. On Arthur Dee see the two articles by John H. Appleby, 'Arthur Dee and Johannes Bánfi Hunyades: Further Information on their Alchemical and Professional Activities', *Ambix*, xxiv (1977), 96–109 and 'Arthur Dee's Associations before Visiting Russia Clarified', *Ambix*, xxvi (1979), 1; also N.A. Figurovski, 'The Alchemist and Physician Arthur Dee (Artemii Ivanovich Dii)', *Ambix*, xiii (1965), 35.
44. Sloane MS 1679, fo. 62ff; cf. Leslie G. Matthews, *The Royal Apothecaries* (London, 1967), p. 173.

Chapter 18 Charles I and the Protestant Débâcle, 1625–1630

1. Lucy Hutchinson, *Memoirs of the Life of Colonel Hutchinson*, ed. James Sutherland (Oxford, 1973), p. 46.
2. BL, Addit. MS 19402, fo. 159.
3. Mayerne wrote to Buckingham from Geneva to congratulate him on forging this alliance: Bodl., Tanner MS 73, fos 485–6.
4. Sloane MS 2068, fo. 31ᵛ.
5. *Mémoires de cardinal de Richelieu*, x (Paris, 1931), p. 246.
6. Above, p. 7.
7. BL, Harleian MS 7000, fo. 206&ᵛ; reproduced in J.H. Wiffen, *Memoirs of the House of Russell* (n.p., 1833), ii. 117.
8. D'Aubigné, *Oeuvres complètes*, i. 331–4.
9. Bouvard was *premier médecin* from 1628 to 1643. According to Amelot de la Houssaie – *Mémoires historiques* (Amsterdam, 1737), ii. 193–4 – in one year he gave Louis XIII 215 purges, 212 enemas, and bled him forty-seven times. He attended Louis XIII at his death, having previously taken steps to ensure that his own office remained in the family: his successor was the same fortunate son-in-law, M. Cousinot. On his bleeding, see also T.H. Reveillé-Parise, *Lettres de Gui Patin* (Paris, 1907), p. 457 (letter of 19 June 1643). But David l'Aigneau, who disapproved of bleeding, had a good word to say for Bouvard, who (he says) will acquire immortal glory if he succeeds in the plan which he has submitted to the king and council, to establish a standing body of physicians and others specialising in the plague, charged 'visiter & assister les seuls pestiférez, avec bons et suffisans gages, en toute saison, soit pestiféré ou non' (L'Aigneau, *Traité de la saignée* (2nd edn, Paris, 1635), p. 325).
10. BL, Addit. MS 20921, fo. 5. Mayerne's copies of his letters to Richelieu, Marie de Médicis, Châteauneuf and other French ministers are in ibid., fos 4–7, 9ᵛ, 27–9, 49&ᵛ; his letter to Edmondes is in BL, Stowe MS 176, fo. 282. The allusion to Polyxena refers to Euripides, *Hecuba*, ll. 571–2.

11. BL, Addit. MS 20921, fo. 7: the letter is dated 21 July 1629. It is addressed merely to 'Monsieur', but the contents suggest a professional acquaintance.
12. BL, Stowe MS 176, fo. 282.
13. BL, Addit. MS 20921, fo. 27&ᵛ.
14. Ibid., fo. 125.
15. D'Aubigné, *Oeuvres complètes*, i. 302. Madame de Mayerne had a pass to go abroad 'for some convenient time' on 12 Aug. 1623 (*APC 1623–5*, p. 79).
16. RPC, 1625, 25 May.
17. D'Aubigné, *Oeuvres complètes*, i. 494.
18. Leiden University Library, MS BPL 885.
19. Carlisle's instructions are in BL, Harleian MS 1584, fos 173, 179.
20. Bodl., Tanner MS 73, fos 173–84.
21. Berne, Bürgerbibliothek MS h.h.XV.24 (6) (29 Mar. 1628).
22. Johannes Dierauer, *Histoire de la confédération Suisse*, iii (Lausanne, 1910), pp. 606–7.
23. The reference is to Virgil, *Aeneid*, X. 108: 'Tros Rutulusne fuat, nullo discrimine habebo'.
24. Berne, Bürgerbibliothek MS. h.h. XV.24 (6).
25. *Letters of Dorothy Osborne* (Folio Soc., 1968), p. 84.
26. BL, Addit. MS 20921, fos 9ᵛ-10.
27. For the marriage licence see *Allegations for Marriage Licenses issued by the Bishop of London 1611 to 1628* (Harleian Society, 1887), ii. 199. The vicar of All Saints, Fulham at the time was Richard Clewet, who would afterwards be ejected by the Puritans. It is difficult to see why Mayerne should have elected to be married there unless it was in order to be married by Laud, who was Dean of the Chapel Royal.
28. [In the 1640s she separated from the Dutch church in London and brought it trouble by attending sectarian meetings in the city. Ole Peter Grell, *Calvinist Exiles in Tudor and Stuart England* (Aldershot, 1996), pp. 88, 91, 131.]
29. Below, ch. 21.

Chapter 19 A New Regime, 1630–1631

1. Samuel Richardson, ed., *Negotiations of Sir Thomas Roe in his Embassy to the Porte, 1621–28* (London, 1740), pp. 694, 719.
2. PRO, SP96/2, fo. 107.
3. Laud's doctor was Sir Simon Baskerville (B. Hamey, 'Bustorum aliquot reliquiae', Sloane MS 2149, fo. 6) – a Catholic. Strafford's doctor was Sir Maurice Williamson. The crisis was when Strafford was ill at York shortly before the meeting of the Long Parliament (RCP, MS 444, pp. 251–3).
4. BL, Addit. MS 20921, fo. 34ᵛ.
5. Ibid., fo. 74ᵛ.
6. Ibid., fo. 117. It is not certain that this letter, of 9 July 1631, was addressed to Mayerne, but if not he was obviously sent a copy; at all events it relates to his requests for recommendations.
7. J[ean] B[ulteel], *A Relation of the Troubles of the Three Foreign Churches in Kent* (London, 1645); J.H. Hessels, *Ecclesiae Londino-Batavae archivum*, iii (1887–97), no. 2353 (for Lady Mayerne see ibid., nos 2500, 3013/3); Ole Peter Grell, *Dutch Calvinists in Early Stuart London* (Leiden, 1989), p. 230. Laud was equally unsympathetic to the appeals for relief of the Bohemian and Palatine refugees organised by the Dutch church at Austin Friars and supported by Mayerne: Grell, *Dutch Calvinists*, pp. 201–2).
8. For public policy in respect of the plague of 1630 see Paul Slack, 'Books of Orders: The Making of English Social Policy 1577–1631', *Transactions of the Royal Historical Society*, 5th series, xxx (1980), 1–22.

9. Printed in *Certain Statutes especially selected and commanded by His Majesty* ... (London, 1630). For the order of the Privy Council to which it is a reply see *Analytical Index to the ... Remembrancia ... of the City of London* (London, 1878), p. 340 (VII. 18).
10. For the composition of the document see G.L. Keynes, *The Writings of William Harvey* (Cambridge, 1928), pp. 189–91.
11. Bodl., Rawlinson MS C. 516, pp. 18, 21, 33, etc.
12. On Bethune's travels in Spain see Sloane MSS 1999, fo. 81; 2050, fo. 70; 2090, fo. 22. On the plague in Spain see B. Bennassar, *Recherches sur les grandes épidémies dans le nord de l'Espagne à la fin du XVIe siècle* (Paris, 1969).
13. PRO, SP16/187, fos 98–116.
14. Sloane MSS 1984, fo. 23ᵛ–26ᵛ; 2044, fo. 9; 2069, fo. 153ᵛ. I have mislaid the reference to snake-root. For his cure for the bites of dogs and snakes see CUL, MS Dd. 5–25, fo. 29ᵛ.
15. On these see Carlo M. Cipolla, *Public Health and the Medical Profession in the Renaissance* (Cambridge, 1976), ch. 1. On the superiority of Italian over English public health organisation see Edward Chaney, 'Philanthropy in Italy', in Thomas Riis, ed., *Aspects of Poverty in Early Modern Europe* (Brussels, 1981), pp. 183–217; [and on the Italian background see too David Gentilcore, *Healers and Healing in Early Modern Italy* (Manchester, 1998)].
16. *APC 1630–1*, p. 274.
17. PRO, SP16/533, fos 26–40.
18. London, Guildhall MSS, 'Remembrancia of the City of London', vii. 19. This document is in English, but its reference to Henri IV as 'Henry the Great of happy memory' suggests that it was originally written by a Frenchman – probably Mayerne.
19. [Nevertheless Mayerne's scheme would be remembered and would be influential in the eighteenth century: Paul Slack, *The Impact of Plague* (London, 1985), pp. 327, 334. See also Slack's *From Reformation to Improvement: Public Welfare in Early Modern England* (Oxford, 1999), pp. 72, 74.]
20. He was converted in 1617. The brothers Haag (*La France protestante* (Paris and Geneva, 1846–59), s.v. 'Monginot') state that he was *médecin ordinaire du roi* from 1635, but this is a mistake: he is already described as such in his justificatory book *Résolution des doubtes ou sommaire décision des controverses* (La Rochelle, 1617) as well as in Mayerne's MSS in 1625 (Sloane MS 2068, fo. 1) and 1630 (2069, fo. 172). Monginot's son, also François, was also a doctor.
21. Above, pp. 123–4.
22. Sloane MS 2069, fos 172–4. It does not seem that Monginot's *Paradox* was published.
23. Cf. below, pp. 326–7.
24. BL, Addit. MS 20921, fo. 7.
25. Sir Oliver Fleming (afterwards Oliver Cromwell's Master of Ceremonies) was sent as first English resident minister to Switzerland in 1629. His instructions are in PRO, SP96/3, fo. 45.
26. Excluded from diplomacy, Biondi wrote three novels, or novelettes, in the reign of Charles I: *L'eromena* (1624), *La donzella desterrada* (1627) and *Il coralbo* (1632).
27. BL, Addit. MS 20921, fo. 19.
28. Ibid., fos 20–2.
29. At least, I presume the name was Benoît: Mayerne always writes it in Latin, Benedictus.
30. The letters concerning James de Mayerne's admission to Oxford are in Sloane MS 2069, fos 76ᵛ–79 (copies in BL, Addit. MS 20921, fos 13–14).
31. BL, Addit. MS 20921, fos 3–4.
32. Sloane MS 2069, fo. 135ᵛ.

Chapter 20   Planting a Dynasty, 1630–1639

1. Auguste Laugel, *Henri de Rohan. Son rôle politique et militaire sous Louis XIII (1579–1638)* (Paris, 1889), pp. 284–5.
2. BL, Addit. MS 20921, fos 11ᵛ, 12ᵛ.
3. Ibid., fo. 71ᵛ.
4. That Chouart was a doctor appears from Sloane MS 3426, fo. 73, 'Adversaria Medica D. Chouart'.
5. BL, Addit. MS 20921, fo. 69&ᵛ.
6. Ibid., fo. 22.
7. Ibid., fo. 19ᵛ.
8. Ibid., fo. 18ᵛ.
9. Ibid., fos 20&ᵛ, 23–4, 26.
10. Ibid., fo. 21.
11. Ibid., fo. 33ᵛ.
12. BN, Carré d'Hozier 423, fos 55–56ᵛ.
13. Louis de Mayerne-Turquet's description of the map was published in 1648 as *Discours sur la carte universelle*. A second edition appeared in 1661. Four copies of the map itself, signed by Louis de Mayerne-Turquet, are in the Bibliothèque Nationale, Département des Cartes et Plans. There is a copy of the second edition in the British Library, and another copy is recorded as being in the Library of the University of Leiden (*Catalogus Bibl. Publ. Univ. Lugd. Bat.*, 1716), p. 198. There is a note on it by Léonard Baulacre, librarian of the city of Geneva, in *Journal helvétique*, Aug. 1752 (reprinted in *Oeuvres historiques et littéraires de Léonard de Baulacre* (Geneva, 1857), i. 166); but Baulacre confused Louis de Mayerne-Turquet with Sir Theodore.
14. BL, Addit. MS 20921, fo. 16.
15. Ibid., fos 20, 26.
16. Ibid., fo. 26.
17. Ibid.
18. Ibid., fo. 32ᵛ.
19. Ibid., fo. 39.
20. Ibid., fo. 41ᵛ.
21. Ibid., fo. 43.
22. *Cal. S.P. Dom. 1636–7*, pp. 17, 21.
23. BL, Addit. MS 20921, fo. 125.
24. 'un berland, un bourdeau, & une bouticque de faux monnoyeurs': d'Aubigné, *Oeuvres complètes*, i. 110: 'Sa vie à ses enfants'.
25. Albert's birth is recorded by Mayerne on 13 Apr. 1634 (RCS, MS 0065, personal record, p. 3); his death by his grandfather Albert Joachimi in a latter to Sir Simonds D'Ewes of 17 Dec. 1637 (BL, Harleian MS 375, fo. 85).
26. Sloane MS 2074, fos 23ᵛ, 30ᵛ.
27. RCP, MS 444, pp. 104, 148.
28. Cambridge University Archives, *Liber Gratiarum* Z. 1620–45, p. 311; J.A. Venn, *Alumni Cantabrigienses*, pt 1, i (1922), p. 371. For Colladon at Norwich see RCP 444, pp. 104–7; Sloane MSS, 2044, fo. 25; CUL, MS Dd 5–25, fo. 40ᵛ. For the apothecary, Mr Byrche ('pharmacopoeus meus', 'pharmacopoeus Norwicensis'): Sloane MSS 2020, fos 2ᵛ, 6, etc; 2022, fos 100ᵛ, 102; 2050, fos 47ᵛ, 71ᵛ.
29. Colladon travelled with a Norfolk friend, perhaps a patient, Edmund Knyvett (*Cal. S.P. Dom. 1636–7*, p. 369).
30. RPC 136, fos 55, 61 (18–27 Feb. 1637); Council Letters 29, fos 158–61. The exchange of letters between the Council and Mayerne is recorded in the Register, but the letters themselves have not been found.
31. RPC, MS 136, fos 436, 504.

32. Sloane MS 1679, fo. 60.
33. Sloane MSS 1988, fo. 209; 1989, fos 71, 177; 1999, fo. 61ᵛ; 2068, fos 56ᵛ–57.
34. Ibid., MS 2072, fo. 56ᵛ.
35. Above, p. 216.
36. BL, Addit. MS 20921, fo. 45.
37. Ibid., fo. 28ᵛ.
38. Ibid., fo. 75.
39. Ibid.
40. Above, p. 102.
41. BL, Addit. MS 20921, fo. 125.
42. Ibid., fo. 26.
43. 'M. de Soubize, Londino discedens in Galliam pereuntem': Sloane MS 2071, fo. 5.
44. Sir Gyles Isham, ed., *The Correspondence of Bishop Brian Duppa and Sir Justinian Isham 1650–1660* (Northamptonshire Record Society, Lamport, 1955), p. 138.
45. BL, Harleian MS 377, fo. 295.

Chapter 21   Entrepreneur and Virtuoso

1. BL, Burney MS 368, fo. 122ᵛ; cf. ibid., fo. 104.
2. *Cal. S.P. Dom. 1619–23*, pp. 102–3, 138; *1623–5*, p. 516; etc.
3. *The Register of the Privy Seal of Scotland 1609–1620*, no. 1437.
4. See BL, Addit. MS 20921, fos 48ᵛ–49.
5. On Sir George Hay's economic ventures see D.W. Kemp, *Notes on Early Iron-Smelting in Sutherland* (Edinburgh, 1887); W. Ivison Macadam, 'Notes on the Ancient Iron Industry of Scotland', *Proceedings of the Society of Antiquaries of Scotland*, xxi (1887), 89, 109–12; *Cal S.P. Dom. 1611–18*, p. 412 [and, now, J. Turnbull, *The Scottish Glass Industry, 1610–1750* (Edinburgh, 2001), esp. ch. 4, and *ODNB*: George Hay, first Earl of Kinnoul].
6. Desmarets to Villeroy, 4 July 1616: BN, MS Fonds français 17975, fos 258ᵛ–259.
7. As had been done, in respect of Newcastle, by Thomas Sutton, who, by acquiring 'the Grand Lease' of the Durham coalfields and selling it to the Newcastle merchants, laid the foundation of a huge personal fortune. See my essay 'The Bishopric of Durham and the Capitalist Reformation', *Durham University Journal*, xxxviii (1945) [revised and reprinted in *Durham Research Review*, xviii (1967)].
8. RCS, MS 0065, Viaticum, p. 157; Mayerne, 'Pictoria, Sculptoria, et quae subalternarum artium', eds, M. Faidutti and C. Versini (Lyon, c. 1970), p. 13; and see CUL, MS Dd. 5-26, fo 99
9. Tillières to Puysieux, 4 Feb. 1620: BN, MS Fonds français 15988, fo. 415.
10. Mayerne to Puysieux, 26 June 1620 (ibid., fo. 476).
11. Mayerne to Puysieux, Dec. 1623: BN, MS Fonds français 15989, fo. 582.
12. BL, Addit. MS 20921, fo. 35ᵛ.
13. Ibid., fo. 36.
14. Ibid., fo. 36ᵛ.
15. BL, Burney MS 369, fo. 103.
16. PRO, SP16/534, fo. 109.
17. Ibid, fo. 110. See too *Cal. S.P. Dom. 1633–4*, pp. 282, 289.
18. The fact appears from a later application for the same post: *Cal. S.P. Dom. 1660–1*, p. 159.
19. Thus the French botanist Vespasien Robin and the Anglo-Dutch scholar John Morris exchanged exotic seeds through Mayerne. See J.A.F. Bekkers, ed., *Correspondence of John Morris with Johannes de Laet 1634–1649* (Assen, 1970), p. 14 (cf. ibid., p. 41).
20. Ibid. p. 28.
21. See Mayerne's introductory puffs to both volumes. Mayerne also received the dedication of *Mercurius botanicus* (1634).

22. *The Distiller of London* (London, 1639); the work was reprinted in 1652.
23. [Trevor-Roper planned a fuller account of Mayerne's activities in the world of distilling. See too now *ODNB*: Sir Thomas Cademan.]
24. Above, pp. 217-8.
25. [Trevor-Roper gives a detailed account of the fate and standing of the document in his essay 'Mayerne and his Manuscript', in Donald Howarth, ed., *Art and Patronage in the Caroline Courts* (Cambridge, 1993), pp. 264-93. See too now Jo Kirby, 'The Painter's Trade in the Seventeenth Century: Theory and Practice', *National Gallery Technical Bulletin*, xx (1999).]
26. Sir Charles Eastlake, *Materials for a History of Oil Painting* (London, 1847), i. ix.
27. Ernst Berger, *Quellen für Maltechnik während der Renaissance und deren Folgezeit (XVI–XVIII Jahrhundert)... nebst dem de Mayerne MS. Beiträge sur Entwicklungsgeschichte der Maltechnik* (Munich, 1901).
28. J.A. van de Graaf, *Het de Mayerne Manuscript als Bron voor de Schildertechniek van de Barok* (Mijdrecht, 1958).
29. M. Faidutti and C. Versini, *Le Manuscrit de Turquet de Mayerne* (Lyon, [1968]), Introduction.
30. Mansfield Kirby Talley, *Portrait Painting in England: Studies in the Technical Literature before 1700* (privately printed for the Paul Mellon Center for Studies in British Art, 1981).
31. R.D. Harley, *Artists' Pigments* (London, 1970), p. 121.
32. On various technical points, I am especially grateful for the help of Miss Jo Kirby, of the National Gallery, London, Mr Edward Chaney and Miss Jennifer Richenberg.
33. Sloane MS 345. On it see Sir Charles Eastlake, *Materials*, i. 281-3.
34. Above, p. 49.
35. BL, Addit. MS 20921, fos 103-4; Sloane MS 2052, fo. 94: 'J'en ay veu à Schwatz'.
36. We may note that although he was interested in miniatures and discussed the technique with Edward Norgate, John Hoskins and Samuel Cooper, Mayerne never cites either Nicholas Hilliard or Isaac Oliver, who were very easily accessible to him since both, like himself, had court appointments. Since Oliver died in September 1617 and Hilliard in January 1619, this also suggests that Mayerne's serious interest only began in 1620.
37. Sloane MS 2057.
38. Sloane MS 2001.
39. Sloane MS 2052, fos 2, 3. Berger, followed by van de Graaf, misreads 'Quaeratur' as 'Inceratur' – with curious consequences to their argument.
40. Sloane MS 2052, fo. 47.
41. Sloane MS 2066, fo. 155.
42. Sloane MS 2052, fo. 31.
43. Sloane MS 2048, fo. 42; 1978, fo. 54: 'ex ore ipsius Huskins, habita confabulatione dum Dominum Mayerne depingeret, 17 Sept 1635'.
44. Sloane MS 2052, fos 29, 77ᵛ, 149.
45. Ibid., fo. 18ᵛ. Berger, Versini and Faidutti misread and mistranslate this passage.
46. Ibid., fo. 328.
47. In French in Sloane MS 2052, fos 143-6; in German in Sloane MS 1990, fos 107ᵛ-25, where he extends his field of expertise to silk-dyeing, confectionary, etc. [Another artist in St Martin's Lane with whom Mayerne discussed painting was Abraham van Blyenberch; see *ODNB*: Paul van Somer.]
48. Norgate's *Miniatura* was not published until 1919 when it was edited by Martin Hardie from the author's fair copy (Bodl., Tanner MS 326). On the evidence of what appears to be the earliest MS (BL, Harleian MS 6000), Hardie concluded that the 'discourse' was written between 1621 and 1626. For Norgate's particular contributions to Mayerne's work see Sloane MSS 2052, fos 22, 40, 97, 160; 2072, fo. 209; 2081, fo. 49ᵛ; and Harley, *Artists' Pigments, passim*.

49. For the interpretation of Mayerne's relations with Petitot see R.W. Lightbown, 'Jean Petitot and Jacques Bordier at the English Court', *The Connoisseur*, clxviii (1968), 82–91; also his 'Les origines de la peinture en émail sur or. Un traité inconnu et des faits nouveaux', *Revue de l'art*, v (1969), 46–54. Lightbown uses the evidence of Sloane MS 1990, fo. 31ᵛ ('crocus Martis corallinus seu <vitriolum Martis> ad summam rubedinem calcinatum'). Other confirmatory references are in Sloane MSS 2020, fo. 35ᵛ ('rubrum ad smaltum Petitot e <vitriolo Martis>'); and 2052, fo. 122, where the same formula – yellow ochre heated in a strong fire – is said to yield 'une couleur rouge presque comme cynabre, excellente pour la carnation et pour la draperie', and is accompanied by a marginal note 'ad smalta'. For Mayerne and Petitot see also appendix B, below.
50. Sloane MSS 1990, fo. 30ᵛ; 2020, fo. 90; 2083, fo. 100.
51. The story is set out, from the archives, by Lightbown, in his article 'Petitot and Bordier'.
52. Petitot's letter is included in Sloane MS 2052, fos 164–5.
53. He is named by Richard Symonds in BL, Egerton MS 1636, fo. 61: printed in Mary Beal, *A Study of Richard Symonds* (New York and London, 1984), p. 243.
54. For the Mantuan paintings, and the cleaning of paintings in general, see Sloane MS 2052, fos 14, 15, 57, 110, 147; for prints, ibid., fo. 59ᵛff; also Mark Stevenson, 'A 17th-Century Manual for the Restoration of Prints', *Print Quarterly*, vii (1990), 420–4.
55. [The other documents, and their relationship to the 'Mayerne manuscript', are discussed in Trevor-Roper, 'Mayerne and his Manuscript'.]
56. The principal one is Sloane MS 1990.
57. Sloane MSS 1989, fo. 302; 2020, fo. 74; 2022, fos 110, 141; 2083, fos 96–8, 101; 3423, *passim*; Prince Rupert: 1990, fo. 99. [Trevor-Roper planned to explore Mayerne's interest in pigment further.]
58. For Hoskins see appendix B. [For Mayerne's artistic contacts see too *ODNB*: Richard Greenbury; Raphael Thorius.]
59. Sloane MS 3423.
60. BL, Egerton MS 2594, fo. 198.

Chapter 22   The Physician and his Late Years, 1640–1655

1. BL, Addit. MS. 78316, fo. 27: N. Le Febvre to John Evelyn, 23 Mar. 1652.
2. 'Tam oraculum artis iatricæ quàm ornamentum': Geo. Bate to Mayerne, RCP, MS 444, p. 254.
3. BL, Sloane MS 2069, fo. 140.
4. 'Mecum habito et novi quam sit mihi curta supellex': a reference to Persius, *Satire IV*, l. 52.
5. BL, Sloane MS 2069, fo. 144.
6. BL, Addit. MS 20921, fo. 46ᵛ.
7. Sloane MS 2069, fos 101ᵛ, 109.
8. Ibid., fo. 65.
9. Cf. the report of Lady Worsley, who, in 1636, had two hard internal humours: 'notanda curatio . . . σύν θεῷ perfecte fuit curata . . . et nunc vivit sana et vegeta, mense Decembri 1642' – afterwards amended to 1650. 'Ναὶ πόνος ἐντελεχὴς πράγματα πάντα τελεῖ' (Truly continuous toil will achieve everything.) (Sloane MS 2072, fos 40ᵛ–41).
10. Sloane MS 2069, fo. 70; fos 69ᵛ–74 and 88ᵛ–90 all deal with the case of Breban.
11. Cf. appendix B, below.
12. Above, p. 58.
13. Edward May, *A Most Certaine and True Relation of a Strange Monster or Serpent Found in the Left Ventricle of the Heart of John Pennant, Gentleman* (London, 1639), dedication to Mayerne, pp. 1–2.

14. Above, p. 285.
15. *Fasciculus chymicus* (Paris, 1631). It was later enlarged as 'Arca Arcanorum, abstrusae Hermeticae scientiae' (Sloane MS 1876).
16. BL, Addit. MS 20921, fo. 42.
17. Above, p. 305.
18. Sloane MS 2060, fo. 17.
19. Sloane MS 2074, fo. 77ᵛ.
20. '. . . maleficium ut certis (at raris) in casibus admitto, sic physicum quamdiu suppetit ipsi naturalium causarum inventio, ad metaphysica relegare, medicumve carminioribus morbea excantare nolim': Sloane MS 2066, fos 158ᵛ–159, 167; cf. Sloane MS 206A, fo. 28, which is a recapitulation of the case.
21. Sloane MS 2074, fos 146&ᵛ.
22. 'ne credas nisi lecto libello . . . ita varia hominum sunt iudicia et non nisi experto crede Roberto': Sloane MS 283, fo. 184.
23. Bodl., Rawlinson MS C. 516, p. 155.
24. John Aubrey, *Brief Lives*, s.v.
25. Sloane MSS 1992, fo. 21ᵛ (Mayerne's treatment of him); 2020, fo. 102 (the diamonds); 2022, fo. 107 (the aphrodisiacs); 2071, fo. 44 (the electuary of vipers).
26. On Hunyadi, whom Mayerne often cites, see Sir Thomas Browne's letter to Elias Ashmole, Mar. 1674, in *Works of Sir Thomas Browne*, ed. Geoffrey Keynes, iv (London, 1931), p. 296; F. Sherwood and C.H. Josten, 'Johannes Banfi Hunyades 1576–1650', *Ambix*, v (1953–6), 44–52, and a 'Supplementary Note' by the same authors in ibid., v. 115; John Appleby, 'Arthur Dee and Johannes Bánfi Hunyades: Further Information on their Alchemical and Professional Activities', *Ambix*, xxiv (1977), 96–109; George Gömöri, 'New Information on János Bánfihunyadi's Life', ibid., 170–4. For Digby and Hunyadi see Vittorio Gabrieli, *Sir Kenelm Digby. Un inglese italianato nell'età della Controriforma* (Rome, 1957), p. 227 n. 4.
27. Sloane MS 2079, fos 47ᵛff.
28. On Digby and Poterius see Gabrieli, *Sir Kenelm Digby*, p. 218. On Poterius see John Ferguson, *Bibliotheca chemica* (Glasgow, 1906), s.v. Mayerne refers often to Poterius as 'insignis chymicus', 'Gallus Bononiae medicinam faciens', etc. Poterius sent a powder to Mayerne in 1636 (Sloane MS 2072, fo. 11), and was alive in 1640, but has not been traced later. He is said to have been murdered by a treacherous friend (see Ferguson, s.v.). Digby's friendship and chemical cooperation with Mayerne acquired, in Digby's hands, a fictional element. Digby's famous chemical discovery was his miraculous 'powder of sympathy', which would cure wounds, without direct contact, by its mere application to a bandage which had touched them. According to Digby, he had learned the secret of this powder from a Carmelite friar who had travelled in the east and whom he had met in Florence in 1622, and he had proved its efficacy soon afterwards by a cure performed in the presence of James I and others, including Francis Bacon – though Bacon, who was interested in such things (Bacon, *Works*, ii. 670), never mentions the episode. Mayerne (according to Digby) asked to be let into the secret, and Digby frankly told it him, 'for in his hands there was no fear that such a secret should be prostituted'. Soon afterwards, Mayerne went to France 'to see some fair territories that he had purchased near Geneva, which was the barony of Aubonne'; and while in France he told the secret to the head of his family, the Duc de Mayerne, who had been a long time his friend and protector. The duke himself performed some miraculous cures with the powder, but was then killed at the siege of Montauban, and so the secret, falling into the hands of his surgeon, was sold by him until it had become, by degrees, 'so divulged that now there is scarce any country barber but knows it'. Sir Kenelm Digby, *A Late Discourse made . . . at Montpellier . . . touching the cure of wounds by the powder of sympathy* (London, 1658), pp. 13–14. Digby's story is pure fantasy. There was no Duc de Mayerne. It was the Duc de Mayenne, who had no connection with

Mayerne, who was killed at Montauban – as leader of the Catholic army fighting against Mayerne's patron Rohan. The 'powder of sympathy' is never mentioned by Mayerne, and although, as a Hermetist, he believed in sympathies, there is no evidence that he went as far as this. His medical patron la Rivière believed in 'the weapon-salve', of which Digby's 'powder of sympathy' is a mere variant; but Mayerne, it seems, did not. (In Sloane MS 2049 Mayerne deals with wounds, and quotes Digby (fo. 109ᵛ; cf. fo. 58ᵛ), but makes no reference to 'sympathetic' cures.)

29. *Opera medica*, i. 286–8.
30. Read – for it is the mirror of a whole society, and deserves to be read in full – Marjorie Hope Nicolson's perfectly edited *Conway Letters* (London, 1930). Not all Mayerne's letters to Conway are printed by Miss Nicolson. The originals, which are in French, are in the State Papers Domestic. [There is an updated edition of Nicolson's *Conway Letters* by Sarah Hutton (Oxford, 1992).]
31. Nicolson, ed., *Conway Letters*, pp. 20–3; cf. ibid., p. 91n.
32. Samuel Pepys also (having read the Duchess of Newcastle's life of her husband) deplored his inability to control her. The book, he remarked, showed her to be 'a mad, conceited, ridiculous woman and he an ass to suffer her to write what she writes to him and of him' (*Diary*, 18 Mar. 1667–8).
33. Nottingham University Library, Portland (Welbeck) MS Pw V 90: 22 May 1649.
34. Ibid.: 24 May 1648.
35. *Isaaci Casauboni epistolae* (Magdeburg, 1656), p. 999.
36. Mayerne recommended the waters of Bath to Queen Anne; those of St Paul near Rouen to Sir William Beecher (*Cal. S.P. Dom. 1641–3*, p. 426); those of Bourbon, Forges and Bougues to the Duchess of Newcastle ('A Book wherein is contained rare mineral receipts'); those of Knaresborough to Lord Livingstone of Almond (*Cal. S.P. Dom. 1637–8*, pp. 526, 600). His papers in the Sloane MSS contain numerous notes on the use of baths and mineral waters.
37. *HMC Cowper*, ii. 289; F.P. Verney, ed., *The Verney Papers*, ii (London, 1892), 106; BL, Sloane MS 1679, fo. 67.
38. Bodl., Tanner MS 173, fo. 484.
39. *HMC 5th Report (House of Lords)*, p. 76; *Journal of the House of Lords*, v. 641, 645.
40. *Journal of the House of Commons*, iii. 198–9.
41. Ibid., iii. 201.
42. Ibid., iii. 230.
43. *Journal of the House of Lords*, vi. 217.
44. For Mayerne's attendance on the king's children, see ibid., vi. 448, 475, etc.
45. For example for Lord Percy: see *Cal. S.P. Dom. 1644–5*, pp. 200, 203.
46. Sloane MS 1679, fo. 71ᵛ.
47. *Journal of the House of Commons*, iii. 488. They left for Exeter on 21 May 1644 and arrived on 28 May (Henry H. Drake, ed., *Hasted's History of Kent, Corrected, Enlarged and Continued*, i (1886), p. 65 n. 8).
48. The history of this order is contained in the entries of the parliamentary journals (*Journal of the House of Commons*, iv. 126–7, 147; *Journal of the House of Lords*, vii. 373), and in Mayerne's petition against it (Bodl., Tanner MS 173, fo. 484). Mayerne paid up: BL, Harleian MS 166, fo. 211.
49. *Journal of the House of Lords*, vii. 373.
50. *Journal of the House of Commons*, iv. 147–8. BL, Harleian MS 166, fo. 211.
51. The Ordinance is in *Journal of the House of Lords*, viii. 24; also *Cal. S.P. Dom. 1645–7*, pp. 247–8.
52. BL, Addit. MS 31,116 (diary of Lawrence Whitaker), fos 77, 207ᵛ.
53. Nicolson, ed., *Conway Letters*, p. 21.
54. PRO, SP25/8, p. 30.
55. Ibid., p. 333.

56. PRO, SP25/70, p. 15. [However, the declaration did not exempt Mayerne from assessments on his landed property, to which, it stated, he had always been subject. He evidently owned, but perhaps never occupied, an estate in Cambridgeshire: PRO, E134/24 Chas 2/Mich 8. A contemporary stated, not necessarily reliably, that Mayerne in his old age had a 'country house': Gideon Harvey, *The Art of Curing Diseases by Expectation* (London, 1689), p. 180.]

57. BL, Addit. MS 20921, fos 120–3. [In pursuit of their own interests, Mayerne, and his nephew Colladon, seem to have carried weight at Whitehall during the interregnum: PRO, SP28/20, fo. 287; cf. *Cal. S.P. Dom. 1649–50*, p. 404, and Ruth Spalding, ed., *The Diary of Bulstrode Whitelocke* (Oxford, 1990), pp. 237, 238, 479, 627. The passage of the declaration of 4 July 1653 by the Council of State in Mayerne's favour suggests the extent of his influence. That was the date on which the radical body chosen by the army officers, 'Barebone's Parliament', assembled. It is a fair guess that the measure was pushed through, at that busy time, so that it would not have to come before Barebone's, where resistance at least as great as that in the Commons in the 1640s could have been expected. The initiative is likely to have come from Cromwell, or at any rate to have had his approval. In 1654 it was at Cromwell's 'desire' that a ship was appointed to carry Lady Mayerne to the Low Countries, and that she was to be exempted, on her return, from the search of her goods: PRO, SP25/75: 8 May 1654. What did Mayerne know, or make, of the involvement of his godson Theodore Naudin in political intrigue against the Cromwellian regime earlier in the same year (S.R. Gardiner, *History of the Commonwealth and Protectorate*, iii. (repr. 1965), p. 125; cf. SP25/75: 7 Aug. 1654)?]

58. See e.g. Sloane MS 206A, fos 62, 64, 83.

59. Ibid., fo. 32. The letter is not signed, but from its character and position I conclude it to be by Mayerne.

60. Atheism being, as Sir Thomas Browne admits at the opening of his *Religio medici*, 'the general scandal of my profession'.

61. Harvey, *Art of Curing Diseases by Expectation*, pp. 179–83.

62. See the letter of the French ambassador, reporting his death, in Thomas Birch, ed., *Thurloe State Papers* (1742), iii. 312.

63. The inscription was solicited by Colladon from Meric Casaubon, the English son of Mayerne's old Huguenot friend and patient: BL, Burney MS 369, fo. 104. [The monument can now be seen at the west end of the crypt.]

64. George Starkey, *Nature's Explication and Helmont's Vindication* (1657), p. 256. (I owe this reference to Mr Charles Webster.)

65. [Dorothy Osborne did not see how Elizabeth could have 'recovered', by her match to 'this buffle-headed marquis', the 'great loss' she had suffered by Hastings's death, but noted that she behaved affectionately to him in public: *Letters of Dorothy Osborne* (Folio Society, 1984), p. 84.]

66. Register of Charenton, July 1637, quoted in the brothers Haag, *La France protestante* (Paris and Geneva, 1846–59), s.v. 'Colladon'.

67. For glimpses of Colladon and the Mayernes in the 1650s see *Cal. S.P. Dom. 1651*, p. 471; *1651–2*, pp. 415, 569; *1655*, p. 582.

68. PRO, PROB 11/245.

69. Spalding, *Diary of Bulstrode Whitelocke*, pp. 479, 627.

70. *Calendar of the Clarendon State Papers*, v. 32: Mordaunt to Hyde, 13 May 1660.

71. Archives Cantonales Vaudoises (Chavannes-près-Renens), cote IB300B, no. 1199.

72. His will is in PRO, PROB 11/349.

73. In 1636 Mayerne's *Ephemerides* contain a note 'à monsieur Colladon à Norwich'. The *consilium* sent by Mayerne in 1635 'for Mr Scottowe alderman of Norwich' was presumably solicited by Colladon. See too Bertram Schofield, ed., *The Knyvett Letters (1620–1644)* (Norfolk Record Society, xx, 1949), p. 137.

Appendix B: Portraits of Mayerne

1. Sloane MS 1978, fo. 54.
2. The statement in the *Catalogue of Engraved British Portraits preserved in the Department of Prints and Drawings in the British Museum* (London, 1908), iii. 215, that this work is based on the portrait in the Royal College of Physicians (below) is wrong. Except for the human skull – a mere stage-property – there is no resemblance.
3. *Praxeos Mayernianae . . . syntagma* (London, 1690).
4. [It now hangs in the Radcliffe Observatory in Green College, Oxford.]
5. For his closeness to Mayerne see above, pp. 344–5.
6. The attribution has been questioned on grounds of style by P.F. Schneeberger, 'Les peintres sur émail genevois au XVIIe siècle', *Geneva*, vi (1958), 134–5. But it was confidently ascribed to Petitot by the miniaturist Bernard Lens, who copied it in 1710, when, as he noted, it belonged to Hans Sloane. Petitot's visit to England in the reign of Charles I, and his connection with Mayerne, were evidently not known at this time, so such an ascription must have rested on positive information; and since Sloane presumably acquired the miniature, as he did Mayerne's books and manuscripts, from the Colladon family, it seems likely that the ascription to Petitot had the authority of Mayerne's family. It has been suggested that the National Portrait Gallery miniature shows Mayerne as an old man, and for that reason a date of 1650 has been suggested. This would rule out Petitot, who evidently left England about 1643. But after his sixtieth year (i.e. 1633) Mayerne was 'heavy with age': above, p. 331.
7. I am grateful to Miss Maria Flemington of Ham House for her help.
8. Augustin Bouvier, 'Un portrait de Theodore de Mayerne attribué à Rubens', *Geneva*, xv (1937), 200–3; Arnold C. Klebs, 'L'Iconographie de Theodore de Mayerne', *Geneva*, xvi (1938), 173–6; Thomas Gibson, 'The Iconography of Sir Theodore Turquet de Mayerne . . .', *Annals of Medical History*, 3rd series, iii (1941), 288–96.
9. The statement that she died in Geneva is based on the fact that a *post mortem* report on her by the Genevese physician Gédeon Chabrey is included in Theophile Bonet's *Sepulchretum* (Geneva, 1679). But Chabrey, an assistant of Mayerne in London, was there in 1655 when Lady Mayerne died.
10. Though dismissed as early as the eighteenth century, the attribution was revived by Gibson, 'Iconography'.
11. Klebs seeks to evade this chronological necessity by suggesting that Diodati did not paint but only engraved the portrait. It could then have been painted from the life by an unidentified older artist. But the inscription on the engraving is clear: 'T. Diodati pinx. sc.', i.e. both painted and engraved by Diodati.
12. The engraving was reprinted in J.J. Manget, *Bibliotheca scriptorum* (Geneva, 1731), ii(1) 281. For the subsequent history of the painting see too Léonard Baulacre, *Oeuvres historiques et littéraires*, ed. E. Mallet (Geneva, 1857), i. 160–9.

Appendix C: Mayerne's Papers

1. [Nance, pp. 30ff and appendix A, supplies much information on the composition and arrangement of the case-notes, and on Mayerne's selection of the material contained in them. He concludes that Mayerne was more likely to record difficult or unusual cases than others – and also more inclined to record the treatment of courtly and aristocratic patients than of others.]
2. I am grateful to Mr Hilton Kelliher for his advice on this subject.

Index